Consumer Reports® cars

NEW CAR BUYING GUIDE 2005-2006

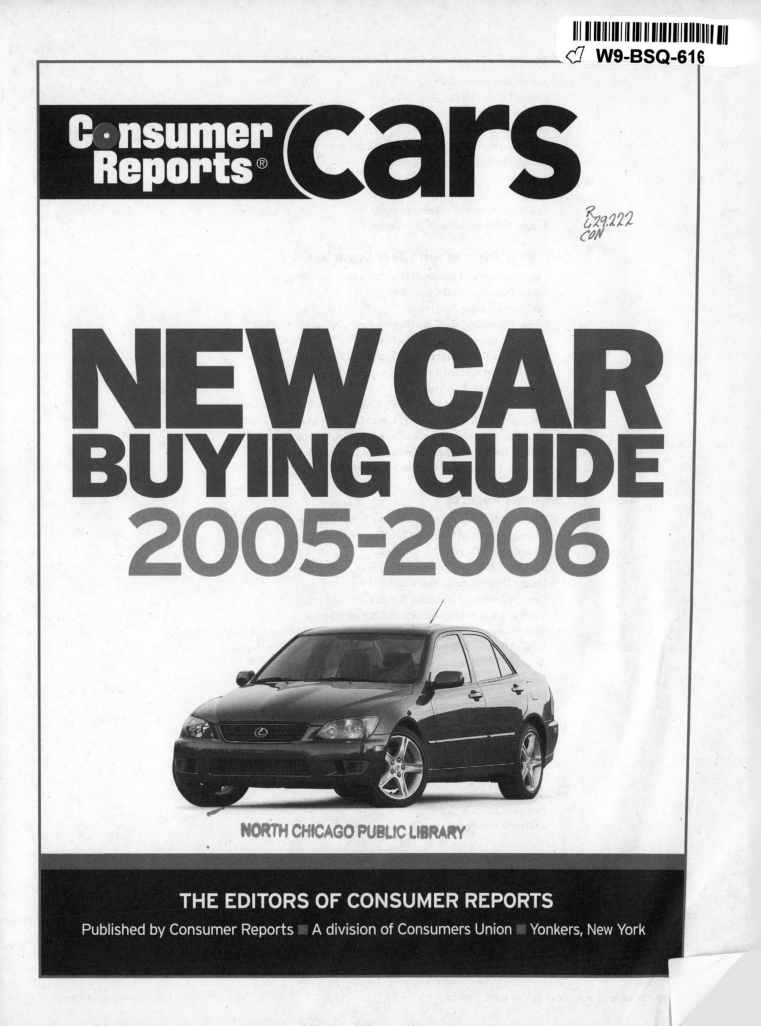

THE EDITORS OF CONSUMER REPORTS

Published by Consumer Reports ■ A division of Consumers Union ■ Yonkers, New York

A Special Publication from Consumer Reports

Automotive Editor Rik Paul
Project Editor Gordon Hard
Deputy Editor, Autos Cliff Weathers
Group Managing Editor Nancy Crowfoot
Coordinating Editor, Autos Jonathan Linkov
Design Manager Rosemary Simmons
Art Director Joseph Ulatowski
Technology Specialist Jennifer Dixon
Production Associate William Breglio
Special Publications Staff Joan Daviet

Consumer Reports Auto Test Department

Vice President and Technical Director Jeffrey A. Asher
Senior Director David Champion
Facilities Manager Alan Hanks
Senior Engineers Jake Fisher, Eugene Petersen, Gabriel Shenhar,
      Richard Small, Jennifer Stockburger
Automotive Data Program Manager Anita Lam
Auto Content Specialist Michael Quincy
Data Analyst Michael Leung
Support Staff Michael Bloch, Frank Chamberlain, Erik Dill, John Ibbotson,
      Mary Reed, Shawn Sinclair, Edward Smith, David Van Cedarfield, Joseph Veselak
Associate Technical Directors Carolyn Clifford-Ferrara, Alan Lefkow
Senior Director, Product Safety and Consumer Science Donald Mays
Director, Statistics and Quality Management Michael Saccucci

Consumer Reports

Vice President and Editorial Director Elizabeth Crow
Associate Editorial Director Christine Arrington
Editor/Senior Director Margot Slade
Director, Editorial Operations David Fox
Design Director, Consumers Union George Arthur
Creative Director, Consumer Reports Tim LaPalme
Vice President, Multimedia Publishing John Sateja
Senior Director & General Manager, CR Information Products Jerry Steinbrink
Senior Director & General Manager, Product & Market Development Paige Amidon
Associate Director, Business Development Carol Lappin
Newsstand Marketing Director Tracey Bowen
Product Manager, Publications Development Lesley Greene
Director, Survey Research Charles Daviet
Research Program Leaders Jacqueline Bruskin, Donato Vaccaro
Manufacturing/Distribution Mark Yatarola
Senior Applications Analyst Usha Srinivasaraghavan

Consumers Union

President James A. Guest
Executive Vice President Joel Gurin

First printing, May 2005
Copyright © 2005 by Consumers Union of United States, Inc., Yonkers, New York 10703.
Published by Consumers Union of United States, Inc., Yonkers, New York 10703.
All rights reserved, including the right of reproduction in whole or in part in any form.
ISSN: 1044-3045
ISBN: 0-89043-999-0

Manufactured in the United States of America

Dodge Grand Caravan

Convertibles & Roadsters

Audi A4
Audi TT
BMW 325Ci/330Ci/**M3**
BMW 6 Series
BMW Z4
Cadillac XLR
Chevrolet Corvette
Chevrolet SSR
Chrysler Crossfire
Chrysler PT Cruiser
Chrysler Sebring
Ford Mustang
Ford Thunderbird
Honda S2000
Lexus SC430
Lotus Elise
Mazda MX-5 Miata
Mercedes-Benz CLK
Mercedes-Benz SLK
Mini Cooper
Mitsubishi Eclipse Spyder
Nissan 350Z
Pontiac Solstice
Porsche Boxster
Saab 9-3
Toyota Camry Solara
Toyota MR2 Spyder
Volkswagen New Beetle

Wagons

Audi A4 Avant
Audi A6 Avant
Audi Allroad
BMW 325i
Chevrolet HHR
Chrysler PT Cruiser
Dodge Magnum
Ford Focus
Ford Taurus
Jaguar X-Type
Kia Rio
Lexus IS300 SportCross
Mazda6
Mercedes-Benz C320
Mercedes-Benz E-Class
Pontiac Vibe
Saab 9-2X
Saab 9-5
Scion xB
Subaru Impreza
Subaru Legacy

Subaru Outback
Saturn Vue
Suzuki Aerio
Suzuki Forenza
Toyota Matrix
Volkswagen Passat
Volvo V50
Volvo V70
Volvo XC70 (Cross Country)

SPORT-UTILITY VEHICLES
Small

Chevrolet Equinox
Chevrolet Tracker
Ford Escape
Honda CR-V
Honda Element
Hyundai Santa Fe
Hyundai Tuscon
Jeep Liberty
Jeep Wrangler
Kia Sorento
Kia Sportage
Land Rover Freelander
Mazda Tribute
Mercury Mariner
Mitsubishi Outlander
Nissan Xterra
Pontiac Aztek
Pontiac Torrent
Saturn Vue
Subaru Forester
Subaru Outback
Suzuki Vitara
Suzuki XL-7
Toyota RAV4

Midsized

Acura MDX
Audi Allroad
BMW X3
BMW X5
Buick Rainier
Buick Rendezvous
Cadillac SRX
Chevrolet TrailBlazer
Chrysler Pacifica
Dodge Durango
Ford Explorer
Ford Freestyle
GMC Envoy
Honda Pilot
Hummer H3
Infiniti FX
Isuzu Ascender
Jeep Grand Cherokee
Land Rover LR3
Land Rover Range Rover
Lexus GX470
Lexus RX330
Lincoln Aviator
Mercedes-Benz M-Class
Mercury Mountaineer

Mitsubishi Endeavor
Mitsubishi Montero
Nissan Murano
Nissan Pathfinder
Porsche Cayenne
Saab 9-7X
Subaru B9 Tribeca
Toyota 4Runner
Toyota Highlander
Volkswagen Touareg
Volvo XC70 (Cross Country)
Volvo XC90

Large

Cadillac Escalade
Chevrolet Suburban
Chevrolet Tahoe
Dodge Durango
Ford Expedition
GMC Yukon
GMC Yukon XL
Infiniti QX56
Hummer H2
Lexus LX470
Lincoln Navigator
Nissan Armada
Toyota Land Cruiser
Toyota Sequoia

MINIVANS

Buick Terazza
Chevrolet Uplander
Chrysler Town & Country
Dodge Caravan/Grand Caravan
Ford Freestar
Honda Odyssey
Kia Sedona
Mazda5
Mazda MPV
Mercury Monterey
Nissan Quest
Pontiac Montana SV6
Saturn Relay
Toyota Sienna

PICKUP TRUCKS
Compact

Chevrolet Colorado
Chevrolet SSR
Dodge Dakota
Ford Explorer Sport Trac
Ford Ranger
GMC Canyon
Honda Ridgeline
Mazda B-Series
Nissan Frontier
Subaru Baja
Toyota Tacoma

Full-sized

Cadillac Escalade EXT
Chevrolet Avalanche
Chevrolet Silverado
Dodge Ram
Ford F-150
GMC Sierra
Lincoln Mark LT
Nissan Titan
Toyota Tundra

7-PASSENGER VEHICLES
All minivans plus these:

Acura MDX
Buick Rendezvous
Cadillac Escalade
Cadillac SRX
Chevrolet Suburban
Chevrolet Tahoe
Chevrolet TrailBlazer EXT
Dodge Durango
Ford Expedition
Ford Explorer
Ford Freestyle
Ford Taurus (wagon)
GMC Envoy XL
GMC Yukon
GMC Yukon XL
Honda Pilot
Isuzu Ascender
Land Rover LR3
Lexus GX470
Lexus LX470
Lincoln Aviator
Lincoln Navigator
Mercedes-Benz E-Class (wagon)
Mercury Mountaineer
Mitsubishi Montero
Nissan Armada
Nissan Pathfinder
Saab 9-7X
Subaru B9 Tribeca
Suzuki XL-7
Toyota 4Runner
Toyota Highlander
Toyota Land Cruiser
Toyota Sequoia
Volvo V70
Volvo XC70 (Cross Country)
Volvo XC90

Nissan Titan

![Consumer Reports cars]

Subaru Legacy

Contents

Introduction

Acura TSX

Ford Focus

CONSUMER REPORTS Auto Resources

CONSUMER REPORTS automotive ratings and information are available in a variety of formats, both in print and online.

CONSUMER REPORTS MAGAZINE. Every monthly issue of CONSUMER REPORTS magazine, except the April Annual Auto Issue, carries a full road-test report comparing a group of competitive vehicles. The April issue is devoted solely to cars.

CONSUMER REPORTS SPECIAL PUBLICATIONS. Throughout the year, CR also produces a number of special auto publications, available in bookstores, on newsstands, or online at *www.ConsumerReports.org*:

- **COMPLETE AUTO PRICING & RATINGS GUIDE**
- **USED CAR BUYING GUIDE**
- **NEW CAR RATINGS & REVIEWS**
- **SUVS, WAGONS, MINIVANS, & TRUCKS**
- **NEW CAR BUYING GUIDE**
- **NEW CAR PREVIEW**
- **BEST & WORST NEW CARS**
- **USED CAR REVIEWS**

CONSUMERREPORTS.ORG features continually updated product Ratings and information. All visitors have free access to helpful advice, safety alerts, recalls, and more. Site subscribers can access all Ratings, reviews, and recent road tests; exclusive reliability information; expert forums and online discussions; and more.

CONSUMER REPORTS CAR PRICE REPORTS. The **New Car Price Service** provides retail and dealer-invoice prices plus current rebates, discounts and unadvertised dealer incentives. It also gives the CR Wholesale Price, which helps you determine what the dealer really paid for the vehicle. The **Used Car Price Service** provides estimates of trade-in values and dealers' selling prices, a worksheet to help you determine a vehicle's value, reliability histories. and more. Call 800-422-1079, or go to *www.ConsumerReports.org*.

CONSUMER REPORTS ONLINE BUYING KITS. The **New Car Buying Kit** is a Web subscription service that provides everything you need to buy your new car. Compare models side by side using customizable interactive Web tools. Get unlimited New Car Price Reports online. Access in-depth, behind-the-scenes reports on all tested cars. All this and more is available at *www.ConsumerReports.org/cr/kit1*. The **Used Car Buying Kit**, another Web subscription service, provides unlimited access to used car pricing, reliability histories, and expert critiques. Available at *www.ConsumerReports.org/cr/ucbk4*.

THE CONSUMERS UNION MISSION: TEST, INFORM, PROTECT

CONSUMER REPORTS publications are produced by Consumers Union, an independent, nonprofit testing and information organization. Founded in 1936, Consumers Union is the largest such organization in the world. We specialize in head-to-head comparison tests of cars and other products, and also provide advice on a broad range of topics of concern to consumers, such as health and nutrition, personal finance, and insurance.

Consumers Union's mission has always been to test products, inform the public, and protect consumers. Our income is derived solely from the sale of CONSUMER REPORTS (in print and online); the sale of our other publications and services; and from nonrestrictive, noncommercial contributions, grants, and fees. We buy all the products we test and accept no free samples. We take no outside advertising and do not let any company use our reports or Ratings for commercial purposes. CONSUMER REPORTS also publishes newsletters on finance and health. Our information appears on TV and radio around the country and in columns found in more than 500 newspapers.

The CONSUMER REPORTS Difference

The New Car Buying Guide is CONSUMER REPORTS' largest, most comprehensive new-car publication. It includes a wealth of information derived from extensive testing, consumer surveys, and professional expertise. In this publication you'll find exclusive vehicle reviews and reliability information, as well as expert buying advice and safety information.

You'll find reviews covering nearly every new model available, Ratings for about 200 tested vehicles, and forecasts of which will likely be the most and the least reliable, as well as safety features and crash-test results, tips on negotiating the best price, and more.

CONSUMER REPORTS has the most comprehensive auto-test program of any U.S. publication, with a full-time staff of auto engineers, technicians, and support staff working at a state-of-the-art, specially equipped, 327-acre auto-test facility in rural Connecticut.

Hands-on, head-to-head testing is at the core of CONSUMER REPORTS' work. By the time a vehicle we've tested earns our "Recommended" check mark, we've driven it on the road and at our track. We've ana-

AT THE TRACK
This test of braking ability on wet pavement is one of the challenging brake tests used to measure stopping distances, pedal feel, and directional control.

lyzed its reliability and factored in accident-avoidance performance and crash- and rollover-test results where that information is available. Unlike competitors that sell their seal of approval to automakers for use in their advertising, we do not put our "Recommended" check mark up for sale.

Interested in how a new car will hold up or in how older cars are faring? CR's latest (2004) annual subscriber survey drew responses for 810,000 vehicles covering 14 trouble spots over eight model years. The reliability information we present is more comprehensive than anything else available and comes from the deepest pool of actual consumer experience.

EMERGENCY HANDLING
Here an SUV is piloted through a zig-zag course of traffic cones at ever increasing speeds. This "avoidance maneuver" helps gauge how a vehicle handles when the driver is attempting to avoid an obstacle in the road.

How CONSUMER REPORTS tests cars

In contrast to other auto publications, which borrow their test vehicles from the auto manufacturers, we buy all the vehicles that go through our rigorous testing program. Posing as ordinary shoppers, CR staffers buy the cars from dealerships, just as you might. Our auto-test staffers anonymously buy 50 or more new vehicles each year, including sedans, minivans, wagons, sporty cars, pickups, and SUVs.

While other reviewers may drive a vehicle for two weeks or less—sometimes only for a few hours—CR's 20-person auto-test staff drives the test cars for six to nine months, sometimes longer. This extended time is sufficient for first impressions to fade and for a car's true character to emerge. The 20-person staff keeps detailed logs of the vehicles' performance, comfort, and convenience-feature operation.

After purchasing a vehicle, CR technicians make a thorough inspection and perform minor adjustments as needed to bring it within the manufacturer's specifications. Any major defects found are repaired by the dealer. CR engineers then conduct more than 50 separate tests and evaluations on each vehicle, including many that aren't typically performed by other reviewers. Track tests include a range of performance tests, such as acceleration, braking, and handling. The engineers push the cars up to and beyond their handling limits to find out how each car behaves under stress. Test engineers also evaluate ride and seat comfort, convenience, interior noise levels, and fuel economy.

Safety is an underlying theme in many of our tests. CR's auto engineers evaluate accident-avoidance capabilities in a series of emergency-handling tests. For crash-test data, CR relies on insurance-industry and government programs. Those results appear with the vehicle profiles that begin on page 38.

Tire testing is another unique offering of CONSUMER REPORTS. CR is the only independent national publication that has a formal, ongoing tire-test program aimed at the consumer. We test a range of tires, including all-season, high-performance, SUV, and winter tires. The key tire tests gauge cornering, emergency handling, and braking performance in wet and dry conditions, as well as evaluating ride comfort, noise levels, and resistance to hydroplaning. All tire types are also tested in snow and on ice.

Expert • Independent • Nonprofit

Buying Advice & Vehicle Ratings

Strategies for getting the right car at the right price.

In an ideal world, a car dealer would exist only to help you find the right vehicle at a fair price with a minimum of fuss. But some dealers are more concerned with selling what they have on the lot than with meeting your particular needs. You can avoid costly pitfalls by following these tips:

5 steps to getting the best price

1. DO YOUR HOMEWORK. Preparation is the key to controlling the process. Going into a showroom without knowing what you want and what it should cost is a good way to get burned. This book can provide you with solid information from our road tests, as well as reliability, safety, and fuel-economy data, but you can consult other sources as well. Since individual preferences vary a lot, you should test drive any car you plan to buy, and consider test driving competing models to familiarize yourself with what else is out there.

If you have a trade-in, learn its approximate worth. That will depend on the vehicle's age, condition, mileage, and equipment, as well as where you trade it in or to whom you sell it. Check local classified-ad publications to see what other people are asking for cars like yours. You can get an idea of your trade-in's value at auto-pricing Web sites such as *www.edmunds.com*, *www.kbb.com*, or with CR's Used Car Price Reports.

ConsumerReports.org offers a free guide to auto-related online services. From CR's home page, type "Autos: Online Resources" in the search field.

2. DON'T PAY STICKER PRICE. Your starting offer should be close to the dealer's actual cost. The dealer invoice price is commonly available on Web sites and in pricing guides. But there are often behind-the-scenes bonuses, such as dealer incentives and hold-backs, that effectively reduce the dealer's cost below the official invoice price.

You can find incentive information at some auto-pricing Web sites, or in CR's New Car Price Reports or New Car Buying Kit (see inside back cover). These include the CR Wholesale Price, which factors in the dealer invoice, holdback, and any incentives or rebates. Start negotiations at 4 to 8 percent over what the dealer paid—or less if the car is not in great demand.

3. NEGOTIATE ONE THING AT A TIME. Salespeople often mix financing, leasing, and trade-in negotiations together. This gives the salesperson an opportunity to play games, inflating one figure while reducing another. Only after you've settled on the price should you discuss financing, leasing, or a trade-in. Negotiate each of those individually.

4. FIGURE FINANCING IN ADVANCE. Compare interest rates at several banks, credit unions, and other lenders along with the dealer's rates. If you are preapproved for a loan, you can keep financial arrangements out of the negotiations. Automakers may offer attractive financing terms, but make sure you qualify for them. Otherwise, the salesperson may sign you up for a higher rate than you could get elsewhere.

5. DON'T PAY FOR EXTRAS YOU DON'T NEED. Dealers often try to sell you extras such as rustproofing, fabric protection, paint sealant, or etching your Vehicle Identification Number (VIN) on windows to deter thieves.

Don't accept those things. If any are pre-printed on the bill of sale, cross them out. You can treat upholstery and apply paint sealant yourself with off-the-shelf products. You can even VIN-etch your windows with a $25 kit.

The incentive game

Automakers have always offered sales incentives, such as cash-back rebates and low-rate financing deals, to sell slow-selling models and end-of-year leftovers. In the past few years, however, rebates and low-cost financing are often found even on newly introduced models.

The key is to pick the car that best suits your needs first and go for the best deal second. A mediocre car is no great bargain at any price. Here are some specific tips:

■ Not everyone qualifies for the low-interest financing offered. Phone the dealer to find out what credit score qualifies a borrower for favorable financing.

■ You can buy your credit scores and reports from the biggest credit-reporting agencies (TransUnion, Equifax, and Experian) for $29.95 from *www.truecredit.com*, or $14.95 each ($44.85 for all three) from *www.myfico.com*. Residents of Western and Midwestern states can get credit reports free from the credit agencies once per year. This service will extend to the rest of the country by September 2005. For details online, see *www.annualcreditreport.com*.

■ Deciding between a low-interest loan and a cash-back rebate can be tricky. Sometimes it can be cheapest to mix and match, say by taking some of the rebate and combining it with a low loan rate. You'll find useful loan calculators at *www.consumerreports.org/wheelingdealing* and *www.bankrate.com*.

■ Don't let an incentive keep you from negotiating. Rebates and low-rate finance deals typically come from the automaker and don't affect the dealer's profit. So don't hesitate to negotiate the final price, just as you would if there were no incentives.

To buy or to lease

Leasing has the advantage of a much lower monthly payment than if you purchased the vehicle with a loan. But leasing is generally more expensive in the long run.

MORE HYBRID VEHICLES COMING

Hybrid powertrains, which combine electric motors with gasoline or diesel engines, have generated a lot of interest since the first one, the Honda Insight, appeared in 1999 as a 2000 model.

At this point there are two types: "mild" and "full" hybrids. A mild hybrid uses a relatively small electric motor as an aid to the gasoline engine, providing extra power when needed. A full hybrid's electric motor (or motors) not only works in tandem with the gasoline engine but can propel the vehicle at low speeds. Full hybrids have more fuel-saving potential than mild hybrids, but much depends on factors such as aerody-namics, vehicle weight, and additional fuel-saving technologies in use.

Toyota introduced the second-generation Prius for 2004. Ford adopted a similar design for the Escape SUV. GM's first hybrids, the full-size Chevrolet Silverado and GMC Sierra pickups, are very mild. They use an integrated 42-volt starter-alternator that allows the engine to shut off when idling and instantly restart when you press the accelerator pedal.

Following is a list of the hybrids available now and in the near future, with the model year of introduction for upcoming models noted in parentheses.

CARS

Full hybrid:
Ford Fusion (2008)
Lexus GS 450h (2007)
Mercury Milan (2008)
Nissan Altima (2006)
Toyota Camry (tentative 2006)
Toyota Prius

Mild hybrid:
Chevrolet Malibu (2007)
Honda Accord Hybrid
Honda Civic Hybrid
Honda Insight

SUVS

Full hybrid:
Chevrolet Tahoe (2007)
Ford Escape Hybrid
GMC Yukon (2007)
Lexus RX400h (2006)
Mazda Tribute (2007)
Mercury Mariner (2005)
Toyota Highlander (2006)

Mild hybrid:
Chevrolet TrailBlazer (2006)
GMC Envoy (2006)
Saturn Vue (2006)

PICKUPS

Mild hybrid:
Chevrolet Silverado 1500
Dodge Ram 2500/3500
 (limited availability) (2005)
GMC Sierra 1500

MINIVANS

Full hybrid:
Toyota Sienna (tentative 2006)

When you lease you're not paying for the entire car, but only for the amount you "use up" while it's in your care, the depreciation. That's why leases have lower monthly payments. With a lease you pay back just the depreciation, plus interest and fees. But worked into the monthly payment is interest on the estimated value of the car at lease end. Why? Because for the years you lease the car you are driving around an asset that belongs to someone else, tying up that capital. Because of the way the finance charges work, you can spend a lot more in interest on a lease than you do with a loan. Leasing generally makes sense only if:

■ You don't exceed the annual mileage allowance—typically 12,000 to 15,000, but sometimes as little as 10,000 miles per year. Extra miles can cost 15 to 25 cents each. It's cheaper to buy more miles up front, but don't buy more than you need.

■ You keep the vehicle in very good shape. "Excess wear and tear" charges can be steep.

■ You plan to turn in your vehicle every two or three years anyway. If you drive your vehicles much longer than that, you're better off buying from the start.

If you think a lease is for you, follow these guidelines:

■ Ask the dealer for the annualized interest rate used to calculate the lease payment. Lease lingo for interest rate is "money factor." Multiply the money factor by 2,400 to get a rough annual percentage rate. Compare that with bank rates. (You can find current rates at *www.bankrate.com.*)

■ Study all the fees. Some contracts make you pay an "acquisition" fee when you initiate the lease and a "disposal fee" at the end. Also ask about "early termination" fees.

MODEL-CHANGE SCORECARD

What's new? What's changed? What's gone?

This rundown includes new and redesigned 2005 and 2006 models, as well as those that have recently passed away.

NEW MODELS

Audi A3 (06)
Audi Q7 (06)
Buick LaCrosse
Buick Lucerne
Buick Terraza
Chevrolet Cobalt
Chevrolet Equinox
Chevrolet HHR (06)
Chevrolet Uplander
Dodge Charger (06)
Dodge Magnum
Ford Five Hundred
Ford Freestyle
Ford Fusion (06)
Honda Ridgeline
Hummer H3 (06)
Hyundai Tucson
Isuzu I-Series pickup ('06)
Land Rover
   Range Rover Sport
Lexus RX400h
Lincoln Mark LT
Lincoln Zephyr (06)

Lotus Elise
Mazda5 (06)
Mercedes-Benz CLS (06)
Mercedes-Benz R-Class (06)
Mercury Mariner
Mercury Milan (06)
Mitsubishi Raider (06)
Pontiac G6
Pontiac Solstice (06)
Pontiac Torrent (06)
Saab 9-2X
Saab 9-7X
Scion tC
Saturn Relay
Subaru B9 Tribeca (06)

REDESIGNED

Acura RL
Audi A6
BMW 3 Series (06)
Cadillac DTS (06)
Cadillac STS
Chevrolet Corvette
Dodge Dakota

Ford Mustang
Honda Civic (06)
Hyundai Accent (06)
Hyundai Elantra (06)
Hyundai Sonata (06)
Infiniti M35/M45
Jeep Grand Cherokee
Kia Sportage
Land Rover LR3 (Discovery)
Lexus IS (06)
Lexus GS300/430
Mazda MX-5 (06)
Mercedes-Benz
   M-Class (06)
Mercedes-Benz SLK
Mitsubishi Eclipse (06)
Nissan Frontier
Nissan Pathfinder
Nissan Xterra
Pontiac Montana SV6
Porsche Boxster
Subaru Legacy/Outback
Toyota Avalon
Toyota Tacoma

Volkswagen Golf (06)
Volkswagen Jetta (06)
Volkswagen Passat (06)
Volvo S40/V50

DISCONTINUED

Buick Century
Buick LeSabre
Buick Park Avenue
Buick Regal
Chevrolet Astro
Chevrolet Cavalier
Chevrolet S-10
Ford Excursion
GMC Envoy XUV
GMC Safari
GMC Sonoma
Isuzu Axiom
Isuzu Rodeo
Mercury Sable
Mitsubishi Diamante
Pontiac Bonneville
Pontiac Sunfire
Toyota Celica
Toyota MR2

■ Check the contract to make sure the monthly payment is derived from the negotiated cost of the car, minus any down payment and trade-in, and not the vehicle's original sticker price.

Extended warranties

When you buy a new car or truck, the salesperson or the dealership's "business manager" will likely urge you to buy, among other add-ons, an extended warranty or service plan. The coverage, which can cost hundreds or even thousands of dollars, kicks in when the manufacturer's basic warranty leaves off, extending warranty coverage for up to several years and/or so-many thousand miles.

CR recommends forgoing an extended warranty, especially if you select a vehicle that has a good reliability record to start with. In any case, don't feel pressured to buy a warranty the same day you buy the car. You can usually buy a plan anytime before the basic warranty expires.

If you do still want an extended warranty, we suggest sticking to a plan offered by the automaker. Third-party coverage a dealer may offer varies enormously in quality, coverage, and price. But you can also buy coverage directly, thus eliminating the dealer altogether. Two well-known direct sellers are Warranty Direct (*WarrantyDirect.com*) and 1 Source Auto Warranty (*1SourceAutoWarranty.com*).

Review any service plan carefully to find out what is and isn't covered, who must perform repairs, and how to file a claim. You also should determine if you need to do anything to keep coverage, such as provide proof you properly maintained the vehicle. If you're buying from a dealer, always negotiate the price. And make sure the plan is transferable if you sell the car.

Owner satisfaction: What hits the spot

A new car is a big expenditure, and we want to be sure it will meet our needs and expectations. Besides performance, reliability, and fuel economy, it's also useful to know how other people who already own the vehicle feel about it. To get a handle on that CR asks its survey respondents whether they would get the same car again if they had it to do all over again.

The car that people most love to love is the Toyota Prius, according to our latest survey of subscribers. About 94 percent of the 1,640 survey respondents who own or lease a redesigned 2004 Prius said they would definitely get one again.

In all, the survey found 32 cars, wagons, minivans, SUVs, and pickups that at least 80 percent of respondents said they would definitely get again. Twenty-five of those vehicles are Japanese makes. Only one U.S. car, the Chevrolet Corvette, made it to the top group. The rest are European luxury sedans and sports cars.

Owner satisfaction doesn't always track with reliability (see page 13). The Mini Cooper and Mercedes-Benz SL, for instance, are among the most satisfying, even though their reliability records are below average. The reason for this might be emotional. Some cars have a certain cache or mystique about them that appeals to their owners. Emotion explains why sporty cars, which are distinctly impractical, make up the largest category of most-satisfied owners.

Among cars that were least satisfying, domestic vehicles accounted for 12 of the 20 in the lineup; Japanese nameplates accounted for 7. The Land Rover Freelander SUV, which has suffered from a woeful reliability record and perhaps other discontents as well, was the only European vehicle in the least-liked lineup.

LIKE IT OR NOT

The owner-satisfaction survey asks

owners and leasers, "Considering all factors (price, performance, reliability, comfort, enjoyment, etc.), would you get this car if you had it to do over again?" Respondents have four choices, ranging from "Definitely would" to "Definitely not" get the same car again. These tables list the percentage of owners who said the would definitely get the same car again.

LEAST SATISFYING

Small sedans	PERCENT
Saturn Ion	49
Mitsubishi Lancer	46
Dodge Neon	44
Chevrolet Cavalier	44
Nissan Sentra	41

Family sedans	
Chrysler Sebring sedan	49
Dodge Stratus sedan	35

Coupes/convertibles	
Chevrolet Cavalier	44
Pontiac Sunfire	44
Mitsubishi Eclipse	42

Minivans	PERCENT
Dodge Caravan (4-cyl.)	38

Midsized SUVs	
Chevrolet TrailBlazer	50
Lincoln Aviator 2WD	50
Chevrolet TrailBlazer EXT	46

Small car-based SUVs	
Mitsubishi Outlander	48
Suzuki Grand Vitara	48
Suzuki XL-7	48
Land Rover Freelander	40

Pickup trucks	
Ford Ranger	49
Mazda B-Series	49

MOST SATISFYING

Small cars	PERCENT
Toyota Prius	94
Scion xB	87
Honda Civic Hybrid	81
Mazda3	80

Family/large sedans	
Toyota Avalon	84
Honda Accord	82

Upscale/luxury sedans	
Lexus LS430	92
Acura TL	87
Acura TSX	83
Jaguar XJ Series	81

Sports/sporty cars	
Honda S2000	89
Chevrolet Corvette	88
Mini Cooper	85
BMW Z4	83
Porsche Boxster	82
BMW M3	82
Subaru Impreza WRX	81
Mazda MX-5 Miata	80

	PERCENT
Coupes/convertibles	
Lexus SC430	85
Mercedes-Benz SL	81
Minivan	
Toyota Sienna	86
Small SUVs	
Honda Element	83
Subaru Forester	81
Midsized SUVs	
Lexus RX330	85
Honda Pilot	83
Toyota Highlander	81
Lexus GX470	81
Toyota 4Runner	80
Large SUVs	
Toyota Land Cruiser	84
Lexus LX470	82
Pickup trucks	
Toyota Tundra	83
Nissan Titan	82

Vehicle Ratings

CONSUMER REPORTS has inaugurated a new and more comprehensive Ratings table that lets you find the scores from CR's road tests with numerous other factors all in one place. The vehicles rated on the following pages are ranked according to how well they performed in CR's formal tests and how, within each category, the vehicles we've tested compare in predicted reliability, safety, owner satisfaction, and fuel economy. Here are some key findings:

■ No vehicles for which we have ratings in all areas did poorly in every area, although the Chevrolet TrailBlazer EXT and GMC Envoy XL SUVs came the closest.

■ There are now 31 vehicles in our Ratings that achieved 25 mpg or better in overall fuel economy. There were 20 last year and only 17 three years ago.

Guide to the ratings

Within each category, vehicles are ranked by their overall test score. Some vehicles appear in multiple categories where appropriate.

Recommended models are divided into two tiers. To earn our first-level recommendation, identified by a ✔ , vehicles have to meet several criteria. They must perform well in our testing; have average or better reliability, according to our latest survey; and, if tested in government and insurance-industry crash tests, provide good overall crash protection based on our crash-protection rating (see below). SUVs and trucks also must not have tipped up in the government's rollover test.

To earn our higher-level and more stringent recommendation, identified by a ✅ , vehicles must meet all of the above requirements and have earned an overall crash-protection rating of very good or excellent (see below). This second tier is intended to provide an extra level of assurance for consumers who place the highest priority on crash protection.

PRICE AS TESTED. This is the approximate Manufacturer's Suggested Retail Price (MSRP) for the version tested, including options and destination charge. Our vehicles are typically equipped with an automatic transmission (unless otherwise noted), power locks/windows/mirrors, air conditioning, and important safety features such as antilock brakes, electronic stability control, and side and side-curtain air bags, when available.

OVERALL TEST SCORE. This is based on the results of more than 45 individual tests that gauge acceleration, braking, handling, comfort, safety, fuel economy, and more.

PREDICTED RELIABILITY. This is our forecast of how well a new car will likely hold up, based on its recent history. We garner that information from our annual subscriber survey, which last year generated 810,000 responses. For more information, see Chapter 2.

OWNER SATISFACTION. This rating also comes from our subscriber survey, and is based on the responses to a question that asks owners and leasers if, considering everything, they would get the same vehicle if they had it to do over again. The scores are based on the percentage of respondents who reported that they would definitely buy the same car again.

A top score of ◉ means 80 percent or more said they would, while a ● means fewer than 50 percent would definitely buy it again. Sometimes we make a prediction about owner satisfaction for a redesigned car if its predecessor had a sterling track record.

ACCIDENT AVOIDANCE. This reflects how capable a vehicle is in helping you avoid an accident through braking, emergency handling, or accelerating out of harm's way. To a lesser extent we also look at driving position, visibility, and seat comfort. All are evaluated in our road tests.

CRASH PROTECTION. This overall rating is given only to vehicles that have been in both IIHS crash tests and at least one NHTSA crash test. **With/Without** indicates whether the vehicle was tested in the IIHS side-crash test with or without side and/or head-protection side air bags.

FUEL ECONOMY. This is the overall fuel economy that a vehicle achieved in CR's real-world tests. The overall mpg figure is based on results from several fuel-economy tests, reflecting a realistic mix of city, country road, and highway driving.

Better ← → Worse (● ◕ ○ ◑ ●)

Within categories, in road test score order

Make & model	Version tested	Price as tested	Road test score (0–100)	Predicted reliability	Owner satisfaction	Accident avoidance	Crash protection	Overall MPG	Highs	Lows
CONVERTIBLES (AUTOMATIC TRANSMISSION)										
✓ Toyota Camry Solara	XLE (V6)	$31,087		○	◑	◕	–	21	Refined powertrain, comfort, quietness, interior quality.	Agility, body quiver, rear visibility.
Ford Mustang	Premium (V6)	28,070		New	New	◑	–	20	Turning circle, solid structure, good looks.	Rear seat, noise, interior materials.
Chrysler Sebring	Limited (V6)	32,715		●	○	◕	–	21	Rear seat, integrated front seat belt.	Acceleration, agility, severe body quiver.
CONVERTIBLES (MANUAL TRANSMISSION)										
Mini Cooper	S	$29,820		◑	●	◕	–	25	Acceleration, handling, fun to drive, turning circle, character, sunroof, easy top operation.	Ride, noise, rear seat, trunk, rear visibility.
Volkswagen New Beetle	GLS 1.8T	27,950		◑	○	◑	–	24	Turning circle, smooth drivetrain, fit and finish.	Rear seat, trunk, rear visibility.
✓ Chrysler PT Cruiser	GT turbo	29,305		◑	○	◑	–	22	Acceleration, rear seat, access.	Rear visibility, turning circle.
SMALL CARS (AUTOMATIC TRANSMISSION)										
✓ Ford Focus	ZX4 SES	$19,080		○	○	●	–/○	24	Agile and fun to drive, steering, braking, ride, interior room, front access.	Interior quality, fuel economy, no rear head rests, IIHS side-crash-test result.
✓ Mazda3	i	18,190		●	●	●	–/○	27	Handling, fuel economy, interior quality, turning circle.	Road noise, small trunk, IIHS side-impact-crash test w/o curtain airbags.
✓ Toyota Prius	–	23,490		●	●	○	–	44	Fuel economy, low emissions, transmission, ride, hatchback versatility, reliability.	Steering feel, multifunction display.
✓ Honda Civic	Hybrid	21,415		●	●	◕	–	36	Fuel economy, low emissions, smooth powertrain, controls.	Acceleration, road noise, trunk.
◔ Toyota Corolla	LE	17,545		●	●	○	◑/○	29	Fuel economy, transmission, controls, reliability, accommodations, access.	Driving position awkward for some, IIHS side-impact-crash test without curtain air bags.
✓ Honda Civic	EX	18,825		●	●	◕	–	29	Engine, fit and finish, fuel economy, controls and displays, reliability.	Ride, road noise.
✓ Hyundai Elantra	GT	17,589		◑	○	◕	○	24	Quietness, ride, warranty, controls and displays.	Lack of agility, fuel economy, optional ABS brakes are hard to find, IIHS side-crash-test result.
Kia Spectra	EX	16,185		NA	NA	○	◑	25	Ride, quietness, fit and finish, standard side and curtain air bags, long warranty.	Acceleration, lack of agility, IIHS side-impact-crash test, ABS may be hard to find.
✓ Subaru Impreza	2.5 RS	20,470		◑	○	◕	◕	22	Handling, ride, all-wheel drive, offset-crash result.	Fuel economy, rear-seat room, no folding rear seat, cargo space.
Nissan Sentra	1.8 S	17,880		◑	●	○	–/◑	26	Fuel economy, interior fit and finish.	Cramped rear seat, braking, IIHS side-impact-crash test.
✓ Scion xB	–	14,995		●	●	◑	–	30	Fuel economy, access, rear seat, cargo capacity, standard stability control, reliability.	Ride, noise, acceleration, turning circle, radio controls.
Suzuki Aerio	LX	16,494		○	NA	○	–	25	Roomy interior, access, driving position, AWD available.	Stiff ride, ABS may be hard to find, IIHS side-impact-crash test.
Chevrolet Cobalt	LS	17,350		New	New	○	◑/○	23	Acceleration, ride.	Steering, engine noise, fuel economy, seat comfort, IIHS side-impact-crash test without side air bags.
Mitsubishi Lancer	ES	16,574		●	●	○	–/○	26	Tight turning circle, fuel economy, offset-crash result.	Handling, acceleration, interior noise, front-seat comfort, IIHS side-impact-crash test.
Scion xA	–	14,445		●	NA	◑	–	30	Fuel economy, access, hatchback versatility.	Ride, noise, acceleration, radio controls.
Saturn Ion	3	18,415		◑	●	○	◑/◑	25	Dent-resistant body panels.	Steering, overall comfort, dash layout, dangerous window switches, fit and finish, IIHS side-impact test.
Suzuki Forenza	S	14,794		NA	NA	○	–	24	Turning circle, audio controls on the steering wheel, fit and finish.	Acceleration, handling, ride, noise, ABS may be hard to find, IIHS side-impact-crash test.
Hyundai Accent	GL	13,779		○	○	○	–	26	Turning circle, fuel economy, long warranty, low price.	Noise, cramped interior, lack of agility, ABS may be hard to find.
Chevrolet Aveo	LS	14,005		NA	NA	○	–	28	Front access, turning circle, fuel economy, hatchback versatility, ABS is widely available.	Acceleration, handling.
Dodge Neon	SXT	17,285		○	●	◑	–/◑	24	Braking, roomy interior.	Ride, noise, fit and finish, turning circle, IIHS side-impact-crash test.

VEHICLE RATINGS

Within categories, in road test score order

Better ◄———► Worse

Make & model	Version tested	Price as tested	Road test score (0–100) P F G VG E	Predicted reliability	Owner satisfaction	Accident avoidance	Crash protection	Overall MPG	Highs	Lows
SMALL CARS (MANUAL TRANSMISSION)										
✓ Mazda3	i	$17,290		◉	◉	◉	–/○	30	Handling, slick manual shifter, fuel economy, interior quality, turning circle.	Road noise, small trunk, IIHS side-impact–crash test w/o curtain air bags.
✓ Toyota Echo	–	13,495		◉	◖	○	–	38	Roomy interior, easy access, fuel economy, interior storage, reliability.	Spartan interior look, ABS may be hard to find.
Kia Spectra	EX	15,185		NA	NA	○	◖	28	Ride, quietness, smooth shifter, fit and finish, standard side and curtain air bags, long warranty.	Lack of agility, IIHS side-impact–crash test, ABS may be hard to find.
✓ Scion xB	–	14,245		◉	◉	◖	–	32	Fuel economy, access, rear seat, cargo capacity, standard stability control, reliability.	Ride, noise, turning circle, radio controls.
Scion xA	–	13,045		◉	NA	◖	–	31	Fuel economy, access, hatchback versatility.	Ride, noise, radio controls.
Suzuki Forenza	S	13,994		NA	NA	○	–	27	Turning circle, audio controls on the steering wheel, fit and finish.	Handling, ride, noise, ABS may be hard to find, IIHS side-impact–crash test.
Honda Insight	–	21,045		NA	NA	◖	–	51	Fuel economy, low emissions.	Ride, noise, cargo room, no air-bag cutoff switch for passenger seat.
Chevrolet Aveo	LS	13,045		NA	NA	○	–	27	Front access, turning circle, fuel economy, hatchback versatility, ABS is widely available.	Acceleration, handling, vague shifter.
FUEL-EFFICIENT CARS										
✓ Toyota Prius	–	$23,490		◉	◉	○	–	44	Fuel economy, low emissions, transmission, ride, hatchback versatility, reliability.	Steering feel, multifunction display.
✓ Honda Civic	Hybrid	21,315		◉	◉	◖	–	36	Fuel economy, low emissions, smooth powertrain, controls.	Acceleration, road noise, trunk.
✓ Toyota Echo	(manual)	13,495		◉	◖	○	–	38	Roomy interior, easy access, fuel economy, interior storage, reliability.	Spartan interior, ABS may be hard to find.
Honda Insight	(manual)	21,045		NA	NA	◖	–	51	Fuel economy, low emissions.	Ride, noise, cargo room, no air-bag cutoff switch for passenger seat.
COMPACT PICKUP										
✓ Ford Explorer Sport Trac	XLT	$29,145		○	◖	○	–	15	Steering feel, composite bed.	Ride, engine noise, off-road ability, tip up of 2WD model in gov't rollover test.
FULL-SIZED PICKUPS										
✓ Toyota Tundra	SR5 (4.7)	$32,100		◉	◉	○	–	14	Ride, quietness, braking, smooth engine, interior quality, reliability.	Turning circle.
✓ Chevrolet Avalanche	1500	40,220		○	◉	○	–	13	Cargo versatility, ride, quietness, full-time four-wheel-drive system.	Fussy to convert midgate, fuel economy, tire grip, visibility, turning circle.
Ford F-150	XLT (5.4)	35,560		●	◉	○	–	14	Ride and handling, quietness, light tailgate, fit and finish, crash-test results.	Braking, access, reliability.
✓ Nissan Titan	SE (5.6)	36,370		○	◉	○	–	13	Powertrain, relatively responsive handling, towing capacity, safety features.	Engine noise, visibility, payload, access, fuel economy, turning circle.
✓ Chevrolet Silverado 1500	Z71 (5.3)	35,610		○	○	○	–	14	Cargo capacity, full-time four-wheel-drive system, quietness.	Ride, turning circle, fit and finish, safety-belt comfort.
✓ GMC Sierra 1500	SLT (5.3)	39,500		○	○	○	–	14	Cargo capacity, full-time four-wheel-drive system, quietness.	Ride, turning circle, fit and finish, safety-belt comfort.
Dodge Ram 1500	SLT (5.7)	36,015		○	○	○	–	11	Large bed, towing, acceleration with the Hemi, crash-test results.	Ride, noise, fuel economy, braking, fit and finish, access, rear seat.
Dodge Ram 1500	SLT (4.7)	33,995		○	○	◖	–	12	Bed size, crash-test results.	Ride, noise, fuel economy, braking, fit and finish, access, rear seat.
FAMILY SEDANS										
✓ Honda Accord	Hybrid (V6)	$30,655		◖	◉	◉	◉	25	Fuel economy, emissions, acceleration, interior room.	No fold-down rear seat.
✓ Volkswagen Passat	GLX (V6)	31,480		○	○	◉	–	21	Safety, comfort, ride, quietness, agility, interior quality.	Premium fuel.
✓ Toyota Camry	XLE (V6)	27,680		◉	◖	◉	◉/○	20	Ride, quietness, powertrain, brakes, access, accommodations, build quality, reliability.	Driver's-seat thigh support, IIHS side-impact-crash test without side air bags.
✓ Honda Accord	EX (V6)	27,365		◖	◉	◉	◉	23	Acceleration, smooth powertrain, driving position, accomodations, ride.	Road noise.

Expert • Independent • Nonprofit

Better ◄———————► Worse

FAMILY SEDANS (continued)

Make & model	Version tested	Price as tested	Road test score (0–100)	Predicted reliability	Owner satisfaction	Accident avoidance	Crash protection	Overall MPG	Highs	Lows
✓ Honda Accord	EX (4-cyl.)	23,515						24	Engine, transmission, ride, fuel economy, accommodations, driving position.	Road noise.
✓ Volkswagen Passat	GLS (4-cyl.)	26,070					–	23	Safety, comfort, ride, handling, interior fit and finish.	Engine hesitation and noise, premium fuel.
✓ Toyota Camry	LE (4-cyl.)	22,065						24	Ride, quietness, transmission, interior room, reliability, fuel economy, controls and displays.	Acceleration, braking, tire grip, IIHS side-impact-crash test without side air bags.
✓ Subaru Legacy	2.5 GT (4-cyl.)	30,370			New			18	Steering, agility, ride, acceleration, transmission, fit and finish.	Fuel economy, at-the-limit handling, no folding rear seat.
✓ Nissan Maxima	3.5 SE (V6)	33,080					–	21	Acceleration, accommodations.	Ride, turning circle, torque steer, windshield reflections, gauges.
✓ Nissan Altima	3.5 SE (V6)	28,280					–/○	20	Acceleration, braking, tire grip, roomy rear seat.	Ride, turning circle, premium fuel, fuel economy, IIHS side-impact-crash test without side air bags.
Volkswagen Passat	GLS TDI (4-cyl.)	26,275		NA	NA		–	28	Fuel economy, cruising range, ride, handling, interior room, fit and finish.	Acceleration, engine noise, emissions.
Mazda6	i (4-cyl.)	21,930					–/○	23	Handling, braking, driving position.	Turning circle, noise, IIHS side-impact-crash test without side air bags.
Mazda6	s (V6)	27,790					–/○	20	Handling, braking, driving position.	Turning circle, ride, fuel economy, IIHS side-impact-crash test without side air bags.
✓ Toyota Prius	(4-cyl.)	23,490					–	44	Fuel economy, low emissions, transmission, ride, hatchback versatility, reliability.	Steering feel, multifunction display.
Chevrolet Malibu	Base (4-cyl.)	21,125					○/○	24	Ride, handling, transmission, interior room, offset-crash result.	Noisy engine, IIHS side-impact-crash test without side air bags.
Chevrolet Malibu	LS (V6)	22,960					○/○	23	Interior space, ride, quietness, offset-crash result.	Driver seat, tire grip, IIHS side-impact-crash test without side air bags.
✓ Nissan Altima	2.5 S (4-cyl.)	24,380					–/○	23	Acceleration, interior room, controls and displays.	Engine noise, turning circle, IIHS side-impact-crash test without side air bags.
Mitsubishi Galant	GTS (V6)	27,094		NA	NA			20	Acceleration, engine and transmission, headlights, crash-test results.	Stiff ride, noise, fuel economy, turning circle, premium fuel.
Volvo S40	2.4i (5-cyl.)	29,145		New	New			23	Turning circle, center console design, available integrated booster seats.	Ride, engine noise, tight rear seat.
Mitsubishi Galant	ES (4-cyl.)	20,944		NA	NA			23	Acceleration, transmission, crash-test results.	Ride, seat comfort, engine noise, turning circle.
✓ Hyundai XG350	L (V6)	25,989					–	19	Ride, braking, long warranty.	Clumsy handling, head room, fuel economy, turning circle.
Kia Optima	EX (V6)	22,745		NA	NA			20	Ride, interior fit and finish, long warranty.	Agility, driving position, fuel economy IIHS side-impact-crash test.
✓ Ford Taurus	SES (V6)	25,445					–	22	Ride, interior room, trunk.	Noise, brakes, turning circle, no rear head restraints.
Chrysler Sebring	Touring (V6)	23,140					–/○	21	Acceleration.	Ride, handling, access, noise, IIHS side-impact-crash test.
Dodge Stratus	ES (V6)	22,585					–/○	21	Acceleration.	Ride, handling, access, noise, IIHS side-impact-crash test.
Pontiac G6	Base (V6)	23,080		New	New		–	21	Transmission, controls and displays, acceleration.	Braking, seat comfort, ride, interior, turning circle.
✓ Chevrolet Impala	LS (V6)	27,520						20	Steering, trunk, crash-test results.	Unsettled ride, road noise, rear seat comfort, fit and finish, fuel economy.
Suzuki Verona	LX (6-cyl.)	19,794		NA	NA			20	Cargo space, seating for seven in a pinch.	Fuel economy, ride, seat comfort, turning circle, IIHS side-impact-crash test.
Pontiac Grand Prix	GT (V6)	28,255					–	20	Controls.	Ride, braking, access, driving position, visibility, rear seat, fuel economy.
Chrysler Sebring	(4-cyl.)	21,080					–/○	21	Government front-crash test results.	Ride, noise, access, rear seat, fit and finish, no rear head restraints, IIHS side-impact-crash test.
Dodge Stratus	SXT (4-cyl.)	20,620					–/○	21	Government front-crash test results.	Ride, noise, access, rear seat, fit and finish, no rear head restraints, IIHS side-impact-crash test.

Within categories, in road test score order

Better ●———————○———————● Worse

Make & model	Version tested	Price as tested	Road test score (0–100, P F G VG E)	Predicted reliability	Owner satisfaction	Accident avoidance	Crash w/wo side air bags	Overall MPG	Highs	Lows
LARGE SEDANS										
✓ Buick Park Avenue	Ultra	$42,805		○	○	◑	–	21	Acceleration, braking, quietness, ride, rear-seat room.	Uncomfortable front shoulder belts, turning circle.
Ford Five Hundred	SEL (FWD)	24,795		New	New	○	–	21	Interior room, trunk, access, visibility, rear-seat comfort.	Engine noise, braking.
Mercury Montego	(FWD)	24,995		New	New	○	–	21	Interior room, trunk, access, visibility, rear-seat comfort.	Engine noise, braking.
Ford Five Hundred	SEL (AWD)	28,800		New	New	○	–	20	Interior room, trunk, access, visibility, rear-seat comfort.	Engine noise, braking, initial acceleration.
Mercury Montego	(AWD)	29,080		New	New	○	–	20	Interior room, trunk, access, visibility, rear-seat comfort.	Engine noise, braking, initial acceleration.
Chrysler 300	C	37,480		New	New	◑	–	16	Rear seat room, acceleration, transmission.	Visibility, suspension noise, ride, fuel economy.
Chrysler 300	Touring	30,255		New	New	◑	–	19	Rear seat room.	Visibility, suspension noise, halogen headlights.
Buick LaCrosse	CXL	31,450		New	New	◑	–	18	Ride, quietness, fit and finish, headlights.	Rear seat room, fuel economy.
Kia Amanti	–	29,740		NA	NA	○	–	18	Isolation, access, fit and finish.	Ride control, clumsy handling, acceleration, braking, fuel economy.
✓ Lincoln Town Car	Signature	42,715		○	○	○	–	17	Spacious trunk, rear seat, crash test results.	Handling, limited rear visibility, noisy engine, fuel economy.
✓ Buick LeSabre	Limited	34,700		○	○	○	–	20	Spacious cabin, smooth transmission.	Wind noise, unsupportive seats.
Ford Crown Victoria	LX	30,900		○	○	○	–	16	Large trunk, crash-test results.	Engine noise, seat comfort, ride, fuel economy.
✓ Mercury Grand Marquis	LSE	32,765		○	○	○	–	16	Large trunk, crash-test results.	Engine noise, seat comfort, ride, fuel economy.
UPSCALE SEDANS										
✓ Acura TL	–	$33,670		○	●	●	●	23	Powertrain, fuel economy, handling, quietness, fit and finish, value.	Turning circle, rear seat doesn't fold.
✓ BMW 3 Series	330i	41,345		○	◑	◑	●	22	Powertrain, agility, ride, brakes, fit and finish, overall safety.	Cramped rear seat.
✓ Lexus IS300	–	33,889		●	◑	◑	–	21	Handling, powertrain, acceleration, braking, reliability.	Ride, tight quarters.
✓ Lexus ES330	–	35,709		●	◑	◑	●	22	Ride, quietness, interior fit and finish, crash-test results.	Lackluster handling, no fore-aft steering-wheel adjustment, no folding rear seat.
Mercedes-Benz C-Class	C320	41,560		◖	○	◑	◑	21	Acceleration, handling, ride, brakes, quietness, safety gear.	Overly complicated controls.
Lincoln LS	Premium (V6)	40,250		◖	◖	○	–	19	Ride, handling, transmission, controls.	Shallow trunk.
✓ Acura TSX	–	29,760		◑	●	◑	–	23	Engine and transmission, fuel economy, handling, driving position, controls, fit and finish, crash-test results.	Ride, turning circle, requires premium fuel.
✓ Audi A4•	1.8T (CVT)	30,370		○	○	◑	–	24	CVT transmission, fuel economy, fit and finish, turning circle.	Rear seat, low-speed ride, requires premium fuel.
✓ Audi A4	3.0 Quattro	38,660		○	○	◑	–	20	Handling, driver's seat comfort, fit and finish, safety gear.	Low-speed ride, tight rear seat.
✓ Cadillac CTS	–	39,425		○	◑	◑	–	20	Handling, engine and transmission.	Rear seat, some confusing controls, pesky oversights.
Saab 9-3	Aero	36,845		●	○	◑	–	21	Handling, braking.	Ride, noise, rear seat, reliability.
✓ Infiniti G35	–	34,960		◑	◑	◑	–	20	Acceleration, engine and transmission, audio sound.	Controls, at-the-limit handling (even with stability control).
Jaguar X-Type	3.0	39,120		●	◖	◑	◑	19	Ride, handling, standard all-wheel drive.	Noise, accommodations, shift gate, reliability.
✓ Saab 9-5	Arc	36,755		◑	○	◑	◑	21	Interior room, crash-test results.	Ride, road and wind noise.
✓ Volvo S60	2.5T	34,980		○	○	◑	–	22	Responsive engine, offset crash-test results.	Ride, rear seat room, visibility, turning circle.

* replaced by 2.0T

Within categories, in road test score order

Make & model	Version tested	Price as tested	Road test score	Predicted reliability	Owner satisfaction	Accident avoidance	Crash protection	Overall MPG	Highs	Lows
LUXURY SEDANS										
✓ Lexus LS430	–	$69,534		◉	◉	◑	–	19	Ride, quietness, powertrain, fit and finish, reliability, turning circle, ergonomics.	Agility.
Mercedes-Benz S-Class	S430	83,800		●	○	◉	–	18	Ride, handling, quietness, seat comfort, interior fit and finish.	Reliability, controls, cup holders.
Mercedes-Benz E-Class	E320	54,570		●	○	◉	–	20	Ride, handling, turning circle, quietness, fit and finish, seat comfort.	Some controls, reliability, brake-pedal feel.
BMW 5 Series	530i	54,770		●	◑	◉	–	20	Engine, transmission, quietness, braking, seat comfort.	Complicated controls, cabin storage, reliability.
Cadillac DeVille	DHS	56,990		◑	◑	○	–	19	Strong and smooth powertrain, ride, roominess, quietness.	Reliability, agility.
Audi A8	L	76,470		NA	NA	◉	–	17	All-wheel drive, spacious rear seat, quietness, fit and finish.	Cumbersome controls, fuel economy.
Jaguar S-Type	4.2	53,170		●	◑	◉	–	19	Acceleration, transmission, controls.	Rear-seat room, trunk, reliability.
Jaguar XJ8	Vanden Plas	73,295		NA	◑	◉	–	19	Powertrain, acceleration, interior ambience, handling, controls.	Ordinary ride, interior room, shallow trunk.
Volvo S80	T6	48,000		◑	○	◉	–	19	Acceleration, interior room, crash-test results.	Ride, agility, shifter, turning circle.
BMW 7 Series	745Li	84,145		●	◑	◑	–	18	Acceleration, quietness, interior room.	Complicated and distracting controls, reliability.
SPORTS/SPORTY CARS										
✓ Audi S4	–	$50,870		○	NA	◉	–	20	Acceleration, braking, interior fit and finish.	Rear seat, handling not much better than other A4s.
✓ BMW M3	–	56,495		○	◉	◉	–	19	Acceleration, handling, braking, fit and finish.	Hard to drive smoothly, noise, rear seat.
✓ Subaru Impreza	WRX STi	32,870		◑	◉	◉	–	20	Acceleration, braking and handling, all-wheel drive, offset-crash result.	Ride, no folding rear seat, noise.
Mazda RX-8	–	31,305		◑	◑	◉	–	18	Smooth-revving engine, handling, ride, shifter, braking, four-passenger capacity.	Fuel economy, reliability
✓ Cadillac CTS-V	–	52,685		○	◉	◉	–	17	Acceleration, powertrain, handling, steering, braking.	Safety belts, fuel economy, complicated multifunction controls, pesky oversights.
Mitsubishi Lancer	Evolution	29,094		NA	NA	◉	–	20	Acceleration, handling, braking, all-wheel drive.	Ride, noise, turning circle, IIHS side-impact-crash test.
✓ Subaru Impreza	WRX	25,470		◑	◑	◑	–	21	Acceleration, handling, all-wheel drive, offset-crash result.	No folding rear seat.
✓ Toyota Celica	GT-S	25,460		◉	◑	◉	–	28	Acceleration, handling, fuel economy, controls, hatchback versatility, reliability.	Rear-seat room.
Ford Mustang	GT (V8)	29,020		New	New	◉	–	20	Acceleration, handling, V8 sound.	Rear seat, low-speed ride, interior quality, trunk space.
Mini Cooper	Base	18,295		◑	◉	◑	–	30	Handling agility, styling, fuel economy, turning circle.	Ride, engine power, tire grip (in Base model), rear seat.
✓ Honda Civic	Si	20,085		◉	◉	◑	–	26	Shifter, controls, fuel economy, engine smoothness and refinement.	Steering, ride, road noise.
✓ Nissan 350Z	Touring	34,800		○	◉	◉	–	22	Acceleration, braking, handling.	Ride, noise, visibility, no cutoff switch for passenger air bag.
✓ Acura RSX	Type-S	24,240		◉	○	◑	–	26	Acceleration, fuel economy, slick shifter action.	Ride, noise, rear accommodations.
Pontiac GTO	–	34,295		NA	NA	◑	–	17	Acceleration, rear-seat comfort, V8 sound.	Imprecise shifter, heavy clutch, access, fuel economy, trunk space.
Chrysler Crossfire	Coupe	29,920		NA	NA	◉	–	22	Engine, acceleration, braking.	Ride, steering feel and response, shifter, controls, visibility, interior room.
Hyundai Tiburon	GT (V6)	21,389		●	○	◑	–	22	Acceleration, fuel economy, long warranty.	Ride, driving position, tight quarters, reliability.
ROADSTERS										
✓ Toyota MR2	–	$25,685		◉	NA	◉	–	31	Acceleration, braking, agility, transmission, fuel economy.	Tiny storage space.
Audi TT	Quattro Convertible	42,320		◑	◑	◉	–	22	Interior craftsmanship, all-wheel drive.	Ride, noise, shifter feel, view out.
✓ Ford Thunderbird	Premium	41,900		○	◑	◑	–	17	Acceleration, braking, style.	Head room, body shake, fuel economy, ordinary handling.

Within categories, in road test score order

Better ← → Worse

Make & model	Version tested	Price as tested	Road test score (0–100) P F G VG E	Survey results: Predicted reliability	Owner satisfaction	Safety: Accident avoidance	Crash protection	Fuel economy: Overall MPG	Highs	Lows
SMALL SPORT-UTILITY VEHICLES										
✔ Subaru Forester	2.5 X	$22,670		◐	◐	◑	◐	21	Ride, agility, steering, fuel economy, controls and displays, crash-test results, reliability.	Gated shifter.
✔ Toyota RAV4	–	22,155		◐	◑	◑	◐/○	21	Interior flexibility, agility, fuel economy, visibility, standard stability control, offset-crash result, reliability.	Narrow cabin, side-opening rear door, no rear bumper, IIHS side-impact-crash test without side air bags.
✔ Pontiac Vibe	(AWD)	22,610		◑	◑	◑	–	24	Interior flexibility, access, rear-seat room, transmission, AWD available.	Noisy engine, acceleration, awkward driving position.
✔ Toyota Matrix	XR (AWD)	20,095		◑	◑	◑	–	24	Interior flexibility, access, rear-seat room, transmission, AWD available.	Noisy engine, acceleration, awkward driving position.
✔ Subaru Baja	–	23,570		◑	◑	◑	–	20	Handling, front-seat comfort, cargo versatility.	Acceleration, bed size.
✔ Honda CR-V	EX	24,065		◐	◑	○	◐	21	Fuel economy, ride, rear seat, reliability, turning circle, fuel economy, value, crash-test results.	Road noise.
Ford Escape	XLT (V6)	26,545		◑	⊖	○	◑◐/○	18	Agility, interior room.	Tire grip, fuel economy, IIHS side-impact-crash test without side air bags, tip up in gov't rollover test.
Mazda Tribute	s (V6)	27,020		◑	⊖	○	◑◐/○	18	Agility, interior room.	Tire grip, fuel economy, IIHS side-impact-crash test without side air bags, tip up in gov't rollover test.
✔ Honda Element	EX	22,240		◐	◑	◑	–/○	20	Braking, transmission, cargo space, reliability.	Ride, road noise, load capacity, visibility, IIHS side-impact-crash test.
✔ Hyundai Santa Fe	GLS (2.7)	22,639		◑	◑	○	◑	18	Ride, quietness, controls, accommodations, long warranty, value.	So-so fuel economy and handling.
✔ Mitsubishi Outlander	XLS	24,524		◑	●	○	–/○	20	Braking, access.	Acceleration, noise, cargo volume, turning circle, IIHS side-impact-crash test.
Saturn Vue	(V6)	26,810		●	○	○	–/○	19	Engine, transmission.	Seats, inconsistent steering, fit and finish, IIHS side-impact-crash test, tip up in gov't rollover test.
Chevrolet Equinox	LT	26,360		New	New	○	–	17	Roomy rear seat, access.	Wind noise, fuel economy, fit and finish, agility, cargo room, tip up in gov't rollover test.
✔ Suzuki XL-7	EX	28,394		○	●	○	–/–	17	Cargo space, seating for seven in a pinch.	Fuel economy, ride, seat comfort, turning circle.
✔ Kia Sorento	LX	24,865		○	◑	○	–	15	Off-road ability, controls, towing capacity, interior quality, long warranty.	Agility, ride, fuel economy.
Land Rover Freelander	SE	27,795		●	●	◑	–	17	Ride, routine handling, braking, seat comfort, off-road ability.	Acceleration, noise, fuel economy, transmission, controls, IIHS side-impact-crash test, reliability.
✔ Jeep Liberty	Sport (V6)	24,310		○	⊖	○	–	15	Turning circle, off-road ability.	Fuel economy, ride, access.
Pontiac Aztek	–	25,410		◑	⊖	○	–	17	Transmission, cargo space.	Visibility, fuel economy, ride, fit and finish, no rear wiper.
MIDSIZED SPORT-UTILITY VEHICLES										
✔ Lexus RX330	–	$44,833		◐	◐	◑	–	18	Ride, quietness, powertrain, interior fit and finish.	Pricey options, cargo capacity.
✔ Honda Pilot	EX-L	34,835		◑	◐	◑	–	17	Powertrain, handling, ride, standard stability control, interior flexibility, fit and finish, access, turning circle.	Road noise.
✔ Toyota Highlander	Limited (V6)	35,155		◐	◑	◑	–	19	Powertrain, access, ride, fuel economy, controls, reliability, standard stability control, optional third-row seat, crash-test results.	Agility.
✔ Nissan Murano	SL	36,240		◑	◑	◑	–	19	Acceleration, transmission, fuel economy, handling, rear seat, access.	Stiff ride, noise, rear visibility, premium fuel.
Cadillac SRX	(V8)	53,730		○	◑	◑	–	16	Ride, handling, acceleration, rear-seat comfort, offset-crash result.	Small third-row seat, seat-mounted shoulder belts, some unintuitive controls.
✔ Volvo XC70	–	43,360		○	◑	◑	–	18	Seat comfort, interior flexibility, safety gear, available integrated booster seats.	Ride, fuel economy.
✔ Acura MDX	Touring	43,045		◐	◑	◑	–	17	Powertrain smoothness, ride, crash-test results, reliability.	Braking, emergency handling.
✔ Infiniti FX35	(V6)	39,960		◑	◑	◑	–	18	Acceleration, handling, transmission.	Ride, rear visibility, cargo capacity, turning circle.

Expert • Independent • Nonprofit

Within categories, in road test score order

Better ◀———————▶ Worse

Make & model	Version tested	Price as tested	Road test score (0–100, P F G VG E)	Predicted reliability	Owner satisfaction	Accident avoidance	Crash w/wo side air bags	Overall MPG	Highs	Lows

MIDSIZED SPORT-UTILITY VEHICLES (continued)

Make & model	Version tested	Price as tested	Road test score	Predicted reliability	Owner satisfaction	Accident avoidance	Crash w/wo side air bags	Overall MPG	Highs	Lows
BMW X5	3.0i	$49,370	(bar)	◖	○	○	–	17	Powertrain, steering, front-seat comfort, fit and finish, crash-test results.	Choppy ride, optional xenon headlights can produce glare to oncoming drivers, reliability.
BMW X3	2.5i	40,195	(bar)	NA	NA	◖	–	17	Handling, engine and transmission.	Ride, so-so acceleration and fuel economy, pricey options.
✓ Lexus GX470	–	51,787	(bar)	○	⊙	◖	–	15	Powertrain, quietness, fit and finish, off-road ability, offset-crash result.	Agility, small third-row seat, fuel economy.
✓ Mitsubishi Endeavor	XLS	32,394	(bar)	⊙	○	○	–	17	Acceleration, transmission, ride, rear seat room, reliability.	Road noise, requires premium fuel.
✓ Toyota 4Runner	SR5 (V6)	33,330	(bar)	◖	⊙	◖	–	16	Quietness, powertrain refinement, off-roading, towing, cargo volume.	Fuel economy.
✓ Chrysler Pacifica	Touring	33,995	(bar)	○	○	◖	–	16	Ride, handling, interior versatility, access, crash-test results.	Powertrain, vision, fuel economy.
Volvo XC90	T6	46,815	(bar)	●	○	○	–	15	Flexible interior, safety features.	Fuel economy, shifter, transmission, reliability.
Volkswagen Touareg	(V6)	43,645	(bar)	●	○	○	–	15	Interior quality, quietness, off-road ability.	Acceleration, fuel economy, controls, reliability.
✓ Ford Explorer	XLT (V6)	34,625	(bar)	○	◖	○	–	16	Interior versatility, standard stability control.	Noisy engine, off-road ability.
✓ Dodge Durango	Limited 5.7 (V8)	39,620	(bar)	○	◖	○	–	12	Ride, interior room, towing capacity.	Fuel economy, braking, location of rear wiper switch, engine noise.
✓ Buick Rendezvous	CXL	36,242	(bar)	○	◖	○	–	16	Transmission, cabin amenities, interior flexibility.	Acceleration, agility, fuel economy, visibility, controls and displays.
Mitsubishi Montero	Limited	36,394	(bar)	NA	NA	○	–	14	Transmission, front seat comfort, view out, interior fit and finish, off-road ability.	Disconcerting emergency handling, ride, fuel economy.
Chevrolet TrailBlazer	LS	33,775	(bar)	●	●	○	–	15	Quiet interior, acceleration, access.	Unimpressive handling, braking, fuel economy, uncomfortable front safety belts, reliability.
GMC Envoy	SLE	34,935	(bar)	●	◖	○	–	15	Quiet interior, acceleration, access.	Unimpressive handling, braking, fuel economy, uncomfortable front safety belts, reliability.
Chevrolet TrailBlazer	EXT LT	36,875	(bar)	●	◖	◖	–	13	Ride, seating capacity.	Handling, braking, fuel economy, fit and finish, front safety belts, turning circle, reliability.
GMC Envoy	XL SLT	39,750	(bar)	●	◖	◖	–	13	Ride, seating capacity.	Handling, braking, fuel economy, fit and finish, front safety belts, turning circle, reliability

LARGE SPORT-UTILITY VEHICLES

Make & model	Version tested	Price as tested	Road test score	Predicted reliability	Owner satisfaction	Accident avoidance	Crash w/wo side air bags	Overall MPG	Highs	Lows
✓ Toyota Land Cruiser	–	$55,590	(bar)	⊙	⊙	○	–	14	Powertrain, ride, quietness, off-road ability, fit and finish, seats up to eight, reliability.	Sloppy emergency handling, fuel economy, price.
Nissan Armada	LE	43,370	(bar)	●	○	○	–	13	Acceleration, transmission, roomy interior, towing, cargo capacity.	Ride, fuel economy, visibility, engine noise, turning circle, reliability.
✓ Toyota Sequoia	Limited	46,705	(bar)	◖	◖	○	–	15	Refined powertrain, standard stability control, rear seat.	Stiff ride, clumsy handling, step-in height.
Ford Expedition	Eddie Bauer	47,335	(bar)	●	○	◖	–	12	Power-folding third-row seats, third-seat comfort, interior flexibility.	Acceleration, braking, fuel economy, reliability.
✓ Dodge Durango	Limited 5.7 (V8)	39,620	(bar)	○	◖	○	–	12	Ride, interior room, towing capacity.	Fuel economy, braking, location of rear wiper switch, engine noise.
✓ Chevrolet Tahoe	LT	48,175	(bar)	○	◖	○	–	13	Acceleration, transmission, ride at low speeds, rear seat.	Fit and finish, fuel economy, third-row comfort, tip up of non-ESC version in gov't rollover test.
✓ GMC Yukon	SLT	48,835	(bar)	○	◖	○	–	13	Acceleration, transmission, ride at low speeds, rear seat.	Fit and finish, fuel economy, third-row comfort, tip up of non-ESC version in gov't rollover test.

VEHICLE RATINGS

Within categories, in road test score order

Better ●——○——● Worse

Make & model	Version tested	Price as tested	Road test score (0–100: P F G VG E)	Predicted reliability	Owner satisfaction	Accident avoidance	Crash protection	Overall MPG	Highs	Lows
MINIVANS										
✓ Honda Odyssey	EX	$32,610		⊖	○	○	–	19	Engine and transmission, ride, handling, interior flexibility, fit and finish, standard safety equipment.	No telescopic steering wheel.
✓ Toyota Sienna	XLE	34,909		⊖	⊙	○	–	19	Ride, quietness, engine and transmission, interior flexibility, fit and finish, headlights, telescoping steering wheel, turning circle, crash-test results, optional all-wheel drive.	Confusing option packages, stopping distances.
Nissan Quest	3.5 SL	26,430		●	○	○	–	18	Spacious and flexible interior, ride, handling, quietness, access, crash-test results.	Turning circle, controls and displays, reliability.
Mazda MPV	ES	32,340		●	○	○	–	19	Compact exterior dimensions, retractable rear side windows.	Ride, interior room, acceleration, reliability.
✓ Chrysler Town & Country	Limited	37,115		○	○	⊖	–	17	Interior flexibility.	Seat comfort, interior trim materials, some controls, coarse engine.
✓ Dodge Grand Caravan	SXT	34,140		○	○	⊖	–	17	Interior flexibility.	Seat comfort, interior trim materials, some controls, coarse engine.
Ford Freestar	SEL	33,285		○	○	⊖	–	17	Access, crash-test results.	Noisy engine, unsettled ride, turning circle, value.
Mercury Monterey	Luxury	35,610		○	NA	○	–	17	Access, crash-test results.	Noisy engine, unsettled ride, turning circle, value.
Buick Terraza	CX	29,845		New	New	○	–	17	Optional all-wheel drive.	Ride, noise, agility, acceleration, interior flexibility, squeaks and rattles, headlights, rear blind spot.
Chevrolet Uplander	LS	27,205		New	New	○	–	17	Optional all-wheel drive.	Ride, noise, agility, acceleration, interior flexibility, squeaks and rattles, headlights, rear blind spot.
Pontiac Montana SV6	–	25,660		New	New	○	–	17	Optional all-wheel drive.	Ride, noise, agility, acceleration, interior flexibility, squeaks and rattles, headlights, rear blind spot.
Saturn Relay	3	30,895		New	New	○	–	17	Optional all-wheel drive.	Ride, noise, agility, acceleration, interior flexibility, squeaks and rattles, headlights, rear blind spot.
Kia Sedona	EX	26,785		⊖	⊖	○	–	16	Long warranty.	Acceleration, fuel economy, ride, handling, turning circle.
WAGONS AND HATCHBACKS										
Volkswagen Passat	GLX 4Motion	$34,230		●	○	⊙	–	18	Ride comfort, quietness, handling, accommodations, safety, fit and finish.	Requires premium fuel, reliability.
✓ Volkswagen Passat	GLS (4-cyl.)	28,945		○	○	⊖	–	21	Roominess, comfort, ride, handling, safety, interior fit and finish.	Requires premium fuel.
✓ Ford Focus	ZXW SE	20,490		○	○	⊖	–	23	Agility, ride, accommodations, ergonomics, value.	Road noise, no handle on rear hatch, IIHS side-impact-crash test.
✓ Subaru Outback	2.5i	28,670		⊖	⊖	○	–	21	Steering, ride, fit and finish, controls, crash-test results.	Acceleration, braking, at-the-limit handling.
Mazda6	s	25,840		⊖	⊖	⊖	–	19	Handling, interior room.	Unresponsive transmission, turning circle, IIHS side-impact-crash test.
✓ Volvo XC70	–	43,360		○	⊖	⊖	–	18	Seat comfort, interior flexibility, safety gear, available integrated booster seats.	Ride, fuel economy.
✓ Pontiac Vibe	Base (FWD)	21,155		⊖	⊖	⊖	–	26	Interior flexibility, fuel economy, access, rear-seat room, transmission, AWD available.	Noisy engine, awkward driving position, acceleration.
✓ Toyota Matrix	XR (AWD)	20,095		⊖	⊖	⊖	–	24	Interior flexibility, access, rear-seat room, transmission, AWD available.	Noisy engine, acceleration, awkward driving position.
✓ Ford Focus	ZX5 SE	18,750		○	○	⊙	–	24	Handling, ride, access.	Road noise, IIHS side-impact-crash test.
Chevrolet Malibu Maxx	LS (V6)	24,085		⊖	○	⊖	–	21	Transmission, rear-seat room, interior versatility, controls and displays, front and rear access.	Tire grip, rear-wiper-switch location, IIHS side-impact-crash test without side air bags.
Volvo V50	T5 (AWD)	35,270		New	New	⊖	–	20	Turning circle, available integrated child-booster seats.	Stiff ride, road noise, tight rear seat, small cargo capacity.
✓ Chrysler PT Cruiser	Limited	23,250		⊖	○	⊖	–	18	Interior flexibility, easy access.	Acceleration with base engine, fuel economy, turning circle.
✓ Subaru Impreza	Outback Sport	20,370		⊖	○	⊖	–	22	All-wheel drive, offset-crash result.	Cargo volume, brake-pedal feel.
Dodge Magnum	SXT	28,895		New	New	○	–	19	Rear seat room.	Visibility, braking, turning circle, modest cargo area.
✓ Scion xB	–	14,995		⊙	⊙	⊖	–	30	Fuel economy, access, rear seat, cargo capacity, standard stability control, reliability.	Ride, noise, acceleration, turning circle, radio controls.

CHAPTER

2

Survey highlights
24

**How automakers
fared**
24

**Reliability
forecast**
27

Reliability:
How Will Today's Cars Hold Up?

While new cars are more reliable than ever, it's the Asian makers that still stand out.

There are few things more aggravating than a new car that starts to fall apart right away or that has to go back to the dealer time and time again. To help you avoid that, CONSUMER REPORTS compiles reliability data that tells you how well older cars are holding up as well as how new cars will likely fare in the future.

To gauge reliability, CONSUMER REPORTS surveys its millions of magazine and online subscribers every year. The respondents are asked about serious problems they have experienced with their own vehicles within the past 12 months. The latest (2004) survey yielded data on some 810,000 vehicles.

The difference between best and worst is quite striking. From the latest survey data CR predicts that the sporty Lexus IS300 and the Mitsubishi Endeavor SUV will likely be the most reliable models, with about 80 percent fewer problems than the average new model. At the other end of the scale is the Lincoln Navigator SUV with about 180 percent more problems than the average.

The gap between Asian makes, particularly Japanese brands, and Detroit's Big Three has been narrowing for years, and last year American cars and trucks continued to edge closer to Asian makes. European vehicles continued to be among the least reliable overall.

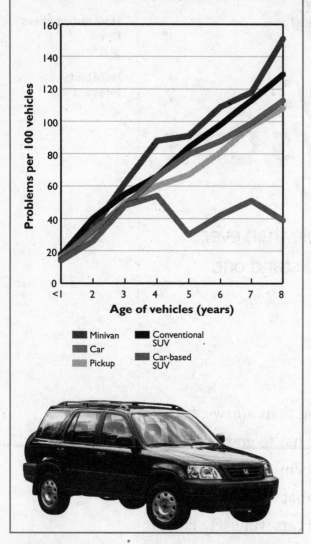
CAR-BASED SUVs
The Honda CR-V, above, and similar models from Subaru and Toyota account for the low problem rate for older car-based SUVs. At the time those reliable makes provided the only members of the segment.

Survey highlights

■ Japanese and Korean automakers once again produced the most trouble-free vehicles overall. See the chart on page 25 for problem-rate comparisons.

■ DaimlerChrysler, Ford, and General Motors inched a little closer to Asian automakers with an overall problem rate of 17 per hundred, down from 18 the year before. Asian makers remained unchanged at 12 problems per 100.

■ European automakers continued to trail behind. BMW, Jaguar, Land Rover, Mercedes-Benz, and Volkswagen had more than their share of problems. Audi and Volvo were slightly better.

■ The first wave of gas/electric hybrids are proving to be very reliable cars. The second-generation Toyota Prius and the Honda Civic Hybrid were among the most trouble-free models.

■ Our surveys indicate that cars often have more problems in their first year after introduction or redesign than they have later on. So in general it's a good idea to wait awhile for manufacturers to address the early teething problems.

While all cars develop more problems as they age, a model that starts out troublesome often stays that way. The graph on page 25 illustrates that point. It compares problem rates across several annual surveys for the Jeep Grand Cherokee. In the first year of its 1999 redesign the Grand Cherokee started with a very high problem rate and continued to have lots of problems as that 1999 version aged. The 2000 and 2001 versions started out with far fewer problems and continued to have fewer problems than the 1999 as they aged.

■ Minivans and car-based SUVs have very different reliability histories from other types of vehicles. (See "Some Types Age Better," above.) The poor showing for minivans is largely the result of the minivan market being dominated by unreliable domestic models for years. Even Honda and Toyota have had trouble making their minivans as trouble-free as their other vehicles. With car-based SUVs, the trend line hops around a bit: The oldest models look better than some of the newer ones. That's because this market segment was dominated by Toyota, Honda, and Subaru between 1997 and 2000, and problem rates were fairly low. In 2001, when domestic makers started building car-based SUVs such as the Ford Escape, subpar reliability increased the trouble rate for that vehicle type. It got even worse when BMW and Land Rover introduced the car-based X5 and Freelander, respectively.

How automakers fared

While domestic makers continue to have an average problem rate about 40 percent higher than that of their Asian counterparts for their newest models, they are improving slightly every year. Here are the specifics, based on predicted reliability for 2005 models:

FORD: A STUDY IN EXTREMES. Some Ford vehicles have proven to be very reliable; others have been extremely trouble-prone. The Ford Focus hatchback, for example, was the most reliable Ford product in our survey—about 26 percent better than the average model. The Ford Focus and Escape continue to improve and are now among the more reliable domestic products. But the Lincoln Navigator, at about 180 percent worse than average, was by far Ford's (and the survey's) worst.

DAIMLERCHRYSLER: AVERAGE PERFORMANCE. The Chrysler part of DaimlerChrysler has been close to the overall industry average, albeit with some highs and lows. The PT Cruiser continued to shine as Chrysler's most reliable vehicle, 33 percent better than average. The Sebring convertible was at the bottom of the Chrysler barrel, at 52 percent worse than the average.

GENERAL MOTORS: SOME IMPROVEMENTS. General Motors has made overall improvements, although the results haven't been uniformly good. GM's compact pickups, the Chevrolet Colorado and GMC Canyon, had a very promising first year—unusual for any carmaker. They and the otherwise lackluster Buick Century were GM's most reliable vehicles. The badly dated Chevrolet Astro and GMC Safari, retired this year, remained unreliable to the end. On the other hand, the Cadillac CTS sedan, which had a poor outing its first year made a significant turnaround in its second and now has improved to average.

EUROPE: STRUGGLING. Volkswagen's Touareg SUV turned in one of the worst records among new vehicles, landing on our charts at 136 percent worse than average. European SUVs in general have had a lot of problems. The BMW X5, Porsche Cayenne, and the first-generation Mercedes-Benz M-Class were worse than average. The Mercedes-Benz E-Class and the turbo version of the Volkswagen New Beetle were also worse than average. Among the few bright spots are the Audi A4 V6, the turbodiesel VW Golf, the outgoing BMW 3 Series, and the Volvo XC70, all with average reliability.

ASIA: ALL NOT QUIET ON THE EASTERN FRONT. Subaru showed significant improvement, with above average reliability for all its vehicles. It suffered last year, largely because of the poor showing of its new Baja truck.

Overall, the best brands are Toyota's which include Scion and Lexus, followed by Subaru, Honda, and Acura.

HOP ON A NEW DESIGN?

It's usually best to wait before buying a newly redesigned model. Problem rates climb as cars age, but the first model year of a redesign is often more troublesome than its successor years. The problem rates of the Jeep Grand Cherokee from its 1999 redesign to 2000 and 2001 models illustrate that.

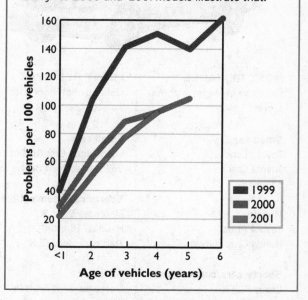

ASIAN BRANDS STILL LEAD

This graph plots average problem rates for vehicles up to eight years old. Detroit edged a little closer to Asian makes last survey while the Europeans lost ground. Asian makers remain comfortably ahead.

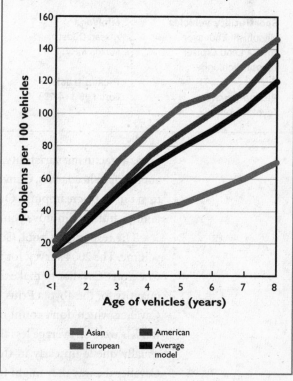

HOW NEW CARS ARE LIKELY TO HOLD UP

MOST RELIABLE
Listed by category with top scorers first.

Small cars
Toyota Echo
Toyota Corolla
Scion xB

Hybrids
Toyota Prius
Honda Civic Hybrid

Sporty cars/convertibles
Lexus SC430
Toyota Celica
Acura RSX

Sedans
Lexus IS300
Toyota Camry
Lexus LS430

Sport-utility vehicles
Mitsubishi Endeavor
Toyota Land Cruiser
Toyota Highlander

Pickup truck
Toyota Tundra

LEAST RELIABLE
Listed by category with worst scorers first

Small cars
Volkswagen Golf (turbo)
Volkswagen New Beetle

Sporty cars/convertibles
Mercedes-Benz SL
Hyundai Tiburon
Mercedes-Benz CLK

Sedans
Mercedes-Benz S-Class
Jaguar S-Type
BMW 7 Series

Sport-utility vehicles
Lincoln Navigator
Land Rover Freelander
Volkswagen Touareg

Minivans
Nissan Quest
Mazda MPV

Pickup truck
Ford F-150 (4WD)

Nissan's showing was disappointing because its new or redesigned models have had high problem rates. The redesigned 2004 Quest minivan and the new Armada SUV were among the worst last year; the Titan pickup was better.

Although Hyundai had much better than average reliability overall, some models trailed. Worst was the Tiburon, at 92 percent worse than the average new car.

The fine print

To be included in the reliability scores, the CR reliability survey requires a minimum sample size of about 100 vehicles. Big sellers such as the Honda Accord or Ford Explorer will generate thousands of responses, while low-volume vehicles such as the Porsche Boxster may barely make the cut.

We compile Reliability Histories (found on the vehicle-profile pages starting on page 38) that span eight model years. We summarize each year's overall score into a composite, the Reliability Verdict.

For Predicted Reliability, CR averages the most recent three years of reliability verdicts (in this case 2002, 2003, and 2004), provided that the 2005 version is substantially identical. If the vehicle doesn't have three years' data available, either because it hasn't been around that long or CR lacks sufficient sample size, then we may base Predicted Reliability on only one or two years' data. In rare cases CR makes a prediction on a newly introduced or redesigned model if the brand or model has had a consistently outstanding track record.

In general a vehicle's recent past is the best indicator of its immediate future. But not infallibly so. An individual vehicle can go either way because of manufacturing variability. With even the most trouble-free models, some examples are apt to create headaches. Conversely, some percentage of the most trouble-prone models will turn out to be creampuffs. Our forecasts, therefore, deal with probabilities rather than certainties, but you improve your odds if you stick with the most reliable models and brands.

The respondent pool, CONSUMER REPORTS subscribers, doesn't always track with sales volume. The 2004 survey, for instance, gathered too few responses on the mass-market 2004 Chevrolet Cavalier to make a reliability judgment for that year, but it gathered a generous quantity for the Toyota Prius, whose sales were much fewer. Possibly, rental-fleet sales of the Cavalier, which don't count in our survey, accounted for the low turnout. Also, the newest models were on average less than six months old at the time of the survey. Consumers don't usually queue up early in the model year to purchase an aging, unchanged car like the Cavalier the way they might for a hot commodity like the second-generation Prius.

RELIABILITY FORECAST

The charts here and on the next page delineate our predictions of reliability for this year's new cars. To create these predictions we calculate an overall reliability score for the past three model years, in this case 2002, 2003, and 2004, provided the vehicle hasn't changed significantly in that time. Extra weight is given to some components, including the engine, transmission, and drive system. Then we average together those three years' worth of reliability scores, and compare the result with the average of all cars in the survey for those three years. The all-car average is the zero line in the charts. The bars represent the percentage by which each vehicle was better or worse than the all-car average.

At the bottom of each chart is a Predicted Reliability score, based on a five-point scale. You will note that average stretches 20 points on either side of the zero line, so it's possible for a car to have average predicted reliability even if its bar is in the negative zone. A broken bar indicates a percentage that extends beyond the chart.

In cases where a model was new or redesigned last year, or where we simply lack data, we may rely on one year's data. Those vehicles are labeled with an asterisk (*).

Most brand-new or redesigned models don't appear here because they are too new to have established a track record. In rare instances we make predictions for a new or redesigned model, if the manufacturer's or model's history has been consistently outstanding.

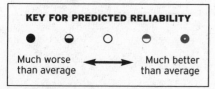

KEY FOR PREDICTED RELIABILITY

● ◗ ○ ◖ ◉

Much worse ←——————→ Much better
than average   than average

SPORTS/SPORTY CARS

	% WORSE	AVERAGE	% BETTER

-80 -40 -20 0 20 40 80

- Toyota Celica
- Acura RSX
- Mazda MX-5 Miata
- Subaru Impreza WRX
- Porsche 911, Carrera
- Ford Thunderbird
- Honda S2000
- BMW Z4
- Nissan 350Z
- Audi TT
- Mazda RX-8*
- Mini Cooper
- Hyundai Tiburon* (-92%)

PREDICTED RELIABILITY ● ◗ ○ ◖ ◉

COUPES & CONVERTIBLES

	% WORSE	AVERAGE	% BETTER

-80 -40 -20 0 20 40 80

- Lexus SC430
- Chevrolet Monte Carlo
- Chrysler Sebring Coupe*
- Dodge Stratus Coupe*
- Toyota Camry Solara*
- Chrysler Sebring Convertible
- Mercedes-Benz CLK (-84%)
- Mercedes-Benz SL* (-135%)

PREDICTED RELIABILITY ● ◗ ○ ◖ ◉

SMALL CARS

	% WORSE	AVERAGE	% BETTER

-80 -40 -20 0 20 40 80

- Toyota Echo
- Toyota Corolla
- Honda Civic
- Mazda3*
- Mitsubishi Lancer (non-turbo)
- Subaru Impreza (non-turbo)
- Hyundai Elantra
- Ford Focus Sedan
- Suzuki Aerio*
- Hyundai Accent
- Dodge Neon
- Nissan Sentra
- Saturn Ion
- Volkswagen Golf
- Volkswagen New Beetle

PREDICTED RELIABILITY ● ◗ ○ ◖ ◉

FAMILY CARS

	% WORSE	AVERAGE	% BETTER

-80 -40 -20 0 20 40 80

- Toyota Prius*
- Toyota Camry
- Pontiac Grand Prix*
- Nissan Maxima*
- Subaru Outback H6
- Subaru Legacy/ Outback (4-cyl.)
- Honda Accord
- Chevrolet Impala
- Hyundai XG350
- Nissan Altima
- Ford Taurus Sedan
- Volkswagen Passat (FWD)
- Mazda6
- Chevrolet Malibu*
- Chrysler Sebring Sedan
- Dodge Stratus Sedan
- Volkswagen Passat (AWD)
- Pontiac Grand Prix (Supercharged)*

PREDICTED RELIABILITY ● ◗ ○ ◖ ◉

LARGE CARS

	% WORSE	AVERAGE	% BETTER

-80 -40 -20 0 20 40 80

- Ford Crown Victoria
- Mercury Grand Marquis
- Lincoln Town Car
- Buick LeSabre
- Buick Park Avenue

PREDICTED RELIABILITY ● ◗ ○ ◖ ◉

LUXURY CARS

	% WORSE	AVERAGE	% BETTER

-80 -40 -20 0 20 40 80

- Lexus LS430
- Infiniti Q45
- Volvo S80
- Cadillac DeVille
- BMW 5 Series*
- Mercedes-Benz E-Class (-85%)
- Jaguar S-Type (-107%)
- BMW 7 Series (-108%)
- Mercedes-Benz S-Class (-124%)

PREDICTED RELIABILITY ● ◗ ○ ◖ ◉

UPSCALE CARS

	% WORSE	AVERAGE	% BETTER

-80 -40 -20 0 20 40 80

Lexus IS300
Acura TSX*
Infiniti G35
Lexus ES330
Saab 9-5
Volvo S60 (FWD)
Cadillac CTS
Acura TL*
BMW 3 Series
Audi A4
Lincoln LS
Mercedes-Benz C-Class
Volvo S60 (AWD)
Saab 9-3
Jaguar X-Type (-89%)

PREDICTED RELIABILITY ● ◐ ○ ◑ ◉

WAGONS & HATCHBACKS

	% WORSE	AVERAGE	% BETTER

-80 -40 -20 0 20 40 80

Scion xB*
Toyota Matrix
Pontiac Vibe
Subaru Impreza Wagon
Subaru Outback H6
Chrysler PT Cruiser
Ford Focus Hatchback
Ford Focus Wagon
Ford Taurus Wagon
Volvo V70/XC70

PREDICTED RELIABILITY ● ◐ ○ ◑ ◉

MINIVANS

	% WORSE	AVERAGE	% BETTER

-80 -40 -20 0 20 40 80

Toyota Sienna*
Chrysler Town & Country (ext, 2WD)
Dodge Grand Caravan (2WD)
Ford Freestar*
Mercury Monterey*
Chrysler Town & Country (reg)
Dodge Caravan
Kia Sedona
Mazda MPV
Nissan Quest* (-115%)

PREDICTED RELIABILITY ● ◐ ○ ◑ ◉

MIDSIZED SUVS

	% WORSE	AVERAGE	% BETTER

-80 -40 -20 0 20 40 80

Mitsubishi Endeavor*
Toyota Highlander
Acura MDX
Honda Pilot
Nissan Murano
Infiniti FX
Toyota 4Runner
Lexus RX330*
Lexus GX470
Chrysler Pacifica*
Buick Rendezvous
Ford Explorer
Mercury Mountaineer
Buick Rainier*
BMW X5
Cadillac SRX*
Lincoln Aviator
Chevrolet TrailBlazer
GMC Envoy
Porsche Cayenne*
Volvo XC90 (-120%)
Volkswagen Touareg* (-136%)

PREDICTED RELIABILITY ● ◐ ○ ◑ ◉

LARGE SUVS

	% WORSE	AVERAGE	% BETTER

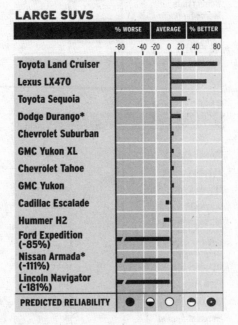

-80 -40 -20 0 20 40 80

Toyota Land Cruiser
Lexus LX470
Toyota Sequoia
Dodge Durango*
Chevrolet Suburban
GMC Yukon XL
Chevrolet Tahoe
GMC Yukon
Cadillac Escalade
Hummer H2
Ford Expedition (-85%)
Nissan Armada* (-111%)
Lincoln Navigator (-181%)

PREDICTED RELIABILITY ● ◐ ○ ◑ ◉

SMALL SUVS

	% WORSE	AVERAGE	% BETTER

-80 -40 -20 0 20 40 80

Toyota RAV4
Honda Element
Honda CR-V
Subaru Forester
Mitsubishi Outlander*
Hyundai Santa Fe
Ford Escape
Mazda Tribute
Kia Sorento
Suzuki Grand Vitara, XL-7
Jeep Liberty
Jeep Wrangler
Pontiac Aztek
Saturn Vue
Land Rover Freelander (-177%)

PREDICTED RELIABILITY ● ◐ ○ ◑ ◉

COMPACT PICKUP TRUCKS

	% WORSE	AVERAGE	% BETTER

-80 -40 -20 0 20 40 80

Chevrolet Colorado*
GMC Canyon*
Subaru Baja*
Ford Ranger
Mazda B-Series
Ford Explorer Sport Trac

PREDICTED RELIABILITY ● ◐ ○ ◑ ◉

FULL-SIZED PICKUP TRUCKS

	% WORSE	AVERAGE	% BETTER

-80 -40 -20 0 20 40 80

Toyota Tundra
Ford F-150 (2WD)*
Dodge Ram 1500
Nissan Titan*
Chevrolet Avalanche
Chevrolet Silverado 1500
GMC Sierra 1500
Ford F-150 (4WD)*

PREDICTED RELIABILITY ● ◐ ○ ◑ ◉

Expert • Independent • Nonprofit

Making Sense of Safety Information

Where to find safety information and what features to look for.

Safety is a key part of any vehicle buying decision, but it's not easy to assess a vehicle's overall safety characteristics. This chapter highlights the various safety issues you should consider and where to find additional information.

Crash protection

How well a vehicle protects its occupants depends mostly on its structural design and safety systems. Using safety belts is the single most important step you can take to protect yourself. Air bags provide additional protection but work best with belted passengers.

No one can say for sure what will happen in an actual crash, but the best indications come from independent crash tests. The two organizations that perform those tests are the federal government's National Highway Traffic Safety Administration (NHTSA) and the Insurance Institute for Highway Safety (IIHS), a private research group supported by auto insurers.

NHTSA conducts two types of crash tests: full frontal and side impact. NHTSA tests are a good indication of how well a vehicle's safety belts and air bags protect occupants in specific types of impact. Crash-test ratings can be found in the "Safety comparisons" chart (page 32) or at *www.nhtsa.dot.gov*.

SIDE IMPACT
Of the 16 small cars initially tested in the new IIHS side-crash test, 14 did poorly, including this Dodge Neon.

PHOTO: IIHS

Offset crash
The IIHS offset-frontal-crash test impacts just part of a vehicle's front end.

The IIHS tests vehicles in an offset-frontal crash, the more common type of head-on crash, and has recently inaugurated a side-crash series as well. Vehicles are rated as Good, Acceptable, Marginal, or Poor.

In the frontal crash a vehicle runs at 40 mph into a deformable barrier. Instead of engaging the whole front end of the car, though, only the part in front of the driver hits the barrier. This test challenges a vehicle's structural integrity and its ability to protect the area around the driver without collapsing. The IIHS side-impact test simulates a T-bone crash where an SUV or pickup crashes at 31 mph into the middle of the driver's-side passenger compartment. Ratings can be found in the "Safety comparisons" chart (page 32) and at the IIHS's Web site, *www.hwysafety.org*.

Both NHTSA and IIHS frontal-crash results are comparable only within a vehicle's weight class. If the vehicle weights are very dissimilar, the results could be very different.

THE SIZE AND WEIGHT FACTOR. All else being equal, larger and heavier vehicles are safer than smaller, lighter ones in a crash. If a big, heavy vehicle crashes into a smaller, lighter one, a lot of the crash energy is transferred to the smaller vehicle. This, in turn, helps to better protect the bigger vehicle's occupants at the expense of the smaller one's.

Accident avoidance

A vehicle's ability to help keep you out of an accident can be just as important as its ability to protect you in a crash. The two most important factors contributing to accident avoidance are braking and emergency handling.

BRAKING. A vehicle's braking system has to stop the vehicle in as short a distance as possible and keep it under control at the same time. CONSUMER REPORTS' tests measure braking performance on both dry and wet pavement and evaluate the effectiveness of a vehicle's antilock brake system (ABS).

EMERGENCY HANDLING. The more controllable and secure a vehicle is when pressed to its handling limits, the better your ability to avoid an accident. CONSUMER REPORTS rates emergency handling on the basis of three tests. One is a series of double-lane-change maneuvers on a course set off with traffic cones. This test is used to evaluate a vehicle's handling in a situation where a driver has to quickly steer around an obstacle on the road. Vehicles are scored on how fast they can execute the maneuver without knocking over any cones, as well as on how controllable and predictable they remained. In the other tests, vehicles are pushed to their cornering limits around a circular blacktop "skid pad" and on a twisty, mile-long handling course.

OTHER ACCIDENT-AVOIDANCE FACTORS. Acceleration, driving position, visibility, and even seat comfort also can affect accident avoidance. Good acceleration helps you merge safely, good visibility lets you see potential hazards better, and a comfortable seat and driving position help limit driver fatigue.

An overall accident-avoidance rating for tested models is included in the vehicle

Expert • Independent • Nonprofit

ratings chart beginning on page 14 and in the vehicle profiles that start on page 38. The profiles also include scores for the individual factors that make up the accident-avoidance rating.

Rollover resistance

NHTSA conducts both static (still) and dynamic (moving vehicle) evaluations to determine how rollover-prone a vehicle might be. The agency uses a five-star rating system of rollover likelihood, called the Rollover Resistance Rating.

In the dynamic test, which was inaugurated with 2004 vehicles, vehicles are subjected to a series of sharp turns that push them to their handling limits. NHTSA's rollover scores predict the probability of a rollover in a single-vehicle crash. One star represents a greater than 40 percent chance of rollover, while five stars represent a less than 10 percent chance. NHTSA's Web site (*www.safercars.gov*) covers many 2001 and newer vehicles. The 2004 and newer vehicle scores include results of the dynamic test.

The static measurement, which is based on a vehicle's track width and center-of-gravity height, accounts for the lion's share of the star rating, regardless of what happens in the dynamic test. NHTSA maintains that its combined scoring system predicts actual rollover propensity better than the old system did. In any event, about a dozen current pickups and SUVs tipped up in NHTSA's dynamic test. CONSUMER REPORTS does not recommend vehicles that tipped up, regardless of how many stars they have earned.

To see if a vehicle tipped, check the tables starting on page 32 or at NHTSA's *www.SaferCar.gov* Web site: Select a 2004 or newer vehicle, click on its name, scroll down to Rollover Details, and then look at "Dynamic Test."

ROLLOVER TEST
In the government's dynamic rollover test, vehicles are equipped with outriggers to prevent them from tipping over completely should they have a tendency to do so. A number of pickups and SUVs have tipped up in this test. If that happens we don't recommend them.

Child safety

Child-safety seats save lives and should be used until a child is big enough to use the vehicle's regular safety belt. However, securing a child seat can sometimes be difficult. If you're buying a child seat, try it in your car first, to make sure it can be cinched up securely and easily. All new vehicles now have a universal system called LATCH (Lower Anchors and Tethers for CHildren) that is designed to make attachment easier and more secure. But CR has found the attachment points in many cars are hard to access. So if you are looking at a new car, check to see if your existing child seat (or any other) can be installed without undue hassle.

BLIND SPOTS. Every year, children are killed because drivers don't see them while backing up. That's mostly because the children are lost in the vehicle's blind spot, the area behind a vehicle that the driver cannot see. The problem is worst with minivans, SUVs, and pickups. To check a vehicle's blind spot, sit in the driver's seat while a friend walks back from the rear, holding a hand at about waist level. When you can see the hand through the back window it'll tell you how large the blind spot is. Before backing up, get out and check behind the vehicle, and keep an eye on any nearby children.

Some SUVs and minivans are equipped with a rear-view video camera that can aid in avoiding a backover accident. They are far more effective than back-up beepers.

Safety features and crash-test ratings

The safety comparisons chart that follows lets you compare safety features and crash-test scores for all available models, listed alphabetically. Here is a guide to each column:

Traction/stability and ABS identify the vehicles with these features. **Traction control** helps maintain traction in slippery conditions. **Electronic stability control** helps prevent skidding sideways. A NHTSA study said that cars equipped with ESC were involved in 30 percent fewer fatal single-vehicle crashes than those without and that SUVs with ESC were involved in 63 percent fewer such crashes. An IIHS study reported that cars and SUVs with ESC were involved in 56 percent fewer fatal single-vehicle crashes than comparable vehicles without it. **ABS** (Antilock Brake System) ensures that a driver can stay on course under hard braking.

Air bags notes the availability of side air bags in the front and rear of the vehicle as well as separate head-protection air bags. The basic side-impact air bag is a cushion that protects the torso. Head-protection side air bags are catching on. The most common design uses curtain-type side air bags, which spread across both the front and rear side windows. Besides providing head protection, they help prevent occupants from being ejected.

Safety-belt pretensioners take up slack on a safety belt during a frontal crash. They help to keep occupants positioned correctly prior to an air-bag deployment. **Center-rear safety belt.** A three-point belt is the safest type, and almost all new vehicles use it. **DRL** (daytime running lights) is a system that runs the low-beam headlights at a reduced intensity, aiding visibility.

Crash tests are our interpretation of published government and insurance-industry results. See page 29 more information.

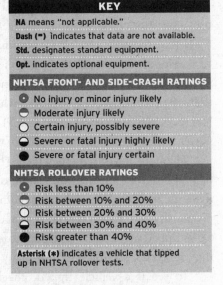

KEY

NA means "not applicable."
Dash (–) indicates that data are not available.
Std. designates standard equipment.
Opt. indicates optional equipment.

NHTSA FRONT- AND SIDE-CRASH RATINGS
- No injury or minor injury likely
- Moderate injury likely
- Certain injury, possibly severe
- Severe or fatal injury highly likely
- Severe or fatal injury certain

NHTSA ROLLOVER RATINGS
- Risk less than 10%
- Risk between 10% and 20%
- Risk between 20% and 30%
- Risk between 30% and 40%
- Risk greater than 40%

Asterisk (∗) indicates a vehicle that tipped up in NHTSA rollover tests.

SAFETY COMPARISONS

MAKE & MODEL	Traction/ stability	ABS	Side F/R	Head protection	Pretensioners	Center-rear belt	DRL	IIHS offset Frontal	IIHS side Side air bags (with/without)	NHTSA front Drv./pass.	NHTSA side Drv./rear pass.	NHTSA rollover rating 2WD/4WD
Acura MDX	Std./std.	Std.	Std./No	Std.	Front	3-point	No	Good	–/–	◉/◉	◉/◉	–/–
Acura RL	Std./std.	Std.	Std./No	Std.	Front	3-point	Std.	–	–/–	◉/◉	◉/◉	–/◉
Acura RSX	No/No	Std.	Std./No	No	Front	NA	No	–	–/–	◉/◉	◒/–	◒/–
Acura TL	Std./std.	Std.	Std./No	Std.	Front	3-point	No	Good	Good/NA	◉/◉	◉/◉	◒/–
Acura TSX	Std./std.	Std.	Std./No	Std.	Front	3-point	No	Good	–/–	◉/◉	◉/◉	◒/–
Audi A3	Std./std.	Std.	Std./No	Std.	Front & rear	3-point	No	–	–/–	–/–	–/–	–/–
Audi A4	Std./std.	Std.	Std./opt.	Std.	Front & rear	3-point	No	Good	–/–	◒/◉	◉/◉	◒/–
Audi A6	Std./std.	Std.	Std./opt.	Std.	Front & rear	3-point	Opt.	–	–/–	–/–	–/–	–/–
Audi A8	Std./std.	Std.	Std./std.	Std.	Front & rear	3-point	Std.	–	–/–	–/–	–/–	–/–
Audi TT	Std./std.	Std.	Std./No	NA	Front	NA	No	–	–/–	–/–	◉/–	◉/–
BMW 3 Series	Std./std.	Std.	Std./opt.	Std.	Front	3-point	Opt.	Good	–/–	◒/◉	○/◉	◒/–
BMW 5 Series	Std./std.	Std.	Std./opt.	Std.	Front	3-point	Opt.	Good	–/–	–/–	–/–	–/–
BMW 6 Series	Std./std.	Std.	Std./No	Std.	Front	NA	Opt.	–	–/–	–/–	–/–	–/–
BMW 7 Series	Std./std.	Std.	Std./opt.	Std.	Front & rear	3-point	No	–	–/–	–/–	–/–	–/–
BMW X3	Std./std.	Std.	Std./opt.	Std.	Front	3-point	Opt.	–	–/–	–/–	–/–	–/–
BMW X5	Std./std.	Std.	Std./opt.	Std.	Front	3-point	Opt.	Good	–/–	◉/◉	◉/◉	◉/–
BMW Z4	Std./std.	Std.	Std./NA	NA	Front	NA	Opt.	–	–/–	◒/◉	○/–	◉/–
Buick LaCrosse	Opt./opt.	Opt.	No/No	Opt.	Front	3-point	Std.	–	–/–	◉/◉	○/○	◒/–

| MAKE & MODEL | AIR BAGS | | | | SAFETY BELTS | | DRL | CRASH & ROLLOVER TESTS | | | | |
| | Traction/ stability | ABS | Side | Head protection | Pretensioners | Center-rear belt | | IIHS offset | IIHS side | NHTSA front | NHTSA side | NHTSA rollover rating |
			F/R					Frontal	Side air bags (with/without)	Drv./pass.	Drv./rear pass.	2WD/4WD
Buick LeSabre	Opt./opt.	Std.	Opt./No	No	No	3-point	Std.	Good	–/–	⊖/○	⊖/⊖	⊖/–
Buick Park Avenue	Opt./opt.	Std.	Std./No	No	No	Lap	Std.	Good	–/–	⊖/○	⊖/⊖	⊖/–
Buick Rainier	Opt./No	Std.	No/No	Opt.	No	3-point	Std.	Marg.	–/–	○/○	⊖/○	○/⊖
Buick Rendezvous	Opt./No	Opt.	Opt./No	No	Front	Lap	Std.	Accept.	–/–	○/○	⊖/○	–/–
Buick Terraza	Opt./No	Std.	Opt./No	No	Front	3-point	Std.	–	–/–	⊖/○	⊖/○	–/–
Cadillac CTS	Std./opt.	Std.	Std./No	Std.	Front	3-point	Std.	Good	–/–	⊖/○	⊖/⊖	–/–
Cadillac DeVille	Std./opt.	Std.	Std./opt.	No	Front	3-point	Std.	–	–/–	⊖/○	–/–	⊖/–
Cadillac Escalade	Std./std.	Std.	Std./No	No	No	3-point	Std.	–	–/–	⊖/○	–/–	–/–
Cadillac SRX	Std./std.	Std.	Std./No	Std.	Front	3-point	Std.	Good	–/–	⊖/○	⊖/○	–/–
Cadillac STS	Std./std.	Std.	Std./No	Std.	Front	3-point	Std.	–	–/–	–/–	–/–	–/–
Cadillac XLR	Std./std.	Std.	Std./NA	NA	Front	NA	Std.	–	–/–	–/–	–/–	–/–
Chevrolet Avalanche	Opt./opt.	Std.	Opt./No	No	No	3-point	Std.	–	–/–	○/○	–/–	–/–
Chevrolet Aveo	No/No	Opt.	No/No	No	Front	3-point	Std.	–	–/–	⊖/○	○/○	⊖/–
Chevrolet Cobalt	Opt./No	Opt.	No/No	Opt.	Front	3-point	Std.	Good	Accept/Poor	⊖/○	–/–	⊖/–
Chevrolet Colorado	Opt./No	Std.	No/No	Opt.	Front	3-point	Std.	–	–/–	⊖/○	⊖/⊖	⊖/⊖
Chevrolet Corvette	Std./std.	Std.	No/NA	NA	No	NA	Std.	–	–/–	–/–	–/–	–/–
Chevrolet Equinox	Opt./No	Opt.	No/No	Opt.	Front	3-point	Std.	–	–/–	⊖/○	⊖/○	⊖*/⊖*
Chevrolet HHR	Opt./No	Opt.	No/No	Opt.	Front	3-point	Std.	–	–/–	–/–	–/–	–/–
Chevrolet Impala	Opt./No	Opt.	Opt./No	No	No	3-point	Std.	Good	–/–	⊖/○	⊖/⊖	–/–
Chevrolet Malibu	Opt./No	Opt.	Opt./No	Opt.	Front	3-point	Std.	Good	Accept./Poor	⊖/○	⊖/○	⊖/–
Chevrolet Monte Carlo	Opt./No	Opt.	Opt./No	No	No	3-point	Std.	–	–/–	⊖/○	○/○	⊖/–
Chevrolet SSR	Opt./No	Std.	Std./NA	NA	Front	NA	Std.	–	–/–	–/–	–/–	–/–
Chevrolet Silverado 1500	Opt./No	Std.	No/No	No	No	3-point	Std.	Marg.	–/–	⊖/○	–/–	⊖/⊖
Chevrolet Suburban	Opt./opt.	Std.	Opt./No	No	No	Lap	Std.	–	–/–	⊖/○	–/–	–/–
Chevrolet Tahoe	Std./Std.	Std.	Opt./No	No	No	Lap	Std.	–	–/–	⊖/○	–/–	○*/○
Chevrolet TrailBlazer	Opt./No	Std.	No/No	Opt.	Front	3-point	Std.	Marg.	–/–	○/○	⊖/○	○/○
Chevrolet Uplander	Opt./opt.	Std.	Opt./No	No	Front	3-point	Std.	–	–/–	⊖/○	⊖/○	–/–
Chrysler 300	Opt./opt.	Opt.	No/No	Opt.	Front	3-point	No	–	–/–	⊖/○	⊖/⊖	⊖/–
Chrysler Crossfire	Std./std.	Std.	Std./NA	NA	Front	NA	No	–	–/–	⊖/○	⊖/○	⊖/–
Chrysler PT Cruiser	Opt./No	Opt.	Opt./No	No	Front	3-point	No	–	–/–	⊖/○	⊖/○	⊖/–
Chrysler Pacifica	Opt./No	Std.	No/No	Opt.	Front	NA	No	Good	–/–	⊖/○	⊖/○	⊖/⊖
Chrysler Sebring	Opt./No	Opt.	Opt./No	Opt.	Front	3-point	No	Accept.	–/Poor	⊖/○	○/○	⊖/–
Chrysler Town & Country	Opt./No	Opt.	No/No	Opt.	Front	Lap	No	Accept.	–/–	⊖/○	⊖/○	⊖/–
Dodge Grand Caravan	Opt./No	Opt.	No/No	Opt.	Front	Lap	No	Accept.	–/–	⊖/○	⊖/○	⊖/–
Dodge Charger	Std./std.	Std.	No/No	Opt.	Front	3-point	No	–	–/–	–/–	–/–	–/–
Dodge Dakota	No/No	Opt.	No/No	Opt.	Front	3-point	No	–	–/–	⊖/○	–/–	–/⊖
Dodge Durango	Opt./No	Opt.	No/No	Opt.	Front	3-point	No	–	–/–	⊖/○	–/–	○/⊖
Dodge Magnum	Opt./opt.	Opt.	No/No	Opt.	Front	3-point	No	–	–/–	⊖/○	⊖/⊖	⊖/–
Dodge Neon	No/No	Opt.	Opt./No	No	No	3-point	No	Marg.	–/Poor	⊖/○	○/○	⊖/–
Dodge Ram 1500	No/No	Opt.	No/No	Opt.	Front	3-point	No	Good	–/–	⊖/○	–/–	⊖/⊖
Dodge Stratus	Opt./No	Opt.	Opt./No	Opt.	Front	3-point	No	Accept.	–/Poor	⊖/○	○/○	⊖/–
Ford Crown Victoria	Opt./No	Std.	Opt./No	No	Front	3-point	No	Good	–/–	⊖/○	⊖/⊖	⊖/–
Ford Escape	No/No	Std.	No/No	No	Front	3-point	No	Accept.	Good/Poor	⊖/○	⊖/○	○*/○*
Ford Expedition	Opt./opt.	Std.	No/No	No	Front	3-point	No	–	–/–	⊖/○	–/–	–/–
Ford Explorer	Opt./std.	Std.	No/No	Opt.	Front	3-point	No	Good	–/–	⊖/○	⊖/○	○/–
Ford Explorer Sport Trac	No/No	Std.	No/No	optn.	No	Lap	No	–	–/–	–/–	–/–	⊖*/○
Ford F-150	No/No	Std.	No/No	No	Front	3-point	No	Good	–/–	⊖/○	–/–	⊖/⊖
Ford Five Hundred	Std./No	Std.	Opt./No	Opt.	Front	3-point	No	–	–/–	⊖/○	⊖/○	⊖/–
Ford Focus	Opt./No	Opt.	Opt./No	No	Front	3-point	No	Good	–/Poor	⊖/○	⊖/⊖	⊖/–
Ford Freestar	Opt./opt.	Std.	Opt./No	Opt.	Front	3-point	No	Good	–/–	⊖/○	⊖/⊖	⊖/–
Ford Freestyle	Std./No	Std.	Opt./No	Opt.	Front	3-point	No	–	–/–	⊖/○	⊖/○	–/–
Ford Fusion ('06)	Opt./No	Opt.	Opt./No	Opt.	Front	3-point	No	–	–/–	–/–	–/–	–/–
Ford Mustang	Opt./No	Opt.	Opt./No	No	Front	NA	No	–	–/–	⊖/○	⊖/–	⊖/–
Ford Ranger	No/No	Std.	No/No	No	Front	NA	No	Accept.	–/–	⊖/○	⊖/–	○/⊖
Ford Taurus	Opt./No	Opt.	Opt./No	No	Front	3-point	No	Good	–/–	⊖/○	○/○	⊖/–
Ford Thunderbird	Std./No	Std.	Std./NA	No	Front	NA	No	–	–/–	⊖/○	⊖/–	⊖/–
GMC Envoy	Opt./No	Std.	No/No	Opt.	No	3-point	Std.	Marg.	–/–	○/○	⊖/○	○/○
GMC Yukon	Std./Std.	Std.	Opt./No	No	No	3-point	Std.	–	–/–	⊖/○	–/–	○*/○
Honda Accord	Opt./No	Std.	Std./No	Std.	Front	3-point	No	Good	Good/NA	⊖/○	⊖/○	⊖/–
Honda CR-V	Std./std.	Std.	Std./No	Std.	Front	3-point	No	Good	Good/NA	⊖/○	⊖/○	–/–
Honda Civic	No/No	Opt.	Opt./No	No	Front	3-point	No	Good	–/–	⊖/○	⊖/○	⊖/–
Honda Element	No/No	Opt.	Opt./No	No	Front	NA	No	Good	–/Poor	⊖/○	⊖/○	–/–
Honda Insight	No/No	Std.	No/NA	No	Front	NA	No	–	–/–	⊖/○	⊖/–	–/–
Honda Odyssey	Std./std.	Std.	Std./No	Std.	Front	3-point	No	–	–/–	⊖/○	⊖/○	⊖/–
Honda Pilot	Std./opt.	Std.	Std./No	No	Front	3-point	No	Good	–/–	⊖/○	⊖/○	–/⊖
Honda Ridgeline	Std./std.	Std.	Std./No	Std.	Front	3-point	No	–	–/–	–/–	–/–	–/–
Honda S2000	No/No	Std.	No/NA	No	Front	NA	No	–	–/–	⊖/○	⊖/–	⊖/–
Hummer H2	Std./No	Std.	No/No	No	No	Lap	Std.	–	–/–	–/–	–/–	–/–
Hummer H3	Std./opt.	Std.	No/No	Std.	No	3-point	Std.	–	–/–	–/–	–/–	–/–
Hyundai Accent	No/No	Opt.	Std./No	No	Front	Lap	No	–	Poor	⊖/○	⊖/○	⊖/–

MAKE & MODEL	AIR BAGS				SAFETY BELTS		DRL	CRASH & ROLLOVER TESTS				
	Traction/ stability	ABS	Side	Head protection	Pretensioners	Center-rear belt		IIHS offset	IIHS side	NHTSA front	NHTSA side	NHTSA rollover rating
			F/R					Frontal	Side air bags (with/without)	Drv./pass.	Drv./rear pass.	2WD/4WD
Hyundai Elantra	Opt./No	Opt.	Std./No	No	Front	3-point	No	Good	Poor/NA	●/●	●/●	●/-
Hyundai Santa Fe	Std./No	Std.	Std./No	No	Front	3-point	No	Good	Accept./NA	●/●	●/●	-/-
Hyundai Sonata ('06)	Std./std.	Std.	Std./No	Std.	Front	3-point	No	-	-/-	-/-	-/-	-/-
Hyundai Tiburon	No/No	Opt.	Std./No	No	Front	NA	No	-	-/-	●/●	●/-	●/-
Hyundai Tucson	Std./std.	Std.	Std./No	Std.	Front	3-point	No	-	-/-	-/-	-/-	-/-
Hyundai XG350	Std./No	Std.	Std./No	No	Front	3-point	No	Good	-/-	●/●	●/●	-/-
Infiniti FX	Std./std.	Std.	Std./No	Std.	Front	3-point	No	Good	-/-	●/●	●/●	●/-
Infiniti G35	Std./std.	Std.	Std./No	Std.	Front	3-point	No	Good	-/-	-/-	-/-	-/-
Infiniti M35/M45 ('06)	Std./std.	Std.	Std./No	Std.	Front	3-point	No	-	-/-	-/-	-/-	-/-
Infiniti Q45	Std./std.	Std.	Std./No	Std.	Front	3-point	No	Good	-/-	-/-	-/-	-/-
Infiniti QX56	Std./std.	Std.	Std./No	Std.	Front & rear	3-point	No	-	-/-	-/-	-/-	-/-
Isuzu Ascender	Opt./No	Std.	No/No	Opt.	No	3-point	Std.	Marg.	-/-	○/●	●/●	○/●
Jaguar S-Type	Std./std.	Std.	Std./No	Std.	Front	3-point	No	-	-/-	-/-	●/●	●/-
Jaguar X-Type	Opt./opt.	Std.	Std./No	Std.	Front	3-point	No	Good	Marg./NA	●/●	●/●	-/●
Jaguar XJ8	Std./std.	Std.	Std./No	Std.	Front & rear	3-point	No	-	-/-	-/-	-/-	-/-
Jeep Grand Cherokee	Opt./opt.	Std.	No/No	Opt.	Front	3-point	No	-	-/-	●/●	●/●	○/●
Jeep Liberty	No/No	Opt.	No/No	Opt.	Front	NA	No	Marg.	-/-	●/●	●/●	○/○
Jeep Wrangler	No/No	Opt.	No/No	No	No	NA	No	Accept.	NA/Marg.	●/●	-/-	-/-
Kia Amanti	Opt./opt.	Std.	Std./std.	Std.	Front	3-point	No	-	-/-	-/-	-/-	-/-
Kia Optima	No/No	Opt.	Std./No	No	Front	3-point	No	Accept.	Poor/NA	●/●	●/●	●/-
Kia Rio	No/No	Opt.	No/No	No	No	Lap	No	-	-/-	●/●	●/●	●/-
Kia Sedona	No/No	Opt.	No/No	No	Front	Lap	No	Accept.	-/-	●/●	●/●	●/-
Kia Sorento	No/No	Opt.	No/No	Std.	Front	3-point	No	Accept.	-/-	●/●	●/●	-/-
Kia Spectra	No/No	Opt.	Std./No	Std.	Front	3-point	No	Accept.	Poor/NA	●/●	●/○	-/-
Kia Sportage	Opt./std.	Std.	Std./No	Std.	Front	3-point	No	-	-/-	-/-	-/-	-/-
Land Rover Freelander	Std./No	Std.	No/No	No	Front	3-point	No	Accept.	-/Poor	-/-	-/-	-/-
Land Rover LR3	Std./std.	Std.	Std./opt.	Std.	Front	3-point	No	-	-/-	-/-	-/-	-/-
Land Rover Range Rover	Std./std.	Std.	Std./std.	Std.	Front	3-point	No	-	-/-	-/-	-/-	-/-
Lexus ES330	Opt./opt.	Std.	Std./No	Std.	Front & rear	3-point	Std.	Good	Good/NA	●/●	●/●	●/-
Lexus GS300/GS430 ('06)	Std./std.	Std.	Std./No	Std.	Front	3-point	Std.	-	-/-	-/-	-/-	-/-
Lexus GX470	Std./std.	Std.	Std./No	Std.	Front	3-point	Std.	Good	-/-	-/-	-/-	-/-
Lexus IS300	Std./opt.	Std.	Std./No	Std.	Front	3-point	Std.	Good	-/-	-/-	●/●	-/-
Lexus LS430	Std./std.	Std.	Std./No	Std.	Front & rear	3-point	Std.	Good	-/-	-/-	-/-	-/-
Lexus LX470	Std./std.	Std.	Std./No	Std.	Front	3-point	Std.	-	-/-	-/-	-/-	-/-
Lexus RX330	Std./std.	Std.	Std./No	Std.	Front	3-point	Std.	Good	-/-	●/●	●/●	-/-
Lexus SC430	Std./std.	Std.	Std./No	No	Front	NA	Std.	-	-/-	-/-	-/-	-/-
Lincoln Aviator	Opt./std.	Std.	No/No	Std.	Front	3-point	No	Good	-/-	●/●	●/●	●/-
Lincoln LS	Std./opt.	Std.	No/No	Opt.	Front	3-point	No	Good	-/-	●/●	●/●	●/-
Lincoln Mark LT ('06)	No/No	Std.	No/No	No	Front	3-point	No	-	-/-	●/●	-/-	-/-
Lincoln Navigator	Opt./std.	Std.	No/No	Std.	Front	3-point	No	-	-/-	●/●	-/-	-/●
Lincoln Town Car	Std./No	Std.	Std./No	No	Front	3-point	No	Good	-/-	●/●	●/●	●/-
Lincoln Zehpyr ('06)	Std./No	Std.	Opt./No	Opt.	Front	3-point	No	-	-/-	-/-	-/-	-/-
Lotus Elise	No/No	Std.	No/NA	No	No	NA	No	-	-/-	-/-	-/-	-/-
Mazda B-Series	No/No	Std.	No/No	No	Front	NA	No	Accept.	-/-	●/●	●/●	○/○
Mazda MPV	Opt./No	Std.	Opt./NA	No	Front	Lap	No	Accept.	-/-	●/●	●/●	●/-
Mazda MX-5 Miata	No/No	Opt.	No/No	No	Front	NA	No	-	-/-	●/●	○/●	●/-
Mazda RX-8	Opt./opt.	Std.	Std./No	Std.	Front	NA	No	-	-/-	●/●	●/●	●/-
Mazda Tribute	No/No	Std.	No/No	Opt.	Front	3-point	No	Accept.	Good/Poor	●/●	●/●	○*/○*
Mazda3	No/No	Opt.	Opt./No	Opt.	Front	3-point	No	Good	-/Poor	●/●	○/○	●/-
Mazda5 ('06)	Std./No	Std.	Opt./No	Opt.	Front	NA	No	-	-/-	-/-	-/-	-/-
Mazda6	Std./opt.	Std.	Opt./No	Opt.	Front	3-point	No	Good	-/Poor	●/●	○/●	●/-
Mercedes-Benz C-Class	Std./std.	Std.	Std./std.	Std.	Front & rear	3-point	Opt.	Good	Accept./NA	●/●	●/●	●/-
Mercedes-Benz CLK	Std./std.	Std.	Std./std.	Std.	Front	NA	Opt.	-	-/-	-/-	●/●	-/-
Mercedes-Benz CLS	Std./std.	Std.	Std./std.	Std.	Front & rear	NA	Opt.	-	-/-	-/-	-/-	-/-
Mercedes-Benz E-Class	Std./std.	Std.	Std./std.	Std.	Front & rear	3-point	Opt.	Good	-/-	●/●	●/●	●/-
Mercedes-Benz M-Class ('06)	Std./std.	Std.	Std./std.	Std.	Front & rear	3-point	Opt.	-	-/-	-/-	-/-	-/-
Mercedes-Benz S-Class	Std./std.	Std.	Std./std.	Std.	Front & rear	3-point	Std.	-	-/-	-/-	-/-	-/-
Mercedes-Benz SLK	Std./std.	Std.	Std./NA	No	Front	NA	No	-	-/-	-/-	-/-	-/-
Mercury Grand Marquis	Std./No	Std.	Opt./No	No	Front	3-point	No	Good	-/-	●/●	●/●	●/-
Mercury Mariner	No/No	Std.	Opt./No	Opt.	Front	3-point	No	Accept.	Good/Poor	●/●	●/●	○*/○*
Mercury Milan ('06)	Opt./No	Opt.	Opt./No	Opt.	Front	3-point	No	-	-/-	-/-	-/-	-/-
Mercury Montego	Std./No	Std.	Opt./No	Opt.	Front	3-point	No	-	-/-	●/●	-/-	●/-
Mercury Monterey	Opt./opt.	Std.	Opt./No	Opt.	Front	3-point	No	Good	-/-	●/●	●/●	●/-
Mercury Mountaineer	Opt./std.	Std.	No/No	Opt.	Front	3-point	No	Good	-/-	●/●	●/●	○/-
Mini Cooper	Opt./opt.	Std.	Std./No	Std.	Front	NA	Opt.	Good	-/-	●/●	●/●	●/-
Mitsubishi Eclipse ('06)	Opt./No	Std.	Std./No	No	Front	NA	Std.	-	-/-	-/-	-/-	-/-
Mitsubishi Endeavor	Opt./No	Opt.	Std./No	No	Front	3-point	Std.	Good	-/-	●/●	●/●	●/-
Mitsubishi Galant	Opt./No	Opt.	Std./No	No	Front	3-point	Std.	Good	Good/NA	●/●	●/●	●/-
Mitsubishi Lancer	No/No	Opt.	Opt./No	No	Front	3-point	No	Good	-/Poor	●/●	●/●	●/-
Mitsubishi Montero	Std./std.	Std.	Opt./No	No	No	3-point	No	Accept.	-/-	-/-	-/-	-/-

MAKE & MODEL	Traction/ stability	ABS	Side F/R	Head protection	Pretensioners	Center-rear belt	DRL	IIHS offset Frontal	IIHS side Side air bags (with/without)	NHTSA front Drv./pass.	NHTSA side Drv./rear pass.	NHTSA rollover rating 2WD/4WD
Mitsubishi Outlander	No/No	Opt.	Opt./No	No	Front	3-point	Std.	Good	–/Poor	●/●	●/●	–/–
Nissan 350Z	Opt./opt.	Std.	Opt./NA	Opt.	Front	NA	No	–	–/–	–/–	●/–	●/–
Nissan Altima	Opt./No	Opt.	Opt./No	Opt.	Front	3-point	No	Good	–/Poor	●/●	○/○	◐/–
Nissan Armada	Std./std.	Std.	Opt./No	Std.	Front	3-point	No	–	–/–	–/–	–/–	–/–
Nissan Frontier	Opt./opt.	Std.	Opt./No	Opt.	Front	3-point	No	–	–/–	●/●	●/●	–/–
Nissan Maxima	Std./opt.	Std.	Std./No	Std.	Front	3-point	No	Good	–/–	●/●	●/●	◐/–
Nissan Murano	Opt./opt.	Std.	Opt./No	Std.	Front	3-point	No	Good	–/–	●/●	●/●	◐/◐
Nissan Pathfinder	Opt./std.	Std.	Opt./No	Opt.	Front	3-point	No	–	–/–	●/●	●/●	–/–
Nissan Quest	Std./opt.	Std.	Opt./No	Std.	Front	3-point	No	Good	–/–	●/●	●/●	◐/–
Nissan Sentra	No/No	Opt.	Opt./No	No	Front	3-point	No	Accept.	–/Poor	●/●	◐/–	◐/–
Nissan Titan	Opt./opt.	Std.	Opt./No	Opt.	Front	3-point	No	Good	–/–	●/●	–/–	–/–
Nissan Xterra	Opt./opt.	Std.	Opt./No	Opt.	Front	3-point	No	–	–/–	–/–	–/–	–/–
Pontiac Aztek	Opt./No	Opt.	Opt./No	No	No	3-point	Std.	Marg.	–/–	○/●	●/○	–/–
Pontiac G6	Opt./No	Opt.	Opt./No	Opt.	Front	3-point	Std.	–	–/–	●/●	○/○	◐/–
Pontiac GTO	Std./No	Std.	Std./No	No	Front	NA	Std.	–	–/–	–/–	–/–	–/–
Pontiac Grand Prix	Opt./opt.	Opt.	No/No	Opt.	Front	3-point	Std.	–	–/–	○/●	○/○	◐/–
Pontiac Montana SV6	Opt./opt.	Std.	Opt./No	No	Front	3-point	Std.	–	–/–	●/●	◐/●	–/–
Pontiac Solstice ('06)	Opt./No	Opt.	No/NA	No	Front	NA	Std.	–	–/–	–/–	–/–	–/–
Pontiac Torrent ('06)	Opt./No	Opt.	Opt./No	Opt.	Front	3-point	Std.	–	–/–	–/–	–/–	–/–
Pontiac Vibe	Opt./opt.	Opt.	Opt./No	No	Front	3-point	Std.	–	–/–	●/●	○/●	◐/◐
Porsche Boxster	Opt./std.	Std.	Std./NA	Opt.	Front	NA	No	–	–/–	–/–	–/–	–/–
Porsche Cayenne	Std./std.	Std.	Std./std.	Std.	Front & rear	3-point	No	–	–/–	–/–	–/–	–/–
Saab 9-2X	No/No	Std.	Std./No	No	Front	3-point	Std.	–	–/–	–/–	–/–	–/–
Saab 9-3	Std./std.	Std.	Std./No	Std.	Front	Good/NA	Std.	Good	Good/NA	–/–	–/–	–/–
Saab 9-5	Std./std.	Std.	Std./No	No	Front	3-point	Std.	Good	Accept./NA	–/–	–/–	–/–
Saab 9-7X	No/No	Std.	No/No	Std.	Front	3-point	Std.	–	–/–	○/●	●/●	◐/–
Saturn Ion	Opt./No	Opt.	No/No	Opt.	Front	3-point	Std.	Accept.	Poor/Poor	●/●	○/●	◐/–
Saturn Relay	Opt./opt.	Std.	Opt./No	No	Front	3-point	Std.	–	–/–	●/●	◐/●	–/–
Saturn Vue	Opt./No	Opt.	No/No	Opt.	Front	3-point	Std.	Good	–/Poor	●/●	●/●	○*/○*
Scion tC	No/No	Std.	Opt./No	Opt.	Front	3-point	No	–	–/–	●/●	●/●	◐/–
Scion xA	Opt./opt.	Std.	Opt./No	Opt.	Front	3-point	No	–	–/–	●/●	●/●	◐/–
Scion xB	Std./std.	Std.	No/No	No	Front	3-point	No	–	–/–	–/–	–/–	–/–
Subaru B9 Tribeca	Std./std.	Std.	Std./No	Std.	Front	3-point	Std.	–	–/–	–/–	–/–	–/–
Subaru Baja	No/No	Std.	No/No	No	Front	NA	Std.	–	–/–	–/–	–/–	–/–
Subaru Forester	No/No	Std.	Std./No	No	Front	3-point	Std.	Good	Good/–	●/●	●/●	–/–
Subaru Impreza	No/No	Std.	Opt./No	No	Front	3-point	Std.	Good	–/–	●/●	◐/–	–/–
Subaru Legacy/Outback	Opt./opt.	Std.	Std./No	Std.	Front	3-point	Std.	Good	Marg./NA	●/●	●/●	–/–
Suzuki Aerio	No/No	Opt.	Std./No	No	Front	3-point	Std.	Good	Poor/NA	–/–	–/–	◐/–
Suzuki Forenza	Opt./No	Opt.	Std./No	No	Front	3-point	Std.	Accept.	Poor/NA	–/–	–/–	◐/–
Suzuki Grand Vitara/XL-7	No/No	Opt.	No/No	No	Front	3-point	Std.	Good	NA/Poor	◐/●	●/●	–/–
Suzuki Verona	Opt./No	Opt.	Std./No	No	Front	3-point	Std.	Accept.	Poor/NA	○/●	◐/○	–/–
Toyota 4Runner	Std./std.	Std.	Opt./No	Opt.	Front & rear	3-point	Opt.	Good	–/–	●/●	●/●	○/○
Toyota Avalon	Opt./opt.	Std.	Std./No	Std.	Front	3-point	Std.	–	–/–	–/–	–/–	–/–
Toyota Camry	Opt./opt.	Std.	Opt./No	Opt.	Front	3-point	Std.[1]	Good	Good/Poor	●/●	●/●	◐/–
Toyota Camry Solara	Opt./opt.	Std.	Opt./No	Opt.	Pretensioners	3-point	Std.[1]	–	–/–	●/●	●/●	◐/–
Toyota Celica	No/No	Opt.	Opt./No	No	Front	NA	Std.	–	–/–	●/●	○/–	–/–
Toyota Corolla	Opt./opt.	Opt.	Opt./No	Opt.	Front	3-point	Std.	Good	Accept./Poor	●/●	◐/●	–/–
Toyota Echo	No/No	Opt.	Opt./No	No	Front	3-point	Opt.	–	–/–	●/●	○/●	◐/–
Toyota Highlander	Std./std.	Std.	Opt./No	Opt.	Front	3-point	Opt.	Good	Accept./Poor	●/●	●/●	◐/◐
Toyota Land Cruiser	Std./std.	Std.	Opt./No	Opt.	Front	3-point	Std.	–	–/–	–/–	–/–	–/–
Toyota MR2	No/No	Std.	No/NA	No	Front	NA	Std.	–	–/–	–/–	–/–	–/–
Toyota Matrix	Opt./opt.	Opt.	Opt./No	Opt.	Front	3-point	Std.	–	–/–	●/●	○/●	◐/◐
Toyota Prius	Std./opt.	Std.	Opt./No	Opt.	Front	3-point	No	–	–/–	●/●	●/●	◐/–
Toyota RAV4	Std./std.	Std.	Opt./No	Opt.	Front	3-point	Opt.	Good	Good/Poor	●/●	●/●	–/–
Toyota Sequoia	Std./std.	Std.	Opt./No	Opt.	Front	3-point	Opt.	–	–/–	●/●	–/–	–/–
Toyota Sienna	Opt./std.	Std.	Opt./No	Opt.	Front	3-point	Opt.	Good	–/–	●/●	●/●	◐/–
Toyota Tacoma	Opt./opt.	Std.	Opt./No	Opt.	Front	3-point	Opt.	–	–/–	●/●	●/–	–/–
Toyota Tundra	Opt./opt.	Std.	Opt./No	Opt.	Front	3-point	Opt.	Good	–/–	●/●	–/–	–/–
Volkswagen Golf	Opt./opt.	Std.	Std./No	Std.	Front	3-point	Std.	Good	–/–	●/●	◐/●	–/–
Volkswagen Jetta ('06)	Std./opt.	Std.	Std./No	Std.	Front	3-point	Std.	–	–/–	–/–	–/–	–/–
Volkswagen New Beetle	Opt./opt.	Std.	Std./No	No	Front	NA	Std.	Good	Poor/NA	●/●	●/○	◐/–
Volkswagen Passat	Std./opt.	Std.	Std./No	Std.	Front & rear	3-point	Std.	Good	–/–	●/●	●/●	◐/–
Volkswagen Phaeton	Std./std.	Std.	Std./No	Std.	Front & rear	3-point	Std.	–	–/–	–/–	–/–	–/–
Volkswagen Touareg	Std./std.	Std.	Std./No	Std.	Front & rear	3-point	Std.	–	–/–	●/●	●/●	–/–
Volvo S40/V50	Std./opt.	Std.	Std./No	Std.	Front & rear	3-point	Std.	Good	Accept./NA	◐/●	●/●	◐/–
Volvo S60	Std./opt.	Std.	Std./No	Std.	Front & rear	3-point	Std.	Good	–/–	●/●	●/●	●/–
Volvo S80	Std./opt.	Std.	Std./No	Std.	Front & rear	3-point	Std.	Good	–/–	●/●	●/●	–/–
Volvo V70/XC70	Std./opt.	Std.	Std./No	Std.	Front & rear	3-point	Std.	–	–/–	●/●	●/●	◐/◐
Volvo XC90	Std./std.	Std.	Std./No	Std.	Front & rear	3-point	Std.	Good	–/–	●/●	●/●	–/◐

[1] DRL (daytime running lights) can be switched off inadvertently.

Profiles

A user's guide

Each profile page contains an array of information and test data about the featured vehicle. This guide details the information in each section and helps you get the most from each profile.

REVIEW ①

CR's overall assessment

The review contains key information about the vehicle, as well as an expert, impartial critique based on CONSUMER REPORTS testing. It also provides a rundown of any major changes or new versions introduced for the new model year.

A model earns a **Recommended** label (below left) if it performed well in our tests, has had average or better reliability according to our annual subscriber survey, and, if crash tested, has performed at least adequately overall in government and/or insurance-industry tests. Some models are not recommended either because CONSUMER REPORTS hasn't tested them recently or because we don't have sufficient reliability data on them. **Recommended Plus** labels (below right) are for vehicles that also stand out in crash protection.

REPORT CARD ②

Scores in key categories

The CONSUMER REPORTS Report Card is a quick summary of a vehicle at a glance, including Highs and Lows and test highlights.

Predicted Reliability is our prediction of how well a model is likely to hold up, derived from responses to CR's 2004 Annual Questionnaire, which garnered 810,000 responses. Detailed Ratings are provided in the Reliability History charts on the opposite page (see No. 7). **Depreciation** predicts how well a new model will hold its value. Average depreciation is 46 percent after the first three years of ownership.

For **Owner Satisfaction** we asked owners in our survey if they would buy their particular vehicle again. A top score (◓) indicates that 80 percent or more would do so. The lowest score (●) indicates fewer than 50 percent would do so. **Accident avoidance, acceleration, ride, front seat comfort,** and **fuel economy** are all described in "From the test track," (see No. 4).

"NA" means data are not available. "New" means we have no data because the model is new or redesigned.

KEY FOR REPORT CARD

● ◓ ○ ◓ ●

Better ◀━━━━▶ Worse

SAFETY INFORMATION ③

Safety equipment and crash-test results

Standard safety equipment on all vehicles now includes dual front air bags, 3-point lap-and-shoulder belts for all outboard seating positions, top-tether child-seat anchors, and lower LATCH anchors for compatible child seats. This section lists the availability of additional safety equipment. "NA" means not applicable.

Antilock brakes refers to the availability of four-wheel systems only. **Traction control, stability control, daytime running lights,** and **tire-pressure monitor** note if these are available. The center-rear belt is either a lap belt or, better, a 3-point belt. **Pretensioners** work instantly to take up slack in the seatbelt during a front crash. Some vehicles have an **occupant-sensing system** that helps control or suppress air-bag deployment depending on several variables, such as the weight and seating position of the front passenger. More vehicles offer **side air bags** as well as head-protection bags (typically side-curtain air bags). An **accident-alert system** calls for help if the air bag deploys in a crash. **Government front- and side-crash-test judgments** are our interpretation of crash results from the National Highway Traffic Safety Administration (NHTSA). Refer to the key at right. The **IIHS offset- and side-crash** tests are the rating that the Insurance Institute for Highway Safety assigns. See the Safety Features and Crash-Test Ratings, starting on page 32, for more information.

KEY FOR NHTSA CRASH-TEST RATINGS

◓	No injury or minor injury likely
◒	Moderate injury likely
○	Certain injury, possibly severe
◓	Severe or fatal injury highly likely
●	Severe or fatal injury certain

(Right-hand side profile card — Acura TL)

Consumer Reports cars

Acura TL — CR RECOMMENDED ✓ — ⑤

THE TL LINE
Body style: sedan
Trim lines: —
Base price range: $33,100

The Honda Accord-based TL is the highest-scoring car we've tested in the upscale-sedan category. The TL is among models in this class that provide a near-ideal blend of comfort, convenience, and sportiness—all at a reasonable price. It delivers taut, agile handling, though ultimately it's not as nimble as a BMW 3 Series or Mercedes C-Class. The car is very quick yet attains commendable fuel economy. The TL has a firm but comfortable and quiet ride. A wide turning circle is one of the few negatives. Interior quality is impressive. — ①

REPORT CARD — ②

○	Predicted reliability
◓	Owner satisfaction
◒	Predicted depreciation
◒	Accident avoidance
◒	Acceleration
◒	Ride
○	Front seat comfort
○	Fuel economy

SAFETY INFORMATION — ③

Active safety features
Antilock brakes .... Standard
Traction control .... Standard
Stability control .... Standard
Daytime running lights .... Not available
Tire pressure monitor .... Not available

Safety belts
Center-rear belt 3-point
Pretensioners, front/rear .... Yes/no

Occupant-sensing system .... Front and Side
Side bags, front/rear .... Standard/no
Inflatable curtain .... Standard
Accident alert system .... Available

Crash tests
Gov't front-crash test, driver/front passenger .... Good
Gov't side-crash test, driver/rear passenger .... Good
IIHS offset crash test .... Good
IIHS side crash test w/ side & curtain airbags .... NA
IIHS side crash test w/o side & curtain airbags .... NA

SPECIFICATIONS — ⑥

Drive wheels front
Seating 2 front, 3 rear
Engines available
3.2-liter V6 (270 hp)
Transmissions available
6-speed manual; 5-speed autom.
Fuel
Fuel type 20/29
EPA city/highway, mpg 17.0
Fuel refill capacity, gal.
Dimensions and weight
Length, in. 196
Width, in. 72
Wheelbase, in. 108
Curb weight, lb. 3,565
Percent weight, front/rear 62/38
Typical towing ability, lb. .... NR

FROM THE TEST TRACK — ④

Tested model
2004 sedan, 3.2-liter V6, 5-speed automatic
Tires as tested
Bridgestone Turanza EL42,
size P235/45SR17 93W
Acceleration
0-30 mph, sec. 2.7
0-60 mph, sec. 6.7
Quarter mile, sec. 15.2
Quarter mile, mph 95
45-65 mph, sec. 4.2
Other findings
Transmission 42
Turning circle, ft. 41
Ground clearance, in. 5.5

Braking and handling
Braking 130
Braking, dry pavement, ft.
Emergency handling
Avoidance maneuver, max. mph 52.5
Convenience and comfort
Ride
Noise
Driving position
Access
Controls and displays
Fit and finish 50.0
Door top to ground, in.
Trunk .... 3+2
Luggage capacity 850
Max. load, lb.

Seating
Front-seat comfort 58.5
Front shoulder room, in. 42.0
Front leg room, in. 3.5
Front head room, in.
Rear-seat comfort 55.0
Rear shoulder room, in. 27.5
Rear leg room, in. 3.5
Rear head room, in.
Fuel economy
CU's overall mileage, mpg 23
CU's city/highway, mpg 16/35
CU's city/highway, mpg 27
CU's 150-mile trip, mpg 31.420
Annual fuel .... 645 gal./$1,420
Cruising range 435

RELIABILITY HISTORY — ⑦

Acura TL

TROUBLE SPOTS

Engine
Cooling
Fuel
Ignition
Transmission
Electrical
Air conditioning
Suspension
Brakes
Exhaust
Paint/trim/rust
Body integrity
Power equipment
Body hardware
RELIABILITY VERDICT

better ◀━━━━▶ worse See page 36 for more information.

FROM THE TEST TRACK ④
Results from CR's testing

CONSUMER REPORTS conducts more than 45 separate evaluations on every vehicle tested. This section provides the key results from those tests. In some cases, CR has tested more than one version of a model. Data for other tested versions are available to subscribers of *ConsumerReports.org.*

All **acceleration** figures except for the 45- to 65-mph passing test are from a standstill with the engine idling. **Other findings** include judgments of **transmission** characteristics and shift quality. **Turning circle** is the bumper clearance needed to make a U-turn. **Ground clearance** is measured to the nearest half-inch with the car loaded with three occupants.

The **braking** judgment is based on several tests performed in dry and wet conditions. The stopping figure is the distance in feet that a vehicle took to stop from 60 mph, with no wheels locked. **Handling** judgments reflect how agile the vehicle is in both routine driving and in emergency handling—how the vehicle performed when pushed to its limits on our track and in a double-lane-change avoidance maneuver. **Avoidance-maneuver** indicates the maximum speed at which a vehicle successfully negotiated the course.

Convenience and comfort includes assessments of ride comfort, overall cabin noise, driving position, ergonomic factors (such as controls and displays), fit and finish, and access. **Cargo volume** is the maximum usable cargo volume with rear seats folded or removed. It's measured using an expanded pipe-frame box to fit the cargo area. Luggage capacity is the number of suitcases plus duffel bags that will fit in the trunk. No volume is given for pickups because there is no height limit. **Maximum load** includes occupants and luggage, and is as specified by the manufacturer or calculated from the difference between the manufacturer's specified gross vehicle weight and our test vehicle weight.

The **seating** section includes comfort judgments and measurements for all seats. Front leg room is the distance from the heel of the accelerator foot to the seatback. Headroom is the clearance above a 5-foot-9-inch tester's head. **Rear leg room** is the horizontal distance from the rear seatback to the back of the front seatback, with front leg room set at 40 inches.

Fuel-economy numbers come from our test measurements and are rounded to the nearest mile per gallon (mpg). The amount and cost of fuel used in 15,000 miles are calculated from equal portions of city and highway driving, and a 150-mile trip, using $2 per gallon for regular, $1.80 for diesel, and $2.20 for premium. Cost is rounded to the nearest $5. Cruising range is calculated based on overall mileage in mixed driving.

KEY FOR TEST JUDGMENTS

Excellent ———————→ Poor

CONFIGURATIONS ⑤
Body styles, trim lines, and price

Models often come in various **body styles** (sedan, coupe, wagon, etc.) and **trim lines**, which are versions that differ mainly in standard equipment, available options, and price. A dash (–) means that only one trim line was available. Pickup trucks are listed by available cab combinations.

Price is the range of base prices for all versions. The base price is the manufacturer's suggested retail price (MSRP) without options or destination charge. An "E" indicates the price is estimated.

SPECIFICATIONS ⑥
Drivetrains, dimensions, and capacities

Look here to find key specifications. **Drive wheels** tells you if the model is available with front-, rear-, all-wheel drive (AWD), or four-wheel drive (4WD). It also shows the type of 4WD system. **Seating** is the maximum number of passengers that can be accommodated in the front, rear, and third-row (if any) seats. Some models are available with different seating configurations; this figure is for the version with the most passenger capacity. **Engines** and **transmissions** show the choices of drivetrain components. **Fuel** includes the recommended type for all of this model's engines, city/highway fuel-economy figures as estimated by the U.S. Environmental Protection Agency, and fuel capacity. Fuel economy and capacity are for the version tested or a typical model. **Dimensions** are as specified by the manufacturer. Most **weight** specifications are as measured by CONSUMER REPORTS. The typical towing ability is for the vehicle version tested or for a typical model. "NR" means not recommended.

RELIABILITY HISTORY ⑦
Trouble spots

This information comes from the same annual survey that lets us forecast reliability. Use it to spot potentially troublesome areas of a vehicle. Our latest data come from our 2004 survey. Respondents were asked to report serious problems in 1997 to 2004 models occurring in the previous 12 months. Data are standardized to minimize the effect of varying mileage. A model might have been redesigned during the eight-year period. Still, past history is a good indication of how a model will age.

In the chart, scores for individual trouble spots represent the percentage of respondents who reported a serious problem in that area. Interpretation depends partly on the car's age. The 2004 models were less than six months old at the time of the survey, with an average of only about 3,000 miles. A score of ○ or worse is not an encouraging sign for a car that new—but it's not so worrisome on older models.

KEY TO RELIABILITY VERDICTS

✔ **Red check** Better-than-average overall reliability for that year.

– **Dash** Average overall reliability for that year.

✗ **Black x** indicates worse-than-average overall reliability for that year.

KEY FOR TROUBLE SPOTS
Percentage of owners reporting problems

◉ 2.0% or less
⊖ 2.0% to 5.0%
○ 5.0% to 9.3%
◑ 9.3% to 14.8%
● More than 14.8%

Acura MDX

CR RECOMMENDED ✓

THE MDX LINE
Body style:
4-door SUV
Trim lines:
Base, Touring
Base price range:
$36,900–$39,725

O ne of CR's top-rated SUVs, the MDX has a strong, refined powertrain and pleasant ride, though road noise is pronounced. The interior features a 50/50-split third-row bench that increases passenger capacity to seven or stows easily into the floor. The MDX feels agile but does not inspire confidence in emergency handling, even with its standard stability control. Braking distances in our tests were also unimpressive. The similar Honda Pilot is less costly and a shade roomier. The optional navigation system works well and incorporates a rear-view camera to assist when backing up.

REPORT CARD

◒	Predicted reliability
⊖	Owner satisfaction
◒	Predicted depreciation
○	Accident avoidance
⊖	Acceleration
⊖	Ride
◒	Front seat comfort
●	Fuel economy

SPECIFICATIONS

Drive wheels AWD

Seating 2 front, 3 rear, 2 third

Engines available
3.5-liter V6 (265 hp)

Transmissions available
5-speed automatic

Fuel
Fuel type ....Premium
EPA city/highway, mpg 17/23
Fuel refill capacity, gal. 20.4

Dimensions and weight
Length, in. 189
Width, in. 77
Wheelbase, in. 106
Curb weight, lb. 4,555
Percent weight, front/rear 56/44
Typical towing ability, lb. 3,500

SAFETY INFORMATION

Active safety features
Antilock brakes ....Standard
Traction control ....Standard
Stability control ....Standard
Daytime running lights ....Not available
Tire pressure monitor ....Available

Safety belts
Center-rear belt 3-point
Pretensioners, front/rear ....Yes/no

Air bags
Occupant-sensing system ....Side
Side bags, front/rear ....Standard/no
Inflatable curtain ....Standard with rollover
Accident alert system ....Available

Crash tests
Gov't front-crash test, driver/front passenger ......◒/◒
Gov't side-crash test, driver/rear passenger ....◒/◒
IIHS offset crash test ....Good
IIHS side crash test w/ side & curtain airbags ....NA
IIHS side crash test w/o side & curtain airbags ....NA

FROM THE TEST TRACK

Tested model
2003 Touring 4-door SUV AWD, 3.5-liter V6, 5-speed automatic

Tires as tested
Michelin Cross Terrain, size P235/65R17 103T

Acceleration ....⊖
0-30 mph, sec. 3.0
0-60 mph, sec. 8.2
Quarter mile, sec. 16.5
Quarter mile, mph 85
45-65 mph, sec. 5.3

Other findings
Transmission ....◒
Turning circle, ft. 40
Ground clearance, in. 5.0

Braking and handling
Braking ....○
Braking, dry pavement, ft. 151
Routine handling ....⊖
Emergency handling ....⊖
Avoidance maneuver, max. mph ...46.0

Convenience and comfort
Ride ....⊖
Noise ....⊖
Driving position ....◒
Access ....⊖
Controls and displays ....⊖
Fit and finish ....⊖
Door top to ground, in. 61.5
Cargo area ....○
Cargo volume, cu.ft. 42.0
Max. load, lb. 1,160

Seating
Front-seat comfort ....◒
Front shoulder room, in. 61.0
Front leg room, in. 41.0
Front head room, in. 4.0
Rear-seat comfort ....⊖
Rear shoulder room, in. 61.0
Rear leg room, in. 30.0
Rear head room, in 4.0
Third-seat comfort ....●
Third shoulder room,in 59.0
Third leg room, in. 24.5
Third head room, in 1.5

Fuel economy ....●
CU's overall mileage, mpg 17
CU's city/highway, mpg 11/26
CU's 150-mile trip, mpg 21
Annual fuel ....875 gal./$1,925
Cruising range 390

RELIABILITY HISTORY

TROUBLE SPOTS	Acura MDX							
	97	98	99	00	01	02	03	04
Engine					●	●	●	●
Cooling					●	●	●	●
Fuel					⊖	●	●	●
Ignition					●	●	●	●
Transmission					⊖	●	●	●
Electrical					⊖	●	●	●
Air conditioning					⊖	●	●	●
Suspension					⊖	●	●	●
Brakes					●	●	●	●
Exhaust					●	●	●	●
Paint/trim/rust					●	●	●	●
Body integrity					⊖	●	●	●
Power equipment					⊖	⊖	●	●
Body hardware					⊖	●	●	●
RELIABILITY VERDICT					✓	✓	✓	

Acura RL

THE RL LINE
Body style:
sedan
Trim lines:
–
Base price range:
$49,100

The RL has been redesigned for the first time in nine years. It is powered by a 300-hp V6 engine mated to an all-wheel-drive system designed to contribute to balanced handling. The navigation system incorporates real-time traffic reports in major metropolitan areas, via XM satellite radio. The center knob that controls the audio and navigation systems isn't particularly intuitive. The powertrain is polished, but ride and handling don't stand out in this class. Interior room is not much better than in the much less expensive TL.

REPORT CARD

⬤	Predicted reliability
New	Owner satisfaction
NA	Predicted depreciation
NA	Accident avoidance
NA	Acceleration
NA	Ride
NA	Front seat comfort
NA	Fuel economy

SPECIFICATIONS

Drive wheels AWD

Seating 2 front, 3 rear

Engines available
3.5-liter V6 (300 hp)

Transmissions available
5-speed automatic

Fuel
Fuel type .Premium
EPA city/highway, mpg 18/26
Fuel refill capacity, gal. 19.6

Dimensions and weight
Length, in. 194
Width, in. 73
Wheelbase, in. .110
Curb weight, lb. 4,035
Percent weight, front/rear 58/42
Typical towing ability, lb. 1,000

SAFETY INFORMATION

Active safety features
Antilock brakes . . . . .Standard
Traction control . . . . .Standard
Stability control . . . . .Standard
Daytime running lights .Standard
Tire pressure monitor .Available

Safety belts
Center-rear belt 3-point
Pretensioners, front/rear . . . . .Yes/no

Air bags
Occupant-sensing system . . . . .Side
Side bags, front/rear . . . . .Standard/no
Inflatable curtain . . . . .Standard
Accident alert system .Available

Crash tests
Gov't front-crash test, driver/front passenger . . . . .◑/◑
Gov't side-crash test, driver/rear passenger . . . .◑/◑
IIHS offset crash test . . . . .NA
IIHS side crash test w/ side & curtain airbags . . . . .NA
IIHS side crash test w/o side & curtain airbags . . . . . . .NA

ANOTHER LOOK

RELIABILITY HISTORY

TROUBLE SPOTS	97 98 99 00 01 02 03 04
Engine	
Cooling	NO
Fuel	
Ignition	
Transmission	DATA
Electrical	
Air conditioning	NEW
Suspension	
Brakes	MODEL
Exhaust	
Paint/trim/rust	
Body integrity	
Power equipment	
Body hardware	
RELIABILITY VERDICT	

⬤ ◑ ○ ◔ ⬤
better ← → worse   See page 36 for more information.

Acura RSX

CR RECOMMENDED ✓

THE RSX LINE
Body style:
2-door hatchback
Trim lines:
Base, Type-S
Base price range:
$20,275-$23,670

The RSX is a Honda Civic-based two-door coupe with a rear hatch. The base model features a 2.0-liter, 160-hp four-cylinder engine. The sportier Type-S variant comes with a 210-hp version that feels invigorating when revved to its 8,000-rpm redline, and complemented by the six-speed manual. Handling is capable but not quite as agile as the Subaru Impreza WRX or discontinued Ford SVT Focus. A stiff, choppy ride and constant road noise make the RSX tiring on long drives. The hatchback and a split fold-down rear seat add versatility, but rear-seat room is very tight.

REPORT CARD

◉	Predicted reliability
○	Owner satisfaction
⊖	Predicted depreciation
⊖	Accident avoidance
⊖	Acceleration
⊜	Ride
⊖	Front seat comfort
⊖	Fuel economy

SPECIFICATIONS

Drive wheels Front

Seating 2 front, 2 rear

Engines available
2.0-liter 4 (160 hp); 2.0-liter 4 (210 hp)

Transmissions available
5-speed manual; 6-speed manual; 5-speed automatic

Fuel
Fuel type . . . . .Regular or premium
EPA city/highway, mpg 23/31
Fuel refill capacity, gal. 13.2

Dimensions and weight
Length, in. 172
Width, in. 68
Wheelbase, in. 101
Curb weight, lb. 2,780
Percent weight, front/rear 61/39
Typical towing ability, lb. 1,000

SAFETY INFORMATION

Active safety features
Antilock brakes . . . . .Standard
Traction control . . . . .Not available
Stability control . . . . .Not available
Daytime running lights . . . . .Not available
Tire pressure monitor . . . . .Not available

Safety belts
Center-rear belt . . . . .NA
Pretensioners, front/rear . . . . .Yes/no

Air bags
Occupant-sensing system . . . . .Side
Side bags, front/rear . . . . .Standard/no
Inflatable curtain . . . . .Not available
Accident alert system . . . . .Not available

Crash tests
Gov't front-crash test, driver/front passenger . . . . . . ◉/◉
Gov't side-crash test, driver/rear passenger . . . . . . ⊖/NA
IIHS offset crash test . . . . .NA
IIHS side crash test w/ side & curtain airbags . . . . .NA
IIHS side crash test w/o side & curtain airbags . . . . .NA

FROM THE TEST TRACK

Tested model
2002 Type-S 2-door hatchback, 2.0-liter Four, 6-speed manual

Tires as tested
Michelin Pilot HX MXM4, size 205/55R16 89V

Acceleration . . . .⊖
0-30 mph, sec. 3.0
0-60 mph, sec. 7.3
Quarter mile, sec. 15.7
Quarter mile, mph 92
45-65 mph, sec. 5.0

Other findings
Transmission . . . . ◉
Turning circle, ft. 40
Ground clearance, in. 5.0

Braking and handling
Braking . . . .○
Braking, dry pavement, ft. 145
Routine handling . . . .⊖
Emergency handling . . . .⊖
Avoidance maneuver, max. mph . . .53.0

Convenience and comfort
Ride . . . . ⊖
Noise . . . .⊖
Driving position . . . .⊖
Access . . . .○
Controls and displays . . . .⊖
Fit and finish . . . .⊖
Door top to ground, in. 49.0
Trunk . . . .⊖
Luggage capacity . . . . .2+2
Max. load, lb. 700

Seating
Front-seat comfort . . . .⊖
Front shoulder room, in. 52.5
Front leg room, in. 41.5
Front head room, in. 3.5
Rear-seat comfort . . . . ●
Rear shoulder room, in. 49.0
Rear leg room, in. 24.0
Rear head room, in 0.0

Fuel economy . . . .⊖
CU's overall mileage, mpg 26
CU's city/highway, mpg 18/37
CU's 150-mile trip, mpg 31
Annual fuel . . . . .570 gal./$1,255
Cruising range 375

RELIABILITY HISTORY

TROUBLE SPOTS	Acura RSX							
	97	98	99	00	01	02	03	04
Engine						◉	◉	◉
Cooling						◉	◉	◉
Fuel						◉	◉	◉
Ignition						◉	◉	◉
Transmission						◉	◉	◉
Electrical						⊖	⊖	◉
Air conditioning						◉	◉	◉
Suspension						◉	◉	◉
Brakes						⊖	⊖	◉
Exhaust						◉	◉	◉
Paint/trim/rust						⊖	◉	◉
Body integrity						○	⊖	⊖
Power equipment						◉	◉	◉
Body hardware						◉	◉	◉
RELIABILITY VERDICT						✓	✓	✓

Acura TL

CR RECOMMENDED ✓

THE TL LINE
Body style:
sedan
Trim lines:
–
Base price range:
$33,100

The Honda Accord-based TL is the highest-scoring car we've tested in the upscale-sedan category. The TL is among the few models in this class that provide a near-ideal blend of comfort, convenience, and sportiness—all at a reasonable price. It delivers taut, agile handling, though ultimately it's not as nimble as a BMW 3 Series or Mercedes C-Class. The car is very quick yet attains commendable fuel economy. The TL has a firm but comfortable and quiet ride. A wide turning circle is one of the few negatives. Interior quality is impressive.

REPORT CARD

○	Predicted reliability
◉	Owner satisfaction
◒	Predicted depreciation
◉	Accident avoidance
◉	Acceleration
◒	Ride
◒	Front seat comfort
○	Fuel economy

SPECIFICATIONS

Drive wheels Front

Seating 2 front, 3 rear

Engines available
3.2-liter V6 (270 hp)

Transmissions available
6-speed manual; 5-speed automatic

Fuel
Fuel type . . . . .Premium
EPA city/highway, mpg 20/29
Fuel refill capacity, gal. 17.0

Dimensions and weight
Length, in. 186
Width, in. 72
Wheelbase, in. .108
Curb weight, lb. 3,565
Percent weight, front/rear 62/38
Typical towing ability, lb. . . . . .NR

SAFETY INFORMATION

Active safety features
Antilock brakes . . . . .Standard
Traction control . . . . .Standard
Stability control . . . . .Standard
Daytime running lights . . . . .Not available
Tire pressure monitor . . . . .Not available

Safety belts
Center-rear belt 3-point
Pretensioners, front/rear . . . . .Yes/no

Air bags
Occupant-sensing system . . . . .Front and Side
Side bags, front/rear . . . . .Standard/no
Inflatable curtain . . . . .Standard
Accident alert system . . . . .Available

Crash tests
Gov't front-crash test, driver/front passenger . . . . .◉/◉
Gov't side-crash test, driver/rear passenger . . . .◒/◉
IIHS offset crash test . . . . .Good
IIHS side crash test w/ side & curtain airbags . . . . .Good
IIHS side crash test w/o side & curtain airbags . . . . .NA

FROM THE TEST TRACK

Tested model
2004 sedan, 3.2-liter V6, 5-speed automatic

Tires as tested
Bridgestone Turanza EL42, size P235/45R17 93W

Acceleration . . . . ◉
0-30 mph, sec. 2.7
0-60 mph, sec. 6.7
Quarter mile, sec. 15.2
Quarter mile, mph 95
45-65 mph, sec. 4.2

Other findings
Transmission . . . . ◉
Turning circle, ft. 42
Ground clearance, in. 5.5

Braking and handling
Braking . . . . ◒
Braking, dry pavement, ft. 130
Routine handling . . . . ◉
Emergency handling . . . . ◒
Avoidance maneuver, max. mph . . .52.5

Convenience and comfort
Ride . . . . ◒
Noise . . . . ◒
Driving position . . . . ◒
Access . . . . ◒
Controls and displays . . . . ◉
Fit and finish . . . . ◉
Door top to ground, in. 50.0
Trunk . . . . ◒
Luggage capacity . . . . .3+2
Max. load, lb. 850

Seating
Front-seat comfort . . . . ◒
Front shoulder room, in. 58.5
Front leg room, in. 42.0
Front head room, in. 3.5
Rear-seat comfort . . . . ◒
Rear shoulder room, in. 55.0
Rear leg room, in. 27.5
Rear head room, in 3.5

Fuel economy . . . . ○
CU's overall mileage, mpg 23
CU's city/highway, mpg 16/35
CU's 150-mile trip, mpg 27
Annual fuel . . . . .645 gal./$1,420
Cruising range 435

RELIABILITY HISTORY

TROUBLE SPOTS	97	98	99	00	01	02	03	04
Engine	◉	◉	◉	◉	◉	◉	◉	◉
Cooling	◉	◉	◉	◉	◉	◉	◉	◉
Fuel	◒	◉	◒	◉	◉	◉	◉	◉
Ignition	◉	◉	◉	◉	◉	◉	◉	◉
Transmission	◉	◉	○	◉	◒	◉	◉	◉
Electrical	○	◒	◉	◉	◉	◉	◉	◉
Air conditioning	◉	◒	◉	◉	◉	◉	◉	◉
Suspension	◉	◒	◉	◉	◉	◉	◉	◉
Brakes	○	○	◉	○	◉	◉	◉	◉
Exhaust	◒	○	◉	◉	◉	◉	◉	◉
Paint/trim/rust	◒	◒	◉	◒	◉	◉	◉	◉
Body integrity	◒	◉	◒	◉	◒	◒	◒	◉
Power equipment	○	◉	◉	◒	◉	◒	◒	◒
Body hardware	◉	◒	◉	◉	◒	◉	◉	◉
RELIABILITY VERDICT	✓	✓	✓	✓	✓	–	✓	–

Acura TSX

CR RECOMMENDED ✔

The TSX is a successor to the Integra sedan, which left the Acura lineup with the introduction of the RSX in 2001. Based on the smaller Accord sold in Japan and Europe, the TSX is positioned below the TL. It features a smooth-revving engine and a slick manual or automatic transmission. Handling is more agile than the Accord's, but the ride is a bit stiff. The rear seat is not that roomy. The optional navigation system is easy to use. The TSX is a pleasant car with a sporty pretense that straddles the family and sporty upscale sedan categories.

THE TSX LINE

Body style:
sedan

Trim lines:
–

Base price range:
$27,190

REPORT CARD

⊖	Predicted reliability
◉	Owner satisfaction
NA	Predicted depreciation
◉	Accident avoidance
○	Acceleration
○	Ride
⊖	Front seat comfort
○	Fuel economy

SPECIFICATIONS

Drive wheels Front

Seating 2 front, 3 rear

Engines available
2.4-liter 4 (200 hp)

Transmissions available
6-speed manual; 5-speed automatic

Fuel
Fuel type .Premium
EPA city/highway, mpg 23/32
Fuel refill capacity, gal. 17.1

Dimensions and weight
Length, in. 183
Width, in. 69
Wheelbase, in. .105
Curb weight, lb. 3,315
Percent weight, front/rear 61/39
Typical towing ability, lb. 1,000

SAFETY INFORMATION

Active safety features
Antilock brakes . . . . .Standard
Traction control . . . . .Standard
Stability control . . . . .Standard
Daytime running lights . . . . .Not available
Tire pressure monitor . . . . .Not available

Safety belts
Center-rear belt 3-point
Pretensioners, front/rear . . . . .Yes/no

Air bags
Occupant-sensing system . . . . .Side
Side bags, front/rear .Standard/no
Inflatable curtain . . . . .Standard
Accident alert system .Available

Crash tests
Gov't front-crash test, driver/front passenger . . . . .◉/◉
Gov't side-crash test, driver/rear passenger . . . . . .◉/⊖
IIHS offset crash test . . . . .Good
IIHS side crash test w/ side & curtain airbags . . . . .NA
IIHS side crash test w/o side & curtain airbags . . . . .NA

FROM THE TEST TRACK

Tested model
2004 sedan, 2.4-liter Four, 5-speed automatic

Tires as tested
Michelin Pilot HX MXM4, size P215/50R17 93V

Acceleration . . . .○
0-30 mph, sec. 3.5
0-60 mph, sec. 9.2
Quarter mile, sec. 17.1
Quarter mile, mph 85
45-65 mph, sec. 5.9

Other findings
Transmission . . . .◉
Turning circle, ft. 40
Ground clearance, in. 5.0

Braking and handling
Braking . . . .⊖
Braking, dry pavement, ft. 136
Routine handling . . . .⊖
Emergency handling . . . .◉
Avoidance maneuver, max. mph . . .52.5

Convenience and comfort
Ride . . . .○
Noise . . . .⊖
Driving position . . . .◉
Access . . . .⊖
Controls and displays . . . .◉
Fit and finish . . . .◉
Door top to ground, in. 51.0
Trunk . . . .○
Luggage capacity . . . . .3+2
Max. load, lb. 850

Seating
Front-seat comfort . . . .⊖
Front shoulder room, in. 55.0
Front leg room, in. 41.0
Front head room, in. 3.0
Rear-seat comfort . . . .⊖
Rear shoulder room, in. 52.5
Rear leg room, in. 27.0
Rear head room, in 2.5

Fuel economy . . . .○
CU's overall mileage, mpg 23
CU's city/highway, mpg 15/36
CU's 150-mile trip, mpg 29
Annual fuel . . . . .650 gal./$1,425
Cruising range 460

RELIABILITY HISTORY

TROUBLE SPOTS	Acura TSX							
	97	98	99	00	01	02	03	04
Engine								◉
Cooling								◉
Fuel								◉
Ignition								◉
Transmission								◉
Electrical								◉
Air conditioning								◉
Suspension								◉
Brakes								◉
Exhaust								◉
Paint/trim/rust								◉
Body integrity								⊖
Power equipment								◉
Body hardware								◉
RELIABILITY VERDICT								✔

Audi A3

THE A3 LINE
Body style:
4-door hatchback
Trim lines:
–
Base price range:
$25,000E

The new A3 is based on the upcoming redesigned Volkswagen Golf. Priced at about $25,000, it is a small, luxurious package with a tasteful interior and generous power output. When it goes on sale this May, this versatile hatchback will be available as a front-wheel drive vehicle only with a 200-hp, turbocharged 2.0-liter four-cylinder engine. Eight months later arrives a powerful all-wheel drive version with a 3.2-liter V6 and a sequential manual that can shift automatically.

REPORT CARD

New	Predicted reliability
New	Owner satisfaction
NA	Predicted depreciation
NA	Accident avoidance
NA	Acceleration
NA	Ride
NA	Front seat comfort
NA	Fuel economy

SPECIFICATIONS

Drive wheels Front

Seating 2 front, 3 rear

Engines available
2.0-liter 4 turbo (200 hp)

Transmissions available
6-speed sequential; 6-speed manual

Fuel
Fuel type ....Premium
EPA city/highway, mpg ....NA
Fuel refill capacity, gal. 14.5

Dimensions and weight
Length, in. 169
Width, in. 70
Wheelbase, in. 102
Curb weight, lb. 2,950
Percent weight, front/rear 60/40
Typical towing ability, lb. ....NA

SAFETY INFORMATION

Active safety features
Antilock brakes ....Standard
Traction control ....Standard
Stability control ....Standard
Daytime running lights ....Optional
Tire pressure monitor ....Available

Safety belts
Center-rear belt 3-point
Pretensioners, front/rear ....Yes/yes

Air bags
Occupant-sensing system ....Not available
Side bags, front/rear ....Standard/no
Inflatable curtain ....Standard
Accident alert system ....Available

Crash tests
Gov't front-crash test, driver/front passenger ....NA/NA
Gov't side-crash test, driver/rear passenger ....NA/NA
IIHS offset crash test ....NA
IIHS side crash test w/ side & curtain airbags ....NA
IIHS side crash test w/o side & curtain airbags ....NA

ANOTHER LOOK

RELIABILITY HISTORY

TROUBLE SPOTS	97 98 99 00 01 02 03 04
Engine	
Cooling	NO
Fuel	
Ignition	
Transmission	DATA
Electrical	
Air conditioning	NEW
Suspension	
Brakes	MODEL
Exhaust	
Paint/trim/rust	
Body integrity	
Power equipment	
Body hardware	
RELIABILITY VERDICT	

● ● ○ ● ●
better ← → worse   See page 36 for more information.

Audi A4

CR RECOMMENDED

THE A4 LINE
Body style: convertible; sedan; wagon
Trim lines: 2.0T, 3.2, S4, S4 Avant
Base price range: $26,000-$53,950E

The recent freshening upgrades the powertrain and includes the MMI interaction system for audio and other functions. The A4 combines agility with style, and the interior boasts superior attention to detail. At low speeds the firm and compliant ride becomes jiggly. The front seats are very comfortable, but the rear is cramped. The 3.2-liter V6 is quiet and delivers readily available power; the 2.0-liter turbo four-cylinder is responsive but a little noisy. The wagon is stylish but lacks spaciousness. A convertible and a muscular, quick, and capable V8-powered S4 are available. Reliability has improved,

REPORT CARD

○	Predicted reliability
○	Owner satisfaction
◉	Predicted depreciation
◉	Accident avoidance
◉	Acceleration
○	Ride
◉	Front seat comfort
○	Fuel economy

SAFETY INFORMATION

Active safety features

Antilock brakes	Standard
Traction control	Standard
Stability control	Standard
Daytime running lights	Not available
Tire pressure monitor	Available

Safety belts

Center-rear belt	3-point
Pretensioners, front/rear	Yes/yes

Air bags

Occupant-sensing system	Not available
Side bags, front/rear	Standard/optional
Inflatable curtain	Standard
Accident alert system	Available

Crash tests

Gov't front-crash test, driver/front passenger	◓/◓
Gov't side-crash test, driver/rear passenger	◉/◓
IIHS offset crash test	Good
IIHS side crash test w/ side & curtain airbags	NA
IIHS side crash test w/o side & curtain airbags	NA

FROM THE TEST TRACK

Tested model
2004 S4 sedan AWD, 4.2-liter V8, 6-speed manual

Tires as tested
Continental SportContact 2, size 235/40ZR18 95Y

Acceleration	◉
0-30 mph, sec.	1.7
0-60 mph, sec.	5.3
Quarter mile, sec.	13.9
Quarter mile, mph	101
45-65 mph, sec.	3.6

Other findings

Transmission	◓
Turning circle, ft.	38
Ground clearance, in.	4.0

Braking and handling

Braking	◉
Braking, dry pavement, ft.	124
Routine handling	◉
Emergency handling	◓
Avoidance maneuver, max. mph	54.5

Convenience and comfort

Ride	○
Noise	◓
Driving position	◓
Access	◓
Controls and displays	◉
Fit and finish	◉
Door top to ground, in.	50.0
Trunk	○
Luggage capacity	4+0
Max. load, lb.	1,145

Seating

Front-seat comfort	◉
Front shoulder room, in.	54.5
Front leg room, in.	43.0
Front head room, in.	3.0
Rear-seat comfort	◒
Rear shoulder room, in.	52.0
Rear leg room, in.	25.5
Rear head room, in	2.0

Fuel economy	○
CU's overall mileage, mpg	20
CU's city/highway, mpg	17/26
CU's 150-mile trip, mpg	21
Annual fuel	730 gal./$1,610
Cruising range	315

SPECIFICATIONS

Drive wheels Front or AWD

Seating 2 front, 3 rear

Engines available
1.8-liter 4 turbo (170 hp); 2.0-liter 4 turbo (200 hp); 3.0-liter V6 (220 hp); 3.2-liter V6 (255 hp); 4.2-liter V8 (340 hp)

Transmissions available
6-speed manual; CVT; 6-speed automatic

Fuel

Fuel type	Premium
EPA city/highway, mpg	15/21
Fuel refill capacity, gal.	16.6

Dimensions and weight

Length, in.	179
Width, in.	70
Wheelbase, in.	104
Curb weight, lb.	3,920
Percent weight, front/rear	60/40
Typical towing ability, lb.	NR

RELIABILITY HISTORY

TROUBLE SPOTS	Audi A4 4-cyl. AWD 97	98	99	00	01	02	03	04
Engine	Insufficient data	◒	◒	◒	○	○	◓	◉
Cooling		○	◓	◓	◉	◉	◉	◉
Fuel		○	○	◒	○	○	◓	◉
Ignition		◓	○	◓	●	◒	◓	◉
Transmission		◓	◓	◓	◉	◉	◉	◉
Electrical		◒	◒	◒	◒	●	◓	◉
Air conditioning		◓	◓	◓	◉	◉	◉	◉
Suspension		◒	◒	◓	◓	◉	◉	◉
Brakes		◒	●	○	○	◓	◉	◉
Exhaust		◉	◓	◓	◉	◉	◉	◉
Paint/trim/rust		○	◓	◉	◉	◉	◉	◉
Body integrity		◒	○	◓	◓	◓	◉	◉
Power equipment		○	○	○	○	○	◓	◉
Body hardware		○	○	◓	◓	○	◓	◉
RELIABILITY VERDICT		✗	✗	✗	-	✗	-	-

Audi A6

THE A6/ALLROAD LINE
Body style:
sedan; wagon
Trim lines:
3.2, 4.2, Allroad 2.7T,
Allroad 4.2
Base price range:
$40,250-$51,500

The A6 received a redesign for the 2005 model year and the new wagon arrives for 2006. Handling is responsive and secure. The ride is firm, yet comfortable, but is no match for the Mercedes E-Class. AWD provides excellent snow traction. The 3.2-liter V6 and six-speed automatic transmission make for a strong, polished powertrain. The seats are excellent and the interior is nicely finished and filled with nice details. The MMI (Multi Media Interface) system with integrated audio and navigation controls is a bit annoying, with some simple functions requiring multiple steps.

REPORT CARD

New	**Predicted reliability**
New	**Owner satisfaction**
NA	**Predicted depreciation**
NA	**Accident avoidance**
NA	**Acceleration**
NA	**Ride**
NA	**Front seat comfort**
NA	**Fuel economy**

SPECIFICATIONS

Drive wheels AWD

Seating 2 front, 3 rear

Engines available
2.7-liter V6 twin-turbo (250 hp); 3.2-liter V6 (255 hp); 4.2-liter V8 (300 hp); 4.2-liter V8 (335 hp)

Transmissions available
6-speed manual; 5-speed automatic; 6-speed automatic

Fuel
Fuel type . . . . .Premium
EPA city/highway, mpg 19/26
Fuel refill capacity, gal. 21.1

Dimensions and weight
Length, in. 194
Width, in. 79
Wheelbase, in. 112
Curb weight, lb. 4,115
Percent weight, front/rear 56/44
Typical towing ability, lb. 2,000

SAFETY INFORMATION

Active safety features
Antilock brakes . . . . .Standard
Traction control . . . . .Standard
Stability control . . . . .Standard
Daytime running lights . . . . .Optional
Tire pressure monitor . . . . .Available

Safety belts
Center-rear belt 3-point
Pretensioners, front/rear . . . . .Yes/yes

Air bags
Occupant-sensing system . . . . .Not available
Side bags, front/rear . . . . .Standard/optional
Inflatable curtain . . . . .Standard
Accident alert system . . . . .Available

Crash tests
Gov't front-crash test, driver/front passenger . . . . . . .NA/NA
Gov't side-crash test, driver/rear passenger . . . . . . .NA/NA
IIHS offset crash test . . . . .NA
IIHS side crash test w/ side & curtain airbags . . . . .NA
IIHS side crash test w/o side & curtain airbags . . . . .NA

ANOTHER LOOK

RELIABILITY HISTORY

TROUBLE SPOTS	97 98 99 00 01 02 03 04
Engine	
Cooling	**NO**
Fuel	
Ignition	**DATA**
Transmission	
Electrical	**NEW**
Air conditioning	
Suspension	
Brakes	**MODEL**
Exhaust	
Paint/trim/rust	
Body integrity	
Power equipment	
Body hardware	
RELIABILITY VERDICT	

● ● ○ ○ ●
better ◄──────► worse   See page 36 for more information.

Audi A8

THE A8 LINE
Body style:
sedan
Trim lines:
Base, L, W12
Base price range:
$66,590-$117,400

The A8 is a very pleasant and capable luxury car with standard AWD. The strong, 4.2-liter V8 and six-speed automatic provide effortless power. A 6.0-liter, 12-cylinder engine is available. Handling is responsive and secure, but ride comfort doesn't match the Mercedes S-Class or Lexus LS430. The interior is very quiet, with impeccable fit and finish. The front seats are extremely comfortable and supportive, and the rear seat is expansive. The MMI (Multi Media Interface) driver interaction system is more intuitive than BMW's iDrive, but not by much.

REPORT CARD

NA	Predicted reliability
NA	Owner satisfaction
NA	Predicted depreciation
◓	Accident avoidance
◓	Acceleration
◓	Ride
◉	Front seat comfort
●	Fuel economy

SPECIFICATIONS

Drive wheels AWD

Seating 2 front, 3 rear

Engines available
4.2-liter V8 (335 hp); 6.0-liter 12 (450 hp)

Transmissions available
6-speed automatic

Fuel
Fuel type ....Premium
EPA city/highway, mpg 18/24
Fuel refill capacity, gal. 23.8

Dimensions and weight
Length, in. 204
Width, in. 75
Wheelbase, in. 121
Curb weight, lb. 4,505
Percent weight, front/rear 56/44
Typical towing ability, lb. 3,500

SAFETY INFORMATION

Active safety features

Antilock brakes ....Standard
Traction control ....Standard
Stability control ....Standard
Daytime running lights ....Standard
Tire pressure monitor ....Available

Safety belts

Center-rear belt 3-point
Pretensioners, front/rear ....Yes/yes

Air bags

Occupant-sensing system ....Not available
Side bags, front/rear ....Standard/standard
Inflatable curtain ....Standard
Accident alert system ....Available

Crash tests

Gov't front-crash test, driver/front passenger ......NA/NA
Gov't side-crash test, driver/rear passenger ....NA/NA
IIHS offset crash test ....NA
IIHS side crash test w/ side & curtain airbags ....NA
IIHS side crash test w/o side & curtain airbags ....NA

FROM THE TEST TRACK

Tested model
2004 L sedan AWD, 4.2-liter V8, 6-speed automatic

Tires as tested
Continental ContiTouring Contact CH95, size 255/45R18 99H

Acceleration ....◓
0-30 mph, sec. 2.9
0-60 mph, sec. 7.6
Quarter mile, sec. 15.9
Quarter mile, mph 93
45-65 mph, sec. 4.4

Other findings
Transmission ....◓
Turning circle, ft. 41
Ground clearance, in. 5.0

Braking and handling
Braking ....◓
Braking, dry pavement, ft. 131
Routine handling ....◓
Emergency handling ....○
Avoidance maneuver, max. mph ...49.5

Convenience and comfort
Ride ....◓
Noise ....◉
Driving position ....◓
Access ....◓
Controls and displays ....○
Fit and finish ....◉
Door top to ground, in. 51.5
Trunk ....○
Luggage capacity ....3+3
Max. load, lb. 1,210

Seating
Front-seat comfort ....◉
Front shoulder room, in. 58.5
Front leg room, in. 43.0
Front head room, in. 3.0
Rear-seat comfort ....◉
Rear shoulder room, in. 55.5
Rear leg room, in. 34.5
Rear head room, in 3.5

Fuel economy ....●
CU's overall mileage, mpg 17
CU's city/highway, mpg 11/26
CU's 150-mile trip, mpg 20
Annual fuel ....885 gal./$1,940
Cruising range 440

RELIABILITY HISTORY

TROUBLE SPOTS	97 98 99 00 01 02 03 04
Engine	
Cooling	
Fuel	NOT
Ignition	
Transmission	ENOUGH
Electrical	
Air conditioning	DATA
Suspension	
Brakes	TO
Exhaust	
Paint/trim/rust	RATE
Body integrity	
Power equipment	
Body hardware	
RELIABILITY VERDICT	

Audi TT

THE TT LINE
Body style:
convertible; coupe
Trim lines:
–
Base price range:
$33,500-$43,150

Based on the Volkswagen New Beetle platform, the TT's handling is responsive and secure but not nearly as agile or enjoyable as that of the Mazda RX-8 or Porsche Boxster. The convertible we tested had a stiff, nervous ride. A gutsy—if noisy—180-hp, turbocharged four-cylinder is standard on FWD editions, while a 225-hp version powers the AWD models. The interior has artful aluminum, stainless-steel, and leather touches. Outward visibility is especially poor. A more potent, better-sounding V6 model arrived for 2004 with a new six-speed automatic transmission or a sequential version.

REPORT CARD

⊖	Predicted reliability
⊖	Owner satisfaction
⊖	Predicted depreciation
◓	Accident avoidance
◓	Acceleration
○	Ride
⊖	Front seat comfort
○	Fuel economy

SPECIFICATIONS

Drive wheels Front or AWD

Seating 2 front, 2 rear

Engines available
1.8-liter 4 turbo (180 hp); 1.8-liter 4 turbo (225 hp); 3.2-liter V6 (250 hp)

Transmissions available
6-speed sequential; 6-speed manual; 6-speed automatic

Fuel
Fuel type . . . . .Premium
EPA city/highway, mpg 20/28
Fuel refill capacity, gal. 16.3

Dimensions and weight
Length, in. 159
Width, in. 73
Wheelbase, in. 96
Curb weight, lb. 3,440
Percent weight, front/rear 59/41
Typical towing ability, lb. . . . . .NR

SAFETY INFORMATION

Active safety features
Antilock brakes . . . . .Standard
Traction control . . . . .Standard
Stability control . . . . .Standard
Daytime running lights . . . . .Not available
Tire pressure monitor . . . . .Not available

Safety belts
Center-rear belt . . . . .NA
Pretensioners, front/rear .Yes/no

Air bags
Occupant-sensing system . . . . .Not available
Side bags, front/rear . . . . .Standard/no
Inflatable curtain . . . . .Not available
Accident alert system . . . . .Not available

Crash tests
Gov't front-crash test, driver/front passenger . . . . . .NA/NA
Gov't side-crash test, driver/rear passenger . . . .◉/NA
IIHS offset crash test . . . . .NA
IIHS side crash test w/ side & curtain airbags . . . . .NA
IIHS side crash test w/o side & curtain airbags . . . . . . .NA

FROM THE TEST TRACK

Tested model
2002 convertible AWD, 1.8-liter Four turbo, 6-speed manual

Tires as tested
Michelin Pilot Sport, size 225/45ZR17 91Y

Acceleration . . . . ◓
0-30 mph, sec. 2.2
0-60 mph, sec. 7.0
Quarter mile, sec. 15.3
Quarter mile, mph 92
45-65 mph, sec. 4.1

Other findings
Transmission . . . . ⊖
Turning circle, ft. 35
Ground clearance, in. 4.5

Braking and handling
Braking . . . . ◓
Braking, dry pavement, ft. 123
Routine handling . . . . ◓
Emergency handling . . . . ⊖
Avoidance maneuver, max. mph . . .55.0

Convenience and comfort
Ride . . . . ○
Noise . . . . ⊖
Driving position . . . . ⊖
Access . . . . ○
Controls and displays . . . . ⊖
Fit and finish . . . . ◕
Door top to ground, in. 46.5
Trunk . . . . ●
Luggage capacity . . . . .1+0
Max. load, lb. 550

Seating
Front-seat comfort . . . . ⊖
Front shoulder room, in. 51.0
Front leg room, in. 41.0
Front head room, in. 3.5

Fuel economy . . . . ○
CU's overall mileage, mpg 22
CU's city/highway, mpg 16/30
CU's 150-mile trip, mpg 25
Annual fuel . . . . .680 gal./$1,490
Cruising range 380

RELIABILITY HISTORY

TROUBLE SPOTS	Audi TT							
	97	98	99	00	01	02	03	04
Engine				⊖	⊖	⊖		
Cooling				⊖	⊖	⊖		
Fuel				●	⊖	⊖		
Ignition				◉	○	○		
Transmission				⊖	⊖	⊖		
Electrical				●	●	●	Insufficient data	Insufficient data
Air conditioning				○	⊖	⊖		
Suspension				⊖	⊖	⊖		
Brakes				○	⊖	⊖		
Exhaust				◉	◉	⊖		
Paint/trim/rust				◉	◉	⊖		
Body integrity				⊖	⊖	⊖		
Power equipment				⊖	⊖	○		
Body hardware				○	⊖	◉		
RELIABILITY VERDICT				–	✗	✗		

BMW 3 Series

CR RECOMMENDED ✓

BMW's 3 Series offers a nearly ideal blend of sportiness, luxury, and safety. Sedan, coupe, wagon, and convertible models are available, as are AWD sedan and wagon xi versions. The 333-hp M3 brings even more performance and sports-car handling to the line. A redesigned sedan arrives in May. It should have agile handling and smooth engines. Both the 325i and 330i use a 3.0-liter engine, with 215 hp for the 330. The rear is less cramped than in previous generations.

THE 3 SERIES LINE

Body style: convertible; coupe; sedan; wagon

Trim lines: 325i, 325xi, 330i, 330xi, 325Ci, 330Ci, M3

Base price range: $29,300-$55,800

REPORT CARD

○	Predicted reliability
⊖	Owner satisfaction
◉	Predicted depreciation
◉	Accident avoidance
◉	Acceleration
○	Ride
◉	Front seat comfort
⊖	Fuel economy

SPECIFICATIONS

Drive wheels Rear or AWD

Seating 2 front, 3 rear

Engines available
2.5-liter 6 (184 hp); 3.0-liter 6 (225 hp); 3.0-liter 6 (235 hp); 3.2-liter 6 (333 hp)

Transmissions available
6-speed sequential; 5-speed manual; 6-speed manual; 5-speed automatic

Fuel
Fuel type .Premium
EPA city/highway, mpg 16/23
Fuel refill capacity, gal. 16.6

Dimensions and weight
Length, in. 177
Width, in. 70
Wheelbase, in. 108
Curb weight, lb. 3,460
Percent weight, front/rear 50/50
Typical towing ability, lb. . . . . .NR

SAFETY INFORMATION

Active safety features
Antilock brakes . . . . .Standard
Traction control . . . . .Standard
Stability control . . . . .Standard
Daytime running lights . . . . .Optional
Tire pressure monitor . . . . .Available

Safety belts
Center-rear belt 3-point
Pretensioners, front/rear . . . . .Yes/no

Air bags
Occupant-sensing system . . . . .Not available
Side bags, front/rear . . . . .Standard/optional
Inflatable curtain . . . . .Standard
Accident alert system . . . . .Available

Crash tests
Gov't front-crash test, driver/front passenger . . . . ⊖/◐
Gov't side-crash test, driver/rear passenger . . . . .NA/NA
IIHS offset crash test . . . . .Good
IIHS side crash test w/ side & curtain airbags . . . . .NA
IIHS side crash test w/o side & curtain airbags . . . . .NA

FROM THE TEST TRACK

Tested model
2004 M3 coupe, 3.2-liter Six, 6-speed manual

Tires as tested
Continental ContiSport Contact M3, size 225/40ZR19 (front), 255/35ZR19 (rear)

Acceleration . . . .◉
0-30 mph, sec. 1.9
0-60 mph, sec. 5.1
Quarter mile, sec. 13.8
Quarter mile, mph 103
45-65 mph, sec. .3.7

Other findings
Transmission . . . .⊖
Turning circle, ft. .36
Ground clearance, in. 4.5

Braking and handling
Braking . . . .◉
Braking, dry pavement, ft. 120
Routine handling . . . .◉
Emergency handling . . . .◉
Avoidance maneuver, max. mph . . .55.5

Convenience and comfort
Ride . . . .○
Noise . . . .○
Driving position . . . .⊖
Access . . . .⊖
Controls and displays . . . .◉
Fit and finish . . . .◉
Door top to ground, in. 50.0
Trunk . . . .⊖
Luggage capacity . . . . .2+1
Max. load, lb. 1,060

Seating
Front-seat comfort . . . .◉
Front shoulder room, in. 54.5
Front leg room, in. 41.0
Front head room, in. 2.0
Rear-seat comfort . . . .⊖
Rear shoulder room, in. 51.5
Rear leg room, in. 25.5
Rear head room, in 1.5

Fuel economy . . . .⊖
CU's overall mileage, mpg 19
  CU's city/highway, mpg 13/27
  CU's 150-mile trip, mpg 23
Annual fuel . . . . .780 gal./$1,715
Cruising range 350

RELIABILITY HISTORY

TROUBLE SPOTS	BMW M3							
	97	98	99	00	01	02	03	04
Engine		○				○	◉	
Cooling		○				◉	◉	
Fuel		◉				◉	◉	
Ignition		◉				◉	◉	
Transmission		○				◉	◉	
Electrical	Insufficient data	○	Insufficient data	Insufficient data	Insufficient data	◉	○	Insufficient data
Air conditioning		○				◉	◉	
Suspension		○				◉	○	
Brakes		○				◉	◉	
Exhaust		○				◉	◉	
Paint/trim/rust		◉				◉	◉	
Body integrity		○				○	○	
Power equipment		○				○	⊖	
Body hardware		○				○	○	
RELIABILITY VERDICT		✓				–	–	

BMW 5 Series

THE 5 SERIES LINE
Body style:
sedan; wagon
Trim lines:
525i, 525xi, 530i,
530xi, 545i, M5
Base price range:
$41,300-$75,000E

The BMW 5 Series is both impressive and frustrating, as well as more expensive. It uses a version of the iDrive control system, which we found tedious to use. Handling is agile and secure, and the ride is comfortable and quiet. The six-speed automatic and the 3.0-liter, six-cylinder engine are smooth and give the car a sporty demeanor. The seats are very comfortable in the front and rear. Interior fit and finish is less impressive than in the previous generation. A powerful M5 arrives for 2005, as well as AWD models, including a wagon. First-year reliability is well below average.

REPORT CARD

●	Predicted reliability
⊖	Owner satisfaction
◐	Predicted depreciation
◐	Accident avoidance
⊖	Acceleration
⊖	Ride
◐	Front seat comfort
⊖	Fuel economy

SPECIFICATIONS

Drive wheels Rear or AWD

Seating 2 front, 3 rear

Engines available
2.5-liter 6 (184 hp); 3.0-liter 6 (225 hp); 4.4-liter V8 (325 hp); 5.0-liter V10 (507 hp)

Transmissions available
6-speed sequential; 7-speed sequential; 6-speed manual; 5-speed automatic; 6-speed automatic

Fuel
Fuel type ....Premium
EPA city/highway, mpg 18/28
Fuel refill capacity, gal. 18.5

Dimensions and weight
Length, in. 191
Width, in. 73
Wheelbase, in. 114
Curb weight, lb. 3,650
Percent weight, front/rear 50/50
Typical towing ability, lb. ....NR

SAFETY INFORMATION

Active safety features
Antilock brakes ....Standard
Traction control ....Standard
Stability control ....Standard
Daytime running lights ....Optional
Tire pressure monitor ....Available

Safety belts
Center-rear belt 3-point
Pretensioners, front/rear ....Yes/no

Air bags
Occupant-sensing system ....Front
Side bags, front/rear ....Standard/optional
Inflatable curtain ....Standard
Accident alert system ....Available

Crash tests
Gov't front-crash test, driver/front passenger ......NA/NA
Gov't side-crash test, driver/rear passenger ....NA/NA
IIHS offset crash test ....Good
IIHS side crash test w/ side & curtain airbags ....NA
IIHS side crash test w/o side & curtain airbags ....NA

FROM THE TEST TRACK

Tested model
2004 530i sedan, 3.0-liter Six, 6-speed automatic

Tires as tested
Continental ContiTouring Contact CV95, size 225/50R17 94V

Acceleration .... ⊖
0-30 mph, sec. 2.7
0-60 mph, sec. 7.4
Quarter mile, sec. 15.7
Quarter mile, mph 92
45-65 mph, sec. 5.1

Other findings
Transmission .... ◐
Turning circle, ft. 39
Ground clearance, in. 5.0

Braking and handling
Braking .... ◐
Braking, dry pavement, ft. 127
Routine handling .... ⊖
Emergency handling .... ⊖
Avoidance maneuver, max. mph ...54.5

Convenience and comfort
Ride .... ⊖
Noise .... ⊖
Driving position .... ⊖
Access .... ⊖
Controls and displays .... ⊖
Fit and finish .... ⊖
Door top to ground, in. 52.0
Trunk .... ○
Luggage capacity ....3+1
Max. load, lb. 1,100

Seating
Front-seat comfort .... ◐
Front shoulder room, in. 57.0
Front leg room, in. 42.0
Front head room, in. 4.5
Rear-seat comfort .... ⊖
Rear shoulder room, in. 56.5
Rear leg room, in. 28.5
Rear head room, in 3.5

Fuel economy .... ⊖
CU's overall mileage, mpg 20
CU's city/highway, mpg 14/29
CU's 150-mile trip, mpg 24
Annual fuel ....740 gal./$1,625
Cruising range 415

RELIABILITY HISTORY

TROUBLE SPOTS	BMW 5 Series							
	97	98	99	00	01	02	03	04
Engine	○	○	●	◐	◐	●	●	●
Cooling	●	◐	◐	◐	◐	◐	●	●
Fuel	◐	◐	◐	◐	○	○	●	●
Ignition	◐	●	◐	◐	●	●	◐	●
Transmission	○	○	◐	◐	●	●	●	●
Electrical	●	●	○	◐	◐	○	◐	●
Air conditioning	○	○	○	◐	◐	●	●	●
Suspension	○	○	○	◐	◐	●	●	●
Brakes	○	○	○	●	●	●	●	◐
Exhaust	○	○	◐	◐	●	●	●	●
Paint/trim/rust	○	○	○	◐	●	●	●	●
Body integrity	○	○	○	◐	◐	●	●	●
Power equipment	●	○	○	◐	●	●	○	●
Body hardware	○	○	◐	◐	◐	●	●	●
RELIABILITY VERDICT	–	–	–	–	✓	✓	✓	✗

● ◐ ○ ⊖ ●
better ◀—————▶ worse   See page 36 for more information.

BMW 6 Series

THE 6 SERIES LINE
Body style:
convertible; coupe
Trim lines:
645Ci, M6
Base price range:
$69,900-$85,000E

The 6 Series revives a tradition of a big BMW coupe, the last of which ended with the demise of the 8 Series in the mid-1990s. Unlike the original 630csi coupe, which was an independent car, the new 6 Series shares a platform with the recently redesigned 5 Series, including the cumbersome iDrive control system. The standard engine is the smooth and punchy 4.4-liter V8 that's also found in the 545i and 745i sedans, thus the designation of 645Ci. A soft-top convertible version is available, defying a trend toward folding metal tops. A limited-production, high-performance V10-powered M6 is new.

REPORT CARD

NA	Predicted reliability
NA	Owner satisfaction
NA	Predicted depreciation
NA	Accident avoidance
NA	Acceleration
NA	Ride
NA	Front seat comfort
NA	Fuel economy

SPECIFICATIONS

Drive wheels Rear

Seating 2 front, 2 rear

Engines available
4.4-liter V8 (325 hp); 5.0-liter V10 (500 hp)

Transmissions available
6-speed sequential; 7-speed sequential; 6-speed manual; 6-speed automatic

Fuel
Fuel type .Premium
EPA city/highway, mpg 17/25
Fuel refill capacity, gal. 18.5

Dimensions and weight
Length, in. 190
Width, in. 73
Wheelbase, in. 109
Curb weight, lb. 3,780
Percent weight, front/rear 52/48
Typical towing ability, lb. . . . . .NR

SAFETY INFORMATION

Active safety features
Antilock brakes . . . . .Standard
Traction control . . . . .Standard
Stability control . . . . .Standard
Daytime running lights . . . . .Optional
Tire pressure monitor . . . . .Available

Safety belts
Center-rear belt . . . . .NA
Pretensioners, front/rear .Yes/no

Air bags
Occupant-sensing system . . . . .Not available
Side bags, front/rear . . . . .Standard/no
Inflatable curtain . . . . .Standard
Accident alert system . . . . .Available

Crash tests
Gov't front-crash test, driver/front passenger . . . . . .NA/NA
Gov't side-crash test, driver/rear passenger . . . . .NA/NA
IIHS offset crash test . . . . .NA
IIHS side crash test w/ side & curtain airbags . . . . .NA
IIHS side crash test w/o side & curtain airbags . . . . .NA

ANOTHER LOOK

RELIABILITY HISTORY

TROUBLE SPOTS	97	98	99	00	01	02	03	04
Engine								
Cooling								
Fuel			NOT					
Ignition								
Transmission			ENOUGH					
Electrical								
Air conditioning			DATA					
Suspension								
Brakes			TO					
Exhaust								
Paint/trim/rust			RATE					
Body integrity								
Power equipment								
Body hardware								
RELIABILITY VERDICT								

BMW 7 Series

THE 7 SERIES LINE
Body style:
sedan
Trim lines:
745i, 745Li, 760i, 760Li
Base price range:
$69,900-$117,300

The 7 Series even makes starting the engine an unusual ceremony. The frustrating iDrive control system uses a single knob to interface with the climate, audio, navigation, and phone systems. Meant to streamline the cabin, it ends up causing stress. A freshening arrives in May. The 745i we tested was very quick, quiet, and agile, with a powerful 325-hp, 4.4-liter V8 mated to a smooth six-speed automatic. The ride is steady but not as absorbent as in the Mercedes S-Class. The cabin is very roomy and well-furnished, but overall the car misses the mark as a luxury sedan. Reliability has been poor.

REPORT CARD

●	Predicted reliability
⊖	Owner satisfaction
◉	Predicted depreciation
⊖	Accident avoidance
◉	Acceleration
⊖	Ride
◉	Front seat comfort
⊖	Fuel economy

SPECIFICATIONS

Drive wheels Rear

Seating 2 front, 3 rear

Engines available
4.4-liter V8 (325 hp); 6.0-liter V12 (438 hp)

Transmissions available
6-speed automatic

Fuel
Fuel type ....Premium
EPA city/highway, mpg 18/26
Fuel refill capacity, gal. 23.3

Dimensions and weight
Length, in. 204
Width, in. 75
Wheelbase, in. 123
Curb weight, lb. 4,505
Percent weight, front/rear 50/50
Typical towing ability, lb. ....NR

SAFETY INFORMATION

Active safety features
Antilock brakes ....Standard
Traction control ....Standard
Stability control ....Standard
Daytime running lights ....Not available
Tire pressure monitor ....Available

Safety belts
Center-rear belt 3-point
Pretensioners, front/rear ....Yes/yes

Air bags
Occupant-sensing system ....Not available
Side bags, front/rear ....Standard/optional
Inflatable curtain ....Standard
Accident alert system ....Available

Crash tests
Gov't front-crash test, driver/front passenger ......NA/NA
Gov't side-crash test, driver/rear passenger ....NA/NA
IIHS offset crash test ....NA
IIHS side crash test w/ side & curtain airbags ....NA
IIHS side crash test w/o side & curtain airbags ....NA

FROM THE TEST TRACK

Tested model
2003 745Li sedan, 4.4-liter V8, 6-speed automatic

Tires as tested
Bridgestone Turanza EL42, size 245/50R18 100V

Acceleration ....◉
0-30 mph, sec. 2.6
0-60 mph, sec. 6.9
Quarter mile, sec. 15.4
Quarter mile, mph 95
45-65 mph, sec. 4.6

Other findings
Transmission ....⊖
Turning circle, ft. 42
Ground clearance, in. 5.0

Braking and handling
Braking ....⊖
Braking, dry pavement, ft. 135
Routine handling ....⊖
Emergency handling ....○
Avoidance maneuver, max. mph ...52.0

Convenience and comfort
Ride ....⊖
Noise ....◉
Driving position ....⊖
Access ....⊖
Controls and displays ....●
Fit and finish ....◉
Door top to ground, in. 52.0
Trunk ....○
Luggage capacity ....3+3
Max. load, lb. 1,060

Seating
Front-seat comfort ....◉
Front shoulder room, in. 59.0
Front leg room, in. 42.0
Front head room, in. 4.0
Rear-seat comfort ....◉
Rear shoulder room, in. 57.0
Rear leg room, in. 35.0
Rear head room, in 3.5

Fuel economy ....⊖
CU's overall mileage, mpg 18
  CU's city/highway, mpg 11/28
  CU's 150-mile trip, mpg 21
Annual fuel ....855 gal./$1,880
Cruising range 465

RELIABILITY HISTORY

TROUBLE SPOTS	97	98	99	00	01	02	03	04
Engine	○	○		◕	●	●	●	
Cooling	●	●		○	◕	○	○	
Fuel	○	○		○	○	○	○	
Ignition	⊖	⊖		◕	●	⊖	⊖	
Transmission	◉	⊖		○	◕	○	○	
Electrical	●	●	Insufficient data	○	○	●	●	Insufficient data
Air conditioning	○	⊖		○	○	○	⊖	
Suspension	⊖	⊖		○	○	⊖	◕	
Brakes	⊖	⊖		◕	●	◕	◕	
Exhaust	○	○		◕	●	○	○	
Paint/trim/rust	○	○		◕	◕	◕	◕	
Body integrity	⊖	⊖		○	○	○	○	
Power equipment	●	●		●	○	●	●	
Body hardware	○	⊖		○	○	○	○	
RELIABILITY VERDICT	✕	✕		✕	−	✕	✕	

● ◕ ○ ⊖ ●
better ◀———▶ worse   See page 36 for more information.

BMW X3

THE X3 LINE
Body style:
4-door SUV
Trim lines:
2.5i, 3.0i
Base price range:
$30,300-$36,300

The X3 SUV is loosely based on the excellent 3 Series wagon but with a considerably roomier rear seat. The X3 has all of the usual BMW comfort and safety equipment. Our X3 has a hard and choppy ride, but BMW claims it was softened as of May 2004. Handling is agile and forgiving. The 184-hp, 2.5-liter engine is adequate, and the 225-hp, 3.0-liter is punchier. Both are mated to a standard six-speed manual or optional five-speed automatic that is very smooth. AWD endows it with good snow traction and capability for light off-road duty. Typical options raise the base price considerably.

REPORT CARD

NA	**Predicted reliability**
NA	**Owner satisfaction**
NA	**Predicted depreciation**
◒	**Accident avoidance**
○	**Acceleration**
◒	**Ride**
◒	**Front seat comfort**
●	**Fuel economy**

SPECIFICATIONS

Drive wheels AWD

Seating 2 front, 3 rear

Engines available
2.5-liter 6 (184 hp); 3.0-liter 6 (225 hp)

Transmissions available
6-speed manual; 5-speed automatic

Fuel
Fuel type . . . . .Premium
EPA city/highway, mpg 17/23
Fuel refill capacity, gal. 17.7

Dimensions and weight
Length, in. 180
Width, in. 73
Wheelbase, in. 110
Curb weight, lb. 4,065
Percent weight, front/rear 51/49
Typical towing ability, lb. 3,500

SAFETY INFORMATION

Active safety features
Antilock brakes . . . . .Standard
Traction control . . . . .Standard
Stability control . . . . .Standard
Daytime running lights . . . . .Optional
Tire pressure monitor . . . . .Available

Safety belts
Center-rear belt 3-point
Pretensioners, front/rear . . . . .Yes/no

Air bags
Occupant-sensing system . . . . .Not available
Side bags, front/rear . . . . .Standard/optional
Inflatable curtain . . . . .Standard
Accident alert system .Available

Crash tests
Gov't front-crash test, driver/front passenger . . . . . . .NA/NA
Gov't side-crash test, driver/rear passenger . . . . .NA/NA
IIHS offset crash test . . . . .NA
IIHS side crash test w/ side & curtain airbags . . . . .NA
IIHS side crash test w/o side & curtain airbags . . . . .NA

FROM THE TEST TRACK

Tested model
2004 2.5i 4-door SUV AWD, 2.5-liter Six, 5-speed automatic

Tires as tested
Bridgestone Turanza EL42, size 235/55R17 99H

Acceleration . . . . ○
0-30 mph, sec. 3.6
0-60 mph, sec. 9.8
Quarter mile, sec. 17.6
Quarter mile, mph 82
45-65 mph, sec. 6.2

Other findings
Transmission . . . . ◉
Turning circle, ft. 39
Ground clearance, in. 7.5

Braking and handling
Braking . . . . ◒
Braking, dry pavement, ft. 130
Routine handling . . . . ◒
Emergency handling . . . . ◒
Avoidance maneuver, max. mph . . .50.5

Convenience and comfort
Ride . . . . ◒
Noise . . . . ◒
Driving position . . . . ◒
Access . . . . ◒
Controls and displays . . . . ◒
Fit and finish . . . . ◒
Door top to ground, in. 59.0
Cargo area . . . . ○
Cargo volume, cu.ft. 33.0
Max. load, lb. 1,005

Seating
Front-seat comfort . . . . ◒
Front shoulder room, in. 55.0
Front leg room, in. 42.0
Front head room, in. 4.0
Rear-seat comfort . . . . ◒
Rear shoulder room, in. 54.0
Rear leg room, in. 27.5
Rear head room, in 3.0

Fuel economy . . . . ●
CU's overall mileage, mpg 17
 CU's city/highway, mpg 12/26
 CU's 150-mile trip, mpg 21
Annual fuel . . . . .860 gal./$1,890
Cruising range 340

RELIABILITY HISTORY

TROUBLE SPOTS	97 98 99 00 01 02 03 04
Engine	
Cooling	NOT
Fuel	
Ignition	ENOUGH
Transmission	
Electrical	
Air conditioning	DATA
Suspension	
Brakes	TO
Exhaust	
Paint/trim/rust	RATE
Body integrity	
Power equipment	
Body hardware	
RELIABILITY VERDICT	

Expert • Independent • Nonprofit

BMW X5

THE X5 LINE
Body style:
4-door SUV
Trim lines:
3.0i, 4.4i, 4.8is
Base price range:
$41,700-$70,100

The car-based X5 delivers agile handling, an impressive drivetrain, and very comfortable front seats. While fun, the 3.0 model feels a bit disconcerting at its cornering limits because of a hopping-sideways sensation. The X5 has good snow traction and can tackle moderate off-road terrain. A hill-descent feature is useful. Below-average reliability, a choppy ride, and modest cargo space are detractions. All of the engines deliver spirited acceleration. The interior is impeccably trimmed and rich-looking, and the rear seat is roomy. The optional HID headlights produce blinding effects on fellow motorists.

REPORT CARD

◖	Predicted reliability
○	Owner satisfaction
◉	Predicted depreciation
○	Accident avoidance
◖	Acceleration
○	Ride
◉	Front seat comfort
●	Fuel economy

SPECIFICATIONS

Drive wheels AWD

Seating 2 front, 3 rear

Engines available
3.0-liter 6 (225 hp); 4.4-liter V8 (315 hp); 4.8-liter V8 (355 hp)

Transmissions available
6-speed manual; 5-speed automatic; 6-speed automatic

Fuel
Fuel type . . . . Premium
EPA city/highway, mpg 16/21
Fuel refill capacity, gal. 24.6

Dimensions and weight
Length, in. 184
Width, in. 74
Wheelbase, in. .111
Curb weight, lb. 4,745
Percent weight, front/rear 49/51
Typical towing ability, lb. 5,000

SAFETY INFORMATION

Active safety features
Antilock brakes . . . . .Standard
Traction control . . . . .Standard
Stability control . . . . .Standard
Daytime running lights . . . . .Optional
Tire pressure monitor . . . . .Not available

Safety belts
Center-rear belt 3-point
Pretensioners, front/rear .Yes/no

Air bags
Occupant-sensing system . . . . .Not available
Side bags, front/rear . . . . .Standard/optional
Inflatable curtain . . . . .Standard
Accident alert system .Available

Crash tests
Gov't front-crash test, driver/front passenger . . . . . . ◖ ◑
Gov't side-crash test, driver/rear passenger . . . . . . ◖ ◑
IIHS offset crash test . . . . .Good
IIHS side crash test w/ side & curtain airbags . . . . .NA
IIHS side crash test w/o side & curtain airbags . . . . .NA

FROM THE TEST TRACK

Tested model
2005 3.0i 4-door SUV AWD, 3.0-liter Six, 5-speed automatic

Tires as tested
Michelin Energy MXV4 Plus, size 235/65R17 104H

Acceleration . . . . ◖
0-30 mph, sec. 3.0
0-60 mph, sec. 8.6
Quarter mile, sec. 16.7
Quarter mile, mph 83
45-65 mph, sec. 5.5

Other findings
Transmission . . . . ◉
Turning circle, ft. 40
Ground clearance, in. 7.5

Braking and handling
Braking . . . . ◖
Braking, dry pavement, ft. 136
Routine handling . . . . ◉
Emergency handling . . . . ◖
Avoidance maneuver, max. mph . . .51.5

Convenience and comfort
Ride . . . . ○
Noise . . . . ○
Driving position . . . . ◖
Access . . . . ◖
Controls and displays . . . . ◖
Fit and finish . . . . ●
Door top to ground, in. 62.5
Cargo area . . . . ◖
Cargo volume, cu.ft. 35.5
Max. load, lb. 1,260

Seating
Front-seat comfort . . . . ◉
Front shoulder room, in. 57.5
Front leg room, in. 42.0
Front head room, in. 4.0
Rear-seat comfort . . . . ◖
Rear shoulder room, in. 56.5
Rear leg room, in. 28.5
Rear head room, in 4.5

Fuel economy . . . . ●
CU's overall mileage, mpg 17
  CU's city/highway, mpg 12/26
  CU's 150-mile trip, mpg 20
Annual fuel . . . . .865 gal./$1,900
Cruising range 465

RELIABILITY HISTORY

TROUBLE SPOTS	BMW X5							
	97	98	99	00	01	02	03	04
Engine					●	●	●	●
Cooling					○	●	●	●
Fuel					◖	◖	◖	●
Ignition					●	●	●	◖
Transmission					◖	◖	●	◖
Electrical					●	◖	○	◖
Air conditioning					○	◖	●	●
Suspension					◖	○	◖	◖
Brakes					◖	◖	◖	◖
Exhaust					●	◖	●	◖
Paint/trim/rust					◖	◖	●	◖
Body integrity					◖	○	○	◖
Power equipment					●	●	○	◖
Body hardware					●	◖	◖	◖
RELIABILITY VERDICT					✗	–	–	✗

(Insufficient data for 97–00)

BMW Z4

THE Z4 LINE
Body style: convertible
Trim lines: 2.5i, 3.0i
Base price range: $34,300-$41,300

The Z4 improves on the Z3, though it's still not as agile as the Porsche Boxster. A roomier cockpit also improves upon the Z3's tight cabin. The two inline six-cylinder engines from the previous version continue to impress. They include a punchy 184-hp, 2.5-liter and a muscular 225-hp, 3.0-liter. The ride is not punishing, fit and finish is good, and the top is well insulated. It is also power operated and, conveniently, requires no manual release of the latches. Electronic stability control and traction control are both standard.

REPORT CARD

○	Predicted reliability
◉	Owner satisfaction
⊖	Predicted depreciation
NA	Accident avoidance
NA	Acceleration
NA	Ride
NA	Front seat comfort
NA	Fuel economy

SPECIFICATIONS

Drive wheels Rear

Seating 2 front

Engines available
2.5-liter 6 (184 hp); 3.0-liter 6 (225 hp)

Transmissions available
6-speed sequential; 5-speed manual; 6-speed manual; 5-speed automatic

Fuel
Fuel type .Premium
EPA city/highway, mpg 20/28
Fuel refill capacity, gal. 14.5

Dimensions and weight
Length, in. 161
Width, in. 70
Wheelbase, in. .98
Curb weight, lb. 3,170
Percent weight, front/rear 52/48
Typical towing ability, lb. . . . . .NR

SAFETY INFORMATION

Active safety features
Antilock brakes . . . . .Standard
Traction control . . . . .Standard
Stability control . . . . .Standard
Daytime running lights . . . . .Optional
Tire pressure monitor . . . . .Available

Safety belts
Center-rear belt . . . . .NA
Pretensioners, front/rear . . . . .Yes/NA

Air bags
Occupant-sensing system . . . . .Not available
Side bags, front/rear . . . . .Standard/NA
Inflatable curtain . . . . .Not available
Accident alert system . . . . .Available

Crash tests
Gov't front-crash test, driver/front passenger . . . . . . ⊖/⊖
Gov't side-crash test, driver/rear passenger . . . . . . ○/NA
IIHS offset crash test . . . . .NA
IIHS side crash test w/ side & curtain airbags . . . . .NA
IIHS side crash test w/o side & curtain airbags . . . . .NA

ANOTHER LOOK

RELIABILITY HISTORY

TROUBLE SPOTS	BMW Z3, Z4							
	97	98	99	00	01	02	03	04
Engine	◒	◒	◒	◒	◉		◉	
Cooling	○	◒	◒	○	◒		◉	
Fuel	◒	○	◒	○	◒		◉	
Ignition	◒	◒	◉	◉	◉		◉	
Transmission	◒	◒	◉	◉	◉		◉	
Electrical	○	◒	◒	◒	○	Insufficient data	○	Insufficient data
Air conditioning	◒	◒	◒	◒	◒		◉	
Suspension	◒	◒	◉	◉	◉		◉	
Brakes	◒	◒	◒	◒	◒		◉	
Exhaust	○	◒	◒	◒	◉		◉	
Paint/trim/rust	●	◒	◒	◒	◉		◉	
Body integrity	●	○	○	◒	○		◒	
Power equipment	●	○	○	○	○		◒	
Body hardware	◒	○	◒	●	○		○	
RELIABILITY VERDICT	—	✓	—	—	—		—	

Expert • Independent • Nonprofit

Buick LaCrosse

THE LACROSSE LINE
Body style:
sedan
Trim lines:
CX, CXL, CXS
Base price range:
$22,835-$28,335

The LaCrosse is a welcome replacement for the outdated Century and Regal, but not a huge leap forward. It preserves Buick's tradition of providing a comfortable and quiet ride, yet offers fairly responsive handling and good attention to interior details, which were sorely missing from its predecessors. Unfortunately, rear-seat room is tight, with meager knee and head room. The standard 3.8-liter V6 engine is thirsty and sounds coarse. The multivalve 3.6-liter V6 in the CXS is much more responsive and refined, but that pushes the price to the low-$30,000 level, where better cars exist.

REPORT CARD

New	Predicted reliability
New	Owner satisfaction
NA	Predicted depreciation
○	Accident avoidance
◕	Acceleration
◕	Ride
◕	Front seat comfort
⊖	Fuel economy

SPECIFICATIONS

Drive wheels Front

Seating 3 front, 3 rear

Engines available
3.8-liter V6 (200 hp); 3.6-liter V6 (240 hp)

Transmissions available
4-speed automatic

Fuel
Fuel type . . . . .Regular
EPA city/highway, mpg 19/27
Fuel refill capacity, gal. 17.5

Dimensions and weight
Length, in. 198
Width, in. 73
Wheelbase, in. 111
Curb weight, lb. 3,565
Percent weight, front/rear 63/37
Typical towing ability, lb. 1,000

SAFETY INFORMATION

Active safety features
Antilock brakes . . . . .Optional (standard on CXS)
Traction control . . . . .Optional (standard on CXS)
Stability control . . . . .Optional on CXS
Daytime running lights . . . . .Standard
Tire pressure monitor . . . . .Not available

Safety belts
Center-rear belt 3-point
Pretensioners, front/rear . . . . .Yes/no

Air bags
Occupant-sensing system . . . . .Front
Side bags, front/rear .No/no
Inflatable curtain . . . . .Optional
Accident alert system . . . . .Available

Crash tests
Gov't front-crash test, driver/front passenger . . . . . .◕/◕
Gov't side-crash test, driver/rear passenger . . . .○/○
IIHS offset crash test . . . . .NA
IIHS side crash test w/ side & curtain airbags . . . . .NA
IIHS side crash test w/o side & curtain airbags . . . . . . .NA

FROM THE TEST TRACK

Tested model
2005 CXL sedan, 3.8-liter V6, 4-speed automatic

Tires as tested
Goodyear Integrity, size P225/60R16 97S

Acceleration . . . . ◕
0-30 mph, sec. 3.1
0-60 mph, sec. 9.0
Quarter mile, sec. 17.0
Quarter mile, mph 83
45-65 mph, sec. 6.3

Other findings
Transmission . . . . ◕
Turning circle, ft. 40
Ground clearance, in. 4.5

Braking and handling
Braking . . . .○
Braking, dry pavement, ft. 146
Routine handling . . . .◕
Emergency handling . . . .○
Avoidance maneuver, max. mph . . .50.0

Convenience and comfort
Ride . . . . ◕
Noise . . . .◕
Driving position . . . .◕
Access . . . .◕
Controls and displays . . . .◕
Fit and finish . . . .◕
Door top to ground, in. 51.5
Trunk . . . .○
Luggage capacity . . . . .4+1
Max. load, lb. 915

Seating
Front-seat comfort . . . . ◕
Front shoulder room, in. 57.0
Front leg room, in. 41.0
Front head room, in. 2.0
Rear-seat comfort . . . .○
Rear shoulder room, in. 56.5
Rear leg room, in. 27.0
Rear head room, in 1.5

Fuel economy . . . . ⊖
CU's overall mileage, mpg 18
CU's city/highway, mpg 12/30
CU's 150-mile trip, mpg 23
Annual fuel . . . . .815 gal./$1,630
Cruising range 375

RELIABILITY HISTORY

TROUBLE SPOTS	97	98	99	00	01	02	03	04
Engine								
Cooling								
Fuel				NO				
Ignition								
Transmission				DATA				
Electrical								
Air conditioning				NEW				
Suspension								
Brakes				MODEL				
Exhaust								
Paint/trim/rust								
Body integrity								
Power equipment								
Body hardware								
RELIABILITY VERDICT								

● ◕ ○ ⊖ ●
better ◄——► worse   See page 36 for more information.

Buick LeSabre

CR RECOMMENDED ✓

THE LESABRE LINE
Body style:
sedan
Trim lines:
Custom, Limited
Base price range:
$26,725-$32,385

This large sedan is distinguished mainly by its spacious cabin and quiet, comfortable low-speed ride. The ride becomes a bit unsettled, and wind noise more pronounced, at highway speeds. The coarse 3.8-liter V6 delivers reasonably brisk acceleration. Handling is ungainly but ultimately secure with the optional stability-control system. The rear seat offers plenty of room, and the trunk is quite large. The front bench is soft and unsupportive, however, and fit and finish is unimpressive. Reliability has consistently been average. The Lucerne replaces the LeSabre and Park Avenue for 2006.

REPORT CARD

○	Predicted reliability
○	Owner satisfaction
◐	Predicted depreciation
○	Accident avoidance
○	Acceleration
◐	Ride
○	Front seat comfort
◐	Fuel economy

SPECIFICATIONS

Drive wheels Front

Seating 3 front, 3 rear

Engines available
3.8-liter V6 (205 hp)

Transmissions available
4-speed automatic

Fuel
Fuel type . . . . .Regular
EPA city/highway, mpg 19/30
Fuel refill capacity, gal. 18.5

Dimensions and weight
Length, in. 200
Width, in. 74
Wheelbase, in. 112
Curb weight, lb. 3,640
Percent weight, front/rear 62/38
Typical towing ability, lb. 1,000

SAFETY INFORMATION

Active safety features
Antilock brakes . . . . .Standard
Traction control . . . . .Optional (standard on Limited)
Stability control .Optional on Limited
Daytime running lights . . . . .Standard
Tire pressure monitor . . . . .Available

Safety belts
Center-rear belt 3-point
Pretensioners, front/rear .No/no

Air bags
Occupant-sensing system . . . . .Not available
Side bags, front/rear .Optional/no
Inflatable curtain . . . . .Not available
Accident alert system . . . . .Available

Crash tests
Gov't front-crash test, driver/front passenger . . . . . .◐/●
Gov't side-crash test, driver/rear passenger . . . .◐/◐
IIHS offset crash test . . . . .Good
IIHS side crash test w/ side & curtain airbags . . . . .NA
IIHS side crash test w/o side & curtain airbags . . . . .NA

FROM THE TEST TRACK

Tested model
2000 Limited sedan, 3.8-liter V6, 4-speed automatic

Tires as tested
Firestone Affinity Touring T2, size P225/60R16 97T

Acceleration . . . .○
0-30 mph, sec. 3.3
0-60 mph, sec. 8.8
Quarter mile, sec. 16.8
Quarter mile, mph 85
45-65 mph, sec. 6.4

Other findings
Transmission . . . .●
Turning circle, ft. 42
Ground clearance, in. 5.5

Braking and handling
Braking . . . .○
Braking, dry pavement, ft. 146
Routine handling . . . .○
Emergency handling . . . .○
Avoidance maneuver, max. mph . . .49.5

Convenience and comfort
Ride . . . .◐
Noise . . . .◐
Driving position . . . .◐
Access . . . .◐
Controls and displays . . . .○
Fit and finish . . . .○
Door top to ground, in. 51.0
Trunk . . . .◐
Luggage capacity . . . . .5+3
Max. load, lb. 1,075

Seating
Front-seat comfort . . . .○
Front shoulder room, in. 59.5
Front leg room, in. 40.5
Front head room, in. 5.0
Rear-seat comfort . . . .○
Rear shoulder room, in. 58.0
Rear leg room, in. 27.5
Rear head room, in 4.5

Fuel economy . . . .◐
CU's overall mileage, mpg 20
CU's city/highway, mpg 13/31
CU's 150-mile trip, mpg 25
Annual fuel . . . . .760 gal./$1,515
Cruising range 405

RELIABILITY HISTORY

TROUBLE SPOTS	Buick LeSabre							
	97	98	99	00	01	02	03	04
Engine	○	◐	○	○	○	○	●	●
Cooling	◐	◐	○	○	◐	◐	●	●
Fuel	◐	◐	○	○	○	●	●	●
Ignition	○	◐	◐	◐	◐	●	●	●
Transmission	○	○	○	○	○	○	●	●
Electrical	○	◐	◐	○	◐	◐	●	●
Air conditioning	○	○	○	○	◐	◐	●	●
Suspension	○	○	○	○	○	○	●	●
Brakes	◐	◐	◐	○	○	○	●	●
Exhaust	◐	◐	●	●	●	●	●	●
Paint/trim/rust	◐	◐	◐	○	○	○	●	●
Body integrity	○	○	○	○	○	◐	●	●
Power equipment	○	○	○	●	○	○	◐	●
Body hardware	◐	◐	◐	○	◐	◐	●	●
RELIABILITY VERDICT	–	–	–	–	–	–	✓	✗

Expert ● Independent ● Nonprofit

Buick Park Avenue

CR RECOMMENDED ✓

THE PARK AVENUE LINE
Body style:
sedan
Trim lines:
Base, Ultra
Base price range:
$35,555-$40,730

uick's flagship delivers expansive seating, a cavernous trunk, and a quiet, compliant ride. Handling with the Gran Touring suspension option (standard on the Ultra) is relatively nimble for such a large car. The base Park Avenue has a 3.8-liter V6 with 205 hp. The Ultra we tested has a responsive 240-hp supercharged version that provides quick and effortless acceleration, along with respectable fuel economy, but it lacks the refinement of modern V6 and V8 engines. Interior ambience is disappointing for a car in this price range. The Park Avenue will be replaced by the Lucerne in fall 2005.

REPORT CARD

○	Predicted reliability
○	Owner satisfaction
◒	Predicted depreciation
◒	Accident avoidance
◒	Acceleration
◒	Ride
◒	Front seat comfort
○	Fuel economy

SPECIFICATIONS

Drive wheels Front

Seating 3 front, 3 rear

Engines available
3.8-liter V6 (205 hp); 3.8-liter V6 supercharged (240 hp)

Transmissions available
4-speed automatic

Fuel
Fuel type . . . . .Regular or premium
EPA city/highway, mpg 18/28
Fuel refill capacity, gal. 18.5

Dimensions and weight
Length, in. 207
Width, in. 75
Wheelbase, in. 114
Curb weight, lb. 3,970
Percent weight, front/rear 61/39
Typical towing ability, lb. 1,000

SAFETY INFORMATION

Active safety features
Antilock brakes . . . . .Standard
Traction control . . . . .Optional (standard on Ultra)
Stability control . . . . .Optional (standard on Ultra)
Daytime running lights . . . . .Standard
Tire pressure monitor . . . . .Available

Safety belts
Center-rear belt . . . . .Lap
Pretensioners, front/rear . . . . .No/no

Air bags
Occupant-sensing system . . . . .Not available
Side bags, front/rear .Standard/no
Inflatable curtain . . . . .Not available
Accident alert system . . . . .Available

Crash tests
Gov't front-crash test, driver/front passenger . . . . . . ◒/◒
Gov't side-crash test, driver/rear passenger . . . . ◒/◒
IIHS offset crash test . . . . .Good
IIHS side crash test w/ side & curtain airbags . . . . .NA
IIHS side crash test w/o side & curtain airbags . . . . .NA

FROM THE TEST TRACK

Tested model
2003 Ultra sedan, 3.8-liter V6 supercharged, 4-speed automatic

Tires as tested
Goodyear Eagle LS, size P235/55R17 98H

Acceleration . . . . ◒
0-30 mph, sec. 2.9
0-60 mph, sec. 7.8
Quarter mile, sec. 16.1
Quarter mile, mph 90
45-65 mph, sec. 5.3

Other findings
Transmission . . . . ◔
Turning circle, ft. 45
Ground clearance, in. 5.5

Braking and handling
Braking . . . . ◒
Braking, dry pavement, ft. 137
Routine handling . . . . ◒
Emergency handling . . . . ○
Avoidance maneuver, max. mph . . .51.0

Convenience and comfort
Ride . . . . ◒
Noise . . . . ◒
Driving position . . . . ◒
Access . . . . ◒
Controls and displays . . . . ◒
Fit and finish . . . . ◒
Door top to ground, in. 52.0
Trunk . . . . ◒
Luggage capacity . . . . .6+2
Max. load, lb. 1,100

Seating
Front-seat comfort . . . . ◒
Front shoulder room, in. 59.0
Front leg room, in. 42.0
Front head room, in. 3.5
Rear-seat comfort . . . . ◔
Rear shoulder room, in. 58.0
Rear leg room, in. 30.5
Rear head room, in 2.5

Fuel economy . . . . ○
CU's overall mileage, mpg 21
 CU's city/highway, mpg 13/32
 CU's 150-mile trip, mpg 26
Annual fuel . . . . .730 gal./$1,605
Cruising range 445

RELIABILITY HISTORY

TROUBLE SPOTS	Buick Park Avenue							
	97	98	99	00	01	02	03	04
Engine	◒	◒	◒	◒	◒	◒	◒	◒
Cooling	○	○	○	◒	◒	◒	◒	◒
Fuel	○	◒	◒	○	◒	◒	◒	◒
Ignition	○	○	○	○	◒	◒	◒	◒
Transmission	○	○	○	○	◒	◒	◒	◒
Electrical	●	◒	◒	◒	○	◒	◒	◒
Air conditioning	○	○	○	○	◒	◒	◒	◒
Suspension	○	○	○	◒	○	◒	◒	◒
Brakes	◒	◒	◒	◒	○	◒	◒	◒
Exhaust	○	○	◒	○	○	◒	◒	◒
Paint/trim/rust	◒	◒	◒	○	◒	◒	◒	◒
Body integrity	○	○	○	○	○	◒	◒	◒
Power equipment	◒	◒	◒	○	○	◒	◒	◒
Body hardware	◒	◒	◒	○	○	◒	◒	◒
RELIABILITY VERDICT	-	✗	-	-	-	-	-	✗

better ● ◒ ○ ◔ ● worse See page 36 for more information.

Buick Rainier

THE RAINIER LINE
Body style:
4-door SUV
Trim lines:
CXL
Base price range:
$33,785-$35,610

The Buick Rainier is a rebadged Chevrolet TrailBlazer/GMC Envoy. With the demise of the Oldsmobile Bravada, Buick takes the baton of the upscale version of these SUVs for GM. The Rainier is available with two engines: the standard 4.2-liter, 275-hp six-cylinder and a 5.3-liter, 300-hp V8. Rear- and all-wheel-drive models are available. The AWD system is permanently engaged and has no low range, which is better suited for slippery roads than serious off-roading. Inflatable curtain air bags are available. Stability control is slated to be standard with 2005 models later this year.

REPORT CARD

◒	**Predicted reliability**
◓	**Owner satisfaction**
NA	**Predicted depreciation**
NA	**Accident avoidance**
NA	**Acceleration**
NA	**Ride**
NA	**Front seat comfort**
NA	**Fuel economy**

SAFETY INFORMATION

Active safety features
Antilock brakes .... Standard
Traction control .... Standard on 2WD
Stability control .... Not available
Daytime running lights .... Standard
Tire pressure monitor .... Available

Safety belts
Center-rear belt 3-point
Pretensioners, front/rear .... No/no

Air bags
Occupant-sensing system .... Front
Side bags, front/rear .... No/no
Inflatable curtain .... Optional
Accident alert system .... Available

Crash tests
Gov't front-crash test, driver/front passenger ..... ○/◓
Gov't side-crash test, driver/rear passenger ...... ⦿/⦿
IIHS offset crash test .... Marginal
IIHS side crash test w/ side & curtain airbags .... NA
IIHS side crash test w/o side & curtain airbags .... NA

SPECIFICATIONS

Drive wheels Rear or AWD

Seating 2 front, 3 rear

Engines available
4.2-liter 6 (275 hp); 5.3-liter V8 (300 hp)

Transmissions available
4-speed automatic

Fuel
Fuel type .... Regular
EPA city/highway, mpg 15/20
Fuel refill capacity, gal. 22.0

Dimensions and weight
Length, in. 193
Width, in. 75
Wheelbase, in. 113
Curb weight, lb. 4,600
Percent weight, front/rear 55/45
Typical towing ability, lb. 6,100

ANOTHER LOOK

RELIABILITY HISTORY

TROUBLE SPOTS	Buick Rainier 97	98	99	00	01	02	03	04
Engine								⦿
Cooling								⦿
Fuel								⦿
Ignition								⦿
Transmission								⦿
Electrical								◓
Air conditioning								⦿
Suspension								⦿
Brakes								⦿
Exhaust								⦿
Paint/trim/rust								⦿
Body integrity								◓
Power equipment								⦿
Body hardware								◓
RELIABILITY VERDICT								✗

Buick Rendezvous

CR RECOMMENDED ✓

THE RENDEZVOUS LINE
Body style:
4-door SUV
Trim lines:
CX, CXL, Ultra
Base price range:
$26,780-$39,415

L ike the Pontiac Aztek, the Rendezvous is derived from GM's minivans. The second-row seating consists of either two captain's chairs or a bench seat. An optional third-row seat that folds into the floor increases seating to seven. The 3.4-liter, pushrod V6 struggles to move this two-ton vehicle. A stronger multivalve, 3.6-liter is available in the Ultra. The interior is made with cheap-looking materials, and the gray-on-gray gauges are hard to read. The ride is fairly comfortable, and handling is secure though a bit reluctant. Reliability has remained average.

REPORT CARD

○	Predicted reliability
◐	Owner satisfaction
○	Predicted depreciation
○	Accident avoidance
◐	Acceleration
○	Ride
◐	Front seat comfort
●	Fuel economy

SPECIFICATIONS

Drive wheels Front or AWD

Seating 2 front, 3 rear, 2 third

Engines available
3.4-liter V6 (185 hp); 3.6-liter V6 (242 hp)

Transmissions available
4-speed automatic

Fuel
Fuel type ....Regular
EPA city/highway, mpg 18/24
Fuel refill capacity, gal. 18.5

Dimensions and weight
Length, in. 187
Width, in. 74
Wheelbase, in. 112
Curb weight, lb. 4,230
Percent weight, front/rear 58/42
Typical towing ability, lb. 3,500

SAFETY INFORMATION

Active safety features
Antilock brakes ....Optional
Traction control ....Optional on FWD
Stability control ....Not available
Daytime running lights ....Standard
Tire pressure monitor ....Available

Safety belts
Center-rear belt ....Lap
Pretensioners, front/rear ....Yes/no

Air bags
Occupant-sensing system ....Front
Side bags, front/rear ....Optional/no
Inflatable curtain ....Not available
Accident alert system ....Available

Crash tests
Gov't front-crash test, driver/front passenger ......○/◐
Gov't side-crash test, driver/rear passenger ....●/◐
IIHS offset crash test ....Acceptable
IIHS side crash test w/ side & curtain airbags ....NA
IIHS side crash test w/o side & curtain airbags ....NA

FROM THE TEST TRACK

Tested model
2002 CXL 4-door SUV AWD, 3.4-liter V6, 4-speed automatic

Tires as tested
Uniroyal Tiger Paw Touring SR, size P215/70R16 99S

Acceleration ....◐
0-30 mph, sec. 4.0
0-60 mph, sec. 11.4
Quarter mile, sec. 18.5
Quarter mile, mph 78
45-65 mph, sec. 7.8

Other findings
Transmission ....◐
Turning circle, ft. 40
Ground clearance, in. 6.0

Braking and handling
Braking ....○
Braking, dry pavement, ft. 142
Routine handling ....○
Emergency handling ....◐
Avoidance maneuver, max. mph 47.0

Convenience and comfort
Ride ....○
Noise ....◐
Driving position ....◐
Access ....◐
Controls and displays ....○
Fit and finish ....○
Door top to ground, in. 62.0
Cargo area ....◐
Cargo volume, cu.ft. 45.0
Max. load, lb. 1,215

Seating
Front-seat comfort ....◐
Front shoulder room, in. 59.0
Front leg room, in. 40.0
Front head room, in. 4.5
Rear-seat comfort ....◐
Rear shoulder room, in. 59.0
Rear leg room, in. 29.5
Rear head room, in 6.0
Third-seat comfort ....◐
Third shoulder room,in 58.5
Third leg room, in. 24.0
Third head room, in 1.0

Fuel economy ....●
CU's overall mileage, mpg 16
CU's city/highway, mpg 11/24
CU's 150-mile trip, mpg 21
Annual fuel ....910 gal./$1,820
Cruising range 350

RELIABILITY HISTORY

TROUBLE SPOTS	Buick Rendezvous							
	97	98	99	00	01	02	03	04
Engine						●	●	●
Cooling						●	●	●
Fuel						◐	◐	◐
Ignition						●	◐	●
Transmission						◐	●	●
Electrical						○	○	●
Air conditioning						○	◐	●
Suspension						◐	◐	●
Brakes						◐	◐	●
Exhaust						●	◐	●
Paint/trim/rust						●	●	●
Body integrity						○	◐	◐
Power equipment						○	◐	◐
Body hardware						○	◐	●
RELIABILITY VERDICT						✗	−	✓

Buick Terraza

The Terraza is one of four freshened GM minivans. As with the Chevrolet Uplander, Pontiac Montana SV6, and Saturn Relay, the Terraza is powered by a coarse 3.5-liter, 200-hp V6 engine. The heavy second-row seats can be folded and removed, while the folding third-row seat stows when not in use. It drives very similar to the Saturn Relay we tested, with a stiff ride and noisy interior. Handling is reluctant. The interior trim is insubstantial. The new snout can't disguise the fact that these are essentially eight-year-old minivans that are not competitive in their class.

THE TERRAZA LINE
Body style:
minivan
Trim lines:
CX, CXL
Base price range:
$28,110-$33,855

REPORT CARD

New	Predicted reliability
New	Owner satisfaction
NA	Predicted depreciation
O	Accident avoidance
O	Acceleration
O	Ride
O	Front seat comfort
●	Fuel economy

SPECIFICATIONS

Drive wheels Front or AWD

Seating 2 front, 2 rear, 3 third

Engines available
3.5-liter V6 (200 hp)

Transmissions available
4-speed automatic

Fuel
Fuel type ....Regular
EPA city/highway, mpg 18/24
Fuel refill capacity, gal. 25.0

Dimensions and weight
Length, in. 205
Width, in..........................72
Wheelbase, in. 121
Curb weight, lb....................4,380
Percent weight, front/rear 56/44
Typical towing ability, lb. 3,500

SAFETY INFORMATION

Active safety features
Antilock brakes ....Standard
Traction control ....Standard on FWD
Stability control ....Optional on FWD
Daytime running lights ....Standard
Tire pressure monitor ....Not available

Safety belts
Center-rear belt 3-point
Pretensioners, front/rear ....Yes/no

Air bags
Occupant-sensing system ....Front
Side bags, front/rear ....Optional/no
Inflatable curtain ....Not available
Accident alert system ....Available

Crash tests
Gov't front-crash test, driver/front passenger ......●/●
Gov't side-crash test, driver/rear passenger ....◐/●
IIHS offset crash test ....NA
IIHS side crash test w/ side & curtain airbags ....NA
IIHS side crash test w/o side & curtain airbags ....NA

FROM THE TEST TRACK

Tested model
2005 Saturn Relay 3 minivan, 3.5-liter V6, 4-speed automatic

Tires as tested
Goodyear Integrity, size P225/60R17 98S

Acceleration ....O
0-30 mph, sec. 3.6
0-60 mph, sec. 10.2
Quarter mile, sec. 17.7
Quarter mile, mph 80
45-65 mph, sec. 7.0

Other findings
Transmission ....◐
Turning circle, ft. 43
Ground clearance, in. 6.0

Braking and handling
Braking ....◐
Braking, dry pavement, ft. 136
Routine handling ....O
Emergency handling ....◐
Avoidance maneuver, max. mph ...48.5

Convenience and comfort
Ride ....O
Noise ....O
Driving position ....O
Access ....●
Controls and displays ....◐
Fit and finish ....O
Door top to ground, in. 62.0
Cargo area ....◐
Cargo volume, cu.ft. 75.5
Max. load, lb. 1,290

Seating
Front-seat comfort ....O
Front shoulder room, in. 59.5
Front leg room, in. 40.5
Front head room, in. 5.0
Rear-seat comfort ....◐
Rear shoulder room, in. 62.0
Rear leg room, in. 26.0
Rear head room, in 4.0
Third-seat comfort ....O
Third shoulder room,in 60.0
Third leg room, in. 28.0
Third head room, in 3.5

Fuel economy ....●
CU's overall mileage, mpg 17
  CU's city/highway, mpg 12/25
  CU's 150-mile trip, mpg 21
Annual fuel ....860 gal./$1,720
Cruising range 510

RELIABILITY HISTORY

TROUBLE SPOTS	97 98 99 00 01 02 03 04
Engine	
Cooling	NO
Fuel	
Ignition	
Transmission	DATA
Electrical	
Air conditioning	NEW
Suspension	
Brakes	MODEL
Exhaust	
Paint/trim/rust	
Body integrity	
Power equipment	
Body hardware	
RELIABILITY VERDICT	

Cadillac CTS

CR RECOMMENDED ✔

THE CTS LINE
Body style:
sedan
Trim lines:
Base, CTS-V
Base price range:
$30,190-$49,490

The rear-wheel-drive CTS feels taut and agile, and it handles like a true sports sedan in the mold of BMW. The ride is firm but supple and effectively absorbs bumps. The cabin is quiet. Some controls are confusing, and details like no passenger grab handle are annoying. The front-seat-mounted safety belts were uncomfortable for some drivers. A new 2.8-liter, entry-level engine arrived for 2005. The 400-hp CTS-V features a Corvette V8, six-speed manual, and tighter suspension, making it a sports car with four-door practicality. Reliability is average, allowing us to recommend the CTS.

REPORT CARD

○	Predicted reliability
⊖	Owner satisfaction
NA	Predicted depreciation
◉	Accident avoidance
◉	Acceleration
○	Ride
◉	Front seat comfort
●	Fuel economy

SAFETY INFORMATION

Active safety features
Antilock brakes . . . . .Standard
Traction control . . . . .Standard
Stability control . . . . .Optional
Daytime running lights . . . . .Standard
Tire pressure monitor . . . . .Available

Safety belts
Center-rear belt 3-point
Pretensioners, front/rear . . . . .Yes/no

Air bags
Occupant-sensing system . . . . .Front
Side bags, front/rear .Standard/no
Inflatable curtain . . . . .Standard
Accident alert system . . . . .Available

Crash tests
Gov't front-crash test, driver/front passenger . . . . .⊖/◉
Gov't side-crash test, driver/rear passenger . . . .⊖/◉
IIHS offset crash test . . . . .Good
IIHS side crash test w/ side & curtain airbags . . . . .NA
IIHS side crash test w/o side & curtain airbags . . . . .NA

FROM THE TEST TRACK

Tested model
2004 CTS-V sedan, 5.7-liter V8, 6-speed manual

Tires as tested
Goodyear Eagle F1 Supercar EMT, size P245/45R18 96W

Acceleration . . . . ◉
0-30 mph, sec. 2.3
0-60 mph, sec. 5.3
Quarter mile, sec. 13.8
Quarter mile, mph 106
45-65 mph, sec. 3.6

Other findings
Transmission . . . . ⊖
Turning circle, ft. 38
Ground clearance, in. 5.5

Braking and handling
Braking . . . . ◉
Braking, dry pavement, ft. 125
Routine handling . . . . ◉
Emergency handling . . . . ⊖
Avoidance maneuver, max. mph . . .53.5

Convenience and comfort
Ride . . . . ○
Noise . . . . ⊖
Driving position . . . . ⊖
Access . . . . ⊖
Controls and displays . . . . ⊖
Fit and finish . . . . ⊖
Door top to ground, in. 51.0
Trunk . . . . ○
Luggage capacity . . . . .3+2
Max. load, lb. 880

Seating
Front-seat comfort . . . . ◉
Front shoulder room, in. 57.0
Front leg room, in. 42.0
Front head room, in. 2.0
Rear-seat comfort . . . . ○
Rear shoulder room, in. 56.0
Rear leg room, in. 29.5
Rear head room, in 2.0

Fuel economy . . . . ●
CU's overall mileage, mpg 17
 CU's city/highway, mpg 11/27
 CU's 150-mile trip, mpg 20
Annual fuel . . . . .880 gal./$1,755
Cruising range 315

SPECIFICATIONS

Drive wheels Rear

Seating 2 front, 3 rear

Engines available
2.8-liter V6 (210 hp); 3.6-liter V6 (255 hp); 5.7-liter V8 (400 hp)

Transmissions available
6-speed manual; 5-speed automatic

Fuel
Fuel type . . . . .Regular
EPA city/highway, mpg 16/25
Fuel refill capacity, gal. 17.5

Dimensions and weight
Length, in. 190
Width, in. 71
Wheelbase, in. 113
Curb weight, lb. 3,950
Percent weight, front/rear 54/46
Typical towing ability, lb. 1,000

RELIABILITY HISTORY

TROUBLE SPOTS	Cadillac CTS								
	97	98	99	00	01	02	03	04
Engine								◉	◉
Cooling								⊖	◉
Fuel								⊖	◉
Ignition								◉	◉
Transmission								◉	◉
Electrical								○	◉
Air conditioning								◉	◉
Suspension								⊖	◉
Brakes								◉	◉
Exhaust								◉	◉
Paint/trim/rust								⊖	◉
Body integrity								○	◉
Power equipment								○	◉
Body hardware								⊖	◉
RELIABILITY VERDICT								✗	✓

Cadillac DeVille

The DeVille's quiet, spacious cabin incorporates many thoughtful details. Rear-seat passengers have plenty of room and can enjoy heated seats, vanity mirrors, a power rear sunshade, and separate climate controls. The smooth Northstar V8 powertrain provides effortless motivation. The DeVille rides comfortably, but handling is less impressive. Many standard safety features are included. Crash-test results have improved, but not up to the competition's level. A freshening incorporating Cadillac's new look arrives for the 2006 model year and will be named DTS.

THE DEVILLE LINE

Body style:
sedan
Trim lines:
Base, DHS, DTS
Base price range:
$45,945-$51,500

REPORT CARD

◖	Predicted reliability
◖	Owner satisfaction
◖	Predicted depreciation
○	Accident avoidance
◖	Acceleration
◉	Ride
◖	Front seat comfort
◖	Fuel economy

SPECIFICATIONS

Drive wheels Front

Seating 3 front, 3 rear

Engines available
4.6-liter V8 (275 hp); 4.6-liter V8 (290 hp)

Transmissions available
4-speed automatic

Fuel
Fuel type . . . . .Regular
EPA city/highway, mpg 18/27
Fuel refill capacity, gal. 18.5

Dimensions and weight
Length, in. . . . . : 207
Width, in. 74
Wheelbase, in. 115
Curb weight, lb. 4,070
Percent weight, front/rear 61/39
Typical towing ability, lb. 2,000

SAFETY INFORMATION

Active safety features
Antilock brakes . . . . .Standard
Traction control . . . . .Standard
Stability control . . . . .Optional (standard on DTS)
Daytime running lights . . . . .Standard
Tire pressure monitor . . . . .Available

Safety belts
Center-rear belt 3-point
Pretensioners, front/rear .Yes/no

Air bags
Occupant-sensing system . . . . .Front
Side bags, front/rear . . . . .Standard/optional
Inflatable curtain . . . . .Not available
Accident alert system . . . . .Available

Crash tests
Gov't front-crash test, driver/front passenger   ◖/◖
Gov't side-crash test, driver/rear passenger   ◖/◖
IIHS offset crash test . . . . .NA
IIHS side crash test w/ side & curtain airbags . . . . .NA
IIHS side crash test w/o side & curtain airbags . . . . .NA

FROM THE TEST TRACK

Tested model
2000 DHS sedan, 4.6-liter V8, 4-speed automatic

Tires as tested
Michelin Symmetry, size P225/60R16 97S

Acceleration . . . . ◖
0-30 mph, sec. 3.1
0-60 mph, sec. 7.4
Quarter mile, sec. 15.7
Quarter mile, mph 92
45-65 mph, sec. 4.7

Other findings
Transmission . . . . ◉
Turning circle, ft. 43
Ground clearance, in. 5.5

Braking and handling
Braking . . . . ○
Braking, dry pavement, ft. 147
Routine handling . . . . ◖
Emergency handling . . . . ○
Avoidance maneuver, max. mph . . .49.0

Convenience and comfort
Ride . . . . ◉
Noise . . . . ◉
Driving position . . . . ◖
Access . . . . ◉
Controls and displays . . . . ◉
Fit and finish . . . . ◉
Door top to ground, in. 51.0
Trunk . . . . ◉
Luggage capacity . . . . .6+1
Max. load, lb. 1,085

Seating
Front-seat comfort . . . . ◖
Front shoulder room, in. 60.5
Front leg room, in. 41.5
Front head room, in. 4.5
Rear-seat comfort . . . . ◉
Rear shoulder room, in. 59.5
Rear leg room, in. 30.0
Rear head room, in 3.0

Fuel economy . . . . ◖
CU's overall mileage, mpg 19
CU's city/highway, mpg 12/29
CU's 150-mile trip, mpg 23
Annual fuel . . . . .810 gal./$1,620
Cruising range 405

RELIABILITY HISTORY

TROUBLE SPOTS	Cadillac DeVille							
	97	98	99	00	01	02	03	04
Engine	◖	○	○	○	○	◖	○	○
Cooling	●	◖	○	◖	○	◉	○	○
Fuel	●	◖	○	◖	○	○	◖	○
Ignition	◖	◖	◖	○	○	○	○	○
Transmission	○	○	◖	○	○	◉	○	○
Electrical	●	●	◖	◖	○	○	○	○
Air conditioning	●	●	○	○	○	○	○	○
Suspension	○	○	○	○	○	○	○	○
Brakes	◖	◖	◖	◖	○	○	◖	○
Exhaust	◉	○	○	○	○	○	○	○
Paint/trim/rust	○	○	○	○	◉	◉	○	○
Body integrity	○	○	○	○	○	◖	◖	◖
Power equipment	◖	◖	◖	○	○	○	○	○
Body hardware	○	○	○	○	○	◖	○	○
RELIABILITY VERDICT	✗	−	−	✗	✗	✗	−	✗

Expert • Independent • Nonprofit

Cadillac Escalade

THE ESCALADE LINE

Body style:
crew cab; 4-door SUV; extended SUV

Trim lines:
Base, ESV, EXT, Platinum

Base price range:
$53,335-$70,175

The big, bulky Escalade is based on the Chevrolet Tahoe/GMC Yukon platform. Rear-drive models use GM's popular 295-hp, 5.3-liter V8, while all-wheel-drive versions get a 345-hp, 6.0-liter version. The interior is a dichotomy of luxurious plushness and cheap materials. A removable split third-row seat brings passenger capacity to eight, but it's uncomfortable in the standard model. Second-row bucket seats are standard, with a bench available. The EXT is a plush version of the Chevrolet Avalanche pickup truck. The longer ESV is based on the Suburban.

REPORT CARD

○	Predicted reliability
◓	Owner satisfaction
◓	Predicted depreciation
NA	Accident avoidance
NA	Acceleration
NA	Ride
NA	Front seat comfort
NA	Fuel economy

SPECIFICATIONS

Drive wheels Rear or AWD

Seating 2 front, 3 rear, 3 third

Engines available
5.3-liter V8 (295 hp); 6.0-liter V8 (345 hp)

Transmissions available
4-speed automatic

Fuel

Fuel type	Regular
EPA city/highway, mpg	13/17
Fuel refill capacity, gal.	26.0

Dimensions and weight

Length, in.	199
Width, in.	79
Wheelbase, in.	116
Curb weight, lb.	5,555
Percent weight, front/rear	52/48
Typical towing ability, lb.	7,800

SAFETY INFORMATION

Active safety features

Antilock brakes	Standard
Traction control	Standard
Stability control	Standard
Daytime running lights	Standard
Tire pressure monitor	Available

Safety belts

Center-rear belt	3-point
Pretensioners, front/rear	No/no

Air bags

Occupant-sensing system	Front
Side bags, front/rear	Standard/no
Inflatable curtain	Not available
Accident alert system	Available

Crash tests

Gov't front-crash test, driver/front passenger	◓/◓
Gov't side-crash test, driver/rear passenger	NA/NA
IIHS offset crash test	NA
IIHS side crash test w/ side & curtain airbags	NA
IIHS side crash test w/o side & curtain airbags	NA

RELIABILITY HISTORY

TROUBLE SPOTS	Cadillac Escalade							
	97	98	99	00	01	02	03	04
Engine			Insufficient data	Insufficient data		⦿	⦿	⦿
Cooling						⦿	⦿	⦿
Fuel						⦿	⦿	⦿
Ignition						⦿	⦿	⦿
Transmission						◓	◓	⦿
Electrical						○	○	⦿
Air conditioning						⦿	◓	⦿
Suspension						◓	◓	⦿
Brakes						◓	⦿	⦿
Exhaust						⦿	⦿	⦿
Paint/trim/rust						◓	⦿	⦿
Body integrity						○	◓	◓
Power equipment						○	○	○
Body hardware						○	◓	⦿
RELIABILITY VERDICT						-	✗	✓

ANOTHER LOOK

⦿ ◓ ○ ◒ ●
better ◄——► worse See page 36 for more information.

Cadillac SRX

THE SRX LINE
Body style:
4-door SUV
Trim lines:
V6, V8
Base price range:
$38,340-$52,035

The SRX is a highly capable tall wagon. It shares the same platform with the CTS sedan and comes as either rear- or all-wheel drive. It is powered by either a 3.6-liter V6 or a 4.6-liter V8, both of which are smooth and powerful. The five-speed automatic is very slick and has manual-shift capability. Like the CTS, the SRX feels taut and agile, and rides comfortably. Fit and finish falls a bit short, and some controls can be confusing. A power-folding third-row seat is optional, pitting the SRX directly against the Acura MDX and Volvo XC90, which also offer seating for seven. First-year reliability is below average.

REPORT CARD

⊖	**Predicted reliability**
⊖	**Owner satisfaction**
NA	**Predicted depreciation**
⊖	**Accident avoidance**
◉	**Acceleration**
⊖	**Ride**
⊖	**Front seat comfort**
●	**Fuel economy**

SPECIFICATIONS

Drive wheels Rear or AWD

Seating 2 front, 3 rear, 2 third

Engines available
3.6-liter V6 (255 hp); 4.6-liter V8 (320 hp)

Transmissions available
5-speed automatic

Fuel
Fuel type . . . . .Regular
EPA city/highway, mpg 15/20
Fuel refill capacity, gal. 20.0

Dimensions and weight
Length, in. 195
Width, in. 73
Wheelbase, in. 116
Curb weight, lb. 4,685
Percent weight, front/rear 53/47
Typical towing ability, lb. 4,250

SAFETY INFORMATION

Active safety features
Antilock brakes . . . . .Standard
Traction control . . . . .Standard
Stability control . . . . .Standard
Daytime running lights .Standard
Tire pressure monitor . . . . .Available

Safety belts
Center-rear belt 3-point
Pretensioners, front/rear . . . . .Yes/no

Air bags
Occupant-sensing system . . . . .Not available
Side bags, front/rear .Standard/no
Inflatable curtain . . . . .Standard
Accident alert system . . . . .Available

Crash tests
Gov't front-crash test, driver/front passenger . . . . .⊖/⊖
Gov't side-crash test, driver/rear passenger . . . .◉/◉
IIHS offset crash test . . . . .Good
IIHS side crash test w/ side & curtain airbags . . . . .NA
IIHS side crash test w/o side & curtain airbags . . . . .NA

FROM THE TEST TRACK

Tested model
2004 V8 4-door SUV AWD, 4.6-liter V8, 5-speed automatic

Tires as tested
Michelin Pilot HX MXM4, size P235/60R18 102V

Acceleration . . . . ◉
0-30 mph, sec. 2.4
0-60 mph, sec. 6.4
Quarter mile, sec. 14.9
Quarter mile, mph 95
45-65 mph, sec. 4.3

Other findings
Transmission . . . . ⊖
Turning circle, ft. 42
Ground clearance, in. 4.0

Braking and handling
Braking . . . . ⊖
Braking, dry pavement, ft. 132
Routine handling . . . . ⊖
Emergency handling . . . . ⊖
Avoidance maneuver, max. mph . . .50.5

Convenience and comfort
Ride . . . . ⊖
Noise . . . . ⊖
Driving position . . . . ○
Access . . . . ○
Controls and displays . . . . ⊖
Fit and finish . . . . ⊖
Door top to ground, in. 59.0
Cargo area . . . . ○
Cargo volume, cu.ft. 40.0
Max. load, lb. 1,200

Seating
Front-seat comfort . . . . ⊖
Front shoulder room, in. 59.0
Front leg room, in. 41.0
Front head room, in. 6.0
Rear-seat comfort . . . . ◉
Rear shoulder room, in. 58.0
Rear leg room, in. 29.0
Rear head room, in 4.0
Third-seat comfort . . . . ●
Third shoulder room,in 44.0
Third leg room, in. 25.5
Third head room, in. 0.0

Fuel economy . . . . ●
CU's overall mileage, mpg 16
CU's city/highway, mpg 11/24
CU's 150-mile trip, mpg 20
Annual fuel . . . . .915 gal./$1,835
Cruising range 360

RELIABILITY HISTORY

TROUBLE SPOTS	Cadillac SRX							
	97	98	99	00	01	02	03	04
Engine								◉
Cooling								◉
Fuel								◉
Ignition								◉
Transmission								◉
Electrical								◉
Air conditioning								◉
Suspension								◉
Brakes								◉
Exhaust								◉
Paint/trim/rust								◉
Body integrity								⊖
Power equipment								⊖
Body hardware								⊖
RELIABILITY VERDICT								✗

Cadillac STS

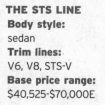

THE STS LINE
Body style:
sedan
Trim lines:
V6, V8, STS-V
Base price range:
$40,525-$70,000E

The STS replaced the Seville and moves Cadillac toward the dynamic prowess reminiscent of BMW and Mercedes-Benz. Based on a new rear-wheel-drive platform, it features Cadillac's contemporary styling. Power comes from either a 3.6-liter V6, found in the CTS and SRX, or the ultra-smooth and powerful 4.6-liter Northstar V8. All-wheel drive is optional on the V8. First impressions indicate that handling is taut and agile and the cabin is very quiet, but the rear seat isn't as sumptuous as the class leaders. A sporty supercharged STS-V joins the line for 2006.

REPORT CARD

New	Predicted reliability
New	Owner satisfaction
NA	Predicted depreciation
NA	Accident avoidance
NA	Acceleration
NA	Ride
NA	Front seat comfort
NA	Fuel economy

SPECIFICATIONS

Drive wheels Rear or AWD

Seating 2 front, 3 rear

Engines available
3.6-liter V6 (255 hp); 4.6-liter V8 (320 hp);
4.4-liter V8 supercharged (440 hp)

Transmissions available
5-speed automatic; 6-speed automatic

Fuel
Fuel type . . . . .Regular or premium
EPA city/highway, mpg 17/26
Fuel refill capacity, gal. 17.5

Dimensions and weight
Length, in. 196
Width, in. 73
Wheelbase, in. 116
Curb weight, lb. 4,030
Percent weight, front/rear 54/46
Typical towing ability, lb. 1,000

SAFETY INFORMATION

Active safety features
Antilock brakes . . . . .Standard
Traction control . . . . .Standard
Stability control . . . . .Standard
Daytime running lights . . . . .Standard
Tire pressure monitor . . . . .Available

Safety belts
Center-rear belt 3-point
Pretensioners, front/rear . . . . .Yes/no

Air bags
Occupant-sensing system . . . . .Front
Side bags, front/rear . . . . .Standard/no
Inflatable curtain . . . . .Standard
Accident alert system .Available

Crash tests
Gov't front-crash test, driver/front passenger . . . . . .NA/NA
Gov't side-crash test, driver/rear passenger . . . . . . .NA/NA
IIHS offset crash test . . . . .NA
IIHS side crash test w/ side & curtain airbags . . . . .NA
IIHS side crash test w/o side & curtain airbags . . . . .NA

ANOTHER LOOK

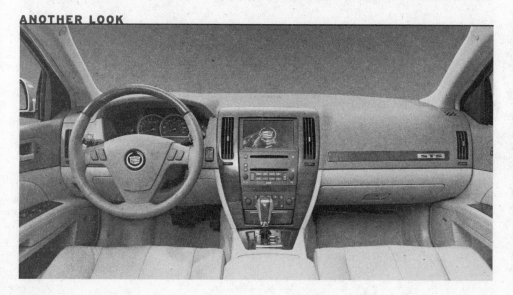

RELIABILITY HISTORY

TROUBLE SPOTS	97 98 99 00 01 02 03 04
Engine	
Cooling	
Fuel	**NO**
Ignition	
Transmission	**DATA**
Electrical	
Air conditioning	**NEW**
Suspension	
Brakes	**MODEL**
Exhaust	
Paint/trim/rust	
Body integrity	
Power equipment	
Body hardware	
RELIABILITY VERDICT	

● ● ○ ○ ◐
better ◀——▶ worse   See page 36 for more information.

Cadillac XLR

THE XLR LINE
Body style:
convertible
Trim lines:
–

Base price range:
$75,835

The XLR is Cadillac's entry in the exclusive luxury convertible niche that includes the Mercedes SL and Jaguar XK8. The XLR is based on the Corvette, but unlike the Corvette it is powered by a sophisticated, smooth Northstar V8 mated to a five-speed automatic. The metal roof is power-retractable—a neat process that's achieved by a press of a button and takes about 30 seconds, similar to the one pioneered by Mercedes in the SLK. The interior is luxuriously appointed. The XLR is quick but doesn't feel as sporty to drive as an SL500. And unlike the Jaguar, it does not offer a small rear seat.

REPORT CARD

NA	Predicted reliability
NA	Owner satisfaction
NA	Predicted depreciation
NA	Accident avoidance
NA	Acceleration
NA	Ride
NA	Front seat comfort
NA	Fuel economy

SPECIFICATIONS

Drive wheels Rear

Seating 2 front

Engines available
4.6-liter V8 (320 hp)

Transmissions available
5-speed automatic

Fuel
Fuel type . . . . .Premium
EPA city/highway, mpg 17/25
Fuel refill capacity, gal. 18.0

Dimensions and weight
Length, in. 178
Width, in. 72
Wheelbase, in. 106
Curb weight, lb. 3,700
Percent weight, front/rear 49/51
Typical towing ability, lb. . . . . .NR

SAFETY INFORMATION

Active safety features
Antilock brakes . . . . .Standard
Traction control . . . . .Standard
Stability control . . . . .Standard
Daytime running lights . . . . .Standard
Tire pressure monitor . . . . .Available

Safety belts
Center-rear belt . . . . .NA
Pretensioners, front/rear .Yes/NA

Air bags
Occupant-sensing system . . . . .Not available
Side bags, front/rear .Standard/NA
Inflatable curtain . . . . .Not available
Accident alert system . . . . .Available

Crash tests
Gov't front-crash test, driver/front passenger . . . . . . .NA/NA
Gov't side-crash test, driver/rear passenger . . . . .NA/NA
IIHS offset crash test . . . . .NA
IIHS side crash test w/ side & curtain airbags . . . . .NA
IIHS side crash test w/o side & curtain airbags . . . . .NA

RELIABILITY HISTORY

TROUBLE SPOTS	97 98 99 00 01 02 03 04
Engine	
Cooling	NOT
Fuel	
Ignition	
Transmission	ENOUGH
Electrical	
Air conditioning	DATA
Suspension	
Brakes	TO
Exhaust	
Paint/trim/rust	RATE
Body integrity	
Power equipment	
Body hardware	
RELIABILITY VERDICT	

ANOTHER LOOK

Chevrolet Avalanche

CR RECOMMENDED ✓

The Avalanche is a full-sized, crew-cab pickup with a unified bed and cab. An innovative "midgate" at the back of the cab can be folded down and the rear glass removed to extend the cargo bed into the rear of the cabin. Along with a standard three-piece removable bed cover, this gives the Avalanche flexibility and versatility. Fussing with all the pieces, however, can be tedious. Rear visibility is very poor. The 5.3-liter V8 provides impressive acceleration but is thirsty. The ride is comfortable and quiet. The four-wheel-drive system can remain engaged indefinitely—a plus. Reliability has been average.

THE AVALANCHE LINE
Body style:
crew cab
Trim lines:
1500
Base price range:
$34,010-$37,010

REPORT CARD

◯	Predicted reliability
⊖	Owner satisfaction
⊖	Predicted depreciation
◯	Accident avoidance
⊖	Acceleration
⊖	Ride
⊖	Front seat comfort
●	Fuel economy

SPECIFICATIONS

Drive wheels Rear or selectable 4WD

Seating 3 front, 3 rear

Engines available
5.3-liter V8 (295 hp)

Transmissions available
4-speed automatic

Fuel
Fuel type . . . . .Regular
EPA city/highway, mpg 14/18
Fuel refill capacity, gal. 31.0

Dimensions and weight
Length, in. 222
Width, in. 80
Wheelbase, in. .130
Curb weight, lb. 5,810
Percent weight, front/rear 52/48
Typical towing ability, lb. 8,100

SAFETY INFORMATION

Active safety features
Antilock brakes . . . . .Standard
Traction control . . . . .Included with stability
Stability control . . . . .Standard
Daytime running lights . . . . .Standard
Tire pressure monitor . . . . .Not available

Safety belts
Center-rear belt 3-point
Pretensioners, front/rear . . . . .No/no

Air bags
Occupant-sensing system . . . . .Front
Side bags, front/rear . . . . .Optional/no
Inflatable curtain . . . . .Not available
Accident alert system .Available

Crash tests
Gov't front-crash test, driver/front passenger . . . . .◯/⊖
Gov't side-crash test, driver/rear passenger . . .NA/NA
IIHS offset crash test . . . . .NA
IIHS side crash test w/ side & curtain airbags . . . . .NA
IIHS side crash test w/o side & curtain airbags . . . . . . .NA

FROM THE TEST TRACK

Tested model
2002 crew cab 4WD, 5.3-liter V8, 4-speed automatic

Tires as tested
Goodyear Wrangler AT/S, size P265/70R17 113S

Acceleration . . . .⊖
0-30 mph, sec. .3.2
0-60 mph, sec. .8.9
Quarter mile, sec. 17.0
Quarter mile, mph 81
45-65 mph, sec. 5.7

Other findings
Transmission . . . .⊖
Turning circle, ft. 47
Ground clearance, in. 8.5

Braking and handling
Braking . . . .◯
Braking, dry pavement, ft. 142
Routine handling . . . .◯
Emergency handling . . . .⊖
Avoidance maneuver, max. mph . . .44.5

Convenience and comfort
Ride . . . .⊖
Noise . . . .⊖
Driving position . . . .⊖
Access . . . .◯
Controls and displays . . . .◉
Fit and finish . . . .◯
Door top to ground, in. 68.0
Cargo area . . . .◯
Max. load, lb. 1,190

Seating
Front-seat comfort . . . .⊖
Front shoulder room, in. 65.0
Front leg room, in. 41.5
Front head room, in. 4.0
Rear-seat comfort . . . .⊖
Rear shoulder room, in. 65.0
Rear leg room, in. 29.0
Rear head room, in 4.0

Fuel economy . . . .●
CU's overall mileage, mpg 13
CU's city/highway, mpg 9/18
CU's 150-mile trip, mpg 16
Annual fuel . . . . .1,150 gal./$2,300
Cruising range 465

RELIABILITY HISTORY

TROUBLE SPOTS	Chevrolet Avalanche							
	97	98	99	00	01	02	03	04
Engine						◉	◉	◉
Cooling						◉	◉	◉
Fuel						⊖	◉	◉
Ignition						◉	◉	◉
Transmission						⊖	◉	◉
Electrical						⊖	⊖	◉
Air conditioning						⊖	⊖	◉
Suspension						⊖	⊖	◉
Brakes						◯	◉	◉
Exhaust						◉	◉	◉
Paint/trim/rust						◯	⊖	◉
Body integrity						◐	◯	◯
Power equipment						◯	⊖	◉
Body hardware						◯	⊖	◉
RELIABILITY VERDICT						✗	–	–

Chevrolet Aveo

THE AVEO LINE
Body style:
4-door hatchback;
sedan
Trim lines:
Special Value, LS, LT
Base price range:
$9,455-$12,865

Even as basic transportation, the Daewoo-produced Aveo falls short. Although an economy car, fuel efficiency is unimpressive. The 1.6-liter engine delivers just adequate performance. Handling lacks agility and confidence, with darty, imprecise steering and lots of body lean. The ride is relatively comfortable, however. Drivers sit fairly high with a good view, and access is relatively easy. Fit and finish is adequate. The ABS option is inexpensive and widely available—a rarity for this class. The hatchback adds versatility, but the sedan version has a roomier trunk.

REPORT CARD

NA	Predicted reliability
NA	Owner satisfaction
NA	Predicted depreciation
◯	Accident avoidance
⊖	Acceleration
◯	Ride
⊖	Front seat comfort
⊖	Fuel economy

SPECIFICATIONS

Drive wheels Front

Seating 2 front, 3 rear

Engines available
1.6-liter 4 (103 hp)

Transmissions available
5-speed manual; 4-speed automatic

Fuel
Fuel type . . . . Regular
EPA city/highway, mpg 26/34
Fuel refill capacity, gal. 11.9

Dimensions and weight
Length, in. 153
Width, in. 66
Wheelbase, in. .98
Curb weight, lb. 2,530
Percent weight, front/rear 63/37
Typical towing ability, lb. . . . . .NR

SAFETY INFORMATION

Active safety features
Antilock brakes . . . . .Optional
Traction control . . . . .Not available
Stability control . . . . .Not available
Daytime running lights . . . . .Standard
Tire pressure monitor .Not available

Safety belts
Center-rear belt 3-point
Pretensioners, front/rear .Yes/no

Air bags
Occupant-sensing system . . . . .Not available
Side bags, front/rear . . . . .No/no
Inflatable curtain . . . . .Not available
Accident alert system . . . . .Not available

Crash tests
Gov't front-crash test, driver/front passenger . . . . . . ◑/◑
Gov't side-crash test, driver/rear passenger . . . . .NA/NA
IIHS offset crash test . . . . .NA
IIHS side crash test w/ side & curtain airbags . . . . .NA
IIHS side crash test w/o side & curtain airbags . . . . .NA

FROM THE TEST TRACK

Tested model
2004 LS 4-door hatchback, 1.6-liter Four,
4-speed automatic

Tires as tested
Kumho Steel Radial 722,
size P185/60R14 82H

Acceleration . . . . ⊖
0-30 mph, sec. 3.9
0-60 mph, sec. 11.7
Quarter mile, sec. 18.8
Quarter mile, mph 73
45-65 mph, sec. 7.3

Other findings
Transmission . . . . ⊖
Turning circle, ft. 35
Ground clearance, in. 4.0

Braking and handling
Braking . . . . ⊖
Braking, dry pavement, ft. 137
Routine handling . . . . ◯
Emergency handling . . . . ◯
Avoidance maneuver, max. mph . . .51.5

Convenience and comfort
Ride . . . . ◯
Noise . . . . ◯
Driving position . . . . ◯
Access . . . . ⊖
Controls and displays . . . . ◯
Fit and finish . . . . ◯
Door top to ground, in. 53.5
Trunk . . . . ●
Luggage capacity . . . . .1+2
Max. load, lb. 860

Seating
Front-seat comfort . . . . ⊖
Front shoulder room, in. 53.5
Front leg room, in. 40.0
Front head room, in. 5.5
Rear-seat comfort . . . . ◯
Rear shoulder room, in. 51.0
Rear leg room, in. 26.0
Rear head room, in 2.0

Fuel economy . . . . ⊖
CU's overall mileage, mpg 28
  CU's city/highway, mpg 19/38
  CU's 150-mile trip, mpg 33
Annual fuel . . . . .545 gal./$1,090
Cruising range 360

RELIABILITY HISTORY

TROUBLE SPOTS	97	98	99	00	01	02	03	04
Engine								
Cooling								
Fuel			**NOT**					
Ignition								
Transmission			**ENOUGH**					
Electrical								
Air conditioning			**DATA**					
Suspension								
Brakes			**TO**					
Exhaust								
Paint/trim/rust			**RATE**					
Body integrity								
Power equipment								
Body hardware								
RELIABILITY VERDICT								

Chevrolet Cobalt

The Cobalt is the successor to the Cavalier, and is based on GM's new Delta platform, which originated with the European Opel Astra. The Cobalt's standard 2.2-liter engine is spirited but noisy and relatively thirsty. The ride is steady, but handling isn't particularly agile. The steering is too light at low speeds. The rear seat is not roomy, even by small-car-class standards. A supercharged 2.0-liter four-cylinder powers the sporty SS model. The optional head-protection curtain air bags resulted in the Cobalt receiving a score of Acceptable in the IIHS side-impact-crash test, and Poor without the option.

THE COBALT LINE

Body style:
coupe; sedan
Trim lines:
Base, LS, LT, SS
Base price range:
$13,625-$21,430

REPORT CARD

New	**Predicted reliability**
New	**Owner satisfaction**
NA	**Predicted depreciation**
○	**Accident avoidance**
◒	**Acceleration**
◒	**Ride**
○	**Front seat comfort**
○	**Fuel economy**

SPECIFICATIONS

Drive wheels Front

Seating 2 front, 3 rear

Engines available
2.2-liter 4 (145 hp); 2.0-liter 4 supercharged (205 hp)

Transmissions available
5-speed manual; 4-speed automatic

Fuel
Fuel type ....Regular
EPA city/highway, mpg 24/32
Fuel refill capacity, gal. 13.5

Dimensions and weight
Length, in. 180
Width, in. 68
Wheelbase, in. 103
Curb weight, lb. 2,850
Percent weight, front/rear 61/39
Typical towing ability, lb. 1,000

SAFETY INFORMATION

Active safety features

Antilock brakes ....Standard (optional on Base)
Traction control ....Optional with automatic & ABS
Stability control ....Not available
Daytime running lights ....Standard
Tire pressure monitor ....Not available

Safety belts

Center-rear belt 3-point
Pretensioners, front/rear ....Yes/no

Air bags

Occupant-sensing system ....Not available
Side bags, front/rear ....No/no
Inflatable curtain ....Optional
Accident alert system ....Available

Crash tests

Gov't front-crash test, driver/front passenger ......◒/◒
Gov't side-crash test, driver/rear passenger ......NA/NA
IIHS offset crash test ....Good
IIHS side crash test w/ side & curtain airbags ...Acceptable
IIHS side crash test w/o side & curtain airbags ....Poor

FROM THE TEST TRACK

Tested model

2005 LS sedan, 2.2-liter Four, 4-speed automatic

Tires as tested

Continental TouringContact AS, size P195/60R15 87S

Acceleration ....◒
0-30 mph, sec. 3.3
0-60 mph, sec. 8.8
Quarter mile, sec. 16.9
Quarter mile, mph 82
45-65 mph, sec. 5.3

Other findings

Transmission ....◒
Turning circle, ft. 37
Ground clearance, in. 5.0

Braking and handling

Braking ....◒
Braking, dry pavement, ft. 141
Routine handling ....○
Emergency handling ....○
Avoidance maneuver, max. mph ...50.5

Convenience and comfort

Ride ....◒
Noise ....○
Driving position ....○
Access ....○
Controls and displays ....◒
Fit and finish ....◒
Door top to ground, in. 51.0
Trunk ....○
Luggage capacity ....3+2
Max. load, lb. 890

Seating

Front-seat comfort ....○
Front shoulder room, in. 53.0
Front leg room, in. 41.5
Front head room, in. 3.5
Rear-seat comfort ....◒
Rear shoulder room, in. 50.0
Rear leg room, in. 27.0
Rear head room, in 3.0

Fuel economy ....○
CU's overall mileage, mpg 23
CU's city/highway, mpg 15/35
CU's 150-mile trip, mpg 29
Annual fuel ....650 gal./$1,295
Cruising range 365

RELIABILITY HISTORY

TROUBLE SPOTS	97 98 99 00 01 02 03 04
Engine	
Cooling	
Fuel	NO
Ignition	
Transmission	DATA
Electrical	
Air conditioning	NEW
Suspension	
Brakes	MODEL
Exhaust	
Paint/trim/rust	
Body integrity	
Power equipment	
Body hardware	
RELIABILITY VERDICT	

Chevrolet Colorado/GMC Canyon

THE COLORADO LINE
Body style:
regular cab; extended
cab; crew cab
Trim lines:
Base, LS
Base price range:
$15,095-$28,550

The Colorado is the replacement for the S-10 compact pickup truck and is a twin of the GMC Canyon—the Sonoma's replacement. Both are available in regular-, extended-, and crew-cab versions. ABS is standard. Four-wheel drive is optional, but it's only a part-time system, unsuitable for use on dry pavement. These new trucks are powered by either a 2.8-liter four-cylinder or 3.5-liter five-cylinder. Both engines are a bit crude and noisy. A V6 isn't offered. The cabin is fairly quiet, and ride and handling are competitive with other current compact pickups.

REPORT CARD

◓	Predicted reliability
○	Owner satisfaction
NA	Predicted depreciation
NA	Accident avoidance
NA	Acceleration
NA	Ride
NA	Front seat comfort
NA	Fuel economy

SPECIFICATIONS

Drive wheels Rear or part-time 4WD

Seating 3 front, 3 rear

Engines available
2.8-liter 4 (175 hp); 3.5-liter 5 (220 hp)

Transmissions available
5-speed manual; 4-speed automatic

Fuel
Fuel type ....Regular
EPA city/highway, mpg 17/22
Fuel refill capacity, gal. 19.6

Dimensions and weight
Length, in. 207
Width, in. 69
Wheelbase, in. 126
Curb weight, lb. 4,240
Percent weight, front/rear 57/43
Typical towing ability, lb. 4,000

SAFETY INFORMATION

Active safety features
Antilock brakes ....Standard
Traction control ....Optional on 2WD
Stability control ....Not available
Daytime running lights ....Standard
Tire pressure monitor ....Not available

Safety belts
Center-rear belt 3-point
Pretensioners, front/rear ....Yes/no

Air bags
Occupant-sensing system ....Not available
Side bags, front/rear ....No/no
Inflatable curtain ....Optional
Accident alert system ....Available

Crash tests
Gov't front-crash test, driver/front passenger .....◓ ◓
Gov't side-crash test, driver/rear passenger ....◓/◓
IIHS offset crash test ....NA
IIHS side crash test w/ side & curtain airbags ....NA
IIHS side crash test w/o side & curtain airbags ....NA

ANOTHER LOOK

RELIABILITY HISTORY

TROUBLE SPOTS	Chevrolet Colorado							
	97	98	99	00	01	02	03	04
Engine								◉
Cooling								◉
Fuel								◉
Ignition								◉
Transmission								◉
Electrical								◉
Air conditioning								◉
Suspension								◉
Brakes								◉
Exhaust								◉
Paint/trim/rust								◉
Body integrity								◓
Power equipment								◉
Body hardware								◉
RELIABILITY VERDICT								✓

Chevrolet Corvette

THE CORVETTE LINE
Body style:
2-door hatchback; convertible
Trim lines:
Base, Z06
Base price range:
$43,710-$60,000E

The redesigned 2005 Corvette is slightly smaller and lighter than the outgoing model. It incorporates traditional Corvette styling cues, including, for the first time since the 1962 model, exposed headlights. Power comes from a revised 6.0-liter, 400-hp V8. A six-speed manual is standard; a four-speed automatic is a no-cost option. Interior trim and materials are improved compared with the outgoing model. Performance is impressive. The previous-generation model we tested hit 60 mph in a head-turning 4.9 seconds. A convertible version arrives for the spring and the Z06 will return with 500 hp.

REPORT CARD

New	**Predicted reliability**
⊙	**Owner satisfaction**
NA	**Predicted depreciation**
NA	**Accident avoidance**
NA	**Acceleration**
NA	**Ride**
NA	**Front seat comfort**
NA	**Fuel economy**

SPECIFICATIONS

Drive wheels Rear

Seating 2 front

Engines available
6.0-liter V8 (400 hp); 7.0-liter V8 (500 hp)

Transmissions available
6-speed manual; 4-speed automatic

Fuel
Fuel type ....Regular
EPA city/highway, mpg 18/28
Fuel refill capacity, gal. 18.0

Dimensions and weight
Length, in. 175
Width, in. 73
Wheelbase, in. 106
Curb weight, lb. 3,180
Percent weight, front/rear 51/49
Typical towing ability, lb. ....NR

SAFETY INFORMATION

Active safety features
Antilock brakes ....Standard
Traction control ....Standard
Stability control ....Standard
Daytime running lights ....Standard
Tire pressure monitor ....Available

Safety belts
Center-rear belt ....NA
Pretensioners, front/rear ....No/NA

Air bags
Occupant-sensing system ....Not available
Side bags, front/rear ....No/NA
Inflatable curtain ....Not available
Accident alert system ....Available

Crash tests
Gov't front-crash test, driver/front passenger ......NA/NA
Gov't side-crash test, driver/rear passenger ....NA/NA
IIHS offset crash test ....NA
IIHS side crash test w/ side & curtain airbags ....NA
IIHS side crash test w/o side & curtain airbags ....NA

ANOTHER LOOK

RELIABILITY HISTORY

TROUBLE SPOTS	97 98 99 00 01 02 03 04
Engine	
Cooling	
Fuel	**NO**
Ignition	
Transmission	**DATA**
Electrical	
Air conditioning	**NEW**
Suspension	
Brakes	**MODEL**
Exhaust	
Paint/trim/rust	
Body integrity	
Power equipment	
Body hardware	
RELIABILITY VERDICT	

better ●◐○●● worse   See page 36 for more information.

Chevrolet Equinox

The Equinox competes against the Ford Escape and Hyundai Santa Fe. The rear seat is roomy and can move fore and aft to increase passenger or cargo room. The quality of interior materials is subpar. The Equinox uses an extended version of the Saturn Vue SUV platform and seats five, with very easy access to the rear seat. However, the 3.4-liter, 185-hp V6 powerplant is an old-tech engine that lacks refinement and returns poor fuel economy. The ride is OK, but handling is clumsy and the turning circle is wide. Wind noise is pronounced. A tip-up in the government rollover test is another negative.

THE EQUINOX LINE

Body style:
4-door SUV
Trim lines:
LS, LT
Base price range:
$21,320-$24,660

SPECIFICATIONS

Drive wheels Front or AWD

Seating 2 front, 3 rear

Engines available
3.4-liter V6 (185 hp)

Transmissions available
5-speed automatic

Fuel
Fuel type . . . . .Regular
EPA city/highway, mpg 19/25
Fuel refill capacity, gal. 16.7

Dimensions and weight
Length, in. 189
Width, in. 71
Wheelbase, in. 113
Curb weight, lb. 3,845
Percent weight, front/rear 56/44
Typical towing ability, lb. 3,500

REPORT CARD

New	Predicted reliability
New	Owner satisfaction
NA	Predicted depreciation
○	Accident avoidance
○	Acceleration
○	Ride
○	Front seat comfort
●	Fuel economy

SAFETY INFORMATION

Active safety features
Antilock brakes . . . . .Optional
Traction control . . . . .Optional on 2WD
Stability control .Not available
Daytime running lights . . . . .Standard
Tire pressure monitor . . . . .Not available

Safety belts
Center-rear belt 3-point
Pretensioners, front/rear .Yes/no

Air bags
Occupant-sensing system . . . . .Not available
Side bags, front/rear . . . . .No/no
Inflatable curtain . . . . .Optional
Accident alert system . . . . .Available

Crash tests
Gov't front-crash test, driver/front passenger . . . . . ◐/◐
Gov't side-crash test, driver/rear passenger . . . . ◐/◐
IIHS offset crash test . . . . .NA
IIHS side crash test w/ side & curtain airbags . . . . .NA
IIHS side crash test w/o side & curtain airbags . . . . .NA

FROM THE TEST TRACK

Tested model
2005 LT 4-door SUV AWD, 3.4-liter V6, 5-speed automatic

Tires as tested
Bridgestone Dueler H/T 684 II, size P235/65R16 101S

Acceleration . . . . ○
0-30 mph, sec. 3.1
0-60 mph, sec. 9.1
Quarter mile, sec. 17.2
Quarter mile, mph 81
45-65 mph, sec. 6.3

Other findings
Transmission . . . . ◐
Turning circle, ft. 44
Ground clearance, in. 6.5

Braking and handling
Braking . . . . ◐
Braking, dry pavement, ft. 142
Routine handling . . . . ○
Emergency handling . . . . ◐
Avoidance maneuver, max. mph . . .47.5

Convenience and comfort
Ride . . . . ○
Noise . . . . ○
Driving position . . . . ◐
Access . . . . ●
Controls and displays . . . . ◐
Fit and finish . . . . ◐
Door top to ground, in. 59.0
Cargo area . . . . ◐
Cargo volume, cu.ft. 33.0
Max. load, lb. 1,230

Seating
Front-seat comfort . . . . ○
Front shoulder room, in. 50.5
Front leg room, in. 42.5
Front head room, in. 6.0
Rear-seat comfort . . . . ◐
Rear shoulder room, in. 52.5
Rear leg room, in. 33.0
Rear head room, in 5.0

Fuel economy . . . . ●
CU's overall mileage, mpg 17
 CU's city/highway, mpg 12/25
 CU's 150-mile trip, mpg 22
Annual fuel . . . . .865 gal./$1,730
Cruising range 330

RELIABILITY HISTORY

TROUBLE SPOTS	97 98 99 00 01 02 03 04
Engine	
Cooling	NO
Fuel	
Ignition	
Transmission	DATA
Electrical	
Air conditioning	NEW
Suspension	
Brakes	MODEL
Exhaust	
Paint/trim/rust	
Body integrity	
Power equipment	
Body hardware	
RELIABILITY VERDICT	

Chevrolet HHR

THE HHR LINE
Body style:
wagon
Trim lines:
LS, 1LT, 2LT
Base price range:
$17,000-$22,000E

The HHR is a raised wagon, similar in concept to the Chrysler PT Cruiser and featuring styling cues of Chevrolet vans from the 1950s. It is based on the same platform as the Cobalt sedan. The five-passenger HHR will be available with 2.2-liter or 2.4-liter four-cylinder engines. A five-speed manual transmission is standard, with a four-speed automatic optional. The split rear seats fold to create a flat load floor.

REPORT CARD

New	**Predicted reliability**
New	**Owner satisfaction**
NA	**Predicted depreciation**
NA	**Accident avoidance**
NA	**Acceleration**
NA	**Ride**
NA	**Front seat comfort**
NA	**Fuel economy**

SPECIFICATIONS

Drive wheels Front

Seating 2 front, 3 rear

Engines available
2.2-liter 4 (143 hp); 2.4-liter 4 (172 hp)

Transmissions available
5-speed manual; 4-speed automatic

Fuel
Fuel type ....Regular
EPA city/highway, mpg ....NA
Fuel refill capacity, gal. 16.2

Dimensions and weight
Length, in. 176
Width, in. 68
Wheelbase, in. 103
Curb weight, lb. ....NA
Percent weight, front/rear ....NA
Typical towing ability, lb. ....NA

SAFETY INFORMATION

Active safety features
Antilock brakes ....Optional
Traction control ....Optional on LS, LT
Stability control ....Not available
Daytime running lights ....Standard
Tire pressure monitor ....NA

Safety belts
Center-rear belt 3-point
Pretensioners, front/rear ....Yes/no

Air bags
Occupant-sensing system ....NA
Side bags, front/rear ....No/no
Inflatable curtain ....Optional
Accident alert system ....Available

Crash tests
Gov't front-crash test, driver/front passenger ......NA/NA
Gov't side-crash test, driver/rear passenger ....NA/NA
IIHS offset crash test ....NA
IIHS side crash test w/ side & curtain airbags ....NA
IIHS side crash test w/o side & curtain airbags ....NA

RELIABILITY HISTORY

TROUBLE SPOTS	97 98 99 00 01 02 03 04		
Engine			
Cooling		NO	
Fuel			
Ignition			
Transmission		DATA	
Electrical			
Air conditioning		NEW	
Suspension			
Brakes		MODEL	
Exhaust			
Paint/trim/rust			
Body integrity			
Power equipment			
Body hardware			
RELIABILITY VERDICT			

ANOTHER LOOK

Chevrolet Impala

CR RECOMMENDED ✓

The Impala will get its first freshening since its 2000 model-year debut, with updated engines and some interior revisions for the 2006 model year. It handles fairly well and has good steering feedback. The coarse 200-hp, 3.8-liter V6 provides very good acceleration. A supercharged V6 is available in the SS model. The Impala's ride is absorbent but unsettled, and road noise is pronounced. The front bench seats lack thigh support, and while the rear seat is roomy, it's too low and short. Interior fit and finish is borderline offensive. The trunk is spacious, though, and crash-test results are impressive.

THE IMPALA LINE
Body style:
sedan
Trim lines:
Base, LS, SS
Base price range:
$22,350-$28,555

REPORT CARD

◖	Predicted reliability
○	Owner satisfaction
◖	Predicted depreciation
○	Accident avoidance
◖	Acceleration
○	Ride
◖	Front seat comfort
◕	Fuel economy

SPECIFICATIONS

Drive wheels Front

Seating 3 front, 3 rear

Engines available
3.4-liter V6 (180 hp); 3.8-liter V6 (200 hp);
3.8-liter V6 supercharged (240 hp)

Transmissions available
4-speed automatic

Fuel
Fuel type . . . . .Regular or premium
EPA city/highway, mpg 20/30
Fuel refill capacity, gal. 17.0

Dimensions and weight
Length, in. 200
Width, in. 73
Wheelbase, in. 111
Curb weight, lb. 3,655
Percent weight, front/rear 63/37
Typical towing ability, lb. 1,000

SAFETY INFORMATION

Active safety features
Antilock brakes . . . . .Standard (optional on Base)
Traction control . . . . .Standard with ABS
Stability control . . . . .Not available
Daytime running lights . . . . .Standard
Tire pressure monitor . . . . .Available

Safety belts
Center-rear belt 3-point
Pretensioners, front/rear . . . . .No/no

Air bags
Occupant-sensing system . . . . .Not available
Side bags, front/rear .Optional/no
Inflatable curtain . . . . .Not available
Accident alert system . . . . .Available

Crash tests
Gov't front-crash test, driver/front passenger . . . . . . ◕/◕
Gov't side-crash test, driver/rear passenger . . . . . . ◖/◖
IIHS offset crash test . . . . .Good
IIHS side crash test w/ side & curtain airbags . . . . .NA
IIHS side crash test w/o side & curtain airbags . . . . .NA

FROM THE TEST TRACK

Tested model
2004 LS sedan, 3.8-liter V6, 4-speed automatic

Tires as tested
Goodyear Eagle GA Touring,
size P225/60R16 97S

Acceleration . . . . ◖
0-30 mph, sec. 3.0
0-60 mph, sec. 8.3
Quarter mile, sec. 16.5
Quarter mile, mph 86
45-65 mph, sec. 5.5

Other findings
Transmission . . . . ◖
Turning circle, ft. 41
Ground clearance, in. 5.5

Braking and handling
Braking . . . . ◖
Braking, dry pavement, ft. 139
Routine handling . . . . ◖
Emergency handling . . . . ○
Avoidance maneuver, max. mph . . .49.0

Convenience and comfort
Ride . . . . ○
Noise . . . . ◖
Driving position . . . . ◖
Access . . . . ◖
Controls and displays . . . . ◖
Fit and finish . . . . ◖
Door top to ground, in. 51.5
Trunk . . . . ◖
Luggage capacity . . . . .5+0
Max. load, lb. 1,095

Seating
Front-seat comfort . . . . ◖
Front shoulder room, in. 58.0
Front leg room, in. 41.5
Front head room, in. 4.0
Rear-seat comfort . . . . ○
Rear shoulder room, in. 58.5
Rear leg room, in. 29.0
Rear head room, in 3.5

Fuel economy . . . . ◕
CU's overall mileage, mpg 20
CU's city/highway, mpg 13/31
CU's 150-mile trip, mpg 24
Annual fuel . . . . .765 gal./$1,530
Cruising range 375

RELIABILITY HISTORY

TROUBLE SPOTS	Chevrolet Impala							
	97	98	99	00	01	02	03	04
Engine				○	◕	◕	◕	◕
Cooling				○	◖	◕	◕	◕
Fuel				○	◕	◖	◕	◕
Ignition				◕	◕	◕	◕	◕
Transmission				◕	○	◖	◕	◕
Electrical				○	○	○	◖	◕
Air conditioning				◕	◕	◕	◕	◕
Suspension				◕	○	◖	◕	◕
Brakes				○	○	◖	◕	◕
Exhaust				◕	◕	◕	◕	◕
Paint/trim/rust				◕	◖	○	◕	◕
Body integrity				○	○	◖	◕	◕
Power equipment				○	◖	◖	◕	◕
Body hardware				◕	◖	◖	◕	◕
RELIABILITY VERDICT		−	✗	−			✓	✓

Chevrolet Malibu

The Malibu is a solid and well-rounded car. The interior offers easy access, but fit and finish is unimpressive. The coarse V6 delivers quick acceleration and 23 mpg in the sedan, but only 21 in the Malibu Maxx. The four-cylinder is noisy and returns 24 mpg. Handling is responsive and secure, and the ride is supple and steady. The seats are so-so. The Maxx is a four-door hatchback with an extended wheelbase for more rear-seat room and the interior flexibility of a wagon or small SUV. Good offset-crash-test result is a plus. First-year reliability has been subpar.

THE MALIBU LINE
Body style:
4-door hatchback; sedan
Trim lines:
Base, LS, LT, Maxx LS, Maxx LT
Base price range:
$19,200–$24,610

REPORT CARD

◖	Predicted reliability
⊖	Owner satisfaction
NA	Predicted depreciation
○	Accident avoidance
⊖	Acceleration
⊖	Ride
○	Front seat comfort
○	Fuel economy

SPECIFICATIONS

Drive wheels Front

Seating 2 front, 3 rear

Engines available
2.2-liter 4 (145 hp); 3.5-liter V6 (200 hp)

Transmissions available
4-speed automatic

Fuel
Fuel type ....Regular
EPA city/highway, mpg 22/32
Fuel refill capacity, gal. 16.1

Dimensions and weight
Length, in. 188
Width, in. 70
Wheelbase, in. 106
Curb weight, lb. 3,290
Percent weight, front/rear 62/38
Typical towing ability, lb. 1,000

SAFETY INFORMATION

Active safety features
Antilock brakes ....Standard (optional on Base)
Traction control ....Standard (optional on Base)
Stability control ....Not available
Daytime running lights ....Standard
Tire pressure monitor ....Not available

Safety belts
Center-rear belt 3-point
Pretensioners, front/rear ....Yes/no

Air bags
Occupant-sensing system ....Not available
Side bags, front/rear ....Optional/no
Inflatable curtain ....Optional
Accident alert system ....Available

Crash tests
Gov't front-crash test, driver/front passenger   ◑/◒
Gov't side-crash test, driver/rear passenger   ◑/◒
IIHS offset crash test ....Good
IIHS side crash test w/ side & curtain airbags ...Acceptable
IIHS side crash test w/o side & curtain airbags ....Poor

FROM THE TEST TRACK

Tested model
2004 LS sedan, 3.5-liter V6, 4-speed automatic

Tires as tested
Bridgestone B450, size P205/65R15 92S
Acceleration ....⊖
0-30 mph, sec. 3.0
0-60 mph, sec. 8.1
Quarter mile, sec. 16.3
Quarter mile, mph 87
45-65 mph, sec. 5.1

Other findings
Transmission ....●
Turning circle, ft. 39
Ground clearance, in. 4.5

Braking and handling
Braking ....○
Braking, dry pavement, ft. 146
Routine handling ....⊖
Emergency handling ....○
Avoidance maneuver, max. mph ..48.0

Convenience and comfort
Ride ....⊖
Noise ....⊖
Driving position ....⊖
Access ....⊖
Controls and displays ....●
Fit and finish ....⊖
Door top to ground, in. 52.0
Trunk ....○
Luggage capacity ....4+1
Max. load, lb. 915

Seating
Front-seat comfort ....○
Front shoulder room, in. 57.0
Front leg room, in. 41.5
Front head room, in. 5.5
Rear-seat comfort ....⊖
Rear shoulder room, in. 55.5
Rear leg room, in. 29.0
Rear head room, in 3.0
Fuel economy ....○
CU's overall mileage, mpg 23
  CU's city/highway, mpg 15/36
  CU's 150-mile trip, mpg 29
Annual fuel ....650 gal./$1,300
Cruising range 430

RELIABILITY HISTORY

TROUBLE SPOTS	Chevrolet Malibu							
	97	98	99	00	01	02	03	04
Engine	●	●	◑	○	○	◑	◑	◑
Cooling	◑	●	●	◑	◑	○	○	○
Fuel	○	○	○	◑	○	◑	○	○
Ignition	○	○	○	◑	◑	◑	○	○
Transmission	○	○	○	○	○	○	○	○
Electrical	●	●	●	●	●	◑	○	◑
Air conditioning	◑	●	◑	◑	◑	○	○	○
Suspension	●	○	○	◑	○	◑	○	○
Brakes	●	●	●	●	●	◑	◑	◑
Exhaust	○	○	◑	○	○	○	○	○
Paint/trim/rust	○	○	○	◑	◑	◑	○	○
Body integrity	◑	◑	○	○	◑	◑	○	○
Power equipment	○	○	○	○	◑	◑	◑	●
Body hardware	○	○	○	○	◑	●	◑	◑
RELIABILITY VERDICT	✗	✗	✗	✗	✗	–	✓	✗

○ better ◖ ○ ◑ ● worse   See page 36 for more information.

Chevrolet Monte Carlo

THE MONTE CARLO LINE
Body style:
coupe
Trim lines:
LS, LT, SS
Base price range:
$22,280-$28,355

This midsized-to-large, pseudo-sporty coupe is based on the Chevrolet Impala and bowed for the 2000 model year. Acceleration is strong, but road noise is pronounced. Handling is not appreciably better than that of the more practical four-door Impala. Some controls look and feel cheap. Rear-seat access is a chore, since you have to duck under the safety belt. Overall, the Monte Carlo offers an underwhelming driving experience. The up-level SS edition has GM's 3.8-liter, 240-hp V6, which benefits from supercharging. A 2006 freshening arrives this summer.

REPORT CARD

⊖	Predicted reliability
⊖	Owner satisfaction
○	Predicted depreciation
NA	Accident avoidance
NA	Acceleration
NA	Ride
NA	Front seat comfort
NA	Fuel economy

SPECIFICATIONS

Drive wheels Front

Seating 2 front, 3 rear

Engines available
3.4-liter V6 (180 hp); 3.8-liter V6 (200 hp); 3.8-liter V6 supercharged (240 hp)

Transmissions available
4-speed automatic

Fuel
Fuel type . . . . .Regular or premium
EPA city/highway, mpg 20/30
Fuel refill capacity, gal. 17.0

Dimensions and weight
Length, in. 198
Width, in. 73
Wheelbase, in. 111
Curb weight, lb. 3,340
Percent weight, front/rear 65/35
Typical towing ability, lb. 1,000

SAFETY INFORMATION

Active safety features
Antilock brakes . . . . .Optional (standard on SS)
Traction control .Standard with ABS
Stability control . . . . .Not available
Daytime running lights .Standard
Tire pressure monitor . . . . .Available

Safety belts
Center-rear belt 3-point
Pretensioners, front/rear . . . . .No/no

Air bags
Occupant-sensing system . . . . .Not available
Side bags, front/rear .Optional/no
Inflatable curtain . . . . .Not available
Accident alert system . . . . .Available

Crash tests
Gov't front-crash test, driver/front passenger . . . . . . ●/◐
Gov't side-crash test, driver/rear passenger . . . . ○/◐
IIHS offset crash test . . . . .NA
IIHS side crash test w/ side & curtain airbags . . . . .NA
IIHS side crash test w/o side & curtain airbags . . . . .NA

ANOTHER LOOK

RELIABILITY HISTORY

TROUBLE SPOTS	Chevrolet Monte Carlo							
	97	98	99	00	01	02	03	04
Engine	⊖	○	○	●	●	●	⊖	
Cooling	○	○	●	○	○	●	⊖	
Fuel	●	●	●	○	○	●	⊖	
Ignition	⊖	●	●	●	●	●	⊖	
Transmission	○	○	⊖	●	●	●	⊖	
Electrical	⊖	●	⊖	⊖	○	○	⊖	
Air conditioning	○	○	○	●	●	●	⊖	
Suspension	●	○	⊖	○	○	●	⊖	
Brakes	●	●	●	○	○	○	⊖	
Exhaust	⊙	⊖	⊖	⊖	●	⊖	⊖	
Paint/trim/rust	○	○	⊖	⊙	●	●	⊖	
Body integrity	○	○	○	○	○	●	⊖	
Power equipment	⊖	⊖	⊖	○	○	○	⊖	
Body hardware	○	○	⊖	⊖	●	●	⊖	
RELIABILITY VERDICT	–	–	✗	–	–	–	–	✓

Insufficient data

Chevrolet SSR

THE SSR LINE
Body style:
regular cab
Trim lines:
–
Base price range:
$42,555

The SSR (Super Sport Roadster) is a pickup truck with a power-retractable hard top that stacks behind the passenger cabin. It is based on the same body-on-frame platform as the TrailBlazer. For 2005, the engine is a 6.0-liter, 390-hp V8, and a six-speed manual is optional. The exhaust and engine sound are certainly invigorating, but the vehicle's weight hampers acceleration and agility. Fit and finish is disappointing. Evoking the styling of Chevy trucks from the 1950s, this two-seater is about nostalgia and open-top motoring, but not much else.

REPORT CARD

NA	**Predicted reliability**
NA	**Owner satisfaction**
NA	**Predicted depreciation**
NA	**Accident avoidance**
NA	**Acceleration**
NA	**Ride**
NA	**Front seat comfort**
NA	**Fuel economy**

SPECIFICATIONS

Drive wheels Rear

Seating 2 front

Engines available
6.0-liter V8 (390 hp)

Transmissions available
6-speed manual; 4-speed automatic

Fuel
Fuel type . . . . .Regular
EPA city/highway, mpg 15/19
Fuel refill capacity, gal. 25.0

Dimensions and weight
Length, in. 191
Width, in. 79
Wheelbase, in. .116
Curb weight, lb. 4,720
Percent weight, front/rear 54/46
Typical towing ability, lb. 2,500

SAFETY INFORMATION

Active safety features
Antilock brakes . . . . .Standard
Traction control . . . . .std. on automatic; NA on manual
Stability control . . . . .Not available
Daytime running lights .Standard
Tire pressure monitor . . . . .Not available

Safety belts
Center-rear belt . . . . .NA
Pretensioners, front/rear . . . . .Yes/NA

Air bags
Occupant-sensing system . . . . .Front
Side bags, front/rear .Standard/NA
Inflatable curtain . . . . .Not available
Accident alert system . . . . .Available

Crash tests
Gov't front-crash test, driver/front passenger . . . . . .NA/NA
Gov't side-crash test, driver/rear passenger . . . . . . .NA/NA
IIHS offset crash test . . . . .NA
IIHS side crash test w/ side & curtain airbags . . . . .NA
IIHS side crash test w/o side & curtain airbags . . . . . . .NA

ANOTHER LOOK

RELIABILITY HISTORY

TROUBLE SPOTS	97 98 99 00 01 02 03 04		
Engine			
Cooling		**NOT**	
Fuel			
Ignition		**ENOUGH**	
Transmission			
Electrical			
Air conditioning		**DATA**	
Suspension			
Brakes		**TO**	
Exhaust			
Paint/trim/rust		**RATE**	
Body integrity			
Power equipment			
Body hardware			
RELIABILITY VERDICT			

● ● ● ○ ● ●
better ◄——► worse   See page 36 for more information.

Chevrolet Silverado/GMC Sierra 1500

CR RECOMMENDED ✓

Our tested Z71 Silverado had a stiff, choppy ride—other trim lines ride slightly better. Braking is adequate, and fit and finish is unimpressive. The powertrain isn't as smooth as competing models from Toyota or Nissan. The Silverado's significant assets are a selectable, full-time, four-wheel-drive system and a generous load capacity. The pricey Quadrasteer four-wheel steering option will be dropped after 2005. A hybrid version is available in some states, with a claimed 12 percent boost to fuel economy. Look for a redesigned Silverado in 2006.

THE SILVERADO 1500 LINE
Body style:
regular cab; extended cab; crew cab
Trim lines:
WT, Base, LS, LS Hybrid, LT, SS
Base price range:
$18,190-$39,490

REPORT CARD

○	Predicted reliability
○	Owner satisfaction
⊖	Predicted depreciation
○	Accident avoidance
⊖	Acceleration
⊖	Ride
○	Front seat comfort
●	Fuel economy

SPECIFICATIONS

Drive wheels Rear, AWD, part-time, or selectable 4WD

Seating 3 front, 3 rear

Engines available
4.3-liter V6 (195 hp); 4.8-liter V8 (285 hp); 5.3-liter V8 (295 hp); 6.0-liter V8 (300 hp); 5.3-liter V8 (310 hp); 6.0-liter V8 (345 hp)

Transmissions available
5-speed manual; 4-speed automatic

Fuel
Fuel type . . . . .Regular
EPA city/highway, mpg 15/18
Fuel refill capacity, gal. 26.0

Dimensions and weight
Length, in. 230
Width, in. 79
Wheelbase, in. 144
Curb weight, lb. 5,300
Percent weight, front/rear 58/42
Typical towing ability, lb. 7,500

SAFETY INFORMATION

Active safety features
Antilock brakes . . . . .Standard
Traction control .Optional on 2WD
Stability control . . . . .Not available
Daytime running lights .Standard
Tire pressure monitor . . . . .Not available

Safety belts
Center-rear belt 3-point
Pretensioners, front/rear .No/no

Air bags
Occupant-sensing system . . . . .Front
Side bags, front/rear . . . . .No/no
Inflatable curtain . . . . .Not available
Accident alert system . . . . .Available

Crash tests
Gov't front-crash test, driver/front passenger . . . . . .◒/○
Gov't side-crash test, driver/rear passenger . . . . .NA/NA
IIHS offset crash test . . . . .Marginal
IIHS side crash test w/ side & curtain airbags . . . . .NA
IIHS side crash test w/o side & curtain airbags . . . . .NA

FROM THE TEST TRACK

Tested model
2004 Z71 crew cab 4WD, 5.3-liter V8, 4-speed automatic

Tires as tested
Bridgestone Dueler A/T, size P265/70R17 113S

Acceleration . . . . ◒
0-30 mph, sec. 3.2
0-60 mph, sec. 8.7
Quarter mile, sec. 16.6
Quarter mile, mph 86
45-65 mph, sec. 5.3

Other findings
Transmission . . . . ◒
Turning circle, ft. 51
Ground clearance, in. 9.0

Braking and handling
Braking . . . . ○
Braking, dry pavement, ft. 146
Routine handling . . . . ○
Emergency handling . . . . ◒
Avoidance maneuver, max. mph . . .46.5

Convenience and comfort
Ride . . . . ◒
Noise . . . . ◒
Driving position . . . . ○
Access . . . . ◒
Controls and displays . . . . ◉
Fit and finish . . . . ◒
Door top to ground, in. 68.0
Cargo area . . . . ○
Max. load, lb. 1,655

Seating
Front-seat comfort . . . . ○
Front shoulder room, in. 65.0
Front leg room, in. 42.0
Front head room, in. 6.5
Rear-seat comfort . . . . ○
Rear shoulder room, in. 65.0
Rear leg room, in. 30.0
Rear head room, in 4.5

Fuel economy
CU's overall mileage, mpg 14
CU's city/highway, mpg 10/19
CU's 150-mile trip, mpg 17
Annual fuel . . . . 1,060 gal./$2,120
Cruising range 420

RELIABILITY HISTORY

TROUBLE SPOTS	Chevrolet Silverado 1500							
	97	98	99	00	01	02	03	04
Engine	◐	◐	●	●	●	●	●	●
Cooling	●	●	●	●	●	●	●	●
Fuel	○	○	◐	◐	●	●	●	●
Ignition	●	●	●	●	●	●	●	●
Transmission	◐	◐	○	○	◐	●	●	●
Electrical	○	○	◐	◐	◐	◐	●	●
Air conditioning	●	●	●	●	◐	●	●	●
Suspension	○	○	◐	◐	◐	◐	●	●
Brakes	●	◐	○	◐	●	●	●	●
Exhaust	●	●	●	●	●	●	●	●
Paint/trim/rust								
Body integrity	◐	◐	○	○	○	◐	●	●
Power equipment	○	○	◐	◐	●	●	●	●
Body hardware	○	○	◐	◐	◐	●	●	●
RELIABILITY VERDICT	-	-	-	✗	✗	-		

Expert • Independent • Nonprofit

Chevrolet Suburban/GMC Yukon XL

The mammoth Suburban SUV can seat eight adults in comfort, tow a heavy trailer, and swallow more cargo than most minivans. Handling is commendable for such a large vehicle, though a wide turning circle hinders parking. Strengths include comfortable seating and a quiet, well-controlled ride. Third-row access is a bit tough, though. A selectable full-time four-wheel-drive system is available and can remain engaged indefinitely. The standard 5.3-liter V8 is powerful but thirsty. Stability control is standard. Reliability has been average.

THE SUBURBAN LINE

Body style:
4-door SUV

Trim lines:
LS, LT

Base price range:
$38,765-$47,155

REPORT CARD

○	Predicted reliability
⊖	Owner satisfaction
⊖	Predicted depreciation
NA	Accident avoidance
NA	Acceleration
NA	Ride
NA	Front seat comfort
NA	Fuel economy

SPECIFICATIONS

Drive wheels Rear or selectable 4WD

Seating 3 front, 3 rear, 3 third

Engines available
5.3-liter V8 (295 hp)

Transmissions available
4-speed automatic

Fuel
Fuel type ....Regular
EPA city/highway, mpg 14/18
Fuel refill capacity, gal. 31.0

Dimensions and weight
Length, in. 219
Width, in. 79
Wheelbase, in. 130
Curb weight, lb. 5,590
Percent weight, front/rear 53/47
Typical towing ability, lb. 8,500

SAFETY INFORMATION

Active safety features
Antilock brakes ....Standard
Traction control ....Optional on 2WD
Stability control ....Optional
Daytime running lights ....Standard
Tire pressure monitor ....Available

Safety belts
Center-rear belt ....Lap
Pretensioners, front/rear ....No/no

Air bags
Occupant-sensing system ....Front
Side bags, front/rear ....Optional/no
Inflatable curtain ....Not available
Accident alert system ....Available

Crash tests
Gov't front-crash test, driver/front passenger ....⊖/○
Gov't side-crash test, driver/rear passenger ....NA/NA
IIHS offset crash test ....NA
IIHS side crash test w/ side & curtain airbags ....NA
IIHS side crash test w/o side & curtain airbags ....NA

ANOTHER LOOK

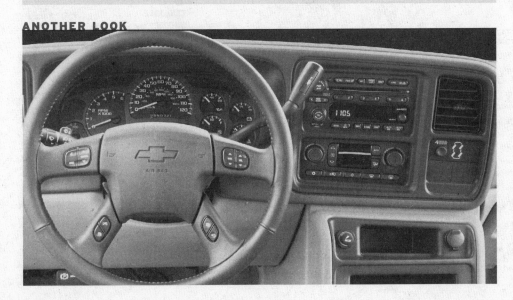

RELIABILITY HISTORY

TROUBLE SPOTS	Chevrolet Suburban							
	97	98	99	00	01	02	03	04
Engine	⊖	○	○	○	●	⊖	⊖	⊖
Cooling	●	⊖	○	⊖	⊖	⊖	⊖	⊖
Fuel	⊖	⊖	⊖	○	○	⊖	⊖	⊖
Ignition	○	○	⊖	⊖	⊖	⊖	⊖	⊖
Transmission	○	⊖	⊖	⊖	●	⊖	○	⊖
Electrical	●	●	●	⊖	○	○	○	⊖
Air conditioning	●	⊖	○	○	⊖	⊖	⊖	⊖
Suspension	⊖	○	○	○	○	⊖	⊖	⊖
Brakes	●	●	●	⊖	○	○	⊖	⊖
Exhaust	⊖	⊖	⊖	⊖	⊖	⊖	⊖	⊖
Paint/trim/rust	⊖	⊖	⊖	⊖	⊖	⊖	⊖	⊖
Body integrity	⊖	○	○	⊖	⊖	⊖	⊖	⊖
Power equipment	○	○	●	●	○	⊖	⊖	⊖
Body hardware	⊖	○	⊖	○	⊖	⊖	⊖	⊖
RELIABILITY VERDICT	✗	✗	✗	–	–	–	–	–

Chevrolet Tahoe

CR RECOMMENDED ✓

THE TAHOE LINE
Body style:
4-door SUV
Trim lines:
LS, LT
Base price range:
$35,915-$46,285

This full-sized SUV offers impressive trailer-towing capability and an absorbant ride at low speeds. The Tahoe seats eight usually but offers little cargo space behind its cramped third-row seat. Handling is imprecise, the steering is vague, and the brakes are so-so. 4WD models have a selectable full-time system that can remain engaged indefinitely. In the initial government rollover tests, models without electronic stability control (ESC) tipped up. All models have standard ESC, which has prevented tip-ups in the test. A redesign arrives in 2006.

REPORT CARD

○	Predicted reliability
◓	Owner satisfaction
◓	Predicted depreciation
○	Accident avoidance
◓	Acceleration
○	Ride
◓	Front seat comfort
●	Fuel economy

SPECIFICATIONS

Drive wheels Rear or selectable 4WD

Seating 3 front, 3 rear, 3 third

Engines available
4.8-liter V8 (285 hp); 5.3-liter V8 (295 hp)

Transmissions available
4-speed automatic

Fuel
Fuel type ....Regular
EPA city/highway, mpg 14/18
Fuel refill capacity, gal. 26.0

Dimensions and weight
Length, in. 199
Width, in. 79
Wheelbase, in. 116
Curb weight, lb. 5,505
Percent weight, front/rear 52/48
Typical towing ability, lb. 7,600

SAFETY INFORMATION

Active safety features
Antilock brakes ....Standard
Traction control ....Standard
Stability control ....Standard
Daytime running lights ....Standard
Tire pressure monitor ....Available

Safety belts
Center-rear belt ....Lap
Pretensioners, front/rear ....No/no

Air bags
Occupant-sensing system ....Front
Side bags, front/rear ....Optional/no
Inflatable curtain ....Not available
Accident alert system ....Available

Crash tests
Gov't front-crash test, driver/front passenger ......◐/◐
Gov't side-crash test, driver/rear passenger ....NA/NA
IIHS offset crash test ....NA
IIHS side crash test w/ side & curtain airbags ....NA
IIHS side crash test w/o side & curtain airbags ....NA

FROM THE TEST TRACK

Tested model
2002 LT 4-door SUV 4WD, 5.3-liter V8, 4-speed automatic

Tires as tested
Firestone Wilderness LE, size P265/70R16 111S

Acceleration ....◓
0-30 mph, sec. 3.3
0-60 mph, sec. 8.7
Quarter mile, sec. 16.7
Quarter mile, mph 85
45-65 mph, sec. 5.6

Other findings
Transmission ....◓
Turning circle, ft. 42
Ground clearance, in. 8.5

Braking and handling
Braking ....◐
Braking, dry pavement, ft. 152
Routine handling ....○
Emergency handling ....◓
Avoidance maneuver, max. mph ...44.5

Convenience and comfort
Ride ....○
Noise ....◓
Driving position ....◓
Access ....○
Controls and displays ....◓
Fit and finish ....○
Door top to ground, in. 67.0
Cargo area ....◐
Cargo volume, cu.ft. 59.0
Max. load, lb. 1,395

Seating
Front-seat comfort ....◐
Front shoulder room, in. 65.0
Front leg room, in. 40.5
Front head room, in. 5.0
Rear-seat comfort ....●
Rear shoulder room, in. 65.0
Rear leg room, in. 29.5
Rear head room, in 4.5
Third-seat comfort ....●
Third shoulder room,in 63.5
Third leg room, in. 28.5
Third head room, in. 0.0

Fuel economy ....●
CU's overall mileage, mpg 13
  CU's city/highway, mpg 9/19
  CU's 150-mile trip, mpg 17
Annual fuel ....1,120 gal./$2,240
Cruising range 405

RELIABILITY HISTORY

TROUBLE SPOTS	Chevrolet Tahoe							
	97	98	99	00	01	02	03	04
Engine	◐	◐	○	◐	●	●	●	●
Cooling	●	●	◐	○	◐	●	◐	◐
Fuel	◐	●	◐	○	◐	◐	◐	◐
Ignition	◐	◐	◐	●	◐	●	◐	◐
Transmission	◐	○	◐	◐	◐	●	◐	◐
Electrical	●	●	●	○	○	◐	◐	◐
Air conditioning	◐	○	○	○	◐	◐	◐	◐
Suspension	◐	○	◐	○	◐	◐	◐	●
Brakes	●	●	●	◐	◐	◐	●	●
Exhaust	◐	○	◐	○	◐	◐	●	●
Paint/trim/rust	●	○	◐	○	◐	●	◐	●
Body integrity	○	○	○	○	◐	◐	○	◐
Power equipment	○	○	○	◐	◐	●	○	◐
Body hardware	○	○	○	○	◐	◐	●	◐
RELIABILITY VERDICT	✗	✗	✗	—	—	—	—	—

Chevrolet TrailBlazer

THE TRAILBLAZER LINE
Body style:
4-door SUV
Trim lines:
LS, LS EXT, LT, LT EXT
Base price range:
$26,465-$32,515

Our tested seven-passenger EXT had a comfortable low-speed ride and a third-row seat that's roomy enough even for adults. Negatives include sloppy handling, uncomfortable seats, ill-fitting trim, and too much wind noise. Despite the seemingly strong 275-hp, six-cylinder engine, acceleration is so-so. Our EXT averaged a dismal 13 mpg. The annoying seat-mounted front safety belts can pull down uncomfortably and are hard to reach. The seats lack support. Reliability and owner satisfaction have been poor, and front- and offset-crash-test results are unimpressive.

REPORT CARD

●	Predicted reliability
●	Owner satisfaction
○	Predicted depreciation
◒	Accident avoidance
○	Acceleration
◒	Ride
○	Front seat comfort
●	Fuel economy

SPECIFICATIONS

Drive wheels Rear or selectable 4WD

Seating 2 front, 3 rear, 2 third

Engines available
4.2-liter 6 (275 hp); 5.3-liter V8 (300 hp)

Transmissions available
4-speed automatic

Fuel
Fuel type . . . . .Regular
EPA city/highway, mpg 15/21
Fuel refill capacity, gal. 25.3

Dimensions and weight
Length, in. 208
Width, in. 75
Wheelbase, in. 129
Curb weight, lb. 5,040
Percent weight, front/rear 53/47
Typical towing ability, lb. 5,300

SAFETY INFORMATION

Active safety features
Antilock brakes . . . . .Standard
Traction control . . . . .Optional on 2WD
Stability control . . . . .Not available
Daytime running lights .Standard
Tire pressure monitor . . . . .Not available

Safety belts
Center-rear belt 3-point
Pretensioners, front/rear . . . . .Yes/no

Air bags
Occupant-sensing system .Front
Side bags, front/rear . . . . .No/no
Inflatable curtain . . . . .Optional
Accident alert system . . . . .Available

Crash tests
Gov't front-crash test, driver/front passenger . . . . . .○/◒
Gov't side-crash test, driver/rear passenger . . . .◑/○
IIHS offset crash test . . . . .Marginal
IIHS side crash test w/ side & curtain airbags . . . . . . .NA
IIHS side crash test w/o side & curtain airbags . . . . . . .NA

FROM THE TEST TRACK

Tested model
2003 EXT LT 4-door SUV 4WD, 4.2-liter Six, 4-speed automatic

Tires as tested
BF Goodrich Rugged Trail T/A, size P245/65R17 105S

Acceleration . . . .○
0-30 mph, sec. 3.4
0-60 mph, sec. 9.8
Quarter mile, sec. 17.4
Quarter mile, mph 82
45-65 mph, sec. 6.9

Other findings
Transmission . . . .◒
Turning circle, ft. 44
Ground clearance, in. 6.5

Braking and handling
Braking . . . .○
Braking, dry pavement, ft. 154
Routine handling . . . .◒
Emergency handling . . . .◒
Avoidance maneuver, max. mph . . .44.5

Convenience and comfort
Ride . . . .○
Noise . . . .○
Driving position . . . .○
Access . . . .◒
Controls and displays . . . .◒
Fit and finish . . . .◒
Door top to ground, in. 63.5
Cargo area . . . .◒
Cargo volume, cu.ft. 42.0
Max. load, lb. 1,360

Seating
Front-seat comfort . . . .○
Front shoulder room, in. 58.5
Front leg room, in. 42.0
Front head room, in. 5.5
Rear-seat comfort . . . .◒
Rear shoulder room, in. 58.0
Rear leg room, in. 27.5
Rear head room, in 4.5
Third-seat comfort . . . .◒
Third shoulder room,in 57.5
Third leg room, in. 27.5
Third head room, in 3.0

Fuel economy . . . .●
CU's overall mileage, mpg 13
 CU's city/highway, mpg 9/20
 CU's 150-mile trip, mpg 16
Annual fuel . . . . .1,115 gal./$2,225
Cruising range 380

RELIABILITY HISTORY

TROUBLE SPOTS	Chevrolet TrailBlazer EXT							
	97	98	99	00	01	02	03	04
Engine						◒	◒	◒
Cooling						◒	◒	◒
Fuel						◒	◒	◒
Ignition						◒	◒	◒
Transmission						○	◒	◒
Electrical						●	◒	◒
Air conditioning						○	◒	○
Suspension						○	◒	◒
Brakes						◒	◒	◒
Exhaust						◒	◒	◒
Paint/trim/rust						○	◒	○
Body integrity						◒	◒	◒
Power equipment						◒	○	◒
Body hardware						◒	○	○
RELIABILITY VERDICT					✗	✗	−	

Chevrolet Uplander

The 2005 Uplander is one of four freshened GM minivans and replaces the Venture. As with the Buick Terraza, Pontiac Montana SV6, and Saturn Relay, the Uplander is powered by a coarse 3.5-liter, 200-hp V6 engine. The heavy second-row seats can be folded and removed, while the folding third-row seat stows flat but raises the level of the floor. The ride is stiff and noisy, the interior trim is flimsy, and handling is vague and reluctant. The new snout can't disguise the fact that these are eight-year-old minivans that were never competitive in their category.

THE UPLANDER LINE
Body style:
minivan
Trim lines:
Base, LS, LT
Base price range:
$23,635-$31,385

REPORT CARD

New	Predicted reliability
New	Owner satisfaction
NA	Predicted depreciation
○	Accident avoidance
○	Acceleration
○	Ride
○	Front seat comfort
●	Fuel economy

SPECIFICATIONS

Drive wheels Front or AWD

Seating 2 front, 2 rear, 3 third

Engines available
3.5-liter V6 (200 hp)

Transmissions available
4-speed automatic

Fuel
Fuel type . . . . .Regular
EPA city/highway, mpg 18/24
Fuel refill capacity, gal. 25.0

Dimensions and weight
Length, in. 205
Width, in. 72
Wheelbase, in. 121
Curb weight, lb. 4,380
Percent weight, front/rear 56/44
Typical towing ability, lb. 3,500

SAFETY INFORMATION

Active safety features
Antilock brakes . . . . .Standard
Traction control . . . . .Optional on LS, LT FWD
Stability control . . . . .Optional on LT FWD
Daytime running lights . . . . .Standard
Tire pressure monitor . . . . .Not available

Safety belts
Center-rear belt 3-point
Pretensioners, front/rear . . . . .Yes/no

Air bags
Occupant-sensing system . . . . .Front
Side bags, front/rear . . . . .Optional/no
Inflatable curtain . . . . .Not available
Accident alert system . . . . .Available

Crash tests
Gov't front-crash test, driver/front passenger . . . . . . ◑/◑
Gov't side-crash test, driver/rear passenger . . . . ◑/◑
IIHS offset crash test . . . . .NA
IIHS side crash test w/ side & curtain airbags . . . . .NA
IIHS side crash test w/o side & curtain airbags . . . . .NA

FROM THE TEST TRACK

Tested model
2005 Saturn Relay 3 minivan, 3.5-liter V6, 4-speed automatic

Tires as tested
Goodyear Integrity, size P225/60R17 98S
Acceleration . . . . ○
0-30 mph, sec. 3.6
0-60 mph, sec. 10.2
Quarter mile, sec. 17.7
Quarter mile, mph 80
45-65 mph, sec. 7.0

Other findings
Transmission . . . . ◑
Turning circle, ft. 43
Ground clearance, in. 6.0

Braking and handling
Braking . . . . ◑
Braking, dry pavement, ft. 136
Routine handling . . . . ○
Emergency handling . . . . ◑
Avoidance maneuver, max. mph . . .48.5

Convenience and comfort
Ride . . . . ○
Noise . . . . ○
Driving position . . . . ○
Access . . . . ●
Controls and displays . . . . ◑
Fit and finish . . . . ○
Door top to ground, in. 62.0
Cargo area . . . . ◑
Cargo volume, cu.ft. 75.5
Max. load, lb. 1,290

Seating
Front-seat comfort . . . . ○
Front shoulder room, in. 59.5
Front leg room, in. 40.5
Front head room, in. 5.0
Rear-seat comfort . . . . ◑
Rear shoulder room, in. 62.0
Rear leg room, in. 26.0
Rear head room, in 4.0
Third-seat comfort . . . . ○
Third shoulder room,in 60.0
Third leg room, in. 28.0
Third head room, in 3.5

Fuel economy . . . . ●
CU's overall mileage, mpg 17
CU's city/highway, mpg 12/25
CU's 150-mile trip, mpg 21
Annual fuel . . . . .860 gal./$1,720
Cruising range 510

RELIABILITY HISTORY

TROUBLE SPOTS	97 98 99 00 01 02 03 04
Engine	
Cooling	NO
Fuel	
Ignition	
Transmission	DATA
Electrical	
Air conditioning	NEW
Suspension	
Brakes	MODEL
Exhaust	
Paint/trim/rust	
Body integrity	
Power equipment	
Body hardware	
RELIABILITY VERDICT	

Chrysler 300

The Chrysler 300's styling draws a lot of attention, but in most ways neither the V8-powered 300C nor the V6-equipped 300 Touring was a standout in our testing. An exception is the acceleration of the 300C, which was very quick but delivered poor fuel economy. The rear suspension and optional all-wheel-drive system come from Mercedes-Benz architecture. Handling is sound but not exceptional. The ride in the Touring is supple and controlled, while the 300C is stiff. Interior materials are OK, but the cabin doesn't stand out in this class. The claustrophobic cabin and limited outward visibility are detractions.

THE 300 LINE
Body style: sedan
Trim lines: Base, Touring, Limited, C, SRT8
Base price range: $23,370-$39,370

REPORT CARD

New	Predicted reliability	
New	Owner satisfaction	
NA	Predicted depreciation	
	Accident avoidance	◖
	Acceleration	◉
	Ride	○
	Front seat comfort	◖
	Fuel economy	●

SPECIFICATIONS

Drive wheels Rear or AWD

Seating 2 front, 3 rear

Engines available
2.7-liter V6 (190 hp); 3.5-liter V6 (250 hp); 5.7-liter V8 (340 hp); 6.1-liter V8 (425 hp)

Transmissions available
4-speed automatic; 5-speed automatic

Fuel
Fuel type ....Regular
EPA city/highway, mpg 17/25
Fuel refill capacity, gal. 19.0

Dimensions and weight
Length, in. 197
Width, in. 74
Wheelbase, in. 120
Curb weight, lb. 4,105
Percent weight, front/rear 54/46
Typical towing ability, lb. 2,000

SAFETY INFORMATION

Active safety features
Antilock brakes ....Standard (optional on Base)
Traction control ....Standard with ABS
Stability control ....Standard (optional on Base)
Daytime running lights ....Not available
Tire pressure monitor ....Available

Safety belts
Center-rear belt 3-point
Pretensioners, front/rear ....Yes/no

Air bags
Occupant-sensing system ....Front
Side bags, front/rear ....No/no
Inflatable curtain ....Optional
Accident alert system ....Not available

Crash tests
Gov't front-crash test, driver/front passenger ......◖/◖
Gov't side-crash test, driver/rear passenger ......◖/◖
IIHS offset crash test ....NA
IIHS side crash test w/ side & curtain airbags ....NA
IIHS side crash test w/o side & curtain airbags ....NA

FROM THE TEST TRACK

Tested model
2005 C sedan, 5.7-liter V8, 5-speed automatic

Tires as tested
Continental ContiTouring Contact CH95 Conti*Seal, size P225/60R18 99H

Acceleration ....◉
0-30 mph, sec. 2.7
0-60 mph, sec. 6.4
Quarter mile, sec. 14.9
Quarter mile, mph. 98
45-65 mph, sec. 3.9

Other findings
Transmission ....◉
Turning circle, ft. 41
Ground clearance, in. 4.0

Braking and handling
Braking ....◖
Braking, dry pavement, ft. 133
Routine handling ....◖
Emergency handling ....○
Avoidance maneuver, max. mph ...51.5

Convenience and comfort
Ride ....○
Noise ....◖
Driving position ....○
Access ....◖
Controls and displays ....◖
Fit and finish ....◖
Door top to ground, in. 52.0
Trunk ....○
Luggage capacity ....4+1
Max. load, lb. 865

Seating
Front-seat comfort ....◖
Front shoulder room, in. 59.5
Front leg room, in. 43.0
Front head room, in. 4.5
Rear-seat comfort ....◖
Rear shoulder room, in. 57.5
Rear leg room, in. 30.5
Rear head room, in 2.5

Fuel economy ....●
CU's overall mileage, mpg 16
CU's city/highway, mpg 10/27
CU's 150-mile trip, mpg 20
Annual fuel ....930 gal./$1,860
Cruising range 350

RELIABILITY HISTORY

TROUBLE SPOTS	97 98 99 00 01 02 03 04
Engine	
Cooling	**NO**
Fuel	
Ignition	**DATA**
Transmission	
Electrical	
Air conditioning	**NEW**
Suspension	
Brakes	**MODEL**
Exhaust	
Paint/trim/rust	
Body integrity	
Power equipment	
Body hardware	
RELIABILITY VERDICT	

Chrysler Crossfire

THE CROSSFIRE LINE
Body style:
convertible; coupe
Trim lines:
Base, Limited, SRT6
Base price range:
$29,045-$49,120

This German-built, two-seat, rear-drive coupe is based on the previous-generation Mercedes-Benz SLK. It competes with the Nissan 350Z and Audi TT. The Crossfire is powered by a punchy 3.2-liter V6 from Mercedes and either a five-speed automatic or a clunky six-speed manual. The outdated steering system makes the handling neither as precise nor as sporty as one would expect. Tenacious tire grip adds security. The ride is stiff, and there's too much wind noise. The interior is cramped, and visibility is poor. A convertible and a supercharged SRT-6 are new.

REPORT CARD

NA	Predicted reliability	
NA	Owner satisfaction	
NA	Predicted depreciation	
◕	Accident avoidance	
◕	Acceleration	
◒	Ride	
◒	Front seat comfort	
○	Fuel economy	

SPECIFICATIONS

Drive wheels Rear

Seating 2 front

Engines available
3.2-liter V6 (215 hp); 3.2-liter V6 supercharged (330 hp)

Transmissions available
6-speed manual; 5-speed automatic

Fuel
Fuel type . . . . .Premium
EPA city/highway, mpg 17/25
Fuel refill capacity, gal. 15.8

Dimensions and weight
Length, in. 160
Width, in. 69
Wheelbase, in. 95
Curb weight, lb. 3,075
Percent weight, front/rear 54/46
Typical towing ability, lb. . . . . .NR

SAFETY INFORMATION

Active safety features
Antilock brakes . . . . .Standard
Traction control . . . . .Standard
Stability control . . . . .Standard
Daytime running lights . . . . .Not available
Tire pressure monitor . . . . .Available

Safety belts
Center-rear belt . . . . .NA
Pretensioners, front/rear . . . . .Yes/NA

Air bags
Occupant-sensing system . . . . .Not available
Side bags, front/rear .Standard/NA
Inflatable curtain . . . . .Not available
Accident alert system .Not available

Crash tests
Gov't front-crash test, driver/front passenger . . . . . .◕/◒
Gov't side-crash test, driver/rear passenger . . . .◕/NA
IIHS offset crash test . . . . .NA
IIHS side crash test w/ side & curtain airbags . . . . .NA
IIHS side crash test w/o side & curtain airbags . . . . .NA

FROM THE TEST TRACK

Tested model
2004 coupe, 3.2-liter V6, 6-speed manual

Tires as tested
Michelin Pilot Sport, size 225/40ZR18 92Y (front), 225/35ZR19 96Y (rear)

Acceleration . . . . ◕
0-30 mph, sec. 2.6
0-60 mph, sec. 7.2
Quarter mile, sec. 15.5
Quarter mile, mph 93
45-65 mph, sec. 4.5

Other findings
Transmission . . . .○
Turning circle, ft. 34
Ground clearance, in. 5.0

Braking and handling
Braking . . . . ●
Braking, dry pavement, ft. 125
Routine handling . . . . ◒
Emergency handling . . . . ◒
Avoidance maneuver, max. mph . . .56.5

Convenience and comfort
Ride . . . . ◒
Noise . . . . ○
Driving position . . . . ◒
Access . . . . ◒
Controls and displays . . . . ○
Fit and finish . . . . ◒
Door top to ground, in. 45.5
Trunk . . . . ◒
Luggage capacity . . . . .2+0
Max. load, lb. 415

Seating
Front-seat comfort . . . . ◒
Front shoulder room, in. 51.5
Front leg room, in. 41.0
Front head room, in. 3.0

Fuel economy . . . . ○
CU's overall mileage, mpg 22
CU's city/highway, mpg 15/30
CU's 150-mile trip, mpg 25
Annual fuel . . . . .695 gal./$1,530
Cruising range 360

RELIABILITY HISTORY

TROUBLE SPOTS	97 98 99 00 01 02 03 04
Engine	
Cooling	
Fuel	**NOT**
Ignition	
Transmission	**ENOUGH**
Electrical	
Air conditioning	**DATA**
Suspension	
Brakes	**TO**
Exhaust	
Paint/trim/rust	**RATE**
Body integrity	
Power equipment	
Body hardware	
RELIABILITY VERDICT	

Chrysler PT Cruiser

CR RECOMMENDED ✓

The PT Cruiser is a tall, front-drive wagon. Strengths include a versatile interior (the rear seats are removable, and the front passenger's seat can be folded flat), easy access, and secure, predictable handling. The brakes work well. Acceleration with the base engine is slow, especially in models equipped with an automatic transmission, and fuel economy is mediocre. The two turbocharged engines rectify the sluggish acceleration, though the 220-hp version needs to be revved. The ride is somewhat stiff and the cabin is a bit noisy, with wind noise particularly evident in the convertible version.

THE PT CRUISER LINE

Body style:
convertible; wagon
Trim lines:
Base, Touring, Limited, GT
Base price range:
$13,405-$27,930

REPORT CARD

⊖	Predicted reliability
○	Owner satisfaction
⊖	Predicted depreciation
⊖	Accident avoidance
◉	Acceleration
○	Ride
⊖	Front seat comfort
○	Fuel economy

SPECIFICATIONS

Drive wheels Front

Seating 2 front, 2 rear

Engines available
2.4-liter 4 (150 hp); 2.4-liter 4 turbo (180 hp); 2.4-liter 4 turbo (220 hp)

Transmissions available
5-speed manual; 4-speed automatic

Fuel
Fuel type . . . . Regular or premium
EPA city/highway, mpg 21/27
Fuel refill capacity, gal. 15.0

Dimensions and weight
Length, in. 169
Width, in. 67
Wheelbase, in. 103
Curb weight, lb. 3,455
Percent weight, front/rear 59/41
Typical towing ability, lb. 1,000

SAFETY INFORMATION

Active safety features
Antilock brakes . . . . .Optional (standard on GT)
Traction control . . . . .Standard with ABS
Stability control .Not available
Daytime running lights . . . . .Not available
Tire pressure monitor . . . . .Not available

Safety belts
Center-rear belt 3-point
Pretensioners, front/rear . . . . .Yes/no

Air bags
Occupant-sensing system . . . . .Not available
Side bags, front/rear . . . . .Optional/no
Inflatable curtain . . . . .Not available
Accident alert system . . . . .Not available

Crash tests
Gov't front-crash test, driver/front passenger . . . . . . ◐ ◐
Gov't side-crash test, driver/rear passenger . . . . .NA/NA
IIHS offset crash test . . . . .NA
IIHS side crash test w/ side & curtain airbags . . . . .NA
IIHS side crash test w/o side & curtain airbags . . . . .NA

FROM THE TEST TRACK

Tested model
2005 GT convertible, 2.4-liter Four turbo, 5-speed manual

Tires as tested
Goodyear Eagle RS-A, size 205/50R17 93H

Acceleration . . . . ◉
0-30 mph, sec. 2.8
0-60 mph, sec. 7.0
Quarter mile, sec. 15.6
Quarter mile, mph 91
45-65 mph, sec. 4.3

Other findings
Transmission . . . . ⊖
Turning circle, ft. 40
Ground clearance, in. 5.0

Braking and handling
Braking . . . . ⊖
Braking, dry pavement, ft. 131
Routine handling . . . . ⊖
Emergency handling . . . . ⊖
Avoidance maneuver, max. mph . .54.0

Convenience and comfort
Ride . . . . ○
Noise . . . . ○
Driving position . . . . ○
Access . . . . ⊖
Controls and displays . . . . ⊖
Fit and finish . . . . ○
Door top to ground, in. 54.0
Cargo area . . . . ●
Luggage capacity . . . . .1+2
Max. load, lb. 715

Seating
Front-seat comfort . . . . ⊖
Front shoulder room, in. 53.0
Front leg room, in. 41.5
Front head room, in. 4.0
Rear-seat comfort . . . . ⊖
Rear shoulder room, in. 41.0
Rear leg room, in. 27.0
Rear head room, in 2.0

Fuel economy . . . . ○
CU's overall mileage, mpg 22
CU's city/highway, mpg 17/27
CU's 150-mile trip, mpg 25
Annual fuel . . . . .685 gal./$1,500
Cruising range 345

RELIABILITY HISTORY

TROUBLE SPOTS	Chrysler PT Cruiser							
	97	98	99	00	01	02	03	04
Engine					◉	◉	◉	
Cooling					◉	◉	◉	◉
Fuel						◉	◉	◉
Ignition					◉	◉	◉	◉
Transmission					◉	◉	●	◉
Electrical					○	◉	●	◉
Air conditioning					◉	◉	◉	◉
Suspension					○	◉	◉	◉
Brakes					◐	○	◉	◉
Exhaust					◉	◉	◉	◉
Paint/trim/rust					◐	◉	◉	◉
Body integrity					◉	◉	◉	◉
Power equipment					◐	◉	◉	◉
Body hardware					◐	◉	◉	◉
RELIABILITY VERDICT					✓	✓	✓	✓

● ◉ ○ ⊖ ●
better ◄——————► worse   See page 36 for more information.

Chrysler Pacifica

CR RECOMMENDED ✓

THE PACIFICA LINE
Body style:
4-door SUV
Trim lines:
Base, Touring, Limited
Base price range:
$24,315-$36,445

The wagonlike Pacifica has a comfortable ride and fairly nimble handling. The noisy and fuel-thirsty 3.5-liter V6 provides only adequate acceleration. The base engine is a 3.8-liter V6. The optional AWD system works well for winter driving. The interior seats six in three rows. The driving position is higher than in most sedans and lower than in most SUVs, but a high beltline compromises the feeling of spaciousness and visibility. When the third row is folded this is a four-seat vehicle. A five-passenger version is new for 2005. Crash-test results are impressive. First-year reliability has been average.

REPORT CARD

○	Predicted reliability
○	Owner satisfaction
NA	Predicted depreciation
⊖	Accident avoidance
○	Acceleration
⊖	Ride
⊖	Front seat comfort
●	Fuel economy

SPECIFICATIONS

Drive wheels Front or AWD

Seating 2 front, 2 rear, 2 third

Engines available
3.8-liter V6 (210 hp); 3.5-liter V6 (250 hp)

Transmissions available
4-speed automatic

Fuel
Fuel type . . . . .Regular
EPA city/highway, mpg 17/22
Fuel refill capacity, gal. 23.0

Dimensions and weight
Length, in. 199
Width, in. 79
Wheelbase, in. 116
Curb weight, lb. 4,635
Percent weight, front/rear 56/44
Typical towing ability, lb. 3,500

SAFETY INFORMATION

Active safety features
Antilock brakes . . . . .Standard
Traction control . . . . .Optional
Stability control . . . . .Not available
Daytime running lights . . . . .Not available
Tire pressure monitor . . . . .Available

Safety belts
Center-rear belt . . . . .NA
Pretensioners, front/rear .Yes/no

Air bags
Occupant-sensing system . . . . .Front
Side bags, front/rear . . . . .No/no
Inflatable curtain . . . . .Optional
Accident alert system .Not available

Crash tests
Gov't front-crash test, driver/front passenger . . . . . .◕/◕
Gov't side-crash test, driver/rear passenger . . . .◕/◕
IIHS offset crash test . . . . .Good
IIHS side crash test w/ side & curtain airbags . . . . .NA
IIHS side crash test w/o side & curtain airbags . . . . .NA

FROM THE TEST TRACK

Tested model
2004 4-door SUV AWD, 3.5-liter V6, 4-speed automatic

Tires as tested
Michelin Energy MXV4 Plus, size P235/65R17 103H

Acceleration . . . . ○
0-30 mph, sec. 3.4
0-60 mph, sec. 9.7
Quarter mile, sec. 17.4
Quarter mile, mph 81
45-65 mph, sec. 6.2

Other findings
Transmission . . . . ⊖
Turning circle, ft. 42
Ground clearance, in. 5.0

Braking and handling
Braking . . . . ⊖
Braking, dry pavement, ft. 134
Routine handling . . . . ⊖
Emergency handling . . . . ○
Avoidance maneuver, max. mph . . .48.0

Convenience and comfort
Ride . . . . ⊖
Noise . . . . ⊖
Driving position . . . . ⊖
Access . . . . ⊖
Controls and displays . . . . ⊖
Fit and finish . . . . ⊖
Door top to ground, in. 57.5
Cargo area . . . . ○
Cargo volume, cu.ft. 36.0
Max. load, lb. 1,165

Seating
Front-seat comfort . . . . ⊖
Front shoulder room, in. 61.0
Front leg room, in. 41.0
Front head room, in. 5.5
Rear-seat comfort . . . . ⊖
Rear shoulder room, in. 59.0
Rear leg room, in. 29.0
Rear head room, in. 5.0
Third-seat comfort . . . . ●
Third shoulder room, in 59.5
Third leg room, in. 25.5
Third head room, in. 0.0

Fuel economy . . . . ●
CU's overall mileage, mpg 16
CU's city/highway, mpg 10/24
CU's 150-mile trip, mpg 19
Annual fuel . . . . .960 gal./$1,920
Cruising range 410

RELIABILITY HISTORY

TROUBLE SPOTS	Chrysler Pacifica								
	97	98	99	00	01	02	03	04
Engine								◒
Cooling								◒
Fuel								◒
Ignition								◒
Transmission								◒
Electrical								◒
Air conditioning								◒
Suspension								◒
Brakes								◒
Exhaust								◒
Paint/trim/rust								◒
Body integrity								◒
Power equipment								◒
Body hardware								◒
RELIABILITY VERDICT								−

Chrysler Sebring

The Sebring is based on the same platform as the Dodge Stratus sedan. The coupe is derived from the Mitsubishi Eclipse. Our tested sedan suffered from too much road noise, lack of handling agility, and a stiff, unsettled ride. Access is difficult, and the rear seat is too low to be comfortable. Emergency handling is secure, braking is competent, and frontal-crash-test performance was good. The four-cylinder engine is slow and thirsty, but the optional 2.7-liter V6 provides quick acceleration with similar fuel economy. Reliability has dropped to below average. A Poor IIHS side-crash score is not encouraging.

THE SEBRING LINE
Body style: convertible; coupe; sedan
Trim lines: Base, GTC, Touring, Limited, TSi
Base price range: $19,460-$31,130

REPORT CARD
◒	Predicted reliability
●	Owner satisfaction
◒	Predicted depreciation
○	Accident avoidance
○	Acceleration
○	Ride
◒	Front seat comfort
○	Fuel economy

SPECIFICATIONS
Drive wheels Front

Seating 2 front, 2 rear

Engines available
2.4-liter 4 (142 hp); 2.4-liter 4 (150 hp); 3.0-liter V6 (198 hp); 2.7-liter V6 (200 hp)

Transmissions available
4-speed automatic

Fuel
Fuel type ....Regular
EPA city/highway, mpg 20/27
Fuel refill capacity, gal. 16.0

Dimensions and weight
Length, in. 194
Width, in. 69
Wheelbase, in. 106
Curb weight, lb. 3,520
Percent weight, front/rear 62/38
Typical towing ability, lb. 1,000

SAFETY INFORMATION

Active safety features
Antilock brakes ....Optional
Traction control ....Optional
Stability control ....Not available
Daytime running lights ....Not available
Tire pressure monitor ....Not available

Safety belts
Center-rear belt 3-point
Pretensioners, front/rear ....Yes/no

Air bags
Occupant-sensing system ....Not available
Side bags, front/rear ....Optional/no
Inflatable curtain ....Optional
Accident alert system ....Not available

Crash tests
Gov't front-crash test, driver/front passenger ......○/○
Gov't side-crash test, driver/rear passenger ....○/◒
IIHS offset crash test ....Acceptable
IIHS side crash test w/ side & curtain airbags ....NA
IIHS side crash test w/o side & curtain airbags ....Poor

FROM THE TEST TRACK

Tested model
2005 Limited convertible, 2.7-liter V6, 4-speed automatic

Tires as tested
Goodyear Eagle LS, size P205/60R16 91T

Acceleration ....○
0-30 mph, sec. 3.5
0-60 mph, sec. 9.4
Quarter mile, sec. 17.3
Quarter mile, mph 82
45-65 mph, sec. 5.9

Other findings
Transmission ....◒
Turning circle, ft. 39
Ground clearance, in. 4.5

Braking and handling
Braking ....◒
Braking, dry pavement, ft. 138
Routine handling ....○
Emergency handling ....○
Avoidance maneuver, max. mph ...51.0

Convenience and comfort
Ride ....○
Noise ....○
Driving position ....○
Access ....○
Controls and displays ....◒
Fit and finish ....○
Door top to ground, in. 50.0
Trunk ....●
Luggage capacity ....1+3
Max. load, lb. 715

Seating
Front-seat comfort ....◒
Front shoulder room, in. 56.0
Front leg room, in. 40.5
Front head room, in. 4.5
Rear-seat comfort ....○
Rear shoulder room, in. 42.5
Rear leg room, in. 26.0
Rear head room, in 2.0

Fuel economy ....○
CU's overall mileage, mpg 21
  CU's city/highway, mpg 14/30
  CU's 150-mile trip, mpg 26
Annual fuel ....715 gal./$1,430
Cruising range 380

RELIABILITY HISTORY

TROUBLE SPOTS	Chrysler Sebring Convertible							
	97	98	99	00	01	02	03	04
Engine	○	○	○	●	●	●	●	●
Cooling	◒	◒	●	●	●	◒	◒	●
Fuel	○	◒	◒	◒	●	◒	◒	●
Ignition	●	◒	●	◒	●	◒	◒	●
Transmission	○	◒	○	◒	○	○	◒	◒
Electrical	●	●	◒	○	○	○	○	●
Air conditioning	◒	○	◒	◒	○	◒	◒	●
Suspension	◒	○	○	◒	◒	◒	●	●
Brakes	●	◒	●	◒	◒	○	◒	●
Exhaust	◒	◒	●	●	○	◒	●	●
Paint/trim/rust	○	○	◒	◒	◒	●	◒	○
Body integrity	◒	◒	◒	●	●	●	◒	●
Power equipment	○	○	○	◒	◒	◒	○	◒
Body hardware	○	◒	◒	◒	◒	◒	●	◒
RELIABILITY VERDICT	✗	–	–	–	✗	–	✗	✗

Chrysler Town & Country

CR RECOMMENDED ✓

THE TOWN & COUNTRY LINE
Body style:
minivan regular; minivan extended
Trim lines:
Base, LX, Touring, Limited
Base price range:
$20,740-$35,445

This more-costly cousin of the Dodge Grand Caravan is pleasant enough, but it is falling behind the competition, especially from Honda and Toyota. Interior flexibility got a boost with the introduction of the 2005 model, which has flat-folding second- and third-row seats. This setup eliminates the AWD model. The minivan rides well enough with a light load and handles securely. Interior noise has become more pronounced. The 3.8-liter V6 isn't as smooth, quiet, or fuel-efficient as the engines in the Odyssey and Sienna. The offset-crash-test result is less impressive. Reliability has improved to average.

REPORT CARD

◯	Predicted reliability
⊖	Owner satisfaction
⊖	Predicted depreciation
◯	Accident avoidance
◯	Acceleration
◯	Ride
◯	Front seat comfort
●	Fuel economy

SAFETY INFORMATION

Active safety features
Antilock brakes ....Standard (optional on Base)
Traction control ....Standard on Touring, Ltd.
Stability control ....Not available
Daytime running lights ....Not available
Tire pressure monitor ....Available

Safety belts
Center-rear belt ....Lap
Pretensioners, front/rear ....Yes/no

Air bags
Occupant-sensing system ....Front
Side bags, front/rear ....No/no
Inflatable curtain ....Optional
Accident alert system ....Not available

Crash tests
Gov't front-crash test, driver/front passenger ......●/●
Gov't side-crash test, driver/rear passenger ....●/●
IIHS offset crash test ....Acceptable
IIHS side crash test w/ side & curtain airbags ....NA
IIHS side crash test w/o side & curtain airbags ....NA

FROM THE TEST TRACK

Tested model
2005 Dodge Caravan/Grand Caravan SXT minivan extended, 3.8-liter V6, 4-speed automatic

Tires as tested
Bridgestone Turanza EL42, size 215/65R16 98T

Acceleration ◯
0-30 mph, sec. 3.4
0-60 mph, sec. 10.1
Quarter mile, sec..............17.7
Quarter mile, mph 79
45-65 mph, sec. 6.3

Other findings
Transmission ....⊖
Turning circle, ft. 41
Ground clearance, in. 5.0

Braking and handling
Braking ....⊖
Braking, dry pavement, ft. 140
Routine handling ....⊖
Emergency handling ....◯
Avoidance maneuver, max. mph ...49.5

Convenience and comfort
Ride ....⊖
Noise ....⊖
Driving position ....⊖
Access ....⊖
Controls and displays ....◯
Fit and finish ....◯
Door top to ground, in. 60.5
Cargo area ....⊖
Cargo volume, cu.ft. 60.0
Max. load, lb. 1,185

Seating
Front-seat comfort ....◯
Front shoulder room, in. 63.0
Front leg room, in. 38.5
Front head room, in. 4.5
Rear-seat comfort ....◯
Rear shoulder room, in. 59.0
Rear leg room, in. 31.0
Rear head room, in. 3.5
Third-seat comfort ....◯
Third shoulder room, in 61.5
Third leg room, in. 26.5
Third head room, in 2.5

Fuel economy ●
CU's overall mileage, mpg 17
CU's city/highway, mpg 11/26
CU's 150-mile trip, mpg 21
Annual fuel ....905 gal./$1,815
Cruising range 390

SPECIFICATIONS

Drive wheels Front

Seating 2 front, 2 rear, 3 third

Engines available
3.3-liter V6 (180 hp); 3.8-liter V6 (205 hp)

Transmissions available
4-speed automatic

Fuel
Fuel type ....Regular
EPA city/highway, mpg 18/25
Fuel refill capacity, gal. 20.0

Dimensions and weight
Length, in. 201
Width, in. 79
Wheelbase, in. 119
Curb weight, lb. 4,515
Percent weight, front/rear 56/44
Typical towing ability, lb. 3,800

RELIABILITY HISTORY

TROUBLE SPOTS	Chrysler Town & Country (ext.)							
	97	98	99	00	01	02	03	04
Engine	◯	⊖	⊖	●	●	●	●	●
Cooling	⊖	⊖	⊖	●	◯	●	●	●
Fuel	◯	⊖	⊖	●	⊖	◯	●	●
Ignition	⊖	⊖	⊖	●	●	◯	⊖	●
Transmission	⊖	⊖	●	⊖	●	◯	⊖	⊖
Electrical	●	●	⊖	◯	◯	⊖	⊖	●
Air conditioning	⊖	⊖	⊖	◯	◯	◯	⊖	●
Suspension	◯	◯	◯	◯	◯	◯	⊖	●
Brakes	⊖	⊖	⊖	◯	◯	⊖	⊖	●
Exhaust	●	●	●	●	●	◯	●	●
Paint/trim/rust	◯	⊖	⊖	●	◯	●	●	●
Body integrity	⊖	◯	◯	◯	⊖	◯	⊖	●
Power equipment	⊖	◯	◯	◯	●	◯	⊖	●
Body hardware	◯	◯	◯	◯	⊖	◯	⊖	●
RELIABILITY VERDICT	✗	—	—	✗	✗	✗	—	—

Dodge Caravan/Grand Caravan

CR RECOMMENDED ✓

THE CARAVAN/GRAND CARAVAN LINE

Body style:
minivan regular; minivan extended

Trim lines:
SE, SXT

Base price range:
$18,330-$26,810

The Caravan and extended-length Grand Caravan are very similar except for the cargo floor behind the third row. Our tested Grand Caravan was pleasant, but it's falling behind the competition. The flat-folding second- and third-row seats improve interior flexibility, but noise levels increased. This setup eliminates the AWD model. The Dodge rides well enough with a light load and handles securely, but it shows its limitations on bumpy corners. The 3.8-liter V6 isn't as smooth, quiet, or fuel-efficient as the engines powering the Toyota Sienna and Honda Odyssey. Reliability has improved to average.

REPORT CARD

○	Predicted reliability
◒	Owner satisfaction
◒	Predicted depreciation
○	Accident avoidance
○	Acceleration
○	Ride
○	Front seat comfort
●	Fuel economy

SPECIFICATIONS

Drive wheels Front

Seating 2 front, 2 rear, 3 third

Engines available
2.4-liter 4 (150 hp); 3.3-liter V6 (180 hp); 3.8-liter V6 (205 hp)

Transmissions available
4-speed automatic

Fuel
Fuel type . . . . Regular
EPA city/highway, mpg 18/25
Fuel refill capacity, gal. 20.0

Dimensions and weight
Length, in. 201
Width, in. 79
Wheelbase, in. 119
Curb weight, lb. 4,515
Percent weight, front/rear 56/44
Typical towing ability, lb. 3,800

SAFETY INFORMATION

Active safety features
Antilock brakes . . . . .Optional (standard on Grand)
Traction control . . . . .Optional
Stability control . . . . Not available
Daytime running lights . . . . .Not available
Tire pressure monitor . . . . .Available

Safety belts
Center-rear belt . . . . .Lap
Pretensioners, front/rear . . . . .Yes/no

Air bags
Occupant-sensing system . . . . .Front
Side bags, front/rear .No/no
Inflatable curtain .Optional
Accident alert system . . . . .Not available

Crash tests
Gov't front-crash test, driver/front passenger . . . . . . ◒/◒
Gov't side-crash test, driver/rear passenger . . . . . . ◒/◒
IIHS offset crash test . . . . .Acceptable
IIHS side crash test w/ side & curtain airbags . . . . .NA
IIHS side crash test w/o side & curtain airbags . . . . .NA

FROM THE TEST TRACK

Tested model
2005 SXT minivan extended, 3.8-liter V6, 4-speed automatic

Tires as tested
Bridgestone Turanza EL42, size 215/65R16 98T

Acceleration . . . . ○
0-30 mph, sec. 3.4
0-60 mph, sec. 10.1
Quarter mile, sec. 17.7
Quarter mile, mph 79
45-65 mph, sec. 6.3

Other findings
Transmission . . . . ◒
Turning circle, ft. 41
Ground clearance, in. 5.0

Braking and handling
Braking . . . . ◒
Braking, dry pavement, ft. 140
Routine handling . . . . ◒
Emergency handling . . . . ○
Avoidance maneuver, max. mph . . .49.5

Convenience and comfort
Ride . . . . ○
Noise . . . . ◒
Driving position . . . . ◒
Access . . . . ◒
Controls and displays . . . . ○
Fit and finish . . . . ○
Door top to ground, in. 60.5
Cargo area . . . . ○
Cargo volume, cu.ft. 60.0
Max. load, lb. 1,185

Seating
Front-seat comfort . . . . ○
Front shoulder room, in. 63.0
Front leg room, in. 38.5
Front head room, in. 4.5
Rear-seat comfort . . . . ○
Rear shoulder room, in. 59.0
Rear leg room, in. 31.0
Rear head room, in 3.5
Third-seat comfort . . . . ○
Third shoulder room,in 61.5
Third leg room, in. 26.5
Third head room, in 2.5
Fuel economy . . . . ●
CU's overall mileage, mpg 17
  CU's city/highway, mpg 11/26
  CU's 150-mile trip, mpg 21
Annual fuel . . . . .905 gal./$1,815
Cruising range 390

RELIABILITY HISTORY

TROUBLE SPOTS	Dodge Grand Caravan V6 2WD							
	97	98	99	00	01	02	03	04
Engine	○	◒	◒	◒	◒	◒	◒	◒
Cooling	◒	◒	◒	◒	◒	◒	◒	●
Fuel	○	○	○	◒	◒	◒	○	◒
Ignition	◒	◒	◒	◒	◒	◒	◒	◒
Transmission	◒	◒	●	◒	◒	◒	◒	◒
Electrical	●	●	◒	◒	◒	◒	◒	◒
Air conditioning	◒	◒	◒	○	◒	◒	◒	◒
Suspension	○	◒	◒	●	◒	◒	○	○
Brakes	●	●	◒	◒	◒	○	○	◒
Exhaust	◒	◒	◒	◒	◒	◒	◒	◒
Paint/trim/rust	○	○	○	○	◒	○	○	◒
Body integrity	◒	◒	○	○	○	○	◒	◒
Power equipment	◒	○	○	●	○	●	◒	◒
Body hardware	○	○	○	○	○	○	◒	◒
RELIABILITY VERDICT	✗	−	−	✗	✗	✗	−	−

○ ◒ ○ ◒ ●
better ◀━━━▶ worse   See page 36 for more information.

Dodge Charger

THE CHARGER LINE
Body style:
sedan
Trim lines:
SE, SXT, R/T, Daytona
R/T, SRT8
Base price range:
$22,000-$35,000E

The Dodge Charger is another vehicle that reintroduces a famous muscle-car name from the 1960s. It has an optional 340-hp Hemi V8, mated to an automatic transmission. Chrysler hopes it will compete with the Ford Mustang and Pontiac GTO, even though it is a sedan and doesn't offer a manual transmission. The Charger is the sedan version of the Dodge Magnum wagon. The Magnum V6 we tested was a sound car but it didn't shine in any particular area. Standard features include ABS and electronic stability control.

REPORT CARD

New	Predicted reliability
New	Owner satisfaction
NA	Predicted depreciation
NA	Accident avoidance
NA	Acceleration
NA	Ride
NA	Front seat comfort
NA	Fuel economy

SPECIFICATIONS

Drive wheels Rear

Seating 2 front, 3 rear

Engines available
3.5-liter V6 (250 hp); 5.7-liter V8 (340 hp);
5.7-liter V8 (350 hp); 6.1-liter V8 (425 hp)

Transmissions available
5-speed automatic

Fuel
Fuel type ....Regular
EPA city/highway, mpg 17/25
Fuel refill capacity, gal. 19.0

Dimensions and weight
Length, in. 200
Width, in. 75
Wheelbase, in. 120
Curb weight, lb. 4,030
Percent weight, front/rear 54/46
Typical towing ability, lb. 2,000

SAFETY INFORMATION

Active safety features
Antilock brakes ....Standard
Traction control ....Standard
Stability control ....Standard
Daytime running lights ....Not available
Tire pressure monitor ....Available

Safety belts
Center-rear belt 3-point
Pretensioners, front/rear ....Yes/no

Air bags
Occupant-sensing system ....Front
Side bags, front/rear ....No/no
Inflatable curtain ....Optional
Accident alert system ....Not available

Crash tests
Gov't front-crash test, driver/front passenger ....NA/NA
Gov't side-crash test, driver/rear passenger ....NA/NA
IIHS offset crash test ....NA
IIHS side crash test w/ side & curtain airbags ....NA
IIHS side crash test w/o side & curtain airbags ....NA

ANOTHER LOOK

RELIABILITY HISTORY

TROUBLE SPOTS	97	98	99	00	01	02	03	04
Engine								
Cooling				NO				
Fuel								
Ignition								
Transmission				DATA				
Electrical								
Air conditioning				NEW				
Suspension								
Brakes				MODEL				
Exhaust								
Paint/trim/rust								
Body integrity								
Power equipment								
Body hardware								
RELIABILITY VERDICT								

Dodge Dakota

THE DAKOTA LINE
Body style:
extended cab; crew cab
Trim lines:
ST, SLT, Laramie
Base price range:
$19,660-$28,965

The new Dakota is based on the redesigned Dodge Durango SUV. Power comes from a standard 210-hp V6. A V8 is optional, but not the Hemi 5.7-liter V8. First impressions indicate that the ride is a bit bouncy and front head room is limited. The available permanent four-wheel-drive system is an advantage. Dodge allows Mitsubishi to share the Dakota platform for its upcoming Raider pickup. The Dakota faces competition from the Chevrolet Colorado, Nissan Frontier, and Toyota Tacoma, as well as the newly-introduced Honda Ridgeline.

REPORT CARD

New	Predicted reliability
New	Owner satisfaction
NA	Predicted depreciation
NA	Accident avoidance
NA	Acceleration
NA	Ride
NA	Front seat comfort
NA	Fuel economy

SPECIFICATIONS

Drive wheels Rear, part-time, or permanent 4WD

Seating 3 front, 3 rear

Engines available
3.7-liter V6 (210 hp); 4.7-liter V8 (230 hp); 4.7-liter V8 (250 hp)

Transmissions available
6-speed manual; 4-speed automatic; 5-speed automatic

Fuel
Fuel type . . . . Regular or premium
EPA city/highway, mpg 15/20
Fuel refill capacity, gal. 22.0

Dimensions and weight
Length, in. 219
Width, in. 74
Wheelbase, in. 131
Curb weight, lb. 4,790
Percent weight, front/rear 58/42
Typical towing ability, lb. 6,700

SAFETY INFORMATION

Active safety features
Antilock brakes . . . . .Optional
Traction control .Not available
Stability control .Not available
Daytime running lights . . . . .Not available
Tire pressure monitor . . , ...Not available

Safety belts
Center-rear belt 3-point
Pretensioners, front/rear . . . . .Yes/no

Air bags
Occupant-sensing system . . . . .Front
Side bags, front/rear .No/no
Inflatable curtain . . . . .Optional
Accident alert system . . . . .Not available

Crash tests
Gov't front-crash test, driver/front passenger . . . . . .NA/NA
Gov't side-crash test, driver/rear passenger . . . . . .NA/NA
IIHS offset crash test . . . . .NA
IIHS side crash test w/ side & curtain airbags . . . . .NA
IIHS side crash test w/o side & curtain airbags . . . . .NA

RELIABILITY HISTORY

TROUBLE SPOTS	97 98 99 00 01 02 03 04
Engine	
Cooling	
Fuel	NO
Ignition	
Transmission	DATA
Electrical	
Air conditioning	NEW
Suspension	
Brakes	MODEL
Exhaust	
Paint/trim/rust	
Body integrity	
Power equipment	
Body hardware	
RELIABILITY VERDICT	

ANOTHER LOOK

better ● ● ○ ● ● worse   See page 36 for more information.

Dodge Durango

CR RECOMMENDED ✓

THE DURANGO LINE
Body style:
4-door SUV
Trim lines:
ST, STX, SLT, Limited
Base price range:
$27,275-$35,915

The Durango straddles the midsized and large SUV classes. It remains a body-on-frame SUV but is much more pleasant than its predecessor. Based on our latest tests, handling is sound and secure and the ride is compliant. The cabin is fairly quiet, but the engine is a bit noisy. The optional 5.7-liter Hemi V8 is responsive, but fuel economy is poor at 12 mpg overall. Towing capacity is the Durango's forte. The third-row seat is more usable than that in the previous generation. Fit and finish is unimpressive. First-year reliability has been average.

REPORT CARD

◯	**Predicted reliability**
⊖	**Owner satisfaction**
NA	**Predicted depreciation**
◯	**Accident avoidance**
⊖	**Acceleration**
⊖	**Ride**
⊖	**Front seat comfort**
●	**Fuel economy**

SPECIFICATIONS

Drive wheels Rear or permanent 4WD

Seating 3 front, 3 rear, 2 third

Engines available
3.7-liter V6 (210 hp); 4.7-liter V8 (230 hp); 5.7-liter V8 (335 hp)

Transmissions available
4-speed automatic; 5-speed automatic

Fuel
Fuel type ....Regular
EPA city/highway, mpg 13/18
Fuel refill capacity, gal. 27.0

Dimensions and weight
Length, in. 201
Width, in. 76
Wheelbase, in. 119
Curb weight, lb. 5,335
Percent weight, front/rear 54/46
Typical towing ability, lb. 8,700

SAFETY INFORMATION

Active safety features
Antilock brakes ....Standard
Traction control ....Optional
Stability control ....Not available
Daytime running lights ....Not available
Tire pressure monitor ....Available

Safety belts
Center-rear belt 3-point
Pretensioners, front/rear ....Yes/no

Air bags
Occupant-sensing system ....Front
Side bags, front/rear ....No/no
Inflatable curtain ....Optional
Accident alert system ....Not available

Crash tests
Gov't front-crash test, driver/front passenger ......◑/◑
Gov't side-crash test, driver/rear passenger ....NA/NA
IIHS offset crash test ....NA
IIHS side crash test w/ side & curtain airbags ....NA
IIHS side crash test w/o side & curtain airbags ....NA

FROM THE TEST TRACK

Tested model
2004 Limited 4-door SUV 4WD, 5.7-liter V8, 5-speed automatic

Tires as tested
Goodyear Wrangler SR-A, size P265/65R17 110S

Acceleration ....⊖
0-30 mph, sec. 2.7
0-60 mph, sec. 7.6
Quarter mile, sec. 15.8
Quarter mile, mph. 87
45-65 mph, sec. 5.2

Other findings
Transmission ....◑
Turning circle, ft. 43
Ground clearance, in. 6.0

Braking and handling
Braking ....◯
Braking, dry pavement, ft. 155
Routine handling ....◯
Emergency handling ....◯
Avoidance maneuver, max. mph ...47.5

Convenience and comfort
Ride ....⊖
Noise ....◯
Driving position ....◯
Access ....⊖
Controls and displays ....⊖
Fit and finish ....◯
Door top to ground, in. 65.5
Cargo area ....⊖
Cargo volume, cu.ft. 44.5
Max. load, lb. 1,260

Seating
Front-seat comfort ....⊖
Front shoulder room, in. 59.0
Front leg room, in. 41.0
Front head room, in. 3.5
Rear-seat comfort ....⊖
Rear shoulder room, in. 59.5
Rear leg room, in. 27.5
Rear head room, in 3.5
Third-seat comfort ....◯
Third shoulder room, in 59.0
Third leg room, in. 28.0
Third head room, in 3.5

Fuel economy ....●
CU's overall mileage, mpg 12
  CU's city/highway, mpg 8/19
  CU's 150-mile trip, mpg 15
Annual fuel ....1,210 gal./$2,420
Cruising range 365

RELIABILITY HISTORY

TROUBLE SPOTS	Dodge Durango							
	97	98	99	00	01	02	03	04
Engine	◯	◯	◑	◑	◑	◑	◑	◑
Cooling	◯	◑	◑	◑	◑	◑	◑	◑
Fuel	◯	◯	◑	◑	◑	◑	◑	◑
Ignition	◑	◑	◑	◑	◑	◑	◑	◑
Transmission	◑	◑	◯	◯	◑	◑	◑	◑
Electrical	◑	◑	◑	◯	◯	◑	◑	◑
Air conditioning	●	◑	◯	◯	◯	◑	◑	◑
Suspension	●	◑	◑	◑	◯	◑	◑	◑
Brakes	◑	●	◑	◑	◯	◯	◑	◑
Exhaust	◑	◑	◑	◑	◑	◑	◑	◑
Paint/trim/rust	◑	◑	◑	◑	◑	◑	◯	◑
Body integrity	◑	◯	◯	◯	◑	◯	◑	◑
Power equipment	●	●	◑	◯	◯	◑	◑	◑
Body hardware	◑	◯	◑	◯	◯	◑	◑	◑
RELIABILITY VERDICT	✗	✗	✗	–	–	–	–	–

Dodge Magnum

THE MAGNUM LINE
Body style:
wagon
Trim lines:
SE, SXT, RT, SRT8
Base price range:
$22,020-$35,500E

The Magnum is a wagon version of the Chrysler 300 sedan. The 3.5-liter V6 version we tested delivered good acceleration. The 5.7-liver Hemi V8 imperceptibly shuts off four cylinders while cruising to conserve fuel. But our 300C got only 16 mpg overall. The architecture relies on Mercedes-Benz hardware but doesn't shine in ride or handling. Fit and finish is acceptable. The view out is compromised by the low roof, high dash, and thick roof pillars. Traction and stability control are available, and optional AWD alleviates concerns about snow traction.

REPORT CARD

New	Predicted reliability
New	Owner satisfaction
NA	Predicted depreciation
◯	Accident avoidance
⊖	Acceleration
⊖	Ride
⊖	Front seat comfort
⊖	Fuel economy

SPECIFICATIONS

Drive wheels Rear or AWD

Seating 2 front, 3 rear

Engines available
2.7-liter V6 (190 hp); 3.5-liter V6 (250 hp);
5.7-liter V8 (340 hp); 6.1-liter V8 (425 hp)

Transmissions available
4-speed automatic; 5-speed automatic

Fuel
Fuel type . . . . .Regular
EPA city/highway, mpg 19/27
Fuel refill capacity, gal. 18.0

Dimensions and weight
Length, in. 198
Width, in. 74
Wheelbase, in. 120
Curb weight, lb. 3,950
Percent weight, front/rear 51/49
Typical towing ability, lb. 2,000

SAFETY INFORMATION

Active safety features
Antilock brakes . . . . .Standard (optional on SE)
Traction control . . . . .Standard with ABS
Stability control . . . . .Standard (optional on SE)
Daytime running lights . . . . .Not available
Tire pressure monitor . . . . .Not available

Safety belts
Center-rear belt 3-point
Pretensioners, front/rear . . . . .Yes/no

Air bags
Occupant-sensing system . . . . .Front
Side bags, front/rear .No/no
Inflatable curtain . . . . .Optional
Accident alert system . . . . .Not available

Crash tests
Gov't front-crash test, driver/front passenger . . .◑/◉
Gov't side-crash test, driver/rear passenger . . . . .⊖/◉
IIHS offset crash test . . . . .NA
IIHS side crash test w/ side & curtain airbags . . . . .NA
IIHS side crash test w/o side & curtain airbags . . . . .NA

FROM THE TEST TRACK

Tested model
2005 SXT wagon, 3.5-liter V6, 4-speed automatic

Tires as tested
Goodyear Integrity, size P215/65R17 98T

Acceleration . . . . ⊖
0-30 mph, sec. 3.1
0-60 mph, sec. 8.8
Quarter mile, sec. 16.7
Quarter mile, mph 85
45-65 mph, sec. 6.2

Other findings
Transmission . . . . ⊖
Turning circle, ft. 41
Ground clearance, in. 5.0

Braking and handling
Braking . . . .◯
Braking, dry pavement, ft. 138
Routine handling . . . .⊖
Emergency handling . . . .◯
Avoidance maneuver, max. mph 48.0

Convenience and comfort
Ride . . . . ⊖
Noise . . . . ⊖
Driving position . . . . ◯
Access . . . . ⊖
Controls and displays . . . . ⊖
Fit and finish . . . . ⊖
Door top to ground, in. 52.0
Cargo area . . . . ⊖
Cargo volume, cu.ft. 29.5
Max. load, lb. 865

Seating
Front-seat comfort . . . .⊖
Front shoulder room, in. 54.0
Front leg room, in. 42.0
Front head room, in. 2.5
Rear-seat comfort . . . .⊖
Rear shoulder room, in. 58.0
Rear leg room, in. 28.5
Rear head room, in 3.0

Fuel economy . . . . ⊖
CU's overall mileage, mpg 19
CU's city/highway, mpg 12/30
CU's 150-mile trip, mpg 23
Annual fuel . . . . .810 gal./$1,615
Cruising range 390

RELIABILITY HISTORY

TROUBLE SPOTS	97 98 99 00 01 02 03 04
Engine	
Cooling	
Fuel	NO
Ignition	
Transmission	DATA
Electrical	
Air conditioning	NEW
Suspension	
Brakes	MODEL
Exhaust	
Paint/trim/rust	
Body integrity	
Power equipment	
Body hardware	
RELIABILITY VERDICT	

Dodge Neon

THE NEON LINE
Body style:
sedan
Trim lines:
SE, SXT, SRT4
Base price range:
$13,700-$20,650

The Neon's strong points include its secure handling, competent braking, and relatively roomy interior. The ride is stiff, choppy, and uncomfortable, however, and wind, engine, and road noise constantly invade the cabin. The four-speed automatic transmission blunts acceleration because it isn't properly coordinated with the engine. A high-performance SRT-4 model with a 230-hp, turbocharged four-cylinder engine and a stiffer suspension is entertaining but crude. Interior fit and finish is decidedly low-rent. The Neon received a Poor rating in the IIHS side-impact-crash test.

REPORT CARD

○	Predicted reliability
●	Owner satisfaction
●	Predicted depreciation
◑	Accident avoidance
○	Acceleration
◑	Ride
○	Front seat comfort
○	Fuel economy

SPECIFICATIONS

Drive wheels Front

Seating 2 front, 3 rear

Engines available
2.0-liter 4 (132 hp); 2.4-liter 4 turbo (230 hp)

Transmissions available
5-speed manual; 4-speed automatic

Fuel
Fuel type . . . . Regular or premium
EPA city/highway, mpg 25/32
Fuel refill capacity, gal. 12.5

Dimensions and weight
Length, in. 174
Width, in. 67
Wheelbase, in. 105
Curb weight, lb. 2,730
Percent weight, front/rear 64/36
Typical towing ability, lb. 1,000

SAFETY INFORMATION

Active safety features
Antilock brakes . . . . .Optional (standard on SRT4)
Traction control . . . . .Not available
Stability control . . . . .Not available
Daytime running lights . . . . .Not available
Tire pressure monitor . . . . .Not available

Safety belts
Center-rear belt 3-point
Pretensioners, front/rear . . . . .No/no

Air bags
Occupant-sensing system . . . . .Not available
Side bags, front/rear . . . . .Optional/no
Inflatable curtain . . . . .Not available
Accident alert system . . . . .Not available

Crash tests
Gov't front-crash test, driver/front passenger . . . . . . ◑/◑
Gov't side-crash test, driver/rear passenger . . . . ○/○
IIHS offset crash test . . . . .Marginal
IIHS side crash test w/ side & curtain airbags . . . . .NA
IIHS side crash test w/o side & curtain airbags . . . . . . .Poor

FROM THE TEST TRACK

Tested model
2003 SXT sedan, 2.0-liter Four, 4-speed automatic

Tires as tested
Goodyear Eagle LS, size P185/60R15 84T

Acceleration . . . . ○
0-30 mph, sec. 3.4
0-60 mph, sec. 9.6
Quarter mile, sec. 17.6
Quarter mile, mph 80
45-65 mph, sec. 6.1

Other findings
Transmission . . . . ◑
Turning circle, ft. 40
Ground clearance, in. 4.5

Braking and handling
Braking . . . . ◑
Braking, dry pavement, ft. 131
Routine handling . . . . ◑
Emergency handling . . . . ○
Avoidance maneuver, max. mph . . .53.0

Convenience and comfort
Ride . . . . ◑
Noise . . . . ◑
Driving position . . . . ○
Access . . . . ○
Controls and displays . . . . ◑
Fit and finish . . . . ◑
Door top to ground, in. 50.5
Trunk . . . . ◑
Luggage capacity . . . . .3+0
Max. load, lb. 865

Seating
Front-seat comfort . . . . ○
Front shoulder room, in. 54.0
Front leg room, in. 41.0
Front head room, in. 4.0
Rear-seat comfort . . . . ◑
Rear shoulder room, in. 53.0
Rear leg room, in. 28.5
Rear head room, in 2.0

Fuel economy . . . . ○
CU's overall mileage, mpg 24
CU's city/highway, mpg 16/34
CU's 150-mile trip, mpg 29
Annual fuel . . . . .630 gal./$1,265
Cruising range 335

RELIABILITY HISTORY

TROUBLE SPOTS	\- Dodge Neon							
	97	98	99	00	01	02	03	04
Engine	●	●	●	◑	○	○	◑	
Cooling	◑	○	◑	○	◑	●	◑	
Fuel	○	◑	◑	◑	○	○	◑	
Ignition	◑	○	◑	○	◑	○	◑	
Transmission	○	○	◑	○	◑	◑	◑	
Electrical	○	◑	◑	◑	◑	○	◑	Insufficient data
Air conditioning	●	●	○	○	◑	○	●	
Suspension	○	○	◑	○	○	○	◑	
Brakes	◑	○	○	◑	◑	◑	◑	
Exhaust	◑	◑	◑	◑	○	◑	◑	
Paint/trim/rust	●	◑	○	○	◑	○	◑	
Body integrity	●	●	◑	○	◑	◑	○	
Power equipment	◑	○	○	○	◑	○	●	
Body hardware	◑	○	◑	○	◑	◑	●	
RELIABILITY VERDICT	✗	✗	✗	✗	✗	✗	✓	

Dodge Ram 1500

T he overly hyped 5.7-liter Hemi V8 makes the Ram fairly quick but also very thirsty, averaging a paltry 11 mpg. The 4.7-liter V8 and automatic transmission make a reasonably smooth combination. The pronounced exhaust note sounds good to some. The Ram falls short of competing trucks, with a jittery ride, cumbersome handling, and a tight rear seat in the crew cab. Braking performance was only adequate, with long stops. The view over the towering hood impeded visibility for short drivers. The cargo bed in the crew-cab version is longer than competing models.

REPORT CARD

○	Predicted reliability
○	Owner satisfaction
◉	Predicted depreciation
○	Accident avoidance
⊖	Acceleration
⊖	Ride
○	Front seat comfort
●	Fuel economy

THE RAM 1500 LINE
Body style:
regular cab; crew cab
Trim lines:
ST, SLT, Laramie, SRT10
Base price range:
$20,455-$50,250

SPECIFICATIONS

Drive wheels Rear, part-time, or permanent 4WD

Seating 3 front, 3 rear

Engines available
3.7-liter V6 (215 hp); 4.7-liter V8 (235 hp); 5.7-liter V8 (345 hp); 8.3-liter V10 (500 hp)

Transmissions available
6-speed manual; 4-speed automatic; 5-speed automatic

Fuel
Fuel type . . . . .Regular or premium
EPA city/highway, mpg 13/17
Fuel refill capacity, gal. 26.0

Dimensions and weight
Length, in. 228
Width, in. 80
Wheelbase, in. .141
Curb weight, lb. 5,380
Percent weight, front/rear 52/48
Typical towing ability, lb. 8,600

SAFETY INFORMATION

Active safety features
Antilock brakes . . . . .Opt. (std. on Laramie, SRT10)
Traction control .Not available
Stability control .Not available
Daytime running lights . . . . .Not available
Tire pressure monitor . . . . .Not available

Safety belts
Center-rear belt 3-point
Pretensioners, front/rear . . . . .Yes/no

Air bags
Occupant-sensing system . . . . .Not available
Side bags, front/rear . . . . .No/no
Inflatable curtain . . . . .Optional
Accident alert system .Not available

Crash tests
Gov't front-crash test, driver/front passenger . . . . . .◉/◉
Gov't side-crash test, driver/rear passenger . . . . . .NA/NA
IIHS offset crash test . . . . .Good
IIHS side crash test w/ side & curtain airbags . . . . .NA
IIHS side crash test w/o side & curtain airbags . . . . .NA

FROM THE TEST TRACK

Tested model
2004 SLT crew cab 4WD, 5.7-liter V8, 5-speed automatic

Tires as tested
Michelin LTX A/S, size P245/70R17 108S

Acceleration . . . . ⊖
0-30 mph, sec. 3.0
0-60 mph, sec. 7.7
Quarter mile, sec. 16.1
Quarter mile, mph 87
45-65 mph, sec. 4.7

Other findings
Transmission . . . . ⊖
Turning circle, ft. 49
Ground clearance, in. 9.5

Braking and handling
Braking . . . . ○
Braking, dry pavement, ft. 152
Routine handling . . . . ⊖
Emergency handling . . . . ⊖
Avoidance maneuver, max. mph . . .47.5

Convenience and comfort
Ride . . . . ⊖
Noise . . . . ○
Driving position . . . . ○
Access . . . . ⊖
Controls and displays . . . . ⊖
Fit and finish . . . . ○
Door top to ground, in. 70.0
Cargo area . . . . ○
Max. load, lb. 1,270

Seating
Front-seat comfort . . . . ○
Front shoulder room, in. 66.5
Front leg room, in. 42.0
Front head room, in. 6.0
Rear-seat comfort . . . . ○
Rear shoulder room, in. 66.5
Rear leg room, in. 27.0
Rear head room, in 3.5

Fuel economy . . . . ●
CU's overall mileage, mpg 11
CU's city/highway, mpg 8/17
CU's 150-mile trip, mpg 13
Annual fuel . . . . .1,325 gal./$2,650
Cruising range 320

RELIABILITY HISTORY

TROUBLE SPOTS	Dodge Ram 1500 4WD							
	97	98	99	00	01	02	03	04
Engine	○	○	○	●	⊖	⊖	⊖	●
Cooling	○	○	○	●	⊖	⊖	●	●
Fuel	●	○	○	●	⊖	⊖	●	●
Ignition	○	○	○	⊘	⊖	⊖	●	●
Transmission	⊖	⊖	⊖	⊖	⊖	⊖	●	●
Electrical	○	⊖	●	○	○	⊖	●	●
Air conditioning	⊖	⊖	○	○	⊖	⊖	●	●
Suspension	○	⊖	⊖	○	○	⊖	●	●
Brakes	○	⊖	⊖	●	○	○	⊖	●
Exhaust	⊖	●	○	●	⊖	⊖	●	●
Paint/trim/rust	○	○	○	○	⊖	⊖	●	●
Body integrity	○	○	○	○	⊖	⊖	⊖	●
Power equipment	●	○	⊖	●	⊖	⊖	●	●
Body hardware	○	⊖	⊖	○	○	⊖	●	●
RELIABILITY VERDICT	✗	✗	✗	✗	✗	✗	−	✓

● ⊖ ○ ⊘ ●
better ◄———► worse   See page 36 for more information.

Dodge Stratus

Though redesigned for 2001, the Stratus feels rough and underdeveloped. The Stratus we tested was noisy and difficult to access. The ride was stiff and unsettled, and handling, though secure, lacked agility. The 2.4-liter, four-cylinder engine is buzzy, slow, and thirsty, making the car feel unrefined. The optional 2.7-liter V6 feels smoother and produces quicker acceleration, as well as similar fuel economy to the four-cylinder. The Stratus offers optional head-protection air bags and has done well in frontal crashes. Reliability has dropped to below average as of late. IIHS side-crash test results are Poor.

THE STRATUS LINE
Body style:
coupe; sedan
Trim lines:
SXT, R/T
Base price range:
$19,255-$23,235

REPORT CARD

⊖	**Predicted reliability**
●	**Owner satisfaction**
●	**Predicted depreciation**
⊖	**Accident avoidance**
○	**Acceleration**
○	**Ride**
⊖	**Front seat comfort**
○	**Fuel economy**

SPECIFICATIONS

Drive wheels Front

Seating 2 front, 3 rear

Engines available
2.4-liter 4 (147 hp); 2.4-liter 4 (150 hp); 2.7-liter V6 (200 hp); 3.0-liter V6 (200 hp)

Transmissions available
5-speed manual; 4-speed automatic

Fuel
Fuel type . . . . .Regular
EPA city/highway, mpg 21/30
Fuel refill capacity, gal. 16.0

Dimensions and weight
Length, in. 191
Width, in. 71
Wheelbase, in. 108
Curb weight, lb. 3,190
Percent weight, front/rear 63/37
Typical towing ability, lb. 1,000

SAFETY INFORMATION

Active safety features
Antilock brakes . . . . .Optional
Traction control . . . . .Standard with ABS
Stability control . . . . .Not available
Daytime running lights . . . . .Not available
Tire pressure monitor . . . . .Not available

Safety belts
Center-rear belt 3-point
Pretensioners, front/rear . . . . .Yes/no

Air bags
Occupant-sensing system . . . . .Not available
Side bags, front/rear . . . . .Optional/no
Inflatable curtain . . . . .Optional
Accident alert system . . . . .Not available

Crash tests
Gov't front-crash test, driver/front passenger . . . . . . ●/⊖
Gov't side-crash test, driver/rear passenger . . . .○/○
IIHS offset crash test . . . . .Acceptable
IIHS side crash test w/ side & curtain airbags . . . . .NA
IIHS side crash test w/o side & curtain airbags . . . . . . .Poor

FROM THE TEST TRACK

Tested model
2004 SXT sedan, 2.4-liter Four, 4-speed automatic

Tires as tested
Goodyear Eagle LS, size P205/60R16 91T
Acceleration . . . . ⊖
0-30 mph, sec. 3.6
0-60 mph, sec. 10.4
Quarter mile, sec. 18.0
Quarter mile, mph 78
45-65 mph, sec. 6.6

Other findings
Transmission . . . . ⊖
Turning circle, ft. 40
Ground clearance, in. 4.5

Braking and handling
Braking . . . . ⊖
Braking, dry pavement, ft. 131
Routine handling . . . . ⊖
Emergency handling . . . . ○
Avoidance maneuver, max. mph . . .50.5

Convenience and comfort
Ride . . . . ⊖
Noise . . . . ○
Driving position . . . . ⊖
Access . . . . ○
Controls and displays . . . . ⊖
Fit and finish . . . . ⊖
Door top to ground, in. 49.0
Trunk . . . . ○
Luggage capacity . . . . .3+3
Max. load, lb. 865

Seating
Front-seat comfort . . . . ⊖
Front shoulder room, in. 55.5
Front leg room, in. 41.5
Front head room, in. 4.0
Rear-seat comfort . . . . ⊖
Rear shoulder room, in. 54.5
Rear leg room, in. 31.5
Rear head room, in 1.5

Fuel economy . . . . ○
CU's overall mileage, mpg 21
CU's city/highway, mpg 14/32
CU's 150-mile trip, mpg 24
Annual fuel . . . . 725 gal./$1,455
Cruising range 360

RELIABILITY HISTORY

TROUBLE SPOTS	Dodge Stratus Sedan V6							
	97	98	99	00	01	02	03	04
Engine	⊖	○	○	○	○	○	●	●
Cooling	⊖	○	⊖	●	○	●	○	●
Fuel	⊖	○	⊖	○	○	●	⊖	●
Ignition	⊖	○	○	○	●	⊖	●	●
Transmission	⊖	○	○	○	○	○	○	○
Electrical	⊖	○	○	○	○	○	●	●
Air conditioning	⊖	○	○	○	○	○	○	●
Suspension	⊖	○	○	○	○	●	○	●
Brakes	●	●	○	⊖	○	○	⊖	●
Exhaust	●	●	●	●	●	○	●	●
Paint/trim/rust	○	○	○	●	●	●	●	●
Body integrity	○	○	○	○	○	○	●	●
Power equipment	○	○	○	○	○	●	●	●
Body hardware	○	○	⊖	○	○	⊖	●	●
RELIABILITY VERDICT	✗	✓	–	–	–	✗	–	✗

Expert • Independent • Nonprofit

Ford Crown Victoria

CR RECOMMENDED ✓

The Crown Victoria/Mercury Grand Marquis twins are among the last big rear-drive sedans with a full frame and a V8 engine. They are both dated despite recent modifications. Both ride too stiffly, and the engines are noisy. Handling is safe enough, but it feels ungainly. Traction control (optional on the Crown Victoria, standard on the Grand Marquis) helps in slippery conditions. The soft front bench seat could use more support, and the rear seat isn't as roomy as you'd expect, though the trunk is suitably cavernous. Crash-test results are impressive.

THE CROWN VICTORIA LINE
Body style: sedan

Trim lines: Base, LX, LX Sport

Base price range: $24,335-$30,420

REPORT CARD

○	Predicted reliability
○	Owner satisfaction
◐	Predicted depreciation
○	Accident avoidance
◐	Acceleration
○	Ride
○	Front seat comfort
●	Fuel economy

SPECIFICATIONS

Drive wheels Rear

Seating 3 front, 3 rear

Engines available
4.6-liter V8 (224 hp); 4.6-liter V8 (239 hp)

Transmissions available
4-speed automatic

Fuel
Fuel type ....Regular
EPA city/highway, mpg 17/25
Fuel refill capacity, gal. 19.0

Dimensions and weight
Length, in. 212
Width, in. 78
Wheelbase, in. 115
Curb weight, lb. 4,180
Percent weight, front/rear 56/44
Typical towing ability, lb. 2,000

SAFETY INFORMATION

Active safety features
Antilock brakes ....Standard
Traction control ....Optional
Stability control ....Not available
Daytime running lights ....Not available
Tire pressure monitor ....Not available

Safety belts
Center-rear belt 3-point
Pretensioners, front/rear ....Yes/no

Air bags
Occupant-sensing system ....Front
Side bags, front/rear ....Optional/no
Inflatable curtain ....Not available
Accident alert system ....Not available

Crash tests
Gov't front-crash test, driver/front passenger   ◐/●
Gov't side-crash test, driver/rear passenger   ◐/●
IIHS offset crash test ....Good
IIHS side crash test w/ side & curtain airbags ....NA
IIHS side crash test w/o side & curtain airbags ....NA

FROM THE TEST TRACK

Tested model
2003 Mercury Grand Marquis LSE sedan, 4.6-liter V8, 4-speed automatic

Tires as tested
Goodyear Integrity, size P225/60R16 97T

Acceleration ....◐
0-30 mph, sec. 3.1
0-60 mph, sec. 8.0
Quarter mile, sec. 16.3
Quarter mile, mph 88
45-65 mph, sec. 5.1

Other findings
Transmission ....◐
Turning circle, ft. 42
Ground clearance, in. 4.5

Braking and handling
Braking ....◐
Braking, dry pavement, ft. 140
Routine handling ....○
Emergency handling ....○
Avoidance maneuver, max. mph ...50.0

Convenience and comfort
Ride ....○
Noise ....◐
Driving position ....◐
Access ....◐
Controls and displays ....◐
Fit and finish ....○
Door top to ground, in. 52.0
Trunk ....●
Luggage capacity ....6+2
Max. load, lb. 1,100

Seating
Front-seat comfort ....○
Front shoulder room, in. 61.0
Front leg room, in. 40.5
Front head room, in. 5.5
Rear-seat comfort ....◐
Rear shoulder room, in. 60.5
Rear leg room, in. 27.5
Rear head room, in 3.0

Fuel economy ....●
CU's overall mileage, mpg 16
CU's city/highway, mpg 10/25
CU's 150-mile trip, mpg 21
Annual fuel ....930 gal./$1,855
Cruising range 365

RELIABILITY HISTORY

TROUBLE SPOTS	Ford Crown Victoria 97	98	99	00	01	02	03	04
Engine	◐	◐	◐	◐	◐	◐	◐	◐
Cooling	○	◐	◐	◐	◐	◐	●	●
Fuel	○	◐	◐	○	○	◐	◐	◐
Ignition	◐	◐	◐	◐	◐	◐	◐	●
Transmission	◐	◐	◐	◐	◐	◐	◐	◐
Electrical	○	○	○	○	◐	◐	◐	●
Air conditioning	◐	◐	◐	◐	◐	◐	●	●
Suspension	○	○	◐	◐	◐	◐	◐	●
Brakes	◐	●	○	○	◐	◐	◐	◐
Exhaust	◐	●	●	●	●	●	●	●
Paint/trim/rust	◐	●	●	●	●	●	●	●
Body integrity	○	◐	◐	○	○	○	○	○
Power equipment	◐	○	○	○	○	◐	◐	●
Body hardware	○	◐	◐	◐	○	◐	◐	●
RELIABILITY VERDICT	-	✓	✓	-	✓	-	X

Ford Escape

The Escape is a sibling of the Mazda Tribute and Mercury Mariner. The roomy interior includes a spacious rear bench. The 3.0-liter V6 provides adequate acceleration, but fuel economy is disappointing. Noise and ride comfort have slightly improved for 2005, and handling is agile. Interior quality has been upgraded, and a more powerful 2.3-liter, four-cylinder engine from Mazda is available. The hybrid model is very noisy on the highway. Offset-crash-test results are improved. Because of a tip-up in the government rollover test, we do not recommend the Escape and its siblings.

THE ESCAPE LINE
Body style:
4-door SUV
Trim lines:
XLS, XLT, XLT Sport, Limited, Hybrid
Base price range:
$19,405-$28,435

REPORT CARD

◔	Predicted reliability
◑	Owner satisfaction
○	Predicted depreciation
○	Accident avoidance
○	Acceleration
○	Ride
◑	Front seat comfort
◕	Fuel economy

SPECIFICATIONS

Drive wheels Front or AWD

Seating 2 front, 3 rear

Engines available
2.3-liter 4 (153 hp); 2.3-liter 4 hybrid (155 hp); 3.0-liter V6 (200 hp)

Transmissions available
5-speed manual; CVT; 4-speed automatic

Fuel
Fuel type . . . . .Regular
EPA city/highway, mpg 18/22
Fuel refill capacity, gal. 16,5

Dimensions and weight
Length, in. 175
Width, in. 70
Wheelbase, in. .103
Curb weight, lb. 3,575
Percent weight, front/rear 59/41
Typical towing ability, lb. 3,500

SAFETY INFORMATION

Active safety features
Antilock brakes . . . . .Standard
Traction control . . . . .Not available
Stability control . . . . .Not available
Daytime running lights . . . . .Not available
Tire pressure monitor .Not available

Safety belts
Center-rear belt 3-point
Pretensioners, front/rear . . . . .Yes/no

Air bags
Occupant-sensing system . . . . .Front
Side bags, front/rear . . . . .No/no
Inflatable curtain . . . . .Optional with rollover
Accident alert system .Not available

Crash tests
Gov't front-crash test, driver/front passenger . . . . . . ◑/◒
Gov't side-crash test, driver/rear passenger . . . . ◑/◒
IIHS offset crash test . . . . .Acceptable
IIHS side crash test w/ side & curtain airbags . . . . .Good
IIHS side crash test w/o side & curtain airbags . . . . . . .Poor

FROM THE TEST TRACK

Tested model
2005 XLT 4-door SUV AWD, 3.0-liter V6, 4-speed automatic

Tires as tested
Continental Contitrac, size P235/70R16 104T

Acceleration . . . . ○
0-30 mph, sec. 3.6
0-60 mph, sec. 10.2
Quarter mile, sec. 17.6
Quarter mile, mph. 82
45-65 mph, sec. 6.7

Other findings
Transmission . . . . ◑
Turning circle, ft. 40
Ground clearance, in. 8.0

Braking and handling
Braking . . . . ○
Braking, dry pavement, ft. 144
Routine handling . . . . ○
Emergency handling . . . . ○
Avoidance maneuver, max. mph . . .47.0

Convenience and comfort
Ride . . . . ○
Noise . . . . ○
Driving position . . . . ◑
Access . . . . ◑
Controls and displays . . . . ◑
Fit and finish . . . . ○
Door top to ground, in. 61.0
Cargo area . . . . ○
Cargo volume, cu.ft. 38.5
Max. load, lb. 950

Seating
Front-seat comfort . . . . ◑
Front shoulder room, in. 56.5
Front leg room, in. 40.5
Front head room, in. 4.5
Rear-seat comfort . . . . ◑
Rear shoulder room, in. 55.0
Rear leg room, in. 28.0
Rear head room, in 5.0

Fuel economy . . . . ◕
CU's overall mileage, mpg 18
  CU's city/highway, mpg 12/27
  CU's 150-mile trip, mpg 22
Annual fuel . . . . .830 gal./$1,660
Cruising range 325

RELIABILITY HISTORY

TROUBLE SPOTS	Ford Escape							
	97	98	99	00	01	02	03	04
Engine					◑	◑	◔	◔
Cooling					◑	◑	◔	◔
Fuel					○	○	◑	◔
Ignition					◑	◑	◔	◔
Transmission					○	◑	◔	◔
Electrical					○	○	◑	◔
Air conditioning					◑	◑	◔	◔
Suspension					◑	◑	◔	◔
Brakes					◑	○	◔	◔
Exhaust					◑	◑	◔	◔
Paint/trim/rust					◑	◑	◔	◔
Body integrity					◑	◑	○	◔
Power equipment					◑	◑	◔	◔
Body hardware					◑	○	◔	◔
RELIABILITY VERDICT		✗	–		✓	✓		

Ford Expedition

The Expedition has a low floor for easy access and loading. Our tested Eddie Bauer model features a power-operated, split third-row seat that can be folded or deployed by pressing a button. It's as comfortable as the second row, and the interior is versatile. Handling is secure and relatively responsive. The ride is fairly steady, though jiggly at low speeds. The standard 5.4-liter V8 isn't particularly smooth. Available safety features include stability control, a tire-pressure monitor, and a rollover-detection system with head-protection air bags. Reliability since the 2003 redesign has been poor.

REPORT CARD

●	Predicted reliability
○	Owner satisfaction
○	Predicted depreciation
◒	Accident avoidance
○	Acceleration
○	Ride
◒	Front seat comfort
●	Fuel economy

THE EXPEDITION LINE

Body style:
4-door SUV
Trim lines:
XLS, XLT, XLT Sport, Eddie Bauer, Limited, King Ranch
Base price range:
$33,030-$45,765

SPECIFICATIONS

Drive wheels Rear or selectable 4WD

Seating 2 front, 3 rear, 3 third

Engines available
5.4-liter V8 (300 hp)

Transmissions available
4-speed automatic

Fuel
Fuel type . . . . .Regular
EPA city/highway, mpg 13/17
Fuel refill capacity, gal. 28.0

Dimensions and weight
Length, in. 206
Width, in. 79
Wheelbase, in. 119
Curb weight, lb. 5,900
Percent weight, front/rear 50/50
Typical towing ability, lb. 8,700

SAFETY INFORMATION

Active safety features
Antilock brakes . . . . .Standard
Traction control . . . . .Included with stability
Stability control . . . . .Optional
Daytime running lights . . . . .Not available
Tire pressure monitor . . . . .Available

Safety belts
Center-rear belt 3-point
Pretensioners, front/rear . . . . .Yes/no

Air bags
Occupant-sensing system .Front
Side bags, front/rear . . . . .No/no
Inflatable curtain . . . . .Optional with rollover
Accident alert system . . . . .Not available

Crash tests
Gov't front-crash test, driver/front passenger . . . . . .◒/◒
Gov't side-crash test, driver/rear passenger . . . . .NA/NA
IIHS offset crash test . . . . .NA
IIHS side crash test w/ side & curtain airbags . . . . .NA
IIHS side crash test w/o side & curtain airbags . . . . .NA

FROM THE TEST TRACK

Tested model
2003 Eddie Bauer 4-door SUV 4WD, 5.4-liter V8, 4-speed automatic

Tires as tested
Continental Contitrac TR, size P265/70R17 113S

Acceleration . . . .○
0-30 mph, sec. 3.7
0-60 mph, sec. 10.5
Quarter mile, sec. 17.9
Quarter mile, mph 79
45-65 mph, sec. 6.6

Other findings
Transmission . . . .○
Turning circle, ft. 42
Ground clearance, in. 7.0

Braking and handling
Braking . . . .◒
Braking, dry pavement, ft. 154
Routine handling . . . .○
Emergency handling . . . .◒
Avoidance maneuver, max. mph . . .44.5

Convenience and comfort
Ride . . . .○
Noise . . . .◒
Driving position . . . .◒
Access . . . .◒
Controls and displays . . . .◒
Fit and finish . . . .◒
Door top to ground, in. 68.0
Cargo area . . . .◒
Cargo volume, cu.ft. 62.0
Max. load, lb. 1,400

Seating
Front-seat comfort . . . .○
Front shoulder room, in. . . .64.0
Front leg room, in. 40.5
Front head room, in. 2.5
Rear-seat comfort . . . .○
Rear shoulder room, in. 65.0
Rear leg room, in. 29.5
Rear head room, in 4.0
Third-seat comfort . . . .○
Third shoulder room,in 50.0
Third leg room, in. 28.0
Third head room, in 3.5

Fuel economy . . . .●
CU's overall mileage, mpg . . .12
CU's city/highway, mpg 8/18
CU's 150-mile trip, mpg 15
Annual fuel . . . . .1,225 gal./$2,445
Cruising range 400

RELIABILITY HISTORY

TROUBLE SPOTS	Ford Expedition							
	97	98	99	00	01	02	03	04
Engine	◒	◒	○	◒	◒	◒	◒	◒
Cooling	●	●	●	◒	◒	◒	◒	◒
Fuel	○	◒	◒	◒	◒	◒	●	●
Ignition	◒	○	◒	◒	◒	●	◒	◒
Transmission	◒	◒	○	○	◒	◒	◒	◒
Electrical	◒	◒	◒	○	○	○	◒	◒
Air conditioning	○	○	○	◒	○	○	◒	◒
Suspension	◒	○	○	○	◒	◒	◒	◒
Brakes	◒	○	◒	○	◒	◒	◒	◒
Exhaust	●	●	●	●	●	◒	◒	○
Paint/trim/rust	○	◒	◒	○	◒	◒	◒	◒
Body integrity	○	○	○	○	◒	○	◒	◒
Power equipment	○	◒	◒	◒	○	○	◒	●
Body hardware	○	○	○	◒	○	○	◒	◒
RELIABILITY VERDICT	✓	–	–	–	–	–	✗	✗

Ford Explorer

CR RECOMMENDED ✓

THE EXPLORER LINE
Body style:
4-door SUV
Trim lines:
XLS, XLS Sport, XLT,
XLT Sport, Eddie Bauer,
Limited
Base price range:
$26,845-$37,605

The Explorer's fully independent suspension gives it a reasonably comfortable ride and fairly responsive handling. Access is easy. Notable options include third-row seats, bringing passenger capacity to seven, and a reverse-sensing system that beeps when the rear bumper nears an object. The versatile interior features useful storage cubbies. The base V6 is noisy and unrefined, and provides only adequate acceleration. The optional V8 is quicker but thirsty. The 4WD system is permanently engaged. Stability control is now standard. Reliability has improved to average.

REPORT CARD

○	Predicted reliability
◒	Owner satisfaction
○	Predicted depreciation
○	Accident avoidance
○	Acceleration
○	Ride
◒	Front seat comfort
●	Fuel economy

SPECIFICATIONS

Drive wheels Rear, permanent 4WD, or AWD

Seating 2 front, 3 rear, 2 third

Engines available
4.0-liter V6 (210 hp); 4.6-liter V8 (239 hp)

Transmissions available
5-speed automatic

Fuel
Fuel type ....Regular
EPA city/highway, mpg 14/20
Fuel refill capacity, gal. 22.2

Dimensions and weight
Length, in. 190
Width, in. 72
Wheelbase, in. 114
Curb weight, lb. 4,515
Percent weight, front/rear 52/48
Typical towing ability, lb. 3,500

SAFETY INFORMATION

Active safety features
Antilock brakes ....Standard
Traction control ....Included with stability
Stability control ....Standard
Daytime running lights ....Not available
Tire pressure monitor ....Available

Safety belts
Center-rear belt 3-point
Pretensioners, front/rear ....Yes/no

Air bags
Occupant-sensing system ....Front
Side bags, front/rear ....No/no
Inflatable curtain ....Optional with rollover
Accident alert system ....Not available

Crash tests
Gov't front-crash test, driver/front passenger .... ◒/◒
Gov't side-crash test, driver/rear passenger .... ●/◒
IIHS offset crash test ....Good
IIHS side crash test w/ side & curtain airbags ....NA
IIHS side crash test w/o side & curtain airbags ....NA

FROM THE TEST TRACK

Tested model
2002 XLT 4-door SUV 4WD, 4.0-liter V6, 5-speed automatic

Tires as tested
Michelin Cross Terrain, size P235/70R16 104S

Acceleration ....○
0-30 mph, sec. 3.1
0-60 mph, sec. 9.3
Quarter mile, sec. 17.1
Quarter mile, mph. 81
45-65 mph, sec. 6.3

Other findings
Transmission ....◒
Turning circle, ft. 39
Ground clearance, in. 7.5

Braking and handling
Braking ....○
Braking, dry pavement, ft. 144
Routine handling ....○
Emergency handling ....◒
Avoidance maneuver, max. mph ..47.0

Convenience and comfort
Ride ....◒
Noise ....◒
Driving position ....◒
Access ....◒
Controls and displays ....◒
Fit and finish ....◒
Door top to ground, in. 63.0
Cargo area ....◒
Cargo volume, cu.ft. 45.5
Max. load, lb. 1,325

Seating
Front-seat comfort ....◒
Front shoulder room, in. 59.5
Front leg room, in. 41.5
Front head room, in. 3.0
Rear-seat comfort ....◒
Rear shoulder room, in. 58.5
Rear leg room, in. 29.0
Rear head room, in 4.5
Third-seat comfort ....◒
Third shoulder room,in 53.5
Third leg room, in. 27.5
Third head room, in 5.5

Fuel economy ....●
CU's overall mileage, mpg 16
CU's city/highway, mpg 11/23
CU's 150-mile trip, mpg 20
Annual fuel ....935 gal./$1,870
Cruising range 410

RELIABILITY HISTORY

TROUBLE SPOTS	Ford Explorer 4WD							
	97	98	99	00	01	02	03	04
Engine	○	○	○	○	◒	●	●	●
Cooling	○	○	◒	○	●	●	●	●
Fuel	○	○	○	○	◒	◒	●	●
Ignition	◒	◒	◒	◒	●	◒	●	●
Transmission	○	○	○	○	○	◒	◒	●
Electrical	○	●	◒	◒	◒	◒	◒	●
Air conditioning	●	◒	○	○	◒	◒	◒	●
Suspension	○	○	◒	○	◒	◒	●	●
Brakes	○	◒	◒	◒	◒	◒	●	●
Exhaust	○	○	○	○	◒	●	●	●
Paint/trim/rust	○	○	◒	○	○	◒	◒	●
Body integrity	○	○	○	○	○	○	○	●
Power equipment	○	○	◒	◒	○	◒	◒	●
Body hardware	○	○	○	○	○	◒	◒	●
RELIABILITY VERDICT	-	X	-	X	-	X	-	-

Expert • Independent • Nonprofit

Ford Explorer Sport Trac

CR RECOMMENDED ✓

The Sport Trac is essentially a crew-cab Ranger pickup. It mates a five-passenger cabin based on the previous-generation Explorer to a short cargo bed. Handling is secure and relatively responsive, but the ride is stiff and choppy. The V6 feels unrefined but is adequately powerful. The cargo box is big enough to handle medium loads and is made out of a tough rustproof plastic material. A powered rear window improves ventilation. A tip-up of the 2WD version in the government rollover test is a concern. Therefore, we recommend only the 4WD version. A redesign arrives in mid-2006.

THE EXPLORER SPORT TRAC LINE

Body style:
crew cab
Trim lines:
XLS, XLT, XLT
Premium, Adrenalin
Base price range:
$23,970-$31,240

REPORT CARD

○	Predicted reliability
◐	Owner satisfaction
◔	Predicted depreciation
○	Accident avoidance
○	Acceleration
◐	Ride
○	Front seat comfort
●	Fuel economy

SPECIFICATIONS

Drive wheels Rear or part-time 4WD

Seating 2 front, 3 rear

Engines available
4.0-liter V6 (210 hp)

Transmissions available
5-speed automatic

Fuel
Fuel type . . . . .Regular
EPA city/highway, mpg 15/20
Fuel refill capacity, gal. 23.0

Dimensions and weight
Length, in. 206
Width, in. 72
Wheelbase, in. 126
Curb weight, lb. 4,410
Percent weight, front/rear 56/44
Typical towing ability, lb. 5,100

SAFETY INFORMATION

Active safety features

Antilock brakes . . . . .Standard
Traction control . . . . .Not available
Stability control . . . . .Not available
Daytime running lights . . . . .Not available
Tire pressure monitor . . . . .Not available

Safety belts

Center-rear belt . . . . .Lap
Pretensioners, front/rear . . . . .No/no

Air bags

Occupant-sensing system . . . . .Not available
Side bags, front/rear . . . . .No/no
Inflatable curtain . . . . .Optional
Accident alert system .Not available

Crash tests

Gov't front-crash test, driver/front passenger . . . . . .NA/NA
Gov't side-crash test, driver/rear passenger . . . . .NA/NA
IIHS offset crash test . . . . .NA
IIHS side crash test w/ side & curtain airbags . . . . .NA
IIHS side crash test w/o side & curtain airbags . . . . .NA

FROM THE TEST TRACK

Tested model
2001 crew cab 4WD, 4.0-liter V6, 5-speed automatic

Tires as tested
Firestone Wilderness AT, size P235/75R15 105S

Acceleration . . . . ○
0-30 mph, sec. 3.2
0-60 mph, sec. 9.6
Quarter mile, sec. 17.4
Quarter mile, mph 79
45-65 mph, sec. .6.2

Other findings
Transmission . . . . ◐
Turning circle, ft. 45
Ground clearance, in. 7.5

Braking and handling
Braking . . . . ○
Braking, dry pavement, ft. 138
Routine handling . . . . ○
Emergency handling . . . . ○
Avoidance maneuver, max. mph . . .50.0

Convenience and comfort
Ride . . . . ◐
Noise . . . . ◐
Driving position . . . . ◐
Access . . . . ◐
Controls and displays . . . . ◐
Fit and finish . . . . ◐
Door top to ground, in. 62.5
Cargo area . . . . ◐
Max. load, lb. 1,190

Seating
Front-seat comfort . . . . ○
Front shoulder room, in. 57.0
Front leg room, in. 41.5
Front head room, in. 4.5
Rear-seat comfort . . . . ◐
Rear shoulder room, in. 57.0
Rear leg room, in. 28.0
Rear head room, in 4.0

Fuel economy . . . . ●
CU's overall mileage, mpg 15
CU's city/highway, mpg 10/21
CU's 150-mile trip, mpg 19
Annual fuel . . . . .985 gal./$1,970
Cruising range 360

RELIABILITY HISTORY

TROUBLE SPOTS	Ford Explorer Sport Trac							
	97	98	99	00	01	02	03	04
Engine					●	●	●	●
Cooling					●	●	●	●
Fuel					○	○	●	●
Ignition					●	●	●	●
Transmission					●	●	●	●
Electrical					○	◐	●	●
Air conditioning					●	●	●	●
Suspension					◐	◐	●	●
Brakes					○	○	●	●
Exhaust					●	●	●	●
Paint/trim/rust					●	◐	●	●
Body integrity					◐	◑	●	●
Power equipment					○	○	◐	●
Body hardware					◐	○	◐	●
RELIABILITY VERDICT					—	—	—	—

Ford F-150

THE F-150 LINE
Body style:
regular cab; extended cab; crew cab
Trim lines:
XL, STX, XLT, Lariat, FX4, King Ranch
Base price range:
$20,480-$39,555

The F-150 rides more comfortably, handles more nimbly, and has a quieter, better-trimmed interior than the previous version. New features include moveable overhead storage bins, a spring-assisted tailgate, and a power-opening rear-window center panel. The four-wheel-drive system is part-time only. The powertrain is not as smooth as that in the Toyota Tundra, but it delivered reasonable acceleration and fuel economy. Braking performance was just adequate, with long stops in our tests. First-year reliability of the 4WD version is below average. The 2WD version is average.

REPORT CARD

●	Predicted reliability
◓	Owner satisfaction
NA	Predicted depreciation
○	Accident avoidance
◓	Acceleration
○	Ride
◓	Front seat comfort
●	Fuel economy

SPECIFICATIONS

Drive wheels Rear or part-time 4WD

Seating 3 front, 3 rear

Engines available
4.2-liter V6 (202 hp); 4.6-liter V8 (231 hp); 5.4-liter V8 (300 hp)

Transmissions available
5-speed manual; 4-speed automatic

Fuel
Fuel type .... Regular
EPA city/highway, mpg 14/18
Fuel refill capacity, gal. 30.0

Dimensions and weight
Length, in. 224
Width, in. 79
Wheelbase, in. 139
Curb weight, lb. 5,690
Percent weight, front/rear 57/43
Typical towing ability, lb. 8,200

SAFETY INFORMATION

Active safety features
Antilock brakes .... Standard
Traction control .... Not available
Stability control .... Not available
Daytime running lights .... Not available
Tire pressure monitor .... Not available

Safety belts
Center-rear belt 3-point
Pretensioners, front/rear .... Yes/no

Air bags
Occupant-sensing system .... Front
Side bags, front/rear .... No/no
Inflatable curtain .... Not available
Accident alert system .... Not available

Crash tests
Gov't front-crash test, driver/front passenger ...... ◓/◓
Gov't side-crash test, driver/rear passenger ...... NA/NA
IIHS offset crash test .... Good
IIHS side crash test w/ side & curtain airbags .... NA
IIHS side crash test w/o side & curtain airbags .... NA

FROM THE TEST TRACK

Tested model
2004 XLT crew cab 4WD, 5.4-liter V8, 4-speed automatic

Tires as tested
General Ameritrac TR, size P255/70R17 110S

Acceleration .... ◓
0-30 mph, sec. 2.8
0-60 mph, sec. 8.3
Quarter mile, sec. 16.4
Quarter mile, mph 85
45-65 mph, sec. 5.6

Other findings
Transmission .... ◓
Turning circle, ft. 47
Ground clearance, in. 8.0

Braking and handling
Braking .... ○
Braking, dry pavement, ft. 149
Routine handling .... ○
Emergency handling .... ◓
Avoidance maneuver, max. mph 45.5

Convenience and comfort
Ride .... ○
Noise .... ◓
Driving position .... ◓
Access .... ◓
Controls and displays .... ◓
Fit and finish .... ◓
Door top to ground, in. 69.0
Cargo area .... ○
Max. load, lb. 1,510

Seating
Front-seat comfort .... ◓
Front shoulder room, in. 66.0
Front leg room, in. 40.0
Front head room, in. 5.0
Rear-seat comfort .... ◓
Rear shoulder room, in. 66.0
Rear leg room, in. 30.0
Rear head room, in 4.0

Fuel economy .... ●
CU's overall mileage, mpg 14
CU's city/highway, mpg 9/20
CU's 150-mile trip, mpg 16
Annual fuel .... 1,090 gal./$2,175
Cruising range 455

RELIABILITY HISTORY

TROUBLE SPOTS	Ford F-150 (new) 4WD							
	97	98	99	00	01	02	03	04
Engine								●
Cooling								●
Fuel								●
Ignition								●
Transmission								●
Electrical								●
Air conditioning								●
Suspension								●
Brakes								◒
Exhaust								●
Paint/trim/rust								●
Body integrity								◒
Power equipment								●
Body hardware								●
RELIABILITY VERDICT								✗

Expert • Independent • Nonprofit

Ford Five Hundred

THE FIVE HUNDRED LINE
Body style:
sedan
Trim lines:
SE, SEL, Limited
Base price range:
$22,145-$28,070

The Ford Five Hundred (and its twin, the Mercury Montego) is a roomy sedan that emphasizes comfort and good ergonomics over performance and style. It features an elevated seating position for good outward vision and cabin access. The rear seat is immense. Power comes from an underpowered and unpolished 3.0-liter V6 engine that is mated to either a six-speed automatic on front-wheel-drive models or a continuously variable transmission. The AWD model was somewhat sluggish at launch. The Five Hundred has a comfortable ride and handles with commendable agility considering its size.

REPORT CARD

New	Predicted reliability
New	Owner satisfaction
NA	Predicted depreciation
○	Accident avoidance
◐	Acceleration
◐	Ride
◐	Front seat comfort
○	Fuel economy

SPECIFICATIONS

Drive wheels Front or AWD

Seating 2 front, 3 rear

Engines available
3.0-liter V6 (203 hp)

Transmissions available
CVT; 6-speed automatic

Fuel
Fuel type ....Regular
EPA city/highway, mpg 21/29
Fuel refill capacity, gal. 19.0

Dimensions and weight
Length, in. 201
Width, in. 75
Wheelbase, in. 113
Curb weight, lb. 3,725
Percent weight, front/rear 60/40
Typical towing ability, lb. 1,000

SAFETY INFORMATION

Active safety features
Antilock brakes ....Standard
Traction control ....Standard
Stability control ....Not available
Daytime running lights ....Not available
Tire pressure monitor ....Not available

Safety belts
Center-rear belt 3-point
Pretensioners, front/rear ....Yes/no

Air bags
Occupant-sensing system ....Front
Side bags, front/rear ....Optional/no
Inflatable curtain ....Optional with rollover
Accident alert system ....Not available

Crash tests
Gov't front-crash test, driver/front passenger ......◐/◐
Gov't side-crash test, driver/rear passenger ......◐/◐
IIHS offset crash test ....NA
IIHS side crash test w/ side & curtain airbags ....NA
IIHS side crash test w/o side & curtain airbags ....NA

FROM THE TEST TRACK

Tested model
2005 SEL sedan, 3.0-liter V6, 6-speed automatic

Tires as tested
Continental ContiTouring Contact CT95, size P215/60R17 95T

Acceleration ....◐
0-30 mph, sec. 3.3
0-60 mph, sec. 8.7
Quarter mile, sec. 16.8
Quarter mile, mph 86
45-65 mph, sec. 5.9

Other findings
Transmission ....◐
Turning circle, ft. 41
Ground clearance, in. 5.0

Braking and handling
Braking ....○
Braking, dry pavement, ft. 147
Routine handling ....◐
Emergency handling ....○
Avoidance maneuver, max. mph ...49.5

Convenience and comfort
Ride ....◐
Noise ....◐
Driving position ....◐
Access ....◐
Controls and displays ....◐
Fit and finish ....◐
Door top to ground, in. 55.0
Trunk ....◐
Luggage capacity ....5+1
Max. load, lb. 950

Seating
Front-seat comfort ....◐
Front shoulder room, in. 58.0
Front leg room, in. 40.0
Front head room, in. 5.0
Rear-seat comfort ....◉
Rear shoulder room, in. 57.5
Rear leg room, in. 31.0
Rear head room, in 3.0

Fuel economy ....○
CU's overall mileage, mpg 21
CU's city/highway, mpg 14/31
CU's 150-mile trip, mpg 26
Annual fuel ......710 gal./$1,420
Cruising range 455

RELIABILITY HISTORY

TROUBLE SPOTS	97	98	99	00	01	02	03	04
Engine								
Cooling				NO				
Fuel								
Ignition								
Transmission				DATA				
Electrical								
Air conditioning				NEW				
Suspension								
Brakes				MODEL				
Exhaust								
Paint/trim/rust								
Body integrity								
Power equipment								
Body hardware								
RELIABILITY VERDICT								

● ◑ ○ ◐ ●
better ◄————► worse   See page 36 for more information.

Ford Focus

CR RECOMMENDED ✓

The Focus has an accomplished ride and good braking. It is agile, fun-to-drive, and handles like a sports car. The seating position is high and commanding, controls are clear and logical and cabin access is easy. The ride is firm, yet supple. Two new, more-refined engines, a 2.0-liter and a 2.3-liter from Mazda, improve acceleration, but fuel economy is not as impressive. Interior quality is still on the cheap side. The roomy wagon is a practical choice. Reliability has remained average. Overall crash protection is good, although it received a Poor rating in the IIHS side-impact-crash test without its optional side airbags.

THE FOCUS LINE
Body style:
2-door hatchback; 4-door hatchback; sedan; wagon
Trim lines:
ZX3 S, ZX3 SE, ZX3 SES, ZX5 S, ZX5 SE, ZX5 SES, ZX4 S, ZX4 SE, ZX4 SES, ZX4 ST, ZXW SE, ZXW SES
Base price range:
$13,315-$18,215

REPORT CARD

○	**Predicted reliability**
○	**Owner satisfaction**
◐	**Predicted depreciation**
◉	**Accident avoidance**
○	**Acceleration**
◐	**Ride**
◐	**Front seat comfort**
○	**Fuel economy**

SPECIFICATIONS

Drive wheels Front

Seating 2 front, 3 rear

Engines available
2.0-liter 4 (130 hp); 2.0-liter 4 (136 hp); 2.3-liter 4 (151 hp)

Transmissions available
5-speed manual; 4-speed automatic

Fuel
Fuel type ....Regular
EPA city/highway, mpg 26/32
Fuel refill capacity, gal. 14.0

Dimensions and weight
Length, in. 175
Width, in. 67
Wheelbase, in. 103
Curb weight, lb. 2,800
Percent weight, front/rear 61/39
Typical towing ability, lb. 1,185

SAFETY INFORMATION

Active safety features
Antilock brakes ....Optional (standard on ST)
Traction control ....Optional with ABS
Stability control ....Not available
Daytime running lights ....Not available
Tire pressure monitor ....Not available

Safety belts
Center-rear belt 3-point
Pretensioners, front/rear ....Yes/no

Air bags
Occupant-sensing system ....Front
Side bags, front/rear ....Optional/no
Inflatable curtain ....Not available
Accident alert system ....Not available

Crash tests
Gov't front-crash test, driver/front passenger ......◉/◐
Gov't side-crash test, driver/rear passenger ....○/◐
IIHS offset crash test ....Good
IIHS side crash test w/ side & curtain airbags ....NA
IIHS side crash test w/o side & curtain airbags ....Poor

FROM THE TEST TRACK

Tested model
2005 ZX4 SES sedan, 2.0-liter Four, 4-speed automatic

Tires as tested
Pirelli Four Seasons, size P205/50R16 87H

Acceleration ....○
0-30 mph, sec. 3.5
0-60 mph, sec. 10.1
Quarter mile, sec. 17.7
Quarter mile, mph 79
45-65 mph, sec. 6.2

Other findings
Transmission ....◐
Turning circle, ft. 37
Ground clearance, in. 5.5

Braking and handling
Braking ....◉
Braking, dry pavement, ft. 128
Routine handling ....◉
Emergency handling ....◐
Avoidance maneuver, max. mph 53.5

Convenience and comfort
Ride ....○
Noise ....○
Driving position ....◐
Access ....◐
Controls and displays ....◐
Fit and finish ....○
Door top to ground, in. 53.5
Trunk ....○
Luggage capacity ....4+0
Max. load, lb. 825

Seating
Front-seat comfort ....◐
Front shoulder room, in. 53.0
Front leg room, in. 39.0
Front head room, in. 5.0
Rear-seat comfort ....○
Rear shoulder room, in. 53.0
Rear leg room, in. 26.5
Rear head room, in 2.0
Fuel economy ....○
CU's overall mileage, mpg 24
  CU's city/highway, mpg 17/32
  CU's 150-mile trip, mpg 28
Annual fuel ....630 gal./$1,260
Cruising range 365

RELIABILITY HISTORY

TROUBLE SPOTS	Ford Focus Sedan							
	97	98	99	00	01	02	03	04
Engine				◐	◉	◉	◉	◉
Cooling				◉	◉	◐	◉	◉
Fuel				●	●	○	◉	◉
Ignition				○	○	◐	◉	◉
Transmission				◐	◐	◉	◐	◉
Electrical				◐	○	◐	◉	◉
Air conditioning				◐	◐	◐	◉	◉
Suspension				○	○	◐	◉	◉
Brakes				●	◐	○	○	◉
Exhaust				◉	◉	◐	◉	◉
Paint/trim/rust				◐	◐	◐	◉	◉
Body integrity				○	○	○	◐	◉
Power equipment				◐	○	◐	◐	◉
Body hardware				◐	○	○	◐	◉
RELIABILITY VERDICT	✗	✗	–	✓	✓			

Ford Freestar

THE FREESTAR LINE
Body style:
minivan
Trim lines:
S, SE, SES, SEL,
Limited
Base price range:
$23,910-$32,735

The Freestar minivan is an extensive freshening of the Windstar rather than a total redesign. Overall, it lags behind the competition and lacks any price advantage. The Freestar (and its Mercury Monterey twin) features a third-row seat that folds flat into the floor when not in use. The second-row seats are too low. Stability control is available. The engines are still noisy, and road noise is pronounced. Handling is more responsive, but the ride is unsettled. Fit and finish trails the class leaders. Crash-test results are impressive. First-year reliability has been average.

REPORT CARD

○	**Predicted reliability**
◐	**Owner satisfaction**
NA	**Predicted depreciation**
○	**Accident avoidance**
◐	**Acceleration**
○	**Ride**
◐	**Front seat comfort**
●	**Fuel economy**

SPECIFICATIONS

Drive wheels Front

Seating 2 front, 2 rear, 3 third

Engines available
3.9-liter V6 (193 hp); 4.2-liter V6 (201 hp)

Transmissions available
4-speed automatic

Fuel
Fuel type . . . . .Regular
EPA city/highway, mpg 17/23
Fuel refill capacity, gal. 26.0

Dimensions and weight
Length, in. 201
Width, in. 77
Wheelbase, in. .121
Curb weight, lb. 4,425
Percent weight, front/rear 59/41
Typical towing ability, lb. 3,500

SAFETY INFORMATION

Active safety features
Antilock brakes . . . . .Standard
Traction control . . . . .Included with stability
Stability control . . . . .Optional
Daytime running lights . . . . .Not available
Tire pressure monitor . . . . .Available

Safety belts
Center-rear belt 3-point
Pretensioners, front/rear . . . . .Yes/no

Air bags
Occupant-sensing system .Front
Side bags, front/rear . . . . .Optional/no
Inflatable curtain . . . . .Optional with rollover
Accident alert system . . . . .Not available

Crash tests
Gov't front-crash test, driver/front passenger . . . . . ◖●/◖●
Gov't side-crash test, driver/rear passenger . . . . . . ◐/◖●
IIHS offset crash test . . . . .Good
IIHS side crash test w/ side & curtain airbags . . . . .NA
IIHS side crash test w/o side & curtain airbags . . . . .NA

FROM THE TEST TRACK

Tested model
2004 SEL minivan, 4.2-liter V6, 4-speed automatic

Tires as tested
Uniroyal Tiger Paw AWP Nail Gard, size P235/60R16 99S

Acceleration . . . . ◐
0-30 mph, sec. 3.1
0-60 mph, sec. 9.2
Quarter mile, sec. 17.2
Quarter mile, mph 80
45-65 mph, sec. 5.9

Other findings
Transmission . . . . ◐
Turning circle, ft. 42
Ground clearance, in. 6.5

Braking and handling
Braking . . . . ◐
Braking, dry pavement, ft. 137
Routine handling . . . . ◐
Emergency handling . . . . ○
Avoidance maneuver, max. mph . . .48.5

Convenience and comfort
Ride . . . . ○
Noise . . . . ○
Driving position . . . . ◐
Access . . . . ◉
Controls and displays . . . . ◐
Fit and finish . . . . ○
Door top to ground, in. 62.0
Cargo area . . . . ○
Cargo volume, cu.ft. 61.5
Max. load, lb. 1,315

Seating
Front-seat comfort . . . . ◖
Front shoulder room, in. 61.0
Front leg room, in. 40.0
Front head room, in. 5.5
Rear-seat comfort . . . . ○
Rear shoulder room, in. 64.0
Rear leg room, in. 29.0
Rear head room, in 6.0
Third-seat comfort . . . . ●
Third shoulder room,in 49.5
Third leg room, in. 27.5
Third head room, in 5.0

Fuel economy . . . . ●
CU's overall mileage, mpg 17
  CU's city/highway, mpg 11/25
  CU's 150-mile trip, mpg 20
Annual fuel . . . . .910 gal./$1,815
Cruising range 495

RELIABILITY HISTORY

TROUBLE SPOTS	Ford Freestar							
	97	98	99	00	01	02	03	04
Engine								●
Cooling								●
Fuel								●
Ignition								●
Transmission								●
Electrical								◐
Air conditioning								●
Suspension								●
Brakes								●
Exhaust								●
Paint/trim/rust								●
Body integrity								◐
Power equipment								◐
Body hardware								◐
RELIABILITY VERDICT								–

● ◖ ○ ◐ ●
better ◄———► worse   See page 36 for more information.

Ford Freestyle

THE FREESTYLE LINE
Body style:
4-door SUV
Trim lines:
SE, SEL, Limited
Base price range:
$25,020-$30,420

This is a wagon version of the Ford Five Hundred sedan. Second- and third-row seats fold flat and offer room for six or seven, depending on the version. A three-row, head-protection curtain air-bag system is available, for protection in a rollover. Power comes from the same unpolished and over-taxed 3.0-liter, 203-hp V6 engine as in the Five Hundred and Mercury Montego. Ride and handling are good. Access and visibility are recommendable. The AWD model feels sluggish, and the engine drones. The Freestyle could potentially be a sensible alternative to a midsized SUV.

REPORT CARD

New	**Predicted reliability**
New	**Owner satisfaction**
NA	**Predicted depreciation**
NA	**Accident avoidance**
NA	**Acceleration**
NA	**Ride**
NA	**Front seat comfort**
NA	**Fuel economy**

SPECIFICATIONS

Drive wheels Front or AWD

Seating 2 front, 3 rear, 2 third

Engines available
3.0-liter V6 (203 hp)

Transmissions available
CVT; 6-speed automatic

Fuel
Fuel type .... Regular
EPA city/highway, mpg 19/24
Fuel refill capacity, gal. 19.0

Dimensions and weight
Length, in. 200
Width, in. 74
Wheelbase, in. 113
Curb weight, lb. 4,280
Percent weight, front/rear 55/45
Typical towing ability, lb. 2,000

SAFETY INFORMATION

Active safety features
Antilock brakes .... Standard
Traction control .... Standard
Stability control .... Not available
Daytime running lights .... Not available
Tire pressure monitor .... Not available

Safety belts
Center-rear belt 3-point
Pretensioners, front/rear .... Yes/no

Air bags
Occupant-sensing system .... Front
Side bags, front/rear .... Optional/no
Inflatable curtain .... Optional with rollover
Accident alert system .... Not available

Crash tests
Gov't front-crash test, driver/front passenger ...... ◐/◐
Gov't side-crash test, driver/rear passenger .... ◐/◐
IIHS offset crash test .... NA
IIHS side crash test w/ side & curtain airbags .... NA
IIHS side crash test w/o side & curtain airbags .... NA

ANOTHER LOOK

RELIABILITY HISTORY

TROUBLE SPOTS	97 98 99 00 01 02 03 04
Engine	
Cooling	
Fuel	NO
Ignition	
Transmission	DATA
Electrical	
Air conditioning	NEW
Suspension	
Brakes	MODEL
Exhaust	
Paint/trim/rust	
Body integrity	
Power equipment	
Body hardware	
RELIABILITY VERDICT	

Ford Fusion

The Fusion is a new midsized sedan that will go on sale this fall. It is a sibling of the upcoming Lincoln Zephyr and Mercury Milan, and all three are based on the Mazda6 platform. The Fusion and larger Five Hundred will become Ford's mainstream sedan offerings. They will replace the Taurus, which is being phased out. The Fusion comes with either a 160-hp, 2.3-liter four-cylinder or a 210-hp, 3.0-liter V6. The fold-flat rear seats use the spring-assist feature found in the Mazda6. In 2006 an all-wheel drive turbo model arrives, and future plans include a hybrid version.

THE FUSION LINE

Body style:
sedan
Trim lines:
–
Base price range:
$19,000-$25,000E

REPORT CARD

New	Predicted reliability
New	Owner satisfaction
NA	Predicted depreciation
NA	Accident avoidance
NA	Acceleration
NA	Ride
NA	Front seat comfort
NA	Fuel economy

SPECIFICATIONS

Drive wheels Front

Seating 2 front, 3 rear

Engines available
2.3-liter 4 (160 hp); 3.0-liter V6 (210 hp)

Transmissions available
5-speed manual; 5-speed automatic; 6-speed automatic

Fuel
Fuel type . . . . .Regular
EPA city/highway, mpg . . . . .NA
Fuel refill capacity, gal. 18.0

Dimensions and weight
Length, in. 190
Width, in. 72
Wheelbase, in. 107
Curb weight, lb. 3,280
Percent weight, front/rear 61/39
Typical towing ability, lb. 1,000

SAFETY INFORMATION

Active safety features
Antilock brakes . . . . .Optional
Traction control . . . . .Optional
Stability control .Not available
Daytime running lights . . . . .Not available
Tire pressure monitor . . . . .Not available

Safety belts
Center-rear belt 3-point
Pretensioners, front/rear . . . . .Yes/no

Air bags
Occupant-sensing system . . . . .Front
Side bags, front/rear .Optional/no
Inflatable curtain . . . . .Optional
Accident alert system .Not available

Crash tests
Gov't front-crash test, driver/front passenger . . . . . .NA/NA
Gov't side-crash test, driver/rear passenger . . . . . . .NA/NA
IIHS offset crash test . . . . .NA
IIHS side crash test w/ side & curtain airbags . . . . .NA
IIHS side crash test w/o side & curtain airbags . . . . .NA

RELIABILITY HISTORY

TROUBLE SPOTS	97 98 99 00 01 02 03 04
Engine	
Cooling	NO
Fuel	
Ignition	
Transmission	DATA
Electrical	
Air conditioning	NEW
Suspension	
Brakes	MODEL
Exhaust	
Paint/trim/rust	
Body integrity	
Power equipment	
Body hardware	
RELIABILITY VERDICT	

ANOTHER LOOK

● ● ○ ◖ ●
better ◄——► worse   See page 36 for more information.

Ford Mustang

THE MUSTANG LINE
Body style:
convertible; coupe
Trim lines:
Deluxe, Premium, GT
Deluxe, GT Premium
Base price range:
$19,145-$30,550

The new Mustang incorporates the look of Mustangs past and replaces an outdated design. Power comes from either a coarse 4.0-liter, 210-hp V6 or a muscular 4.6-liter, 300-hp V8. The latter is very quick and sounds inspiring. The manual shifter works well. The suspension still features a live rear axle rather than an independent rear setup. The ride is a bit stiff. Handling is fairly nimble but lacks finesse at the limits. Fit and finish of the retro-look interior is unimpressive. The convertible version features a well-insulated, power-operated top. The body is fairly free of quiver over rough roads.

REPORT CARD

New	Predicted reliability
New	Owner satisfaction
NA	Predicted depreciation
◒	Accident avoidance
◒	Acceleration
○	Ride
◓	Front seat comfort
◒	Fuel economy

SPECIFICATIONS

Drive wheels Rear

Seating 2 front, 2 rear

Engines available
4.0-liter V6 (210 hp); 4.6-liter V8 (300 hp)

Transmissions available
5-speed manual; 5-speed automatic

Fuel
Fuel type . . . . .Regular
EPA city/highway, mpg 17/25
Fuel refill capacity, gal. 16.0

Dimensions and weight
Length, in. 188
Width, in. 74
Wheelbase, in. 107
Curb weight, lb. 3,585
Percent weight, front/rear 53/47
Typical towing ability, lb. 1,000

SAFETY INFORMATION

Active safety features

Antilock brakes . . . . .Standard (optional on Base)
Traction control . . . . .Standard (optional on Base)
Stability control . . . . .Not available
Daytime running lights . . . . .Not available
Tire pressure monitor . . . . .Not available

Safety belts

Center-rear belt . . . . .NA
Pretensioners, front/rear . . . . .Yes/no

Air bags

Occupant-sensing system . . . . .Front
Side bags, front/rear . . . . .Optional/no
Inflatable curtain . . . . .Not available
Accident alert system . . . . .Not available

Crash tests

Gov't front-crash test, driver/front passenger . . . . . .◒/◒
Gov't side-crash test, driver/rear passenger . . . .◓/NA
IIHS offset crash test . . . . .NA
IIHS side crash test w/ side & curtain airbags . . . . .NA
IIHS side crash test w/o side & curtain airbags . . . . .NA

FROM THE TEST TRACK

Tested model
2005 GT Premium coupe, 4.6-liter V8, 5-speed manual

Tires as tested
Pirelli PZero Nero, size P235/55R17 98W

Acceleration . . . .◒
0-30 mph, sec. 2.2
0-60 mph, sec. 5.5
Quarter mile, sec. 14.2
Quarter mile, mph 100
45-65 mph, sec. 4.1

Other findings
Transmission . . . .◓
Turning circle, ft. 39
Ground clearance, in. 4.5

Braking and handling
Braking . . . .◓
Braking, dry pavement, ft. 131
Routine handling . . . .◓
Emergency handling . . . .◓
Avoidance maneuver, max. mph . . .55.0

Convenience and comfort
Ride . . . .○
Noise . . . .○
Driving position . . . .◓
Access . . . .○
Controls and displays . . . .◓
Fit and finish . . . .○
Door top to ground, in. 47.5
Trunk . . . .◓
Luggage capacity . . . . .2+1
Max. load, lb. 720

Seating
Front-seat comfort . . . .◓
Front shoulder room, in. 55.5
Front leg room, in. 40.5
Front head room, in. 5.0
Rear-seat comfort . . . .●
Rear shoulder room, in. 52.5
Rear leg room, in. 23.5
Rear head room, in 0.0

Fuel economy . . . .◒
CU's overall mileage, mpg 20
CU's city/highway, mpg 15/28
CU's 150-mile trip, mpg 23
Annual fuel . . . . .735 gal./$1,475
Cruising range 330

RELIABILITY HISTORY

TROUBLE SPOTS	97 98 99 00 01 02 03 04
Engine	
Cooling	
Fuel	NO
Ignition	
Transmission	DATA
Electrical	
Air conditioning	NEW
Suspension	
Brakes	MODEL
Exhaust	
Paint/trim/rust	
Body integrity	
Power equipment	
Body hardware	
RELIABILITY VERDICT	

Ford Ranger

The Ranger received some minor styling changes over the years, but underneath it's the same vehicle. The Ranger and its clone, the Mazda B-Series, never let you forget you're driving a truck. Handling is fairly responsive, but the ride is stiff and choppy. The 3.0-liter V6 is pleasant enough and adequately powerful. The extended-cab models offer two small, rear-hinged doors, but the rear-seat area is fit for cargo only. The front seats are thinly padded and mounted too low. The Explorer Sport Trac is a crew-cab version of the Ranger.

THE RANGER LINE
Body style:
regular cab; extended cab
Trim lines:
XL, Edge, STX, XLT, FX4
Base price range:
$14,425-$26,465

REPORT CARD

○	Predicted reliability
●	Owner satisfaction
○	Predicted depreciation
NA	Accident avoidance
NA	Acceleration
NA	Ride
NA	Front seat comfort
NA	Fuel economy

SPECIFICATIONS

Drive wheels Rear or part-time 4WD

Seating 3 front, 2 rear

Engines available
2.3-liter 4 (143 hp); 3.0-liter V6 (148 hp); 4.0-liter V6 (207 hp)

Transmissions available
5-speed manual; 5-speed automatic

Fuel
Fuel type . . . . .Regular
EPA city/highway, mpg 15/19
Fuel refill capacity, gal. 20.0

Dimensions and weight
Length, in. 202
Width, in. 70
Wheelbase, in. 126
Curb weight, lb. 3,870
Percent weight, front/rear 60/40
Typical towing ability, lb. 3,180

SAFETY INFORMATION

Active safety features
Antilock brakes . . . . .Standard
Traction control . . . . .Not available
Stability control . . . . .Not available
Daytime running lights . . . . .Not available
Tire pressure monitor . . . . .Not available

Safety belts
Center-rear belt . . . . .NA
Pretensioners, front/rear . . . . .Yes/no

Air bags
Occupant-sensing system . . . . .Not available
Side bags, front/rear . . . . .No/no
Inflatable curtain . . . . .Not available
Accident alert system .Not available

Crash tests
Gov't front-crash test, driver/front passenger . . . . . . ◒/◒
Gov't side-crash test, driver/rear passenger . . . .◒/NA
IIHS offset crash test . . . . .Acceptable
IIHS side crash test w/ side & curtain airbags . . . . .NA
IIHS side crash test w/o side & curtain airbags . . . . .NA

ANOTHER LOOK

RELIABILITY HISTORY

TROUBLE SPOTS	Ford Ranger 4WD							
	97	98	99	00	01	02	03	04
Engine	○	○	○	○	◒	◒	●	●
Cooling	◒	◒	○	◒	◒	◒	●	◒
Fuel	◒	○	○	◒	◒	◒	●	◒
Ignition	○	○	○	◒	○	◒	●	●
Transmission	○	○	○	○	○	●	◒	◒
Electrical	●	●	◒	○	○	○	◒	○
Air conditioning	◒	○	○	◒	○	●	●	●
Suspension	●	◒	◒	◒	○	◒	●	●
Brakes	◒	○	●	●	○	◒	●	◒
Exhaust	○	◒	○	◒	◒	◒	◒	◒
Paint/trim/rust	◒	◒	◒	◒	◒	◒	◒	◒
Body integrity	◒	○	◒	◒	◒	◒	◒	●
Power equipment	◒	◒	○	◒	○	◒	●	●
Body hardware	◒	◒	○	○	○	●	◒	◒
RELIABILITY VERDICT	✗	−	−	−	✗	✗	✓	✗

Ford Taurus

CR RECOMMENDED ✓

The current Taurus dates back to 1996 and is showing its age. It's roomy, with a decent ride and a spacious rear seat and trunk. Handling is sound but not agile, and braking distances were long. The optional 3.0-liter, 201-hp V6, which we prefer to the base V6, performs adequately, but it is nowhere near as responsive or quiet as those from Honda, Nissan, or Toyota. The interior is bland. The wagon offers a small third-row seat. However, its days are numbered, as its Mercury Sable twin has been discontinued. A smaller sedan called the Fusion and the larger Five Hundred will eventually replace the Taurus.

THE TAURUS LINE

Body style:
sedan; wagon
Trim lines:
SE, SEL
Base price range:
$20,935-$23,690

REPORT CARD

○	Predicted reliability
◒	Owner satisfaction
●	Predicted depreciation
○	Accident avoidance
◒	Acceleration
◒	Ride
◒	Front seat comfort
○	Fuel economy

SPECIFICATIONS

Drive wheels Front

Seating 3 front, 3 rear, 2 third

Engines available
3.0-liter V6 (153 hp); 3.0-liter V6 (201 hp)

Transmissions available
4-speed automatic

Fuel
Fuel type . . . . .Regular
EPA city/highway, mpg 20/27
Fuel refill capacity, gal. 18.0

Dimensions and weight
Length, in. 198
Width, in. 73
Wheelbase, in. 109
Curb weight, lb. 3,325
Percent weight, front/rear 64/36
Typical towing ability, lb. 1,750

SAFETY INFORMATION

Active safety features

Antilock brakes . . . . .Optional
Traction control . . . . .Optional
Stability control .Not available
Daytime running lights . . . . .Not available
Tire pressure monitor . . . . .Not available

Safety belts

Center-rear belt 3-point
Pretensioners, front/rear . . . . .Yes/no

Air bags

Occupant-sensing system .Front
Side bags, front/rear . . . . .Optional/no
Inflatable curtain .Not available
Accident alert system . . . . .Not available

Crash tests

Gov't front-crash test, driver/front passenger . . . . . ◒/◐
Gov't side-crash test, driver/rear passenger . . . .○/○
IIHS offset crash test . . . . .Good
IIHS side crash test w/ side & curtain airbags . . . . .NA
IIHS side crash test w/o side & curtain airbags . . . . .NA

FROM THE TEST TRACK

Tested model
2004 SES sedan, 3.0-liter V6, 4-speed automatic

Tires as tested
Continental TouringContact AS, size P215/60R16 94T

Acceleration . . . . ◒
0-30 mph, sec. 3.2
0-60 mph, sec. 8.3
Quarter mile, sec. 16.4
Quarter mile, mph 88
45-65 mph, sec. 4.9

Other findings
Transmission . . . . ◒
Turning circle, ft. 42
Ground clearance, in. 5.5

Braking and handling
Braking . . . . ◒
Braking, dry pavement, ft. 154
Routine handling . . . . ◒
Emergency handling . . . .○
Avoidance maneuver, max. mph . . .48.5

Convenience and comfort
Ride . . . . ◒
Noise . . . .○
Driving position . . . . ◒
Access . . . . ◒
Controls and displays . . . . ◒
Fit and finish . . . .○
Door top to ground, in. 51.0
Trunk . . . . ◒
Luggage capacity . . . . .5+0
Max. load, lb. 1,100

Seating
Front-seat comfort . . . . ◒
Front shoulder room, in. 58.0
Front leg room, in. 41.5
Front head room, in. 6.5
Rear-seat comfort . . . . ◒
Rear shoulder room, in. 57.0
Rear leg room, in. 30.5
Rear head room, in 3.0

Fuel economy . . . . ○
CU's overall mileage, mpg 22
CU's city/highway, mpg 15/31
CU's 150-mile trip, mpg 26
Annual fuel . . . . .680 gal./$1,360
Cruising range 445

RELIABILITY HISTORY

TROUBLE SPOTS	Ford Taurus Sedan							
	97	98	99	00	01	02	03	04
Engine	○	○	○	○	○	◒	○	○
Cooling	○	○	○	◒	◒	◒	◒	◒
Fuel	○	○	○	○	◒	◒	◒	○
Ignition	◒	◒	○	◒	◒	◒	◒	◒
Transmission	◒	○	○	○	○	○	○	○
Electrical	●	●	◒	◒	◒	○	○	○
Air conditioning	○	○	○	○	○	◒	○	○
Suspension	○	○	◒	○	○	○	◒	○
Brakes	◒	●	●	●	◒	○	○	◒
Exhaust	◒	○	◒	◒	○	◒	○	◒
Paint/trim/rust	○	◒	◒	◒	◒	◒	○	◒
Body integrity	○	○	○	○	◒	◒	◒	◒
Power equipment	◒	○	○	○	○	○	◒	◒
Body hardware	○	○	○	◒	◒	○	◒	○
RELIABILITY VERDICT	–	–	–	–	–	–	–	–

Ford Thunderbird

CR RECOMMENDED ✓

After decades spent as a big, mundane coupe, the Thunderbird was reinvented for 2002 as a retro-revival two-seater. The rear-wheel-drive chassis is shared with the Lincoln LS and Jaguar S-Type. It's powered by a strong 280-hp, 3.9-liter V8 with a smooth-shifting automatic. While the car accelerates quickly and steers well, it isn't particularly sporty. The ride is supple but slightly floaty, and body flex is pronounced. Head room is meager. The power soft top is easy to operate, but the heavy optional hard top takes two people to install and remove. This is the last year for the T-Bird.

THE THUNDERBIRD LINE

Body style:
convertible
Trim lines:
Deluxe, Premium
Base price range:
$37,895-$38,940

REPORT CARD

○	Predicted reliability
⊖	Owner satisfaction
⊖	Predicted depreciation
⊖	Accident avoidance
◉	Acceleration
○	Ride
⊖	Front seat comfort
●	Fuel economy

SPECIFICATIONS

Drive wheels Rear

Seating 2 front

Engines available
3.9-liter V8 (280 hp)

Transmissions available
5-speed automatic

Fuel
Fuel type .... Premium
EPA city/highway, mpg 17/23
Fuel refill capacity, gal. 18.0

Dimensions and weight
Length, in. .... .186
Width, in. .... .72
Wheelbase, in. .... .107
Curb weight, lb. 3,905
Percent weight, front/rear 52/48
Typical towing ability, lb. 1,000

SAFETY INFORMATION

Active safety features
Antilock brakes .... Standard
Traction control .... Standard
Stability control .... Not available
Daytime running lights .... Not available
Tire pressure monitor .... Not available

Safety belts
Center-rear belt .... NA
Pretensioners, front/rear .... Yes/NA

Air bags
Occupant-sensing system .... Not available
Side bags, front/rear .... Standard/NA
Inflatable curtain .... Not available
Accident alert system .... Not available

Crash tests
Gov't front-crash test, driver/front passenger ..... ⊖/◑
Gov't side-crash test, driver/rear passenger .... ◑/NA
IIHS offset crash test .... NA
IIHS side crash test w/ side & curtain airbags .... NA
IIHS side crash test w/o side & curtain airbags .... NA

FROM THE TEST TRACK

Tested model
2002 Premium convertible, 3.9-liter V8, 5-speed automatic

Tires as tested
Michelin Pilot HX MXM4, size P235/50R17 95V

Acceleration .... ◉
0-30 mph, sec. 2.7
0-60 mph, sec. 7.3
Quarter mile, sec. 15.6
Quarter mile, mph .... .92
45-65 mph, sec. 4.5

Other findings
Transmission .... ◉
Turning circle, ft. .... .38
Ground clearance, in. 5.0

Braking and handling
Braking .... ◉
Braking, dry pavement, ft. .... .126
Routine handling .... ⊖
Emergency handling .... ○
Avoidance maneuver, max. mph 53.5

Convenience and comfort
Ride .... ○
Noise .... ○
Driving position .... ○
Access .... ○
Controls and displays .... ⊖
Fit and finish .... ⊖
Door top to ground, in. 46.5
Trunk .... ●
Luggage capacity .... .1+0
Max. load, lb. 455

Seating
Front-seat comfort .... ⊖
Front shoulder room, in. 57.5
Front leg room, in. 40.5
Front head room, in. 2.0

Fuel economy .... ●
CU's overall mileage, mpg .... .17
  CU's city/highway, mpg 12/25
  CU's 150-mile trip, mpg .... .21
Annual fuel .... .870 gal./$1,915
Cruising range .... .345

RELIABILITY HISTORY

TROUBLE SPOTS	Ford Thunderbird							
	97	98	99	00	01	02	03	04
Engine	⊖					◑	◑	
Cooling	●					◑	◑	
Fuel	○					◑	◑	
Ignition	⊖					◑	◑	
Transmission	⊖					◑	◑	
Electrical	○					◑	◑	
Air conditioning	⊖					◑	◑	
Suspension	○					◑	◑	
Brakes	◑					◑	◑	
Exhaust	⊖					◑	◑	
Paint/trim/rust	○				○	◑		
Body integrity	⊖				○	●		
Power equipment	◑					◑	◑	
Body hardware	○				○	◑		
RELIABILITY VERDICT	−					✓	−	

Insufficient data

better ◀—▶ worse
● ◉ ○ ⊖ ●   See page 36 for more information.

GMC Envoy

THE ENVOY LINE
Body style:
4-door SUV
Trim lines:
SLE, SLT, XL, Denali
Base price range:
$28,525-$40,235

Available in both five- and seven-passenger (XL) body styles, the Envoy has an absorbant low-speed ride. However, overall it falls short due to sloppy handling, uncomfortable seats, ill-fitting trim, and too much wind noise. The 275-hp engine needs to be revved to supply thrust, and it averaged a dismal 13 mpg in the long-wheelbase XL and 15 in the standard-length model. Off-roading is not a strength. The annoying seat-mounted front safety belts are hard to reach. The important crash-test results are unimpressive. The XUV, which featured a sliding rear roof, will end in March 2005.

REPORT CARD

●	Predicted reliability
◒	Owner satisfaction
○	Predicted depreciation
○	Accident avoidance
◒	Acceleration
○	Ride
○	Front seat comfort
●	Fuel economy

SPECIFICATIONS

Drive wheels Rear or selectable 4WD

Seating 2 front, 3 rear, 2 third

Engines available
4.2-liter 6 (275 hp); 5.3-liter V8 (300 hp)

Transmissions available
4-speed automatic

Fuel
Fuel type . . . . .Regular
EPA city/highway, mpg 15/21
Fuel refill capacity, gal. 22.0

Dimensions and weight
Length, in. 192
Width, in. 75
Wheelbase, in. .113
Curb weight, lb. 4,660
Percent weight, front/rear 54/46
Typical towing ability, lb. 6,100

SAFETY INFORMATION

Active safety features
Antilock brakes . . . . .Standard
Traction control . . . . .Standard on 2WD
Stability control . . . . .Not available
Daytime running lights .Standard
Tire pressure monitor . . . . .Not available

Safety belts
Center-rear belt 3-point
Pretensioners, front/rear . . . . .No/no

Air bags
Occupant-sensing system . . . . .Not available
Side bags, front/rear . . . . .No/no
Inflatable curtain . . . . .Optional
Accident alert system . . . . .Available

Crash tests
Gov't front-crash test, driver/front passenger . . . ○/◑
Gov't side-crash test, driver/rear passenger . . . . . ●/◑
IIHS offset crash test . . . . .Marginal
IIHS side crash test w/ side & curtain airbags . . . . .NA
IIHS side crash test w/o side & curtain airbags . . . . .NA

FROM THE TEST TRACK

Tested model
2002 SLE 4-door SUV 4WD, 4.2-liter Six, 4-speed automatic

Tires as tested
Michelin Cross Terrain, size P245/65R17 105S

Acceleration . . . .◒
0-30 mph, sec. 3.0
0-60 mph, sec. 8.3
Quarter mile, sec. 16.4
Quarter mile, mph 85
45-65 mph, sec. 5.7

Other findings
Transmission . . . .◒
Turning circle, ft. 39
Ground clearance, in. 7.0

Braking and handling
Braking . . . .○
Braking, dry pavement, ft. 152
Routine handling . . . .○
Emergency handling . . . .◒
Avoidance maneuver, max. mph . . .47.0

Convenience and comfort
Ride . . . .○
Noise . . . .◒
Driving position . . . .◒
Access . . . .◒
Controls and displays . . . .◒
Fit and finish . . . .○
Door top to ground, in. 64.0
Cargo area . . . .○
Cargo volume, cu.ft. 39.0
Max. load, lb. 1,090

Seating
Front-seat comfort . . . .○
Front shoulder room, in. 59.0
Front leg room, in. 41.0
Front head room, in. 5.5
Rear-seat comfort . . . .◒
Rear shoulder room, in. 59.0
Rear leg room, in. 27.5
Rear head room, in. 4.0

Fuel economy . . . .●
CU's overall mileage, mpg 15
CU's city/highway, mpg 10/22
CU's 150-mile trip, mpg 19
Annual fuel . . . . .1,005 gal./$2,010
Cruising range 315

RELIABILITY HISTORY

TROUBLE SPOTS	GMC Envoy							
	97	98	99	00	01	02	03	04
Engine						◒	●	●
Cooling						●	●	●
Fuel						◒	●	●
Ignition						◒	●	●
Transmission						◑	●	◒
Electrical						●	○	○
Air conditioning						◒	●	○
Suspension						◒	◒	●
Brakes						◒	●	●
Exhaust						●	●	●
Paint/trim/rust						◒	●	◒
Body integrity						◒	◑	◒
Power equipment						◑	◒	◒
Body hardware						○	○	◒
RELIABILITY VERDICT						✗	✗	✗

GMC Yukon

CR RECOMMENDED ✓

T he Yukon is a full-sized SUV that offers impressive towing capability and a smooth, quiet ride—at low speeds. The V8s feel strong. The Yukon can accommodate nine passengers. There is very little cargo space behind its cramped third-row seat. Handling is vague and imprecise. Braking performance is unimpressive. Models with 4WD have a selectable system that can remain engaged indefinitely. All models have standard ESC, which has prevented tip-ups in the government test. Look for a redesign to arrive in 2006.

THE YUKON LINE
Body style:
4-door SUV
Trim lines:
SLE, SLT, Denali
Base price range:
$36,405-$50,285

REPORT CARD

○	Predicted reliability
⊖	Owner satisfaction
⊖	Predicted depreciation
○	Accident avoidance
⊖	Acceleration
○	Ride
⊖	Front seat comfort
●	Fuel economy

SPECIFICATIONS

Drive wheels Rear, selectable 4WD, or AWD

Seating 3 front, 3 rear, 3 third

Engines available
4.8-liter V8 (285 hp); 5.3-liter V8 (295 hp); 6.0-liter V8 (335 hp)

Transmissions available
4-speed automatic

Fuel
Fuel type ....Regular
EPA city/highway, mpg 14/18
Fuel refill capacity, gal. 26.0

Dimensions and weight
Length, in. 199
Width, in. 79
Wheelbase, in. 116
Curb weight, lb. 5,505
Percent weight, front/rear 52/48
Typical towing ability, lb. 7,600

SAFETY INFORMATION

Active safety features
Antilock brakes ....Standard
Traction control ....Standard
Stability control ....Standard
Daytime running lights ....Standard
Tire pressure monitor ....Available

Safety belts
Center-rear belt 3-point
Pretensioners, front/rear ....No/no

Air bags
Occupant-sensing system ....Front
Side bags, front/rear ....Optional/no
Inflatable curtain ....Not available
Accident alert system ....Available

Crash tests
Gov't front-crash test, driver/front passenger ....⊖/⊖
Gov't side-crash test, driver/rear passenger ....NA/NA
IIHS offset crash test ....NA
IIHS side crash test w/ side & curtain airbags ....NA
IIHS side crash test w/o side & curtain airbags ....NA

FROM THE TEST TRACK

Tested model
2002 Chevrolet Tahoe LT 4-door SUV 4WD, 5.3-liter V8, 4-speed automatic

Tires as tested
Firestone Wilderness LE, size P265/70R16 111S

Acceleration ....⊖
0-30 mph, sec. 3.3
0-60 mph, sec. 8.7
Quarter mile, sec. 16.7
Quarter mile, mph 85
45-65 mph, sec. 5.6

Other findings
Transmission ....●
Turning circle, ft. 42
Ground clearance, in. 8.5

Braking and handling
Braking ....⊖
Braking, dry pavement, ft. 152
Routine handling ....○
Emergency handling ....⊖
Avoidance maneuver, max. mph ...44.5

Convenience and comfort
Ride ....○
Noise ....⊖
Driving position ....⊖
Access ....⊖
Controls and displays ....⊖
Fit and finish ....○
Door top to ground, in. 67.0
Cargo area ....⊖
Cargo volume, cu.ft. 59.0
Max. load, lb. 1,395

Seating
Front-seat comfort ....⊖
Front shoulder room, in. 65.0
Front leg room, in. 40.5
Front head room, in. 5.0
Rear-seat comfort ....●
Rear shoulder room, in. 65.0
Rear leg room, in. 29.5
Rear head room, in 4.5
Third-seat comfort ....●
Third shoulder room,in 63.5
Third leg room, in. 28.5
Third head room, in. 0.0

Fuel economy ....●
CU's overall mileage, mpg 13
CU's city/highway, mpg 9/19
CU's 150-mile trip, mpg 17
Annual fuel ....1,120 gal./$2,240
Cruising range 405

RELIABILITY HISTORY

TROUBLE SPOTS	GMC Yukon							
	97	98	99	00	01	02	03	04
Engine	⊖	○	○	⊖	●	●	●	●
Cooling	●	⊖	○	●	●	●	●	●
Fuel	⊖	⊖	○	●	●	●	●	●
Ignition	⊖	⊖	○	⊖	⊖	●	●	●
Transmission	⊖	○	○	○	⊖	●	●	⊖
Electrical	●	●	●	○	○	○	●	○
Air conditioning	⊖	○	○	○	⊖	⊖	●	●
Suspension	⊖	○	○	⊖	●	●	●	●
Brakes	●	●	●	⊖	○	⊖	●	●
Exhaust	⊖	○	○	○	●	●	●	●
Paint/trim/rust	⊖	○	○	●	●	●	●	●
Body integrity	○	○	○	○	⊖	●	●	⊖
Power equipment	○	○	○	⊖	○	⊖	●	●
Body hardware	○	○	○	⊖	⊖	●	●	●
RELIABILITY VERDICT	✗	✗	✗	–	–	–	–	–

Honda Accord

CR RECOMMENDED ✓

THE ACCORD LINE
Body style:
coupe; sedan
Trim lines:
DX, LX, EX, Hybrid
Base price range:
$16,295-$30,140

The Accord is our Top Pick family sedan. Handling is fairly agile, and the ride is steady and compliant. The cabin is roomy, and controls are intuitive. A telescoping steering column facilitates an ideal driving position. The Accord is quiet, though less so than the Toyota Camry and VW Passat because of some road noise. The automatic shifts very smoothly and responsively. The four-cylinder engine is smoother than many V6s. Curtain air bags are standard. The V6 model is very quick and relatively fuel-efficient. The hybrid version is even quicker and gets 25 mpg. Crash-test results are impressive.

REPORT CARD

⊖	Predicted reliability
⊙	Owner satisfaction
⊖	Predicted depreciation
⊙	Accident avoidance
⊙	Acceleration
⊖	Ride
⊙	Front seat comfort
⊖	Fuel economy

SPECIFICATIONS

Drive wheels Front

Seating 2 front, 3 rear

Engines available
2.4-liter 4 (160 hp); 3.0-liter V6 (240 hp); 3.0-liter V6 hybrid (255 hp)

Transmissions available
5-speed manual; 6-speed manual; 5-speed automatic

Fuel
Fuel type .... Regular
EPA city/highway, mpg 29/37
Fuel refill capacity, gal. 17.1

Dimensions and weight
Length, in. .... .190
Width, in. .... .72
Wheelbase, in. .... .108
Curb weight, lb. 3,475
Percent weight, front/rear 62/38
Typical towing ability, lb. 1,000

SAFETY INFORMATION

Active safety features
Antilock brakes .... .Standard
Traction control .... .Standard on V6
Stability control .... .Not available
Daytime running lights .... .Not available
Tire pressure monitor .... .Not available

Safety belts
Center-rear belt 3-point
Pretensioners, front/rear .... .Yes/no

Air bags
Occupant-sensing system .... .Side
Side bags, front/rear .... .Standard/no
Inflatable curtain .... .Standard
Accident alert system .... .Not available

Crash tests
Gov't front-crash test, driver/front passenger ...... ⊙/⊙
Gov't side-crash test, driver/rear passenger .... ⊖/⊖
IIHS offset crash test .... .Good
IIHS side crash test w/ side & curtain airbags .... .Good
IIHS side crash test w/o side & curtain airbags .... .NA

FROM THE TEST TRACK

Tested model
2005 Hybrid sedan, 3.0-liter V6 hybrid, 5-speed automatic

Tires as tested
Michelin Energy MXV4, P215/60R16 94V

Acceleration .... ⊙
0-30 mph, sec. 2.6
0-60 mph, sec. 6.9
Quarter mile, sec. 15.6
Quarter mile, mph .... .93
45-65 mph, sec. 4.5

Other findings
Transmission .... ⊖
Turning circle, ft. .... .39
Ground clearance, in. 5.0

Braking and handling
Braking .... ⊙
Braking, dry pavement, ft. .... .130
Routine handling .... ⊖
Emergency handling .... ⊖
Avoidance maneuver, max. mph ...52.0

Convenience and comfort
Ride .... ⊖
Noise .... ⊖
Driving position .... ⊙
Access .... ⊖
Controls and displays .... ⊙
Fit and finish .... ⊙
Door top to ground, in. 51.0
Trunk .... ⊖
Luggage capacity .... .3+1
Max. load, lb. 850

Seating
Front-seat comfort .... ⊙
Front shoulder room, in. 57.0
Front leg room, in. 42.0
Front head room, in. 3.0
Rear-seat comfort .... ⊖
Rear shoulder room, in. 55.5
Rear leg room, in. 30.5
Rear head room, in 3.5

Fuel economy
CU's overall mileage, mpg .... .25
CU's city/highway, mpg 18/37
CU's 150-mile trip, mpg .... .29
Annual fuel .... .590 gal./$1,180
Cruising range .... .460

RELIABILITY HISTORY

TROUBLE SPOTS	Honda Accord V6							
	97	98	99	00	01	02	03	04
Engine								
Cooling								
Fuel								
Ignition								
Transmission								
Electrical								
Air conditioning								
Suspension								
Brakes								
Exhaust								
Paint/trim/rust								
Body integrity								
Power equipment								
Body hardware								
RELIABILITY VERDICT	✓	✓	✓	✓	✓	✓	✓	✓

Expert • Independent • Nonprofit

Honda CR-V

CR RECOMMENDED ✓

THE CR-V LINE
Body style:
4-door SUV
Trim lines:
LX, EX, SE
Base price range:
$20,195–$25,250

This is one of the best car-based SUVs on the market. The ride is supple and controlled. The steering feel is good and handling is secure. Stability control, side and curtain air bags, and ABS are standard for 2005. The 2.4-liter four-cylinder is more energetic, refined, and economical than the V6s of some competitors. The five-speed automatic transmission is very smooth and responsive. The rear seat is roomy. Road noise is a bit pronounced. The cargo floor folds out to double as a picnic table. The rear gate swings open to the side and the window can be opened separately. Crash-test results are impressive.

REPORT CARD

◉	Predicted reliability
⊖	Owner satisfaction
◉	Predicted depreciation
○	Accident avoidance
○	Acceleration
⊖	Ride
⊖	Front seat comfort
○	Fuel economy

SPECIFICATIONS

Drive wheels Front or AWD

Seating 2 front, 3 rear

Engines available
2.4-liter 4 (160 hp)

Transmissions available
5-speed manual; 5-speed automatic

Fuel
Fuel type ....Regular
EPA city/highway, mpg 22/27
Fuel refill capacity, gal. 15.3

Dimensions and weight
Length, in. 179
Width, in. 70
Wheelbase, in. 103
Curb weight, lb. 3,375
Percent weight, front/rear 55/45
Typical towing ability, lb. 1,500

SAFETY INFORMATION

Active safety features
Antilock brakes ....Standard
Traction control ....Standard
Stability control ....Standard
Daytime running lights ....Not available
Tire pressure monitor ....Not available

Safety belts
Center-rear belt 3-point
Pretensioners, front/rear ....Yes/no

Air bags
Occupant-sensing system ....Side
Side bags, front/rear ....Standard/no
Inflatable curtain ....Standard with rollover
Accident alert system ....Not available

Crash tests
Gov't front-crash test, driver/front passenger ...... ◉/◉
Gov't side-crash test, driver/rear passenger ...... ◉/◉
IIHS offset crash test ....Good
IIHS side crash test w/ side & curtain airbags ....Good
IIHS side crash test w/o side & curtain airbags ....NA

FROM THE TEST TRACK

Tested model
2002 EX 4-door SUV AWD, 2.4-liter Four, 4-speed automatic

Tires as tested
Bridgestone Dueler H/T 684, size P205/70R15 95S

Acceleration ....○
0-30 mph, sec. 3.4
0-60 mph, sec. 9.6
Quarter mile, sec. 17.6
Quarter mile, mph 78
45-65 mph, sec. 6.1

Other findings
Transmission ....●
Turning circle, ft. 37
Ground clearance, in. 6.5

Braking and handling
Braking ....⊖
Braking, dry pavement, ft. 135
Routine handling ....⊖
Emergency handling ....○
Avoidance maneuver, max. mph ...48.5

Convenience and comfort
Ride ....⊖
Noise ....⊖
Driving position ....⊖
Access ....⊖
Controls and displays ....⊖
Fit and finish ....⊖
Door top to ground, in. 60.0
Cargo area ....○
Cargo volume, cu.ft. 32.0
Max. load, lb. 850

Seating
Front-seat comfort ....⊖
Front shoulder room, in. 57.0
Front leg room, in. 40.0
Front head room, in. 4.5
Rear-seat comfort ....⊖
Rear shoulder room, in. 56.5
Rear leg room, in. 30.0
Rear head room, in 4.0

Fuel economy ....○
CU's overall mileage, mpg 21
CU's city/highway, mpg 15/27
CU's 150-mile trip, mpg 24
Annual fuel ....715 gal./$1,430
Cruising range 340

RELIABILITY HISTORY

TROUBLE SPOTS	Honda CR-V							
	97	98	99	00	01	02	03	04
Engine	◉	◉	◉	◉	◉	◉	◉	◉
Cooling	◉	◉	◉	◉	◉	◉	◉	◉
Fuel	◉	○	◉	◉	◉	◉	◉	◉
Ignition	◉	◉	◉	◉	◉	◉	◉	◉
Transmission	◉	◉	◉	◉	◉	◉	◉	◉
Electrical	○	◉	◉	◉	◉	◉	◉	◉
Air conditioning	◉	◉	◉	◉	◉	◉	◉	◉
Suspension	◉	◉	◉	◉	◉	◉	◉	◉
Brakes	⊖	◉	⊖	◉	◉	◉	◉	◉
Exhaust	◉	◉	◉	◉	◉	◉	◉	◉
Paint/trim/rust	◉	○	◉	◉	◉	◉	◉	◉
Body integrity	◉	◉	◉	◉	◉	◉	◉	◉
Power equipment	◉	◉	◉	◉	◉	◉	◉	◉
Body hardware	◉	◉	◉	◉	◉	◉	◉	◉
RELIABILITY VERDICT	✓	✓	✓	✓	✓	✓	✓	✓

● ◐ ○ ⊖ ● better ◄———► worse   See page 36 for more information.

Honda Civic

CR RECOMMENDED ✓

Good performance, fuel economy, and interior space help make the Civic one of the better small sedans. The standard 1.7-liter, 115-hp four-cylinder and the EX's 127-hp version are sprightly. The HX has a fuel-efficient, lean-burn engine. The automatic works very well. Handling is fairly nimble, though not quite as agile as the Ford Focus or Mazda3. The ride is a bit too firm, and road noise is pronounced. Good crash-test results are a plus. The Si drives similarly despite its 160-hp engine. The Hybrid model is slower and averaged 36 mpg in CR tests with the CVT. A redesign arrives in the fall.

THE CIVIC LINE
Body style:
2-door hatchback; coupe; sedan
Trim lines:
DX, VP, HX, LX, EX, Si, SE, Hybrid
Base price range:
$13,260-$19,900

REPORT CARD

◉	Predicted reliability
⊖	Owner satisfaction
○	Predicted depreciation
⊖	Accident avoidance
○	Acceleration
○	Ride
⊖	Front seat comfort
⊖	Fuel economy

SPECIFICATIONS

Drive wheels Front

Seating 2 front, 3 rear

Engines available
1.3-liter 4 hybrid (93 hp); 1.7-liter 4 (115 hp); 1.7-liter 4 (117 hp); 1.7-liter 4 (127 hp); 2.0-liter 4 (160 hp)

Transmissions available
5-speed manual; CVT; 4-speed automatic

Fuel
Fuel type .... Regular
EPA city/highway, mpg 31/38
Fuel refill capacity, gal. 13.2

Dimensions and weight
Length, in. 175
Width, in. 68
Wheelbase, in. 103
Curb weight, lb. 2,645
Percent weight, front/rear 61/39
Typical towing ability, lb. .... NR

SAFETY INFORMATION

Active safety features
Antilock brakes .... Std. on EX, Si, SE, Hybrid
Traction control .... Not available
Stability control .... Not available
Daytime running lights .... Not available
Tire pressure monitor .... Not available

Safety belts
Center-rear belt 3-point
Pretensioners, front/rear .... Yes/no

Air bags
Occupant-sensing system .... Side
Side bags, front/rear .... Optional/no
Inflatable curtain .... Not available
Accident alert system .... Not available

Crash tests
Gov't front-crash test, driver/front passenger ..... ◐/◕
Gov't side-crash test, driver/rear passenger .... ◑/◔
IIHS offset crash test .... Good
IIHS side crash test w/ side & curtain airbags .... NA
IIHS side crash test w/o side & curtain airbags .... NA

FROM THE TEST TRACK

Tested model
2005 EX sedan, 1.7-liter Four, 4-speed automatic

Tires as tested
Bridgestone Potenza RE92, size 195/60R15 87H

Acceleration .... ○
0-30 mph, sec. 3.8
0-60 mph, sec. 10.5
Quarter mile, sec. 18.1
Quarter mile, mph 78
45-65 mph, sec. 6.4

Other findings
Transmission .... ⊖
Turning circle, ft. 39
Ground clearance, in. 4.5

Braking and handling
Braking .... ⊖
Braking, dry pavement, ft. 129
Routine handling .... ⊖
Emergency handling .... ○
Avoidance maneuver, max. mph ... 51.0

Convenience and comfort
Ride .... ○
Noise .... ○
Driving position .... ⊖
Access .... ⊖
Controls and displays .... ◉
Fit and finish .... ⊖
Door top to ground, in. 50.0
Trunk .... ○
Luggage capacity .... 3+2
Max. load, lb. 850

Seating
Front-seat comfort .... ⊖
Front shoulder room, in. 52.5
Front leg room, in. 41.5
Front head room, in. 3.0
Rear-seat comfort .... ○
Rear shoulder room, in. 52.0
Rear leg room, in. 28.0
Rear head room, in 2.0

Fuel economy .... ⊖
CU's overall mileage, mpg 29
  CU's city/highway, mpg 21/40
  CU's 150-mile trip, mpg 35
Annual fuel .... 510 gal./$1,020
Cruising range 425

RELIABILITY HISTORY

TROUBLE SPOTS	Honda Civic							
	97	98	99	00	01	02	03	04
Engine	◉	◉	◉	◉	◉	◉	◉	◉
Cooling	◉	◉	◐	◉	◉	◐	◉	◉
Fuel	◐	◐	◐	◉	◉	◉	◉	◉
Ignition	◉	◉	◐	◐	◉	◉	◉	◉
Transmission	◐	◉	◉	◐	◉	◉	◐	◉
Electrical	◐	◐	◐	◐	◐	◐	◐	◐
Air conditioning	◐	◉	◐	◉	◉	◉	◉	◉
Suspension	◉	◉	◐	◐	◐	◉	◉	◉
Brakes	◐	◐	◐	◑	◐	◐	◉	◐
Exhaust	○	○	○	◐	◐	◉	◉	◉
Paint/trim/rust	◐	◐	◐	◐	◉	◐	◉	◉
Body integrity	○	◐	◐	◐	○	○	◐	◐
Power equipment	◐	◐	◐	◐	◉	◉	◉	◉
Body hardware	◐	◐	◐	◐	◉	◉	◐	◉
RELIABILITY VERDICT	✓	✓	✓	✓	✓	✓	✓	✓

Honda Element

CR RECOMMENDED ✓

This boxy, small SUV shares underpinnings with the CR-V. Handling is responsive, but the ride is very choppy and road noise is pronounced. The large roof pillars compromise visibility. There's no center roof pillar between the front and rear-hinged rear doors, so opening both creates a wide path for loading and unloading cargo. The spacious interior has a plastic-covered floor that's easy to wash. All four seats can fold back flat, making a bed of sorts. The rear seats can fold up against the side or be removed. a Overall crash protection is ok, although it received a Poor rating in the IIHS side-impact-crash test.

THE ELEMENT LINE
Body style:
4-door SUV
Trim lines:
LX, EX
Base price range:
$17,450-$20,925

REPORT CARD

◓	Predicted reliability
◓	Owner satisfaction
NA	Predicted depreciation
⊖	Accident avoidance
○	Acceleration
⊖	Ride
⊖	Front seat comfort
⊖	Fuel economy

SPECIFICATIONS

Drive wheels Front or AWD

Seating 2 front, 2 rear

Engines available
2.4-liter 4 (160 hp)

Transmissions available
5-speed manual; 4-speed automatic

Fuel
Fuel type ....Regular
EPA city/highway, mpg 21/24
Fuel refill capacity, gal. 15.9

Dimensions and weight
Length, in. 169
Width, in. 72
Wheelbase, in. 101
Curb weight, lb. 3,560
Percent weight, front/rear 55/45
Typical towing ability, lb. 1,500

SAFETY INFORMATION

Active safety features
Antilock brakes ....Std. on EX; NA on LX
Traction control ....Not available
Stability control ....Not available
Daytime running lights ....Not available
Tire pressure monitor ....Not available

Safety belts
Center-rear belt ....NA
Pretensioners, front/rear ....Yes/no

Air bags
Occupant-sensing system ....Side
Side bags, front/rear ....Optional/no
Inflatable curtain ....Not available
Accident alert system ....Not available

Crash tests
Gov't front-crash test, driver/front passenger .....◔/◒
Gov't side-crash test, driver/rear passenger .....◔/◒
IIHS offset crash test ....Good
IIHS side crash test w/ side & curtain airbags ....NA
IIHS side crash test w/o side & curtain airbags ....Poor

FROM THE TEST TRACK

Tested model
2003 EX 4-door SUV AWD, 2.4-liter Four, 4-speed automatic

Tires as tested
Goodyear Wrangler HP, size P215/70R16 99S

Acceleration ....○
0-30 mph, sec. 3.6
0-60 mph, sec. 10.5
Quarter mile, sec. 18.0
Quarter mile, mph 78
45-65 mph, sec. 6.7

Other findings
Transmission ....◓
Turning circle, ft. 37
Ground clearance, in. 6.0

Braking and handling
Braking ....⊖
Braking, dry pavement, ft. 134
Routine handling ....⊖
Emergency handling ....○
Avoidance maneuver, max. mph 50.5

Convenience and comfort
Ride ....⊖
Noise ....⊖
Driving position ....○
Access ....⊖
Controls and displays ....⊖
Fit and finish ....⊖
Door top to ground, in. 63.5
Cargo area ....⊖
Cargo volume, cu.ft. 47.0
Max. load, lb. 675

Seating
Front-seat comfort ....⊖
Front shoulder room, in. 57.0
Front leg room, in. 41.5
Front head room, in. 8.5
Rear-seat comfort ....○
Rear shoulder room, in. 52.0
Rear leg room, in. 34.5
Rear head room, in 3.0

Fuel economy ....⊖
CU's overall mileage, mpg 20
CU's city/highway, mpg 14/26
CU's 150-mile trip, mpg 24
Annual fuel ....750 gal./$1,500
Cruising range 345

RELIABILITY HISTORY

TROUBLE SPOTS	Honda Element	
	97 98 99 00 01 02	03 04
Engine		◓ ◓
Cooling		◓ ◓
Fuel		◓ ◓
Ignition		◓ ◓
Transmission		◓ ◓
Electrical		◓ ◓
Air conditioning		◓ ◓
Suspension		◓ ◓
Brakes		◓ ◓
Exhaust		◓ ◓
Paint/trim/rust		◓ ◓
Body integrity		○ ○
Power equipment		◓ ◓
Body hardware		◑ ◑
RELIABILITY VERDICT		✓ ✓

● ◓ ○ ⊖ ●
better ◄————► worse See page 36 for more information.

Honda Insight

The Insight is a two-seat gasoline/electric hybrid that is a true fuel miser; we managed 51 mpg in mixed driving with a five-speed manual model. Unfortunately, the Insight sacrifices a lot for its superior fuel economy. It rides stiffly, handles less than nimbly, and has a very noisy cabin. The battery pack hogs a lot of trunk space. The 1.0-liter, three-cylinder gasoline engine is coupled with an electric motor that provides extra power when needed. In turn, the gas engine recharges the batteries while the car is driven. The four-door Honda Civic Hybrid and the Toyota Prius are more-practical hybrid choices.

THE INSIGHT LINE

Body style:
2-door hatchback
Trim lines:
–

Base price range:
$19,330

REPORT CARD

NA	**Predicted reliability**
NA	**Owner satisfaction**
⊖	**Predicted depreciation**
⊖	**Accident avoidance**
⊜	**Acceleration**
⊜	**Ride**
⊖	**Front seat comfort**
●	**Fuel economy**

SPECIFICATIONS

Drive wheels Front

Seating 2 front

Engines available
1.0-liter 3 hybrid (73 hp)

Transmissions available
5-speed manual; CVT

Fuel
Fuel type . . . . .Regular
EPA city/highway, mpg 61/66
Fuel refill capacity, gal. 10.6

Dimensions and weight
Length, in. 155
Width, in. 67
Wheelbase, in. .95
Curb weight, lb. 1,875
Percent weight, front/rear 60/40
Typical towing ability, lb. . . . . .NR

SAFETY INFORMATION

Active safety features
Antilock brakes . . . . .Standard
Traction control . . . . .Not available
Stability control . . . . .Not available
Daytime running lights . . . . .Not available
Tire pressure monitor . . . . .Not available

Safety belts
Center-rear belt . . . . .NA
Pretensioners, front/rear .Yes/NA

Air bags
Occupant-sensing system . . . . .Not available
Side bags, front/rear . . . . .No/NA
Inflatable curtain . . . . .Not available
Accident alert system . . . . .Not available

Crash tests
Gov't front-crash test, driver/front passenger . . . . . .⊖/⊖
Gov't side-crash test, driver/rear passenger . . . .⊖/NA
IIHS offset crash test . . . . .NA
IIHS side crash test w/ side & curtain airbags . . . . .NA
IIHS side crash test w/o side & curtain airbags . . . . .NA

FROM THE TEST TRACK

Tested model
2000 2-door hatchback, 1.0-liter Three, 5-speed manual

Tires as tested
Bridgestone Potenza RE92, size P165/65R14 78S

Acceleration . . . . ⊜
0-30 mph, sec. 3.8
0-60 mph, sec. 11.2
Quarter mile, sec. 18.4
Quarter mile, mph 75
45-65 mph, sec. 7.9

Other findings
Transmission . . . .○
Turning circle, ft. 34
Ground clearance, in. 5.0

Braking and handling
Braking . . . . ⊖
Braking, dry pavement, ft. 132
Routine handling . . . .○
Emergency handling . . . .○
Avoidance maneuver, max. mph . . .52.0

Convenience and comfort
Ride . . . . ⊜
Noise . . . . ⊜
Driving position . . . .○
Access . . . .○
Controls and displays . . . . ⊖
Fit and finish . . . . ⊖
Door top to ground, in. 46.5
Trunk . . . . ●
Luggage capacity . . . . .2+1
Max. load, lb. 365

Seating
Front-seat comfort . . . . ⊖
Front shoulder room, in. 49.5
Front leg room, in. 41.5
Front head room, in. 3.5

Fuel economy . . . . ●
CU's overall mileage, mpg 51
CU's city/highway, mpg 36/66
CU's 150-mile trip, mpg 61
Annual fuel . . . . 295 gal./$590
Cruising range 620

RELIABILITY HISTORY

TROUBLE SPOTS	Honda Insight							
	97	98	99	00	01	02	03	04
Engine				●				
Cooling				●				
Fuel			○					
Ignition				●				
Transmission			●	●				
Electrical			○	●				
Air conditioning					Insufficient data	Insufficient data	Insufficient data	Insufficient data
Suspension				●				
Brakes				●				
Exhaust				●				
Paint/trim/rust				●				
Body integrity			○					
Power equipment			⊖					
Body hardware			⊖					
RELIABILITY VERDICT			✓					

Expert ● Independent ● Nonprofit

Honda Odyssey

CR RECOMMENDED ✓

THE ODYSSEY LINE
Body style:
minivan
Trim lines:
LX, EX, Touring
Base price range:
$25,195-$34,695

The redesigned Odyssey is our Top Pick minivan. In our most recent test, it outscored the Toyota Sienna by a small margin. It has improved interior flexibility, and fit and finish. The third row folds into the floor in sections. The cabin features many well-designed details. Road noise has been reduced. Handling is agile and precise, and the ride is supple and steady. The V6 is smooth, punchy, and quiet. The engine in the high-end models imperceptibly shuts off three cylinders when cruising in order to save fuel. Overall this is a very slick vehicle that is every bit as capable as a midluxury sedan.

REPORT CARD

⊖	Predicted reliability
⊖	Owner satisfaction
NA	Predicted depreciation
⊖	Accident avoidance
⊖	Acceleration
⊖	Ride
◉	Front seat comfort
◐	Fuel economy

SAFETY INFORMATION

Active safety features

Antilock brakes	Standard
Traction control	Standard
Stability control	Standard
Daytime running lights	Not available
Tire pressure monitor	Available

Safety belts

Center-rear belt	3-point
Pretensioners, front/rear	Yes/no

Air bags

Occupant-sensing system	Front and Side
Side bags, front/rear	Standard/no
Inflatable curtain	Standard with rollover
Accident alert system	Not available

Crash tests

Gov't front-crash test, driver/front passenger	◉/◉
Gov't side-crash test, driver/rear passenger	◉/◉
IIHS offset crash test	NA
IIHS side crash test w/ side & curtain airbags	NA
IIHS side crash test w/o side & curtain airbags	NA

SPECIFICATIONS

Drive wheels Front

Seating 2 front, 3 rear, 3 third

Engines available
3.5-liter V6 (255 hp)

Transmissions available
5-speed automatic

Fuel

Fuel type	Regular
EPA city/highway, mpg	20/28
Fuel refill capacity, gal.	21.0

Dimensions and weight

Length, in.	201
Width, in.	77
Wheelbase, in.	118
Curb weight, lb.	4,615
Percent weight, front/rear	55/45
Typical towing ability, lb.	3,500

FROM THE TEST TRACK

Tested model
2005 EX minivan, 3.5-liter V6, 5-speed automatic

Tires as tested
Michelin Energy LX4, size 235/65R16 103T

Acceleration ⊖

0-30 mph, sec.	3.3
0-60 mph, sec.	8.6
Quarter mile, sec.	16.9
Quarter mile, mph	84
45-65 mph, sec.	5.3

Other findings

Transmission	◉
Turning circle, ft.	40
Ground clearance, in.	5.0

Braking and handling

Braking	⊖
Braking, dry pavement, ft.	136
Routine handling	⊖
Emergency handling	⊖
Avoidance maneuver, max. mph	50.0

Convenience and comfort

Ride	⊖
Noise	⊖
Driving position	⊖
Access	◉
Controls and displays	⊖
Fit and finish	⊖
Door top to ground, in.	62.0
Cargo area	⊖
Cargo volume, cu.ft.	66.5
Max. load, lb.	1,320

Seating

Front-seat comfort	◉
Front shoulder room, in.	62.5
Front leg room, in.	41.5
Front head room, in.	4.5
Rear-seat comfort	◉
Rear shoulder room, in.	62.0
Rear leg room, in.	31.0
Rear head room, in	5.5
Third-seat comfort	○
Third shoulder room, in	54.0
Third leg room, in.	28.0
Third head room, in	2.0

Fuel economy ◐

CU's overall mileage, mpg	19
CU's city/highway, mpg	12/28
CU's 150-mile trip, mpg	23
Annual fuel	805 gal./$1,605
Cruising range	450

RELIABILITY HISTORY

TROUBLE SPOTS	Honda Odyssey							
	97	98	99	00	01	02	03	04
Engine	◉	◉	◉	◉	◉	◉	◉	◉
Cooling	◉	◉	◉	◉	◉	◉	◉	◉
Fuel	◉	◉	◉	◉	◉	◉	◉	◉
Ignition	⊖	◉	◉	◉	◉	◉	◉	◉
Transmission	◉	◉	○	◉	○	○	◉	◉
Electrical	◉	⊖	⊖	◉	◉	◉	◉	◉
Air conditioning	◉	◉	◉	◉	◉	◉	◉	◉
Suspension	◉	◉	◉	◉	◉	◉	◉	◉
Brakes	○	◐	○	○	○	◉	◉	◉
Exhaust	◉	◉	◉	◉	◉	◉	◉	◉
Paint/trim/rust	⊖	⊖	⊖	◉	◉	◉	◉	◉
Body integrity	⊖	⊖	○	○	○	⊖	⊖	⊖
Power equipment	⊖	⊖	◐	⊖	◉	◉	◉	◉
Body hardware	⊖	⊖	◐	⊖	◉	◉	◉	◉
RELIABILITY VERDICT	✓	✓	–	✓	–	✓	✓	✓

Honda Pilot

CR RECOMMENDED ✓

The Pilot combines the best of a wagon, SUV, and minivan at an affordable price, and is our Top Pick SUV for this price bracket. It has V6 similar to that of the Acura MDX and shares its full-time AWD system. The engine is smooth and quiet, and it delivers respectable fuel economy. A comfortable ride and secure handling are assets. Although quiet overall, road noise was pronounced. The standard split third-row seat folds flat, creating ample cargo space. Access is easy, and fit and finish is impeccable. Crash-test results are impressive. Stability control is standard on the EX with leather.

THE PILOT LINE
Body style:
4-door SUV
Trim lines:
LX, EX, EX-L
Base price range:
$27,550–$32,320

REPORT CARD

◖	Predicted reliability
◑	Owner satisfaction
NA	Predicted depreciation
◖	Accident avoidance
◖	Acceleration
◖	Ride
◖	Front seat comfort
●	Fuel economy

SPECIFICATIONS

Drive wheels AWD

Seating 2 front, 3 rear, 3 third

Engines available
3.5-liter V6 (255 hp)

Transmissions available
5-speed automatic

Fuel
Fuel type . . . . Regular
EPA city/highway, mpg 17/22
Fuel refill capacity, gal. 20.4

Dimensions and weight
Length, in. 188
Width, in. 78
Wheelbase, in. .107
Curb weight, lb. 4,535
Percent weight, front/rear 55/45
Typical towing ability, lb. 3,500

SAFETY INFORMATION

Active safety features
Antilock brakes . . . . .Standard
Traction control . . . . .Standard
Stability control . . . . .Standard on EX-L
Daytime running lights . . . . .Not available
Tire pressure monitor . . . . .Available

Safety belts
Center-rear belt 3-point
Pretensioners, front/rear . . . . .Yes/no

Air bags
Occupant-sensing system . . . . .Front and Side
Side bags, front/rear . . . . .Standard/no
Inflatable curtain . . . . .Not available
Accident alert system .Not available

Crash tests
Gov't front-crash test, driver/front passenger . . . . . ◑/◑
Gov't side-crash test, driver/rear passenger . . . . ◑/◑
IIHS offset crash test . . . . .Good
IIHS side crash test w/ side & curtain airbags . . . . .NA
IIHS side crash test w/o side & curtain airbags . . . . .NA

FROM THE TEST TRACK

Tested model
2005 EX-L 4-door SUV AWD, 3.5-liter V6, 5-speed automatic

Tires as tested
Goodyear Integrity, size P235/70R16 104S

Acceleration . . . . ◖
0-30 mph, sec. 3.2
0-60 mph, sec. 8.2
Quarter mile, sec. 16.5
Quarter mile, mph 85
45-65 mph, sec. 5.2

Other findings
Transmission . . . . ●
Turning circle, ft. 40
Ground clearance, in. 5.0

Braking and handling
Braking . . . . ◖
Braking, dry pavement, ft. 131
Routine handling . . . . ◖
Emergency handling . . . . ○
Avoidance maneuver, max. mph . . .48.0

Convenience and comfort
Ride . . . . ◖
Noise . . . . ◖
Driving position . . . . ◖
Access . . . . ●
Controls and displays . . . . ●
Fit and finish . . . . ●
Door top to ground, in. 53.0
Cargo area . . . . ◖
Cargo volume, cu.ft. 42.5
Max. load, lb. 1,320

Seating
Front-seat comfort . . . . ◖
Front shoulder room, in. 61.0
Front leg room, in. 41.0
Front head room, in. 7.5
Rear-seat comfort . . . . ◖
Rear shoulder room, in. 61.0
Rear leg room, in. 29.0
Rear head room, in 6.0
Third-seat comfort . . . . ◐
Third shoulder room,in 58.5
Third leg room, in. 24.5
Third head room, in 2.5

Fuel economy . . . . ●
CU's overall mileage, mpg 17
  CU's city/highway, mpg 12/25
  CU's 150-mile trip, mpg 20
Annual fuel . . . . .875 gal./$1,750
Cruising range 385

RELIABILITY HISTORY

TROUBLE SPOTS	Honda Pilot							
	97	98	99	00	01	02	03	04
Engine							●	●
Cooling							●	●
Fuel							●	◑
Ignition							●	●
Transmission							●	●
Electrical							◐	◐
Air conditioning							●	●
Suspension							●	●
Brakes							●	●
Exhaust							●	●
Paint/trim/rust							●	●
Body integrity							◐	◐
Power equipment							●	●
Body hardware							◐	●
RELIABILITY VERDICT							✓	✓

Honda Ridgeline

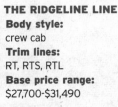

THE RIDGELINE LINE
Body style:
crew cab
Trim lines:
RT, RTS, RTL
Base price range:
$27,700-$31,490

The Ridgeline, Honda's first pickup truck, is a crew-cab based on the Honda Pilot. Unlike traditional pickups, the ride is supple and steady, and handling is quite agile. It includes a five-foot-long cargo bed that's made from a composite material and has no wheel arch intrusion. The cab is roomy and the rear seats flip up to create storage space. Below the cargo bed is an all-weather, lockable trunk. The tailgate can open two ways: down and sideways. Towing is rated at 5,000 pounds, and payload is a generous 1,500 pounds. The AWD system is permanent and lacks a low range. Stability control is standard.

REPORT CARD

New	**Predicted reliability**
New	**Owner satisfaction**
NA	**Predicted depreciation**
NA	**Accident avoidance**
NA	**Acceleration**
NA	**Ride**
NA	**Front seat comfort**
NA	**Fuel economy**

SPECIFICATIONS

Drive wheels AWD

Seating 2 front, 3 rear

Engines available
3.5-liter V6 (255 hp)

Transmissions available
5-speed automatic

Fuel
Fuel type ....Regular
EPA city/highway, mpg 16/21
Fuel refill capacity, gal. 22.0

Dimensions and weight
Length, in. 207
Width, in. 76
Wheelbase, in. 122
Curb weight, lb. 4,490
Percent weight, front/rear 58/42
Typical towing ability, lb. 5,000

SAFETY INFORMATION

Active safety features
Antilock brakes ....Standard
Traction control ....Standard
Stability control ....Standard
Daytime running lights ....Not available
Tire pressure monitor ....Available

Safety belts
Center-rear belt 3-point
Pretensioners, front/rear ....Yes/no

Air bags
Occupant-sensing system ....Side
Side bags, front/rear ....Standard/no
Inflatable curtain ....Standard
Accident alert system ....Not available

Crash tests
Gov't front-crash test, driver/front passenger ......NA/NA
Gov't side-crash test, driver/rear passenger ....NA/NA
IIHS offset crash test ....NA
IIHS side crash test w/ side & curtain airbags ....NA
IIHS side crash test w/o side & curtain airbags ....NA

ANOTHER LOOK

RELIABILITY HISTORY

TROUBLE SPOTS	97 98 99 00 01 02 03 04
Engine	
Cooling	NO
Fuel	
Ignition	
Transmission	DATA
Electrical	
Air conditioning	NEW
Suspension	
Brakes	MODEL
Exhaust	
Paint/trim/rust	
Body integrity	
Power equipment	
Body hardware	
RELIABILITY VERDICT	

better ●◐○◑● worse   See page 36 for more information.

Honda S2000

THE S2000 LINE
Body style:
convertible
Trim lines:
–

Base price range:
$33,150

This rear-drive roadster is an uncompromising sports car, with a relatively small four-cylinder engine that delivers an impressive 240 hp without turbo- or supercharging. It's complemented by a crisp-shifting six-speed manual transmission. The engine feels exhilarating when stretched but a bit ordinary in normal driving. Displacement grew to 2.2-liters for 2004, which might help engine flexibility. Handling is precise, and tire grip is outstanding. The ride, however, is hard and noisy, which can get tiresome in everyday driving. The power top is easy to operate. A glass rear window is standard.

REPORT CARD

○	Predicted reliability
◉	Owner satisfaction
⊖	Predicted depreciation
NA	Accident avoidance
NA	Acceleration
NA	Ride
NA	Front seat comfort
NA	Fuel economy

SPECIFICATIONS

Drive wheels Rear

Seating 2 front

Engines available
2.2-liter 4 (240 hp)

Transmissions available
6-speed manual

Fuel
Fuel type . . . . .Premium
EPA city/highway, mpg 20/26
Fuel refill capacity, gal. 13.2

Dimensions and weight
Length, in. 162
Width, in. 69
Wheelbase, in. .95
Curb weight, lb. 2,790
Percent weight, front/rear 49/51
Typical towing ability, lb. . . . . .NR

SAFETY INFORMATION

Active safety features
Antilock brakes . . . . .Standard
Traction control .Not available
Stability control . . . . .Not available
Daytime running lights . . . . .Not available
Tire pressure monitor . . . . .Not available

Safety belts
Center-rear belt . . . . .NA
Pretensioners, front/rear . . . . .Yes/NA

Air bags
Occupant-sensing system . . . . .Not available
Side bags, front/rear . . . . .No/NA
Inflatable curtain . . . . .Not available
Accident alert system . . . . .Not available

Crash tests
Gov't front-crash test, driver/front passenger . . . . . . ◔/◔
Gov't side-crash test, driver/rear passenger . . . . . . ◉ /NA
IIHS offset crash test . . . . .NA
IIHS side crash test w/ side & curtain airbags . . . . .NA
IIHS side crash test w/o side & curtain airbags . . . . .NA

ANOTHER LOOK

RELIABILITY HISTORY

TROUBLE SPOTS	Honda S2000							
	97	98	99	00	01	02	03	04
Engine				◉	○	◉	◉	
Cooling				◉	◉	◉	◉	
Fuel				◉	◉	◉	◉	
Ignition				◉	◉	◉	◉	
Transmission				◉	○	◉	◉	
Electrical				◉	◑	◉	◉	
Air conditioning				◉	◉	◉	◉	
Suspension				◉	◉	◉	◉	
Brakes				◉	◉	◉	◉	
Exhaust				◉	◉	◉	◉	
Paint/trim/rust				◑	◉	◉	◉	
Body integrity				◑	◐	○	◉	
Power equipment				◉	◑	◐	◉	
Body hardware				◑	◉	◉	◉	
RELIABILITY VERDICT				✓	✓	✓	✓	

Insufficient data

Hummer H2

THE H2 LINE
Body style:
crew cab; 4-door SUV
Trim lines:
Base, Adventure,
Luxury, SUT
Base price range:
$52,430-$56,670

The Hummer H2, based on the Chevrolet Tahoe, has much more usable interior space (six seats) than the grossly impractical—at least for everyday civilian use—original Hummer, now called the H1. The engine is GM's 6.0-liter V8. Fuel economy is not the H2's strength. The full-time four-wheel-drive system with locking center and rear differentials offers exceptional off-road ability. Ride and handling are fairly civilized. With a short windshield, wide roof pillars, and a huge spare tire, the view out is wanting. The SUT offers a short pickup bed with a foldable partition.

REPORT CARD

○	**Predicted reliability**
◒	**Owner satisfaction**
NA	**Predicted depreciation**
NA	**Accident avoidance**
NA	**Acceleration**
NA	**Ride**
NA	**Front seat comfort**
NA	**Fuel economy**

SPECIFICATIONS

Drive wheels Permanent 4WD

Seating 2 front, 3 rear, 1 third

Engines available
6.0-liter V8 (325 hp)

Transmissions available
4-speed automatic

Fuel
Fuel type ....Regular
EPA city/highway, mpg ....NA
Fuel refill capacity, gal. 32.0

Dimensions and weight
Length, in. 190
Width, in. 81
Wheelbase, in. 123
Curb weight, lb. 6,700
Percent weight, front/rear 54/46
Typical towing ability, lb. 6,700

SAFETY INFORMATION

Active safety features
Antilock brakes ....Standard
Traction control ....Standard
Stability control ....Not available
Daytime running lights ....Standard
Tire pressure monitor ....Not available

Safety belts
Center-rear belt ....Lap
Pretensioners, front/rear ....No/no

Air bags
Occupant-sensing system ....Not available
Side bags, front/rear ....No/no
Inflatable curtain ....Not available
Accident alert system ....Available

Crash tests
Gov't front-crash test, driver/front passenger .....NA/NA
Gov't side-crash test, driver/rear passenger ......NA/NA
IIHS offset crash test ....NA
IIHS side crash test w/ side & curtain airbags ....NA
IIHS side crash test w/o side & curtain airbags ....NA

ANOTHER LOOK

RELIABILITY HISTORY

TROUBLE SPOTS	Hummer H2							
	97	98	99	00	01	02	03	04
Engine							◐	
Cooling							◐	
Fuel							◐	
Ignition							◐	
Transmission							◐	
Electrical							○	
Air conditioning							◐	
Suspension							◐	
Brakes							◐	
Exhaust							◐	
Paint/trim/rust							◐	
Body integrity							○	
Power equipment							○	
Body hardware							◐	
RELIABILITY VERDICT							-	

Insufficient data

○ ● ○ ◐ ●
better ← → worse   See page 36 for more information.

Hummer H3

THE H3 LINE
Body style:
4-door SUV
Trim lines:
–
Base price range:
$34,000-$37,000E

The H3 is based on the Chevrolet Colorado/GMC Canyon pickup trucks. General Motors is trying to bring Hummer style and off-road ability to the masses, as well as compete directly with the Jeep Grand Cherokee. The 3.5-liter, 220-hp inline five-cylinder engine that we have found coarse and unimpressive in the GM pickups provides power. The four-wheel-drive system is permanently engaged and has a low range. Stability control is available. An optional ultra-low-range gear is available and promises even more off-road capability.

REPORT CARD

New	**Predicted reliability**
New	**Owner satisfaction**
NA	**Predicted depreciation**
NA	**Accident avoidance**
NA	**Acceleration**
NA	**Ride**
NA	**Front seat comfort**
NA	**Fuel economy**

SPECIFICATIONS

Drive wheels Permanent 4WD

Seating 2 front, 3 rear

Engines available
3.5-liter 5 (220 hp)

Transmissions available
5-speed manual; 4-speed automatic

Fuel
Fuel type ....Regular
EPA city/highway, mpg ....NA
Fuel refill capacity, gal. 23.0

Dimensions and weight
Length, in. 187
Width, in. 75
Wheelbase, in. 112
Curb weight, lb. 4,700
Percent weight, front/rear ....NA
Typical towing ability, lb. 4,500

SAFETY INFORMATION

Active safety features
Antilock brakes ....Standard
Traction control ....Standard
Stability control ....Optional
Daytime running lights ....Standard
Tire pressure monitor ....Available

Safety belts
Center-rear belt 3-point
Pretensioners, front/rear ....Yes/no

Air bags
Occupant-sensing system ....Front
Side bags, front/rear ....No/no
Inflatable curtain ....Optional with rollover
Accident alert system ....Available

Crash tests
Gov't front-crash test, driver/front passenger ......NA/NA
Gov't side-crash test, driver/rear passenger ....NA/NA
IIHS offset crash test ....NA
IIHS side crash test w/ side & curtain airbags ....NA
IIHS side crash test w/o side & curtain airbags ....NA

RELIABILITY HISTORY

TROUBLE SPOTS	97 98 99 00 01 02 03 04
Engine	
Cooling	NO
Fuel	
Ignition	
Transmission	DATA
Electrical	
Air conditioning	NEW
Suspension	
Brakes	MODEL
Exhaust	
Paint/trim/rust	
Body integrity	
Power equipment	
Body hardware	
RELIABILITY VERDICT	

ANOTHER LOOK

Hyundai Accent

THE ACCENT LINE
Body style:
2-door hatchback;
sedan
Trim lines:
GLS, GT, GL
Base price range:
$9,999-$10,799

Hyundai's entry-level model comes as either a sedan or a two-door hatchback. All versions are now powered by a 1.6-liter, four-cylinder engine. The Accent is one of the least expensive cars on the road, but it's well equipped at a list price of just under $10,000. It is slow and noisy, although the ride is tolerable. Handling is secure, but not agile. Antilock brakes are optional on 2005 models. Overall, the Accent is a little more pleasant than competitors such as the Kia Rio, but it's no better than a used Honda Civic. It's basic transportation and no more. A redesign arrives for 2006.

REPORT CARD

○	**Predicted reliability**
◒	**Owner satisfaction**
●	**Predicted depreciation**
○	**Accident avoidance**
○	**Acceleration**
○	**Ride**
◒	**Front seat comfort**
◒	**Fuel economy**

SPECIFICATIONS

Drive wheels Front

Seating 2 front, 3 rear

Engines available
1.6-liter 4 (104 hp)

Transmissions available
5-speed manual; 4-speed automatic

Fuel
Fuel type . . . . .Regular
EPA city/highway, mpg 26/35
Fuel refill capacity, gal. 11.9

Dimensions and weight
Length, in. 167
Width, in. 66
Wheelbase, in. .96
Curb weight, lb. 2,525
Percent weight, front/rear 62/38
Typical towing ability, lb. . . . . .NR

SAFETY INFORMATION

Active safety features
Antilock brakes . . . . .Optional
Traction control . . . . .Not available
Stability control . . . . .Not available
Daytime running lights . . . . .Not available
Tire pressure monitor . . . . .Not available

Safety belts
Center-rear belt . . . . .Lap
Pretensioners, front/rear . . . . .Yes/no

Air bags
Occupant-sensing system . . . . .Front
Side bags, front/rear .Standard/no
Inflatable curtain . . . . .Not available
Accident alert system . . . . .Not available

Crash tests
Gov't front-crash test, driver/front passenger . . . . . ◒/◒
Gov't side-crash test, driver/rear passenger . . . . . . ●/◒
IIHS offset crash test . . . . .NA
IIHS side crash test w/ side & curtain airbags . . . . .NA
IIHS side crash test w/o side & curtain airbags . . . . .NA

FROM THE TEST TRACK

Tested model
2003 GL sedan, 1.6-liter Four, 4-speed automatic

Tires as tested
Kumho Steel Radial 722, size P175/70R13 82T

Acceleration . . . .○
0-30 mph, sec. 3.5
0-60 mph, sec. 10.8
Quarter mile, sec. 18.3
Quarter mile, mph 76
45-65 mph, sec. 7.1

Other findings
Transmission . . . .◒
Turning circle, ft. 36
Ground clearance, in. 4.0

Braking and handling
Braking . . . .◒
Braking, dry pavement, ft. 151
Routine handling . . . .○
Emergency handling . . . .○
Avoidance maneuver, max. mph . . .51.5

Convenience and comfort
Ride . . . .○
Noise . . . .◐
Driving position . . . .◒
Access . . . .○
Controls and displays . . . .◒
Fit and finish . . . .○
Door top to ground, in. 50.0
Trunk . . . .◒
Luggage capacity . . . . .3+1
Max. load, lb. 850

Seating
Front-seat comfort . . . .◒
Front shoulder room, in. 53.0
Front leg room, in. 40.5
Front head room, in. 4.0
Rear-seat comfort . . . .◒
Rear shoulder room, in. 52.5
Rear leg room, in. 25.5
Rear head room, in 1.5

Fuel economy . . . .◒
CU's overall mileage, mpg 26
CU's city/highway, mpg 18/38
CU's 150-mile trip, mpg 33
Annual fuel . . . . .565 gal./$1,130
Cruising range 360

RELIABILITY HISTORY

TROUBLE SPOTS	Hyundai Accent							
	97	98	99	00	01	02	03	04
Engine					○	◒	●	
Cooling					○	◒	●	
Fuel				○	○	◒	●	
Ignition					○	◒	●	
Transmission				○	○	◒		
Electrical	Insufficient data	Insufficient data	Insufficient data	Insufficient data	○	○	◒	Insufficient data
Air conditioning					◒	●	●	
Suspension					◒	◒	●	
Brakes				○	◒	◐	●	
Exhaust					◒	●	●	
Paint/trim/rust					◒	◒	●	
Body integrity				○	○	○		
Power equipment					◒	●	●	
Body hardware				○	◒	●		
RELIABILITY VERDICT					–	–	✓	

Hyundai Elantra

CR RECOMMENDED ✓

The Elantra competes well overall with the Mitsubishi Lancer and Nissan Sentra, and reliability has been above average. It rides relatively comfortably and quietly. The cabin is fairly spacious. The engine feels refined and provides adequate acceleration, but fuel economy is unimpressive. The automatic transmission works well. Handling is secure but not particularly agile. A GT model with a firmer suspension and more standard equipment is also available. IIHS offset-crash results are Good. It received a Poor rating in the IIHS side-impact-crash test.

THE ELANTRA LINE
Body style:
4-door hatchback; sedan
Trim lines:
GLS, GT
Base price range:
$13,299-$14,849

REPORT CARD

⊖	Predicted reliability
○	Owner satisfaction
⊖	Predicted depreciation
⊖	Accident avoidance
○	Acceleration
⊖	Ride
⊖	Front seat comfort
○	Fuel economy

SPECIFICATIONS

Drive wheels Front

Seating 2 front, 3 rear

Engines available
2.0-liter 4 (138 hp)

Transmissions available
5-speed manual; 4-speed automatic

Fuel
Fuel type . . . . .Regular
EPA city/highway, mpg 24/32
Fuel refill capacity, gal. 14.5

Dimensions and weight
Length, in. 177
Width, in. 68
Wheelbase, in. .103
Curb weight, lb. 2,980
Percent weight, front/rear 63/37
Typical towing ability, lb. 2,000

SAFETY INFORMATION

Active safety features
Antilock brakes . . . . .Optional
Traction control . . . . .Optional
Stability control . . . . .Not available
Daytime running lights . . . . .Not available
Tire pressure monitor . . . . .Not available

Safety belts
Center-rear belt 3-point
Pretensioners, front/rear . . . . .Yes/no

Air bags
Occupant-sensing system . . . . .Front
Side bags, front/rear . . . . .Standard/no
Inflatable curtain . . . . .Not available
Accident alert system . . . . .Not available

Crash tests
Gov't front-crash test, driver/front passenger . . . . . .◑/⊖
Gov't side-crash test, driver/rear passenger . . . .◑/⊖
IIHS offset crash test . . . . .Good
IIHS side crash test w/ side & curtain airbags . . . . .Poor
IIHS side crash test w/o side & curtain airbags . . . . .NA

FROM THE TEST TRACK

Tested model
2005 GT sedan, 2.0-liter Four, 4-speed automatic

Tires as tested
Michelin Energy MXV4 Plus, size 195/60R15 88H

Acceleration . . . .○
0-30 mph, sec. 3.5
0-60 mph, sec. 10.3
Quarter mile, sec. 17.7
Quarter mile, mph 79
45-65 mph, sec. 6.4

Other findings
Transmission . . . .⊖
Turning circle, ft. 37
Ground clearance, in. 5.0

Braking and handling
Braking . . . .⊖
Braking, dry pavement, ft. 133
Routine handling . . . .⊖
Emergency handling . . . .○
Avoidance maneuver, max. mph . . .52.5

Convenience and comfort
Ride . . . .⊖
Noise . . . .⊖
Driving position . . . .⊖
Access . . . .⊖
Controls and displays . . . .◑
Fit and finish . . . .⊖
Door top to ground, in. 51.0
Trunk . . . .○
Luggage capacity . . . . .3+2
Max. load, lb. 850

Seating
Front-seat comfort . . . .⊖
Front shoulder room, in. 54.5
Front leg room, in. 40.0
Front head room, in. 2.5
Rear-seat comfort . . . .○
Rear shoulder room, in. 53.5
Rear leg room, in. 27.5
Rear head room, in 2.0

Fuel economy . . . .○
CU's overall mileage, mpg 24
CU's city/highway, mpg 16/33
CU's 150-mile trip, mpg 28
Annual fuel . . . . .635 gal./$1,270
Cruising range 375

RELIABILITY HISTORY

TROUBLE SPOTS	Hyundai Elantra							
	97	98	99	00	01	02	03	04
Engine			●	●	●	●	●	●
Cooling			●	●	○	●	●	●
Fuel			○	○	○	●	●	●
Ignition			○	○	○	●	●	●
Transmission			◐	○	○	●	●	●
Electrical	Insufficient data	Insufficient data	○	○	○	●	●	●
Air conditioning			○	○	●	●	●	●
Suspension			●	●	◐	●	●	●
Brakes			○	●	○	○	●	●
Exhaust			●	●	○	●	●	●
Paint/trim/rust			○	○	○	○	◐	●
Body integrity			○	○	○	◐	◐	●
Power equipment			●	●	○	●	●	●
Body hardware			○	○	○	◐	●	●
RELIABILITY VERDICT			–	–	–	–	✓	✓

Hyundai Santa Fe

CR RECOMMENDED ✓

THE SANTA FE LINE

Body style:
4-door SUV

Trim lines:
Base, GLS, LX

Base price range:
$21,649-$26,099

The Santa Fe is a good car-based SUV with a four-wheel independent suspension. Fit and finish is good, and the controls are logically placed. The ride is supple and quiet. Handling is secure, though not very agile, and the AWD system works effectively and transparently. The 2.7-liter V6 feels refined, but weight takes a toll on acceleration and fuel economy—we managed only 18 mpg overall. A 3.5-liter V6 with a five-speed automatic is available. The steeply raked windshield can make the cockpit feel a bit confining. The four-cylinder was dropped for 2005 with the introduction of the smaller Tucson.

REPORT CARD

⊖	Predicted reliability
⊖	Owner satisfaction
⊖	Predicted depreciation
○	Accident avoidance
○	Acceleration
⊖	Ride
⊖	Front seat comfort
⊖	Fuel economy

SPECIFICATIONS

Drive wheels Front or AWD

Seating 2 front, 3 rear

Engines available
2.7-liter V6 (170 hp); 3.5-liter V6 (200 hp)

Transmissions available
4-speed automatic; 5-speed automatic

Fuel
Fuel type . . . . .Regular
EPA city/highway, mpg 18/23
Fuel refill capacity, gal. 19.0

Dimensions and weight
Length, in. 177
Width, in. 73
Wheelbase, in. .103
Curb weight, lb. 3,875
Percent weight, front/rear 58/42
Typical towing ability, lb. 2,200

SAFETY INFORMATION

Active safety features

Antilock brakes . . . . .Standard
Traction control . . . . , ...Standard
Stability control . . . . .Not available
Daytime running lights . . . . .Not available
Tire pressure monitor . . . . .Not available

Safety belts

Center-rear belt 3-point
Pretensioners, front/rear . . . . .Yes/no

Air bags

Occupant-sensing system . . . . .Not available
Side bags, front/rear . . . . .Standard/no
Inflatable curtain . . . . .Not available
Accident alert system .Not available

Crash tests

Gov't front-crash test, driver/front passenger . . . . ⊜/◉
Gov't side-crash test, driver/rear passenger . . . . . . ◉/◉
IIHS offset crash test . . . . .Good
IIHS side crash test w/ side & curtain airbags . . .Acceptable
IIHS side crash test w/o side & curtain airbags . . . . .NA

FROM THE TEST TRACK

Tested model
2001 GLS 4-door SUV AWD, 2.7-liter V6, 4-speed automatic

Tires as tested
BF Goodrich Radial Long Trail T/A, size P225/70R16 101T

Acceleration . . . . ○
0-30 mph, sec. 3.8
0-60 mph, sec. 10.8
Quarter mile, sec. 18.2
Quarter mile, mph 77
45-65 mph, sec. 6.8

Other findings
Transmission . . . . ⊖
Turning circle, ft. 40
Ground clearance, in. 6.0

Braking and handling
Braking . . . . ⊖
Braking, dry pavement, ft. 137
Routine handling . . . . ⊖
Emergency handling . . . . ⊖
Avoidance maneuver, max. mph . . .49.0

Convenience and comfort
Ride . . . . ⊖
Noise . . . . ⊖
Driving position . . . . ⊖
Access . . . . ⊖
Controls and displays . . . . ◉
Fit and finish . . . . ⊖
Door top to ground, in. 60.0
Cargo area . . . . ○
Cargo volume, cu.ft. 33.5
Max. load, lb. 880

Seating
Front-seat comfort . . . . ⊖
Front shoulder room, in. 56.0
Front leg room, in. 40.0
Front head room, in. 4.0
Rear-seat comfort . . . . ○
Rear shoulder room, in. 56.0
Rear leg room, in. 29.0
Rear head room, in 4.0

Fuel economy . . . . ⊖
CU's overall mileage, mpg 18
  CU's city/highway, mpg 13/23
  CU's 150-mile trip, mpg 22
Annual fuel . . . . .840 gal./$1,680
Cruising range 345

RELIABILITY HISTORY

TROUBLE SPOTS	97	98	99	00	01	02	03	04
Engine					⊖	⊖	⊖	⊖
Cooling				◉	⊖	◉	⊖	◉
Fuel				⊖	⊜	⊖	⊖	◉
Ignition				◉	⊖	◉	⊖	◉
Transmission				⊖	⊖	⊖	⊖	◉
Electrical				⊜	◉	⊖	◉	⊖
Air conditioning				⊖	⊖	◉	⊖	◉
Suspension				◉	⊖	⊖	⊖	◉
Brakes				○	○	⊖	⊖	◉
Exhaust				◉	◉	◉	⊖	◉
Paint/trim/rust				⊖	◉	⊖	◉	◉
Body integrity				○	⊖	⊖	⊖	◉
Power equipment				○	⊖	◉	◉	◉
Body hardware				⊖	⊖	◉	⊖	◉
RELIABILITY VERDICT					–	✓	✓	✓

Hyundai Sonata

THE SONATA LINE
Body style:
sedan
Trim lines:
GL, GLS, LX
Base price range:
$18,000-$22,000E

The Sonata has always been a low-cost alternative to the refined Toyota Camry and Honda Accord. The outgoing model competed well with domestic entries like the Chrysler Sebring and Chevrolet Malibu. A redesigned 2006 Sonata has just been introduced. Built in Alabama, it features new, more powerful engines and better interior quality, in addition to increased interior room. Comprehensive safety gear, including stability control, is standard.

REPORT CARD

New	**Predicted reliability**
New	**Owner satisfaction**
NA	**Predicted depreciation**
NA	**Accident avoidance**
NA	**Acceleration**
NA	**Ride**
NA	**Front seat comfort**
NA	**Fuel economy**

SPECIFICATIONS

Drive wheels Front

Seating 2 front, 3 rear

Engines available
2.4-liter 4 (162 hp); 3.3-liter V6 (237 hp)

Transmissions available
5-speed manual; 4-speed automatic; 5-speed automatic

Fuel
Fuel type ....Regular
EPA city/highway, mpg ....NA
Fuel refill capacity, gal. 17.7

Dimensions and weight
Length, in. 189
Width, in. 72
Wheelbase, in. 107
Curb weight, lb. 3,460
Percent weight, front/rear ....NA
Typical towing ability, lb. 2,000

SAFETY INFORMATION

Active safety features
Antilock brakes ....Standard
Traction control ....Standard
Stability control ....Standard
Daytime running lights ....Not available
Tire pressure monitor ....Not available

Safety belts
Center-rear belt 3-point
Pretensioners, front/rear ....Yes/no

Air bags
Occupant-sensing system ....Front
Side bags, front/rear ....Standard/no
Inflatable curtain ....Standard
Accident alert system ....Not available

Crash tests
Gov't front-crash test, driver/front passenger ....NA/NA
Gov't side-crash test, driver/rear passenger ....NA/NA
IIHS offset crash test ....NA
IIHS side crash test w/ side & curtain airbags ....NA
IIHS side crash test w/o side & curtain airbags ....NA

ANOTHER LOOK

RELIABILITY HISTORY

TROUBLE SPOTS	97 98 99 00 01 02 03 04
Engine	
Cooling	
Fuel	NO
Ignition	
Transmission	DATA
Electrical	
Air conditioning	NEW
Suspension	
Brakes	MODEL
Exhaust	
Paint/trim/rust	
Body integrity	
Power equipment	
Body hardware	
RELIABILITY VERDICT	

Hyundai Tiburon

THE TIBURON LINE
Body style:
coupe
Trim lines:
GS, GT, SE
Base price range:
$15,999-$19,999

The Tiburon is a sporty coupe with tiny rear seats and a hatchback rear gate. The 2003 redesign brought more-elegant styling but head room is meager. The cockpit has a higher-quality feel. The GT model we tested comes with a six-speed manual transmission that shifts pretty well but not precisely. The GT's 2.7-liter V6 is smooth and refined but isn't all that eager to rev. Base models continue to use a 2.0-liter, four-cylinder engine. Handling is fairly nimble but not as involving as you might expect. The car feels nose-heavy, and the steering isn't particularly quick. The ride is very stiff, even for a sporty car.

REPORT CARD

●	Predicted reliability
○	Owner satisfaction
NA	Predicted depreciation
◓	Accident avoidance
◓	Acceleration
◑	Ride
○	Front seat comfort
○	Fuel economy

SPECIFICATIONS

Drive wheels Front

Seating 2 front, 2 rear

Engines available
2.0-liter 4 (138 hp); 2.7-liter V6 (172 hp)

Transmissions available
5-speed manual; 6-speed manual; 4-speed automatic

Fuel
Fuel type . . . . .Regular
EPA city/highway, mpg 18/26
Fuel refill capacity, gal. 14.5

Dimensions and weight
Length, in. 173
Width, in. 69
Wheelbase, in. 100
Curb weight, lb. 3,110
Percent weight, front/rear 62/38
Typical towing ability, lb. 1,000

SAFETY INFORMATION

Active safety features
Antilock brakes . . . . .Optional on GT; standard on SE
Traction control . . . . .Not available
Stability control . . . . .Not available
Daytime running lights .Not available
Tire pressure monitor . . . . .Not available

Safety belts
Center-rear belt . . . . .NA
Pretensioners, front/rear . . . . .Yes/no

Air bags
Occupant-sensing system . . . . .Not available
Side bags, front/rear .Standard/no
Inflatable curtain . . . . .Not available
Accident alert system .Not available

Crash tests
Gov't front-crash test, driver/front passenger . . . ◑/◓
Gov't side-crash test, driver/rear passenger . . . . ◑/NA
IIHS offset crash test . . . . .NA
IIHS side crash test w/ side & curtain airbags . . . . .NA
IIHS side crash test w/o side & curtain airbags . . . . .NA

FROM THE TEST TRACK

Tested model
2003 GT V6 coupe, 2.7-liter V6, 6-speed manual

Tires as tested
Michelin Pilot Sport, size 215/45R17 87Y

Acceleration . . . . ◓
0-30 mph, sec. .2.7
0-60 mph, sec. .7.9
Quarter mile, sec. 16.2
Quarter mile, mph 86
45-65 mph, sec. 4.9

Other findings
Transmission . . . . ◓
Turning circle, ft. 38
Ground clearance, in. 5.0

Braking and handling
Braking . . . . ◓
Braking, dry pavement, ft. 137
Routine handling . . . . ◓
Emergency handling . . . . ◓
Avoidance maneuver, max. mph . . .52.5

Convenience and comfort
Ride . . . . ◑
Noise . . . . ○
Driving position . . . . ◓
Access . . . . ◓
Controls and displays . . . . ◐
Fit and finish . . . . ◑
Door top to ground, in. 47.0
Trunk . . . . ●
Luggage capacity . . . . .1+2
Max. load, lb. 700

Seating
Front-seat comfort . . . . ○
Front shoulder room, in. 54.0
Front leg room, in. 41.5
Front head room, in. 2.0
Rear-seat comfort . . . . ●
Rear shoulder room, in. 47.0
Rear leg room, in. 25.0
Rear head room, in 0.0

Fuel economy . . . . ○
CU's overall mileage, mpg 22
CU's city/highway, mpg 15/30
CU's 150-mile trip, mpg 25
Annual fuel . . . . .695 gal./$1,395
Cruising range 335

RELIABILITY HISTORY

TROUBLE SPOTS	Hyundai Tiburon							
	97	98	99	00	01	02	03	04
Engine							●	
Cooling							●	
Fuel							◑	
Ignition							●	
Transmission							●	
Electrical	Insufficient data	Insufficient data	Insufficient data	Insufficient data	Insufficient data	Insufficient data	○	Insufficient data
Air conditioning							◐	
Suspension							◐	
Brakes							◐	
Exhaust							●	
Paint/trim/rust							○	
Body integrity							◑	
Power equipment							●	
Body hardware							◑	
RELIABILITY VERDICT							✗	

● ◑ ○ ◓ ●
better ← → worse   See page 36 for more information.

Hyundai Tucson

THE TUCSON LINE
Body style:
4-door SUV
Trim lines:
GL, GLS, LX
Base price range:
$17,499-$22,799

The Tucson is a small SUV designed to compete with the Honda CR-V and Toyota RAV4. It is based on the Elantra sedan and is smaller than the Santa Fe SUV. Power comes from a 2.0-liter, 140-hp four-cylinder engine. The 2.7-liter, 173-hp V6 version is priced similarly to the four-cylinder Honda and Toyota offerings. The Tucson is not very agile. The ride is reasonably comfortable, but suspension noise is pronounced. Cabin access is easy and the rear is relatively roomy. Antilock brakes, stability control, and side- and head-protection air bags are standard. The Kia Sportage is the Tucson's sister vehicle.

REPORT CARD

New	**Predicted reliability**
New	**Owner satisfaction**
NA	**Predicted depreciation**
NA	**Accident avoidance**
NA	**Acceleration**
NA	**Ride**
NA	**Front seat comfort**
NA	**Fuel economy**

SPECIFICATIONS

Drive wheels Front or AWD

Seating 2 front, 3 rear

Engines available
2.0-liter 4 (140 hp); 2.7-liter V6 (173 hp)

Transmissions available
5-speed manual; 4-speed automatic

Fuel
Fuel type . . . . .Regular
EPA city/highway, mpg 19/24
Fuel refill capacity, gal. 17.2

Dimensions and weight
Length, in. 170
Width, in. 71
Wheelbase, in. 104
Curb weight, lb. 3,800
Percent weight, front/rear 60/40
Typical towing ability, lb. 1,500

SAFETY INFORMATION

Active safety features
Antilock brakes . . . . .Standard
Traction control . . . . .Standard
Stability control . . . . .Standard
Daytime running lights . . . . .Not available
Tire pressure monitor .Not available

Safety belts
Center-rear belt 3-point
Pretensioners, front/rear . . . . .Yes/no

Air bags
Occupant-sensing system . . . . .Not available
Side bags, front/rear .Standard/no
Inflatable curtain . . . . .Standard
Accident alert system .Not available

Crash tests
Gov't front-crash test, driver/front passenger . . . . . . .NA/NA
Gov't side-crash test, driver/rear passenger . . . . .NA/NA
IIHS offset crash test . . . . .NA
IIHS side crash test w/ side & curtain airbags . . . . .NA
IIHS side crash test w/o side & curtain airbags . . . . .NA

ANOTHER LOOK

RELIABILITY HISTORY

TROUBLE SPOTS	97	98	99	00	01	02	03	04
Engine								
Cooling								
Fuel				NO				
Ignition								
Transmission				DATA				
Electrical								
Air conditioning				NEW				
Suspension								
Brakes				MODEL				
Exhaust								
Paint/trim/rust								
Body integrity								
Power equipment								
Body hardware								
RELIABILITY VERDICT								

Hyundai XG350

CR RECOMMENDED ✓

THE XG350 LINE
Body style:
sedan
Trim lines:
Base, L
Base price range:
$24,899-$26,499

I f you want to reminisce about a brand-new Buick from the 1960s, this is it. Handling is ungainly, with pronounced body roll and slow steering. The ride, while comfortable and isolated, can get floaty on undulations, especially at higher speeds. The XG350 has a torquey, 3.5-liter V6 engine. The interior is roomy and fairly quiet, although head room is tight. Inside, amenities include automatic climate control and heated, powered leather seats. The car is invitingly priced for its size and content, and fit and finish is commendable. A replacement called the Azera goes on sale in November.

REPORT CARD

○	Predicted reliability
◐	Owner satisfaction
◒	Predicted depreciation
○	Accident avoidance
◐	Acceleration
◐	Ride
◐	Front seat comfort
◒	Fuel economy

SPECIFICATIONS

Drive wheels Front

Seating 2 front, 3 rear

Engines available
3.5-liter V6 (194 hp)

Transmissions available
5-speed automatic

Fuel
Fuel type . . . . .Regular
EPA city/highway, mpg 17/26
Fuel refill capacity, gal. 18.5

Dimensions and weight
Length, in. 192
Width, in. 72
Wheelbase, in. .108
Curb weight, lb. 3,750
Percent weight, front/rear 62/38
Typical towing ability, lb. 2,000

SAFETY INFORMATION

Active safety features
Antilock brakes . . . . .Standard
Traction control . . . . .Standard
Stability control . . . . .Not available
Daytime running lights . . . . .Not available
Tire pressure monitor . . . . .Not available

Safety belts
Center-rear belt 3-point
Pretensioners, front/rear . . . . .Yes/no

Air bags
Occupant-sensing system . . . . .Not available
Side bags, front/rear .Standard/no
Inflatable curtain . . . . .Not available
Accident alert system . . . . .Not available

Crash tests
Gov't front-crash test, driver/front passenger . . . . .◐/◐
Gov't side-crash test, driver/rear passenger . . . . . .◒/◒
IIHS offset crash test . . . . .Good
IIHS side crash test w/ side & curtain airbags . . . . .NA
IIHS side crash test w/o side & curtain airbags . . . . .NA

FROM THE TEST TRACK

Tested model
2003 L sedan, 3.5-liter V6, 5-speed automatic

Tires as tested
Michelin Energy MXV4 Plus, size P205/60R16 91H

Acceleration . . . . ◐
0-30 mph, sec. 2.9
0-60 mph, sec. 8.0
Quarter mile, sec. 16.4
Quarter mile, mph. 87
45-65 mph, sec. 5.2

Other findings
Transmission . . . . ◐
Turning circle, ft. 41
Ground clearance, in. 6.5

Braking and handling
Braking . . . .◐
Braking, dry pavement, ft. 137
Routine handling . . . .◐
Emergency handling . . . .◒
Avoidance maneuver, max. mph . . .49.5

Convenience and comfort
Ride . . . . ◐
Noise . . . . ◐
Driving position . . . . ◐
Access . . . . ◐
Controls and displays . . . . ◐
Fit and finish . . . . ◐
Door top to ground, in. 51.0
Trunk . . . . ○
Luggage capacity . . . . .3+3
Max. load, lb. 860

Seating
Front-seat comfort . . . . ◐
Front shoulder room, in. 57.0
Front leg room, in. 39.0
Front head room, in. 2.5
Rear-seat comfort . . . . ◐
Rear shoulder room, in. 56.0
Rear leg room, in. 29.5
Rear head room, in 2.5

Fuel economy . . . . ◒
CU's overall mileage, mpg 19
CU's city/highway, mpg 13/30
CU's 150-mile trip, mpg 23
Annual fuel . . . . .785 gal./$1,570
Cruising range 390

RELIABILITY HISTORY

TROUBLE SPOTS	Hyundai XG300, XG350							
	97	98	99	00	01	02	03	04
Engine					◐	◐	●	●
Cooling					●	●	●	●
Fuel				○	◒	●	●	●
Ignition				○	●	●	●	●
Transmission				○	●	●	●	●
Electrical				●	○	◐	◐	●
Air conditioning					◐	●	●	●
Suspension					◐	●	●	●
Brakes					◐	●	●	●
Exhaust					●	●	●	●
Paint/trim/rust					●	●	●	●
Body integrity				○	○	◐	●	●
Power equipment				○	◐	●	●	●
Body hardware				◐	●	○	◐	●
RELIABILITY VERDICT					--	--	✓	✗

Infiniti FX

CR RECOMMENDED ✓

THE FX LINE
Body style:
4-door SUV
Trim lines:
FX35, FX45
Base price range:
$34,950-$45,450

The FX35 we tested drove more like a a sports sedan than an SUV. The strong, smooth V6, coupled with an excellent five-speed automatic, provides impressive performance. The FX45 features a gutsy, 315-hp V8. Handling is nimble and remains stable and secure at its limits. A stiff ride that transmits bumps and pavement flaws to the passengers is one of its drawbacks. The pronounced exhaust note can be tiresome. The cabin feels snug, partly because of the high doorsills and low roof. Rear visibility is poor. The wide turning circle makes parking cumbersome. Cargo volume is modest.

REPORT CARD

⊖	Predicted reliability
⊖	Owner satisfaction
NA	Predicted depreciation
⊖	Accident avoidance
⊖	Acceleration
○	Ride
◑	Front seat comfort
⊖	Fuel economy

SPECIFICATIONS

Drive wheels Rear or AWD

Seating 2 front, 3 rear

Engines available
3.5-liter V6 (280 hp); 4.5-liter V8 (315 hp)

Transmissions available
5-speed automatic

Fuel
Fuel type ....Premium
EPA city/highway, mpg 16/22
Fuel refill capacity, gal. 23.8

Dimensions and weight
Length, in. 189
Width, in. 77
Wheelbase, in. 112
Curb weight, lb. 4,295
Percent weight, front/rear 52/48
Typical towing ability, lb. 3,500

SAFETY INFORMATION

Active safety features
Antilock brakes ....Standard
Traction control ....Standard
Stability control ....Standard
Daytime running lights ....Not available
Tire pressure monitor ....Available

Safety belts
Center-rear belt 3-point
Pretensioners, front/rear ....Yes/no

Air bags
Occupant-sensing system ....Front
Side bags, front/rear ....Standard/no
Inflatable curtain ....Standard with rollover
Accident alert system ....Not available

Crash tests
Gov't front-crash test, driver/front passenger ......◑/◑
Gov't side-crash test, driver/rear passenger ......◑/◑
IIHS offset crash test ....Good
IIHS side crash test w/ side & curtain airbags ....NA
IIHS side crash test w/o side & curtain airbags ....NA

FROM THE TEST TRACK

Tested model
2003 FX35 4-door SUV AWD, 3.5-liter V6, 5-speed automatic

Tires as tested
Bridgestone Potenza RE92A, size P265/60R18 109V

Acceleration ....⊖
0-30 mph, sec. 2.9
0-60 mph, sec. 7.4
Quarter mile, sec. 15.8
Quarter mile, mph. 90
45-65 mph, sec. 4.8

Other findings
Transmission ....◑
Turning circle, ft. 42
Ground clearance, in. 7.0

Braking and handling
Braking ....⊖
Braking, dry pavement, ft. 135
Routine handling ....◑
Emergency handling ....○
Avoidance maneuver, max. mph ...49.0

Convenience and comfort
Ride ....○
Noise ....⊖
Driving position ....○
Access ....⊖
Controls and displays ....⊖
Fit and finish ....⊖
Door top to ground, in. 58.0
Cargo area ....⊖
Cargo volume, cu.ft. 29.0
Max. load, lb. 950

Seating
Front-seat comfort ....◑
Front shoulder room, in. 55.5
Front leg room, in. 42.5
Front head room, in. 4.5
Rear-seat comfort ....⊖
Rear shoulder room, in. 56.0
Rear leg room, in. 29.0
Rear head room, in 4.0

Fuel economy ....⊖
CU's overall mileage, mpg 18
CU's city/highway, mpg 13/25
CU's 150-mile trip, mpg 21
Annual fuel ....835 gal./$1,840
Cruising range 470

RELIABILITY HISTORY

TROUBLE SPOTS	Infiniti FX							
	97	98	99	00	01	02	03	04
Engine							◑	◑
Cooling							◑	◑
Fuel							◑	◑
Ignition							◑	◑
Transmission							◑	◑
Electrical							⊖	◑
Air conditioning							◑	◑
Suspension							◑	◑
Brakes							⊖	◑
Exhaust							◑	◑
Paint/trim/rust							⊖	◑
Body integrity							◑	◑
Power equipment							○	◑
Body hardware							○	◑
RELIABILITY VERDICT							✓	✓

Infiniti G35

CR RECOMMENDED ✓

THE G35 LINE
Body style:
coupe; sedan
Trim lines:
Base, X, Sport
Base price range:
$30,450-$33,000

The G35 is a pleasant car but has some drawbacks. Its 3.5-liter V6 is strong, and the automatic is exceptionally smooth. Routine handling is fairly agile, but at its limits the tail slid out unexpectedly on our test car—even with the standard stability control. The ride is comfortable and quiet. The power seat controls are poorly marked and confusing to use, as are a few other controls. A coupe version with a six-speed manual is available. All-wheel drive on the sedan aids snow traction. For 2005, Infiniti revised the interior with better materials and a tilt-and-telescoping steering wheel.

REPORT CARD

⊖	**Predicted reliability**
⊖	**Owner satisfaction**
NA	**Predicted depreciation**
⊖	**Accident avoidance**
⊙	**Acceleration**
⊖	**Ride**
⊖	**Front seat comfort**
◖	**Fuel economy**

SAFETY INFORMATION

Active safety features
Antilock brakes . . . . .Standard
Traction control . . . . .Standard
Stability control . . . . .Standard
Daytime running lights . . . . .Not available
Tire pressure monitor . . . . .Available

Safety belts
Center-rear belt 3-point
Pretensioners, front/rear . . . . .Yes/no

Air bags
Occupant-sensing system . . . . .Not available
Side bags, front/rear . . . . .Standard/no
Inflatable curtain . . . . .Standard
Accident alert system . . . . .Not available

Crash tests
Gov't front-crash test, driver/front passenger . . . . . .NA/NA
Gov't side-crash test, driver/rear passenger . . . . . .NA/NA
IIHS offset crash test . . . . .Good
IIHS side crash test w/ side & curtain airbags . . . . .NA
IIHS side crash test w/o side & curtain airbags . . . . .NA

SPECIFICATIONS

Drive wheels Rear or AWD

Seating 2 front, 3 rear

Engines available
3.5-liter V6 (280 hp); 3.5-liter V6 (298 hp)

Transmissions available
6-speed manual; 5-speed automatic

Fuel
Fuel type . . . . .Premium
EPA city/highway, mpg 18/26
Fuel refill capacity, gal. 20.0

Dimensions and weight
Length, in. 187
Width, in. 69
Wheelbase, in. 112
Curb weight, lb. 3,515
Percent weight, front/rear 53/47
Typical towing ability, lb. 1,000

FROM THE TEST TRACK

Tested model
2003 sedan, 3.5-liter V6, 5-speed automatic

Tires as tested
Bridgestone Turanza EL42,
size P215/55R17 93V

Acceleration . . . . ⊙
0-30 mph, sec. 2.8
0-60 mph, sec. 6.8
Quarter mile, sec. 15.4
Quarter mile, mph 93
45-65 mph, sec. 4.3

Other findings
Transmission . . . . ⊙
Turning circle, ft. 39
Ground clearance, in. 3.5

Braking and handling
Braking . . . . ⊖
Braking, dry pavement, ft. 133
Routine handling . . . . ⊖
Emergency handling . . . . ○
Avoidance maneuver, max. mph . . .54.0

Convenience and comfort
Ride . . . . ⊖
Noise . . . . ⊖
Driving position . . . . ⊖
Access . . . . ⊖
Controls and displays . . . . ○
Fit and finish . . . . ⊖
Door top to ground, in. 51.5
Trunk . . . . ◖
Luggage capacity . . . . .3+2
Max. load, lb. 900

Seating
Front-seat comfort . . . . ⊖
Front shoulder room, in. 56.5
Front leg room, in. 41.5
Front head room, in. 3.0
Rear-seat comfort . . . . ⊖
Rear shoulder room, in. 55.0
Rear leg room, in. 29.0
Rear head room, in 2.5

Fuel economy . . . . ◖
CU's overall mileage, mpg 20
 CU's city/highway, mpg 14/29
 CU's 150-mile trip, mpg 26
Annual fuel . . . . .740 gal./$1,630
Cruising range 480

RELIABILITY HISTORY

TROUBLE SPOTS	Infiniti G35							
	97	98	99	00	01	02	03	04
Engine							◒	◒
Cooling							◒	◒
Fuel							◒	◒
Ignition							◒	◒
Transmission							◒	◒
Electrical							◐	◒
Air conditioning							◒	◒
Suspension							◒	◒
Brakes							◐	◒
Exhaust							◒	◒
Paint/trim/rust							◒	◒
Body integrity							◐	◒
Power equipment							◐	◒
Body hardware							◒	◒
RELIABILITY VERDICT							–	✓

Infiniti M35/M45

THE M35/M45 LINE
Body style:
sedan
Trim lines:
M35, M35 X, M35
Sport, M45, M45 Sport
Base price range:
$39,900-$49,550

The original, short-lived M45 was slotted between the midsized G35 and large Q45. It was a conservatively styled sedan with a notably tight interior. The 2006 redesign is a much roomier, more contemporary design that is competitive with the Acura RL and Audi A6. Even with all-wheel drive the 3.5-liter V6 of the M35 is gutsy. Ride and handling are good and the interior is plush and well constructed. Audio and navigation functions are relatively easy to master, and are controlled via a dash-top knob or voice activation.

REPORT CARD

New	Predicted reliability
New	Owner satisfaction
NA	Predicted depreciation
NA	Accident avoidance
NA	Acceleration
NA	Ride
NA	Front seat comfort
NA	Fuel economy

SPECIFICATIONS

Drive wheels Rear or AWD

Seating 2 front, 3 rear

Engines available
3.5-liter V6 (280 hp); 4.5-liter V8 (335 hp)

Transmissions available
5-speed automatic

Fuel
Fuel type ....Premium
EPA city/highway, mpg 18/25
Fuel refill capacity, gal. 20.0

Dimensions and weight
Length, in. 193
Width, in. 71
Wheelbase, in. 114
Curb weight, lb. 3,950
Percent weight, front/rear 54/46
Typical towing ability, lb. 1,000

SAFETY INFORMATION

Active safety features
Antilock brakes ....Standard
Traction control ....Standard
Stability control ....Standard
Daytime running lights ....Not available
Tire pressure monitor ....Available

Safety belts
Center-rear belt 3-point
Pretensioners, front/rear ....Yes/no

Air bags
Occupant-sensing system ....Front
Side bags, front/rear ....Standard/no
Inflatable curtain ....Standard
Accident alert system ....Not available

Crash tests
Gov't front-crash test, driver/front passenger ......NA/NA
Gov't side-crash test, driver/rear passenger ....NA/NA
IIHS offset crash test ....NA
IIHS side crash test w/ side & curtain airbags ....NA
IIHS side crash test w/o side & curtain airbags ....NA

ANOTHER LOOK

RELIABILITY HISTORY

TROUBLE SPOTS	97 98 99 00 01 02 03 04		
Engine			
Cooling		NO	
Fuel			
Ignition			
Transmission		DATA	
Electrical			
Air conditioning		NEW	
Suspension			
Brakes		MODEL	
Exhaust			
Paint/trim/rust			
Body integrity			
Power equipment			
Body hardware			
RELIABILITY VERDICT			

Infiniti Q45

THE Q45 LINE
Body style:
sedan
Trim lines:
–
Base price range:
$56,200

The Q has a smooth, refined V8, but the ride and handling of this big rear-drive sedan are not quite world-class. Rear-seat room is also disappointing. As is common to the class, comprehensive safety equipment is standard. An optional voice-activated system allows the driver to control audio, climate-control, and navigation functions. Mastering this system takes patience, practice, and a good deal of frustration. Other options include a rear-view camera system to aid visibility when backing up and distance-sensing cruise control.

REPORT CARD

○	Predicted reliability
○	Owner satisfaction
⊖	Predicted depreciation
NA	Accident avoidance
NA	Acceleration
NA	Ride
NA	Front seat comfort
NA	Fuel economy

SPECIFICATIONS

Drive wheels Rear

Seating 2 front, 3 rear

Engines available
4.5-liter V8 (340 hp)

Transmissions available
5-speed automatic

Fuel
Fuel type ....Premium
EPA city/highway, mpg 17/25
Fuel refill capacity, gal. 21.4

Dimensions and weight
Length, in. 200
Width, in. 73
Wheelbase, in. 113
Curb weight, lb. 4,050
Percent weight, front/rear 53/47
Typical towing ability, lb. 1,000

SAFETY INFORMATION

Active safety features
Antilock brakes ....Standard
Traction control ....Standard
Stability control ....Standard
Daytime running lights ....Not available
Tire pressure monitor ....Available

Safety belts
Center-rear belt 3-point
Pretensioners, front/rear ....Yes/no

Air bags
Occupant-sensing system ....Not available
Side bags, front/rear ....Standard/no
Inflatable curtain ....Standard
Accident alert system ....Not available

Crash tests
Gov't front-crash test, driver/front passenger .....NA/NA
Gov't side-crash test, driver/rear passenger ....NA/NA
IIHS offset crash test ....Good
IIHS side crash test w/ side & curtain airbags ....NA
IIHS side crash test w/o side & curtain airbags ....NA

ANOTHER LOOK

RELIABILITY HISTORY

TROUBLE SPOTS	Infiniti Q45							
	97	98	99	00	01	02	03	04
Engine	●	●			●			
Cooling	●	●	○		●			
Fuel	⊖	⊖	○		●			
Ignition	●	●	●		●			
Transmission	●	●	●		●			
Electrical	⊖	Insufficient data	Insufficient data	Insufficient data	⊖	Insufficient data	Insufficient data	Insufficient data
Air conditioning	●				●			
Suspension	○				⊖			
Brakes	⊖				●			
Exhaust	●				●			
Paint/trim/rust	⊖	●		●				
Body integrity	⊖	⊖		⊖				
Power equipment	●	●		⊖				
Body hardware	●	●		⊖				
RELIABILITY VERDICT	✓	✓		⊝				

Infiniti QX56

THE QX56 LINE
Body style:
4-door SUV
Trim lines:
–
Base price range:
$48,000-$51,000

This large SUV is Infiniti's version of the Nissan Armada, which is based on the Titan pickup. The roughly $10,000 premium over the Nissan buys a more-luxurious interior with a standard navigation system; a DVD entertainment system is optional. The V8 in our tested Armada was smooth and powerful, linked to a slick five-speed automatic. These SUVs feature an independent rear suspension, and handling was quite responsive for a vehicle this large and tall. The ride was quite stiff, and engine noise was pronounced. The interior is spacious, but the third-row seat is small.

REPORT CARD

NA	**Predicted reliability**
NA	**Owner satisfaction**
NA	**Predicted depreciation**
NA	**Accident avoidance**
NA	**Acceleration**
NA	**Ride**
NA	**Front seat comfort**
NA	**Fuel economy**

SPECIFICATIONS

Drive wheels Rear or permanent 4WD

Seating 2 front, 3 rear, 3 third

Engines available
5.6-liter V8 (315 hp)

Transmissions available
5-speed automatic

Fuel
Fuel type ....Premium
EPA city/highway, mpg 13/18
Fuel refill capacity, gal. 28.0

Dimensions and weight
Length, in. 207
Width, in. 79
Wheelbase, in. 123
Curb weight, lb. 5,630
Percent weight, front/rear 52/48
Typical towing ability, lb. 8,900

SAFETY INFORMATION

Active safety features
Antilock brakes ....Standard
Traction control ....Standard
Stability control ....Standard
Daytime running lights ....Not available
Tire pressure monitor ....Available

Safety belts
Center-rear belt 3-point
Pretensioners, front/rear ....Yes/yes

Air bags
Occupant-sensing system ....Front
Side bags, front/rear ....Standard/no
Inflatable curtain ....Standard with rollover
Accident alert system ....Not available

Crash tests
Gov't front-crash test, driver/front passenger ......NA/NA
Gov't side-crash test, driver/rear passenger ....NA/NA
IIHS offset crash test ....NA
IIHS side crash test w/ side & curtain airbags ....NA
IIHS side crash test w/o side & curtain airbags ....NA

ANOTHER LOOK

RELIABILITY HISTORY

TROUBLE SPOTS	97 98 99 00 01 02 03 04
Engine	
Cooling	
Fuel	NOT
Ignition	
Transmission	ENOUGH
Electrical	
Air conditioning	DATA
Suspension	
Brakes	TO
Exhaust	
Paint/trim/rust	RATE
Body integrity	
Power equipment	
Body hardware	
RELIABILITY VERDICT	

Expert • Independent • Nonprofit

Isuzu Ascender

The Ascender, Isuzu's only remaining vehicle in its lineup, is the Trooper's successor. It is essentially a rebadged Chevrolet TrailBlazer/GMC Envoy. An available third-row seat makes it a seven-passenger vehicle. Our tested Envoy and TrailBlazer offered a compliant if somewhat jiggly ride. The standard 4.2-liter inline six-cylinder needs to be revved for thrust. The Limited model comes standard with a 5.3-liter V8. Handling is clumsy. Emergency handling is sloppy, and braking is mediocre. The front seats aren't comfortable, and the hard-to-reach seat-mounted front safety belts are a nuisance.

THE ASCENDER LINE

Body style:
4-door SUV
Trim lines:
S, LS, Limited
Base price range:
$25,959-$38,914

REPORT CARD

NA	**Predicted reliability**
NA	**Owner satisfaction**
NA	**Predicted depreciation**
NA	**Accident avoidance**
NA	**Acceleration**
NA	**Ride**
NA	**Front seat comfort**
NA	**Fuel economy**

SAFETY INFORMATION

Active safety features

Antilock brakes	Standard
Traction control	Optional on 2WD
Stability control	Not available
Daytime running lights	Standard
Tire pressure monitor	Not available

Safety belts

Center-rear belt	3-point
Pretensioners, front/rear	No/no

Air bags

Occupant-sensing system	Not available
Side bags, front/rear	No/no
Inflatable curtain	Optional
Accident alert system	Available

Crash tests

Gov't front-crash test, driver/front passenger	◐/◓
Gov't side-crash test, driver/rear passenger	●/◓
IIHS offset crash test	Marginal
IIHS side crash test w/ side & curtain airbags	NA
IIHS side crash test w/o side & curtain airbags	NA

SPECIFICATIONS

Drive wheels Rear or selectable 4WD

Seating 2 front, 3 rear, 2 third

Engines available
4.2-liter 6 (275 hp); 5.3-liter V8 (300 hp)

Transmissions available
4-speed automatic

Fuel

Fuel type	Regular
EPA city/highway, mpg	16/21
Fuel refill capacity, gal.	25.0

Dimensions and weight

Length, in.	208
Width, in.	76
Wheelbase, in.	129
Curb weight, lb.	4,965
Percent weight, front/rear	54/46
Typical towing ability, lb.	5,500

ANOTHER LOOK

RELIABILITY HISTORY

TROUBLE SPOTS	97	98	99	00	01	02	03	04
Engine								
Cooling				NOT				
Fuel								
Ignition								
Transmission				ENOUGH				
Electrical								
Air conditioning				DATA				
Suspension								
Brakes				TO				
Exhaust								
Paint/trim/rust				RATE				
Body integrity								
Power equipment								
Body hardware								
RELIABILITY VERDICT								

● ● ○ ● ●
better ◄——► worse   See page 36 for more information.

Jaguar S-Type

The S-Type lacks the outstanding interior quality and quietness of its major competitors from BMW, Lexus, and Mercedes-Benz. The 3.0-liter V6 doesn't feel very responsive, particularly at low revs. The 4.2-liter V8, mated to a six-speed automatic, makes for a strong powertrain. The ride is supple and well-controlled but can't match the BMW 5 Series or Mercedes-Benz E-Class in comfort and quietness. Handling is sound, with recently improved steering and body control. The rear seat and trunk are cramped. The R model gets a supercharged, 390-hp engine. Reliability continues to be poor.

THE S-TYPE LINE

Body style: sedan
Trim lines: 3.0, 4.2, VDP, R
Base price range: $44,230-$58,330

REPORT CARD

●	Predicted reliability
◓	Owner satisfaction
○	Predicted depreciation
◉	Accident avoidance
◉	Acceleration
◓	Ride
◉	Front seat comfort
◓	Fuel economy

SPECIFICATIONS

Drive wheels Rear

Seating 2 front, 3 rear

Engines available
3.0-liter V6 (235 hp); 4.2-liter V8 (294 hp); 4.2-liter V8 supercharged (390 hp)

Transmissions available
6-speed automatic

Fuel
Fuel type . . . . Premium
EPA city/highway, mpg 18/26
Fuel refill capacity, gal. 18.4

Dimensions and weight
Length, in. 192
Width, in. 72
Wheelbase, in. .115
Curb weight, lb. 3,880
Percent weight, front/rear 53/47
Typical towing ability, lb. 4,070

SAFETY INFORMATION

Active safety features
Antilock brakes . . . . .Standard
Traction control . . . . .Standard
Stability control . . . . .Standard
Daytime running lights . . . . .Not available
Tire pressure monitor . . . . .Not available

Safety belts
Center-rear belt 3-point
Pretensioners, front/rear .Yes/no

Air bags
Occupant-sensing system . . . . .Front
Side bags, front/rear .Standard/no
Inflatable curtain . . . . .Standard
Accident alert system . . . . .Available

Crash tests
Gov't front-crash test, driver/front passenger . . . . . .NA/NA
Gov't side-crash test, driver/rear passenger . . . . . .◓/◉
IIHS offset crash test . . . . .NA
IIHS side crash test w/ side & curtain airbags . . . . .NA
IIHS side crash test w/o side & curtain airbags . . . . .NA

FROM THE TEST TRACK

Tested model
2004 4.2 sedan, 4.2-liter V8, 6-speed automatic

Tires as tested
Michelin Pilot HX MXM4, size 235/50R17 96H

Acceleration . . . . ◉
0-30 mph, sec. 2.4
0-60 mph, sec. 6.3
Quarter mile, sec. 14.9
Quarter mile, mph 97
45-65 mph, sec. 4.2

Other findings
Transmission . . . . ◉
Turning circle, ft. 40
Ground clearance, in. 4.5

Braking and handling
Braking . . . .◓
Braking, dry pavement, ft. 129
Routine handling . . . .◓
Emergency handling . . . .◓
Avoidance maneuver, max. mph . . .51.5

Convenience and comfort
Ride . . . .◓
Noise . . . .◓
Driving position . . . .◓
Access . . . .◓
Controls and displays . . . .◓
Fit and finish . . . .◓
Door top to ground, in. 51.0
Trunk . . . .◓
Luggage capacity . . . . .2+1
Max. load, lb. 905

Seating
Front-seat comfort . . . . ◉
Front shoulder room, in. 55.0
Front leg room, in. 41.0
Front head room, in. 4.0
Rear-seat comfort . . . . ○
Rear shoulder room, in. 55.0
Rear leg room, in. 27.5
Rear head room, in 1.0

Fuel economy . . . . ◓
CU's overall mileage, mpg 19
CU's city/highway, mpg 12/29
CU's 150-mile trip, mpg 24
Annual fuel . . . . .795 gal./$1,755
Cruising range 405

RELIABILITY HISTORY

TROUBLE SPOTS	97	98	99	00	01	02	03	04
Engine			○	○			◓	
Cooling			◓	◓			◉	
Fuel			◓	◓			◓	
Ignition			◓	○			◓	
Transmission			○	○			◓	
Electrical			●	◓			◓	
Air conditioning			○	◓	Insufficient data		Insufficient data	
Suspension			◓	◓			◉	
Brakes			○	◓			◓	
Exhaust			◉	◉			○	
Paint/trim/rust			◓	◓			◉	
Body integrity			◓	○			○	
Power equipment			◓	◓			◓	
Body hardware			◓	◓			○	
RELIABILITY VERDICT			X	X			X	

Jaguar X-Type

The X-Type is Jaguar's entry model and the second developed on a Ford platform. All-wheel drive is standard. The 3.0-liter V6 is a lively performer, and the automatic shifts smoothly. Handling is fairly nimble and ultimately forgiving. The ride is supple. The cabin is a bit tight, road noise is pronounced, and fit and finish falls a little short of luxury-car expectations. Overall, the car isn't as well-rounded as competitors from Audi and BMW, even though it's almost as expensive. Reliability continues to be poor. A wagon version joins the lineup for 2005. The 2.5-liter engine has been dropped.

THE X-TYPE LINE
Body style:
sedan; wagon
Trim lines:
3.0, Sport, VDP
Base price range:
$30,330-$38,080

REPORT CARD

●	Predicted reliability
◒	Owner satisfaction
○	Predicted depreciation
◉	Accident avoidance
◒	Acceleration
◒	Ride
◒	Front seat comfort
◒	Fuel economy

SPECIFICATIONS

Drive wheels AWD

Seating 2 front, 3 rear

Engines available
3.0-liter V6 (227 hp)

Transmissions available
5-speed manual; 5-speed automatic

Fuel
Fuel type ....Premium
EPA city/highway, mpg 18/25
Fuel refill capacity, gal. 16.2

Dimensions and weight
Length, in. 184
Width, in. 70
Wheelbase, in. 107
Curb weight, lb. 3,625
Percent weight, front/rear 60/40
Typical towing ability, lb. 3,306

SAFETY INFORMATION

Active safety features
Antilock brakes ....Standard
Traction control ....Included with stability
Stability control ......Optional (standard on Sport, wagon)
Daytime running lights ....Not available
Tire pressure monitor ....Not available

Safety belts
Center-rear belt 3-point
Pretensioners, front/rear ....Yes/no

Air bags
Occupant-sensing system ....Front
Side bags, front/rear ....Standard/no
Inflatable curtain ....Standard
Accident alert system ....Available

Crash tests
Gov't front-crash test, driver/front passenger ...... ◒/◒
Gov't side-crash test, driver/rear passenger ...... ◒/◒
IIHS offset crash test ....Good
IIHS side crash test w/ side & curtain airbags .....Marginal
IIHS side crash test w/o side & curtain airbags ....NA

FROM THE TEST TRACK

Tested model
2002 3.0 sedan AWD, 3.0-liter V6, 5-speed automatic

Tires as tested
Continental ContiTouring Contact, size 205/55R16 91H

Acceleration ....◒
0-30 mph, sec. 2.8
0-60 mph, sec. 7.8
Quarter mile, sec. 16.1
Quarter mile, mph 89
45-65 mph, sec. 5.2

Other findings
Transmission ....◒
Turning circle, ft. 38
Ground clearance, in. 4.5

Braking and handling
Braking ....◒
Braking, dry pavement, ft. 136
Routine handling ....●
Emergency handling ....◒
Avoidance maneuver, max. mph ..53.0

Convenience and comfort
Ride ....◒
Noise ....○
Driving position ....◒
Access ....◒
Controls and displays ....◒
Fit and finish ....◒
Door top to ground, in. 50.0
Trunk ....◒
Luggage capacity ....3+3
Max. load, lb. 880

Seating
Front-seat comfort ....◒
Front shoulder room, in. 54.0
Front leg room, in. 41.0
Front head room, in. 2.5
Rear-seat comfort ....○
Rear shoulder room, in. 53.0
Rear leg room, in. 27.0
Rear head room, in 2.0

Fuel economy ....◒
CU's overall mileage, mpg 19
 CU's city/highway, mpg 13/29
 CU's 150-mile trip, mpg 24
Annual fuel ....770 gal./$1,695
Cruising range 355

RELIABILITY HISTORY

TROUBLE SPOTS	Jaguar X-Type							
	97	98	99	00	01	02	03	04
Engine						◒	◒	●
Cooling						○	◒	◒
Fuel						○	◒	●
Ignition						●	◒	●
Transmission						●	◒	◒
Electrical						◒	◒	◒
Air conditioning						◒	◒	●
Suspension						◒	●	●
Brakes						○	◒	●
Exhaust						●	●	●
Paint/trim/rust						◒	◒	●
Body integrity						◒	●	◒
Power equipment						○	◒	◒
Body hardware						●	●	◒
RELIABILITY VERDICT						✗	✗	-

Jaguar XJ8

The XJ8 maintains the big Jaguar's chic, classic looks. Its aluminum body weighs considerably less than the old model. The refined and powerful V8 engine pumps out 294 hp. The six-speed automatic is very smooth, and the interior features luxurious leather and wood. The ride, however, isn't as comfortable as it should be in a large luxury car, nor as quiet as the leaders in this class. Handling is fairly nimble, though the steering is too light. The rear seat is relatively cramped, but better in the long-wheelbase L model. The intuitive controls are a positive departure from Jaguar tradition.

REPORT CARD

NA	Predicted reliability
⊙	Owner satisfaction
NA	Predicted depreciation
⊙	Accident avoidance
⊙	Acceleration
⊖	Ride
⊖	Front seat comfort
⊖	Fuel economy

THE XJ8 LINE
Body style: sedan
Trim lines: Base, XJ8L, Vanden Plas, XJR, Super V8
Base price range: $60,830-$89,330

SPECIFICATIONS

Drive wheels Rear

Seating 2 front, 3 rear

Engines available
4.2-liter V8 (294 hp); 4.2-liter V8 supercharged (390 hp)

Transmissions available
6-speed automatic

Fuel
Fuel type ....Premium
EPA city/highway, mpg 18/28
Fuel refill capacity, gal. 22.4

Dimensions and weight
Length, in. 200
Width, in. 73
Wheelbase, in. 119
Curb weight, lb. 3,860
Percent weight, front/rear 52/48
Typical towing ability, lb. 4,180

SAFETY INFORMATION

Active safety features
Antilock brakes ....Standard
Traction control ....Standard
Stability control ....Standard
Daytime running lights ....Not available
Tire pressure monitor ....Not available

Safety belts
Center-rear belt 3-point
Pretensioners, front/rear ....Yes/yes

Air bags
Occupant-sensing system ....Front
Side bags, front/rear ....Standard/no
Inflatable curtain ....Standard
Accident alert system ....Not available

Crash tests
Gov't front-crash test, driver/front passenger ......NA/NA
Gov't side-crash test, driver/rear passenger ....NA/NA
IIHS offset crash test ....NA
IIHS side crash test w/ side & curtain airbags ....NA
IIHS side crash test w/o side & curtain airbags ....NA

FROM THE TEST TRACK

Tested model
2004 Vanden Plas sedan, 4.2-liter V8, 6-speed automatic

Tires as tested
Continental ContiTouring Contact CH95, size 235/50R18 97H

Acceleration .... ⊙
0-30 mph, sec. 2.8
0-60 mph, sec. 7.1
Quarter mile, sec. 15.6
Quarter mile, mph 93
45-65 mph, sec. 4.4

Other findings
Transmission .... ⊙
Turning circle, ft. 41
Ground clearance, in. 4.5

Braking and handling
Braking .... ⊖
Braking, dry pavement, ft. 133
Routine handling .... ⊖
Emergency handling .... ⊖
Avoidance maneuver, max. mph ..52.0

Convenience and comfort
Ride .... ⊖
Noise .... ⊖
Driving position .... ⊖
Access .... ⊖
Controls and displays .... ⊖
Fit and finish .... ⊙
Door top to ground, in. 51.0
Trunk .... ⊖
Luggage capacity ....2+2
Max. load, lb. 880

Seating
Front-seat comfort .... ⊖
Front shoulder room, in. 58.0
Front leg room, in. 41.5
Front head room, in. 4.0
Rear-seat comfort .... ⊖
Rear shoulder room, in. 58.5
Rear leg room, in. 29.5
Rear head room, in 3.5

Fuel economy
CU's overall mileage, mpg 19
CU's city/highway, mpg 12/30
CU's 150-mile trip, mpg 23
Annual fuel ....785 gal./$1,725
Cruising range 490

RELIABILITY HISTORY

TROUBLE SPOTS	Jaguar XJ Series							
	97	98	99	00	01	02	03	04
Engine		○	○	○				
Cooling		○	●	○				
Fuel		○	○	○				
Ignition		⊙	○	○				
Transmission		◑	●	○				
Electrical	●	○	●	○				
Air conditioning		◑	●	○				
Suspension		◑	○	○				
Brakes	◑	○	○	○				
Exhaust		○	○	○				
Paint/trim/rust		○	○	○				
Body integrity		○	◑	○				
Power equipment		○	○	●				
Body hardware		○	○	◑				
RELIABILITY VERDICT	✗	–	✗					

Columns 01, 02, 03, 04: Insufficient data

Expert • Independent • Nonprofit

Jeep Grand Cherokee

THE GRAND CHEROKEE LINE

Body style:
4-door SUV
Trim lines:
Laredo, Limited, SRT8
Base price range:
$26,230-$37,500E

The Grand Cherokee got its first thorough redesign in over a decade. The front suspension is now independent, and the steering adopts a modern rack-and-pinion setup. Handling is more precise and the ride is much improved. Rear-seat space, however, is only slightly improved. The base engine is a lackluster 3.7-liter V6. A stronger 4.7-liter V8 and the much-hyped 5.7-liter Hemi V8 are also available. Fit and finish isn't on par with its competitors. Unlike other SUVs in this class, a third-row seat isn't offered. The upcoming Commander will have three rows.

REPORT CARD

New	**Predicted reliability**
New	**Owner satisfaction**
NA	**Predicted depreciation**
NA	**Accident avoidance**
NA	**Acceleration**
NA	**Ride**
NA	**Front seat comfort**
NA	**Fuel economy**

SPECIFICATIONS

Drive wheels Rear or permanent 4WD

Seating 2 front, 3 rear

Engines available
3.7-liter V6 (210 hp); 4.7-liter V8 (230 hp);
5.7-liter V8 (325 hp); 6.1-liter V8 (415 hp)

Transmissions available
5-speed automatic

Fuel
Fuel type . . . . Regular
EPA city/highway, mpg 15/20
Fuel refill capacity, gal. 20.6

Dimensions and weight
Length, in. 186
Width, in. 84
Wheelbase, in. 109
Curb weight, lb. 4,725
Percent weight, front/rear 54/46
Typical towing ability, lb. 6,500

SAFETY INFORMATION

Active safety features
Antilock brakes . . . . .Standard
Traction control . . . . .Included with stability
Stability control . . . . .Optional on 4WD
Daytime running lights . . . . .Not available
Tire pressure monitor . . . . .Available

Safety belts
Center-rear belt 3-point
Pretensioners, front/rear . . . . .Yes/no

Air bags
Occupant-sensing system . . . . .Front
Side bags, front/rear . . . . .No/no
Inflatable curtain . . . . .Optional
Accident alert system . . . . .Not available

Crash tests
Gov't front-crash test, driver/front passenger . . . . . . ●/●
Gov't side-crash test, driver/rear passenger . . . .●/●
IIHS offset crash test . . . . .NA
IIHS side crash test w/ side & curtain airbags . . . . .NA
IIHS side crash test w/o side & curtain airbags . . . . .NA

ANOTHER LOOK

RELIABILITY HISTORY

TROUBLE SPOTS	97 98 99 00 01 02 03 04
Engine	
Cooling	NO
Fuel	
Ignition	DATA
Transmission	
Electrical	
Air conditioning	NEW
Suspension	
Brakes	MODEL
Exhaust	
Paint/trim/rust	
Body integrity	
Power equipment	
Body hardware	
RELIABILITY VERDICT	

● ● ○ ◑ ●
better ◀—— ——▶ worse   See page 36 for more information.

Jeep Liberty

CR RECOMMENDED ✓

THE LIBERTY LINE
Body style:
4-door SUV
Trim lines:
Sport, Renegade,
Limited
Base price range:
$19,380-$25,225

The Liberty was the first 4WD Jeep to adopt an independent front suspension and a modern rack-and-pinion steering setup. The 4WD model we tested handled soundly and proved secure and predictable in our testing. The ride is jittery, even on smooth roads, and road noise is pronounced. The available 3.7-liter, 210-hp V6 is responsive, though not fuel-efficient. The cockpit is rather narrow, and access is awkward. With low-range gearing, it did quite well in our tough off-road courses. We recommend the Selec-Trac 4WD system, which can remain engaged indefinitely. A diesel version is new for 2005.

REPORT CARD

○	Predicted reliability
⊖	Owner satisfaction
◉	Predicted depreciation
○	Accident avoidance
○	Acceleration
○	Ride
⊖	Front seat comfort
●	Fuel economy

SPECIFICATIONS

Drive wheels Rear, part-time, or permanent 4WD

Seating 2 front, 3 rear

Engines available
2.4-liter 4 (150 hp); 2.8-liter 4 turbodiesel (160 hp); 3.7-liter V6 (210 hp)

Transmissions available
6-speed manual; 4-speed automatic; 5-speed automatic

Fuel
Fuel type . . . . .Regular or diesel
EPA city/highway, mpg 17/22
Fuel refill capacity, gal. 20.5

Dimensions and weight
Length, in. 174
Width, in. 72
Wheelbase, in. 104
Curb weight, lb. 4,125
Percent weight, front/rear 55/45
Typical towing ability, lb. 2,000

SAFETY INFORMATION

Active safety features
Antilock brakes . . . . .Optional (standard with diesel)
Traction control . . . . .Not available
Stability control . . . . .Not available
Daytime running lights . . . . .Not available
Tire pressure monitor . . . . .Available

Safety belts
Center-rear belt 3-point
Pretensioners, front/rear . . . . .Yes/no

Air bags
Occupant-sensing system . . . . .Not available
Side bags, front/rear . . . . .No/no
Inflatable curtain . . . . .Optional
Accident alert system .Not available

Crash tests
Gov't front-crash test, driver/front passenger . . . . . .◉/○
Gov't side-crash test, driver/rear passenger . . . .◉/○
IIHS offset crash test . . . . .Marginal
IIHS side crash test w/ side & curtain airbags . . . . .NA
IIHS side crash test w/o side & curtain airbags . . . . .NA

FROM THE TEST TRACK

Tested model
2002 Sport 4-door SUV 4WD, 3.7-liter V6, 4-speed automatic

Tires as tested
Goodyear Wrangler SR-A, size P235/70R16 104S

Acceleration . . . .○
0-30 mph, sec. 3.2
0-60 mph, sec. 9.2
Quarter mile, sec. 17.1
Quarter mile, mph 80
45-65 mph, sec. 6.1

Other findings
Transmission . . . .⊖
Turning circle, ft. 37
Ground clearance, in. 6.5

Braking and handling
Braking . . . .○
Braking, dry pavement, ft. 139
Routine handling . . . .○
Emergency handling . . . .○
Avoidance maneuver, max. mph . .49.5

Convenience and comfort
Ride . . . .○
Noise . . . .○
Driving position . . . .○
Access . . . .○
Controls and displays . . . .⊖
Fit and finish . . . .○
Door top to ground, in. 61.5
Cargo area . . . .○
Cargo volume, cu.ft. 35.0
Max. load, lb. 1,150

Seating
Front-seat comfort . . . .⊖
Front shoulder room, in. 56.0
Front leg room, in. 40.0
Front head room, in. 6.0
Rear-seat comfort . . . .○
Rear shoulder room, in. 56.0
Rear leg room, in. 28.5
Rear head room, in 7.0

Fuel economy . . . .●
CU's overall mileage, mpg 15
CU's city/highway, mpg 10/21
CU's 150-mile trip, mpg 18
Annual fuel . . . . .1,000 gal./$1,995
Cruising range 310

RELIABILITY HISTORY

TROUBLE SPOTS	Jeep Liberty							
	97	98	99	00	01	02	03	04
Engine						◉	◉	◉
Cooling						◉	◉	◉
Fuel						◉	◉	◉
Ignition						◉	◉	◉
Transmission						⊖	⊖	◉
Electrical						⊖	◉	◉
Air conditioning						◉	◉	◉
Suspension						○	⊖	◉
Brakes						○	○	◉
Exhaust						◉	◉	◉
Paint/trim/rust						◉	◉	◉
Body integrity						◐	◐	◉
Power equipment						⊖	◉	◉
Body hardware						◐	◉	◉
RELIABILITY VERDICT						−	−	−

Jeep Wrangler

Consider the Wrangler a vehicle for off-road use rather than highway travel. While its off-pavement credentials are impeccable, this smallest and crudest Jeep is perhaps a bit too true to its roots. The ride is noisy and uncomfortable, and the steering is vague and imprecise. Outward visibility is poor, and opening the canvas top is a nuisance. The cramped rear seat is better suited to carrying cargo than passengers, but the longer wheelbase in the Unlimited model helps alleviate that problem. ABS is not available on most versions. Reliability has been average.

THE WRANGLER LINE

Body style:
2-door SUV

Trim lines:
SE, X, Sport, Unlimited, Rubicon, Unlimited Rubicon

Base price range:
$17,970-$28,365

REPORT CARD

○	Predicted reliability
⊖	Owner satisfaction
⊙	Predicted depreciation
NA	Accident avoidance
NA	Acceleration
NA	Ride
NA	Front seat comfort
NA	Fuel economy

SPECIFICATIONS

Drive wheels Part-time 4WD

Seating 2 front, 2 rear

Engines available
2.4-liter 4 (147 hp); 4.0-liter 6 (190 hp)

Transmissions available
5-speed manual; 6-speed manual; 4-speed automatic

Fuel
Fuel type ....Regular
EPA city/highway, mpg 16/19
Fuel refill capacity, gal. 19.0

Dimensions and weight
Length, in. 155
Width, in. 67
Wheelbase, in. 93
Curb weight, lb. 3,510
Percent weight, front/rear 50/50
Typical towing ability, lb. 2,000

SAFETY INFORMATION

Active safety features
Antilock brakes ....Optional on Sport only
Traction control ....Not available
Stability control ....Not available
Daytime running lights ....Not available
Tire pressure monitor ....Not available

Safety belts
Center-rear belt ....NA
Pretensioners, front/rear ....No/no

Air bags
Occupant-sensing system ....Not available
Side bags, front/rear ....No/no
Inflatable curtain ....Not available
Accident alert system ....Not available

Crash tests
Gov't front-crash test, driver/front passenger ......⊖/⊖
Gov't side-crash test, driver/rear passenger ....NA/NA
IIHS offset crash test ....Acceptable
IIHS side crash test w/ side & curtain airbags ....NA
IIHS side crash test w/o side & curtain airbags ....Marginal

ANOTHER LOOK

RELIABILITY HISTORY

TROUBLE SPOTS	Jeep Wrangler							
	97	98	99	00	01	02	03	04
Engine	⊖	⊖	⊖	⊖	⊖	○	○	○
Cooling	⊖	⊖	⊖	○	○	○	○	○
Fuel	○	○	○	○	○	○	○	○
Ignition	○	○	○	○	○	○	○	○
Transmission	○	○	○	○	○	○	○	○
Electrical	⊖	●	⊖	⊖	○	○	○	○
Air conditioning	⊖	⊖	⊖	⊖	○	○	○	○
Suspension	○	○	○	○	○	○	○	○
Brakes	⊖	○	○	○	○	○	○	○
Exhaust	●	⊖	⊖	○	○	○	○	○
Paint/trim/rust	○	⊖	○	○	○	⊖	○	○
Body integrity	⊖	⊖	⊖	⊖	⊖	○	○	○
Power equipment	○	○	○	○	○	○	○	○
Body hardware	○	○	○	○	⊖	○	○	○
RELIABILITY VERDICT	-	X	-	-	-	-	X	-

better ●—○—● worse   See page 36 for more information.

Kia Amanti

The Amanti, based on the Hyundai XG350, is not up to the level of the better cars in this class. Its soft ride isolates the cabin from road imperfections, but the car feels too buoyant to be comfortable. The Amanti is the worst-handling sedan we've recently tested, although its optional ESC keeps it secure at its handling limits. Stops in our braking tests were a bit long on wet surfaces. The V6 delivers only adequate performance, and its 18-mpg fuel economy is unexceptional. The interior boasts good fit and finish.

THE AMANTI LINE
Body style:
sedan
Trim lines:
–
Base price range:
$25,500

REPORT CARD

NA	Predicted reliability
NA	Owner satisfaction
NA	Predicted depreciation
○	Accident avoidance
○	Acceleration
◑	Ride
◑	Front seat comfort
◒	Fuel economy

SPECIFICATIONS

Drive wheels Front

Seating 2 front, 3 rear

Engines available
3.5-liter V6 (200 hp)

Transmissions available
5-speed automatic

Fuel
Fuel type ....Regular
EPA city/highway, mpg 17/25
Fuel refill capacity, gal. 18.5

Dimensions and weight
Length, in. 196
Width, in. 73
Wheelbase, in. 110
Curb weight, lb. 4,020
Percent weight, front/rear 62/38
Typical towing ability, lb. 2,000

SAFETY INFORMATION

Active safety features
Antilock brakes ....Standard
Traction control ....Optional
Stability control ....Optional
Daytime running lights ....Not available
Tire pressure monitor ....Not available

Safety belts
Center-rear belt 3-point
Pretensioners, front/rear ....Yes/no

Air bags
Occupant-sensing system ....Not available
Side bags, front/rear ....Standard/standard
Inflatable curtain ....Standard
Accident alert system ....Not available

Crash tests
Gov't front-crash test, driver/front passenger ......NA/NA
Gov't side-crash test, driver/rear passenger ....NA/NA
IIHS offset crash test ....NA
IIHS side crash test w/ side & curtain airbags ....NA
IIHS side crash test w/o side & curtain airbags ....NA

FROM THE TEST TRACK

Tested model
2004 sedan, 3.5-liter V6, 5-speed automatic

Tires as tested
Hankook Optimo H417, size P225/60R16 97H

Acceleration ....○
0-30 mph, sec. 3.2
0-60 mph, sec. 9.1
Quarter mile, sec. 17.2
Quarter mile, mph 83
45-65 mph, sec. 6.1

Other findings
Transmission ....◑
Turning circle, ft. 41
Ground clearance, in. 5.5

Braking and handling
Braking ....○
Braking, dry pavement, ft. 143
Routine handling ....○
Emergency handling ....◑
Avoidance maneuver, max. mph ...50.0

Convenience and comfort
Ride ....◑
Noise ....◑
Driving position ....◑
Access ....◑
Controls and displays ....○
Fit and finish ....●
Door top to ground, in. 52.5
Trunk ....○
Luggage capacity ....4+1
Max. load, lb. 860

Seating
Front-seat comfort ....◑
Front shoulder room, in. 58.0
Front leg room, in. 40.5
Front head room, in. 3.0
Rear-seat comfort ....◑
Rear shoulder room, in. 57.0
Rear leg room, in. 29.5
Rear head room, in 4.0

Fuel economy ....◒
CU's overall mileage, mpg 18
CU's city/highway, mpg 11/29
CU's 150-mile trip, mpg 22
Annual fuel ....840 gal./$1,675
Cruising range 385

RELIABILITY HISTORY

TROUBLE SPOTS	97 98 99 00 01 02 03 04
Engine	
Cooling	NOT
Fuel	
Ignition	
Transmission	ENOUGH
Electrical	
Air conditioning	DATA
Suspension	
Brakes	TO
Exhaust	
Paint/trim/rust	RATE
Body integrity	
Power equipment	
Body hardware	
RELIABILITY VERDICT	

Kia Optima

THE OPTIMA LINE

Body style:
sedan

Trim lines:
LX, EX

Base price range:
$15,900-$19,900

The Optima comes well equipped at a competitive price. It has a comfortable ride, quiet cabin, and very good fit and finish. The 2.7-liter V6 performs smoothly but isn't very fuel-efficient—it averaged just 20 mpg overall. Handling is not the Optima's strength, as the car corners with pronounced body lean, and steering is slow and uncommunicative. The front seats lacked lower back support for some of our drivers. Head room is tight, requiring some drivers to recline the seat. A Poor in the IIHS side-crash test is another negative. Four-cylinder models can't be equipped with antilock brakes.

REPORT CARD

NA	Predicted reliability
NA	Owner satisfaction
●	Predicted depreciation
○	Accident avoidance
◒	Acceleration
◒	Ride
◒	Front seat comfort
◔	Fuel economy

SPECIFICATIONS

Drive wheels Front

Seating 2 front, 3 rear

Engines available
2.4-liter 4 (138 hp); 2.7-liter V6 (170 hp)

Transmissions available
5-speed manual; 4-speed automatic

Fuel
Fuel type ....Regular
EPA city/highway, mpg 19/26
Fuel refill capacity, gal. 17.2

Dimensions and weight
Length, in. 186
Width, in. 72
Wheelbase, in. 106
Curb weight, lb. 3,410
Percent weight, front/rear 61/39
Typical towing ability, lb. ....NR

SAFETY INFORMATION

Active safety features

Antilock brakes ....Optional with V6
Traction control ....Not available
Stability control ....Not available
Daytime running lights ....Not available
Tire pressure monitor ....Not available

Safety belts

Center-rear belt 3-point
Pretensioners, front/rear ....Yes/no

Air bags

Occupant-sensing system ....Not available
Side bags, front/rear ....Standard/no
Inflatable curtain ....Not available
Accident alert system ....Not available

Crash tests

Gov't front-crash test, driver/front passenger .....◒/◔
Gov't side-crash test, driver/rear passenger ......◒/◔
IIHS offset crash test ....Acceptable
IIHS side crash test w/ side & curtain airbags ....Poor
IIHS side crash test w/o side & curtain airbags ....NA

FROM THE TEST TRACK

Tested model
2004 EX sedan, 2.7-liter V6, 4-speed automatic

Tires as tested
Michelin Energy MXV4 Plus, size P205/55R16 89V

Acceleration ....◔
0-30 mph, sec. 3.4
0-60 mph, sec. 9.1
Quarter mile, sec. 17.1
Quarter mile, mph 83
45-65 mph, sec. 5.7

Other findings
Transmission ....◒
Turning circle, ft. 38
Ground clearance, in. 5.5

Braking and handling
Braking ....◒
Braking, dry pavement, ft. 141
Routine handling ....○
Emergency handling ....○
Avoidance maneuver, max. mph ...50.0

Convenience and comfort
Ride ....◒
Noise ....○
Driving position ....○
Access ....◒
Controls and displays ....◒
Fit and finish ....◒
Door top to ground, in. 50.0
Trunk ....○
Luggage capacity ....3+2
Max. load, lb. 860

Seating
Front-seat comfort ....◒
Front shoulder room, in. 57.0
Front leg room, in. 41.0
Front head room, in. 3.0
Rear-seat comfort ....◒
Rear shoulder room, in. 55.0
Rear leg room, in. 28.5
Rear head room, in 3.0

Fuel economy ....◔
CU's overall mileage, mpg 20
CU's city/highway, mpg 13/29
CU's 150-mile trip, mpg 23
Annual fuel ....765 gal./$1,530
Cruising range 375

RELIABILITY HISTORY

TROUBLE SPOTS	97 98 99 00 01 02 03 04
Engine	
Cooling	NOT
Fuel	
Ignition	ENOUGH
Transmission	
Electrical	DATA
Air conditioning	
Suspension	TO
Brakes	
Exhaust	RATE
Paint/trim/rust	
Body integrity	
Power equipment	
Body hardware	
RELIABILITY VERDICT	

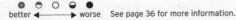
better ◀——▶ worse   See page 36 for more information.

Kia Rio

THE RIO LINE
Body style:
sedan; wagon
Trim lines:
Base, Cinco
Base price range:
$9,995-$11,500

The Rio is one of the lowest-priced cars sold in the U.S. Expect to get what you pay for. It's based on the dreadful Ford Aspire, which was made for Ford by Kia in the mid-1990s. A five-door wagon model named the Cinco is also available. Like the sedan, the cheapest wagon in the U.S. competes with other low-end economy cars as well as midpriced used vehicles. Kia's 10-year/100,000-mile powertrain warranty is one of the Rio's few selling points. A 1.6-liter engine from the Hyundai Accent is standard. The 2006 redesign, in the form of a sedan and hatchback, arrives soon.

REPORT CARD

NA	Predicted reliability
NA	Owner satisfaction
●	Predicted depreciation
NA	Accident avoidance
NA	Acceleration
NA	Ride
NA	Front seat comfort
NA	Fuel economy

SPECIFICATIONS

Drive wheels Front

Seating 2 front, 3 rear

Engines available
1.6-liter 4 (104 hp)

Transmissions available
5-speed manual; 4-speed automatic

Fuel
Fuel type . . . . .Regular
EPA city/highway, mpg 25/32
Fuel refill capacity, gal. 11.9

Dimensions and weight
Length, in. 166
Width, in. 66
Wheelbase, in. 95
Curb weight, lb. 2,295
Percent weight, front/rear 64/36
Typical towing ability, lb. . . . . .NR

SAFETY INFORMATION

Active safety features
Antilock brakes . . . . .Optional
Traction control . . . . .Not available
Stability control . . . . .Not available
Daytime running lights . . . . .Not available
Tire pressure monitor . . . . .Not available

Safety belts
Center-rear belt . . . . .Lap
Pretensioners, front/rear . . . . .No/no

Air bags
Occupant-sensing system . . . . .Not available
Side bags, front/rear . . . . .No/no
Inflatable curtain . . . . .Not available
Accident alert system . . . . .Not available

Crash tests
Gov't front-crash test, driver/front passenger . . . . .◐/◐
Gov't side-crash test, driver/rear passenger . . . .◐/◐
IIHS offset crash test . . . . .NA
IIHS side crash test w/ side & curtain airbags . . . . .NA
IIHS side crash test w/o side & curtain airbags . . . . .NA

ANOTHER LOOK

RELIABILITY HISTORY

TROUBLE SPOTS	97 98 99 00 01 02 03 04
Engine	
Cooling	NOT
Fuel	
Ignition	
Transmission	ENOUGH
Electrical	
Air conditioning	DATA
Suspension	
Brakes	TO
Exhaust	
Paint/trim/rust	RATE
Body integrity	
Power equipment	
Body hardware	
RELIABILITY VERDICT	

Kia Sedona

THE SEDONA LINE
Body style:
minivan
Trim lines:
LX, EX
Base price range:
$20,350-$22,950

The Sedona's 3.5-liter V6 is fairly refined, and the five-speed automatic shifts smoothly. However, the ride is stiff and uncomfortable, and the Sedona corners reluctantly and clumsily. Wind noise is excessive. The interior shows commendable attention to detail, with lots of storage bins and good fit and finish. Convenience features include dual sliding doors, but they lack power operation. The third-row seat is a 50/50-split bench. The van's heavy weight takes a toll on acceleration and fuel economy—only 16 mpg overall. Reliability has dropped to below average. A redesign arrives for 2006.

REPORT CARD

⊖	Predicted reliability
⊖	Owner satisfaction
○	Predicted depreciation
○	Accident avoidance
○	Acceleration
○	Ride
⊖	Front seat comfort
●	Fuel economy

SPECIFICATIONS

Drive wheels Front

Seating 2 front, 2 rear, 3 third

Engines available
3.5-liter V6 (195 hp)

Transmissions available
5-speed automatic

Fuel
Fuel type ....Regular
EPA city/highway, mpg 16/22
Fuel refill capacity, gal. 19.5

Dimensions and weight
Length, in. 194
Width, in. 75
Wheelbase, in. 115
Curb weight, lb. 4,800
Percent weight, front/rear 58/42
Typical towing ability, lb. 3,500

SAFETY INFORMATION

Active safety features
Antilock brakes ....Optional
Traction control ....Not available
Stability control ....Not available
Daytime running lights ....Not available
Tire pressure monitor ....Not available

Safety belts
Center-rear belt ....Lap
Pretensioners, front/rear ....Yes/no

Air bags
Occupant-sensing system ....Not available
Side bags, front/rear ....No/no
Inflatable curtain ....Not available
Accident alert system ....Not available

Crash tests
Gov't front-crash test, driver/front passenger   ○/○
Gov't side-crash test, driver/rear passenger   ○/○
IIHS offset crash test ....Acceptable
IIHS side crash test w/ side & curtain airbags ....NA
IIHS side crash test w/o side & curtain airbags ....NA

FROM THE TEST TRACK

Tested model
2003 EX minivan, 3.5-liter V6, 5-speed automatic

Tires as tested
Hankook RA07, size 215/70R15 98H

Acceleration ....○
0-30 mph, sec. 3.5
0-60 mph, sec. 10.5
Quarter mile, sec. 18.1
Quarter mile, mph 78
45-65 mph, sec. 6.9

Other findings
Transmission ....⊖
Turning circle, ft. 44
Ground clearance, in. 5.5

Braking and handling
Braking ....○
Braking, dry pavement, ft. 143
Routine handling ....○
Emergency handling ....⊖
Avoidance maneuver, max. mph ...47.5

Convenience and comfort
Ride ....○
Noise ....○
Driving position ....○
Access ....⊖
Controls and displays ....○
Fit and finish ....○
Door top to ground, in. 61.5
Cargo area ....○
Cargo volume, cu.ft. 62.0
Max. load, lb. 1,160

Seating
Front-seat comfort ....⊖
Front shoulder room, in. 62.0
Front leg room, in. 39.0
Front head room, in. 4.0
Rear-seat comfort ....○
Rear shoulder room, in. 63.0
Rear leg room, in. 28.5
Rear head room, in 4.5
Third-seat comfort ....⊖
Third shoulder room,in 58.0
Third leg room, in. 30.5
Third head room, in 1.0

Fuel economy ....●
CU's overall mileage, mpg 16
  CU's city/highway, mpg 10/25
  CU's 150-mile trip, mpg 20
Annual fuel ......955 gal./$1,905
Cruising range 350

RELIABILITY HISTORY

TROUBLE SPOTS	Kia Sedona							
	97	98	99	00	01	02	03	04
Engine						●	⊖	
Cooling						●	⊖	
Fuel						○	○	
Ignition						●	●	
Transmission						⊖	⊖	
Electrical						●	○	
Air conditioning						○	⊖	
Suspension						○	●	
Brakes						⊖	●	
Exhaust						●	○	
Paint/trim/rust						○	⊖	
Body integrity						⊖	○	
Power equipment						○	⊖	
Body hardware						●	○	
RELIABILITY VERDICT						✗	−	

Insufficient data

Kia Sorento

CR RECOMMENDED ✓

THE SORENTO LINE
Body style:
4-door SUV
Trim lines:
LX, EX
Base price range:
$18,995-$25,900

The Sorento competes among small SUVs even though it's larger than most of its competitors. It's an old-style body-on-frame truck powered by a 3.5-liter, 192-hp engine from Hyundai. Acceleration is quite spirited and the engine sounds civilized, but fuel economy is abysmal. The interior is fairly roomy, with good fit and finish. With its low-range gearing and ample ground clearance, the Sorento is competent off-road. The ride is stiff and handling is clumsy, though ultimately secure. A 10-year/100,000-mile warranty is a plus.

REPORT CARD

○	Predicted reliability
⊖	Owner satisfaction
NA	Predicted depreciation
○	Accident avoidance
○	Acceleration
⊖	Ride
⊖	Front seat comfort
●	Fuel economy

SPECIFICATIONS

Drive wheels Rear, part-time, or selectable 4WD

Seating 2 front, 3 rear

Engines available
3.5-liter V6 (192 hp)

Transmissions available
5-speed manual; 5-speed automatic

Fuel
Fuel type ....Regular
EPA city/highway, mpg 15/20
Fuel refill capacity, gal. 21.1

Dimensions and weight
Length, in. 180
Width, in. 74
Wheelbase, in. 107
Curb weight, lb. 4,500
Percent weight, front/rear 56/44
Typical towing ability, lb. 3,500

SAFETY INFORMATION

Active safety features
Antilock brakes ....Optional
Traction control ....Not available
Stability control ....Not available
Daytime running lights ....Not available
Tire pressure monitor ....Available

Safety belts
Center-rear belt 3-point
Pretensioners, front/rear ....Yes/no

Air bags
Occupant-sensing system ....Not available
Side bags, front/rear ....No/no
Inflatable curtain ....Standard
Accident alert system ....Not available

Crash tests
Gov't front-crash test, driver/front passenger .....⊖/⊖
Gov't side-crash test, driver/rear passenger ....◑/◑
IIHS offset crash test ....Acceptable
IIHS side crash test w/ side & curtain airbags ....NA
IIHS side crash test w/o side & curtain airbags ....NA

FROM THE TEST TRACK

Tested model
2004 LX 4-door SUV 4WD, 3.5-liter V6, 4-speed automatic

Tires as tested
Michelin Cross Terrain, size P245/70R16 106H

Acceleration ....○
0-30 mph, sec. 3.1
0-60 mph, sec. 9.5
Quarter mile, sec. 17.4
Quarter mile, mph 80
45-65 mph, sec. 5.8

Other findings
Transmission ....⊖
Turning circle, ft. 39
Ground clearance, in. 7.0

Braking and handling
Braking ....○
Braking, dry pavement, ft. 144
Routine handling ....○
Emergency handling ....○
Avoidance maneuver, max. mph ...48.0

Convenience and comfort
Ride ....⊖
Noise ....⊖
Driving position ....○
Access ....⊖
Controls and displays ....◑
Fit and finish ....⊖
Door top to ground, in. 62.5
Cargo area ....⊖
Cargo volume, cu.ft. 30.5
Max. load, lb. 1,145

Seating
Front-seat comfort ....⊖
Front shoulder room, in. 58.5
Front leg room, in. 40.0
Front head room, in. 3.0
Rear-seat comfort ....○
Rear shoulder room, in. 57.5
Rear leg room, in. 27.5
Rear head room, in 3.5

Fuel economy ....●
CU's overall mileage, mpg 15
  CU's city/highway, mpg 10/21
  CU's 150-mile trip, mpg 17
Annual fuel ....1,015 gal./$2,030
Cruising range 340

RELIABILITY HISTORY

TROUBLE SPOTS	Kia Sorento							
	97	98	99	00	01	02	03	04
Engine							◑	●
Cooling							◑	●
Fuel							⊖	●
Ignition							◑	●
Transmission							◑	●
Electrical							⊖	●
Air conditioning							◑	●
Suspension							◑	●
Brakes							⊖	●
Exhaust							◑	●
Paint/trim/rust							○	○
Body integrity							○	○
Power equipment							◑	●
Body hardware							⊖	●
RELIABILITY VERDICT							−	✓

Kia Spectra

THE SPECTRA LINE
Body style:
4-door hatchback;
sedan
Trim lines:
LX, EX, SX, Spectra5
Base price range:
$12,700-$15,150

The Kia Spectra, now based on the Hyundai Elantra, is better than its predecessor. It offers a comfortable ride, quiet interior, and good fit and finish. But it still trails the better cars in this category, with reluctant cornering and mediocre acceleration and fuel economy. The Spectra comes with standard side- and head-protection air bags, but it still got a Poor in the IIHS side-crash test. ABS can be extremely hard to find. The 138-hp, 2.0-liter four-cylinder engine delivers lackluster acceleration with the automatic and unimpressive fuel economy. A Spectra5 hatchback is available.

REPORT CARD

NA	Predicted reliability
NA	Owner satisfaction
NA	Predicted depreciation
○	Accident avoidance
◑	Acceleration
◑	Ride
◑	Front seat comfort
◑	Fuel economy

SPECIFICATIONS

Drive wheels Front

Seating 2 front, 3 rear

Engines available
2.0-liter 4 (138 hp)

Transmissions available
5-speed manual; 4-speed automatic

Fuel
Fuel type . . . . .Regular
EPA city/highway, mpg 24/32
Fuel refill capacity, gal. 14.5

Dimensions and weight
Length, in. 176
Width, in. 68
Wheelbase, in. .103
Curb weight, lb. 2,875
Percent weight, front/rear 64/36
Typical towing ability, lb. 1,874

SAFETY INFORMATION

Active safety features
Antilock brakes . . . . .Optional
Traction control . . . . .Not available
Stability control . . . . .Not available
Daytime running lights . . . . .Not available
Tire pressure monitor . . . . .Not available

Safety belts
Center-rear belt 3-point
Pretensioners, front/rear . . . . .Yes/no

Air bags
Occupant-sensing system .Front
Side bags, front/rear . . . . .Standard/no
Inflatable curtain . . . . .Standard
Accident alert system . . . . .Not available

Crash tests
Gov't front-crash test, driver/front passenger . . . . . ◔/◑
Gov't side-crash test, driver/rear passenger . . . . . . ◑/○
IIHS offset crash test .Acceptable
IIHS side crash test w/ side & curtain airbags . . . . .Poor
IIHS side crash test w/o side & curtain airbags . . . . .NA

FROM THE TEST TRACK

Tested model
2004 EX sedan, 2.0-liter Four, 4-speed automatic

Tires as tested
Goodyear Eagle LS, size P195/60R15 87H

Acceleration . . . . ◑
0-30 mph, sec. 3.8
0-60 mph, sec. 11.4
Quarter mile, sec. 18.4
Quarter mile, mph 76
45-65 mph, sec. 7.0

Other findings
Transmission . . . . ◑
Turning circle, ft. 37
Ground clearance, in. 5.5

Braking and handling
Braking . . . . ○
Braking, dry pavement, ft. 144
Routine handling . . . . ○
Emergency handling . . . . ○
Avoidance maneuver, max. mph . . .50.0

Convenience and comfort
Ride . . . . ◑
Noise . . . . ◑
Driving position . . . . ◑
Access . . . . ◑
Controls and displays . . . . ●
Fit and finish . . . . ◑
Door top to ground, in. 52.5
Trunk . . . . ○
Luggage capacity . . . . .3+1
Max. load, lb. 850

Seating
Front-seat comfort . . . . ◑
Front shoulder room, in. 55.0
Front leg room, in. 41.0
Front head room, in. 5.0
Rear-seat comfort . . . . ○
Rear shoulder room, in. 54.0
Rear leg room, in. 28.0
Rear head room, in 2.5

Fuel economy . . . . ◑
CU's overall mileage, mpg 25
 CU's city/highway, mpg 18/36
 CU's 150-mile trip, mpg 29
Annual fuel . . . . .590 gal./$1,180
Cruising range 395

RELIABILITY HISTORY

TROUBLE SPOTS	97 98 99 00 01 02 03 04
Engine	
Cooling	
Fuel	NOT
Ignition	
Transmission	ENOUGH
Electrical	
Air conditioning	DATA
Suspension	
Brakes	TO
Exhaust	
Paint/trim/rust	RATE
Body integrity	
Power equipment	
Body hardware	
RELIABILITY VERDICT	

● ● ○ ◑ ●
better ◄——► worse   See page 36 for more information.

Kia Sportage

THE SPORTAGE LINE
Body style:
4-door SUV
Trim lines:
LX, EX
Base price range:
$15,900-$21,400

Kia revives the Sportage name in this sister vehicle to the Hyundai Tucson, which is based on the Elantra. The base model comes equipped with a 2.0-liter four-cylinder engine, front-wheel drive, and a five-speed manual transmission. A four-speed automatic is optional. The 2.7-liter V6 model is priced below or on par with the four-cylinder versions from competitors. It is very similar to the Hyundai Tucson other than interior and exterior styling details. ABS, stability control, and head-protection side-curtain air bags are all standard.

REPORT CARD

New	Predicted reliability
New	Owner satisfaction
NA	Predicted depreciation
NA	Accident avoidance
NA	Acceleration
NA	Ride
NA	Front seat comfort
NA	Fuel economy

SPECIFICATIONS

Drive wheels Front or AWD

Seating 2 front, 3 rear

Engines available
2.0-liter 4 (140 hp); 2.7-liter V6 (173 hp)

Transmissions available
5-speed manual; 4-speed automatic

Fuel
Fuel type ....Regular
EPA city/highway, mpg 19/24
Fuel refill capacity, gal. 17.2

Dimensions and weight
Length, in. 171
Width, in. 71
Wheelbase, in. 104
Curb weight, lb. 3,520
Percent weight, front/rear 59/41
Typical towing ability, lb. 1,500

SAFETY INFORMATION

Active safety features
Antilock brakes ....Standard
Traction control ....Included with stability
Stability control ....Standard
Daytime running lights ....Not available
Tire pressure monitor ....Not available

Safety belts
Center-rear belt 3-point
Pretensioners, front/rear ....Yes/no

Air bags
Occupant-sensing system ....Front
Side bags, front/rear ....Standard/no
Inflatable curtain ....Standard
Accident alert system ....Not available

Crash tests
Gov't front-crash test, driver/front passenger ......NA/NA
Gov't side-crash test, driver/rear passenger ....NA/NA
IIHS offset crash test ....NA
IIHS side crash test w/ side & curtain airbags ....NA
IIHS side crash test w/o side & curtain airbags ....NA

ANOTHER LOOK

RELIABILITY HISTORY

TROUBLE SPOTS	97 98 99 00 01 02 03 04
Engine	
Cooling	NO
Fuel	
Ignition	
Transmission	DATA
Electrical	
Air conditioning	NEW
Suspension	
Brakes	MODEL
Exhaust	
Paint/trim/rust	
Body integrity	
Power equipment	
Body hardware	
RELIABILITY VERDICT	

Land Rover Freelander

THE FREELANDER LINE
Body style:
2-door SUV; 4-door SUV
Trim lines:
SE, SE3
Base price range:
$26,830

This small SUV has independent suspension and all-wheel drive. With traction control and an effective hill-descent system, it's one of the few unibody SUVs that's capable off-road. Ride and handling are quite good, and the brakes are strong. The seats are comfortable, and the rear is roomy. When we tested it in 2002, we found many controls were cryptic. The V6 is neither energetic nor fuel-efficient. The automatic didn't shift smoothly. Interior quality was unimpressive, and the air conditioning was marginal. A recent freshening has addressed some of those flaws. Reliability has been poor.

REPORT CARD

●	Predicted reliability
●	Owner satisfaction
○	Predicted depreciation
⊖	Accident avoidance
○	Acceleration
⊖	Ride
⊖	Front seat comfort
●	Fuel economy

SPECIFICATIONS

Drive wheels AWD

Seating 2 front, 3 rear

Engines available
2.5-liter V6 (174 hp)

Transmissions available
5-speed automatic

Fuel
Fuel type .... Premium
EPA city/highway, mpg 18/21
Fuel refill capacity, gal. 16.9

Dimensions and weight
Length, in. 175
Width, in. 71
Wheelbase, in. 101
Curb weight, lb. 3,640
Percent weight, front/rear 57/43
Typical towing ability, lb. 2,500

SAFETY INFORMATION

Active safety features
Antilock brakes .... Standard
Traction control .... Standard
Stability control .... Not available
Daytime running lights .... Not available
Tire pressure monitor .... Not available

Safety belts
Center-rear belt 3-point
Pretensioners, front/rear .... Yes/no

Air bags
Occupant-sensing system .... Not available
Side bags, front/rear .... No/no
Inflatable curtain .... Not available
Accident alert system .... Not available

Crash tests
Gov't front-crash test, driver/front passenger ..... NA/NA
Gov't side-crash test, driver/rear passenger ...... NA/NA
IIHS offset crash test .... Acceptable
IIHS side crash test w/ side & curtain airbags .... NA
IIHS side crash test w/o side & curtain airbags ...... Poor

FROM THE TEST TRACK

Tested model
2002 SE 4-door SUV 4WD, 2.5-liter V6, 5-speed automatic

Tires as tested
Michelin 4X4 Synchrone, size 225/55R17 97H

Acceleration .... ○
0-30 mph, sec. 3.6
0-60 mph, sec. 10.7
Quarter mile, sec. 18.0
Quarter mile, mph. 77
45-65 mph, sec. 7.3

Other findings
Transmission .... ○
Turning circle, ft. 40
Ground clearance, in. 6.5

Braking and handling
Braking .... ●
Braking, dry pavement, ft. 127
Routine handling .... ⊖
Emergency handling .... ○
Avoidance maneuver, max. mph ... 52.5

Convenience and comfort
Ride .... ⊖
Noise .... ○
Driving position .... ⊖
Access .... ⊖
Controls and displays .... ⊖
Fit and finish .... ○
Door top to ground, in. 59.0
Cargo area .... ⊖
Cargo volume, cu.ft. 29.0
Max. load, lb. 905

Seating
Front-seat comfort .... ⊖
Front shoulder room, in. 55.5
Front leg room, in. 40.5
Front head room, in. 2.5
Rear-seat comfort .... ⊖
Rear shoulder room, in. 55.0
Rear leg room, in. 28.0
Rear head room, in 3.0

Fuel economy .... ●
CU's overall mileage, mpg 17
CU's city/highway, mpg 13/22
CU's 150-mile trip, mpg 20
Annual fuel .... 870 gal./$1,740
Cruising range 305

RELIABILITY HISTORY

TROUBLE SPOTS	Land Rover Freelander							
	97	98	99	00	01	02	03	04
Engine						⊖		
Cooling						⊖		
Fuel						○		
Ignition						⊖		
Transmission						○		
Electrical						●	Insufficient data	Insufficient data
Air conditioning						⊖		
Suspension						○		
Brakes						●		
Exhaust						⊖		
Paint/trim/rust						⊖		
Body integrity						⊖		
Power equipment						●		
Body hardware						⊖		
RELIABILITY VERDICT						✗		

Land Rover LR3

THE LR3 LINE
Body style:
4-door SUV
Trim lines:
SE, HSE
Base price range:
$44,330-$49,330

The LR3 is the replacement for the Discovery. It follows in the tracks of the current Range Rover with fully independent suspension, but unlike the Range Rover, the LR3 is technically a body-on-frame design. A smooth, Jaguar-derived V8 supplies power, but is taxed with moving a heavy vehicle. Cabin access and interior quality have been improved. The ride is comfortable and handling is responsive. The optional third-row seat is usable now. With the turn of a knob, the Terrain Response system adjusts for snow, sand, or boulders by choosing or suggesting the appropriate setting.

REPORT CARD

New	**Predicted reliability**
New	**Owner satisfaction**
NA	**Predicted depreciation**
NA	**Accident avoidance**
NA	**Acceleration**
NA	**Ride**
NA	**Front seat comfort**
NA	**Fuel economy**

SPECIFICATIONS

Drive wheels Permanent 4WD

Seating 2 front, 3 rear, 2 third

Engines available
4.4-liter V8 (300 hp)

Transmissions available
6-speed automatic

Fuel
Fuel type . . . . .Premium
EPA city/highway, mpg 14/18
Fuel refill capacity, gal. 22.8

Dimensions and weight
Length, in. 191
Width, in. 75
Wheelbase, in. 114
Curb weight, lb. 5,705
Percent weight, front/rear 48/52
Typical towing ability, lb. 7,700

SAFETY INFORMATION

Active safety features
Antilock brakes . . . . .Standard
Traction control . . . . .Standard
Stability control . . . . .Standard
Daytime running lights . . . . .Not available
Tire pressure monitor .Not available

Safety belts
Center-rear belt 3-point
Pretensioners, front/rear .Yes/no

Air bags
Occupant-sensing system . . . . .Not available
Side bags, front/rear . . . . .Standard/optional
Inflatable curtain . . . . .Standard
Accident alert system . . . . .Not available

Crash tests
Gov't front-crash test, driver/front passenger . . . . . .NA/NA
Gov't side-crash test, driver/rear passenger . . . . .NA/NA
IIHS offset crash test . . . . .NA
IIHS side crash test w/ side & curtain airbags . . . . .NA
IIHS side crash test w/o side & curtain airbags . . . . .NA

ANOTHER LOOK

RELIABILITY HISTORY

TROUBLE SPOTS	97 98 99 00 01 02 03 04
Engine	
Cooling	
Fuel	NO
Ignition	
Transmission	DATA
Electrical	
Air conditioning	NEW
Suspension	
Brakes	MODEL
Exhaust	
Paint/trim/rust	
Body integrity	
Power equipment	
Body hardware	
RELIABILITY VERDICT	

Land Rover Range Rover

THE RANGE ROVER LINE
Body style:
4-door SUV
Trim lines:
HSE, Westminster
Base price range:
$73,085-$85,335

The current Range Rover luxury SUV comes with a host of high-end amenities and safety features. Developed by former-owner BMW and powered by a BMW V8, it delivers smooth, strong acceleration; mechanical refinement; and a very comfortable ride, although handling isn't quite BMW-agile. For 2006 the BMW engine is replaced by a Jaguar-sourced V8. Even though it's now a unibody construction with a fully independent suspension, it remains good off-road. The seats are very comfortable, and the wood and leather interior is tasteful.

REPORT CARD

NA	**Predicted reliability**
NA	**Owner satisfaction**
NA	**Predicted depreciation**
NA	**Accident avoidance**
NA	**Acceleration**
NA	**Ride**
NA	**Front seat comfort**
NA	**Fuel economy**

SPECIFICATIONS

Drive wheels Permanent 4WD

Seating 2 front, 3 rear

Engines available
4.4-liter V8 (282 hp)

Transmissions available
5-speed automatic

Fuel
Fuel type .Premium
EPA city/highway, mpg 12/16
Fuel refill capacity, gal. 26.4

Dimensions and weight
Length, in. 195
Width, in. 76
Wheelbase, in. 113
Curb weight, lb. 5,670
Percent weight, front/rear 48/52
Typical towing ability, lb. 7,700

SAFETY INFORMATION

Active safety features
Antilock brakes . . . . .Standard
Traction control . . . . .Standard
Stability control . . . . .Standard
Daytime running lights . . . . .Not available
Tire pressure monitor . . . . .Not available

Safety belts
Center-rear belt 3-point
Pretensioners, front/rear . . . . .Yes/no

Air bags
Occupant-sensing system . . . . .Not available
Side bags, front/rear . . . . .Standard/standard
Inflatable curtain . . . . .Standard
Accident alert system .Not available

Crash tests
Gov't front-crash test, driver/front passenger . . . . .NA/NA
Gov't side-crash test, driver/rear passenger . . . . . .NA/NA
IIHS offset crash test . . . . .NA
IIHS side crash test w/ side & curtain airbags . . . . .NA
IIHS side crash test w/o side & curtain airbags . . . . .NA

ANOTHER LOOK

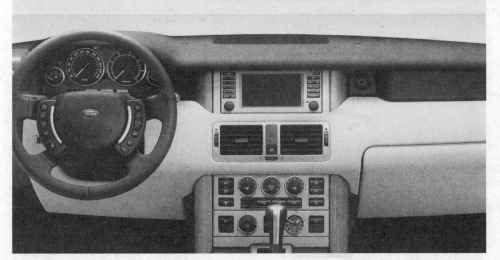

RELIABILITY HISTORY

TROUBLE SPOTS	97 98 99 00 01 02 03 04
Engine	
Cooling	**NOT**
Fuel	
Ignition	
Transmission	**ENOUGH**
Electrical	
Air conditioning	**DATA**
Suspension	
Brakes	**TO**
Exhaust	
Paint/trim/rust	**RATE**
Body integrity	
Power equipment	
Body hardware	
RELIABILITY VERDICT	

better ●○●○●─● worse   See page 36 for more information.

Lexus ES330

CR RECOMMENDED ✓

The ES330 provides the most comfortable and quiet driving experience in its class but isn't particularly engaging to drive. It has a refined powertrain, impressive fit and finish, and a comfortable interior. The ride is smooth and very quiet. The 3.3-liter V6 provides respectable acceleration and fuel economy. Handling is lackluster, with pronounced body lean in corners. The lack of a telescoping steering wheel is a significant omission in this price class, which makes finding a comfortable driving position difficult for some. Stability control is a worthwhile option.

THE ES330 LINE
Body style:
sedan
Trim lines:
–

Base price range:
$32,175

REPORT CARD

◒	Predicted reliability
◒	Owner satisfaction
◉	Predicted depreciation
◒	Accident avoidance
◒	Acceleration
◒	Ride
◉	Front seat comfort
○	Fuel economy

SPECIFICATIONS

Drive wheels Front

Seating 2 front, 3 rear

Engines available
3.3-liter V6 (225 hp)

Transmissions available
5-speed automatic

Fuel
Fuel type . . . . .Regular
EPA city/highway, mpg 21/29
Fuel refill capacity, gal. 18.5

Dimensions and weight
Length, in. 191
Width, in. 71
Wheelbase, in. .107
Curb weight, lb. 3,525
Percent weight, front/rear 61/39
Typical towing ability, lb. 2,000

SAFETY INFORMATION

Active safety features
Antilock brakes . . . . .Standard
Traction control . . . . .Included with stability
Stability control . . . . .Optional
Daytime running lights . . . . .Standard
Tire pressure monitor .Not available

Safety belts
Center-rear belt 3-point
Pretensioners, front/rear . . . . .Yes/yes

Air bags
Occupant-sensing system . . . . .Front
Side bags, front/rear . . . . .Standard/no
Inflatable curtain . . . . .Standard
Accident alert system .Not available

Crash tests
Gov't front-crash test, driver/front passenger . . . . . .◉/◉
Gov't side-crash test, driver/rear passenger . . . .◉/◒
IIHS offset crash test . . . . .Good
IIHS side crash test w/ side & curtain airbags . . . . .Good
IIHS side crash test w/o side & curtain airbags . . . . .NA

FROM THE TEST TRACK

Tested model
2004 sedan, 3.3-liter V6, 5-speed automatic

Tires as tested
Bridgestone Potenza RE92, size P215/60R16 94V

Acceleration . . . . ◒
0-30 mph, sec. 2.8
0-60 mph, sec. 7.9
Quarter mile, sec. 16.2
Quarter mile, mph 88
45-65 mph, sec. 5.5

Other findings
Transmission . . . . ◒
Turning circle, ft. 39
Ground clearance, in. 5.0

Braking and handling
Braking . . . . ◒
Braking, dry pavement, ft. 132
Routine handling . . . . ◒
Emergency handling . . . . ○
Avoidance maneuver, max. mph . . .47.5

Convenience and comfort
Ride . . . . ◒
Noise . . . . ◒
Driving position . . . . ◒
Access . . . . ◒
Controls and displays . . . . ◉
Fit and finish . . . . ◉
Door top to ground, in. 52.0
Trunk . . . . ○
Luggage capacity . . . . .4+1
Max. load, lb. 900

Seating
Front-seat comfort . . . . ◉
Front shoulder room, in. 56.5
Front leg room, in. 41.5
Front head room, in. 2.5
Rear-seat comfort . . . . ◒
Rear shoulder room, in. 55.0
Rear leg room, in. 27.0
Rear head room, in 2.5

Fuel economy . . . . ○
CU's overall mileage, mpg 22
 CU's city/highway, mpg 14/33
 CU's 150-mile trip, mpg 26
Annual fuel . . . . .695 gal./$1,390
Cruising range 460

RELIABILITY HISTORY

TROUBLE SPOTS	Lexus ES300, ES330							
	97	98	99	00	01	02	03	04
Engine	◒	◉	◉	◉	◉	◉	◉	◉
Cooling	◉	◉	◉	◉	◉	◉	◉	◉
Fuel	◒	◉	◉	◉	◉	◉	◉	◉
Ignition	◉	◉	◉	◉	◉	◉	◉	◉
Transmission	◉	◉	◉	◉	◉	◉	◉	◉
Electrical	◒	◒	○	◒	◒	◒	◒	◉
Air conditioning	◉	◉	◉	◉	◉	◉	◉	◉
Suspension	○	◒	◒	◉	◉	◉	◉	◉
Brakes	◒	◒	◒	○	○	◒	◒	◉
Exhaust	◉	◉	◉	◉	◉	◉	◉	◉
Paint/trim/rust	◉	◉	◉	◒	◉	◉	◉	◉
Body integrity	◒	◒	◒	◒	◒	◒	◒	◉
Power equipment	◒	◒	◒	◉	◉	◉	◉	◉
Body hardware	◉	◉	◉	◉	◉	◉	◉	◉
RELIABILITY VERDICT	✓	✓	✓	✓	✓	✓	✓	–

Expert • Independent • Nonprofit

Lexus GS300/GS430

THE GS300/GS430 LINE
Body style:
sedan
Trim lines:
GS300, GS430
Base price range:
$42,900-$51,125

The outgoing GS was a quiet and polished luxury sedan. Though competent, it always lacked the optimal ride-and-handling balance of the BMW 5 Series and Mercedes-Benz E-Class. A redesign featuring a move to a new V6 engine recently arrived. The V6 will offer optional all-wheel drive. A 4.3-liter V8 continues in the GS430 model, with a six-speed automatic transmission and a host of safety and high-tech features. The new car has the potential to be more competitive in its class. A GS450h hybrid-powered version is also planned.

REPORT CARD

⊖	Predicted reliability
⊖	Owner satisfaction
NA	Predicted depreciation
NA	Accident avoidance
NA	Acceleration
NA	Ride
NA	Front seat comfort
NA	Fuel economy

SPECIFICATIONS

Drive wheels Rear or AWD

Seating 2 front, 3 rear

Engines available
3.0-liter V6 (245 hp); 4.3-liter V8 (300 hp)

Transmissions available
6-speed automatic

Fuel
Fuel type . . . . .Premium
EPA city/highway, mpg 18/23
Fuel refill capacity, gal. 18.8

Dimensions and weight
Length, in. 190
Width, in. 72
Wheelbase, in. 112
Curb weight, lb. 3,535
Percent weight, front/rear 53/47
Typical towing ability, lb. 2,000

SAFETY INFORMATION

Active safety features

Antilock brakes . . . . .Standard
Traction control . . . . .Standard
Stability control . . . . .Standard
Daytime running lights . . . . .Standard
Tire pressure monitor .Available

Safety belts

Center-rear belt 3-point
Pretensioners, front/rear . . . . .Yes/no

Air bags

Occupant-sensing system . . . . .Front
Side bags, front/rear .Standard/no
Inflatable curtain . . . . .Standard
Accident alert system . . . . .Not available

Crash tests

Gov't front-crash test, driver/front passenger . . . . .NA/NA
Gov't side-crash test, driver/rear passenger . . . . . . .NA/NA
IIHS offset crash test . . . . .NA
IIHS side crash test w/ side & curtain airbags . . . . .NA
IIHS side crash test w/o side & curtain airbags . . . . .NA

ANOTHER LOOK

RELIABILITY HISTORY

TROUBLE SPOTS	Lexus GS300/GS400,							
	97	98	99	00	01	02	03	04
Engine		⊙	⊙	⊙	⊙	⊙	⊙	⊙
Cooling		⊙	⊙	⊙	⊙	⊙	⊙	⊙
Fuel		⊙	◒	◒	⊙	⊙	⊙	⊙
Ignition		⊙	⊙	⊙	⊙	⊙	⊙	⊙
Transmission		⊙	⊙	⊙	⊙	⊙	⊙	⊙
Electrical	Insufficient data	⊙	⊙	⊙	⊙	◒	⊙	⊙
Air conditioning		⊙	⊙	⊙	⊙	⊙	⊙	⊙
Suspension		⊙	⊙	⊙	⊙	⊙	⊙	⊙
Brakes		⊙	⊙	◒	◒	⊙	⊙	⊙
Exhaust		⊙	⊙	⊙	⊙	⊙	⊙	⊙
Paint/trim/rust		◒	⊙	⊙	⊙	⊙	⊙	⊙
Body integrity		○	◒	◒	◒	◒	◒	⊙
Power equipment		○	○	⊙	⊙	⊙	⊙	⊙
Body hardware		⊙	◒	⊙	⊙	⊙	⊙	⊙
RELIABILITY VERDICT		✓	✓	✓	✓	✓	✓	✓

⬤ ◕ ○ ◓ ⬤
better ← → worse   See page 36 for more information.

Lexus GX470

CR RECOMMENDED ✓

The GX470 luxury SUV shares its body-on-frame platform with the Toyota 4Runner. It has three rows of seats, but the third seat is tiny. It shares the luxurious Lexus LX470's smooth and quiet drivetrain, as well as many of its appointments. For 2005 horsepower grew to 270. The ride is comfortable and quiet, but it gets unsettled. Cornering is less than agile, though ultimately secure. Interior fit and finish is impressive. Typical options push the price to the low-$50,000 range. The GX is very competent off-road. An optional active suspension reduces lean in corners.

THE GX470 LINE
Body style:
4-door SUV
Trim lines:
–
Base price range:
$46,225

REPORT CARD

○	Predicted reliability
◉	Owner satisfaction
NA	Predicted depreciation
⊖	Accident avoidance
⊖	Acceleration
⊖	Ride
⊖	Front seat comfort
●	Fuel economy

SPECIFICATIONS

Drive wheels Permanent 4WD

Seating 2 front, 3 rear, 3 third

Engines available
4.7-liter V8 (270 hp)

Transmissions available
5-speed automatic

Fuel
Fuel type ....Regular
EPA city/highway, mpg 15/19
Fuel refill capacity, gal. 23.0

Dimensions and weight
Length, in. 188
Width, in. 74
Wheelbase, in. 110
Curb weight, lb. 4,825
Percent weight, front/rear 53/47
Typical towing ability, lb. 6,500

SAFETY INFORMATION

Active safety features
Antilock brakes ....Standard
Traction control ....Standard
Stability control ....Standard
Daytime running lights ....Standard
Tire pressure monitor ....Available

Safety belts
Center-rear belt 3-point
Pretensioners, front/rear ....Yes/no

Air bags
Occupant-sensing system ....Not available
Side bags, front/rear ....Standard/no
Inflatable curtain ....Standard with rollover
Accident alert system ....Available

Crash tests
Gov't front-crash test, driver/front passenger ......NA/NA
Gov't side-crash test, driver/rear passenger ......NA/NA
IIHS offset crash test ....Good
IIHS side crash test w/ side & curtain airbags ....NA
IIHS side crash test w/o side & curtain airbags ....NA

FROM THE TEST TRACK

Tested model
2004 4-door SUV 4WD, 4.7-liter V8, 5-speed automatic

Tires as tested
Bridgestone Dueler H/T B40, size P265/65R17 110S

Acceleration ....⊖
0-30 mph, sec. 2.7
0-60 mph, sec. 8.0
Quarter mile, sec. 16.4
Quarter mile, mph 83
45-65 mph, sec. 5.5

Other findings
Transmission ....◉
Turning circle, ft. 41
Ground clearance, in. 7.5

Braking and handling
Braking ....⊖
Braking, dry pavement, ft. 135
Routine handling ....○
Emergency handling ....⊖
Avoidance maneuver, max. mph ...49.0

Convenience and comfort
Ride ....⊖
Noise ....⊖
Driving position ....⊖
Access ....⊖
Controls and displays ....⊖
Fit and finish ....◉
Door top to ground, in. 66.0
Cargo area ....○
Cargo volume, cu.ft. 39.5
Max. load, lb. 1,225

Seating
Front-seat comfort ....⊖
Front shoulder room, in. 57.5
Front leg room, in. 41.5
Front head room, in. 4.0
Rear-seat comfort ....⊖
Rear shoulder room, in. 57.0
Rear leg room, in. 29.0
Rear head room, in 6.0
Third-seat comfort ....●
Third shoulder room,in 56.0
Third leg room, in. 24.0

Fuel economy ....●
CU's overall mileage, mpg 15
CU's city/highway, mpg 11/21
CU's 150-mile trip, mpg 18
Annual fuel ....995 gal./$1,990
Cruising range 380

RELIABILITY HISTORY

TROUBLE SPOTS	Lexus GX470							
	97	98	99	00	01	02	03	04
Engine							◉	◉
Cooling							◉	◉
Fuel							◉	◉
Ignition							◉	◉
Transmission							◉	◉
Electrical							◉	◉
Air conditioning							◉	◉
Suspension							○	⊖
Brakes							◉	◉
Exhaust							◉	◉
Paint/trim/rust							◉	◉
Body integrity							○	◉
Power equipment							○	◉
Body hardware							◉	◉
RELIABILITY VERDICT							✗	✓

Lexus IS300

CR RECOMMENDED ✓

The rear-drive IS300 is a compact sports sedan competing with the BMW 3 Series. The IS300's ride is firm but too jittery, lacking the compliance found in its German competitors. Power comes from a silky-smooth, 215-hp, six-cylinder engine mated to a five-speed automatic or manual transmission. Handling is very capable, though ultimately less agile or satisfying to drive than the 3 Series. The interior is snug, and the rear is tight. A 2006 redesign arrives this fall with 2.5- and 3.5-liter V6 engines. The 2.5 offers AWD.

THE IS300 LINE
Body style:
4-door hatchback; sedan
Trim lines:
Base, SportCross
Base price range:
$29,735-$31,105

REPORT CARD

◕	Predicted reliability
⊖	Owner satisfaction
⊖	Predicted depreciation
◕	Accident avoidance
◕	Acceleration
○	Ride
◕	Front seat comfort
○	Fuel economy

SPECIFICATIONS

Drive wheels Rear

Seating 2 front, 3 rear

Engines available
3.0-liter 6 (215 hp)

Transmissions available
5-speed manual; 5-speed automatic

Fuel
Fuel type ....Premium
EPA city/highway, mpg 18/25
Fuel refill capacity, gal. 17.5

Dimensions and weight
Length, in. 177
Width, in. 68
Wheelbase, in. 105
Curb weight, lb. 3,390
Percent weight, front/rear 54/46
Typical towing ability, lb. ....NR

SAFETY INFORMATION

Active safety features
Antilock brakes ....Standard
Traction control ....Standard
Stability control ....Optional
Daytime running lights ....Standard
Tire pressure monitor ....Not available

Safety belts
Center-rear belt 3-point
Pretensioners, front/rear ....Yes/no

Air bags
Occupant-sensing system ....Not available
Side bags, front/rear ....Standard/no
Inflatable curtain ....Standard
Accident alert system ....Not available

Crash tests
Gov't front-crash test, driver/front passenger .....NA/NA
Gov't side-crash test, driver/rear passenger ......◕/◕
IIHS offset crash test ....Good
IIHS side crash test w/ side & curtain airbags ....NA
IIHS side crash test w/o side & curtain airbags ....NA

FROM THE TEST TRACK

Tested model
2001 sedan, 3.0-liter Six, 5-speed automatic

Tires as tested
Goodyear Eagle GS-D, size 215/45R17 87W

Acceleration ....◕
0-30 mph, sec. 2.7
0-60 mph, sec. 7.4
Quarter mile, sec. 15.7
Quarter mile, mph 91
45-65 mph, sec. 4.4

Other findings
Transmission ....◕
Turning circle, ft. 37
Ground clearance, in. 3.5

Braking and handling
Braking ....◕
Braking, dry pavement, ft. 128
Routine handling ....◕
Emergency handling ....◕
Avoidance maneuver, max. mph ...57.0

Convenience and comfort
Ride ....○
Noise ....⊖
Driving position ....⊖
Access ....⊖
Controls and displays ....◕
Fit and finish ....◕
Door top to ground, in. 49.5
Trunk ....⊖
Luggage capacity ....3+1
Max. load, lb. 860

Seating
Front-seat comfort ....◕
Front shoulder room, in. 54.5
Front leg room, in. 41.5
Front head room, in. 2.0
Rear-seat comfort ....○
Rear shoulder room, in. 53.5
Rear leg room, in. 28.0
Rear head room, in 2.5

Fuel economy ....○
CU's overall mileage, mpg 21
CU's city/highway, mpg 15/28
CU's 150-mile trip, mpg 25
Annual fuel ....710 gal./$1,555
Cruising range 410

RELIABILITY HISTORY

TROUBLE SPOTS	Lexus IS300							
	97	98	99	00	01	02	03	04
Engine					◕	◕	◕	
Cooling					◕	◕	◕	
Fuel					◕	◕	◕	
Ignition					◕	◕	◕	
Transmission					◕	◕	◕	
Electrical					◕	◕	◕	
Air conditioning					◕	◕	◕	
Suspension					◕	◕	◕	
Brakes					⊖	◕	◕	
Exhaust					◕	◕	◕	
Paint/trim/rust					◕	⊖	⊖	
Body integrity					◕	⊖	◕	
Power equipment					◕	⊖	◕	
Body hardware					◕	⊖	◕	
RELIABILITY VERDICT					✓	✓	✓	Insufficient data

◕ ◑ ○ ⊖ ●
better ← → worse   See page 36 for more information.

Lexus LS430

CR RECOMMENDED ✓

The Lexus flagship surpasses the world's best when it comes to quietness and refinement. The LS430 is a stress-free and relaxing car. The 4.3-liter V8 delivers quick, effortless motivation. The ride is very comfortable and serene in an ultrahushed cabin, though not quite as absorbent as the Mercedes S-Class. Unlike most of its competitors, the controls are user-friendly. Fit and finish is exceptional. Optional heated seats that recline and massage pamper rear passengers. Handling is secure but lacks agility. An excellent reliability record and low depreciation make this car a standout.

THE LS430 LINE
Body style:
sedan
Trim lines:
–
Base price range:
$56,225

REPORT CARD

☺	Predicted reliability
☺	Owner satisfaction
☺	Predicted depreciation
⊖	Accident avoidance
☺	Acceleration
☺	Ride
☺	Front seat comfort
⊖	Fuel economy

SPECIFICATIONS

Drive wheels Rear

Seating 2 front, 3 rear

Engines available
4.3-liter V8 (290 hp)

Transmissions available
6-speed automatic

Fuel
Fuel type .... Premium
EPA city/highway, mpg 19/25
Fuel refill capacity, gal. 22.2

Dimensions and weight
Length, in. 197
Width, in. 72
Wheelbase, in. 115
Curb weight, lb. 4,205
Percent weight, front/rear 51/49
Typical towing ability, lb. 2,000

SAFETY INFORMATION

Active safety features
Antilock brakes .... Standard
Traction control .... Standard
Stability control .... Standard
Daytime running lights .... Standard
Tire pressure monitor .... Available

Safety belts
Center-rear belt 3-point
Pretensioners, front/rear .... Yes/yes

Air bags
Occupant-sensing system .... Not available
Side bags, front/rear .... Standard/no
Inflatable curtain .... Standard
Accident alert system .... Available

Crash tests
Gov't front-crash test, driver/front passenger ...... NA/NA
Gov't side-crash test, driver/rear passenger .... NA/NA
IIHS offset crash test .... Good
IIHS side crash test w/ side & curtain airbags .... NA
IIHS side crash test w/o side & curtain airbags .... NA

FROM THE TEST TRACK

Tested model
2003 sedan, 4.3-liter V8, 5-speed automatic

Tires as tested
Dunlop SP Sport 5000M, size P225/55R17 95H

Acceleration .... ☺
0-30 mph, sec. 2.8
0-60 mph, sec. 7.1
Quarter mile, sec. 15.6
Quarter mile, mph 93
45-65 mph, sec. 4.5

Other findings
Transmission .... ☺
Turning circle, ft. 37
Ground clearance, in. 6.0

Braking and handling
Braking .... ⊖
Braking, dry pavement, ft. 134
Routine handling .... ⊖
Emergency handling .... ○
Avoidance maneuver, max. mph ...49.0

Convenience and comfort
Ride .... ☺
Noise .... ☺
Driving position .... ☺
Access .... ☺
Controls and displays .... ☺
Fit and finish .... ☺
Door top to ground, in. 54.0
Trunk .... ○
Luggage capacity .... 4+1
Max. load, lb. 900

Seating
Front-seat comfort .... ☺
Front shoulder room, in. 59.0
Front leg room, in. 42.0
Front head room, in. 3.0
Rear-seat comfort .... ☺
Rear shoulder room, in. 57.0
Rear leg room, in. 30.5
Rear head room, in 3.0

Fuel economy .... ⊖
CU's overall mileage, mpg 19
CU's city/highway, mpg 12/29
CU's 150-mile trip, mpg 23
Annual fuel .... 795 gal./$1,755
Cruising range 490

RELIABILITY HISTORY

TROUBLE SPOTS	Lexus LS400, LS430							
	97	98	99	00	01	02	03	04
Engine	●	●	●	●	●	●	●	●
Cooling	●	●	●	●	●	●	●	●
Fuel	●	◐	●	●	●	●	●	◐
Ignition	●	●	●	●	●	●	●	●
Transmission	●	●	●	●	●	●	●	●
Electrical	◐	●	◐	○	●	●	●	●
Air conditioning	●	●	●	●	●	●	●	●
Suspension	●	●	●	●	●	●	●	●
Brakes	●	◐	◐	●	◐	●	●	●
Exhaust	●	●	●	●	●	●	●	●
Paint/trim/rust	●	●	●	●	●	●	●	●
Body integrity	●	●	●	◐	●	●	●	●
Power equipment	●	●	◐	○	◐	●	◐	●
Body hardware	●	●	●	●	●	●	●	●
RELIABILITY VERDICT	✓	✓	✓	✓	✓	✓	✓	

Lexus LX470

THE LX470 LINE
Body style:
4-door SUV
Trim lines:
–
Base price range:
$65,225

This luxury SUV competes at the top of the SUV market. It's based on the big, imposing Toyota Land Cruiser—itself hardly plebeian with its slick powertrain, comfortable ride, and quiet, nicely appointed cabin. Added features include a height-adjustable suspension and a power-adjustable steering wheel. The LX470 is one of the few SUVs that manages to be both capable off-road and civilized on pavement. Electronic stability control is standard, as is full-time four-wheel drive. Generous cargo space and a folding 50/50-split third seat add versatility.

REPORT CARD

◕	Predicted reliability
◔	Owner satisfaction
◕	Predicted depreciation
NA	Accident avoidance
NA	Acceleration
NA	Ride
NA	Front seat comfort
NA	Fuel economy

SPECIFICATIONS

Drive wheels Permanent 4WD

Seating 2 front, 3 rear, 3 third

Engines available
4.7-liter V8 (235 hp)

Transmissions available
5-speed automatic

Fuel
Fuel type ....Regular
EPA city/highway, mpg 13/17
Fuel refill capacity, gal. 25.4

Dimensions and weight
Length, in. 193
Width, in. 76
Wheelbase, in. 112
Curb weight, lb. 5,400
Percent weight, front/rear 51/49
Typical towing ability, lb. 6,500

SAFETY INFORMATION

Active safety features
Antilock brakes ....Standard
Traction control ....Standard
Stability control ....Standard
Daytime running lights ....Standard
Tire pressure monitor ....Not available

Safety belts
Center-rear belt 3-point
Pretensioners, front/rear ....Yes/no

Air bags
Occupant-sensing system ....Not available
Side bags, front/rear ....Standard/no
Inflatable curtain ....Standard with rollover
Accident alert system ....Available

Crash tests
Gov't front-crash test, driver/front passenger .....NA/NA
Gov't side-crash test, driver/rear passenger ......NA/NA
IIHS offset crash test ....NA
IIHS side crash test w/ side & curtain airbags ....NA
IIHS side crash test w/o side & curtain airbags ....NA

ANOTHER LOOK

RELIABILITY HISTORY

TROUBLE SPOTS	Lexus LX450, LX470							
	97	98	99	00	01	02	03	04
Engine			●	●	●	●	●	
Cooling			●	●	●	●	●	
Fuel			◖	●	●	●	●	
Ignition			◖	●	●	●	●	
Transmission			●	●	●	●	●	
Electrical	Insufficient data	Insufficient data	◖	○	●	●	●	Insufficient data
Air conditioning			●	●	●	●	●	
Suspension			●	●	●	●	●	
Brakes			○	◖	◖	◖	●	
Exhaust			●	●	●	●	●	
Paint/trim/rust			◖	◖	●	●	●	
Body integrity			◖	◖	●	●	◖	
Power equipment			○	●	○	◖	◖	
Body hardware			●	◖	●	●	●	
RELIABILITY VERDICT			✓	✓	✓	✓	✓	

● ◔ ○ ◕ ●
better ◄——► worse   See page 36 for more information.

Lexus RX330

CR RECOMMENDED ✓

THE RX330 LINE
Body style:
4-door SUV
Trim lines:
Base, 400h
Base price range:
$36,025–$48,535

The RX330 is our top-pick midsized SUV. The refined and responsive 230-hp, 3.3-liter V6 and smooth five-speed automatic work well. Handling is fairly agile. Emergency handling is forgiving and secure. The ride is very comfortable. The well-detailed interior is as plush and quiet as in many luxury cars. The rear seat is roomy, but cargo capacity is modest. The rear roof pillars create a large blind spot. An optional rear-view camera that helps when backing up is bundled with the navigation system. The RX400h hybrid version is beginning to arrive at dealers.

REPORT CARD

⊖	Predicted reliability
◉	Owner satisfaction
◉	Predicted depreciation
⊖	Accident avoidance
◐	Acceleration
⊖	Ride
◉	Front seat comfort
⊖	Fuel economy

SPECIFICATIONS

Drive wheels Front or AWD

Seating 2 front, 3 rear

Engines available
3.3-liter V6 (230 hp); 3.3-liter V6 hybrid (268 hp)

Transmissions available
CVT; 5-speed automatic

Fuel
Fuel type ....Regular
EPA city/highway, mpg 18/24
Fuel refill capacity, gal. 19.2

Dimensions and weight
Length, in. 186
Width, in. 73
Wheelbase, in. 107
Curb weight, lb. 4,200
Percent weight, front/rear 57/43
Typical towing ability, lb. 3,500

SAFETY INFORMATION

Active safety features
Antilock brakes ....Standard
Traction control ....Standard
Stability control ....Standard
Daytime running lights ....Standard
Tire pressure monitor ....Available

Safety belts
Center-rear belt 3-point
Pretensioners, front/rear ....Yes/no

Air bags
Occupant-sensing system ....Front
Side bags, front/rear ....Standard/no
Inflatable curtain ....Standard with rollover
Accident alert system ....Available

Crash tests
Gov't front-crash test, driver/front passenger ......◉/⊖
Gov't side-crash test, driver/rear passenger ....◉/⊖
IIHS offset crash test ....Good
IIHS side crash test w/ side & curtain airbags ....NA
IIHS side crash test w/o side & curtain airbags ....NA

FROM THE TEST TRACK

Tested model
2004 4-door SUV AWD, 3.3-liter V6, 5-speed automatic

Tires as tested
Goodyear Eagle RS-A,
size P235/55R18 99V

Acceleration ....⊖
0-30 mph, sec. 2.9
0-60 mph, sec. 8.8
Quarter mile, sec. 17.0
Quarter mile, mph 83
45-65 mph, sec. 6.2

Other findings
Transmission ....◉
Turning circle, ft. 40
Ground clearance, in. 5.5

Braking and handling
Braking ....⊖
Braking, dry pavement, ft. 134
Routine handling ....⊖
Emergency handling ....○
Avoidance maneuver, max. mph ...52.0

Convenience and comfort
Ride ....⊖
Noise ....◉
Driving position ....◉
Access ....◉
Controls and displays ....◉
Fit and finish ....◉
Door top to ground, in. 59.5
Cargo area ....○
Cargo volume, cu.ft. 34.5
Max. load, lb. 925

Seating
Front-seat comfort ....◉
Front shoulder room, in. 57.5
Front leg room, in. 41.0
Front head room, in. 3.0
Rear-seat comfort ....⊖
Rear shoulder room, in. 56.5
Rear leg room, in. 29.5
Rear head room, in 4.0

Fuel economy ....⊖
CU's overall mileage, mpg 18
CU's city/highway, mpg 12/26
CU's 150-mile trip, mpg 21
Annual fuel ....850 gal./$1,700
Cruising range 370

RELIABILITY HISTORY

TROUBLE SPOTS	Lexus RX300, RX330							
	97	98	99	00	01	02	03	04
Engine			◐	◐	◉	◉	◉	◉
Cooling			◉	◉	◉	◉	◉	◉
Fuel			◐	◐	◉	◉	◉	◉
Ignition			◉	◉	◉	◉	◉	◉
Transmission			◐	◉	◉	◉	◉	◉
Electrical			○	◐	◉	◉	◉	◉
Air conditioning			◉	◉	◉	◉	◉	◉
Suspension			◐	◉	◉	◉	◉	◉
Brakes			◐	◉	◉	◉	◉	◉
Exhaust			◉	◉	◉	◉	◉	◉
Paint/trim/rust			◐	◉	◉	◉	◉	◉
Body integrity			◐	◐	◐	◐	◐	◐
Power equipment			◐	◉	◉	◉	◉	◉
Body hardware			◐	◉	◉	◉	◉	◉
RELIABILITY VERDICT			✓	✓	✓	✓	✓	

Expert • Independent • Nonprofit

Lexus SC430

THE SC430 LINE
Body style:
convertible
Trim lines:
–

Base price range:
$63,575

This luxury coupe-cum-convertible features an electrically operated metal roof that retracts into the trunk at the touch of a button, much like the one found on the Mercedes-Benz SL500. While theoretically a 2+2, the SC430 has a tiny rear seat best suited to a pocketbook or briefcase. Power comes from a 300-hp version of the same refined 4.3-liter V8 found in Lexus' GS and LS sedans. Expect quiet, smooth, powerful acceleration. Handling is less sporty than in some competing models, however. The list of standard features is quite comprehensive, including DVD navigation.

REPORT CARD

◓	**Predicted reliability**
◓	**Owner satisfaction**
◓	**Predicted depreciation**
NA	**Accident avoidance**
NA	**Acceleration**
NA	**Ride**
NA	**Front seat comfort**
NA	**Fuel economy**

SPECIFICATIONS

Drive wheels Rear

Seating 2 front, 2 rear

Engines available
4.3-liter V8 (300 hp)

Transmissions available
5-speed automatic

Fuel
Fuel type . . . . .Premium
EPA city/highway, mpg 18/23
Fuel refill capacity, gal. 19.8

Dimensions and weight
Length, in. 178
Width, in. 72
Wheelbase, in. .103
Curb weight, lb. 3,840
Percent weight, front/rear 53/47
Typical towing ability, lb. . . . . .NR

SAFETY INFORMATION

Active safety features
Antilock brakes . . . . .Standard
Traction control . . . . .Standard
Stability control . . . . .Standard
Daytime running lights . . . . .Standard
Tire pressure monitor . . . . .Available

Safety belts
Center-rear belt . . . . .NA
Pretensioners, front/rear . . . . .Yes/no

Air bags
Occupant-sensing system . . . . .Not available
Side bags, front/rear .Standard/no
Inflatable curtain . . . . .Not available
Accident alert system . . . . .Available

Crash tests
Gov't front-crash test, driver/front passenger . . . . .NA/NA
Gov't side-crash test, driver/rear passenger . . . . . . .NA/NA
IIHS offset crash test . . . . .NA
IIHS side crash test w/ side & curtain airbags . . . . .NA
IIHS side crash test w/o side & curtain airbags . . . . .NA

ANOTHER LOOK

RELIABILITY HISTORY

TROUBLE SPOTS	Lexus SC300/SC400,							
	97	98	99	00	01	02	03	04
Engine						◒	◒	
Cooling						◒	◒	
Fuel						◒	◒	
Ignition						◒	◒	
Transmission						◒	◒	
Electrical	Insufficient data	Insufficient data	Insufficient data	Insufficient data		◒	◒	Insufficient data
Air conditioning						◒	◒	
Suspension						◒	◒	
Brakes						◒	◒	
Exhaust						◒	◒	
Paint/trim/rust						◒	◒	
Body integrity						○	◒	
Power equipment						◒	◒	
Body hardware						◒	◒	
RELIABILITY VERDICT						✓	✓	

● ◐ ○ ◑ ●
better ◄——► worse   See page 36 for more information.

Lincoln Aviator

THE AVIATOR LINE
Body style:
4-door SUV
Trim lines:
Luxury
Base price range:
$40,615-$43,565

The Aviator is Lincoln's version of the Mercury Mountaineer and Ford Explorer. It's made for people who find the Lincoln Navigator too imposing and expensive. It comes with a smooth, strong 302-hp V8 that is mated to a five-speed automatic. Without low-range gearing, it's not meant for serious off-roading, but it is appropriate for snow. The ride is stiffer than that of the Explorer and handling is more nimble. Some controls are less intuitive. A standard third row expands seating to seven. The premium price buys more power, amenities, and plushness than in the Explorer.

REPORT CARD

⊖	**Predicted reliability**
○	**Owner satisfaction**
NA	**Predicted depreciation**
NA	**Accident avoidance**
NA	**Acceleration**
NA	**Ride**
NA	**Front seat comfort**
NA	**Fuel economy**

SPECIFICATIONS

Drive wheels Rear or AWD

Seating 2 front, 3 rear, 2 third

Engines available
4.6-liter V8 (302 hp)

Transmissions available
5-speed automatic

Fuel
Fuel type ....Premium
EPA city/highway, mpg 13/17
Fuel refill capacity, gal. 22.5

Dimensions and weight
Length, in. 193
Width, in. 76
Wheelbase, in. 114
Curb weight, lb. 5,085
Percent weight, front/rear 52/48
Typical towing ability, lb. 7,100

SAFETY INFORMATION

Active safety features
Antilock brakes ....Standard
Traction control ....Included with stability
Stability control ....Standard
Daytime running lights ....Not available
Tire pressure monitor ....Available

Safety belts
Center-rear belt 3-point
Pretensioners, front/rear ....Yes/no

Air bags
Occupant-sensing system ....Front
Side bags, front/rear ....No/no
Inflatable curtain ....Standard with rollover
Accident alert system ....Not available

Crash tests
Gov't front-crash test, driver/front passenger ......NA/NA
Gov't side-crash test, driver/rear passenger ....NA/NA
IIHS offset crash test ....Good
IIHS side crash test w/ side & curtain airbags ....NA
IIHS side crash test w/o side & curtain airbags ....NA

RELIABILITY HISTORY

TROUBLE SPOTS	Lincoln Aviator							
	97	98	99	00	01	02	03	04
Engine							○	○
Cooling							○	○
Fuel							○	○
Ignition							○	○
Transmission							○	○
Electrical							○	○
Air conditioning							○	○
Suspension							○	○
Brakes							⊖	○
Exhaust							○	○
Paint/trim/rust							○	○
Body integrity							○	○
Power equipment							⊖	○
Body hardware							○	○
RELIABILITY VERDICT							✗	✗

ANOTHER LOOK

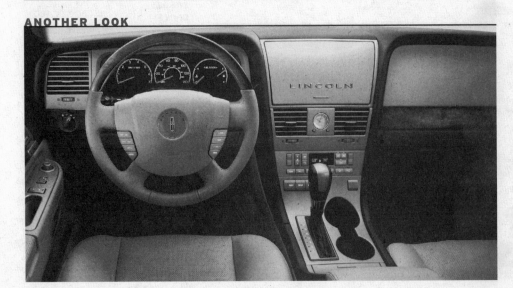

Expert ● Independent ● Nonprofit

Lincoln LS

THE LS LINE
Body style:
sedan
Trim lines:
V6 Luxury, V6
Appearance, V6
Premium, V8 Sport, V8
Ultimate
Base price range:
$32,620-$43,570

The rear-drive LS strikes a nice balance between luxury and sportiness, delivering fairly agile handling, a comfortable ride, and a quiet cabin. The 232-hp V6 and automatic provide smooth performance. The optional V8 provides more readily available power and effortless acceleration. The interior is pleasant. Power-adjustable pedals and a tilt/telescope steering wheel facilitate a good driving position. The rear seats fold to expand trunk capacity. The LS shares its platform with the Ford Thunderbird and Jaguar S-Type. Reliability has dropped to below average.

REPORT CARD

◖	Predicted reliability
○	Owner satisfaction
◖	Predicted depreciation
◕	Accident avoidance
◕	Acceleration
◕	Ride
◉	Front seat comfort
◖	Fuel economy

SPECIFICATIONS

Drive wheels Rear

Seating 2 front, 3 rear

Engines available
3.0-liter V6 (232 hp); 3.9-liter V8 (280 hp)

Transmissions available
5-speed automatic

Fuel
Fuel type . . . . .Premium
EPA city/highway, mpg 20/26
Fuel refill capacity, gal. 18.1

Dimensions and weight
Length, in. 194
Width, in. 73
Wheelbase, in. 115
Curb weight, lb. 3,700
Percent weight, front/rear 52/48
Typical towing ability, lb. . . . . .NR

SAFETY INFORMATION

Active safety features

Antilock brakes . . . . .Standard
Traction control . . . . .Standard
Stability control . . . . .Optional
Daytime running lights . . . . .Not available
Tire pressure monitor . . . . .Not available

Safety belts

Center-rear belt 3-point
Pretensioners, front/rear . . . . .Yes/no

Air bags

Occupant-sensing system . . . . .Front
Side bags, front/rear .Standard/no
Inflatable curtain . . . . .Optional
Accident alert system . . . . .Available

Crash tests

Gov't front-crash test, driver/front passenger . . . . . ◉/◕
Gov't side-crash test, driver/rear passenger . . . . . . ◕/◉
IIHS offset crash test . . . . .Good
IIHS side crash test w/ side & curtain airbags . . . . .NA
IIHS side crash test w/o side & curtain airbags . . . . .NA

FROM THE TEST TRACK

Tested model
2003 Premium sedan, 3.0-liter V6, 5-speed automatic

Tires as tested
Continental ContiTouring Contact, size P225/55R16 94V

Acceleration . . . . ◕
0-30 mph, sec. 3.1
0-60 mph, sec. 8.3
Quarter mile, sec. 16.4
Quarter mile, mph 87
45-65 mph, sec. 5.4

Other findings
Transmission . . . . ◕
Turning circle, ft. 40
Ground clearance, in. 3.5

Braking and handling

Braking . . . . ◕
Braking, dry pavement, ft. 142
Routine handling . . . . ◕
Emergency handling . . . . ◕
Avoidance maneuver, max. mph 53.0

Convenience and comfort

Ride . . . . ◕
Noise . . . . ◕
Driving position . . . . ◉
Access . . . . ◕
Controls and displays . . . . ◉
Fit and finish . . . . ◕
Door top to ground, in. 50.5
Trunk . . . . ◕
Luggage capacity . . . . .3+0
Max. load, lb. 900

Seating

Front-seat comfort . . . . ◉
Front shoulder room, in. 58.0
Front leg room, in. 41.0
Front head room, in. 3.5
Rear-seat comfort . . . . ◕
Rear shoulder room, in. 57.0
Rear leg room, in. 28.5
Rear head room, in 2.5

Fuel economy . . . . ◖
CU's overall mileage, mpg 19
  CU's city/highway, mpg 13/29
  CU's 150-mile trip, mpg 23
Annual fuel . . . . .785 gal./$1,725
Cruising range 385

RELIABILITY HISTORY

TROUBLE SPOTS	97	98	99	00	01	02	03	04
Engine			○	○	◕	◕	◕	
Cooling			◕	◕	◕	◕	◕	
Fuel			◕	◕	◕	◕	◕	
Ignition			◕	◕	◕	◕	◕	
Transmission			○	○	◕	◖	◕	
Electrical			○	○	○	◕	◕	
Air conditioning			◕	◕	◕	◕	◕	
Suspension			◕	◕	◕	◕	◕	
Brakes			○	◕	◕	◕	◕	
Exhaust			◕	◕	◕	◕	◕	
Paint/trim/rust			◕	◕	◕	◕	◕	
Body integrity			○	○	○	○	◕	
Power equipment			●	●	○	○	◕	
Body hardware			◕	○	◕	◕	◕	
RELIABILITY VERDICT			✗	–	–	✗	–	

Lincoln Mark LT

THE MARK LT LINE
Body style:
crew cab
Trim lines:
—
Base price range:
$39,200-$42,700

The Mark LT is Lincoln's second attempt at a luxury pickup truck. The first attempt, the Blackwood, was pulled from the market after one model year. The Mark LT is based on the new Ford F-150 pickup, which was redesigned for 2004. In our testing we found the F-150 to ride more comfortably, handle more nimbly, and have a quieter, better-trimmed interior than the previous version. Braking performance was just adequate, with long stops in our tests. The Mark LT sports a luxurious interior, but the 4WD system is part-time only.

REPORT CARD

New	**Predicted reliability**
New	**Owner satisfaction**
NA	**Predicted depreciation**
NA	**Accident avoidance**
NA	**Acceleration**
NA	**Ride**
NA	**Front seat comfort**
NA	**Fuel economy**

SPECIFICATIONS

Drive wheels Rear or part-time 4WD

Seating 2 front, 3 rear

Engines available
5.4-liter V8 (300 hp)

Transmissions available
4-speed automatic

Fuel
Fuel type ....Regular
EPA city/highway, mpg 14/18
Fuel refill capacity, gal. 30.0

Dimensions and weight
Length, in. 224
Width, in. 79
Wheelbase, in. 139
Curb weight, lb. 5,675
Percent weight, front/rear ....NA
Typical towing ability, lb. 8,600

SAFETY INFORMATION

Active safety features
Antilock brakes ....Standard
Traction control ....Not available
Stability control ....Not available
Daytime running lights ....Not available
Tire pressure monitor ....Not available

Safety belts
Center-rear belt 3-point
Pretensioners, front/rear ....Yes/no

Air bags
Occupant-sensing system ....Front
Side bags, front/rear ....No/no
Inflatable curtain ....Not available
Accident alert system ....Not available

Crash tests
Gov't front-crash test, driver/front passenger   ◐/◐
Gov't side-crash test, driver/rear passenger   NA/NA
IIHS offset crash test ....NA
IIHS side crash test w/ side & curtain airbags ....NA
IIHS side crash test w/o side & curtain airbags ....NA

ANOTHER LOOK

RELIABILITY HISTORY

TROUBLE SPOTS	97 98 99 00 01 02 03 04
Engine	
Cooling	NO
Fuel	
Ignition	
Transmission	DATA
Electrical	
Air conditioning	NEW
Suspension	
Brakes	MODEL
Exhaust	
Paint/trim/rust	
Body integrity	
Power equipment	
Body hardware	
RELIABILITY VERDICT	

Lincoln Navigator

THE NAVIGATOR LINE
Body style:
4-door SUV
Trim lines:
Luxury, Ultimate
Base price range:
$50,305-$56,955

This is a luxury version of the Ford Expedition, with a plusher, warmer interior. Its 5.4-liter V8 isn't particularly smooth. With a fully independent suspension and lower step-in height, access is easier than in the previous generation. The power-operated split third-row seat folds flat into the floor by pressing a button. The cabin is quiet, and both ride and handling are commendable. The steering is responsive and the ride supple. The center section of the 40/20/40 second-row seat slides forward so a child can sit closer to front-seat occupants. Reliability since the redesign has been poor.

REPORT CARD

●	**Predicted reliability**
⊖	**Owner satisfaction**
○	**Predicted depreciation**
NA	**Accident avoidance**
NA	**Acceleration**
NA	**Ride**
NA	**Front seat comfort**
NA	**Fuel economy**

SPECIFICATIONS

Drive wheels Rear or selectable 4WD

Seating 2 front, 3 rear, 3 third

Engines available
5.4-liter V8 (300 hp)

Transmissions available
6-speed automatic

Fuel
Fuel type . . . . .Premium
EPA city/highway, mpg 11/16
Fuel refill capacity, gal. 28.0

Dimensions and weight
Length, in. 206
Width, in. 79
Wheelbase, in. 119
Curb weight, lb. 5,900
Percent weight, front/rear 50/50
Typical towing ability, lb. 8,700

SAFETY INFORMATION

Active safety features
Antilock brakes . . . . .Standard
Traction control . . . . .Included with stability
Stability control . . . . .Standard
Daytime running lights . . . . .Not available
Tire pressure monitor . . . . .Available

Safety belts
Center-rear belt 3-point
Pretensioners, front/rear .Yes/no

Air bags
Occupant-sensing system . . . . .Front
Side bags, front/rear . . . . .No/no
Inflatable curtain . . . . .Standard with rollover
Accident alert system . . . . .Not available

Crash tests
Gov't front-crash test, driver/front passenger . . . . . . ⊖/⊖
Gov't side-crash test, driver/rear passenger . . . . .NA/NA
IIHS offset crash test . . . . .NA
IIHS side crash test w/ side & curtain airbags . . . . .NA
IIHS side crash test w/o side & curtain airbags . . . . .NA

ANOTHER LOOK

RELIABILITY HISTORY

TROUBLE SPOTS	Lincoln Navigator							
	97	98	99	00	01	02	03	04
Engine	○	⊖	⊖	⊖	⊖	●	⊖	
Cooling	⊖	●	⊖	⊖	●	⊖	●	
Fuel	⊖	●	⊖	⊖	⊖	⊖	●	
Ignition	⊖	⊖	○	⊖	⊖	⊖	●	
Transmission	⊖	○	○	○	○	⊖	●	
Electrical	○	○	○	○	○	○	○	
Air conditioning	⊖	○	⊖	○	○	⊖	○	
Suspension	⊖	⊖	○	○	○	○	⊖	
Brakes	●	⊖	⊖	○	⊖	⊖	⊖	
Exhaust	●	●	●	⊖	⊖	●	⊖	
Paint/trim/rust	⊖	○	⊖	⊖	○	⊖	○	
Body integrity	○	⊖	○	○	⊖	⊖	○	
Power equipment	⊖	⊖	⊖	⊖	⊖	●	○	
Body hardware	○	○	○	○	○	○	○	
RELIABILITY VERDICT	–	–	–	–	X	X	X	

Lincoln Town Car

CR RECOMMENDED ✓

The big, traditional Town Car delivers a fairly comfortable ride, though it's not up to luxury-car standards. Handling is rather clumsy but secure. The 4.6-liter V8 is too noisy for a luxury car and isn't as muscular or refined as the V8 in its major competitor, the Cadillac DeVille. The rear seat can hold three adults comfortably, and even more room is available in the extended Signature model. Reliability has been average, but depreciation is steep. On the whole, its stately appearance isn't backed up by true luxury attributes. At least crash-test results are impressive.

THE TOWN CAR LINE

Body style:
sedan
Trim lines:
Signature, Signature Limited, Signature L
Base price range:
$42,035-$50,505

REPORT CARD

○	Predicted reliability
○	Owner satisfaction
◓	Predicted depreciation
○	Accident avoidance
◒	Acceleration
◒	Ride
◒	Front seat comfort
●	Fuel economy

SPECIFICATIONS

Drive wheels Rear

Seating 3 front, 3 rear

Engines available
4.6-liter V8 (239 hp)

Transmissions available
4-speed automatic

Fuel
Fuel type . . . . .Regular
EPA city/highway, mpg 17/25
Fuel refill capacity, gal. 19.0

Dimensions and weight
Length, in. 215
Width, in. 78
Wheelbase, in. 118
Curb weight, lb. 4,415
Percent weight, front/rear 54/46
Typical towing ability, lb. 2,000

SAFETY INFORMATION

Active safety features

Antilock brakes . . . . .Standard
Traction control . . . . .Standard
Stability control . . . . .Not available
Daytime running lights . . . . .Not available
Tire pressure monitor . . . . .Not available

Safety belts

Center-rear belt 3-point
Pretensioners, front/rear . . . . .Yes/no

Air bags

Occupant-sensing system . . . . .Front
Side bags, front/rear . . . . .Standard/no
Inflatable curtain . . . . .Not available
Accident alert system . . . . .Available

Crash tests

Gov't front-crash test, driver/front passenger . . . . . . ◓/◓
Gov't side-crash test, driver/rear passenger . . . . ◓/◓
IIHS offset crash test . . . . .Good
IIHS side crash test w/ side & curtain airbags . . . . .NA
IIHS side crash test w/o side & curtain airbags . . . . .NA

FROM THE TEST TRACK

Tested model

2003 Signature sedan, 4.6-liter V8, 4-speed automatic

Tires as tested

Michelin Energy LX4, size P225/60R17 98T

Acceleration . . . . ◒

0-30 mph, sec. 3.1
0-60 mph, sec. 8.7
Quarter mile, sec. 16.7
Quarter mile, mph 84
45-65 mph, sec. 5.8

Other findings

Transmission . . . . ◒
Turning circle, ft. 42
Ground clearance, in. 5.0

Braking and handling

Braking . . . . ○
Braking, dry pavement, ft. 143
Routine handling . . . . ○
Emergency handling . . . . ◒
Avoidance maneuver, max. mph . . .47.5

Convenience and comfort

Ride . . . . ◒
Noise . . . . ◒
Driving position . . . . ◒
Access . . . . ◒
Controls and displays . . . . ◒
Fit and finish . . . . ◒
Door top to ground, in. 52.5
Trunk . . . . ◒
Luggage capacity . . . . .7+2
Max. load, lb. 1,100

Seating

Front-seat comfort . . . . ◒
Front shoulder room, in. 60.5
Front leg room, in. 42.0
Front head room, in. 3.0
Rear-seat comfort . . . . ◒
Rear shoulder room, in. 60.0
Rear leg room, in. 30.0
Rear head room, in 3.5

Fuel economy . . . . ●

CU's overall mileage, mpg 17
CU's city/highway, mpg 11/27
CU's 150-mile trip, mpg 22
Annual fuel . . . . .860 gal./$1,725
Cruising range 390

RELIABILITY HISTORY

TROUBLE SPOTS	Lincoln Town Car							
	97	98	99	00	01	02	03	04
Engine	◒	●	●	●	●	●	●	●
Cooling	◒	◒	●	●	●	●	●	●
Fuel	○	◒	●	●	○	○	●	●
Ignition		◒	◒	●	●	○	●	●
Transmission		◒	●	●	●	●	●	●
Electrical	○	◒	○	●	○	○	●	●
Air conditioning	○	◒	○	●	●	●	●	●
Suspension	○	◒	○	●	○	●	●	●
Brakes	◐	○	◒	○	○	●	●	●
Exhaust	◒	◒	●	◒	●	●	●	●
Paint/trim/rust	○	◒	○	○	○	●	●	●
Body integrity	○	◒	○	○	○	◒	●	●
Power equipment	◐	●	●	○	○	○	●	●
Body hardware	○	◒	○	○	○	◒	●	●
RELIABILITY VERDICT	✓	✓	✓	✓	✓	✓	–	–

Lincoln Zephyr

THE ZEPHYR LINE
Body style:
sedan
Trim lines:
–
Base price range:
$29,000-$34,000E

The Zephyr is a new midsized sedan that will go on sale this fall, and expected to retail in the low $30,000 range, just below the Lincoln LS. It is the upscale sibling of the upcoming Ford Fusion and Mercury Milan, and all three are based on the Mazda6 platform. The Lincoln is powered by a 210-hp 3.0-liter V6 mated to a six-speed automatic transmission. The interior will be trimmed in standard leather and wood. ABS and traction control are standard, but stability control is not offered. The fold-flat rear seats use the spring-assist feature found in the Mazda6.

REPORT CARD

New	**Predicted reliability**
New	**Owner satisfaction**
NA	**Predicted depreciation**
NA	**Accident avoidance**
NA	**Acceleration**
NA	**Ride**
NA	**Front seat comfort**
NA	**Fuel economy**

SPECIFICATIONS

Drive wheels Front

Seating 2 front, 3 rear

Engines available
3.0-liter V6 (210 hp)

Transmissions available
6-speed automatic

Fuel
Fuel type . . . . .Regular
EPA city/highway, mpg . . . . .NA
Fuel refill capacity, gal. 18.0

Dimensions and weight
Length, in. 190
Width, in. 72
Wheelbase, in. 107
Curb weight, lb. 3,405
Percent weight, front/rear 61/39
Typical towing ability, lb. 1,000

SAFETY INFORMATION

Active safety features
Antilock brakes . . . . .Standard
Traction control . . . . .Standard
Stability control .Not available
Daytime running lights . . . . .Not available
Tire pressure monitor . . . . .Not available

Safety belts
Center-rear belt 3-point
Pretensioners, front/rear . . . . .Yes/no

Air bags
Occupant-sensing system . . . . .Front
Side bags, front/rear . . . . .Standard/no
Inflatable curtain . . . . .Standard
Accident alert system . . . . .Not available

Crash tests
Gov't front-crash test, driver/front passenger . . . . . .NA/NA
Gov't side-crash test, driver/rear passenger . . . . . .NA/NA
IIHS offset crash test . . . . .NA
IIHS side crash test w/ side & curtain airbags . . . . .NA
IIHS side crash test w/o side & curtain airbags . . . . .NA

ANOTHER LOOK

RELIABILITY HISTORY

TROUBLE SPOTS	97 98 99 00 01 02 03 04
Engine	
Cooling	
Fuel	NO
Ignition	
Transmission	DATA
Electrical	
Air conditioning	NEW
Suspension	
Brakes	MODEL
Exhaust	
Paint/trim/rust	
Body integrity	
Power equipment	
Body hardware	
RELIABILITY VERDICT	

● ◐ ○ ○ ○
better ◀ ──── ▶ worse   See page 36 for more information.

Lotus Elise

THE ELISE LINE
Body style:
convertible
Trim lines:
–
Base price range:
$42,990

After eight years of being available only in Europe, the Lotus Elise is now available in the U.S., but the waiting list is long filled. This midengine roadster is quick because of its light weight. It doesn't even need power steering. Power comes from a high-revving, 190-hp, 1.8-liter four-cylinder plucked out of the Toyota Celica GT-S. For about $43,000 owners will get legendary, Lotus agility; a tight, spartan, driver-focused interior; difficult access; and exclusivity, as it will be imported in limited numbers.

REPORT CARD

New	Predicted reliability
New	Owner satisfaction
NA	Predicted depreciation
NA	Accident avoidance
NA	Acceleration
NA	Ride
NA	Front seat comfort
NA	Fuel economy

SPECIFICATIONS

Drive wheels Rear

Seating 2 front

Engines available
1.8-liter 4 (190 hp)

Transmissions available
6-speed manual

Fuel
Fuel type .Premium
EPA city/highway, mpg 23/27
Fuel refill capacity, gal. 10.5

Dimensions and weight
Length, in. 149
Width, in. 68
Wheelbase, in. .91
Curb weight, lb. 2,000
Percent weight, front/rear 38/62
Typical towing ability, lb. . . . . .NR

SAFETY INFORMATION

Active safety features
Antilock brakes . . . . .Standard
Traction control . . . . .Not available
Stability control . . . . .Not available
Daytime running lights . . . . .Not available
Tire pressure monitor . . . . .Not available

Safety belts
Center-rear belt . . . . .NA
Pretensioners, front/rear .No/NA

Air bags
Occupant-sensing system . . . . .Not available
Side bags, front/rear . . . . .No/NA
Inflatable curtain . . . . .Not available
Accident alert system . . . . .Not available

Crash tests
Gov't front-crash test, driver/front passenger . . . . . .NA/NA
Gov't side-crash test, driver/rear passenger . . . . . . .NA/NA
IIHS offset crash test . . . . .NA
IIHS side crash test w/ side & curtain airbags . . . . .NA
IIHS side crash test w/o side & curtain airbags . . . . .NA

ANOTHER LOOK

RELIABILITY HISTORY

TROUBLE SPOTS	97 98 99 00 01 02 03 04
Engine	
Cooling	
Fuel	NO
Ignition	
Transmission	DATA
Electrical	
Air conditioning	NEW
Suspension	
Brakes	MODEL
Exhaust	
Paint/trim/rust	
Body integrity	
Power equipment	
Body hardware	
RELIABILITY VERDICT	

Expert • Independent • Nonprofit

Mazda B-Series

The B-Series, a clone of the Ford Ranger, never lets you forget you're driving a truck. Handling is fairly responsive, but the ride is stiff and choppy. The 3.0-liter V6 is pleasant enough and adequately powerful. An overhead-cam 4.0-liter V6 and a 2.3-liter four-cylinder are also available. A smooth-shifting five-speed automatic is available across the line. Extended-cab models offer two small rear-hinged doors, but the rear seat is fit only for cargo, not people. The front seats are thinly padded and mounted too low. A crew-cab model isn't offered.

THE B-SERIES LINE

Body style:
regular cab; extended cab

Trim lines:
B2300, B3000, B3000 Dual Sport, B4000, B4000 SE

Base price range:
$15,340-$26,440

REPORT CARD

○	Predicted reliability
●	Owner satisfaction
○	Predicted depreciation
NA	Accident avoidance
NA	Acceleration
NA	Ride
NA	Front seat comfort
NA	Fuel economy

SPECIFICATIONS

Drive wheels Rear or part-time 4WD

Seating 3 front, 2 rear

Engines available
2.3-liter 4 (143 hp); 3.0-liter V6 (148 hp); 4.0-liter V6 (207 hp)

Transmissions available
5-speed manual; 5-speed automatic

Fuel
Fuel type . . . . .Regular
EPA city/highway, mpg 15/19
Fuel refill capacity, gal. 20.0

Dimensions and weight
Length, in. 202
Width, in. 70
Wheelbase, in. 126
Curb weight, lb. 3,870
Percent weight, front/rear 60/40
Typical towing ability, lb. 3,180

SAFETY INFORMATION

Active safety features
Antilock brakes . . . . .Standard
Traction control . . . . .Not available
Stability control . . . . .Not available
Daytime running lights . . . . .Not available
Tire pressure monitor . . . . .Not available

Safety belts
Center-rear belt . . . . .NA
Pretensioners, front/rear .Yes/no

Air bags
Occupant-sensing system . . . . .Not available
Side bags, front/rear . . . . .No/no
Inflatable curtain . . . . .Not available
Accident alert system .Not available

Crash tests
Gov't front-crash test, driver/front passenger . . . . .◑/◑
Gov't side-crash test, driver/rear passenger . . . . . .◑/NA
IIHS offset crash test . . . . .Acceptable
IIHS side crash test w/ side & curtain airbags . . . . .NA
IIHS side crash test w/o side & curtain airbags . . . . .NA

ANOTHER LOOK

RELIABILITY HISTORY

TROUBLE SPOTS	Mazda B-Series 2WD							
	97	98	99	00	01	02	03	04
Engine	○	○	○	○	○	○	●	●
Cooling	◑	◑	○	○	○	○	●	●
Fuel	●	○	○	○	◑	◑	●	●
Ignition	○	○	◑	◑	◑	◑	●	●
Transmission	◑	○	○	○	◑	◑	●	●
Electrical	●	●	◑	○	○	○	●	●
Air conditioning	◑	○	◑	◑	◑	◑	●	●
Suspension	○	○	◑	◑	◑	◑	●	●
Brakes	○	○	○	◑	◑	◑	●	●
Exhaust	○	◑	◑	◑	◑	◑	●	●
Paint/trim/rust	◑	◑	◑	◑	◑	◑	●	●
Body integrity	○	○	◑	◑	◑	◑	●	●
Power equipment	○	○	◑	◑	◑	◑	●	●
Body hardware	○	○	◑	◑	◑	◑	●	●
RELIABILITY VERDICT	✓	✓	✓	✓	✓	-	-	-

better ●◑○◑● worse   See page 36 for more information.

Mazda MPV

The MPV is shorter and narrower than most minivans, which helps give it an almost carlike driving experience. Handling is secure, but the ride is stiff. Braking is very good. The noisy Ford-supplied 3.0-liter V6 delivers lackluster performance. The five-speed automatic shifts reasonably smoothly. Side windows that retract into the two sliding rear doors are a plus. The well-finished interior includes a flat-folding third-row seat. The middle-row seats are cramped, and the third-row bench is uncomfortable and hard to access. Reliability has declined, so we can't recommend the MPV.

THE MPV LINE
Body style:
minivan
Trim lines:
LX, ES
Base price range:
$22,940-$28,505

REPORT CARD

●	Predicted reliability
○	Owner satisfaction
○	Predicted depreciation
◒	Accident avoidance
○	Acceleration
○	Ride
◒	Front seat comfort
◔	Fuel economy

SPECIFICATIONS

Drive wheels Front

Seating 2 front, 2 rear, 3 third

Engines available
3.0-liter V6 (200 hp)

Transmissions available
5-speed automatic

Fuel
Fuel type . . . . Regular
EPA city/highway, mpg 18/25
Fuel refill capacity, gal. 19.8

Dimensions and weight
Length, in. 188
Width, in. 72
Wheelbase, in. 112
Curb weight, lb. 3,925
Percent weight, front/rear 58/42
Typical towing ability, lb. 3,000

SAFETY INFORMATION

Active safety features
Antilock brakes . . . . .Standard
Traction control . . . . .Optional
Stability control . . . . .Not available
Daytime running lights . . . . .Not available
Tire pressure monitor . . . . .Not available

Safety belts
Center-rear belt . . . . .Lap
Pretensioners, front/rear . . . . .Yes/no

Air bags
Occupant-sensing system . . . . .Front
Side bags, front/rear . . . . .Optional/no
Inflatable curtain .Not available
Accident alert system . . . . .Not available

Crash tests
Gov't front-crash test, driver/front passenger . . . . . ◒/◒
Gov't side-crash test, driver/rear passenger . . . . ◒/◒
IIHS offset crash test . . . . .Acceptable
IIHS side crash test w/ side & curtain airbags . . . . . . .NA
IIHS side crash test w/o side & curtain airbags . . . . .NA

FROM THE TEST TRACK

Tested model
2003 ES minivan, 3.0-liter V6, 5-speed automatic

Tires as tested
Dunlop SP Sport 4000, size P215/60R17 95H

Acceleration . . . .○
0-30 mph, sec. 3.7
0-60 mph, sec. 10.0
Quarter mile, sec. 17.9
Quarter mile, mph 80
45-65 mph, sec. 6.3

Other findings
Transmission . . . .◒
Turning circle, ft. 41
Ground clearance, in. 7.0

Braking and handling
Braking . . . .◒
Braking, dry pavement, ft. 135
Routine handling . . . .◒
Emergency handling . . . .○
Avoidance maneuver, max. mph 49.5

Convenience and comfort
Ride . . . .○
Noise . . . .○
Driving position . . . .○
Access . . . .●
Controls and displays . . . .●
Fit and finish . . . .●
Door top to ground, in. 61.0
Cargo area . . . .○
Cargo volume, cu.ft. 56.0
Max. load, lb. 1,305

Seating
Front-seat comfort . . . .◒
Front shoulder room, in. 60.0
Front leg room, in. 41.0
Front head room, in. 6.5
Rear-seat comfort . . . .◒
Rear shoulder room, in. 60.5
Rear leg room, in. 27.5
Rear head room, in. 5.0
Third-seat comfort . . . .◔
Third shoulder room, in 57.5
Third leg room, in. 27.5
Third head room, in 3.0

Fuel economy . . . .◔
CU's overall mileage, mpg 19
CU's city/highway, mpg 12/28
CU's 150-mile trip, mpg 23
Annual fuel . . . . .805 gal./$1,610
Cruising range 425

RELIABILITY HISTORY

TROUBLE SPOTS	Mazda MPV							
	97	98	99	00	01	02	03	04
Engine			●	●	●	●	●	
Cooling			●	●	●	◒	●	
Fuel			◒	◒	○	●	●	
Ignition			●	●	●	●	●	
Transmission			●	●	●	○	●	
Electrical	Insufficient data	Insufficient data	◒	●	●	●	●	
Air conditioning			●	●	●	●	●	
Suspension			●	●	●	●	●	
Brakes			●	◒	◒	◒	●	
Exhaust			●	●	●	●	●	
Paint/trim/rust			●	●	●	●	●	
Body integrity			◒	◒	◒	◒	●	
Power equipment			◒	●	●	●	●	
Body hardware			○	◒	●	●	●	
RELIABILITY VERDICT			✓	✓	–	✗	✗	

Mazda MX-5 Miata

The look and feel of classic 1960s British sports cars and Japanese quality and reliability converge in this nimble, fun-to-drive roadster. Though it leans in corners a bit more than did earlier Miatas, the latest version rides marginally better. The engine is willing and responsive, if not overly powerful, and the stubby manual shifter is a joy to use. The manually operated convertible top has a glass rear window. The interior is cramped for tall people, however, and driving the Miata on a long cross-country trip can prove tiring. A redesign (shown) arrives for 2006.

THE MX-5 MIATA LINE
Body style: convertible
Trim lines: Base, LS, Mazdaspeed
Base price range: $22,098-$25,780

REPORT CARD

◐	Predicted reliability
◉	Owner satisfaction
○	Predicted depreciation
NA	Accident avoidance
NA	Acceleration
NA	Ride
NA	Front seat comfort
NA	Fuel economy

SPECIFICATIONS

Drive wheels Rear

Seating 2 front

Engines available
1.8-liter 4 (142 hp); 1.8-liter 4 turbo (178 hp)

Transmissions available
5-speed manual; 6-speed manual; 4-speed automatic

Fuel
Fuel type . . . . .Regular or premium
EPA city/highway, mpg 23/28
Fuel refill capacity, gal. 12.7

Dimensions and weight
Length, in. 155
Width, in. 66
Wheelbase, in. .89
Curb weight, lb. 2,365
Percent weight, front/rear 53/47
Typical towing ability, lb. . . . . .NR

SAFETY INFORMATION

Active safety features
Antilock brakes . . . . .Opt. on LS; std. on MazdaSpeed
Traction control . . . . .Not available
Stability control . . . . .Not available
Daytime running lights . . . . .Not available
Tire pressure monitor . . . . .Not available

Safety belts
Center-rear belt . . . . .NA
Pretensioners, front/rear . . . . .Yes/NA

Air bags
Occupant-sensing system . . . . .Not available
Side bags, front/rear . . . . .No/NA
Inflatable curtain . . . . .Not available
Accident alert system .Not available

Crash tests
Gov't front-crash test, driver/front passenger . . . . .◐/◉
Gov't side-crash test, driver/rear passenger . . . . . .○/NA
IIHS offset crash test . . . . .NA
IIHS side crash test w/ side & curtain airbags . . . . .NA
IIHS side crash test w/o side & curtain airbags . . . . .NA

ANOTHER LOOK

RELIABILITY HISTORY

TROUBLE SPOTS	Mazda MX-5 Miata							
	97	98	99	00	01	02	03	04
Engine	◉		◉	◉	◉	◉		
Cooling	◐		◐	◐	◐	◐		
Fuel	◉		○	◐	◐	◐		
Ignition	◉		◐	◐	◐	◐		
Transmission	◉		◉	◐	◐	◐		
Electrical	◐		○	◐	◐	◐		
Air conditioning	◐		◐	◐	◐	◐		
Suspension	◉		◉	◐	◐	◐		
Brakes	◉		◐	◐	◐	◐		
Exhaust	◉		◐	◐	◐	◐		
Paint/trim/rust	○		◐	◐	◐	◐		
Body integrity	◐		○	○	○	○		
Power equipment	◉		◐	◐	◐	◐		
Body hardware	◐		◉	◐	◐	◐		
RELIABILITY VERDICT	✓		✓	✓	✓	✓	✓	

(Insufficient data)

● ◉ ○ ◐ ●
better ◀——▶ worse   See page 36 for more information.

Mazda RX-8

THE RX-8 LINE
Body style:
coupe
Trim lines:
Base, Shinka
Base price range:
$25,375-$32,470

The RX-8 is a sporty coupe and successor to the RX-7. While acceleration is not explosive, the Wankel rotary engine is exceptionally smooth and responsive, provided you keep it at mid-revs, which becomes natural and sounds invigorating. Handling is super agile, with quick, communicative steering, and is forgiving at the limits. Unlike some competitors, the ride is fairly comfortable. This truly fun-to-drive car doesn't beat you up and seats four. The rear-hinged rear doors with no center roof pillar make backseat access relatively easy. Fuel economy is disappointing, as is first-year reliability.

REPORT CARD

⊖	Predicted reliability
⊖	Owner satisfaction
NA	Predicted depreciation
◉	Accident avoidance
◉	Acceleration
○	Ride
◉	Front seat comfort
⊖	Fuel economy

SPECIFICATIONS

Drive wheels Rear

Seating 2 front, 2 rear

Engines available
1.3-liter rotary (197 hp); 1.3-liter rotary (238 hp)

Transmissions available
6-speed manual; 4-speed automatic

Fuel
Fuel type . . . . .Premium
EPA city/highway, mpg 18/24
Fuel refill capacity, gal. 15.9

Dimensions and weight
Length, in. 174
Width, in. 70
Wheelbase, in. 106
Curb weight, lb. 3,085
Percent weight, front/rear 52/48
Typical towing ability, lb. . . . . .NR

SAFETY INFORMATION

Active safety features
Antilock brakes . . . . .Standard
Traction control . . . . .Included with stability
Stability control . . . . .Optional
Daytime running lights . . . . .Not available
Tire pressure monitor . . . . .Available

Safety belts
Center-rear belt . . . . .NA
Pretensioners, front/rear .Yes/no

Air bags
Occupant-sensing system . . . . .Not available
Side bags, front/rear . . . . .Standard/no
Inflatable curtain . . . . .Standard
Accident alert system . . . . .Not available

Crash tests
Gov't front-crash test, driver/front passenger . . . . .⊖/◉
Gov't side-crash test, driver/rear passenger . . . .⊖/⊖
IIHS offset crash test . . . . .NA
IIHS side crash test w/ side & curtain airbags . . . . .NA
IIHS side crash test w/o side & curtain airbags . . . . .NA

FROM THE TEST TRACK

Tested model
2004 coupe, 1.3-liter rotary, 6-speed manual

Tires as tested
Bridgestone Potenza RE040, size 225/45R18 91W

Acceleration ◉
0-30 mph, sec. 2.2
0-60 mph, sec. 6.7
Quarter mile, sec. 15.2
Quarter mile, mph 92
45-65 mph, sec. 4.9

Other findings
Transmission . . . . ◉
Turning circle, ft. 38
Ground clearance, in. 4.0

Braking and handling
Braking . . . . ◉
Braking, dry pavement, ft. 117
Routine handling . . . . ◉
Emergency handling . . . . ◉
Avoidance maneuver, max. mph . . .56.0

Convenience and comfort
Ride . . . . ○
Noise . . . . ○
Driving position . . . . ⊖
Access . . . . ○
Controls and displays . . . . ◉
Fit and finish . . . . ◉
Door top to ground, in. 47.5
Trunk . . . . ⊖
Luggage capacity . . . . .2+0
Max. load, lb. 680

Seating
Front-seat comfort . . . . ◉
Front shoulder room, in. 54.5
Front leg room, in. 40.0
Front head room, in. 1.5
Rear-seat comfort . . . . ⊖
Rear shoulder room, in. 50.5
Rear leg room, in. 26.0
Rear head room, in 1.5

Fuel economy ⊖
CU's overall mileage, mpg 18
  CU's city/highway, mpg 14/22
  CU's 150-mile trip, mpg 20
Annual fuel . . . . .840 gal./$1,850
Cruising range 280

RELIABILITY HISTORY

TROUBLE SPOTS	Mazda RX-8							
	97	98	99	00	01	02	03	04
Engine								⊖
Cooling								◉
Fuel								⊖
Ignition								⊖
Transmission								⊖
Electrical								◉
Air conditioning								⊖
Suspension								◉
Brakes								◉
Exhaust								◉
Paint/trim/rust								◉
Body integrity								◉
Power equipment								◉
Body hardware								◉
RELIABILITY VERDICT								✗

Mazda Tribute

THE TRIBUTE LINE
Body style:
4-door SUV
Trim lines:
i, s
Base price range:
$19,765-$24,600

The Tribute is a mechanical twin of the Ford Escape and Mercury Mariner. The interior is roomy, and the rear seat is spacious. A 2005 freshening brought a revised interior; a more powerful 2.3-liter, four-cylinder engine; and improvements to noise suppression. The Ford-supplied 3.0-liter V6 serves up adequate acceleration, but unimpressive fuel economy. Handling is quite nimble, but the ride is stiff. Frontal-offset-crash-test results recently improved to acceptable. Because of a tip-up in the government rollover test, we do not recommend the Escape and its siblings.

REPORT CARD

◓	Predicted reliability
◖	Owner satisfaction
◓	Predicted depreciation
○	Accident avoidance
○	Acceleration
○	Ride
◓	Front seat comfort
◖	Fuel economy

SPECIFICATIONS

Drive wheels Front or AWD

Seating 2 front, 3 rear

Engines available
2.3-liter 4 (153 hp); 3.0-liter V6 (200 hp)

Transmissions available
5-speed manual; 4-speed automatic

Fuel
Fuel type . . . . .Regular
EPA city/highway, mpg 18/22
Fuel refill capacity, gal. 16.5

Dimensions and weight
Length, in. 175
Width, in. 70
Wheelbase, in. 103
Curb weight, lb. 3,575
Percent weight, front/rear 59/41
Typical towing ability, lb. 3,500

SAFETY INFORMATION

Active safety features
Antilock brakes .Standard
Traction control . . . . .Not available
Stability control . . . . .Not available
Daytime running lights . . . . .Not available
Tire pressure monitor . . . . .Not available

Safety belts
Center-rear belt 3-point
Pretensioners, front/rear . . . . .Yes/no

Air bags
Occupant-sensing system . . . . .Front
Side bags, front/rear . . . . .No/no
Inflatable curtain . . . . .Optional with rollover
Accident alert system . . . . .Not available

Crash tests
Gov't front-crash test, driver/front passenger . . . . . .◖/◖
Gov't side-crash test, driver/rear passenger . . . .●/◖
IIHS offset crash test . . . . .Acceptable
IIHS side crash test w/ side & curtain airbags . . . . .Good
IIHS side crash test w/o side & curtain airbags . . . . . . .Poor

FROM THE TEST TRACK

Tested model
2005 Ford Escape XLT 4-door SUV AWD,
3.0-liter V6, 4-speed automatic

Tires as tested
Continental Contitrac,
size P235/70R16 104T

Acceleration . . . .○
0-30 mph, sec. 3.6
0-60 mph, sec. 10.2
Quarter mile, sec. 17.6
Quarter mile, mph 82
45-65 mph, sec. 6.7

Other findings
Transmission . . . .◓
Turning circle, ft. 40
Ground clearance, in. 8.0

Braking and handling
Braking . . . .○
Braking, dry pavement, ft. 144
Routine handling . . . .◖
Emergency handling . . . .○
Avoidance maneuver, max. mph . . .47.0

Convenience and comfort
Ride . . . .○
Noise . . . .○
Driving position . . . .◓
Access . . . .◓
Controls and displays . . . .◓
Fit and finish . . . .◓
Door top to ground, in. 61.0
Cargo area . . . .◓
Cargo volume, cu.ft. 38.5
Max. load, lb. 950

Seating
Front-seat comfort . . . .◓
Front shoulder room, in. 56.5
Front leg room, in. 40.5
Front head room, in. 4.5
Rear-seat comfort . . . .◓
Rear shoulder room, in. 55.0
Rear leg room, in. 28.0
Rear head room, in 5.0

Fuel economy . . . .◖
CU's overall mileage, mpg 18
CU's city/highway, mpg 12/27
CU's 150-mile trip, mpg 22
Annual fuel . . . . .830 gal./$1,660
Cruising range 325

RELIABILITY HISTORY

TROUBLE SPOTS	97	98	99	00	01	02	03	04
Engine					●	◓	●	●
Cooling					●	●	●	●
Fuel					○	◖	●	●
Ignition					●	●	●	●
Transmission					○	◓	●	●
Electrical					○	◖	●	●
Air conditioning					●	●	●	●
Suspension					◖	◓	●	●
Brakes					◖	○	●	●
Exhaust					●	●	●	●
Paint/trim/rust					●	●	●	●
Body integrity					◖	○	◖	◖
Power equipment					◓	◖	●	●
Body hardware					◖	○	●	●
RELIABILITY VERDICT					✗	–	✓	✓

Mazda3

CR RECOMMENDED ✓

The very pleasant Mazda3 shares its underpinnings with the new Volvo S40. The standard 2.0-liter engine is relatively quick, refined, and sparing with fuel. The 2.3-liter engine is punchy. The slick manual transmission augments the sporty character. The 3 also has precise, responsive handling and a firm, relatively comfortable ride, though road noise is pronounced. Interior quality is very good. The rear-seat room is competitive in this class, but the trunk is a bit small. We recommend getting the optional curtain airbags. Without them the Mazda3 received a Poor in the IIHS side-crash test.

THE 3 LINE
Body style:
4-door hatchback; sedan
Trim lines:
i, s, SP23
Base price range:
$13,680-$18,685

REPORT CARD

◉	Predicted reliability
◉	Owner satisfaction
NA	Predicted depreciation
◉	Accident avoidance
○	Acceleration
○	Ride
⊖	Front seat comfort
⊖	Fuel economy

SPECIFICATIONS

Drive wheels Front

Seating 2 front, 3 rear

Engines available
2.0-liter 4 (148 hp); 2.3-liter 4 (160 hp)

Transmissions available
5-speed manual; 4-speed automatic

Fuel
Fuel type ....Regular
EPA city/highway, mpg 28/35
Fuel refill capacity, gal. 14.5

Dimensions and weight
Length, in. 178
Width, in. 69
Wheelbase, in. 104
Curb weight, lb. 2,815
Percent weight, front/rear 62/38
Typical towing ability, lb. ....NR

SAFETY INFORMATION

Active safety features
Antilock brakes ....Optional
Traction control ....Not available
Stability control ....Not available
Daytime running lights ....Not available
Tire pressure monitor ....Available

Safety belts
Center-rear belt 3-point
Pretensioners, front/rear ....Yes/no

Air bags
Occupant-sensing system ....Front
Side bags, front/rear ....Optional/no
Inflatable curtain ....Optional
Accident alert system ....Not available

Crash tests
Gov't front-crash test, driver/front passenger .....⊖/⊖
Gov't side-crash test, driver/rear passenger ......○/○
IIHS offset crash test ....Good
IIHS side crash test w/ side & curtain airbags ....NA
IIHS side crash test w/o side & curtain airbags ....Poor

FROM THE TEST TRACK

Tested model
2004 i sedan, 2.0-liter Four, 4-speed automatic

Tires as tested
Toyo Proxes A05, size P205/55R16 89H

Acceleration ....○
0-30 mph, sec. 3.6
0-60 mph, sec. 9.6
Quarter mile, sec. 17.4
Quarter mile, mph 83
45-65 mph, sec.................6.7

Other findings
Transmission ....⊖
Turning circle, ft. 36
Ground clearance, in. 5.0

Braking and handling
Braking ....⊖
Braking, dry pavement, ft. 132
Routine handling ....◉
Emergency handling ....⊖
Avoidance maneuver, max. mph ..52.5

Convenience and comfort
Ride ....○
Noise ....○
Driving position ....⊖
Access ....⊖
Controls and displays ....◉
Fit and finish ....⊖
Door top to ground, in. ..52.0
Trunk ....◖
Luggage capacity ....2+3
Max. load, lb. 850

Seating
Front-seat comfort ....⊖
Front shoulder room, in. 55.0
Front leg room, in. 41.5
Front head room, in. 5.5
Rear-seat comfort ....○
Rear shoulder room, in. 53.0
Rear leg room, in. 27.0
Rear head room, in 2.0

Fuel economy
CU's overall mileage, mpg 27
CU's city/highway, mpg 18/38
CU's 150-mile trip, mpg 32
Annual fuel ....560 gal./$1,120
Cruising range 440

RELIABILITY HISTORY

TROUBLE SPOTS	Mazda3
	97 98 99 00 01 02 03 04
Engine	◉
Cooling	◉
Fuel	◉
Ignition	◉
Transmission	◉
Electrical	◉
Air conditioning	◉
Suspension	◉
Brakes	⊖
Exhaust	◉
Paint/trim/rust	◉
Body integrity	◉
Power equipment	◉
Body hardware	◉
RELIABILITY VERDICT	✓

Mazda5

THE 5 LINE
Body style:
minivan
Trim lines:
Sport, Touring
Base price range:
$20,000-$30,000E

The Mazda5 is a six-passenger minivan based on the Mazda3, which performed very well in our testing. It is designed to provide the utility of a minivan with easy maneuverability in tight spaces, all at an affordable price. Seating is for six, and the second- and third-row seats can easily be folded to provide a flat loading space.

REPORT CARD

New	**Predicted reliability**
New	**Owner satisfaction**
NA	**Predicted depreciation**
NA	**Accident avoidance**
NA	**Acceleration**
NA	**Ride**
NA	**Front seat comfort**
NA	**Fuel economy**

SPECIFICATIONS

Drive wheels Front

Seating 2 front, 2 rear, 2 third

Engines available
2.3-liter 4 (157 hp)

Transmissions available
4-speed automatic; 5-speed manual

Fuel
Fuel type ....Regular
EPA city/highway, mpg ....NA
Fuel refill capacity, gal. ....NA

Dimensions and weight
Length, in. 177
Width, in. 69
Wheelbase, in. 108
Curb weight, lb. ....NA
Percent weight, front/rear ....NA
Typical towing ability, lb. ....NA

SAFETY INFORMATION

Active safety features
Antilock brakes ....Optional
Traction control ....Not available
Stability control ....Not available
Daytime running lights ....Not available
Tire pressure monitor ....Available

Safety belts
Center-rear belt ....NA
Pretensioners, front/rear ....Yes/no

Air bags
Occupant-sensing system ....Not available
Side bags, front/rear ....Optional/no
Inflatable curtain ....Optional
Accident alert system ....Not available

Crash tests
Gov't front-crash test, driver/front passenger ......NA/NA
Gov't side-crash test, driver/rear passenger ....NA/NA
IIHS offset crash test ....NA
IIHS side crash test w/ side & curtain airbags ....NA
IIHS side crash test w/o side & curtain airbags ....NA

ANOTHER LOOK

RELIABILITY HISTORY

TROUBLE SPOTS	97 98 99 00 01 02 03 04
Engine	
Cooling	NO
Fuel	
Ignition	
Transmission	DATA
Electrical	
Air conditioning	NEW
Suspension	
Brakes	MODEL
Exhaust	
Paint/trim/rust	
Body integrity	
Power equipment	
Body hardware	
RELIABILITY VERDICT	

better ◀━━━▶ worse   See page 36 for more information.

Mazda6

THE 6 LINE
Body style:
4-door hatchback;
sedan; wagon
Trim lines:
i, s, Mazdaspeed
Base price range:
$18,995-$27,995

The Mazda6 is competitive with the better family sedans. The slow-responding five-speed automatic was replaced by a six-speed for 2005, while the four-cylinder model makes due with a four-speed. The split folding rear seatback has a spring-loaded release mechanism to fold the seats. Handling is fairly nimble. The ride is firm yet compliant. The engines aren't as punchy or refined as those in the Accord or Camry. The Ford-supplied V6 is relatively thirsty. The turning circle is wide, making parking maneuvers tedious. Reliability has dropped to below average, so we no longer recommend the Mazda6.

REPORT CARD

⬒	Predicted reliability
⬒	Owner satisfaction
NA	Predicted depreciation
⬒	Accident avoidance
⬒	Acceleration
⬒	Ride
⬒	Front seat comfort
⬒	Fuel economy

SPECIFICATIONS

Drive wheels Front

Seating 2 front, 3 rear

Engines available
2.3-liter 4 (160 hp); 3.0-liter V6 (220 hp);
2.3-liter 4 turbo (274 hp)

Transmissions available
5-speed manual; 6-speed manual; 4-speed automatic; 6-speed automatic

Fuel
Fuel type . . . . .Regular or premium
EPA city/highway, mpg 20/27
Fuel refill capacity, gal. 18.0

Dimensions and weight
Length, in. 187
Width, in. 70
Wheelbase, in. 105
Curb weight, lb. 3,510
Percent weight, front/rear 59/41
Typical towing ability, lb. . . . . .NR

SAFETY INFORMATION

Active safety features
Antilock brakes . . . . .Standard
Traction control . . . . .Standard
Stability control . . . . .Std. on MazdaSpeed
Daytime running lights . . . . .Not available
Tire pressure monitor . . . . .Not available

Safety belts
Center-rear belt 3-point
Pretensioners, front/rear . . . . .Yes/no

Air bags
Occupant-sensing system . . . . .Front
Side bags, front/rear . . . . .Optional/no
Inflatable curtain . . . . .Optional
Accident alert system . . . . .Not available

Crash tests
Gov't front-crash test, driver/front passenger . . . . . . ◐/◐
Gov't side-crash test, driver/rear passenger . . . . ○/◐
IIHS offset crash test . . . . .Good
IIHS side crash test w/ side & curtain airbags . . . . .NA
IIHS side crash test w/o side & curtain airbags . . . . . . .Poor

FROM THE TEST TRACK

Tested model
2004 s wagon, 3.0-liter V6, 5-speed
automatic

Tires as tested
Michelin Pilot HX MXM4,
size P215/50R17 93V

Acceleration . . . . ◐
0-30 mph, sec. 3.3
0-60 mph, sec. 8.8
Quarter mile, sec. 17.0
Quarter mile, mph 85
45-65 mph, sec. 5.9

Other findings
Transmission . . . . ○
Turning circle, ft. 41
Ground clearance, in. 5.0

Braking and handling
Braking . . . . ◐
Braking, dry pavement, ft. 133
Routine handling . . . . ◐
Emergency handling . . . . ◐
Avoidance maneuver, max. mph . . .52.0

Convenience and comfort
Ride . . . . ◐
Noise . . . . ◐
Driving position . . . . ◐
Access . . . . ◐
Controls and displays . . . . ◐
Fit and finish . . . . ◐
Door top to ground, in. 51.0
Trunk . . . . ○
Cargo volume, cu.ft. 33.5
Max. load, lb. 850

Seating
Front-seat comfort . . . . ◐
Front shoulder room, in. 56.0
Front leg room, in. 41.0
Front head room, in. 3.0
Rear-seat comfort . . . . ◐
Rear shoulder room, in. 55.0
Rear leg room, in. 28.0
Rear head room, in 4.0

Fuel economy . . . . ⬒
CU's overall mileage, mpg 19
  CU's city/highway, mpg 13/30
  CU's 150-mile trip, mpg 23
Annual fuel . . . . .775 gal./$1,550
Cruising range 390

RELIABILITY HISTORY

TROUBLE SPOTS	Mazda6							
	97	98	99	00	01	02	03	04
Engine							●	●
Cooling							●	●
Fuel							○	●
Ignition							●	●
Transmission							●	●
Electrical							●	●
Air conditioning							●	●
Suspension							●	●
Brakes							○	●
Exhaust							●	●
Paint/trim/rust							●	●
Body integrity							○	●
Power equipment							●	●
Body hardware							●	●
RELIABILITY VERDICT							✗	✗

Mercedes-Benz C-Class

THE C-CLASS LINE
Body style:
sedan; wagon
Trim lines:
C230, C240, C320, C55
AMG
Base price range:
$29,250-$53,900

The Mercedes-Benz C-Class competes well with the best-in-class Acura TL and BMW 3 Series. The C320 is quick, with a very quiet interior and a comfortable ride. Handling is agile and secure, and the steering is very precise and communicative. AWD versions are available. The seats are exceptionally comfortable and supportive, but the rear is tight. Some controls are overly complicated, although they're slightly improved for 2005. The wagon is nicely detailed. All versions are fun to drive, not only the track-ready 362-hp C55 AMG. The Coupe was dropped for 2005. Reliability has been below average.

REPORT CARD

⊖	Predicted reliability
◯	Owner satisfaction
⊖	Predicted depreciation
◉	Accident avoidance
◉	Acceleration
⊖	Ride
◉	Front seat comfort
◯	Fuel economy

SPECIFICATIONS

Drive wheels Rear or AWD

Seating 2 front, 3 rear

Engines available
2.6-liter V6 (168 hp); 1.8-liter 4 super-charged (189 hp); 3.2-liter V6 (215 hp); 5.5-liter V8 (362 hp)

Transmissions available
6-speed manual; 5-speed automatic

Fuel
Fuel type . . . . .Premium
EPA city/highway, mpg 19/25
Fuel refill capacity, gal. 16.2

Dimensions and weight
Length, in. 178
Width, in. 68
Wheelbase, in. 107
Curb weight, lb. 3,445
Percent weight, front/rear 53/47
Typical towing ability, lb. . . . . .NR

SAFETY INFORMATION

Active safety features
Antilock brakes . . . . .Standard
Traction control . . . . .Standard
Stability control .Standard
Daytime running lights . . . . .Optional
Tire pressure monitor . . . . .Not available

Safety belts
Center-rear belt 3-point
Pretensioners, front/rear . . . . .Yes/yes

Air bags
Occupant-sensing system . . . . .Front
Side bags, front/rear . . . . .Standard/standard
Inflatable curtain .Standard
Accident alert system . . . . .Available

Crash tests
Gov't front-crash test, driver/front passenger . . . . . ◒/◒
Gov't side-crash test, driver/rear passenger . . . . ◉/◉
IIHS offset crash test . . . . .Good
IIHS side crash test w/ side & curtain airbags . . .Acceptable
IIHS side crash test w/o side & curtain airbags . . . . . . .NA

FROM THE TEST TRACK

Tested model
2001 C320 sedan, 3.2-liter V6, 5-speed automatic

Tires as tested
Continental ContiTouring Contact, size 205/55R16 91H

Acceleration . . . . ◉
0-30 mph, sec. 2.6
0-60 mph, sec. 7.0
Quarter mile, sec. 15.5
Quarter mile, mph 92
45-65 mph, sec. 5.0

Other findings
Transmission . . . . ◉
Turning circle, ft. 35
Ground clearance, in. 5.0

Braking and handling
Braking . . . . ◒
Braking, dry pavement, ft. 132
Routine handling . . . . ◉
Emergency handling . . . . ◒
Avoidance maneuver, max. mph . . .53.5

Convenience and comfort
Ride . . . . ◒
Noise . . . . ◒
Driving position . . . . ◒
Access . . . . ◯
Controls and displays . . . . ◯
Fit and finish . . . . ◉
Door top to ground, in. 51.0
Trunk . . . . ⊖
Luggage capacity . . . . .3+1
Max. load, lb. 865

Seating
Front-seat comfort . . . . ◉
Front shoulder room, in. 53.0
Front leg room, in. 42.5
Front head room, in. 3.0
Rear-seat comfort . . . . ◯
Rear shoulder room, in. 53.5
Rear leg room, in. 27.5
Rear head room, in 4.0

Fuel economy . . . . ◯
CU's overall mileage, mpg 21
CU's city/highway, mpg 15/29
CU's 150-mile trip, mpg 25
Annual fuel . . . . .710 gal./$1,560
Cruising range 380

RELIABILITY HISTORY

TROUBLE SPOTS	Mercedes-Benz C-Class V6							
	97	98	99	00	01	02	03	04
Engine			◯		◒	◒	◒	◒
Cooling			●		◒	◯	◯	◒
Fuel			●		◯	◯	◒	◒
Ignition			◯		◯	◯	◒	◒
Transmission			◯		◒	◒	◒	◒
Electrical	Insufficient data	Insufficient data	●	Insufficient data	●	●	◒	◒
Air conditioning			◯		◯	◯	◒	◒
Suspension			◯		◯	◯	◒	◒
Brakes			◯		◯	◯	◯	◒
Exhaust			◯		◯	◯	◒	◒
Paint/trim/rust			◯		◯	◯	◒	◒
Body integrity			◯		◯	◯	◒	◒
Power equipment			●		●	●	◒	◒
Body hardware			◒		◒	◒	◒	◒
RELIABILITY VERDICT			-		✗	✗	✗	✗

Mercedes-Benz CLK

Redesigned for 2003, the CLK is based on the current-generation C-Class sedan, which lends it more exuberance and more agile handling than the previous generation. The CLK's steering has a more modern and direct design now. The V6 is nice, but the muscular 5.0-liter V8 mated to a seven-speed automatic provides abundant thrust. The CLK55 AMG has a brawny 362-hp V8. The two-person rear seating is comfortable for a coupe. In the front, a belt "presenter" moves the seat belt toward you. A convertible is also available.

THE CLK LINE

Body style:
convertible; coupe
Trim lines:
CLK320, CLK500, CLK55 AMG
Base price range:
$46,000-$82,000

REPORT CARD

●	Predicted reliability
⊖	Owner satisfaction
◉	Predicted depreciation
NA	Accident avoidance
NA	Acceleration
NA	Ride
NA	Front seat comfort
NA	Fuel economy

SPECIFICATIONS

Drive wheels Rear

Seating 2 front, 2 rear

Engines available
3.2-liter V6 (215 hp); 5.0-liter V8 (302 hp); 5.5-liter V8 (362 hp)

Transmissions available
5-speed automatic; 7-speed automatic

Fuel
Fuel type .Premium
EPA city/highway, mpg 20/26
Fuel refill capacity, gal. 16.4

Dimensions and weight
Length, in. 183
Width, in. 68
Wheelbase, in. 107
Curb weight, lb. 3,515
Percent weight, front/rear 54/46
Typical towing ability, lb. . . . . .NR

SAFETY INFORMATION

Active safety features
Antilock brakes . . . . .Standard
Traction control . . . . .Standard
Stability control . . . . .Standard
Daytime running lights . . . . .Optional
Tire pressure monitor . . . . .Not available

Safety belts
Center-rear belt . . . . .NA
Pretensioners, front/rear .Yes/no

Air bags
Occupant-sensing system . . . . .Front
Side bags, front/rear . . . . .Standard/no
Inflatable curtain . . . . .Standard
Accident alert system . . . . .Available

Crash tests
Gov't front-crash test, driver/front passenger . . . . . .NA/NA
Gov't side-crash test, driver/rear passenger . . . . .NA/NA
IIHS offset crash test . . . . .NA
IIHS side crash test w/ side & curtain airbags . . . . .NA
IIHS side crash test w/o side & curtain airbags . . . . .NA

ANOTHER LOOK

RELIABILITY HISTORY

TROUBLE SPOTS	Mercedes-Benz CLK							
	97	98	99	00	01	02	03	04
Engine			○	○	○	○	○	○
Cooling			○	○	○	○	○	○
Fuel			○	○	○	○	○	○
Ignition			○	○	○	○	○	○
Transmission			○	○	○	○	○	○
Electrical			○	●	○	○	○	○
Air conditioning			○	○	○	○	○	○
Suspension			○	○	○	○	○	○
Brakes			○	○	○	○	○	○
Exhaust			○	○	○	○	○	○
Paint/trim/rust			○	○	○	○	○	○
Body integrity			○	○	○	○	○	○
Power equipment			○	○	●	●	○	○
Body hardware			○	○	●	●	○	○
RELIABILITY VERDICT			X	X	-	X	X	X

(Columns 97–98: Insufficient data)

Mercedes-Benz CLS

THE CLS LINE
Body style:
sedan
Trim lines:
CLS500, CLS55 AMG
Base price range:
$64,900-$86,800

The new CLS is a four-door sedan with a swoopy, stream-lined roof that leads Mercedes-Benz to refer to it as a coupe. Based on the E-Class platform, the luxurious CLS features seating for just four passengers. Even so, rear seat room is tight for tall passengers, and the angle of the roof cuts into head room. The CLS comes with a powerful V8 powerplant. The AMG version will be even more powerful. A seven-speed automatic transmission is standard. Other features include an air suspension, four-zone automatic climate control, and finely-stitched leather surfaces.

REPORT CARD

New	**Predicted reliability**
New	**Owner satisfaction**
NA	**Predicted depreciation**
NA	**Accident avoidance**
NA	**Acceleration**
NA	**Ride**
NA	**Front seat comfort**
NA	**Fuel economy**

SPECIFICATIONS

Drive wheels Rear

Seating 2 front, 2 rear

Engines available
5.0-liter V8 (302 hp); 5.5-liter V8 super-charged (469 hp)

Transmissions available
5-speed automatic; 7-speed automatic

Fuel
Fuel type . . . . .Premium
EPA city/highway, mpg 17/21
Fuel refill capacity, gal. 21.1

Dimensions and weight
Length, in. 194
Width, in. 74
Wheelbase, in. 112
Curb weight, lb. 4,050
Percent weight, front/rear . . . . .NA
Typical towing ability, lb. . . . . .NR

SAFETY INFORMATION

Active safety features

Antilock brakes . . . . .Standard
Traction control . . . . .Standard
Stability control . . . . .Standard
Daytime running lights . . . . .Optional
Tire pressure monitor . . . . .Available

Safety belts

Center-rear belt . . . . .NA
Pretensioners, front/rear . . . . .Yes/yes

Air bags

Occupant-sensing system . . . . .Front and Side
Side bags, front/rear . . . . .Standard/standard
Inflatable curtain . . . . .Standard
Accident alert system . . . . .Available

Crash tests

Gov't front-crash test, driver/front passenger . . . . .NA/NA
Gov't side-crash test, driver/rear passenger . . . . . . .NA/NA
IIHS offset crash test . . . . .NA
IIHS side crash test w/ side & curtain airbags . . . . .NA
IIHS side crash test w/o side & curtain airbags . . . . .NA

ANOTHER LOOK

RELIABILITY HISTORY

TROUBLE SPOTS	97 98 99 00 01 02 03 04
Engine	
Cooling	
Fuel	**NO**
Ignition	
Transmission	**DATA**
Electrical	
Air conditioning	**NEW**
Suspension	
Brakes	**MODEL**
Exhaust	
Paint/trim/rust	
Body integrity	
Power equipment	
Body hardware	
RELIABILITY VERDICT	

Mercedes-Benz E-Class

The E-Class is a pleasure to drive, blending spirited acceleration and respectable fuel economy. The car is remarkable for its ability to deliver a magic-carpet ride and still offer agile, sporty handling. The 3.2-liter V6 has just been replaced by a stronger 3.5-liter unit mated to a seven-speed automatic. The high-performance E55 AMG is powered by a supercharged V8. Seat comfort and driving position are first class. Rear seat and trunk room are commendable. Wagon, diesel, and all-wheel-drive models are also available. Reliability has been poor.

THE E-CLASS LINE
Body style: sedan; wagon
Trim lines: E350, E320 CDI, E500, E55 AMG
Base price range: $50,050-$82,600

REPORT CARD

●	Predicted reliability
○	Owner satisfaction
◐	Predicted depreciation
◓	Accident avoidance
◐	Acceleration
◓	Ride
◓	Front seat comfort
◒	Fuel economy

SPECIFICATIONS

Drive wheels Rear or AWD

Seating 2 front, 3 rear, 2 third

Engines available
3.2-liter 6 turbodiesel (201 hp); 3.5-liter V6 (268 hp); 5.0-liter V8 (302 hp); 5.5-liter V8 supercharged (469 hp)

Transmissions available
5-speed automatic; 7-speed automatic

Fuel
Fuel type . . . . .Diesel or premium
EPA city/highway, mpg 20/28
Fuel refill capacity, gal. 21.1

Dimensions and weight
Length, in. 190
Width, in. 71
Wheelbase, in. 112
Curb weight, lb. 3,745
Percent weight, front/rear 51/49
Typical towing ability, lb. . . . . .NR

SAFETY INFORMATION

Active safety features
Antilock brakes . . . . .Standard
Traction control . . . . .Standard
Stability control . . . . .Standard
Daytime running lights .Optional
Tire pressure monitor . . . . .Available

Safety belts
Center-rear belt 3-point
Pretensioners, front/rear . . . . .Yes/yes

Air bags
Occupant-sensing system . . . . .Front
Side bags, front/rear . . . . .Standard/standard
Inflatable curtain . . . . .Standard with rollover
Accident alert system . . . . .Available

Crash tests
Gov't front-crash test, driver/front passenger . . . . . .◐/◐
Gov't side-crash test, driver/rear passenger . . . .◓/◐
IIHS offset crash test . . . . .Good
IIHS side crash test w/ side & curtain airbags . . . . .NA
IIHS side crash test w/o side & curtain airbags . . . . .NA

FROM THE TEST TRACK

Tested model
2004 E320 sedan, 3.2-liter V6, 5-speed automatic

Tires as tested
Continental ContiTouring Contact CH95, size 225/55R16 95H

Acceleration . . . .◒
0-30 mph, sec. 2.9
0-60 mph, sec. 7.6
Quarter mile, sec. 16.0
Quarter mile, mph 89
45-65 mph, sec. 4.9

Other findings
Transmission . . . .◒
Turning circle, ft. 38
Ground clearance, in. 4.5

Braking and handling
Braking . . . .◒
Braking, dry pavement, ft. 128
Routine handling . . . .◓
Emergency handling . . . .◒
Avoidance maneuver, max. mph . . .54.0

Convenience and comfort
Ride . . . .◓
Noise . . . .◓
Driving position . . . .◓
Access . . . .◒
Controls and displays . . . .○
Fit and finish . . . .◓
Door top to ground, in. 51.5
Trunk . . . .○
Luggage capacity . . . . .4+1
Max. load, lb. 965

Seating
Front-seat comfort . . . .◓
Front shoulder room, in. 56.0
Front leg room, in. 43.0
Front head room, in. 3.5
Rear-seat comfort . . . .◒
Rear shoulder room, in. 54.5
Rear leg room, in. 27.5
Rear head room, in 4.0

Fuel economy . . . .◒
CU's overall mileage, mpg 20
CU's city/highway, mpg 14/28
CU's 150-mile trip, mpg 25
Annual fuel . . . . .745 gal./$1,645
Cruising range 490

RELIABILITY HISTORY

TROUBLE SPOTS	Mercedes-Benz E-Class							
	97	98	99	00	01	02	03	04
Engine	◐	○	○	○	◐	●	◐	◐
Cooling	◐	◐	◐	◐	●	◐	◐	●
Fuel	○	◐	○	○	◐	◐	◐	◐
Ignition	◐	○	○	◓	◐	◐	◐	◐
Transmission	○	○	○	○	◐	◐	◐	◐
Electrical	●	●	●	◐	◐	◐	◐	◐
Air conditioning	●	◐	○	○	○	◐	◐	◐
Suspension	○	◐	○	○	○	◐	◐	◐
Brakes	○	○	○	○	◐	◐	◐	◐
Exhaust	○	◐	◐	○	○	◐	◐	◐
Paint/trim/rust	◐	◐	◐	◐	◐	◐	◐	◐
Body integrity	○	○	○	◐	○	◐	○	◐
Power equipment	●	●	●	●	◐	○	◐	◐
Body hardware	◐	◐	○	○	○	◐	○	◐
RELIABILITY VERDICT	-	-	X	-	X	X	X	X

Expert • Independent • Nonprofit

Mercedes-Benz M-Class

THE M-CLASS LINE

Body style:
4-door SUV

Trim lines:
ML350, ML500

Base price range:
$39,750-$48,500

The redesigned M-Class debuted this past spring. Unlike the outgoing version, it uses unibody construction. The M-Class will not offer a third-row seat. The pricey upcoming R-Class will offer a third row. The new M-Class won't have low-range gearing, just an electronic hill-descent system, unless the off-road option is chosen. Both V6 and V8 engines use a seven-speed automatic. The second-row seats fold flat for carrying cargo. The M-Class will include Mercedes' Pre-Safe system, which proactively adjusts the seats and closes windows prior to an anticipated crash.

REPORT CARD

New	**Predicted reliability**
New	**Owner satisfaction**
NA	**Predicted depreciation**
NA	**Accident avoidance**
NA	**Acceleration**
NA	**Ride**
NA	**Front seat comfort**
NA	**Fuel economy**

SPECIFICATIONS

Drive wheels Permanent 4WD

Seating 2 front, 3 rear

Engines available
3.5-liter V6 (268 hp); 5.0-liter V8 (302 hp)

Transmissions available
7-speed automatic

Fuel
Fuel type . . . . Premium
EPA city/highway, mpg 15/18
Fuel refill capacity, gal. 25.1

Dimensions and weight
Length, in. 189
Width, in. 75
Wheelbase, in. 115
Curb weight, lb. 4,790
Percent weight, front/rear . . . . .NA
Typical towing ability, lb. 5,000

SAFETY INFORMATION

Active safety features

Antilock brakes . . . . .Standard
Traction control . . . . .Standard
Stability control . . . . .Standard
Daytime running lights . . . . .Optional
Tire pressure monitor . . . . .Available

Safety belts

Center-rear belt 3-point
Pretensioners, front/rear . . . . .Yes/yes

Air bags

Occupant-sensing system . . . . .Front
Side bags, front/rear . . . . .Standard/standard
Inflatable curtain . . . . .Standard with rollover
Accident alert system . . . . .Available

Crash tests

Gov't front-crash test, driver/front passenger . . . . . .NA/NA
Gov't side-crash test, driver/rear passenger . . . . . . .NA/NA
IIHS offset crash test . . . . .NA
IIHS side crash test w/ side & curtain airbags . . . . .NA
IIHS side crash test w/o side & curtain airbags . . . . . . .NA

ANOTHER LOOK

RELIABILITY HISTORY

TROUBLE SPOTS	97 98 99 00 01 02 03 04
Engine	
Cooling	**NO**
Fuel	
Ignition	
Transmission	**DATA**
Electrical	
Air conditioning	**NEW**
Suspension	
Brakes	**MODEL**
Exhaust	
Paint/trim/rust	
Body integrity	
Power equipment	
Body hardware	
RELIABILITY VERDICT	

● ◐ ○ ○ ●
better ◀——▶ worse   See page 36 for more information.

Mercedes-Benz S-Class

THE S-CLASS LINE
Body style:
sedan
Trim lines:
S350, S430, S500, S55
AMG, S600, S65 AMG
Base price range:
$64,900-$169,000

The S-Class line is stately and advanced. The V8 and V12 engines are smooth, powerful, and refined. The S430 we tested is quiet and luxurious. Despite its size, it handles with surprising agility, making it a delight to drive. The cushy ride is extremely comfortable and the best we've tested. The heated and ventilated seats are supportive, and the sumptuous rear is roomy. AWD is a no-cost option. V8 models feature a seven-speed automatic in an effort to improve acceleration, response, and fuel economy. Despite its very high ranking in our tests, reliability remains below par, so we can't recommend it.

REPORT CARD

●	Predicted reliability
○	Owner satisfaction
◒	Predicted depreciation
◔	Accident avoidance
◒	Acceleration
◔	Ride
◔	Front seat comfort
◓	Fuel economy

SPECIFICATIONS

Drive wheels Rear or AWD

Seating 2 front, 3 rear

Engines available
3.7-liter V6 (241 hp); 4.3-liter V8 (275 hp); 5.0-liter V8 (302 hp); 5.5-liter V12 twin-turbo (493 hp); 5.5-liter V8 supercharged (493 hp); 6.0-liter V12 twin-turbo (604 hp)

Transmissions available
5-speed automatic; 7-speed automatic

Fuel
Fuel type ....Premium
EPA city/highway, mpg 18/26
Fuel refill capacity, gal. 23.2

Dimensions and weight
Length, in. 203
Width, in. 73
Wheelbase, in. 122
Curb weight, lb. 4,195
Percent weight, front/rear 50/50
Typical towing ability, lb. ....NR

SAFETY INFORMATION

Active safety features
Antilock brakes ....Standard
Traction control ....Standard
Stability control ....Standard
Daytime running lights ....Standard
Tire pressure monitor ....Available

Safety belts
Center-rear belt 3-point
Pretensioners, front/rear ....Yes/yes

Air bags
Occupant-sensing system ....Front and Side
Side bags, front/rear ....Standard/standard
Inflatable curtain ....Standard with rollover
Accident alert system ....Available

Crash tests
Gov't front-crash test, driver/front passenger ......NA/NA
Gov't side-crash test, driver/rear passenger ....NA/NA
IIHS offset crash test ....NA
IIHS side crash test w/ side & curtain airbags ....NA
IIHS side crash test w/o side & curtain airbags ....NA

FROM THE TEST TRACK

Tested model
2003 S430 sedan, 4.3-liter V8, 5-speed automatic

Tires as tested
Michelin Energy MXV4 Plus, size 225/55R17 97H

Acceleration ....◒
0-30 mph, sec. 3.1
0-60 mph, sec. 7.7
Quarter mile, sec. 16.0
Quarter mile, mph 91
45-65 mph, sec. 4.6

Other findings
Transmission ....◔
Turning circle, ft. 40
Ground clearance, in. 6.5

Braking and handling
Braking ....◒
Braking, dry pavement, ft. 135
Routine handling ....◔
Emergency handling ....◒
Avoidance maneuver, max. mph . .51.5

Convenience and comfort
Ride ....◔
Noise ....◔
Driving position ....◔
Access ....○
Controls and displays ....○
Fit and finish ....◔
Door top to ground, in. 53.0
Trunk ....◒
Luggage capacity ....3+2
Max. load, lb. 970

Seating
Front-seat comfort ....◔
Front shoulder room, in. 58.5
Front leg room, in. 44.0
Front head room, in. 3.0
Rear-seat comfort ....◔
Rear shoulder room, in. 58.0
Rear leg room, in. 34.0
Rear head room, in 3.5

Fuel economy ....◓
CU's overall mileage, mpg 18
  CU's city/highway, mpg 11/28
  CU's 150-mile trip, mpg 22
Annual fuel ....850 gal./$1,875
Cruising range 475

RELIABILITY HISTORY

TROUBLE SPOTS	Mercedes-Benz S-Class							
	97	98	99	00	01	02	03	04
Engine				◒	◔	◔	◔	
Cooling				◔	◔	◔	◔	
Fuel				○	◔	◔	◔	
Ignition				◒	◔	◔	◔	
Transmission				◒	◔	◔	◔	
Electrical	Insufficient data	Insufficient data	Insufficient data	●	●	●	○	Insufficient data
Air conditioning				◔	○	◒	◔	
Suspension				◔	◒	◒	◒	
Brakes				◒	○	○	◒	
Exhaust				◔	◔	◔	◔	
Paint/trim/rust				◔	◔	◔		
Body integrity				○	○	○	○	
Power equipment				●	○	●	●	
Body hardware				○	○	○	○	
RELIABILITY VERDICT				✗	–	✗	✗	

Mercedes-Benz SLK

THE SLK LINE
Body style:
convertible
Trim lines:
SLK350, SLK55 AMG
Base price range:
$46,250-$60,500

Redesigned for 2005, the SLK convertible continues to offer top-down motoring without the usual compromises of poor rear visibility and pronounced wind noise. An electrically retractable hardtop stows itself in the trunk. The SLK comes with a strong 3.5-liter V6. First impressions indicate the manual shifter and clutch are more user-friendly than in the first-generation SLK. Handling is more agile than the previous version, yet the ride is relatively comfortable. One worthwhile option is the vent in the headrest, which blows warm air around your neck.

REPORT CARD

New	**Predicted reliability**
New	**Owner satisfaction**
NA	**Predicted depreciation**
NA	**Accident avoidance**
NA	**Acceleration**
NA	**Ride**
NA	**Front seat comfort**
NA	**Fuel economy**

SPECIFICATIONS

Drive wheels Rear

Seating 2 front

Engines available
3.5-liter V6 (268 hp); 5.5-liter V8 (355 hp)

Transmissions available
6-speed manual; 7-speed automatic

Fuel
Fuel type . . . . .Premium
EPA city/highway, mpg 18/25
Fuel refill capacity, gal. 18.5

Dimensions and weight
Length, in. 161
Width, in. 70
Wheelbase, in. 96
Curb weight, lb. 3,315
Percent weight, front/rear 52/48
Typical towing ability, lb. . . . . .NR

SAFETY INFORMATION

Active safety features
Antilock brakes . . . . .Standard
Traction control . . . . .Standard
Stability control . . . . .Standard
Daytime running lights . . . . .Not available
Tire pressure monitor . . . . .Not available

Safety belts
Center-rear belt . . . . .NA
Pretensioners, front/rear . . . . .Yes/NA

Air bags
Occupant-sensing system . . . . .Front
Side bags, front/rear . . . . .Standard/NA
Inflatable curtain .Not available
Accident alert system . . . . .Available

Crash tests
Gov't front-crash test, driver/front passenger . . . . .NA/NA
Gov't side-crash test, driver/rear passenger . . . . . .NA/NA
IIHS offset crash test . . . . .NA
IIHS side crash test w/ side & curtain airbags . . . . .NA
IIHS side crash test w/o side & curtain airbags . . . . .NA

RELIABILITY HISTORY

TROUBLE SPOTS	97	98	99	00	01	02	03	04
Engine								
Cooling								
Fuel				NO				
Ignition								
Transmission				DATA				
Electrical								
Air conditioning				NEW				
Suspension								
Brakes				MODEL				
Exhaust								
Paint/trim/rust								
Body integrity								
Power equipment								
Body hardware								
RELIABILITY VERDICT								

ANOTHER LOOK

● ● ○ ○ ●
better ◄——► worse   See page 36 for more information.

Mercury Grand Marquis

CR RECOMMENDED ✓

THE GRAND MARQUIS LINE
Body style:
sedan
Trim lines:
GS, GS Convenience,
LS Premium, LS
Ultimate
Base price range:
$24,565-$30,920

The Mercury Grand Marquis/Ford Crown Victoria twins are among the last big rear-drive sedans with a full frame and a noisy V8. Both are a bit dated. The ride is stiff and jiggly. Handling is safe enough but feels ungainly despite a revised suspension and steering gear that arrived for 2003. Standard traction control helps in slippery conditions. The soft front bench seat could use more support, and the rear seat isn't as roomy as you'd expect, though the trunk is suitably cavernous. Crash-test results are impressive.

REPORT CARD

○	Predicted reliability
○	Owner satisfaction
◐	Predicted depreciation
○	Accident avoidance
◐	Acceleration
○	Ride
○	Front seat comfort
●	Fuel economy

SPECIFICATIONS

Drive wheels Rear

Seating 3 front, 3 rear

Engines available
4.6-liter V8 (224 hp); 4.6-liter V8 (239 hp)

Transmissions available
4-speed automatic

Fuel
Fuel type ....Regular
EPA city/highway, mpg 17/25
Fuel refill capacity, gal. 19.0

Dimensions and weight
Length, in. 212
Width, in. 78
Wheelbase, in. 115
Curb weight, lb. 4,180
Percent weight, front/rear 56/44
Typical towing ability, lb. 2,000

SAFETY INFORMATION

Active safety features
Antilock brakes ....Standard
Traction control ....Standard
Stability control ....Not available
Daytime running lights ....Not available
Tire pressure monitor ....Not available

Safety belts
Center-rear belt 3-point
Pretensioners, front/rear ....Yes/no

Air bags
Occupant-sensing system ....Front
Side bags, front/rear ....Optional/no
Inflatable curtain ....Not available
Accident alert system ....Not available

Crash tests
Gov't front-crash test, driver/front passenger .....◐/●
Gov't side-crash test, driver/rear passenger ....◐/●
IIHS offset crash test ....Good
IIHS side crash test w/ side & curtain airbags ....NA
IIHS side crash test w/o side & curtain airbags ....NA

FROM THE TEST TRACK

Tested model
2003 LSE sedan, 4.6-liter V8, 4-speed automatic

Tires as tested
Goodyear Integrity, size P225/60R16 97T
Acceleration ....◐
0-30 mph, sec. 3.1
0-60 mph, sec. 8.0
Quarter mile, sec. 16.3
Quarter mile, mph 88
45-65 mph, sec. 5.1

Other findings
Transmission ....◐
Turning circle, ft. 42
Ground clearance, in. 4.5

Braking and handling
Braking ....◐
Braking, dry pavement, ft. 140
Routine handling ....○
Emergency handling ....○
Avoidance maneuver, max. mph . .50.0

Convenience and comfort
Ride ....○
Noise ....◐
Driving position ....○
Access ....◐
Controls and displays ....◐
Fit and finish ....○
Door top to ground, in. 52.0
Trunk ....◐
Luggage capacity ....6+2
Max. load, lb. 1,100

Seating
Front-seat comfort ....○
Front shoulder room, in. 61.0
Front leg room, in. 40.5
Front head room, in. 5.5
Rear-seat comfort ....◐
Rear shoulder room, in. 60.5
Rear leg room, in. 27.5
Rear head room, in 3.0

Fuel economy ....●
CU's overall mileage, mpg 16
CU's city/highway, mpg 10/25
CU's 150-mile trip, mpg 21
Annual fuel ....930 gal./$1,855
Cruising range 365

RELIABILITY HISTORY

TROUBLE SPOTS	Mercury Grand Marquis							
	97	98	99	00	01	02	03	04
Engine	◐	◐	◐	◐	◐	◐	◐	◐
Cooling	○	◐	◐	◐	◐	◐	◐	◐
Fuel	○	◐	○	○	○	○	◐	◐
Ignition	◐	◐	◐	◐	◐	◐	◐	◐
Transmission	◐	◐	◐	◐	◐	◐	◐	◐
Electrical	○	○	○	○	○	○	◐	◐
Air conditioning	◐	○	○	◐	○	○	◐	◐
Suspension	○	○	○	○	◐	◐	◐	◐
Brakes	◐	○	○	◐	○	○	○	◐
Exhaust	◐	◐	◐	◐	◐	◐	◐	◐
Paint/trim/rust	◐	◐	◐	◐	◐	◐	◐	◐
Body integrity	○	◐	○	○	○	○	○	○
Power equipment	◐	○	○	○	○	○	◐	◐
Body hardware	○	◐	○	○	○	○	◐	◐
RELIABILITY VERDICT	–	✓	✓	✓	–	✓	–	✗

Expert • Independent • Nonprofit

Mercury Mariner

THE MARINER LINE
Body style:
4-door SUV
Trim lines:
Convenience, Luxury, Premier
Base price range:
$21,405-$26,765

The Mariner is a rebadged twin of the Ford Escape and Mazda Tribute. All are unibody SUVs with a fully independent suspension. Our tested Ford Escape had a roomy interior that included a spacious rear bench. Handling is relatively nimble. The 3.0-liter, 200-hp V6 serves up adequate acceleration. Fuel economy was disappointing at just 18 mpg overall. Because of a tip-up in the government rollover test, we do not recommend the Escape and its siblings. A hybrid version like in the Escape will be available for the Mariner as well.

REPORT CARD

New	**Predicted reliability**
New	**Owner satisfaction**
NA	**Predicted depreciation**
NA	**Accident avoidance**
NA	**Acceleration**
NA	**Ride**
NA	**Front seat comfort**
NA	**Fuel economy**

SPECIFICATIONS

Drive wheels Front or AWD

Seating 2 front, 3 rear

Engines available
2.3-liter 4 (153 hp); 3.0-liter V6 (200 hp)

Transmissions available
4-speed automatic

Fuel
Fuel type ....Regular
EPA city/highway, mpg 18/23
Fuel refill capacity, gal. 16.5

Dimensions and weight
Length, in. 174
Width, in. 70
Wheelbase, in. 103
Curb weight, lb. 3,465
Percent weight, front/rear 59/41
Typical towing ability, lb. 3,500

SAFETY INFORMATION

Active safety features
Antilock brakes ....Standard
Traction control ....Not available
Stability control ....Not available
Daytime running lights ....Not available
Tire pressure monitor ....Available

Safety belts
Center-rear belt 3-point
Pretensioners, front/rear ....Yes/no

Air bags
Occupant-sensing system ....Front
Side bags, front/rear ....Optional/no
Inflatable curtain ....Optional with rollover
Accident alert system ....Not available

Crash tests
Gov't front-crash test, driver/front passenger ....◔/◔
Gov't side-crash test, driver/rear passenger ......◑/◔
IIHS offset crash test ....Acceptable
IIHS side crash test w/ side & curtain airbags ....Good
IIHS side crash test w/o side & curtain airbags ....Poor

RELIABILITY HISTORY

TROUBLE SPOTS	97 98 99 00 01 02 03 04
Engine	
Cooling	**NO**
Fuel	
Ignition	
Transmission	**DATA**
Electrical	
Air conditioning	**NEW**
Suspension	
Brakes	**MODEL**
Exhaust	
Paint/trim/rust	
Body integrity	
Power equipment	
Body hardware	
RELIABILITY VERDICT	

ANOTHER LOOK

● ◔ ○ ◑ ●
better ◄——► worse   See page 36 for more information.

Mercury Milan

THE MILAN LINE
Body style:
sedan
Trim lines:
–
Base price range:
$20,000-$26,000E

The Milan midsized sedan will go on sale this fall. It is the sibling of the upcoming Ford Fusion, and will be less expensive than the Lincoln Zephyr variant. All three are based on the Mazda6 platform. The Mercury will come with either a 160-hp, 2.3-liter four-cylinder or a 210-hp 3.0-liter V6. Now that Mercury has discontinued the Sable, the Milan and larger Montego revive the sedan lineup. The fold-flat rear seats use the spring-assist feature found in the Mazda6. Future plans include a hybrid version.

REPORT CARD

New	**Predicted reliability**
New	**Owner satisfaction**
NA	**Predicted depreciation**
NA	**Accident avoidance**
NA	**Acceleration**
NA	**Ride**
NA	**Front seat comfort**
NA	**Fuel economy**

SPECIFICATIONS

Drive wheels Front

Seating 2 front, 3 rear

Engines available
2.3-liter 4 (160 hp); 3.0-liter V6 (210 hp)

Transmissions available
5-speed manual; 5-speed automatic; 6-speed automatic

Fuel
Fuel type . . . . .Regular
EPA city/highway, mpg . . . . .NA
Fuel refill capacity, gal. 18.0

Dimensions and weight
Length, in. 190
Width, in. 72
Wheelbase, in. .107
Curb weight, lb. 3,305
Percent weight, front/rear 61/39
Typical towing ability, lb. 1,000

SAFETY INFORMATION

Active safety features
Antilock brakes . . . . .Optional
Traction control . . . . .Optional
Stability control .Not available
Daytime running lights . . . . .Not available
Tire pressure monitor . . . . .Not available

Safety belts
Center-rear belt 3-point
Pretensioners, front/rear . . . . .Yes/no

Air bags
Occupant-sensing system . . . . .Front
Side bags, front/rear . . . . .No/no
Inflatable curtain . . . . .Optional
Accident alert system .Not available

Crash tests
Gov't front-crash test, driver/front passenger . . . . .NA/NA
Gov't side-crash test, driver/rear passenger . . . . . . .NA/NA
IIHS offset crash test . . . . .NA
IIHS side crash test w/ side & curtain airbags . . . . .NA
IIHS side crash test w/o side & curtain airbags . . . . .NA

ANOTHER LOOK

RELIABILITY HISTORY

TROUBLE SPOTS

	97	98	99	00	01	02	03	04
Engine								
Cooling								
Fuel				**NO**				
Ignition								
Transmission				**DATA**				
Electrical								
Air conditioning				**NEW**				
Suspension								
Brakes				**MODEL**				
Exhaust								
Paint/trim/rust								
Body integrity								
Power equipment								
Body hardware								
RELIABILITY VERDICT								

Mercury Montego

THE MONTEGO LINE
Body style:
sedan
Trim lines:
Luxury, Premier
Base price range:
$24,345-$28,570

The Mercury Montego (and its twin, the Ford Five Hundred) is a roomy sedan that emphasizes comfort and good ergonomics over performance and pizzazz. It features an elevated seating position for good outward vision and cabin access. The rear seat is immense. Power comes from an over-taxed and unpolished 3.0-liter V6 engine that is mated to either a six-speed automatic on front-wheel-drive models or a continuously variable transmission (CVT). The AWD model was sluggish at launch. Handling is agile, especially considering the Montego's size. The ride is comfortable.

REPORT CARD

New	Predicted reliability
New	Owner satisfaction
NA	Predicted depreciation
○	Accident avoidance
○	Acceleration
◖	Ride
◖	Front seat comfort
◐	Fuel economy

SPECIFICATIONS

Drive wheels Front or AWD

Seating 2 front, 3 rear

Engines available
3.0-liter V6 (203 hp)

Transmissions available
CVT; 6-speed automatic

Fuel
Fuel type . . . . .Regular
EPA city/highway, mpg 21/29
Fuel refill capacity, gal. 19.0

Dimensions and weight
Length, in. 201
Width, in. 75
Wheelbase, in. 113
Curb weight, lb. 3,950
Percent weight, front/rear 60/40
Typical towing ability, lb. 1,000

SAFETY INFORMATION

Active safety features
Antilock brakes . . . . .Standard
Traction control . . . . .Standard
Stability control . . . . .Not available
Daytime running lights . . . . .Not available
Tire pressure monitor . . . . .Not available

Safety belts
Center-rear belt 3-point
Pretensioners, front/rear . . . . .Yes/no

Air bags
Occupant-sensing system . . . . .Front
Side bags, front/rear . . . . .Optional/no
Inflatable curtain . . . . .Optional with rollover
Accident alert system . . . . .Not available

Crash tests
Gov't front-crash test, driver/front passenger . . .◒/◒
Gov't side-crash test, driver/rear passenger . . . . .◒/◒
IIHS offset crash test . . . . .NA
IIHS side crash test w/ side & curtain airbags . . . . .NA
IIHS side crash test w/o side & curtain airbags . . . . .NA

FROM THE TEST TRACK

Tested model
2005 Ford Five Hundred SEL sedan AWD, 3.0-liter V6, CVT

Tires as tested
Continental ContiTouring Contact CT95, size P215/60R17 95T

Acceleration . . . .○
0-30 mph, sec. 3.6
0-60 mph, sec. 8.7
Quarter mile, sec. 16.9
Quarter mile, mph 86
45-65 mph, sec. 5.7

Other findings
Transmission . . . .◑
Turning circle, ft. 42
Ground clearance, in. 5.0

Braking and handling
Braking . . . .○
Braking, dry pavement, ft. 144
Routine handling . . . .◖
Emergency handling . . . .○
Avoidance maneuver, max. mph . . .48.5

Convenience and comfort
Ride . . . .◖
Noise . . . .◖
Driving position . . . .◖
Access . . . .◖
Controls and displays . . . .◖
Fit and finish . . . .◖
Door top to ground, in. . . .55.0
Trunk . . . .◖
Luggage capacity . . . . .5+1
Max. load, lb. 950

Seating
Front-seat comfort . . . .◖
Front shoulder room, in. 58.0
Front leg room, in. 40.0
Front head room, in. 5.0
Rear-seat comfort . . . .◑
Rear shoulder room, in. 57.5
Rear leg room, in. 31.0
Rear head room, in 3.0

Fuel economy . . . .◐
CU's overall mileage, mpg 20
CU's city/highway, mpg 13/30
CU's 150-mile trip, mpg 25
Annual fuel . . . . .760 gal./$1,515
Cruising range 440

RELIABILITY HISTORY

TROUBLE SPOTS	97 98 99 00 01 02 03 04	
Engine		
Cooling		NO
Fuel		
Ignition		DATA
Transmission		
Electrical		
Air conditioning		NEW
Suspension		
Brakes		MODEL
Exhaust		
Paint/trim/rust		
Body integrity		
Power equipment		
Body hardware		
RELIABILITY VERDICT		

● ◑ ○ ◖ ●
better ◄——► worse   See page 36 for more information.

Mercury Monterey

The Monterey is the successor to the Villager, which was a Nissan product. The Monterey is an upscale version of the Ford Freestar, itself an evolution of the Windstar. The standard 4.2-liter V6 is noisy and unrefined. The ride is a bit unsettled, but handling is secure. The Monterey features a third-row seat that folds flat into the floor. The second-row seats are too low. The optional head-protection curtain air bags cover all three rows. Stability control and adjustable pedals are available, as well as parking-assist warning sensors. Crash-test results are impressive.

THE MONTEREY LINE
Body style: minivan
Trim lines: Convenience, Luxury, Premier
Base price range: $29,010-$34,935

REPORT CARD

O	Predicted reliability
NA	Owner satisfaction
NA	Predicted depreciation
O	Accident avoidance
⊖	Acceleration
O	Ride
⊖	Front seat comfort
●	Fuel economy

SPECIFICATIONS

Drive wheels Front

Seating 2 front, 2 rear, 3 third

Engines available
4.2-liter V6 (201 hp)

Transmissions available
4-speed automatic

Fuel
Fuel type .... Regular
EPA city/highway, mpg 16/23
Fuel refill capacity, gal. 26.0

Dimensions and weight
Length, in. 201
Width, in. 77
Wheelbase, in. 121
Curb weight, lb. 4,425
Percent weight, front/rear 59/41
Typical towing ability, lb. 3,500

SAFETY INFORMATION

Active safety features
Antilock brakes .... Standard
Traction control .... Included with stability
Stability control .... Optional
Daytime running lights .... Not available
Tire pressure monitor .... Available

Safety belts
Center-rear belt 3-point
Pretensioners, front/rear .... Yes/no

Air bags
Occupant-sensing system .... Front
Side bags, front/rear .... Optional/no
Inflatable curtain .... Optional with rollover
Accident alert system .... Not available

Crash tests
Gov't front-crash test, driver/front passenger ...... ⊖/O
Gov't side-crash test, driver/rear passenger .... ⊖/O
IIHS offset crash test .... Good
IIHS side crash test w/ side & curtain airbags .... NA
IIHS side crash test w/o side & curtain airbags .... NA

FROM THE TEST TRACK

Tested model
2004 Ford Freestar SEL minivan, 4.2-liter V6, 4-speed automatic

Tires as tested
Uniroyal Tiger Paw AWP Nail Gard, size P235/60R16 99S

Acceleration .... ⊖
0-30 mph, sec. 3.1
0-60 mph, sec. 9.2
Quarter mile, sec. 17.2
Quarter mile, mph 80
45-65 mph, sec. 5.9

Other findings
Transmission .... ⊖
Turning circle, ft. 42
Ground clearance, in. 6.5

Braking and handling
Braking .... ⊖
Braking, dry pavement, ft. 137
Routine handling .... ⊖
Emergency handling .... O
Avoidance maneuver, max. mph ... 48.5

Convenience and comfort
Ride .... O
Noise .... O
Driving position .... ⊖
Access .... ●
Controls and displays .... ⊖
Fit and finish .... O
Door top to ground, in. 62.0
Cargo area .... O
Cargo volume, cu.ft. 61.5
Max. load, lb. 1,315

Seating
Front-seat comfort .... ⊖
Front shoulder room, in. 61.0
Front leg room, in. 40.0
Front head room, in. 5.5
Rear-seat comfort .... O
Rear shoulder room, in. 64.0
Rear leg room, in. 29.0
Rear head room, in 6.0
Third-seat comfort .... O
Third shoulder room, in 49.5
Third leg room, in. 27.5
Third head room, in 5.0

Fuel economy
CU's overall mileage, mpg 17
CU's city/highway, mpg 11/25
CU's 150-mile trip, mpg 20
Annual fuel .... 910 gal./$1,815
Cruising range 495

RELIABILITY HISTORY

TROUBLE SPOTS	Mercury Monterey
	97 98 99 00 01 02 03 04
Engine	●
Cooling	●
Fuel	●
Ignition	●
Transmission	●
Electrical	⊖
Air conditioning	●
Suspension	●
Brakes	●
Exhaust	●
Paint/trim/rust	⊖
Body integrity	⊖
Power equipment	⊖
Body hardware	⊖
RELIABILITY VERDICT	−

Mercury Mountaineer

The Mountaineer is a clone of the Ford Explorer. The standard engine is an adequate-performing but coarse-sounding 4.0-liter V6; a more powerful 4.6-liter V8 is available. The ride is firm and controlled. Handling is sound, if unexceptional. The interior is versatile, with various folding seat arrangements. Unlike the Explorer, the Mountaineer uses a permanent AWD system without a low range. Standard stability control for 2005 alleviates concerns of a tip-up in a past government rollover test. A 2006 freshening, with a more powerful V8 engine and six-speed automatic transmission, arrives in the fall.

THE MOUNTAINEER LINE
Body style:
4-door SUV
Trim lines:
Convenience, Luxury, Premier
Base price range:
$29,685-$38,530

REPORT CARD

○	Predicted reliability
◖	Owner satisfaction
○	Predicted depreciation
NA	Accident avoidance
NA	Acceleration
NA	Ride
NA	Front seat comfort
NA	Fuel economy

SPECIFICATIONS

Drive wheels Rear or AWD

Seating 2 front, 3 rear, 2 third

Engines available
4.0-liter V6 (210 hp); 4.6-liter V8 (239 hp)

Transmissions available
5-speed automatic

Fuel
Fuel type ....Regular
EPA city/highway, mpg 14/18
Fuel refill capacity, gal. 22.5

Dimensions and weight
Length, in. 190
Width, in. 72
Wheelbase, in. 114
Curb weight, lb. 4,760
Percent weight, front/rear 52/48
Typical towing ability, lb. 3,500

SAFETY INFORMATION

Active safety features
Antilock brakes ....Standard
Traction control ....Included with stability
Stability control ....Standard
Daytime running lights ....Not available
Tire pressure monitor ....Available

Safety belts
Center-rear belt 3-point
Pretensioners, front/rear ....Yes/no

Air bags
Occupant-sensing system ....Front
Side bags, front/rear ....No/no
Inflatable curtain ....Optional with rollover
Accident alert system ....Not available

Crash tests
Gov't front-crash test, driver/front passenger .....◖/◉
Gov't side-crash test, driver/rear passenger ....◉/◉
IIHS offset crash test ....Good
IIHS side crash test w/ side & curtain airbags ....NA
IIHS side crash test w/o side & curtain airbags ....NA

ANOTHER LOOK

RELIABILITY HISTORY

TROUBLE SPOTS	Mercury Mountaineer 4WD							
	97	98	99	00	01	02	03	04
Engine	○	○	○	◖	◖	◖	◖	◖
Cooling	○	○	◖	○	◖	◖	◖	◖
Fuel	○	○	○	○	◖	◖	◖	◖
Ignition	◖	◖	◖	◖	◖	◖	◖	◖
Transmission	○	○	○	○	◖	◖	◖	◖
Electrical	◖	●	●	◖	◖	○	○	◖
Air conditioning	●	◖	○	◖	◖	◖	◖	◖
Suspension	○	○	◖	◖	◖	○	◖	◖
Brakes	◖	◖	◖	◖	◖	◖	◖	◖
Exhaust	◖	○	○	○	○	○	◖	◖
Paint/trim/rust	○	◖	◖	◖	◖	○	◖	◖
Body integrity	○	◖	○	◖	◖	◖	◖	◖
Power equipment	○	◖	●	●	◖	◖	◖	◖
Body hardware	○	◖	◖	◖	◖	○	◖	◖
RELIABILITY VERDICT	-	✗	-	✗	-	✗	-	-

Mini Cooper

THE COOPER LINE
Body style:
2-door hatchback; convertible
Trim lines:
Base, S, JCW
Base price range:
$16,950-$25,050

The Mini, developed by BMW, blends 1960s charm with modern levels of amenities and safety. The 1.6-liter engine is paired with either a slick manual or a continuously variable transmission (CVT). Handling is agile, with quick, precise steering and hardly any body roll, making it truly fun to drive. The ride is a bit choppy. The base engine lacks oomph, but the supercharged Cooper S is strong. The rear is very tight and some controls are unintuitive. Reliability remained below average. The convertible incorporates a partial-open sunroof stage and lowering the top requires no manual latch release.

REPORT CARD

⊖	Predicted reliability
◉	Owner satisfaction
◉	Predicted depreciation
◉	Accident avoidance
◉	Acceleration
⊖	Ride
⊖	Front seat comfort
⊖	Fuel economy

SPECIFICATIONS

Drive wheels Front

Seating 2 front, 2 rear

Engines available
1.6-liter 4 (115 hp); 1.6-liter 4 supercharged (168 hp); 1.6-liter 4 supercharged (207 hp)

Transmissions available
5-speed manual; 6-speed manual; CVT; 6-speed automatic

Fuel
Fuel type . . . . .Premium
EPA city/highway, mpg 24/33
Fuel refill capacity, gal. 13.2

Dimensions and weight
Length, in. 144
Width, in. 58
Wheelbase, in. .97
Curb weight, lb. 2,900
Percent weight, front/rear 59/41
Typical towing ability, lb. . . . . .NR

SAFETY INFORMATION

Active safety features
Antilock brakes . . . . .Standard
Traction control . . . . .Standard on S
Stability control . . . . .Optional
Daytime running lights . . . . .Optional
Tire pressure monitor . . . . .Available

Safety belts
Center-rear belt . . . . .NA
Pretensioners, front/rear . . . . .Yes/no

Air bags
Occupant-sensing system . . . . .Not available
Side bags, front/rear . . . . .Standard/no
Inflatable curtain . . . . .Standard
Accident alert system . . . . .Not available

Crash tests
Gov't front-crash test, driver/front passenger . . . . . .◐/◐
Gov't side-crash test, driver/rear passenger . . . . . . .NA/NA
IIHS offset crash test . . . . .Good
IIHS side crash test w/ side & curtain airbags . . . . .NA
IIHS side crash test w/o side & curtain airbags . . . . .NA

FROM THE TEST TRACK

Tested model
2005 S convertible, 1.6-liter Four supercharged, 6-speed manual

Tires as tested
Dunlop SP Sport 9000 DSST, size 205/45R17 84V

Acceleration . . . . ◉
0-30 mph, sec. 2.9
0-60 mph, sec. 7.1
Quarter mile, sec. 15.7
Quarter mile, mph 92
45-65 mph, sec. 4.6

Other findings
Transmission . . . . ⊖
Turning circle, ft. 36
Ground clearance, in. 5.0

Braking and handling
Braking . . . . ◉
Braking, dry pavement, ft. 122
Routine handling . . . . ◉
Emergency handling . . . . ◉
Avoidance maneuver, max. mph . . .57.5

Convenience and comfort
Ride . . . . ⊖
Noise . . . . ⊖
Driving position . . . . ○
Access . . . . ○
Controls and displays . . . . ⊖
Fit and finish . . . . ⊖
Door top to ground, in. 50.0
Trunk . . . . ●
Luggage capacity . . . . .0+2
Max. load, lb. 815

Seating
Front-seat comfort . . . . ⊖
Front shoulder room, in. 50.0
Front leg room, in. 41.0
Front head room, in. 5.0
Rear-seat comfort . . . . ●
Rear shoulder room, in. 38.0
Rear leg room, in. 24.0
Rear head room, in 3.0

Fuel economy . . . . ⊖
CU's overall mileage, mpg 25
CU's city/highway, mpg 19/32
CU's 150-mile trip, mpg 28
Annual fuel . . . . .605 gal./$1,330
Cruising range 335

RELIABILITY HISTORY

TROUBLE SPOTS	Mini Cooper							
	97	98	99	00	01	02	03	04
Engine						◉	◉	◉
Cooling						◐	◐	◉
Fuel						◐	◐	◉
Ignition						◉	◉	◉
Transmission						○	◉	◉
Electrical						○	○	◉
Air conditioning						◉	◉	◉
Suspension						◉	◉	◉
Brakes						◉	◉	◉
Exhaust						◉	◉	◉
Paint/trim/rust						◉	◉	◉
Body integrity						◐	○	◐
Power equipment						○	○	◉
Body hardware						◐	○	◐
RELIABILITY VERDICT						✗	✗	–

Mitsubishi Eclipse

THE ECLIPSE LINE

Body style:
2-door hatchback
Trim lines:
GS, GT
Base price range:
$19,000-$27,000

Although it offered a powerful 3.0-liter V6 engine and lots of sporty styling cues, the outgoing Eclipse didn't feel very sporty to drive. A redesign for 2006, based on the current Galant, has just been rolled out. The 2.4-liter engine is strong, but noisy. The optional engine is a powerful 3.8-liter V6. We found that in the Galant this engine overwhelmed the front tires while trying to put the power down to the ground.

REPORT CARD

New	**Predicted reliability**
New	**Owner satisfaction**
NA	**Predicted depreciation**
NA	**Accident avoidance**
NA	**Acceleration**
NA	**Ride**
NA	**Front seat comfort**
NA	**Fuel economy**

SPECIFICATIONS

Drive wheels Front

Seating 2 front, 2 rear

Engines available
2.4-liter 4 (162 hp); 3.8-liter V6 (263 hp)

Transmissions available
5-speed manual; 6-speed manual; 4-speed automatic; 5-speed automatic

Fuel
Fuel type . . . . .Regular or premium
EPA city/highway, mpg . . . . .NA
Fuel refill capacity, gal. 17.7

Dimensions and weight
Length, in. 180
Width, in. 72
Wheelbase, in. 101
Curb weight, lb. 3,470
Percent weight, front/rear 62/38
Typical towing ability, lb. . . . . .NR

SAFETY INFORMATION

Active safety features
Antilock brakes . . . . .Standard
Traction control . . . . .Optional
Stability control . . . . .Not available
Daytime running lights . . . . .Standard
Tire pressure monitor . . . . .Not available

Safety belts
Center-rear belt . . . . .NA
Pretensioners, front/rear . . . . .No/no

Air bags
Occupant-sensing system . . . . .Not available
Side bags, front/rear . . . . .Optional/no
Inflatable curtain .Not available
Accident alert system . . . . .Not available

Crash tests
Gov't front-crash test, driver/front passenger . . . . .NA/NA
Gov't side-crash test, driver/rear passenger . . . . . . .NA/NA
IIHS offset crash test . . . . .NA
IIHS side crash test w/ side & curtain airbags . . . . .NA
IIHS side crash test w/o side & curtain airbags . . . . .NA

ANOTHER LOOK

RELIABILITY HISTORY

TROUBLE SPOTS	97	98	99	00	01	02	03	04
Engine								
Cooling				NO				
Fuel								
Ignition								
Transmission				DATA				
Electrical								
Air conditioning				NEW				
Suspension								
Brakes				MODEL				
Exhaust								
Paint/trim/rust								
Body integrity								
Power equipment								
Body hardware								
RELIABILITY VERDICT								

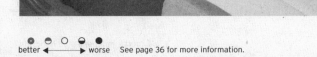

better ◄——► worse   See page 36 for more information.

Mitsubishi Endeavor

CR RECOMMENDED ✓

THE ENDEAVOR LINE
Body style:
4-door SUV
Trim lines:
LS, XLS, Limited
Base price range:
$25,699–$33,499

The Endeavor competes well with other midsized car-based SUVs. It shares the same platform with the Galant. The Endeavor has a fairly comfortable, quiet ride and secure handling, but cornering isn't particularly agile. The refined 3.8-liter V6 provides strong acceleration. The responsive automatic transmission provides very smooth shifts. Like most car-based SUVs, the Endeavor doesn't come with low-range gearing, but the AWD is appropriate for snow and sand. The rear seat is spacious, and the seatback is easy to fold. First-year reliability has been outstanding.

REPORT CARD

◉	Predicted reliability
○	Owner satisfaction
NA	Predicted depreciation
○	Accident avoidance
◒	Acceleration
◒	Ride
◒	Front seat comfort
●	Fuel economy

SPECIFICATIONS

Drive wheels Front or AWD

Seating 2 front, 3 rear

Engines available
3.8-liter V6 (225 hp)

Transmissions available
4-speed automatic

Fuel
Fuel type . . . . .Premium
EPA city/highway, mpg 17/22
Fuel refill capacity, gal. 21.4

Dimensions and weight
Length, in. 190
Width, in. 74
Wheelbase, in. .108
Curb weight, lb. 4,195
Percent weight, front/rear 55/45
Typical towing ability, lb. 3,500

SAFETY INFORMATION

Active safety features
Antilock brakes . . . . .Opt. (std. on AWD, Limited)
Traction control . . . . .Optional on 2WD
Stability control .Optional on 4WD
Daytime running lights . . . . .Standard
Tire pressure monitor . . . . .Available

Safety belts
Center-rear belt 3-point
Pretensioners, front/rear .Yes/no

Air bags
Occupant-sensing system . . . . .Not available
Side bags, front/rear .Standard/no
Inflatable curtain . . . . .Not available
Accident alert system . . . . .Not available

Crash tests
Gov't front-crash test, driver/front passenger . . . . . ◒/◒
Gov't side-crash test, driver/rear passenger . . . . ◒/◒
IIHS offset crash test . . . . .Good
IIHS side crash test w/ side & curtain airbags . . . . .NA
IIHS side crash test w/o side & curtain airbags . . . . . . .NA

FROM THE TEST TRACK

Tested model
2004 XLS 4-door SUV AWD, 3.8-liter V6, 4-speed automatic

Tires as tested
Bridgestone Turanza EL42, size P235/65R17 103T

Acceleration . . . . ◒
0-30 mph, sec. 3.1
0-60 mph, sec. 8.2
Quarter mile, sec. 16.6
Quarter mile, mph 84
45-65 mph, sec. 5.2

Other findings
Transmission . . . . ◉
Turning circle, ft. 41
Ground clearance, in. 7.0

Braking and handling
Braking . . . . ◒
Braking, dry pavement, ft. 137
Routine handling . . . . ○
Emergency handling . . . . ○
Avoidance maneuver, max. mph . . .48.5

Convenience and comfort
Ride . . . . ◒
Noise . . . . ○
Driving position . . . . ◒
Access . . . . ◒
Controls and displays . . . . ◒
Fit and finish . . . . ◒
Door top to ground, in. 61.0
Cargo area . . . . ○
Cargo volume, cu.ft. 40.0
Max. load, lb. 970

Seating
Front-seat comfort . . . . ◒
Front shoulder room, in. 58.5
Front leg room, in. 41.5
Front head room, in. 4.5
Rear-seat comfort . . . . ◒
Rear shoulder room, in. 58.0
Rear leg room, in. 30.0
Rear head room, in 4.5

Fuel economy . . . . ●
CU's overall mileage, mpg 17
  CU's city/highway, mpg 12/22
  CU's 150-mile trip, mpg 20
Annual fuel . . . . .870 gal./$1,915
Cruising range 405

RELIABILITY HISTORY

TROUBLE SPOTS	Mitsubishi Endeavor							
	97	98	99	00	01	02	03	04
Engine								◉
Cooling								◉
Fuel								◉
Ignition								◉
Transmission								◉
Electrical								◉
Air conditioning								◉
Suspension								◉
Brakes								◉
Exhaust								◉
Paint/trim/rust								◉
Body integrity								◉
Power equipment								◉
Body hardware								◉
RELIABILITY VERDICT								✓

Mitsubishi Galant

THE GALANT LINE
Body style:
sedan
Trim lines:
DE, ES, LS, GTS
Base price range:
$18,999-$26,499

A redesigned Galant was introduced in 2004, but we were not impressed with the four-cylinder model we tested. The GTS V6 model, however, is quick and nicely trimmed. The drivetrain is smooth and strong. It may be too strong, as the Galant struggles for front traction. Fuel economy is so-so. Handling is secure but not agile. The 2.4-liter four-cylinder engine is spirited but noisy. The Galant's ride is choppy and stiff even on smooth pavement, more so with the V6. Its wide turning circle makes parking awkward. The Galant still isn't competitive with the best in this class.

REPORT CARD

NA	Predicted reliability
NA	Owner satisfaction
NA	Predicted depreciation
⊖	Accident avoidance
◉	Acceleration
○	Ride
⊖	Front seat comfort
⊜	Fuel economy

SPECIFICATIONS

Drive wheels Front

Seating 2 front, 3 rear

Engines available
2.4-liter 4 (160 hp); 3.8-liter V6 (230 hp)

Transmissions available
4-speed automatic

Fuel
Fuel type . . . . .Regular or premium
EPA city/highway, mpg 19/27
Fuel refill capacity, gal. 17.7

Dimensions and weight
Length, in. 190
Width, in. 72
Wheelbase, in. 108
Curb weight, lb. 3,715
Percent weight, front/rear 62/38
Typical towing ability, lb. . . . . .NR

SAFETY INFORMATION

Active safety features
Antilock brakes .Opt. ES; std. LS, GTS
Traction control . . . . .Opt. ES; std. LS, GTS
Stability control . . . . .Not available
Daytime running lights . . . . .Standard
Tire pressure monitor .Not available

Safety belts
Center-rear belt 3-point
Pretensioners, front/rear . . . . .Yes/no

Air bags
Occupant-sensing system . . . . .Front
Side bags, front/rear .Standard/no
Inflatable curtain . . . . .Not available
Accident alert system .Not available

Crash tests
Gov't front-crash test, driver/front passenger . . . . . ◉/◉
Gov't side-crash test, driver/rear passenger . . . . . . ◉/◉
IIHS offset crash test . . . . .Good
IIHS side crash test w/ side & curtain airbags . . . . . . .Good
IIHS side crash test w/o side & curtain airbags . . . . . . .NA

FROM THE TEST TRACK

Tested model
2005 GTS sedan, 3.8-liter V6, 4-speed automatic

Tires as tested
Goodyear Eagle RS-A, size P215/55R17 93V

Acceleration . . . . ◉
0-30 mph, sec. 2.8
0-60 mph, sec. 7.2
Quarter mile, sec. 15.7
Quarter mile, mph 90
45-65 mph, sec. 4.5

Other findings
Transmission . . . . ◉
Turning circle, ft. 43
Ground clearance, in. 5.5

Braking and handling
Braking . . . . ⊖
Braking, dry pavement, ft. 144
Routine handling . . . . ⊖
Emergency handling . . . . ⊖
Avoidance maneuver, max. mph . . .52.5

Convenience and comfort
Ride . . . . ○
Noise . . . . ○
Driving position . . . . ⊖
Access . . . . ⊖
Controls and displays . . . . ⊖
Fit and finish . . . . ⊖
Door top to ground, in. 52.0
Trunk . . . . ○
Luggage capacity . . . . .4+1
Max. load, lb. 825

Seating
Front-seat comfort . . . . ⊖
Front shoulder room, in. 57.0
Front leg room, in. 41.0
Front head room, in. 2.5
Rear-seat comfort . . . . ⊖
Rear shoulder room, in. 55.5
Rear leg room, in. 29.5
Rear head room, in 2.0

Fuel economy . . . . ⊜
CU's overall mileage, mpg 20
  CU's city/highway, mpg 14/28
  CU's 150-mile trip, mpg 24
Annual fuel . . . . .755 gal./$1,665
Cruising range 390

RELIABILITY HISTORY

TROUBLE SPOTS	Mitsubishi Galant							
	97	98	99	00	01	02	03	04
Engine	○		⊖	◉	◉	◉	⊖	
Cooling	○		◉	◉	◉	◉	○	
Fuel	⊖		⊖	◉	◉	◉	◉	
Ignition	⊖		⊖	◉	◉	◉	◉	
Transmission	●		⊖	◉	◉	◉	◉	
Electrical	⊖	Insufficient data	⊖	◉	◉	◉	⊖	Insufficient data
Air conditioning	○		⊖	◉	◉	◉	⊖	
Suspension	○		○	⊖	◉	⊖	⊖	
Brakes	⊖		●	●	○	○	○	
Exhaust	⊖		⊖	○	○	⊖	○	
Paint/trim/rust	●		○	○	⊖	◉	⊖	
Body integrity	●		○	○	○	⊖	⊖	
Power equipment	⊖		⊖	◉	◉	◉	⊖	
Body hardware	○		○	○	⊖	⊖		
RELIABILITY VERDICT	✗		✓	✓	✓	✓		

Mitsubishi Lancer

THE LANCER LINE
Body style:
sedan
Trim lines:
ES, OZ-Rally, Ralliart, Evolution RS, Evolution VIII, Evolution MR
Base price range:
$14,299-$34,699

The Lancer is Mitsubishi's entry-level sedan. Interior appointments look and feel insubstantial. Handling with the base model is clumsy, the ride is just tolerable, and road noise is pronounced. The powerplant is a relatively spirited (but noisy) 2.0-liter four-cylinder. A turbocharged, all-wheel-drive Evolution rally-race-car model with 276 hp is also available and competes well with the extreme Subaru Impreza WRX STi. The Evolution is super fast, agile, and fun, but with a harsh ride. We lack reliability and ownership data for the Evo. The Lancer received a Poor rating in the IIHS side-impact-crash test.

REPORT CARD

NA	**Predicted reliability**
NA	**Owner satisfaction**
●	**Predicted depreciation**
◒	**Accident avoidance**
◒	**Acceleration**
●	**Ride**
⊖	**Front seat comfort**
⊖	**Fuel economy**

SPECIFICATIONS

Drive wheels Front or AWD

Seating 2 front, 3 rear

Engines available
2.0-liter 4 (120 hp); 2.4-liter 4 (162 hp); 2.0-liter 4 turbo (276 hp)

Transmissions available
5-speed manual; 6-speed manual; 4-speed automatic

Fuel
Fuel type . . . . Regular or premium
EPA city/highway, mpg 18/26
Fuel refill capacity, gal. 14.0

Dimensions and weight
Length, in. 179
Width, in. 70
Wheelbase, in. .103
Curb weight, lb. 3,340
Percent weight, front/rear 60/40
Typical towing ability, lb. . . . . .NR

SAFETY INFORMATION

Active safety features
Antilock brakes . . . . .Opt.; std. Evo, Ralliart
Traction control . . . . .Not available
Stability control . . . . .Not available
Daytime running lights . . . . .Not available
Tire pressure monitor . . . . .Not available

Safety belts
Center-rear belt 3-point
Pretensioners, front/rear . . . . .Yes/no

Air bags
Occupant-sensing system . . . . .Not available
Side bags, front/rear . . . . .Optional/no
Inflatable curtain . . . . .Not available
Accident alert system . . . . .Not available

Crash tests
Gov't front-crash test, driver/front passenger . . . . . . ⊖/⊖
Gov't side-crash test, driver/rear passenger . . . . . . ⊖/⊖
IIHS offset crash test . . . . .Good
IIHS side crash test w/ side & curtain airbags . . . . .NA
IIHS side crash test w/o side & curtain airbags . . . . . . .Poor

FROM THE TEST TRACK

Tested model
2003 Evolution sedan AWD, 2.0-liter Four turbo, 5-speed manual

Tires as tested
Yokohama Advan A-046, size P235/45R17 93W

Acceleration . . . . ●
0-30 mph, sec. 1.7
0-60 mph, sec. 5.3
Quarter mile, sec. 14.0
Quarter mile, mph 98
45-65 mph, sec. 3.5

Other findings
Transmission . . . . ◒
Turning circle, ft. 42
Ground clearance, in. 3.5

Braking and handling
Braking . . . . ●
Braking, dry pavement, ft. 119
Routine handling . . . . ●
Emergency handling . . . . ◒
Avoidance maneuver, max. mph . . .54.5

Convenience and comfort
Ride . . . . ●
Noise . . . . ⊖
Driving position . . . . ◒
Access . . . . ○
Controls and displays . . . . ◒
Fit and finish . . . . ○
Door top to ground, in. 51.0
Trunk . . . . ⊖
Luggage capacity . . . . .3+0
Max. load, lb. 825

Seating
Front-seat comfort . . . . ⊖
Front shoulder room, in. 54.0
Front leg room, in. 40.5
Front head room, in. 4.5
Rear-seat comfort . . . . ○
Rear shoulder room, in. 53.0
Rear leg room, in. 27.5
Rear head room, in 1.5

Fuel economy . . . . ⊖
CU's overall mileage, mpg 20
CU's city/highway, mpg 15/26
CU's 150-mile trip, mpg 23
Annual fuel . . . . .745 gal./$1,640
Cruising range 285

RELIABILITY HISTORY

TROUBLE SPOTS

	97 98 99 00 01 02 03 04
Engine	
Cooling	
Fuel	**NOT**
Ignition	
Transmission	**ENOUGH**
Electrical	
Air conditioning	**DATA**
Suspension	
Brakes	**TO**
Exhaust	
Paint/trim/rust	**RATE**
Body integrity	
Power equipment	
Body hardware	
RELIABILITY VERDICT	

Expert • Independent • Nonprofit

Mitsubishi Montero

THE MONTERO LINE

Body style:
4-door SUV

Trim lines:
Limited

Base price range:
$35,799

The Montero is a pleasant SUV that's marred by clumsy and disconcerting handling. Helped by its standard stability-control system, it performed slightly better in our avoidance maneuver tests compared with that of the 2001 Limited model, which earned a "Not Acceptable" Rating. This moved the 2003 Montero from Not Acceptable to a poor Rating in our emergency handling tests. The interior has very good fit and finish, comfortable seats, and well-designed controls. The powertrain is polished, and the Montero performed well in our off-road tests. The ride is a bit jittery, and fuel economy is poor.

REPORT CARD

NA	Predicted reliability
NA	Owner satisfaction
◒	Predicted depreciation
○	Accident avoidance
○	Acceleration
○	Ride
◉	Front seat comfort
●	Fuel economy

SPECIFICATIONS

Drive wheels Selectable 4WD

Seating 2 front, 3 rear, 2 third

Engines available
3.8-liter V6 (215 hp)

Transmissions available
5-speed automatic

Fuel
Fuel type ....Premium
EPA city/highway, mpg 15/19
Fuel refill capacity, gal. 23.8

Dimensions and weight
Length, in. 190
Width, in. 75
Wheelbase, in. 110
Curb weight, lb. 4,955
Percent weight, front/rear 47/53
Typical towing ability, lb. 5,000

SAFETY INFORMATION

Active safety features

Antilock brakes ....Standard
Traction control ....Standard
Stability control ....Standard
Daytime running lights ....Not available
Tire pressure monitor ....Available

Safety belts

Center-rear belt 3-point
Pretensioners, front/rear ....Yes/no

Air bags

Occupant-sensing system ....Not available
Side bags, front/rear ....Optional/no
Inflatable curtain ....Not available
Accident alert system ....Not available

Crash tests

Gov't front-crash test, driver/front passenger ......NA/NA
Gov't side-crash test, driver/rear passenger ....NA/NA
IIHS offset crash test ....Acceptable
IIHS side crash test w/ side & curtain airbags ....NA
IIHS side crash test w/o side & curtain airbags ....NA

FROM THE TEST TRACK

Tested model
2003 Limited 4-door SUV 4WD, 3.8-liter V6, 5-speed automatic

Tires as tested
Yokohama Geolandar G039, size 265/70R16 112S

Acceleration ....○
0-30 mph, sec. 3.2
0-60 mph, sec. 9.7
Quarter mile, sec. 17.5
Quarter mile, mph 79
45-65 mph, sec. 6.7

Other findings
Transmission ....◉
Turning circle, ft. 40
Ground clearance, in. 8.0

Braking and handling
Braking ....◒
Braking, dry pavement, ft. 132
Routine handling ....◒
Emergency handling ....●
Avoidance maneuver, max. mph 47.0

Convenience and comfort
Ride ....○
Noise ....○
Driving position ....◒
Access ....◒
Controls and displays ....◒
Fit and finish ....◉
Door top to ground, in. 65.0
Cargo area ....○
Cargo volume, cu.ft. 45.0
Max. load, lb. 1,180

Seating
Front-seat comfort ....◉
Front shoulder room, in. 58.0
Front leg room, in. 41.0
Front head room, in. 4.5
Rear-seat comfort ....○
Rear shoulder room, in. 57.5
Rear leg room, in. 30.5
Rear head room, in 3.0
Third-seat comfort ....●
Third shoulder room, in 54.5
Third leg room, in. 24.0
Third head room, in 3.0

Fuel economy ....●
CU's overall mileage, mpg 14
CU's city/highway, mpg 10/19
CU's 150-mile trip, mpg 17
Annual fuel ....1,085 gal./$2,390
Cruising range 365

RELIABILITY HISTORY

TROUBLE SPOTS	Mitsubishi Montero							
	97	98	99	00	01	02	03	04
Engine	Insufficient data	Insufficient data	Insufficient data	Insufficient data	◉	Insufficient data	Insufficient data	Insufficient data
Cooling					◉			
Fuel					◒			
Ignition					◉			
Transmission					◉			
Electrical								
Air conditioning					◉			
Suspension					◉			
Brakes					◉			
Exhaust					◉			
Paint/trim/rust					◒			
Body integrity					○			
Power equipment					○			
Body hardware					○			
RELIABILITY VERDICT					–			

◉ ◒ ○ ◐ ●
better ◄——► worse   See page 36 for more information.

Mitsubishi Outlander

CR RECOMMENDED ✓

The Outlander is a small SUV made in the mold of the successful Honda CR-V, Subaru Forester, and Toyota RAV4. It's based on the Lancer. The Outlander is powered by an adequate but noisy 2.4-liter four-cylinder linked to a responsive four-speed automatic. Acceleration and fuel economy were so-so. The ride is reasonably comfortable. Handling is less nimble than the RAV4 and Forester because of its overly light steering and pronounced body lean, though it's ultimately secure. Interior fit and finish is unimpressive. The Outlander received a Poor rating in the IIHS side-impact-crash test.

THE OUTLANDER LINE
Body style:
4-door SUV
Trim lines:
LS, XLS, Limited
Base price range:
$17,999-$25,479

REPORT CARD

⊖	Predicted reliability
●	Owner satisfaction
NA	Predicted depreciation
○	Accident avoidance
⊖	Acceleration
○	Ride
⊖	Front seat comfort
⊖	Fuel economy

SPECIFICATIONS

Drive wheels Front or AWD

Seating 2 front, 3 rear

Engines available
2.4-liter 4 (160 hp)

Transmissions available
5-speed manual; 4-speed automatic

Fuel
Fuel type ....Regular
EPA city/highway, mpg 21/25
Fuel refill capacity, gal. 15.7

Dimensions and weight
Length, in. 179
Width, in. 69
Wheelbase, in. 103
Curb weight, lb. 3,525
Percent weight, front/rear 58/42
Typical towing ability, lb. 1,500

SAFETY INFORMATION

Active safety features
Antilock brakes ....Optional (NA on LS)
Traction control ....Not available
Stability control ....Not available
Daytime running lights ....Standard
Tire pressure monitor ....Not available

Safety belts
Center-rear belt 3-point
Pretensioners, front/rear ....Yes/no

Air bags
Occupant-sensing system ....Not available
Side bags, front/rear ....Optional/no
Inflatable curtain ....Not available
Accident alert system ....Not available

Crash tests
Gov't front-crash test, driver/front passenger .... ◐/◖
Gov't side-crash test, driver/rear passenger .... ●/◖
IIHS offset crash test ....Good
IIHS side crash test w/ side & curtain airbags ....NA
IIHS side crash test w/o side & curtain airbags ....Poor

FROM THE TEST TRACK

Tested model
2003 XLS 4-door SUV AWD, 2.4-liter Four, 4-speed automatic

Tires as tested
Yokohama Geolandar G035, size P225/60R16 97H

Acceleration ....⊖
0-30 mph, sec. 3.6
0-60 mph, sec. 11.6
Quarter mile, sec. 18.7
Quarter mile, mph 74
45-65 mph, sec. 7.8

Other findings
Transmission ....⊖
Turning circle, ft. 41
Ground clearance, in. 5.5

Braking and handling
Braking ....⊖
Braking, dry pavement, ft. 137
Routine handling ....○
Emergency handling ....○
Avoidance maneuver, max. mph ..50.5

Convenience and comfort
Ride ....○
Noise ....○
Driving position ....⊖
Access ....⊖
Controls and displays ....⊖
Fit and finish ....○
Door top to ground, in. 57.0
Cargo area ....●
Cargo volume, cu.ft. 24.0
Max. load, lb. 825

Seating
Front-seat comfort ....⊖
Front shoulder room, in. 56.0
Front leg room, in. 40.5
Front head room, in. 3.0
Rear-seat comfort ....○
Rear shoulder room, in. 54.5
Rear leg room, in. 28.5
Rear head room, in 4.0

Fuel economy ....⊖
CU's overall mileage, mpg 20
CU's city/highway, mpg 14/26
CU's 150-mile trip, mpg 23
Annual fuel ....765 gal./$1,530
Cruising range 330

RELIABILITY HISTORY

TROUBLE SPOTS	Mitsubishi Outlander							
	97	98	99	00	01	02	03	04
Engine							●	
Cooling							●	
Fuel							●	
Ignition							●	
Transmission							●	
Electrical							●	
Air conditioning							●	
Suspension							⊖	
Brakes							⊖	
Exhaust							●	
Paint/trim/rust							●	
Body integrity							⊖	
Power equipment							●	
Body hardware							⊖	
RELIABILITY VERDICT							✓	

Insufficient data

Nissan 350Z

CR RECOMMENDED ✓

The 350Z two-seater revives Nissan's now-classic Z series of sports cars that started its dynasty in the early 1970s, when Nissan was still called Datsun. It shares mechanical components with the Infiniti G35, including a wonderfully strong and smooth V6. Acceleration is very quick, and fuel economy is respectable. The six-speed manual shifter feels slightly notchy. Handling is fairly agile but less so than the Mazda RX-8. The ride is harsh and uncomfortable. Rear visibility is poor. Interior fit and finish is disappointing. A convertible with a power-operated top is also available.

REPORT CARD

○	Predicted reliability
⊖	Owner satisfaction
NA	Predicted depreciation
◑	Accident avoidance
◑	Acceleration
●	Ride
⊖	Front seat comfort
○	Fuel economy

THE 350Z LINE

Body style:
convertible; coupe
Trim lines:
Base, Enthusiast, Performance, Touring, Track, 35th Anniversary, Grand Touring
Base price range:
$26,700-$39,200

SPECIFICATIONS

Drive wheels Rear

Seating 2 front

Engines available
3.5-liter V6 (287 hp); 3.5-liter V6 (300 hp)

Transmissions available
6-speed manual; 5-speed automatic

Fuel
Fuel type .... Premium
EPA city/highway, mpg 20/26
Fuel refill capacity, gal. 20.0

Dimensions and weight
Length, in. 170
Width, in. 72
Wheelbase, in. 104
Curb weight, lb. 3,345
Percent weight, front/rear 53/47
Typical towing ability, lb. 1,000

SAFETY INFORMATION

Active safety features
Antilock brakes .... Standard
Traction control .... Optional
Stability control .... Optional
Daytime running lights .... Not available
Tire pressure monitor .... Available

Safety belts
Center-rear belt .... NA
Pretensioners, front/rear .... Yes/NA

Air bags
Occupant-sensing system .... Not available
Side bags, front/rear .... Optional/NA
Inflatable curtain .... Optional
Accident alert system .... Not available

Crash tests
Gov't front-crash test, driver/front passenger ...... NA/NA
Gov't side-crash test, driver/rear passenger .... ◑/NA
IIHS offset crash test .... NA
IIHS side crash test w/ side & curtain airbags .... NA
IIHS side crash test w/o side & curtain airbags .... NA

FROM THE TEST TRACK

Tested model
2003 Touring coupe, 3.5-liter V6, 6-speed manual

Tires as tested
Bridgestone Potenza RE 040, size 225/45R18 91W (front), 245/45R18 96W (rear)

Acceleration .... ◑
0-30 mph, sec. 2.1
0-60 mph, sec. 5.4
Quarter mile, sec. 14.0
Quarter mile, mph 102
45-65 mph, sec. 3.7

Other findings
Transmission .... ⊖
Turning circle, ft. 37
Ground clearance, in. 3.5

Braking and handling
Braking .... ◑
Braking, dry pavement, ft. 116
Routine handling .... ◑
Emergency handling .... ◑
Avoidance maneuver, max. mph ... 55.0

Convenience and comfort
Ride .... ●
Noise .... ⊖
Driving position .... ○
Access .... ⊖
Controls and displays .... ⊖
Fit and finish .... ○
Door top to ground, in. 46.0
Trunk .... ⊖
Luggage capacity .... 1+1
Max. load, lb. 450

Seating
Front-seat comfort .... ⊖
Front shoulder room, in. 53.0
Front leg room, in. 41.0
Front head room, in. 3.0

Fuel economy .... ○
CU's overall mileage, mpg 22
  CU's city/highway, mpg 16/30
  CU's 150-mile trip, mpg 24
Annual fuel .... 690 gal./$1,515
Cruising range 460

RELIABILITY HISTORY

TROUBLE SPOTS	Nissan 350Z
	97 98 99 00 01 02 03 04
Engine	◑ ◑
Cooling	◑ ◑
Fuel	◑ ◑
Ignition	◑ ◑
Transmission	⊖ ◑
Electrical	⊖ ◑
Air conditioning	◑ ◑
Suspension	● ◑
Brakes	⊖ ◑
Exhaust	◑ ◑
Paint/trim/rust	⊖ ◑
Body integrity	○ ⊖
Power equipment	◐ ◑
Body hardware	⊖ ◑
RELIABILITY VERDICT	✗ ✓

Nissan Altima

CR RECOMMENDED ✓

The 2.5 S model's handling is sound but not nimble. It accelerates quickly though the four-cylinder engine is noisy. The ride lacks the superb isolation found in the Toyota Camry. With its firmer suspension and wider tires, the pricier—and quicker—3.5 SE, which we also tested, offers more tire grip but suffers from a stiff, jittery ride. The front seats are fairly comfortable, and the spacious rear seats offer plentiful leg room and support. A wide turning circle hampers maneuverability. We recommend the optional curtain airbags. Without them the Altima received a Poor rating in the IIHS side-impact-crash test.

THE ALTIMA LINE
Body style: sedan
Trim lines: 2.5, 2.5 S, 3.5 SE, 3.5 SL, SE-R
Base price range: $17,350-$29,300

REPORT CARD

○	Predicted reliability
○	Owner satisfaction
◐	Predicted depreciation
◐	Accident avoidance
◐	Acceleration
◐	Ride
◐	Front seat comfort
○	Fuel economy

SPECIFICATIONS

Drive wheels Front

Seating 2 front, 3 rear

Engines available
2.5-liter 4 (175 hp); 3.5-liter V6 (250 hp); 3.5-liter V6 (260 hp)

Transmissions available
5-speed manual; 6-speed manual; 4-speed automatic; 5-speed automatic

Fuel
Fuel type . . . . Regular or premium
EPA city/highway, mpg 23/29
Fuel refill capacity, gal. 20.0

Dimensions and weight
Length, in. 192
Width, in. 70
Wheelbase, in. 110
Curb weight, lb. 3,235
Percent weight, front/rear 60/40
Typical towing ability, lb. 1,000

SAFETY INFORMATION

Active safety features
Antilock brakes . . . . .Optional (standard on SE-R)
Traction control . . . . .Optional (NA on 2.5, 2.5 S)
Stability control . . . . .Not available
Daytime running lights . . . . .Not available
Tire pressure monitor . . . . .Not available

Safety belts
Center-rear belt 3-point
Pretensioners, front/rear . . . . .Yes/no

Air bags
Occupant-sensing system . . . . .Not available
Side bags, front/rear . . . . .Optional/no
Inflatable curtain . . . . .Optional
Accident alert system . . . . .Not available

Crash tests
Gov't front-crash test, driver/front passenger . . . . . . ◉/◉
Gov't side-crash test, driver/rear passenger . . . . . . ○/○
IIHS offset crash test . . . . .Good
IIHS side crash test w/ side & curtain airbags . . . . .NA
IIHS side crash test w/o side & curtain airbags . . . . . . .Poor

FROM THE TEST TRACK

Tested model
2005 2.5 S sedan, 2.5-liter Four, 4-speed automatic

Tires as tested
Continental TouringContact AS, size P215/60R16 94T

Acceleration . . . . ◐
0-30 mph, sec. 3.2
0-60 mph, sec. 8.9
Quarter mile, sec. 17.1
Quarter mile, mph 82
45-65 mph, sec. 5.5

Other findings
Transmission . . . . ◐
Turning circle, ft. 41
Ground clearance, in. 4.5

Braking and handling
Braking . . . . ◐
Braking, dry pavement, ft. 144
Routine handling . . . . ◐
Emergency handling . . . . ○
Avoidance maneuver, max. mph . . .50.5

Convenience and comfort
Ride . . . . ◐
Noise . . . . ○
Driving position . . . . ◐
Access . . . . ◐
Controls and displays . . . . ◉
Fit and finish . . . . ◐
Door top to ground, in. 52.0
Trunk . . . . ○
Luggage capacity . . . . .4+1
Max. load, lb. 860

Seating
Front-seat comfort . . . . ◐
Front shoulder room, in. 54.5
Front leg room, in. 40.5
Front head room, in. 3.0
Rear-seat comfort . . . . ◐
Rear shoulder room, in. 55.5
Rear leg room, in. 30.0
Rear head room, in 2.0

Fuel economy . . . . ○
CU's overall mileage, mpg 23
CU's city/highway, mpg 16/30
CU's 150-mile trip, mpg 28
Annual fuel . . . . .655 gal./$1,310
Cruising range 520

RELIABILITY HISTORY

TROUBLE SPOTS	Nissan Altima 4-cyl.							
	97	98	99	00	01	02	03	04
Engine	○	◐	◐	◐	●	◐	◉	◉
Cooling	◐	◐	●	◐	◐	◐	◐	◉
Fuel	◐	◐	◐	◐	◐	○	◐	◉
Ignition	◐	◐	◐	◐	◐	◐	◐	◉
Transmission	◐	◐	◐	◐	◐	◐	◐	◉
Electrical	○	◐	◐	○	◐	◐	◐	◉
Air conditioning	○	◐	◐	◐	◐	◐	◐	◉
Suspension	○	◐	○	◐	◐	◐	◐	◉
Brakes	○	○	○	◐	◐	◐	◐	◉
Exhaust	○	◉	◐	◐	◐	◐	◐	◉
Paint/trim/rust	●	◐	◐	◐	◐	◐	◉	◉
Body integrity	○	○	○	◐	◐	○	◐	◉
Power equipment	○	◐	◐	●	◐	◐	◐	◉
Body hardware	○	◐	◐	◐	◐	◐	◐	◉
RELIABILITY VERDICT	✓	✓	✓	✓	✗	–	✓	

Nissan Armada

The Armada, based on the Titan pickup, is a large SUV with seating for eight. Unlike the Titan, it features an independent rear suspension. Power comes from a smooth-revving but noisy 5.6-liter, 305-hp V8 engine coupled with a slick five-speed automatic. This powertrain makes the Armada quick. Handling is relatively responsive, but the ride is quite stiff. As in other new Nissans, interior quality is disappointing. It is hard for children to reach the rear door handles. The Armada boasts a high towing capacity with the optional tow package. Rear cargo space is generous. First-year reliability has been poor.

THE ARMADA LINE
Body style:
4-door SUV
Trim lines:
SE, LE
Base price range:
$33,800-$41,700

REPORT CARD

●	Predicted reliability
○	Owner satisfaction
NA	Predicted depreciation
○	Accident avoidance
◉	Acceleration
○	Ride
⊖	Front seat comfort
●	Fuel economy

SPECIFICATIONS

Drive wheels Rear or selectable 4WD

Seating 2 front, 3 rear, 3 third

Engines available
5.6-liter V8 (305 hp)

Transmissions available
5-speed automatic

Fuel
Fuel type . . . . .Regular
EPA city/highway, mpg 13/18
Fuel refill capacity, gal. 28.0

Dimensions and weight
Length, in. 207
Width, in. 79
Wheelbase, in. 123
Curb weight, lb. 5,715
Percent weight, front/rear 50/50
Typical towing ability, lb. 9,100

SAFETY INFORMATION

Active safety features
Antilock brakes . . . . .Standard
Traction control . . . . .Standard
Stability control . . . . .Standard
Daytime running lights . . . . .Not available
Tire pressure monitor . . . . .Available

Safety belts
Center-rear belt 3-point
Pretensioners, front/rear .Yes/no

Air bags
Occupant-sensing system . . . . .Front
Side bags, front/rear .Optional/no
Inflatable curtain . . . . .Standard with rollover
Accident alert system .Not available

Crash tests
Gov't front-crash test, driver/front passenger . . .NA/NA
Gov't side-crash test, driver/rear passenger . . . . . .NA/NA
IIHS offset crash test . . . . .NA
IIHS side crash test w/ side & curtain airbags . . . . .NA
IIHS side crash test w/o side & curtain airbags . . . . .NA

FROM THE TEST TRACK

Tested model
2004 LE 4-door SUV 4WD, 5.6-liter V8, 5-speed automatic

Tires as tested
Goodyear Wrangler SR-A, size P265/70R18 114S

Acceleration . . . . ◉
0-30 mph, sec. 2.5
0-60 mph, sec. 7.2
Quarter mile, sec. 15.8
Quarter mile, mph 88
45-65 mph, sec. 4.8

Other findings
Transmission . . . . ◉
Turning circle, ft. 44
Ground clearance, in. 9.0

Braking and handling
Braking . . . . ⊖
Braking, dry pavement, ft. 132
Routine handling . . . . ○
Emergency handling . . . . ○
Avoidance maneuver, max. mph . . .46.0

Convenience and comfort
Ride . . . . ○
Noise . . . . ○
Driving position . . . . ○
Access . . . . ◔
Controls and displays . . . . ◔
Fit and finish . . . . ◔
Door top to ground, in. 69.0
Cargo area . . . . ◔
Cargo volume, cu.ft. 58.5
Max. load, lb. 1,375

Seating
Front-seat comfort . . . . ⊖
Front shoulder room, in. 65.0
Front leg room, in. 41.5
Front head room, in. 6.0
Rear-seat comfort . . . . ◉
Rear shoulder room, in. 64.0
Rear leg room, in. 33.5
Rear head room, in 5.0
Third-seat comfort . . . . ⊖
Third shoulder room,in 63.0
Third leg room, in. 27.0
Third head room, in 0.5

Fuel economy . . . . ●
CU's overall mileage, mpg 13
CU's city/highway, mpg 9/19
CU's 150-mile trip, mpg 16
Annual fuel . . . . .1,145 gal./$2,290
Cruising range 415

RELIABILITY HISTORY

TROUBLE SPOTS	Nissan Armada							
	97	98	99	00	01	02	03	04
Engine								◉
Cooling								◉
Fuel								◉
Ignition								◉
Transmission								◉
Electrical								⊖
Air conditioning								⊖
Suspension								○
Brakes								○
Exhaust								◉
Paint/trim/rust								⊖
Body integrity								⊖
Power equipment								⊖
Body hardware								○
RELIABILITY VERDICT								✗

● ◔ ○ ◑ ⊖
better ◀—→ worse See page 36 for more information.

Nissan Frontier

THE FRONTIER LINE
Body style:
extended cab; crew cab
Trim lines:
XE, SE, Nismo, LE
Base price range:
$15,500-$26,750

The previous-generation Frontier was crude, underpowered, and cramped. A thorough redesign, based on the Titan pickup architecture, brings plenty of power, thanks to the very strong and smooth 265-hp, 4.0-liter V6. Base models are powered by a 154-hp, 2.5-liter four-cylinder. Handling is relatively nimble and the ride is stiff, but tolerable. The optional stability control helps on slippery and washboard surfaces. Only crew- and extended-cab body styles are offered. A part-time four-wheel drive system comes on 4WD models.

REPORT CARD

New	Predicted reliability
New	Owner satisfaction
NA	Predicted depreciation
NA	Accident avoidance
NA	Acceleration
NA	Ride
NA	Front seat comfort
NA	Fuel economy

SPECIFICATIONS

Drive wheels Rear or part-time 4WD

Seating 2 front, 3 rear

Engines available
2.5-liter 4 (154 hp); 4.0-liter V6 (265 hp)

Transmissions available
5-speed manual; 6-speed manual; 5-speed automatic

Fuel
Fuel type .... Regular
EPA city/highway, mpg 15/20
Fuel refill capacity, gal. 21.1

Dimensions and weight
Length, in. 206
Width, in. 73
Wheelbase, in. 126
Curb weight, lb. 4,435
Percent weight, front/rear 57/43
Typical towing ability, lb. 6,100

SAFETY INFORMATION

Active safety features
Antilock brakes ....Standard
Traction control ....Included with stability
Stability control ....Optional
Daytime running lights ....Not available
Tire pressure monitor ....Available

Safety belts
Center-rear belt 3-point
Pretensioners, front/rear ....Yes/no

Air bags
Occupant-sensing system ....Front
Side bags, front/rear ....Optional/no
Inflatable curtain ....Optional with rollover
Accident alert system ....Not available

Crash tests
Gov't front-crash test, driver/front passenger .....
Gov't side-crash test, driver/rear passenger ....
IIHS offset crash test ....NA
IIHS side crash test w/ side & curtain airbags ....NA
IIHS side crash test w/o side & curtain airbags ....NA

ANOTHER LOOK

RELIABILITY HISTORY

TROUBLE SPOTS	97 98 99 00 01 02 03 04
Engine	
Cooling	
Fuel	**NO**
Ignition	
Transmission	**DATA**
Electrical	
Air conditioning	**NEW**
Suspension	
Brakes	**MODEL**
Exhaust	
Paint/trim/rust	
Body integrity	
Power equipment	
Body hardware	
RELIABILITY VERDICT	

Expert • Independent • Nonprofit

Nissan Maxima

CR RECOMMENDED ✓

THE MAXIMA LINE
Body style:
sedan
Trim lines:
3.5 SE, 3.5 SL
Base price range:
$27,350-$29,600

Several shortcomings keep the Maxima from being among the best in either the upscale- or family-sedan categories. The quick and refined 265-hp, 3.5-liter V6 gets high marks, but that power produces a fair amount of torque steer in this front-wheel-drive sedan, which causes a tug on the steering wheel. The ride is stiff and jiggly, and while handling has improved, the car still feels less agile than its competitors. A 44-foot turning circle hampers maneuverability. The interior lacks an upscale feel befit a $30,000 car. The rear seating is very spacious.

REPORT CARD

⊖	Predicted reliability
⊖	Owner satisfaction
○	Predicted depreciation
⊖	Accident avoidance
●	Acceleration
○	Ride
●	Front seat comfort
○	Fuel economy

SPECIFICATIONS

Drive wheels Front

Seating 2 front, 3 rear

Engines available
3.5-liter V6 (265 hp)

Transmissions available
6-speed manual; 4-speed automatic; 5-speed automatic

Fuel
Fuel type .... Premium
EPA city/highway, mpg 20/28
Fuel refill capacity, gal. 20.0

Dimensions and weight
Length, in. 194
Width, in. 72
Wheelbase, in. 111
Curb weight, lb. 3,545
Percent weight, front/rear 61/39
Typical towing ability, lb. 1,000

SAFETY INFORMATION

Active safety features

Antilock brakes .... Standard
Traction control .... Standard
Stability control .... Optional
Daytime running lights .... Not available
Tire pressure monitor .... Not available

Safety belts

Center-rear belt 3-point
Pretensioners, front/rear .... Yes/no

Air bags

Occupant-sensing system .... Not available
Side bags, front/rear .... Standard/no
Inflatable curtain .... Standard
Accident alert system .... Not available

Crash tests

Gov't front-crash test, driver/front passenger ..... ●/⊖
Gov't side-crash test, driver/rear passenger ...... ⊖/⊖
IIHS offset crash test .... Good
IIHS side crash test w/ side & curtain airbags .... NA
IIHS side crash test w/o side & curtain airbags .... NA

FROM THE TEST TRACK

Tested model
2004 3.5 SE sedan, 3.5-liter V6, 5-speed automatic

Tires as tested
Goodyear Eagle RS-A, size P245/45R18 96V

Acceleration .... ●
0-30 mph, sec. 2.8
0-60 mph, sec. 6.8
Quarter mile, sec. 15.5
Quarter mile, mph 93
45-65 mph, sec. 4.4

Other findings
Transmission .... ⊖
Turning circle, ft. 44
Ground clearance, in. 3.5

Braking and handling
Braking .... ⊖
Braking, dry pavement, ft. 137
Routine handling .... ⊖
Emergency handling .... ⊖
Avoidance maneuver, max. mph ... 52.5

Convenience and comfort
Ride .... ○
Noise .... ⊖
Driving position .... ⊖
Access .... ⊖
Controls and displays .... ⊖
Fit and finish .... ⊖
Door top to ground, in. 51.5
Trunk .... ○
Luggage capacity .... 3+3
Max. load, lb. 860

Seating
Front-seat comfort .... ●
Front shoulder room, in. 57.0
Front leg room, in. 42.0
Front head room, in. 3.0
Rear-seat comfort .... ●
Rear shoulder room, in. 55.0
Rear leg room, in. 29.5
Rear head room, in. 2.5

Fuel economy .... ○
CU's overall mileage, mpg 21
CU's city/highway, mpg 14/32
CU's 150-mile trip, mpg 26
Annual fuel .... 710 gal./$1,560
Cruising range 490

RELIABILITY HISTORY

TROUBLE SPOTS	Nissan Maxima							
	97	98	99	00	01	02	03	04
Engine	⊖	●	●	●	●	●	●	●
Cooling	●	●	●	⊖	⊖	●	●	●
Fuel	○	⊖	●	○	○	⊖	●	●
Ignition	●	⊖	◑	○	●	⊖	●	●
Transmission	●	●	●	●	⊖	●	●	●
Electrical	⊖	○	○	○	⊖	●	●	●
Air conditioning	⊖	●	●	⊖	●	●	●	●
Suspension	⊖	⊖	●	⊖	●	●	●	●
Brakes	○	○	⊖	◑	○	⊖	●	●
Exhaust	●	●	●	●	⊖	●	●	●
Paint/trim/rust	⊖	●	●	⊖	●	●	●	●
Body integrity	⊖	⊖	⊖	⊖	○	○	⊖	●
Power equipment	⊖	⊖	⊖	⊖	○	○	⊖	●
Body hardware	●	⊖	⊖	⊖	⊖	●	●	●
RELIABILITY VERDICT	✓	✓	✓	✓	✓	✓	✓	✓

better ●◐○◑● worse   See page 36 for more information.

Nissan Murano

CR RECOMMENDED ✓

THE MURANO LINE
Body style:
4-door SUV
Trim lines:
S, SL, SE
Base price range:
$27,000-$31,050

The Murano is one of the better car-based SUVs we've test-ed. Its powerful 3.5-liter V6 is mated to a continuously variable transmission (CVT), delivering strong performance and respectable fuel economy. Handling is responsive, secure, and forgiving with optional stability control. A stiff and noisy ride is a significant drawback. The interior is stylish, but does-n't offer the quality to match the price. The rear seat is roomy. Reliability has been above average. The steering defect problem we experienced in our first test vehicle has been rectified in the 2005 model we tested, enabling us to recommend the Murano.

REPORT CARD

⊖	Predicted reliability
⊖	Owner satisfaction
NA	Predicted depreciation
⊖	Accident avoidance
⊖	Acceleration
○	Ride
⊖	Front seat comfort
◒	Fuel economy

SPECIFICATIONS

Drive wheels Front or AWD

Seating 2 front, 3 rear

Engines available
3.5-liter V6 (245 hp)

Transmissions available
CVT

Fuel
Fuel type ....Premium
EPA city/highway, mpg 20/24
Fuel refill capacity, gal. 21.7

Dimensions and weight
Length, in. 188
Width, in. 74
Wheelbase, in. 111
Curb weight, lb. 4,090
Percent weight, front/rear 59/41
Typical towing ability, lb. 3,500

SAFETY INFORMATION

Active safety features
Antilock brakes ....Standard
Traction control ....Included with stability
Stability control ....Optional
Daytime running lights ....Not available
Tire pressure monitor ....Available

Safety belts
Center-rear belt 3-point
Pretensioners, front/rear ....Yes/no

Air bags
Occupant-sensing system ....Not available
Side bags, front/rear ....Standard/no
Inflatable curtain ....Standard with rollover
Accident alert system ....Not available

Crash tests
Gov't front-crash test, driver/front passenger ......⊖/⊖
Gov't side-crash test, driver/rear passenger ....◉/○
IIHS offset crash test ....Good
IIHS side crash test w/ side & curtain airbags ....NA
IIHS side crash test w/o side & curtain airbags ....NA

FROM THE TEST TRACK

Tested model
2005 SL 4-door SUV AWD, 3.5-liter V6, CVT

Tires as tested
Goodyear Eagle LS, size P235/65R18 104T

Acceleration ....◒
0-30 mph, sec. 3.0
0-60 mph, sec. 8.0
Quarter mile, sec. 16.4
Quarter mile, mph 86
45-65 mph, sec. 5.4

Other findings
Transmission ....◉
Turning circle, ft. 40
Ground clearance, in. 5.5

Braking and handling
Braking ....◒
Braking, dry pavement, ft. 134
Routine handling ....◒
Emergency handling ....○
Avoidance maneuver, max. mph ..50.0

Convenience and comfort
Ride ....○
Noise ....○
Driving position ....◒
Access ....◉
Controls and displays ....◉
Fit and finish ....◒
Door top to ground, in. 60.0
Cargo area ....○
Cargo volume, cu.ft. 35.0
Max. load, lb. 860

Seating
Front-seat comfort ....◒
Front shoulder room, in. 60.0
Front leg room, in. 40.0
Front head room, in. 3.5
Rear-seat comfort ....◉
Rear shoulder room, in. 58.5
Rear leg room, in. 29.0
Rear head room, in 5.0

Fuel economy ....◒
CU's overall mileage, mpg 19
CU's city/highway, mpg 14/26
CU's 150-mile trip, mpg 22
Annual fuel ....785 gal./$1,725
Cruising range 445

RELIABILITY HISTORY

TROUBLE SPOTS	Nissan Murano							
	97	98	99	00	01	02	03	04
Engine							◉	◉
Cooling							◉	◉
Fuel							◉	◉
Ignition							◉	◉
Transmission							◉	◉
Electrical							◒	◒
Air conditioning							◉	◉
Suspension							◉	◉
Brakes							◉	◉
Exhaust							◉	◉
Paint/trim/rust							◉	◉
Body integrity							○	○
Power equipment							◉	◉
Body hardware							◉	◉
RELIABILITY VERDICT							✓	✓

Nissan Pathfinder

THE PATHFINDER LINE
Body style:
4-door SUV
Trim lines:
XE, SE, LE
Base price range:
$24,650-$34,750

The outgoing Pathfinder has been around since 1996, and never felt as contemporary as some newer unibody SUVs. A redesign with a new 4.0-liter V6, independent-rear suspension, and third-row seat arrived this past fall. The 270-hp V6 is smooth and strong, on par with some V8s, though the engine is somewhat loud. The ride is a bit stiff but handling is responsive. The third-row seat is tolerable for short trips. Side and head-protection air bags are optional, and stability control is standard.

REPORT CARD

New	**Predicted reliability**
New	**Owner satisfaction**
NA	**Predicted depreciation**
NA	**Accident avoidance**
NA	**Acceleration**
NA	**Ride**
NA	**Front seat comfort**
NA	**Fuel economy**

SPECIFICATIONS

Drive wheels Rear, part-time, or selectable 4WD

Seating 2 front, 3 rear, 2 third

Engines available
4.0-liter V6 (270 hp)

Transmissions available
5-speed automatic

Fuel
Fuel type ....Regular
EPA city/highway, mpg 15/21
Fuel refill capacity, gal. 21.1

Dimensions and weight
Length, in. 188
Width, in. 73
Wheelbase, in. 112
Curb weight, lb. 4,875
Percent weight, front/rear 51/49
Typical towing ability, lb. 6,000

SAFETY INFORMATION

Active safety features
Antilock brakes ....Standard
Traction control ....\....Included with stability
Stability control ....Standard
Daytime running lights ....Not available
Tire pressure monitor ....Available

Safety belts
Center-rear belt 3-point
Pretensioners, front/rear ....Yes/no

Air bags
Occupant-sensing system ....Front
Side bags, front/rear ....Optional/no
Inflatable curtain ....Optional with rollover
Accident alert system ....Not available

Crash tests
Gov't front-crash test, driver/front passenger .....⊘/◯
Gov't side-crash test, driver/rear passenger ....◑/◐
IIHS offset crash test ....NA
IIHS side crash test w/ side & curtain airbags ....NA
IIHS side crash test w/o side & curtain airbags ....NA

ANOTHER LOOK

RELIABILITY HISTORY

TROUBLE SPOTS	97	98	99	00	01	02	03	04
Engine								
Cooling				NO				
Fuel								
Ignition								
Transmission				DATA				
Electrical								
Air conditioning				NEW				
Suspension								
Brakes				MODEL				
Exhaust								
Paint/trim/rust								
Body integrity								
Power equipment								
Body hardware								
RELIABILITY VERDICT								

● ◔ ◯ ◑ ●
better ◄———► worse   See page 36 for more information.

Nissan Quest

THE QUEST LINE
Body style:
minivan
Trim lines:
3.5, 3.5 S, 3.5 SL, 3.5 SE
Base price range:
$23,450-$32,350

The Quest is a competitive minivan that's sensibly priced. Based on the Altima, it's powered by a 240-hp V6, but acceleration is only adequate. Both the second- and third-row seats fold flat when not in use. The ride is supple and steady, with responsive and secure handling. The interior is roomy, with easy access to all rows. The instrument cluster is located in the center of the dash, which is a nuisance and makes some gauges difficult to read. Nissan claims the instrument panel will be redesigned soon. Reliability has been poor. Crash-test results are impressive.

REPORT CARD

●	Predicted reliability
○	Owner satisfaction
NA	Predicted depreciation
○	Accident avoidance
○	Acceleration
◓	Ride
◓	Front seat comfort
◒	Fuel economy

SPECIFICATIONS

Drive wheels Front

Seating 2 front, 2 rear, 3 third

Engines available
3.5-liter V6 (240 hp)

Transmissions available
4-speed automatic; 5-speed automatic

Fuel
Fuel type . . . . .Regular
EPA city/highway, mpg 19/26
Fuel refill capacity, gal. 20.0

Dimensions and weight
Length, in. 204
Width, in. 78
Wheelbase, in. 124
Curb weight, lb. 4,410
Percent weight, front/rear 58/42
Typical towing ability, lb. 3,500

SAFETY INFORMATION

Active safety features
Antilock brakes . . . . .Standard
Traction control . . . . .Standard
Stability control . . . . .Standard on SE
Daytime running lights . . . . .Not available
Tire pressure monitor . . . . .Available

Safety belts
Center-rear belt 3-point
Pretensioners, front/rear . . . . .Yes/no

Air bags
Occupant-sensing system . . . . .Front
Side bags, front/rear .Optional/no
Inflatable curtain . . . . .Standard
Accident alert system .Not available

Crash tests
Gov't front-crash test, driver/front passenger . . . . . .◐/◐
Gov't side-crash test, driver/rear passenger . . . .◐/◐
IIHS offset crash test . . . . .Good
IIHS side crash test w/ side & curtain airbags . . . . .NA
IIHS side crash test w/o side & curtain airbags . . . . .NA

FROM THE TEST TRACK

Tested model
2004 3.5 SL minivan, 3.5-liter V6, 4-speed automatic

Tires as tested
Goodyear Eagle LS 2, size P225/65R16 99H

Acceleration . . . .○
0-30 mph, sec. 3.7
0-60 mph, sec. 9.9
Quarter mile, sec. 17.5
Quarter mile, mph 84
45-65 mph, sec. 6.5

Other findings
Transmission . . . .◓
Turning circle, ft. 44
Ground clearance, in. 4.0

Braking and handling
Braking . . . .○
Braking, dry pavement, ft. 148
Routine handling . . . .◓
Emergency handling . . . .○
Avoidance maneuver, max. mph . . .47.0

Convenience and comfort
Ride . . . .◓
Noise . . . .◓
Driving position . . . .◓
Access . . . .●
Controls and displays . . . .○
Fit and finish . . . .◓
Door top to ground, in. 61.0
Cargo area . . . .◓
Cargo volume, cu.ft. 60.0
Max. load, lb. 1,205

Seating
Front-seat comfort . . . .◓
Front shoulder room, in. 64.0
Front leg room, in. 40.0
Front head room, in. 6.5
Rear-seat comfort . . . .●
Rear shoulder room, in. 66.5
Rear leg room, in. 28.0
Rear head room, in 7.5
Third-seat comfort . . . .○
Third shoulder room,in 61.0
Third leg room, in. 32.0
Third head room, in 3.0

Fuel economy . . . .◒
CU's overall mileage, mpg 18
CU's city/highway, mpg 12/28
CU's 150-mile trip, mpg 21
Annual fuel . . . . .845 gal./$1,695
Cruising range 390

RELIABILITY HISTORY

TROUBLE SPOTS	Nissan Quest							
	97	98	99	00	01	02	03	04
Engine	◐	◐	●	●	●			●
Cooling	◐	◒	◐	●	●			◒
Fuel	◒	○	○	◐	◐			◒
Ignition	◐	●	●	●	●			○
Transmission	◐	●	◐	●	●			◒
Electrical	◐	◒	◒	◐	○			◒
Air conditioning	◒	◐	◒	◐	●			◒
Suspension	○	○	○	◐	◒			○
Brakes	◒	◒	○	◒	◒			●
Exhaust	◒	●	●	◒	●			◒
Paint/trim/rust	◒	◒	◒	◒	◒			●
Body integrity	◒	◒	○	◒	◒			◒
Power equipment	●	●	●	◒	○			○
Body hardware	●	●	○	○	●			◒
RELIABILITY VERDICT	–	–	–	✓	–	–		✗

Nissan Sentra

THE SENTRA LINE
Body style:
sedan
Trim lines:
1.8, 1.8 S, SE-R, SE-R
Spec V
Base price range:
$12,700-$17,800

The aging Sentra is facing some very good competition. Its responsive 1.8-liter engine and optional automatic transmission work well together. Handling is sound, though not as agile as that of the Ford Focus or Mazda3. The ride is stiff. Braking is so-so, with long stopping distances. The front seats are reasonably comfortable, though the rear seat is cramped. The sporty SE-R has a 165-hp engine and firmer suspension. The SE-R Spec V model gets a six-speed manual transmission and 175 hp. Reliability has remained below average. The Sentra received a Poor rating in the IIHS side-impact-crash test.

REPORT CARD

◒	Predicted reliability
●	Owner satisfaction
○	Predicted depreciation
○	Accident avoidance
○	Acceleration
○	Ride
◒	Front seat comfort
◒	Fuel economy

SPECIFICATIONS

Drive wheels Front

Seating 2 front, 3 rear

Engines available
1.8-liter 4 (126 hp); 2.5-liter 4 (165 hp); 2.5-liter 4 (175 hp)

Transmissions available
5-speed manual; 6-speed manual; 4-speed automatic

Fuel
Fuel type . . . . .Regular or premium
EPA city/highway, mpg 27/35
Fuel refill capacity, gal. 13.2

Dimensions and weight
Length, in. .178
Width, in. 67
Wheelbase, in. 100
Curb weight, lb. 2,695
Percent weight, front/rear 62/38
Typical towing ability, lb. 1,000

SAFETY INFORMATION

Active safety features
Antilock brakes . . . . .Optional
Traction control . . . . .Not available
Stability control . . . . .Not available
Daytime running lights . . . . .Not available
Tire pressure monitor . . . . .Not available

Safety belts
Center-rear belt 3-point
Pretensioners, front/rear . . . . .Yes/no

Air bags
Occupant-sensing system . . . . .Not available
Side bags, front/rear . . . . .Optional/no
Inflatable curtain .Not available
Accident alert system . . . . .Not available

Crash tests
Gov't front-crash test, driver/front passenger . . . . .◒/◒
Gov't side-crash test, driver/rear passenger . . . .◒/NA
IIHS offset crash test . . . . .Acceptable
IIHS side crash test w/ side & curtain airbags . . . . .NA
IIHS side crash test w/o side & curtain airbags . . . . . . .Poor

FROM THE TEST TRACK

Tested model
2000 GXE sedan, 1.8-liter Four, 4-speed automatic

Tires as tested
Bridgestone Potenza RE92, size P195/60R15 87H

Acceleration . . . .○
0-30 mph, sec. 3.7
0-60 mph, sec. 10.9
Quarter mile, sec. 18.3
Quarter mile, mph 76
45-65 mph, sec. 6.8

Other findings
Transmission . . . .◒
Turning circle, ft. 38
Ground clearance, in. 4.0

Braking and handling
Braking . . . .○
Braking, dry pavement, ft. 150
Routine handling . . . .◒
Emergency handling . . . .○
Avoidance maneuver, max. mph . . .51.0

Convenience and comfort
Ride . . . .○
Noise . . . .◒
Driving position . . . .◒
Access . . . .○
Controls and displays . . . .◒
Fit and finish . . . .◒
Door top to ground, in. 51.0
Trunk . . . .○
Luggage capacity . . . . .4+1
Max. load, lb. 825

Seating
Front-seat comfort . . . .◒
Front shoulder room, in. 52.5
Front leg room, in. 40.0
Front head room, in. 4.0
Rear-seat comfort . . . .◒
Rear shoulder room, in. 51.5
Rear leg room, in. 25.0
Rear head room, in 1.5

Fuel economy
CU's overall mileage, mpg 26
CU's city/highway, mpg 18/36
CU's 150-mile trip, mpg 32
Annual fuel . . . . . . .570 gal./$1,140
Cruising range 390

RELIABILITY HISTORY

TROUBLE SPOTS	97	98	99	00	01	02	03	04
Engine	◒	◒	◒	○	○	○	○	●
Cooling	●	●	●	●	●	●	●	●
Fuel	○	○	●	◒	○	◒	◒	●
Ignition	◒	◒	◒	●	◒	◒	●	●
Transmission	●	●	●	●	○	○	◒	●
Electrical	◒	◒	◒	○	○	◒	◒	◒
Air conditioning	○	○	◒	◒	◒	◒	◒	●
Suspension	◒	◒	◒	◒	◒	◒	●	●
Brakes	◒	●	◒	◒	○	○	◒	◒
Exhaust	◒	◒	◒	◒	◒	●	●	●
Paint/trim/rust	◒	◒	◒	◒	◒	◒	●	◒
Body integrity	●	●	◒	◒	○	○	◒	◒
Power equipment	◒	◒	●	◒	○	◒	◒	●
Body hardware	○	○	◒	◒	◒	◒	◒	◒
RELIABILITY VERDICT	✓	✓	✓	–	–	✗	✗	–

Nissan Titan

CR RECOMMENDED ✓

The Titan is Nissan's first entry into the full-sized truck category and it more than holds its own against the competition. It has an impressively large cabin, is relatively agile, and has a fairly comfortable ride and a very smooth transmission. Safety features include optional electronic stability control (ESC) and head-protection air bags. The crew cab's cargo bed is fairly small compared to the competition, and payload capacity is a meager 1,105 pounds. The Titan's muscular V8 provides strong acceleration, but the constant engine and exhaust noise can become tiresome.

THE TITAN LINE

Body style:
extended cab; crew cab

Trim lines:
XE, SE, LE

Base price range:
$22,800-$35,250

REPORT CARD

○	Predicted reliability
◉	Owner satisfaction
NA	Predicted depreciation
○	Accident avoidance
⊖	Acceleration
○	Ride
⊖	Front seat comfort
●	Fuel economy

SPECIFICATIONS

Drive wheels Rear or part-time 4WD

Seating 3 front, 3 rear

Engines available
5.6-liter V8 (305 hp)

Transmissions available
5-speed automatic

Fuel
Fuel type ....Regular
EPA city/highway, mpg 14/18
Fuel refill capacity, gal. 28.0

Dimensions and weight
Length, in. 224
Width, in. 79
Wheelbase, in. 140
Curb weight, lb. 5,380
Percent weight, front/rear 55/45
Typical towing ability, lb. 9,400

SAFETY INFORMATION

Active safety features

Antilock brakes ....Standard
Traction control ....Included with stability
Stability control ....Optional
Daytime running lights ....Not available
Tire pressure monitor ....Available

Safety belts

Center-rear belt 3-point
Pretensioners, front/rear ....Yes/no

Air bags

Occupant-sensing system ....Front
Side bags, front/rear ....Optional/no
Inflatable curtain ....Optional
Accident alert system ....Not available

Crash tests

Gov't front-crash test, driver/front passenger .....◑/◒
Gov't side-crash test, driver/rear passenger ....NA/NA
IIHS offset crash test ....Good
IIHS side crash test w/ side & curtain airbags ....NA
IIHS side crash test w/o side & curtain airbags ....NA

FROM THE TEST TRACK

Tested model
2004 SE crew cab 4WD, 5.6-liter V8, 5-speed automatic

Tires as tested
Goodyear Wrangler SR-A, size P265/70R18 114S

Acceleration ....⊖
0-30 mph, sec. 2.6
0-60 mph, sec...................7.3
Quarter mile, sec. 16.0
Quarter mile, mph 88
45-65 mph, sec. 4.9

Other findings
Transmission ....●
Turning circle, ft. 49
Ground clearance, in. 10.0

Braking and handling
Braking ....⊖
Braking, dry pavement, ft. 139
Routine handling ....○
Emergency handling ....⊖
Avoidance maneuver, max. mph ...47.5

Convenience and comfort
Ride ....○
Noise ....○
Driving position ....○
Access ....⊖
Controls and displays ....⊖
Fit and finish ....⊖
Door top to ground, in. 70.0
Cargo area ....⊖
Max. load, lb. 1,105

Seating
Front-seat comfort ....⊖
Front shoulder room, in. 65.0
Front leg room, in. 41.5
Front head room, in. 5.5
Rear-seat comfort ....○
Rear shoulder room, in. 64.5
Rear leg room, in. 32.0
Rear head room, in 5.0

Fuel economy ....●
CU's overall mileage, mpg 13
CU's city/highway, mpg 9/18
CU's 150-mile trip, mpg 16
Annual fuel ....1,170 gal./$2,340
Cruising range 415

RELIABILITY HISTORY

TROUBLE SPOTS	Nissan Titan							
	97	98	99	00	01	02	03	04
Engine								◉
Cooling								◉
Fuel								◉
Ignition								◉
Transmission								◉
Electrical								◉
Air conditioning								◉
Suspension								◉
Brakes								◑
Exhaust								◉
Paint/trim/rust								◑
Body integrity								◑
Power equipment								◑
Body hardware								◑
RELIABILITY VERDICT								⊟

Nissan Xterra

THE XTERRA LINE
Body style:
4-door SUV
Trim lines:
S, Off-Road, SE
Base price range:
$20,800–$27,300

The original Xterra, based on Nissan's unimpressive and outdated Frontier pickup, was basic and trucklike. A redesign based on the new Frontier arrived in February. It should retain its off-road capability but be more civilized on the road. Power will come from a new, strong 4.0-liter, 265-hp V6 engine. The four-wheel-drive system is still part-time. The Off-Road model comes with a hill-descent system. The spartan interior looks rugged and has a few handy tie-down rings. Side- and head-protection air bags, as well as stability control, are available.

REPORT CARD

New	Predicted reliability
New	Owner satisfaction
NA	Predicted depreciation
NA	Accident avoidance
NA	Acceleration
NA	Ride
NA	Front seat comfort
NA	Fuel economy

SPECIFICATIONS

Drive wheels Rear or part-time 4WD

Seating 2 front, 3 rear

Engines available
4.0-liter V6 (265 hp)

Transmissions available
6-speed manual; 5-speed automatic

Fuel
Fuel type ....Regular
EPA city/highway, mpg 16/21
Fuel refill capacity, gal. 21.1

Dimensions and weight
Length, in. 179
Width, in. 73
Wheelbase, in. 106
Curb weight, lb. 4,350
Percent weight, front/rear 56/44
Typical towing ability, lb. 5,000

SAFETY INFORMATION

Active safety features
Antilock brakes ....Standard
Traction control ....Included with stability
Stability control ....Optional
Daytime running lights ....Not available
Tire pressure monitor ....Available

Safety belts
Center-rear belt 3-point
Pretensioners, front/rear ....Yes/no

Air bags
Occupant-sensing system ....Front
Side bags, front/rear ....Optional/no
Inflatable curtain ....Optional with rollover
Accident alert system ....Not available

Crash tests
Gov't front-crash test, driver/front passenger ......NA/NA
Gov't side-crash test, driver/rear passenger ....NA/NA
IIHS offset crash test ....NA
IIHS side crash test w/ side & curtain airbags ....NA
IIHS side crash test w/o side & curtain airbags ....NA

ANOTHER LOOK

RELIABILITY HISTORY

TROUBLE SPOTS	97 98 99 00 01 02 03 04
Engine	
Cooling	NO
Fuel	
Ignition	
Transmission	DATA
Electrical	
Air conditioning	NEW
Suspension	
Brakes	MODEL
Exhaust	
Paint/trim/rust	
Body integrity	
Power equipment	
Body hardware	
RELIABILITY VERDICT	

better ◄——► worse   See page 36 for more information.

Pontiac Aztek

THE AZTEK LINE
Body style:
4-door SUV
Trim lines:
–
Base price range:
$21,530-$24,445

The minivan-based Aztek is available with either front- or all-wheel drive. The coarse 3.4-liter, 185-hp V6 is shared with the Buick Rendezvous, delivering so-so acceleration and poor fuel economy. Options such as a removable center-console cooler and a tent that attaches onto the rear of the vehicle are features unique to the Aztek. The ride is uncomfortable, and handling is clumsy but secure. Other flaws include a rear seat that's too low, an awkward and heavy split rear gate, and poor side and rear visibility. The lack of a rear wiper hurts visibility in inclement weather. Crash-test results are unimpressive.

REPORT CARD

⊖	Predicted reliability
⊖	Owner satisfaction
⊖	Predicted depreciation
○	Accident avoidance
○	Acceleration
⊖	Ride
○	Front seat comfort
●	Fuel economy

SPECIFICATIONS

Drive wheels Front or AWD

Seating 2 front, 3 rear

Engines available
3.4-liter V6 (185 hp)

Transmissions available
4-speed automatic

Fuel
Fuel type . . . . .Regular
EPA city/highway, mpg 18/24
Fuel refill capacity, gal. 18.0

Dimensions and weight
Length, in. 182
Width, in. 74
Wheelbase, in. 108
Curb weight, lb. 4,170
Percent weight, front/rear 59/41
Typical towing ability, lb. 3,500

SAFETY INFORMATION

Active safety features
Antilock brakes . . . . .Optional (standard on AWD)
Traction control . . . . .Optional on 2WD
Stability control .Not available
Daytime running lights . . . . .Standard
Tire pressure monitor . . . . .Not available

Safety belts
Center-rear belt 3-point
Pretensioners, front/rear . . . . .No/no

Air bags
Occupant-sensing system . . . . .Not available
Side bags, front/rear . . . . .Optional/no
Inflatable curtain . . . . .Not available
Accident alert system . . . . .Available

Crash tests
Gov't front-crash test, driver/front passenger . . . . . ○/⊖
Gov't side-crash test, driver/rear passenger . . . . ●/○
IIHS offset crash test . . . . .Marginal
IIHS side crash test w/ side & curtain airbags . . . . .NA
IIHS side crash test w/o side & curtain airbags . . . . .NA

FROM THE TEST TRACK

Tested model
2003 4-door SUV AWD, 3.4-liter V6, 4-speed automatic

Tires as tested
Goodyear Eagle RS-A, size P235/55R17 98H

Acceleration . . . . ○
0-30 mph, sec. 3.7
0-60 mph, sec. 11.3
Quarter mile, sec. 18.3
Quarter mile, mph 76
45-65 mph, sec. 6.9

Other findings
Transmission . . . . ●
Turning circle, ft. 39
Ground clearance, in. 6.5

Braking and handling
Braking . . . . ○
Braking, dry pavement, ft. 150
Routine handling . . . . ○
Emergency handling . . . . ○
Avoidance maneuver, max. mph . . .49.0

Convenience and comfort
Ride . . . . ⊖
Noise . . . . ⊖
Driving position . . . . ⊖
Access . . . . ⊖
Controls and displays . . . . ⊖
Fit and finish . . . . ⊖
Door top to ground, in. 61.0
Cargo area . . . . ⊖
Cargo volume, cu.ft. 49.0
Max. load, lb. 1,185

Seating
Front-seat comfort . . . . ○
Front shoulder room, in. 59.0
Front leg room, in. 41.0
Front head room, in. 3.5
Rear-seat comfort . . . . ○
Rear shoulder room, in. 59.0
Rear leg room, in. 29.0
Rear head room, in 4.0

Fuel economy . . . . ●
CU's overall mileage, mpg 17
CU's city/highway, mpg 12/24
CU's 150-mile trip, mpg 20
Annual fuel . . . . .880 gal./$1,755
Cruising range 330

RELIABILITY HISTORY

TROUBLE SPOTS	Pontiac Aztek							
	97	98	99	00	01	02	03	04
Engine					○	●	⊖	
Cooling					⊖	⊖	●	
Fuel					⊖	⊖	●	
Ignition					⊖	●	●	
Transmission					○	●	●	
Electrical					●	⊖	⊖	
Air conditioning					●	⊖	⊖	
Suspension					⊖	⊖	●	
Brakes					○	⊖	○	
Exhaust					●	⊖	●	
Paint/trim/rust					⊖	●	⊖	
Body integrity					○	⊖	○	
Power equipment					○	○	○	
Body hardware					○	○	○	
RELIABILITY VERDICT					✗	✗	✗	

Insufficient data

Expert • Independent • Nonprofit

Pontiac G6

THE G6 LINE
Body style:
sedan
Trim lines:
Base, GT
Base price range:
$20,675-$23,300

The Pontiac G6 is the long-awaited replacement to the Grand Am. It shares its underpinnings with the Chevrolet Malibu, but it isn't as well-rounded. The V6 provides ample power and acceptable fuel economy but sounds coarse. The base model lacks agility and tire grip, and the ride is stiff. The coupelike styling impedes rear access and visibility. Interior quality is unimpressive. Some drivers found the seats too confining. Coupe and convertible models arrive later. A 2.4-liter, 170-hp four-cylinder and a 3.9-liter, 240-hp V6 will be added to the lineup in 2006.

REPORT CARD

New	**Predicted reliability**
New	**Owner satisfaction**
NA	**Predicted depreciation**
○	**Accident avoidance**
⊖	**Acceleration**
○	**Ride**
○	**Front seat comfort**
○	**Fuel economy**

SPECIFICATIONS

Drive wheels Front

Seating 2 front, 3 rear

Engines available
3.5-liter V6 (200 hp)

Transmissions available
4-speed automatic

Fuel
Fuel type ....Regular
EPA city/highway, mpg 22/32
Fuel refill capacity, gal. 16.3

Dimensions and weight
Length, in. 189
Width, in. 71
Wheelbase, in. 112
Curb weight, lb. 3,475
Percent weight, front/rear 62/38
Typical towing ability, lb. 1,000

SAFETY INFORMATION

Active safety features
Antilock brakes ....Standard (optional on Base)
Traction control ....Optional
Stability control ....Not available
Daytime running lights ....Standard
Tire pressure monitor ....Not available

Safety belts
Center-rear belt 3-point
Pretensioners, front/rear ....Yes/no

Air bags
Occupant-sensing system ....Not available
Side bags, front/rear ....Optional/no
Inflatable curtain ....Optional
Accident alert system ....Available

Crash tests
Gov't front-crash test, driver/front passenger .....◑/◔
Gov't side-crash test, driver/rear passenger ......○/◑
IIHS offset crash test ....NA
IIHS side crash test w/ side & curtain airbags ....NA
IIHS side crash test w/o side & curtain airbags ....NA

FROM THE TEST TRACK

Tested model
2005 Base sedan, 3.5-liter V6, 4-speed automatic

Tires as tested
Uniroyal Tiger Paw Touring SR, size P215/60R16 94S

Acceleration ....⊖
0-30 mph, sec. 3.1
0-60 mph, sec. 8.1
Quarter mile, sec. 16.3
Quarter mile, mph 88
45-65 mph, sec. 5.3

Other findings
Transmission ....◑
Turning circle, ft. 41
Ground clearance, in. 5.0

Braking and handling
Braking ....○
Braking, dry pavement, ft. 146
Routine handling ....◑
Emergency handling ....○
Avoidance maneuver, max. mph ..52.0

Convenience and comfort
Ride ....○
Noise ....◑
Driving position ....◑
Access ....○
Controls and displays ....◑
Fit and finish ....○
Door top to ground, in. 50.0
Trunk ....○
Luggage capacity ....3+1
Max. load, lb. 890

Seating
Front-seat comfort ....○
Front shoulder room, in. 54.5
Front leg room, in. 42.0
Front head room, in. 4.0
Rear-seat comfort ....○
Rear shoulder room, in. 51.5
Rear leg room, in. 31.0
Rear head room, in 2.0
Fuel economy ....○
CU's overall mileage, mpg 21
  CU's city/highway, mpg 13/34
  CU's 150-mile trip, mpg 27
Annual fuel ....710 gal./$1,420
Cruising range 410

RELIABILITY HISTORY

TROUBLE SPOTS	97	98	99	00	01	02	03	04
Engine								
Cooling				NO				
Fuel								
Ignition								
Transmission				DATA				
Electrical								
Air conditioning				NEW				
Suspension								
Brakes				MODEL				
Exhaust								
Paint/trim/rust								
Body integrity								
Power equipment								
Body hardware								
RELIABILITY VERDICT								

● ◑ ○ ◔ ●
better ◀ ━━▶ worse   See page 36 for more information.

Pontiac GTO

THE GTO LINE
Body style:
coupe
Trim lines:
–
Base price range:
$32,295

The rear-drive Pontiac GTO is a slightly modified Holden Monaro, a car produced by GM's Australian subsidiary. For 2005 it uses a version of the Corvette's 6.0-liter V8 engine that produces 400 hp. The GTO competes primarily with the redesigned Ford Mustang. The GTO is quick, and the engine sounds and feels muscular. Handling isn't overtly sporty, but it is entertaining at its limits for driving enthusiasts. The manual shifter isn't slick, and the clutch is heavy. The ride is fairly compliant. The seats are comfortable, and the interior has good fit and finish.

REPORT CARD

NA	**Predicted reliability**
NA	**Owner satisfaction**
NA	**Predicted depreciation**
⊖	**Accident avoidance**
◉	**Acceleration**
○	**Ride**
⊖	**Front seat comfort**
●	**Fuel economy**

SPECIFICATIONS

Drive wheels Rear

Seating 2 front, 2 rear

Engines available
6.0-liter V8 (400 hp)

Transmissions available
6-speed manual; 4-speed automatic

Fuel
Fuel type . . . . .Premium
EPA city/highway, mpg 17/25
Fuel refill capacity, gal. 18.5

Dimensions and weight
Length, in. 190
Width, in. 73
Wheelbase, in. .110
Curb weight, lb. 3,770
Percent weight, front/rear 55/45
Typical towing ability, lb. . . . . .NR

SAFETY INFORMATION

Active safety features
Antilock brakes . . . . .Standard
Traction control . . . . .Standard
Stability control . . . . .Not available
Daytime running lights . . . . .Standard
Tire pressure monitor .Available

Safety belts
Center-rear belt . . . . .NA
Pretensioners, front/rear .Yes/no

Air bags
Occupant-sensing system . . . . .Not available
Side bags, front/rear . . . . .Standard/no
Inflatable curtain . . . . .Not available
Accident alert system . . . . .Available

Crash tests
Gov't front-crash test, driver/front passenger . . . . . .NA/NA
Gov't side-crash test, driver/rear passenger . . . . . . .NA/NA
IIHS offset crash test . . . . .NA
IIHS side crash test w/ side & curtain airbags . . . . .NA
IIHS side crash test w/o side & curtain airbags . . . . .NA

FROM THE TEST TRACK

Tested model
2004 coupe, 5.7-liter V8, 6-speed manual

Tires as tested
BF Goodrich g-Force T/A KDWS,
size 245/45ZR17 95W

Acceleration . . . . ◉
0-30 mph, sec. 2.3
0-60 mph, sec. 5.5
Quarter mile, sec. 14.2
Quarter mile, mph 102
45-65 mph, sec. 3.5

Other findings
Transmission . . . . ○
Turning circle, ft. 37
Ground clearance, in. 4.5

Braking and handling
Braking . . . . ⊖
Braking, dry pavement, ft. 143
Routine handling . . . . ⊖
Emergency handling . . . . ⊖
Avoidance maneuver, max. mph . . .50.0

Convenience and comfort
Ride . . . . ○
Noise . . . . ⊖
Driving position . . . . ○
Access . . . . ○
Controls and displays . . . . ⊖
Fit and finish . . . . ⊖
Door top to ground, in. 48.5
Trunk . . . . ●
Luggage capacity . . . . .1+2
Max. load, lb. 740

Seating
Front-seat comfort . . . . ⊖
Front shoulder room, in. 59.0
Front leg room, in. 41.0
Front head room, in. 3.0
Rear-seat comfort . . . . ⊖
Rear shoulder room, in. 50.5
Rear leg room, in. 26.0
Rear head room, in 1.5

Fuel economy . . . . ●
CU's overall mileage, mpg 17
CU's city/highway, mpg 11/27
CU's 150-mile trip, mpg 21
Annual fuel . . . . .870 gal./$1,915
Cruising range 350

RELIABILITY HISTORY

TROUBLE SPOTS	97 98 99 00 01 02 03 04
Engine	
Cooling	
Fuel	NOT
Ignition	
Transmission	ENOUGH
Electrical	
Air conditioning	DATA
Suspension	
Brakes	TO
Exhaust	
Paint/trim/rust	RATE
Body integrity	
Power equipment	
Body hardware	
RELIABILITY VERDICT	

Pontiac Grand Prix

Despite a redesign for 2004, the Grand Prix is a mediocre sedan. Its ride, rear-seat comfort, and 20 mpg overall fuel economy aren't competitive. The 3.8-liter, 200-hp V6 in our test car was fairly quick but noisy; the high-end GTP model features a supercharged 3.8-liter V6, producing 260 hp. The ride is very stiff, and braking was only adequate. The coupelike styling limits visibility and access, particularly to the rear. The low roofline limits head room. The rear seats are very cramped and lack thigh support. The base V6 version has excellent reliability, but reliability of the supercharged model is poor.

THE GRAND PRIX LINE
Body style:
sedan
Trim lines:
Base, GT, GTP, GXP
Base price range:
$23,060-$29,335

REPORT CARD

◉	Predicted reliability
○	Owner satisfaction
NA	Predicted depreciation
○	Accident avoidance
⊖	Acceleration
○	Ride
⊖	Front seat comfort
⊖	Fuel economy

SPECIFICATIONS

Drive wheels Front

Seating 2 front, 3 rear

Engines available
3.8-liter V6 (200 hp); 3.8-liter V6 super-charged (260 hp); 5.3-liter V8 (303 hp)

Transmissions available
4-speed automatic

Fuel
Fuel type . . . . .Regular or premium
EPA city/highway, mpg 20/30
Fuel refill capacity, gal. 17.0

Dimensions and weight
Length, in. 198
Width, in. 72
Wheelbase, in. 111
Curb weight, lb. 3,630
Percent weight, front/rear 63/37
Typical towing ability, lb. 1,000

SAFETY INFORMATION

Active safety features
Antilock brakes . . . . .Standard (optional on Base)
Traction control .Standard with ABS
Stability control . . . . .Optional on GTP
Daytime running lights . . . . .Standard
Tire pressure monitor . . . . .Available

Safety belts
Center-rear belt 3-point
Pretensioners, front/rear .Yes/no

Air bags
Occupant-sensing system . . . . .Not available
Side bags, front/rear . . . . .No/no
Inflatable curtain . . . . .Optional
Accident alert system .Available

Crash tests
Gov't front-crash test, driver/front passenger . . . . . ○/⊖
Gov't side-crash test, driver/rear passenger . . . . . . ○/○
IIHS offset crash test . . . . .NA
IIHS side crash test w/ side & curtain airbags . . . . .NA
IIHS side crash test w/o side & curtain airbags . . . . .NA

FROM THE TEST TRACK

Tested model
2004 GT2 sedan, 3.8-liter V6, 4-speed automatic

Tires as tested
Goodyear Eagle LS, size P225/60R16 97S

Acceleration . . . . ⊖
0-30 mph, sec. 2.9
0-60 mph, sec. 8.3
Quarter mile, sec. 16.4
Quarter mile, mph 86
45-65 mph, sec. 5.8

Other findings
Transmission . . . . ⊖
Turning circle, ft. 41
Ground clearance, in. 5.5

Braking and handling
Braking . . . .○
Braking, dry pavement, ft. 153
Routine handling . . . .⊖
Emergency handling . . . .○
Avoidance maneuver, max. mph . . .49.0

Convenience and comfort
Ride . . . .○
Noise . . . .⊖
Driving position . . . .○
Access . . . .○
Controls and displays . . . .◉
Fit and finish . . . .○
Door top to ground, in. . . .50.0
Trunk . . . .○
Luggage capacity . . . . .3+3
Max. load, lb. 915

Seating
Front-seat comfort . . . . ⊖
Front shoulder room, in. 57.5
Front leg room, in. 41.5
Front head room, in. 2.0
Rear-seat comfort . . . . ⊖
Rear shoulder room, in. 57.5
Rear leg room, in. 28.0
Rear head room, in 2.0

Fuel economy . . . . ⊖
CU's overall mileage, mpg 20
CU's city/highway, mpg . . .13/31
CU's 150-mile trip, mpg 25
Annual fuel . . . . .745 gal./$1,495
Cruising range 390

RELIABILITY HISTORY

TROUBLE SPOTS	Pontiac Grand Prix								
	97	98	99	00	01	02	03	04
Engine	⊖	○	⊖	○	○	●	●	●
Cooling	●	⊖	○	●	●	●	●	●
Fuel	○	○	○	○	⊖	●	●	●
Ignition	○	○	⊖	○	○	○	◉	●
Transmission	○	○	○	○	○	◉	●	●
Electrical	●	●	○	⊖	○	◉	●	●
Air conditioning	⊖	○	○	○	○	◉	●	●
Suspension	○	○	○	○	⊖	●	●	●
Brakes	○	○	○	○	○	◉	●	●
Exhaust	⊖	⊖	⊖	⊖	⊖	●	●	●
Paint/trim/rust	○	○	○	○	○	◉	●	●
Body integrity	⊖	⊖	○	○	○	◉	●	●
Power equipment	●	●	●	○	○	◉	●	●
Body hardware	○	○	○	○	○	◉	●	●
RELIABILITY VERDICT	✗	✗	–	–	–	–	–	✓

Pontiac Montana SV6

THE MONTANA SV6 LINE
Body style:
minivan
Trim lines:
–
Base price range:
$24,520-$30,210

The 2005 Montana SV6 is a freshened version of a family of GM minivans that have been in production for eight years. Along with the Buick Terraza, Chevrolet Uplander, and Saturn Relay, all four are powered by a coarse 3.5-liter, 200-hp V6 engine. The ride is stiff and noisy. Interior fit and finish is insubstantial. The second-row seats can be folded and removed, but the seat is cumbersome. The folding third-row seat folds flat on the floor, rather than into a well under the floor. All-wheel drive is optional. The revised styling doesn't obscure the fact that this is an outdated design.

REPORT CARD

New	Predicted reliability
New	Owner satisfaction
NA	Predicted depreciation
○	Accident avoidance
○	Acceleration
○	Ride
○	Front seat comfort
●	Fuel economy

SPECIFICATIONS

Drive wheels Front or AWD

Seating 2 front, 2 rear, 3 third

Engines available
3.5-liter V6 (200 hp)

Transmissions available
4-speed automatic

Fuel
Fuel type . . . . .Regular
EPA city/highway, mpg 18/24
Fuel refill capacity, gal. 25.0

Dimensions and weight
Length, in. 205
Width, in. 72
Wheelbase, in. 121
Curb weight, lb. 4,380
Percent weight, front/rear 56/44
Typical towing ability, lb. 3,500

SAFETY INFORMATION

Active safety features
Antilock brakes . . . . .Standard
Traction control . . . . .Optional on FWD
Stability control . . . . .Optional on FWD
Daytime running lights . . . . .Standard
Tire pressure monitor . . . . .Not available

Safety belts
Center-rear belt 3-point
Pretensioners, front/rear . . . . .Yes/no

Air bags
Occupant-sensing system .Front
Side bags, front/rear . . . . .Optional/no
Inflatable curtain .Not available
Accident alert system . . . . .Available

Crash tests
Gov't front-crash test, driver/front passenger . . . . . ◑/◑
Gov't side-crash test, driver/rear passenger . . . . . . ◑/◑
IIHS offset crash test . . . . .NA
IIHS side crash test w/ side & curtain airbags . . . . .NA
IIHS side crash test w/o side & curtain airbags . . . . . . .NA

FROM THE TEST TRACK

Tested model
2005 Saturn Relay 3 minivan, 3.5-liter V6, 4-speed automatic

Tires as tested
Goodyear Integrity, size P225/60R17 98S

Acceleration . . . . ○
0-30 mph, sec. 3.6
0-60 mph, sec. 10.2
Quarter mile, sec. 17.7
Quarter mile, mph 80
45-65 mph, sec. 7.0

Other findings
Transmission . . . . ◑
Turning circle, ft. 43
Ground clearance, in. 6.0

Braking and handling
Braking . . . . ◑
Braking, dry pavement, ft. 136
Routine handling . . . . ○
Emergency handling . . . . ◑
Avoidance maneuver, max. mph . . .48.5

Convenience and comfort
Ride . . . . ○
Noise . . . . ○
Driving position . . . . ○
Access . . . . ●
Controls and displays . . . . ◑
Fit and finish . . . . ○
Door top to ground, in. 62.0
Cargo area . . . . ◑
Cargo volume, cu.ft. 75.5
Max. load, lb. 1,290

Seating
Front-seat comfort . . . . ○
Front shoulder room, in. 59.5
Front leg room, in. 40.5
Front head room, in. 5.0
Rear-seat comfort . . . . ◑
Rear shoulder room, in. 62.0
Rear leg room, in. 26.0
Rear head room, in 4.0
Third-seat comfort . . . . ○
Third shoulder room,in 60.0
Third leg room, in. 28.0
Third head room, in 3.5

Fuel economy . . . . ●
CU's overall mileage, mpg 17
CU's city/highway, mpg 12/25
CU's 150-mile trip, mpg 21
Annual fuel . . . . .860 gal./$1,720
Cruising range 510

RELIABILITY HISTORY

TROUBLE SPOTS	97 98 99 00 01 02 03 04
Engine	
Cooling	NO
Fuel	
Ignition	
Transmission	DATA
Electrical	
Air conditioning	NEW
Suspension	
Brakes	MODEL
Exhaust	
Paint/trim/rust	
Body integrity	
Power equipment	
Body hardware	
RELIABILITY VERDICT	

Expert • Independent • Nonprofit

Pontiac Solstice

Nearly three years after the concept was shown, the 2006 Pontiac Solstice roadster arrives in dealerships this fall. It is expected to cost about $20,000. The Solstice is a rear-wheel drive, two-seat convertible powered by a 2.4-liter four-cylinder engine that produces about 170 hp. A five-speed manual will be the only transmission offered initially. ABS will be optional. Saturn will also get a version named the Sky.

THE SOLSTICE LINE
Body style:
convertible
Trim lines:
–
Base price range:
$19,420

REPORT CARD

New	**Predicted reliability**
New	**Owner satisfaction**
NA	**Predicted depreciation**
NA	**Accident avoidance**
NA	**Acceleration**
NA	**Ride**
NA	**Front seat comfort**
NA	**Fuel economy**

SPECIFICATIONS

Drive wheels Rear

Seating 2 front

Engines available
2.4-liter 4 (170 hp)

Transmissions available
5-speed manual

Fuel
Fuel type . . . . .Regular
EPA city/highway, mpg . . . . .NA
Fuel refill capacity, gal. . . . . .NA

Dimensions and weight
Length, in. 157
Width, in. 72
Wheelbase, in. 95
Curb weight, lb. 2,860
Percent weight, front/rear 50/50
Typical towing ability, lb. . . . . .NR

SAFETY INFORMATION

Active safety features
Antilock brakes . . . . .Standard
Traction control . . . . .N.A.
Stability control . . . . .Not available
Daytime running lights .Standard
Tire pressure monitor .Available

Safety belts
Center-rear belt . . . . .NA
Pretensioners, front/rear . . . . .NA/NA

Air bags
Occupant-sensing system . . . .
Side bags, front/rear . . . . .No/NA
Inflatable curtain . . . . .Not available
Accident alert system . . . . .Available

Crash tests
Gov't front-crash test, driver/front passenger . . . .NA/NA
Gov't side-crash test, driver/rear passenger . . . . . .NA/NA
IIHS offset crash test . . . . .NA
IIHS side crash test w/ side & curtain airbags . . . . .NA
IIHS side crash test w/o side & curtain airbags . . . . .NA

ANOTHER LOOK

RELIABILITY HISTORY

TROUBLE SPOTS	97 98 99 00 01 02 03 04
Engine	
Cooling	**NO**
Fuel	
Ignition	
Transmission	**DATA**
Electrical	
Air conditioning	**NEW**
Suspension	
Brakes	**MODEL**
Exhaust	
Paint/trim/rust	
Body integrity	
Power equipment	
Body hardware	
RELIABILITY VERDICT	

Pontiac Torrent

THE TORRENT LINE
Body style:
4-door SUV
Trim lines:
–
Base price range:
$22,000-$26,000E

The Torrent is Pontiac's rebadged version of the Chevrolet Equinox. Both use an extended version of the Saturn Vue platform. In our tests of the Equinox we found the rear seat to be quite roomy. It can can move fore and aft to increase passenger or cargo room. However, the quality of the interior materials is subpar and the 3.4-liter, 185-hp V6 powerplant is an old-tech engine that lacks refinement and returns poor fuel economy. The ride was OK, but handling was clumsy and the turning circle wide. Wind noise was pronounced. A tip-up in the government rollover test is another negative.

REPORT CARD

New	**Predicted reliability**
New	**Owner satisfaction**
NA	**Predicted depreciation**
NA	**Accident avoidance**
NA	**Acceleration**
NA	**Ride**
NA	**Front seat comfort**
NA	**Fuel economy**

SPECIFICATIONS

Drive wheels Front or AWD

Seating 2 front, 3 rear

Engines available
3.4-liter V6 (185 hp)

Transmissions available
5-speed automatic

Fuel
Fuel type . . . . .Regular
EPA city/highway, mpg 19/25
Fuel refill capacity, gal. 16.7

Dimensions and weight
Length, in. 189
Width, in. 71
Wheelbase, in. .113
Curb weight, lb. 3,845
Percent weight, front/rear 56/44
Typical towing ability, lb. 3,500

SAFETY INFORMATION

Active safety features
Antilock brakes . . . . .Optional
Traction control . . . . .Optional
Stability control .Not available
Daytime running lights . . . . .Standard
Tire pressure monitor . . . . .Available

Safety belts
Center-rear belt 3-point
Pretensioners, front/rear . . . . .Yes/no

Air bags
Occupant-sensing system . . . .
Side bags, front/rear .No/no
Inflatable curtain . . . . .Optional
Accident alert system .Available

Crash tests
Gov't front-crash test, driver/front passenger . . . .NA/NA
Gov't side-crash test, driver/rear passenger . . . . . . .NA/NA
IIHS offset crash test . . . . .NA
IIHS side crash test w/ side & curtain airbags . . . . .NA
IIHS side crash test w/o side & curtain airbags . . . . .NA

ANOTHER LOOK

RELIABILITY HISTORY

TROUBLE SPOTS	97 98 99 00 01 02 03 04
Engine	
Cooling	
Fuel	**NO**
Ignition	
Transmission	**DATA**
Electrical	
Air conditioning	**NEW**
Suspension	
Brakes	**MODEL**
Exhaust	
Paint/trim/rust	
Body integrity	
Power equipment	
Body hardware	
RELIABILITY VERDICT	

Pontiac Vibe

CR RECOMMENDED ✓

The Vibe is a tall, small wagon. It is a twin of the Toyota Matrix, and both are based on the Toyota Corolla. The 1.8-liter four-cylinder drones loudly and performs modestly. GT models use a 170-hp version and come only with a manual. Handling is fairly nimble, and the ride is compliant if a little jittery. Access is very easy, and the rear seat is quite roomy. The driving position is only so-so. The optional AWD system works well but hurts acceleration and fuel economy. Folding the rear seats creates a large, flat load floor. This is a sensible alternative to a small SUV. Stability control is optional for 2005.

THE VIBE LINE
Body style:
wagon
Trim lines:
Base, GT
Base price range:
$17,130–$20,455

REPORT CARD

⊖	Predicted reliability
○	Owner satisfaction
NA	Predicted depreciation
○	Accident avoidance
⊖	Acceleration
○	Ride
⊖	Front seat comfort
⊖	Fuel economy

SPECIFICATIONS

Drive wheels Front or AWD

Seating 2 front, 3 rear

Engines available
1.8-liter 4 (123 hp); 1.8-liter 4 (130 hp); 1.8-liter 4 (170 hp)

Transmissions available
5-speed manual; 6-speed manual; 4-speed automatic

Fuel
Fuel type . . . . .Regular or premium
EPA city/highway, mpg 29/34
Fuel refill capacity, gal. 13.2

Dimensions and weight
Length, in. 172
Width, in. 70
Wheelbase, in. 102
Curb weight, lb. 2,805
Percent weight, front/rear 59/41
Typical towing ability, lb. 1,500

SAFETY INFORMATION

Active safety features
Antilock brakes . . . . .Standard (optional on Base)
Traction control . . . . .Included with stability
Stability control . . . . .Optional
Daytime running lights .Standard
Tire pressure monitor .Available

Safety belts
Center-rear belt 3-point
Pretensioners, front/rear . . . . .Yes/no

Air bags
Occupant-sensing system . . . . .Not available
Side bags, front/rear . . . . .Optional/no
Inflatable curtain . . . . .Not available
Accident alert system . . . . .Not available

Crash tests
Gov't front-crash test, driver/front passenger . . . .◉/⊖
Gov't side-crash test, driver/rear passenger . . . .○/⊖
IIHS offset crash test . . . . .NA
IIHS side crash test w/ side & curtain airbags . . . . .NA
IIHS side crash test w/o side & curtain airbags . . . . .NA

FROM THE TEST TRACK

Tested model
2003 Base wagon, 1.8-liter Four, 4-speed automatic

Tires as tested
Goodyear Eagle RSA, size P205/55R16 89H

Acceleration . . . . ⊖
0-30 mph, sec. 4.1
0-60 mph, sec. 11.2
Quarter mile, sec. 18.5
Quarter mile, mph 76
45-65 mph, sec. 6.7

Other findings
Transmission . . . .◉
Turning circle, ft. 39
Ground clearance, in. 5.0

Braking and handling
Braking . . . . ⊖
Braking, dry pavement, ft. 139
Routine handling . . . . ⊖
Emergency handling . . . . ○
Avoidance maneuver, max. mph . . .51.0

Convenience and comfort
Ride . . . . ○
Noise . . . . ○
Driving position . . . . ○
Access . . . . ◉
Controls and displays . . . . ◉
Fit and finish . . . . ⊖
Door top to ground, in. 55.0
Cargo area . . . . ⊖
Cargo volume, cu.ft. 25.0
Max. load, lb. 860

Seating
Front-seat comfort . . . . ⊖
Front shoulder room, in. 53.0
Front leg room, in. 41.5
Front head room, in. 6.0
Rear-seat comfort . . . . ⊖
Rear shoulder room, in. 52.0
Rear leg room, in. 28.5
Rear head room, in 5.5

Fuel economy . . . . ⊖
CU's overall mileage, mpg 26
 CU's city/highway, mpg . . .18/36
 CU's 150-mile trip, mpg 32
Annual fuel . . . . .570 gal./$1,140
Cruising range 380

RELIABILITY HISTORY

TROUBLE SPOTS	Pontiac Vibe							
	97	98	99	00	01	02	03	04
Engine							◉	◉
Cooling							◉	◉
Fuel							◉	◉
Ignition							◉	◉
Transmission							◉	◉
Electrical							⊖	◉
Air conditioning							◉	◉
Suspension							◉	⊖
Brakes							◉	◉
Exhaust							◉	◉
Paint/trim/rust							⊖	⊖
Body integrity							○	⊖
Power equipment							◉	◉
Body hardware							⊖	⊖
RELIABILITY VERDICT							✓	✓

Porsche Boxster

THE BOXSTER LINE
Body style:
convertible
Trim lines:
Base, S
Base price range:
$43,800-$53,100

The Boxster's agile handling is fun and forgiving, with precise, communicative steering and excellent tire grip. Braking is top-notch, and the ride is firm and well-controlled yet not punishing. The horizontally opposed boxer engine is mated to a crisp-shifting, five-speed manual transmission in the standard Boxster or a six-speed in the S. Throttle response is sharp, and the unique engine sound is invigorating. The two fore-and-aft trunks are both small. The power top is easy to operate. The 2005 redesign brings more power, a nicer interior, and subtle exterior styling changes.

REPORT CARD

New	**Predicted reliability**
●	**Owner satisfaction**
New	**Predicted depreciation**
NA	**Accident avoidance**
NA	**Acceleration**
NA	**Ride**
NA	**Front seat comfort**
NA	**Fuel economy**

SPECIFICATIONS

Drive wheels Rear

Seating 2 front

Engines available
2.7-liter 6 (240 hp); 3.2-liter 6 (280 hp)

Transmissions available
5-speed manual; 6-speed manual; 5-speed automatic

Fuel
Fuel type .... Premium
EPA city/highway, mpg 20/29
Fuel refill capacity, gal. 16.9

Dimensions and weight
Length, in. 172
Width, in. 70
Wheelbase, in. 95
Curb weight, lb. 2,960
Percent weight, front/rear 47/53
Typical towing ability, lb. .... NR

SAFETY INFORMATION

Active safety features
Antilock brakes .... Standard
Traction control .... Optional
Stability control .... Standard
Daytime running lights .... Not available
Tire pressure monitor .... Not available

Safety belts
Center-rear belt .... NA
Pretensioners, front/rear .... Yes/NA

Air bags
Occupant-sensing system .... Not available
Side bags, front/rear .... Standard/NA
Inflatable curtain .... Optional
Accident alert system .... Not available

Crash tests
Gov't front-crash test, driver/front passenger ..... NA/NA
Gov't side-crash test, driver/rear passenger .... NA/NA
IIHS offset crash test .... NA
IIHS side crash test w/ side & curtain airbags .... NA
IIHS side crash test w/o side & curtain airbags .... NA

ANOTHER LOOK

RELIABILITY HISTORY

TROUBLE SPOTS	97 98 99 00 01 02 03 04
Engine	
Cooling	NO
Fuel	
Ignition	
Transmission	DATA
Electrical	
Air conditioning	NEW
Suspension	
Brakes	MODEL
Exhaust	
Paint/trim/rust	
Body integrity	
Power equipment	
Body hardware	
RELIABILITY VERDICT	

Porsche Cayenne

THE CAYENNE LINE
Body style:
4-door SUV
Trim lines:
Base, S, Turbo
Base price range:
$41,100-$109,200

The Cayenne is a luxury midsized, unibody SUV. Developed with the Volkswagen Touareg, it comes with a choice of a Porsche V8 engine or a Volkswagen-based V6. Low-range gearing and advanced electronics promise some off-road capability. The powerful V8 of the Turbo grows to 500 hp with the Technique package. The S and Turbo are very fast but lack the trademark agility of a Porsche. Some controls are overly complicated. Like the Range Rover, the Turbo has an automatically adjustable ride height. Poor first-year reliability is a disappointment.

REPORT CARD

●	Predicted reliability
⊖	Owner satisfaction
NA	Predicted depreciation
NA	Accident avoidance
NA	Acceleration
NA	Ride
NA	Front seat comfort
NA	Fuel economy

SPECIFICATIONS

Drive wheels AWD

Seating 2 front, 3 rear

Engines available
3.2-liter V6 (247 hp); 4.5-liter V8 (340 hp); 4.5-liter V8 twin-turbo (450 hp); 4.5-liter V8 twin-turbo (500 hp)

Transmissions available
6-speed manual; 6-speed automatic

Fuel
Fuel type ....Premium
EPA city/highway, mpg 14/18
Fuel refill capacity, gal. 26.2

Dimensions and weight
Length, in. 188
Width, in. 76
Wheelbase, in. 112
Curb weight, lb. 4,950
Percent weight, front/rear ....NA
Typical towing ability, lb. 7,700

SAFETY INFORMATION

Active safety features
Antilock brakes ....Standard
Traction control ....Standard
Stability control ....Standard
Daytime running lights ....Not available
Tire pressure monitor ....Not available

Safety belts
Center-rear belt 3-point
Pretensioners, front/rear ....Yes/yes

Air bags
Occupant-sensing system ....Not available
Side bags, front/rear ....Standard/standard
Inflatable curtain ....Standard
Accident alert system ....Not available

Crash tests
Gov't front-crash test, driver/front passenger ......NA/NA
Gov't side-crash test, driver/rear passenger ....NA/NA
IIHS offset crash test ....NA
IIHS side crash test w/ side & curtain airbags ....NA
IIHS side crash test w/o side & curtain airbags ....NA

ANOTHER LOOK

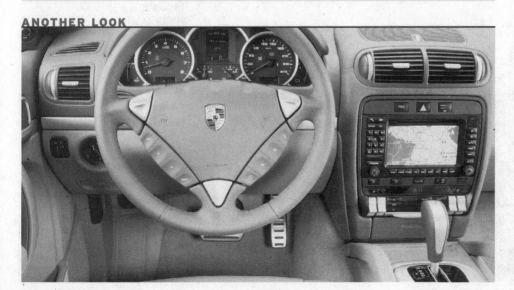

RELIABILITY HISTORY

TROUBLE SPOTS	Porsche Cayenne							
	97	98	99	00	01	02	03	04
Engine								●
Cooling								●
Fuel								●
Ignition								●
Transmission								●
Electrical								○
Air conditioning								●
Suspension								●
Brakes								●
Exhaust								●
Paint/trim/rust								●
Body integrity								⊖
Power equipment							⊖	
Body hardware								○
RELIABILITY VERDICT								✗

Insufficient data

Saab 9-2X

THE 9-2X LINE
Body style:
wagon
Trim lines:
Linear, Aero
Base price range:
$22,990-$26,950

The 9-2X is a thinly disguised Subaru Impreza wagon. All-wheel drive is standard, and power comes from the Subaru's standard 2.5-liter, 165-hp four-cylinder, which is just adequate. The strong 2.0-liter, 227-hp turbocharged four-cylinder from the WRX comes in the Aero trim line. Handling is quite agile, and the ride is supple. This peculiar crossbreeding is a result of GM owning Saab and partly owning Subaru.

REPORT CARD

New	Predicted reliability
New	Owner satisfaction
NA	Predicted depreciation
NA	Accident avoidance
NA	Acceleration
NA	Ride
NA	Front seat comfort
NA	Fuel economy

SPECIFICATIONS

Drive wheels AWD

Seating 2 front, 3 rear

Engines available
2.5-liter 4 (165 hp); 2.0-liter 4 turbo (227 hp)

Transmissions available
5-speed manual; 4-speed automatic

Fuel
Fuel type . . . . .Regular or premium
EPA city/highway, mpg 22/29
Fuel refill capacity, gal. 15.9

Dimensions and weight
Length, in. 176
Width, in. 67
Wheelbase, in. 99
Curb weight, lb. 3,110
Percent weight, front/rear 56/44
Typical towing ability, lb. 2,000

SAFETY INFORMATION

Active safety features
Antilock brakes . . . . .Standard
Traction control . . . . .Not available
Stability control . . . . .Not available
Daytime running lights . . . . .Standard
Tire pressure monitor . . . . .Not available

Safety belts
Center-rear belt 3-point
Pretensioners, front/rear . . . . .Yes/no

Air bags
Occupant-sensing system . . . . .Not available
Side bags, front/rear . . . . .Standard/no
Inflatable curtain . . . . .Not available
Accident alert system . . . . .Available

Crash tests
Gov't front-crash test, driver/front passenger . . . . . .NA/NA
Gov't side-crash test, driver/rear passenger . . . . .NA/NA
IIHS offset crash test . . . . .NA
IIHS side crash test w/ side & curtain airbags . . . . .NA
IIHS side crash test w/o side & curtain airbags . . . . .NA

ANOTHER LOOK

RELIABILITY HISTORY

TROUBLE SPOTS	97 98 99 00 01 02 03 04
Engine	
Cooling	NO
Fuel	
Ignition	
Transmission	DATA
Electrical	
Air conditioning	NEW
Suspension	
Brakes	MODEL
Exhaust	
Paint/trim/rust	
Body integrity	
Power equipment	
Body hardware	
RELIABILITY VERDICT	

Saab 9-3

The 9-3 is a huge improvement over its predecessor, but it doesn't match up to the class best. Handling is sporty, capable, and enjoyable. Braking performance was exceptionally good. A stiff ride transmits each road flaw to the passengers, especially in the Aero model we tested with 17-inch performance tires. A lot of road rumble further detracted from comfort. The 210-hp, turbocharged engine delivers relatively quick performance but lacks the low-end punch of competitive V6s. The front seats are well-sculpted. Rear seat room is tight. Reliability has dropped to well below average.

THE 9-3 LINE
Body style: convertible; sedan
Trim lines: Linear, Arc, Aero
Base price range: $26,850-$42,600

REPORT CARD

●	Predicted reliability
○	Owner satisfaction
○	Predicted depreciation
◉	Accident avoidance
⊖	Acceleration
◒	Ride
⊖	Front seat comfort
○	Fuel economy

SPECIFICATIONS

Drive wheels Front

Seating 2 front, 3 rear

Engines available
2.0-liter 4 turbo (175 hp); 2.0-liter 4 turbo (210 hp)

Transmissions available
5-speed manual; 6-speed manual; 5-speed automatic

Fuel
Fuel type . . . . .Premium
EPA city/highway, mpg 22/30
Fuel refill capacity, gal. 16.3

Dimensions and weight
Length, in. 182
Width, in. 68
Wheelbase, in. .105
Curb weight, lb. 3,420
Percent weight, front/rear 60/40
Typical towing ability, lb. 880

SAFETY INFORMATION

Active safety features
Antilock brakes . . . . .Standard
Traction control . . . . .Standard
Stability control . . . . .Standard
Daytime running lights . . . . .Standard
Tire pressure monitor . . . . .Available

Safety belts
Center-rear belt 3-point
Pretensioners, front/rear . . . . .Yes/no

Air bags
Occupant-sensing system . . . . .Front
Side bags, front/rear . . . . .Standard/no
Inflatable curtain . . . . .Standard
Accident alert system .Available

Crash tests
Gov't front-crash test, driver/front passenger . . . . . .NA/NA
Gov't side-crash test, driver/rear passenger . . . . . . .NA/NA
IIHS offset crash test . . . . .Good
IIHS side crash test w/ side & curtain airbags . . . . .Good
IIHS side crash test w/o side & curtain airbags . . . . .NA

FROM THE TEST TRACK

Tested model
2003 Vector sedan, 2.0-liter Four turbo, 5-speed automatic

Tires as tested
Pirelli P Zero Rosso, size 225/45R17 94W

Acceleration . . . . ⊖
0-30 mph, sec. 3.3
0-60 mph, sec. 8.1
Quarter mile, sec. 16.4
Quarter mile, mph 89
45-65 mph, sec. 5.2

Other findings
Transmission . . . . ◒
Turning circle, ft. 37
Ground clearance, in. 4.0

Braking and handling
Braking . . . . ◉
Braking, dry pavement, ft. 120
Routine handling . . . . ◒
Emergency handling . . . . ◒
Avoidance maneuver, max. mph . . .56.0

Convenience and comfort
Ride . . . . ◒
Noise . . . . ○
Driving position . . . . ○
Access . . . . ○
Controls and displays . . . . ◒
Fit and finish . . . . ◒
Door top to ground, in. 50.0
Trunk . . . . ○
Luggage capacity . . . . .4+1
Max. load, lb. 920

Seating
Front-seat comfort . . . . ⊖
Front shoulder room, in. 55.0
Front leg room, in. 41.0
Front head room, in. 3.0
Rear-seat comfort . . . . ○
Rear shoulder room, in. 54.5
Rear leg room, in. 25.5
Rear head room, in 2.5

Fuel economy . . . . ○
CU's overall mileage, mpg 21
CU's city/highway, mpg 14/32
CU's 150-mile trip, mpg 25
Annual fuel . . . . .715 gal./$1,570
Cruising range 380

RELIABILITY HISTORY

TROUBLE SPOTS	97	98	99	00	01	02	03	04
Engine			⊖	○	○	●	○	●
Cooling			◒	◒	●	●	◒	◒
Fuel			◒	◒	○	●	◒	●
Ignition			◒	○	○	●	●	●
Transmission			●	●	●	◒	◒	●
Electrical			◒	◒	◒	○	◒	●
Air conditioning			◒	●	●	○	◒	●
Suspension			●	○	●	●	◒	◒
Brakes			○	●	●	◒	○	○
Exhaust			○	◒	◒	◒	●	◒
Paint/trim/rust			○	○	○	◒	●	◒
Body integrity			○	○	○	○	●	●
Power equipment			◒	○	●	◒	◒	○
Body hardware			○	○	○	◒	●	●
RELIABILITY VERDICT			-	-	-	-	✗	✗

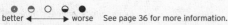

Saab 9-5

CR RECOMMENDED ✓

THE 9-5 LINE
Body style:
sedan; wagon
Trim lines:
Linear, Arc, Aero
Base price range:
$32,550-$40,750

The Saab 9-5 is a good car but has received only a few updates since its 1998 introduction. Handling is sound and secure, but not very agile. The ride is stiff and buoyant. The cabin is relatively noisy for a car in this class. The 220-hp, turbocharged four-cylinder in our tested Arc model provides spirited performance but sounds coarse and unrefined. The front seats are comfortable, and the rear is quite roomy. The wagon is competent and well-rounded but doesn't offer a third-row seat or all-wheel drive, unlike the Volvo V70. Excellent crash-test results are a plus.

REPORT CARD

◒	Predicted reliability
○	Owner satisfaction
○	Predicted depreciation
◒	Accident avoidance
◒	Acceleration
○	Ride
◒	Front seat comfort
○	Fuel economy

SPECIFICATIONS

Drive wheels Front

Seating 2 front, 3 rear

Engines available
2.3-liter 4 turbo (185 hp); 2.3-liter 4 turbo (220 hp); 2.3-liter 4 turbo (250 hp)

Transmissions available
5-speed manual; 5-speed automatic

Fuel
Fuel type . . . . .Premium
EPA city/highway, mpg 19/28
Fuel refill capacity, gal. 18.5

Dimensions and weight
Length, in. 190
Width, in. 71
Wheelbase, in. .106
Curb weight, lb. 3,540
Percent weight, front/rear 62/38
Typical towing ability, lb. 3,500

SAFETY INFORMATION

Active safety features
Antilock brakes . . . . .Standard
Traction control . . . . .Standard
Stability control . . . . .Standard
Daytime running lights . . . . .Standard
Tire pressure monitor . . . . .Not available

Safety belts
Center-rear belt 3-point
Pretensioners, front/rear . . . . .Yes/no

Air bags
Occupant-sensing system . . . . .Not available
Side bags, front/rear . . . . .Standard/no
Inflatable curtain . . . . .Not available
Accident alert system . . . . .Available

Crash tests
Gov't front-crash test, driver/front passenger . . . . . .◑/◑
Gov't side-crash test, driver/rear passenger . . . .◑/◑
IIHS offset crash test . . . . .Good
IIHS side crash test w/ side & curtain airbags . . .Acceptable
IIHS side crash test w/o side & curtain airbags . . . . . . .NA

FROM THE TEST TRACK

Tested model
2004 Arc sedan, 2.3-liter Four turbo, 5-speed automatic

Tires as tested
Pirelli P6 Four Seasons, size 215/55R16 93V

Acceleration . . . . ◒
0-30 mph, sec. 2.9
0-60 mph, sec. 7.4
Quarter mile, sec. 15.8
Quarter mile, mph 92
45-65 mph, sec. 5.3

Other findings
Transmission . . . .◒
Turning circle, ft. 39
Ground clearance, in. 6.0

Braking and handling
Braking . . . .◒
Braking, dry pavement, ft. 133
Routine handling . . . .◒
Emergency handling . . . . ○
Avoidance maneuver, max. mph . . .52.0

Convenience and comfort
Ride . . . . ○
Noise . . . . ○
Driving position . . . . ○
Access . . . . ○
Controls and displays . . . . ◒
Fit and finish . . . . ○
Door top to ground, in. 51.5
Trunk . . . . ◒
Luggage capacity . . . . .4+1
Max. load, lb. 930

Seating
Front-seat comfort . . . . ◒
Front shoulder room, in. 57.0
Front leg room, in. 41.5
Front head room, in. 3.5
Rear-seat comfort . . . . ◒
Rear shoulder room, in. 56.0
Rear leg room, in. 28.5
Rear head room, in 3.0

Fuel economy . . . . ○
CU's overall mileage, mpg 21
CU's city/highway, mpg 14/33
CU's 150-mile trip, mpg 26
Annual fuel . . . . .715 gal./$1,570
Cruising range 450

RELIABILITY HISTORY

TROUBLE SPOTS	Saab 9-5							
	97	98	99	00	01	02	03	04
Engine			●	○	○	◒	◒	●
Cooling			◒	●	◒	◒	◒	●
Fuel			○	○	◒	◒	●	●
Ignition			○	○	○	◒	◒	●
Transmission			◒	◒	◒	◒	◒	●
Electrical			●	●	●	○	◒	●
Air conditioning			○	○	◒	◒	◒	●
Suspension			○	◒	○	◒	◒	●
Brakes			○	○	◒	◒	◒	●
Exhaust			◒	◒	●	●	◒	●
Paint/trim/rust			◒	◒	◒	◒	◒	●
Body integrity			◒	◒	◒	◒	◒	●
Power equipment			○	○	○	◒	◒	●
Body hardware			◒	◒	◒	◒	◒	●
RELIABILITY VERDICT		✗	–	–	–	–	–	✓

Expert • Independent • Nonprofit

Saab 9-7X

THE 9-7X LINE
Body style:
4-door SUV
Trim lines:
Linear, Arc
Base price range:
$38,270-$40,270

The Saab 9-7X is Saab's first SUV, but it is really just a Chevrolet TrailBlazer with upgraded interior and exterior appointments. It even has a traditional Saab ignition key on the center console. The suspension is calibrated differently from the TrailBlazer. The all-wheel-drive system is permanent and lacks a low range. The 9-7X is also the first "Saab" to have a V8. Reliability of the TrailBlazer has been poor, and the off-set crash-test results of the Chevrolet are unimpressive.

REPORT CARD

New	Predicted reliability
New	Owner satisfaction
NA	Predicted depreciation
NA	Accident avoidance
NA	Acceleration
NA	Ride
NA	Front seat comfort
NA	Fuel economy

SPECIFICATIONS

Drive wheels AWD

Seating 2 front, 3 rear

Engines available
4.2-liter 6 (275 hp); 5.3-liter V8 (300 hp)

Transmissions available
4-speed automatic

Fuel
Fuel type .... Regular
EPA city/highway, mpg 15/21
Fuel refill capacity, gal. 22.0

Dimensions and weight
Length, in. .... .193
Width, in. .... .75
Wheelbase, in. .... .113
Curb weight, lb. 4,610
Percent weight, front/rear 53/47
Typical towing ability, lb. 6,500

SAFETY INFORMATION

Active safety features
Antilock brakes .... Standard
Traction control .... Not available
Stability control .... Not available
Daytime running lights .... Standard
Tire pressure monitor .... Not available

Safety belts
Center-rear belt 3-point
Pretensioners, front/rear .... Yes/no

Air bags
Occupant-sensing system .... Front
Side bags, front/rear .... No/no
Inflatable curtain .... Standard
Accident alert system .... Available

Crash tests
Gov't front-crash test, driver/front passenger ..... ◯/◖
Gov't side-crash test, driver/rear passenger .... NA/NA
IIHS offset crash test .... NA
IIHS side crash test w/ side & curtain airbags .... NA
IIHS side crash test w/o side & curtain airbags .... NA

ANOTHER LOOK

RELIABILITY HISTORY

TROUBLE SPOTS	97	98	99	00	01	02	03	04
Engine								
Cooling			**NO**					
Fuel								
Ignition								
Transmission			**DATA**					
Electrical								
Air conditioning			**NEW**					
Suspension								
Brakes			**MODEL**					
Exhaust								
Paint/trim/rust								
Body integrity								
Power equipment								
Body hardware								
RELIABILITY VERDICT								

● ● ◯ ◖ ●
better ◄——► worse   See page 36 for more information.

Saturn Ion

THE ION LINE

Body style:
coupe; sedan

Trim lines:
1, 2, 3, Red Line

Base price range:
$11,430-$20,885

The Ion is Saturn's disappointing small car. It comes as either a sedan or four-door coupe. The sedan has an acceptable ride and capable handling except for its inconsistent steering. The noisy, 2.2-liter, 4-cylinder engine returned less-than-exceptional fuel economy but acceleration is adequate. The interior is cramped, with uncomfortable seats, ill-fitting pieces, and cheap-feeling materials. The hard-to-read gauges are located in the center of the dash, which requires taking your eyes off the road frequently. Reliability has dropped below average. The Ion received a Poor rating in the IIHS side-impact-crash test.

REPORT CARD

◗	Predicted reliability
●	Owner satisfaction
NA	Predicted depreciation
○	Accident avoidance
○	Acceleration
○	Ride
○	Front seat comfort
◗	Fuel economy

SPECIFICATIONS

Drive wheels Front

Seating 2 front, 3 rear

Engines available
2.2-liter 4 (140 hp); 2.0-liter 4 supercharged (205 hp)

Transmissions available
5-speed manual; 4-speed automatic

Fuel
Fuel type . . . . .Regular or premium
EPA city/highway, mpg 24/32
Fuel refill capacity, gal. 13.5

Dimensions and weight
Length, in. 185
Width, in. 67
Wheelbase, in. 103
Curb weight, lb. 2,865
Percent weight, front/rear 61/39
Typical towing ability, lb. 1,000

SAFETY INFORMATION

Active safety features
Antilock brakes . . . . .Optional (std. on Red Line)
Traction control . . . . .Optional (NA on Red Line)
Stability control . . . . .Not available
Daytime running lights . . . . .Standard
Tire pressure monitor . . . . .Not available

Safety belts
Center-rear belt 3-point
Pretensioners, front/rear . . . . .Yes/no

Air bags
Occupant-sensing system . . . . .Not available
Side bags, front/rear . . . . .No/no
Inflatable curtain . . . . .Optional
Accident alert system . . . . .Available

Crash tests
Gov't front-crash test, driver/front passenger . . . . . . ●/●
Gov't side-crash test, driver/rear passenger . . . .○/◗
IIHS offset crash test . . . . .Acceptable
IIHS side crash test w/ side & curtain airbags . . . . . . .Poor
IIHS side crash test w/o side & curtain airbags . . . . . . .Poor

FROM THE TEST TRACK

Tested model
2005 3 sedan, 2.2-liter Four, 4-speed automatic

Tires as tested
Firestone Firehawk GTA 03, size P205/55R16 89H

Acceleration . . . . ○
0-30 mph, sec. 3.3
0-60 mph, sec. 9.2
Quarter mile, sec. 19.9
Quarter mile, mph 81
45-65 mph, sec. 5.4

Other findings
Transmission . . . . ◗
Turning circle, ft. 37
Ground clearance, in. 5.0

Braking and handling
Braking . . . . ◗
Braking, dry pavement, ft. 130
Routine handling . . . . ◗
Emergency handling . . . . ○
Avoidance maneuver, max. mph . . .51.5

Convenience and comfort
Ride . . . . ○
Noise . . . . ○
Driving position . . . . ○
Access . . . . ○
Controls and displays . . . . ○
Fit and finish . . . . ◗
Door top to ground, in. 51.5
Trunk . . . . ○
Luggage capacity . . . . .3+2
Max. load, lb. 900

Seating
Front-seat comfort . . . . ○
Front shoulder room, in. 54.0
Front leg room, in. 40.0
Front head room, in. 5.5
Rear-seat comfort . . . . ◗
Rear shoulder room, in. 52.5
Rear leg room, in. 25.5
Rear head room, in 1.0

Fuel economy . . . . ◗
CU's overall mileage, mpg 25
  CU's city/highway, mpg 17/35
  CU's 150-mile trip, mpg 30
Annual fuel . . . . .600 gal./$1,195
Cruising range 375

RELIABILITY HISTORY

TROUBLE SPOTS	Saturn Ion							
	97	98	99	00	01	02	03	04
Engine							●	●
Cooling							●	●
Fuel							◗	●
Ignition							●	●
Transmission							◗	◗
Electrical							○	◗
Air conditioning							◗	●
Suspension							●	●
Brakes							◗	◗
Exhaust							●	●
Paint/trim/rust							●	●
Body integrity							◗	●
Power equipment							◗	●
Body hardware							○	◗
RELIABILITY VERDICT							✗	−

Expert • Independent • Nonprofit

Saturn Relay

THE RELAY LINE
Body style: minivan
Trim lines: 2, 3
Base price range: $23,770-$29,855

Saturn's first minivan, the 2005 Relay, is a freshened version of a family of GM minivans that have been in production for eight years. As with the Buick Terraza, Chevrolet Uplander, and Pontiac Montana SV6, the Relay is powered by a coarse 3.5-liter, 200-hp V6 engine. The ride is stiff and noisy, handling is reluctant, and fit and finish is insubstantial. The second-row seats can be folded and removed, but they are heavy. The folding third-row seat folds flat on the floor, rather than into a well under the floor. Despite the new nameplate, this is basically an outdated and uncompetitive minivan.

REPORT CARD

New	**Predicted reliability**
New	**Owner satisfaction**
NA	**Predicted depreciation**
○	**Accident avoidance**
○	**Acceleration**
○	**Ride**
○	**Front seat comfort**
●	**Fuel economy**

SPECIFICATIONS

Drive wheels Front or AWD

Seating 2 front, 2 rear, 3 third

Engines available
3.5-liter V6 (200 hp)

Transmissions available
4-speed automatic

Fuel

Fuel type	Regular
EPA city/highway, mpg	18/24
Fuel refill capacity, gal.	25.0

Dimensions and weight

Length, in.	205
Width, in.	72
Wheelbase, in.	121
Curb weight, lb.	4,380
Percent weight, front/rear	56/44
Typical towing ability, lb.	3,500

SAFETY INFORMATION

Active safety features

Antilock brakes	Standard
Traction control	Optional on FWD
Stability control	Optional on FWD
Daytime running lights	Standard
Tire pressure monitor	Not available

Safety belts

Center-rear belt	3-point
Pretensioners, front/rear	Yes/no

Air bags

Occupant-sensing system	Front
Side bags, front/rear	Optional/no
Inflatable curtain	Not available
Accident alert system	Available

Crash tests

Gov't front-crash test, driver/front passenger	◉/◉
Gov't side-crash test, driver/rear passenger	◓/◉
IIHS offset crash test	NA
IIHS side crash test w/ side & curtain airbags	NA
IIHS side crash test w/o side & curtain airbags	NA

RELIABILITY HISTORY

TROUBLE SPOTS	97 98 99 00 01 02 03 04
Engine	NO DATA NEW MODEL
Cooling	
Fuel	
Ignition	
Transmission	
Electrical	
Air conditioning	
Suspension	
Brakes	
Exhaust	
Paint/trim/rust	
Body integrity	
Power equipment	
Body hardware	
RELIABILITY VERDICT	

FROM THE TEST TRACK

Tested model
2005 3 minivan, 3.5-liter V6, 4-speed automatic

Tires as tested
Goodyear Integrity, size P225/60R17 98S

Acceleration	○
0-30 mph, sec.	3.6
0-60 mph, sec.	10.2
Quarter mile, sec.	17.7
Quarter mile, mph	80
45-65 mph, sec.	7.0

Other findings

Transmission	◓
Turning circle, ft.	43
Ground clearance, in.	6.0

Braking and handling

Braking	◓
Braking, dry pavement, ft.	136
Routine handling	○
Emergency handling	◒
Avoidance maneuver, max. mph	48.5

Convenience and comfort

Ride	○
Noise	○
Driving position	○
Access	◉
Controls and displays	◓
Fit and finish	○
Door top to ground, in.	62.0
Cargo area	◓
Cargo volume, cu.ft.	75.5
Max. load, lb.	1,290

Seating

Front-seat comfort	○
Front shoulder room, in.	59.5
Front leg room, in.	40.5
Front head room, in.	5.0
Rear-seat comfort	◓
Rear shoulder room, in.	62.0
Rear leg room, in.	26.0
Rear head room, in	4.0
Third-seat comfort	○
Third shoulder room,in	60.0
Third leg room, in.	28.0
Third head room, in	3.5

Fuel economy	●
CU's overall mileage, mpg	17
CU's city/highway, mpg	12/25
CU's 150-mile trip, mpg	21
Annual fuel	860 gal./$1,720
Cruising range	510

◉ ◓ ○ ◒ ●
better ◄——► worse See page 36 for more information.

Saturn Vue

THE VUE LINE
Body style:
4-door SUV
Trim lines:
4, V6, Red Line
Base price range:
$17,055-$26,625

Saturn's first SUV has a unibody platform offering a low step-in height, four-wheel independent suspension, and an acceptable ride. Handling is secure, but the steering is too light at low speeds. We found the AWD system slow to respond; the front wheels spun noticeably before the rear wheels engaged. The 3.0-liter V6 has been replaced by a smooth, powerful 3.5-liter from Honda. Interior fit and finish is subpar, the front seats lack support, and the rear bench is too low. The Vue received a rating of Poor in the IIHS side-impact-crash test, and a tip-up in government rollover tests is cause for concern.

REPORT CARD

●	Predicted reliability
○	Owner satisfaction
◒	Predicted depreciation
○	Accident avoidance
◒	Acceleration
○	Ride
◒	Front seat comfort
◒	Fuel economy

SPECIFICATIONS

Drive wheels Front or AWD

Seating 2 front, 3 rear

Engines available
2.2-liter 4 (143 hp); 3.5-liter V6 (250 hp)

Transmissions available
5-speed manual; CVT; 4-speed automatic; 5-speed automatic

Fuel
Fuel type . . . . .Regular
EPA city/highway, mpg 19/25
Fuel refill capacity, gal. 16.5

Dimensions and weight
Length, in. 181
Width, in. 72
Wheelbase, in. 107
Curb weight, lb. 3,740
Percent weight, front/rear 58/42
Typical towing ability, lb. 3,500

SAFETY INFORMATION

Active safety features
Antilock brakes . . . . .Optional
Traction control .Optional on 2WD
Stability control . . . . .Not available
Daytime running lights .Standard
Tire pressure monitor . . . . .Not available

Safety belts
Center-rear belt 3-point
Pretensioners, front/rear . . . . .Yes/no

Air bags
Occupant-sensing system . . . . .Not available
Side bags, front/rear . . . . .No/no
Inflatable curtain . . . . .Optional
Accident alert system . . . . .Available

Crash tests
Gov't front-crash test, driver/front passenger . . . . . ◒/◒
Gov't side-crash test, driver/rear passenger . . . . . . ◒/◒
IIHS offset crash test . . . . .Good
IIHS side crash test w/ side & curtain airbags . . . . .NA
IIHS side crash test w/o side & curtain airbags . . . . . . .Poor

FROM THE TEST TRACK

Tested model
2004 V6 4-door SUV AWD, 3.5-liter V6, 5-speed automatic

Tires as tested
Bridgestone Dueler H/T 684 II, size P235/60R17 100S

Acceleration . . . . ◒
0-30 mph, sec. 3.2
0-60 mph, sec. 7.9
Quarter mile, sec. 16.3
Quarter mile, mph 87
45-65 mph, sec. 5.1

Other findings
Transmission . . . . ●
Turning circle, ft. 42
Ground clearance, in. 6.5

Braking and handling
Braking . . . . ◒
Braking, dry pavement, ft. 135
Routine handling . . . . ○
Emergency handling . . . . ◒
Avoidance maneuver, max. mph . . .49.0

Convenience and comfort
Ride . . . . ○
Noise . . . . ○
Driving position . . . . ◒
Access . . . . ◒
Controls and displays . . . . ◒
Fit and finish . . . . ◒
Door top to ground, in. 60.5
Cargo area . . . . ○
Cargo volume, cu.ft. 36.5
Max. load, lb. 1,175

Seating
Front-seat comfort . . . . ◒
Front shoulder room, in. 56.0
Front leg room, in. 42.0
Front head room, in. 6.0
Rear-seat comfort . . . . ○
Rear shoulder room, in. 56.0
Rear leg room, in. 28.5
Rear head room, in 6.0

Fuel economy . . . . ◒
CU's overall mileage, mpg 19
CU's city/highway, mpg 12/27
CU's 150-mile trip, mpg 23
Annual fuel . . . . .810 gal./$1,615
Cruising range 345

RELIABILITY HISTORY

TROUBLE SPOTS	Saturn Vue							
	97	98	99	00	01	02	03	04
Engine						○	●	●
Cooling						○	●	●
Fuel						○	●	●
Ignition						●	●	●
Transmission						◒	●	●
Electrical						○	◒	●
Air conditioning						●	●	●
Suspension						○	○	●
Brakes						◒	●	●
Exhaust						●	●	●
Paint/trim/rust						●	●	●
Body integrity					◒	○	○	●
Power equipment					◒	◒	●	●
Body hardware					○	◒	●	●
RELIABILITY VERDICT						✗	✗	✗

Scion tC

THE TC LINE
Body style:
coupe
Trim lines:
–

Base price range:
$16,000

Scion is a new brand from Toyota, aimed at young buyers. The tC is a small coupe that joins the xA and xB as the third Scion model. The tC is powered by a spirited 160-hp, 2.4-liter four-cylinder engine, with the choice of a slick five-speed manual or four-speed automatic. The tC is based on the Toyota Avensis family sedan sold overseas. Fit and finish is impressive. As in the xA and aB, the radio is unintuitive. A dealer-installed supercharger increases power to 200 hp. The 60/40-split rear seats fold to enlarge cargo room, and the seat-backs can recline for passenger comfort.

REPORT CARD

New	Predicted reliability
New	Owner satisfaction
NA	Predicted depreciation
NA	Accident avoidance
NA	Acceleration
NA	Ride
NA	Front seat comfort
NA	Fuel economy

SPECIFICATIONS

Drive wheels Front

Seating 2 front, 3 rear

Engines available
2.4-liter 4 (160 hp); 2.4-liter 4 supercharged (200 hp)

Transmissions available
5-speed manual; 4-speed automatic

Fuel
Fuel type . . . . Regular or premium
EPA city/highway, mpg 22/29
Fuel refill capacity, gal. 14.5

Dimensions and weight
Length, in. 174
Width, in. 69
Wheelbase, in. 106
Curb weight, lb. 2,890
Percent weight, front/rear 60/40
Typical towing ability, lb. . . . . .NR

SAFETY INFORMATION

Active safety features
Antilock brakes . . . . .Standard
Traction control . . . . .Not available
Stability control .Not available
Daytime running lights . . . . .Not available
Tire pressure monitor . . . . .Not available

Safety belts
Center-rear belt 3-point
Pretensioners, front/rear . . . . .Yes/no

Air bags
Occupant-sensing system . . . . .Not available
Side bags, front/rear . . . . .Optional/no
Inflatable curtain . . . . .Optional
Accident alert system . . . . .Not available

Crash tests
Gov't front-crash test, driver/front passenger . . . . . ◐◖
Gov't side-crash test, driver/rear passenger . . . .◐◖
IIHS offset crash test . . . . .NA
IIHS side crash test w/ side & curtain airbags . . . . .NA
IIHS side crash test w/o side & curtain airbags . . . . .NA

ANOTHER LOOK

RELIABILITY HISTORY

TROUBLE SPOTS	97 98 99 00 01 02 03 04
Engine	
Cooling	**NO**
Fuel	
Ignition	
Transmission	**DATA**
Electrical	
Air conditioning	**NEW**
Suspension	
Brakes	**MODEL**
Exhaust	
Paint/trim/rust	
Body integrity	
Power equipment	
Body hardware	
RELIABILITY VERDICT	

better ●◐○◖● worse   See page 36 for more information.

Scion xA

THE XA LINE
Body style:
4-door hatchback
Trim lines:
–
Base price range:
$12,530

The xA is a small hatchback powered by a 108-hp, 1.5-liter four-cylinder engine that it shares with the Scion xB and Toyota Echo. While the rear hatchback provides cargo-carrying versatility, the xA lacks the xB's spacious interior. Drivers sit high and upright, with good visibility. The firm and supportive seats are well contoured, with good side bolsters. Handling is fairly nimble and stability control is optional. The stiff, choppy ride is very uncomfortable. Acceleration is so-so and the engine is buzzy, but the xA is affordable and gets good mileage. The cargo area is small.

REPORT CARD

⊕	**Predicted reliability**
NA	**Owner satisfaction**
NA	**Predicted depreciation**
⊖	**Accident avoidance**
⊖	**Acceleration**
●	**Ride**
⊖	**Front seat comfort**
⊖	**Fuel economy**

SPECIFICATIONS

Drive wheels Front

Seating 2 front, 3 rear

Engines available
1.5-liter 4 (108 hp)

Transmissions available
5-speed manual; 4-speed automatic

Fuel
Fuel type . . . . Regular
EPA city/highway, mpg 32/38
Fuel refill capacity, gal. 11.9

Dimensions and weight
Length, in. 154
Width, in. 67
Wheelbase, in. 93
Curb weight, lb. 2,400
Percent weight, front/rear 60/40
Typical towing ability, lb. . . . . .NR

SAFETY INFORMATION

Active safety features
Antilock brakes . . . . .Standard
Traction control . . . . .Included with stability
Stability control . . . . .Optional (with RS 1.0 package)
Daytime running lights . . . . .Not available
Tire pressure monitor . . . . .Not available

Safety belts
Center-rear belt 3-point
Pretensioners, front/rear . . . . .Yes/no

Air bags
Occupant-sensing system . . . . .Not available
Side bags, front/rear . . . . .Optional/no
Inflatable curtain . . . . .Optional
Accident alert system .Not available

Crash tests
Gov't front-crash test, driver/front passenger . . . . . ⊖/⊖
Gov't side-crash test, driver/rear passenger . . . .⊖/⊖
IIHS offset crash test . . . . .NA
IIHS side crash test w/ side & curtain airbags . . . . .NA
IIHS side crash test w/o side & curtain airbags . . . . .NA

FROM THE TEST TRACK

Tested model
2004 4-door hatchback, 1.5-liter Four, 4-speed automatic

Tires as tested
Goodyear Eagle LS, size P185/60R15 84T
Acceleration . . . . ⊖
0-30 mph, sec. 4.0
0-60 mph, sec. 11.1
Quarter mile, sec. 18.6
Quarter mile, mph 75
45-65 mph, sec. 7.3

Other findings
Transmission . . . . ⊖
Turning circle, ft. 38
Ground clearance, in. 5.5

Braking and handling
Braking . . . . ⊖
Braking, dry pavement, ft. 135
Routine handling . . . . ⊖
Emergency handling . . . . ○
Avoidance maneuver, max. mph . . .52.0

Convenience and comfort
Ride . . . . ●
Noise . . . . ○
Driving position . . . . ○
Access . . . . ⊖
Controls and displays . . . . ○
Fit and finish . . . . ⊖
Door top to ground, in. 55.0
Trunk . . . . ●
Luggage capacity . . . . .1+2
Max. load, lb. 825

Seating
Front-seat comfort . . . . ⊖
Front shoulder room, in. 52.0
Front leg room, in. 39.5
Front head room, in. 4.5
Rear-seat comfort . . . . ○
Rear shoulder room, in. 50.5
Rear leg room, in. 26.0
Rear head room, in 2.5

Fuel economy
CU's overall mileage, mpg 30
CU's city/highway, mpg 20/40
CU's 150-mile trip, mpg 37
Annual fuel . . . . .505 gal./$1,010
Cruising range 410

RELIABILITY HISTORY

TROUBLE SPOTS	97	98	99	00	01	02	03	04
Engine								
Cooling								
Fuel			NOT					
Ignition								
Transmission			ENOUGH					
Electrical								
Air conditioning			DATA					
Suspension								
Brakes			TO					
Exhaust								
Paint/trim/rust			RATE					
Body integrity								
Power equipment								
Body hardware								
RELIABILITY VERDICT								

Scion xB

CR RECOMMENDED ✓

THE XB LINE
Body style:
wagon
Trim lines:
–
Base price range:
$13,730

The cube-like xB is a brilliant concept in space efficiency, and offers an exceptionally roomy interior. Rear-seat room compares favorably with large sedans. The low floor and high roof make access very easy. Antilock brakes and stability control are standard. Handling is fairly nimble. Good visibility and compact dimensions make the xB a great city car. The 108-hp, 1.5-liter four-cylinder engine delivers poky performance but respectable fuel economy. High levels of wind and engine noise; the stiff, choppy ride; and hard-to-work radio controls make the xB fatiguing on a long drive.

REPORT CARD

◐	Predicted reliability
◐	Owner satisfaction
NA	Predicted depreciation
⊖	Accident avoidance
◒	Acceleration
●	Ride
⊖	Front seat comfort
⊖	Fuel economy

SPECIFICATIONS

Drive wheels Front

Seating 2 front, 3 rear

Engines available
1.5-liter 4 (108 hp)

Transmissions available
5-speed manual; 4-speed automatic

Fuel
Fuel type . . . . .Regular
EPA city/highway, mpg 30/34
Fuel refill capacity, gal. 11.9

Dimensions and weight
Length, in. 155
Width, in. 67
Wheelbase, in. 98
Curb weight, lb. 2,485
Percent weight, front/rear 59/41
Typical towing ability, lb. . . . . .NR

SAFETY INFORMATION

Active safety features
Antilock brakes . . . . .Standard
Traction control . . . . .Standard
Stability control . . . . .Standard
Daytime running lights . . . . .Not available
Tire pressure monitor . . . . .Not available

Safety belts
Center-rear belt 3-point
Pretensioners, front/rear . . . . .Yes/no

Air bags
Occupant-sensing system . . . . .Not available
Side bags, front/rear . . . . .No/no
Inflatable curtain . . . . .Not available
Accident alert system . . . . .Not available

Crash tests
Gov't front-crash test, driver/front passenger . . . . . .NA/NA
Gov't side-crash test, driver/rear passenger . . . . .NA/NA
IIHS offset crash test . . . . .NA
IIHS side crash test w/ side & curtain airbags . . . . .NA
IIHS side crash test w/o side & curtain airbags . . . . . . .NA

FROM THE TEST TRACK

Tested model
2004 wagon, 1.5-liter Four, 4-speed automatic

Tires as tested
Goodyear Eagle LS, size P185/60R15 84T

Acceleration . . . . ◒
0-30 mph, sec. 4.0
0-60 mph, sec. 11.4
Quarter mile, sec. 18.7
Quarter mile, mph 74
45-65 mph, sec. 7.3

Other findings
Transmission . . . . ◒
Turning circle, ft. 40
Ground clearance, in. 6.0

Braking and handling
Braking . . . . ⊖
Braking, dry pavement, ft. 134
Routine handling . . . . ⊖
Emergency handling . . . . ○
Avoidance maneuver, max. mph . . .51.5

Convenience and comfort
Ride . . . . ●
Noise . . . . ○
Driving position . . . . ⊖
Access . . . . ◒
Controls and displays . . . . ○
Fit and finish . . . . ⊖
Door top to ground, in. 57.5
Cargo area . . . . ○
Cargo volume, cu.ft. 33.5
Max. load, lb. 825

Seating
Front-seat comfort . . . . ⊖
Front shoulder room, in. 52.5
Front leg room, in. 40.5
Front head room, in. 6.0
Rear-seat comfort . . . . ◒
Rear shoulder room, in. 52.0
Rear leg room, in. 31.0
Rear head room, in 6.5

Fuel economy . . . . ⊖
CU's overall mileage, mpg 30
 CU's city/highway, mpg 23/37
 CU's 150-mile trip, mpg 35
Annual fuel . . . . .500 gal./$1,000
Cruising range 385

RELIABILITY HISTORY

TROUBLE SPOTS	Scion xB							
	97	98	99	00	01	02	03	04
Engine								◉
Cooling								◉
Fuel								◉
Ignition								◉
Transmission								◉
Electrical								◉
Air conditioning								◉
Suspension								◉
Brakes								◉
Exhaust								◉
Paint/trim/rust								◉
Body integrity								◒
Power equipment								◉
Body hardware								◒
RELIABILITY VERDICT								✓

● ◒ ○ ⊖ ●
better ◄——————► worse   See page 36 for more information.

Subaru B9 Tribeca

THE B9 TRIBECA LINE
Body style:
4-door SUV
Trim lines:
Base, Limited
Base price range:
$30,695-$33,895

Loosely based on the Legacy/Outback platform, this car-based SUV is Subaru's first that is not a raised wagon. It competes directly with the Honda Pilot and Toyota Highlander. A five-passenger model and a seven-passenger one are available. The latter comes with a 50/50-split third-row seat. The Tribeca, which goes on sale in May, will come standard with a 250-hp, 3.0-liter horizontally opposed six-cylinder engine; head-protection air bags; electronic stability control; and all-wheel drive. A rear DVD entertainment system and navigation system will be optional.

REPORT CARD

New	Predicted reliability
New	Owner satisfaction
NA	Predicted depreciation
NA	Accident avoidance
NA	Acceleration
NA	Ride
NA	Front seat comfort
NA	Fuel economy

SPECIFICATIONS

Drive wheels AWD

Seating 2 front, 3 rear, 2 third

Engines available
3.0-liter 6 (250 hp)

Transmissions available
5-speed automatic

Fuel
Fuel type . . . . .Premium
EPA city/highway, mpg . . . . .NA
Fuel refill capacity, gal. 16.9

Dimensions and weight
Length, in. 190
Width, in. 74
Wheelbase, in. .108
Curb weight, lb. 4,245
Percent weight, front/rear . . . . .NA
Typical towing ability, lb. 3,500

SAFETY INFORMATION

Active safety features
Antilock brakes . . . . .Standard
Traction control . . . . .Standard
Stability control . . . . .Standard
Daytime running lights . . . . .Standard
Tire pressure monitor . . . . .Available

Safety belts
Center-rear belt 3-point
Pretensioners, front/rear . . . . .Yes/no

Air bags
Occupant-sensing system . . . . .Front
Side bags, front/rear . . . . .Standard/no
Inflatable curtain . . . . .Standard
Accident alert system . . . . .Available

Crash tests
Gov't front-crash test, driver/front passenger . . . . . .NA/NA
Gov't side-crash test, driver/rear passenger . . . . .NA/NA
IIHS offset crash test . . . . .NA
IIHS side crash test w/ side & curtain airbags . . . . .NA
IIHS side crash test w/o side & curtain airbags . . . . .NA

ANOTHER LOOK

RELIABILITY HISTORY

TROUBLE SPOTS	97 98 99 00 01 02 03 04
Engine	
Cooling	
Fuel	**NO**
Ignition	
Transmission	**DATA**
Electrical	
Air conditioning	**NEW**
Suspension	
Brakes	**MODEL**
Exhaust	
Paint/trim/rust	
Body integrity	
Power equipment	
Body hardware	
RELIABILITY VERDICT	

Expert • Independent • Nonprofit

Subaru Baja

CR RECOMMENDED ✓

THE BAJA LINE
Body style:
crew cab
Trim lines:
Sport, Turbo
Base price range:
$22,195-$24,195

The Baja is a car-based pickup truck, sort of a successor to the old Brat. The Baja is a Legacy from the cabin forward and a pickup truck aft of the rear seats. It can accommodate only four people, limiting its family appeal. The rear seats fold down, exposing a pass-through to the open cargo bed. Like the Legacy, it rides comfortably and feels agile with precise steering. Acceleration is not brisk with the standard engine. A 210-hp turbocharged model is also available. Reliability has improved to above average.

REPORT CARD

⊖	Predicted reliability
⊖	Owner satisfaction
NA	Predicted depreciation
⊖	Accident avoidance
○	Acceleration
○	Ride
◉	Front seat comfort
⊖	Fuel economy

SPECIFICATIONS

Drive wheels AWD

Seating 2 front, 2 rear

Engines available
2.5-liter 4 (165 hp); 2.5-liter 4 turbo (210 hp)

Transmissions available
5-speed manual; 4-speed automatic

Fuel
Fuel type . . . . .Regular or premium
EPA city/highway, mpg 21/28
Fuel refill capacity, gal. 16.9

Dimensions and weight
Length, in. 193
Width, in. 70
Wheelbase, in. 104
Curb weight, lb. 3,575
Percent weight, front/rear 54/46
Typical towing ability, lb. 2,400

SAFETY INFORMATION

Active safety features
Antilock brakes . . . . .Standard
Traction control . . . . .Not available
Stability control . . . . .Not available
Daytime running lights . . . . .Standard
Tire pressure monitor . . . . .Not available

Safety belts
Center-rear belt . . . . .NA
Pretensioners, front/rear . . . . .Yes/no

Air bags
Occupant-sensing system . . . . .Not available
Side bags, front/rear . . . . .No/no
Inflatable curtain . . . . .Not available
Accident alert system . . . . .Not available

Crash tests
Gov't front-crash test, driver/front passenger . . . . .NA/NA
Gov't side-crash test, driver/rear passenger . . . . . . .NA/NA
IIHS offset crash test . . . . .NA
IIHS side crash test w/ side & curtain airbags . . . . .NA
IIHS side crash test w/o side & curtain airbags . . . . .NA

FROM THE TEST TRACK

Tested model
2003 Base crew cab AWD, 2.5-liter Four, 4-speed automatic

Tires as tested
Bridgestone Potenza, size P225/60R16 97H

Acceleration . . . . ○
0-30 mph, sec. 3.5
0-60 mph, sec. 10.7
Quarter mile, sec. 18.2
Quarter mile, mph 76
45-65 mph, sec. 7.1

Other findings
Transmission . . . . ⊖
Turning circle, ft. 41
Ground clearance, in. 6.0

Braking and handling
Braking . . . . ⊖
Braking, dry pavement, ft. 138
Routine handling . . . . ⊖
Emergency handling . . . . ○
Avoidance maneuver, max. mph . . .50.5

Convenience and comfort
Ride . . . . ○
Noise . . . . ⊖
Driving position . . . . ⊖
Access . . . . ⊖
Controls and displays . . . . ◉
Fit and finish . . . . ⊖
Door top to ground, in. 53.5
Cargo area . . . . ⊖
Max. load, lb. 800

Seating
Front-seat comfort . . . . ◉
Front shoulder room, in. 54.0
Front leg room, in. 41.0
Front head room, in. 2.5
Rear-seat comfort . . . . ○
Rear shoulder room, in. 53.5
Rear leg room, in. 27.0
Rear head room, in 1.5

Fuel economy . . . . ⊖
CU's overall mileage, mpg 20
CU's city/highway, mpg 14/28
CU's 150-mile trip, mpg 24
Annual fuel . . . . . . .745 gal./$1,485
Cruising range 380

RELIABILITY HISTORY

TROUBLE SPOTS	Subaru Baja
	97 98 99 00 01 02 03 04
Engine	◉
Cooling	◉
Fuel	◉
Ignition	◉
Transmission	◉
Electrical	⊖
Air conditioning	◉
Suspension	◉
Brakes	⊖
Exhaust	◉
Paint/trim/rust	◉
Body integrity	○
Power equipment	◉
Body hardware	◉
RELIABILITY VERDICT	✓

(Insufficient data)

◉ ⊖ ○ ⊖ ⊖
better ◄——► worse   See page 36 for more information.

Subaru Forester

CR RECOMMENDED ✓

THE FORESTER LINE
Body style:
4-door SUV
Trim lines:
2.5 X, 2.5 XS, 2.5 XT,
2.5 XS L.L. Bean
Base price range:
$21,295-$26,395

The Forester is our Top Pick in the small SUV class. This car-based SUV/wagon rides compliantly and handles well, with good steering feel. Braking is very good. The engine provides adequate acceleration, and the optional automatic transmission shifts responsively. Standard all-wheel drive helps in slippery road conditions and in moderate off-road driving. The front seats are firm and well-shaped, and the rear has been improved slightly. The square cargo space is very usable. The 2.5 X is an excellent value at around $22,000. Crash-test results are impressive. A 210-hp turbo model is available.

REPORT CARD

◉	Predicted reliability
◉	Owner satisfaction
⊖	Predicted depreciation
⊖	Accident avoidance
○	Acceleration
⊖	Ride
⊖	Front seat comfort
○	Fuel economy

SPECIFICATIONS

Drive wheels AWD

Seating 2 front, 3 rear

Engines available
2.5-liter 4 (165 hp); 2.5-liter 4 turbo (210 hp)

Transmissions available
5-speed manual; 4-speed automatic

Fuel
Fuel type . . . . Regular or premium
EPA city/highway, mpg 22/28
Fuel refill capacity, gal. 15.9

Dimensions and weight
Length, in. 175
Width, in. 68
Wheelbase, in. 99
Curb weight, lb. 3,215
Percent weight, front/rear 56/44
Typical towing ability, lb. 2,000

SAFETY INFORMATION

Active safety features
Antilock brakes . . . . .Standard
Traction control . . . . .Not available
Stability control . . . . .Not available
Daytime running lights .Standard
Tire pressure monitor . . . . .Not available

Safety belts
Center-rear belt 3-point
Pretensioners, front/rear . . . . .Yes/no

Air bags
Occupant-sensing system . . . . .Not available
Side bags, front/rear . . . . .Standard/no
Inflatable curtain . . . . .Not available
Accident alert system . . . . .Not available

Crash tests
Gov't front-crash test, driver/front passenger . . . . . . ◉/◉
Gov't side-crash test, driver/rear passenger . . . . ◉/◉
IIHS offset crash test . . . . .Good
IIHS side crash test w/ side & curtain airbags . . . . .Good
IIHS side crash test w/o side & curtain airbags . . . . .NA

FROM THE TEST TRACK

Tested model
2003 2.5 X 4-door SUV AWD, 2.5-liter
Four, 4-speed automatic

Tires as tested
Yokohama Geolandar G900,
size P215/60R16 94H

Acceleration . . . . ○
0-30 mph, sec. 3.2
0-60 mph, sec. 9.7
Quarter mile, sec. 17.6
Quarter mile, mph 78
45-65 mph, sec. 6.6

Other findings
Transmission . . . . ⊖
Turning circle, ft. 38
Ground clearance, in. 5.5

Braking and handling
Braking . . . . ⊖
Braking, dry pavement, ft. 137
Routine handling . . . . ⊖
Emergency handling . . . . ○
Avoidance maneuver, max. mph . . .50.5

Convenience and comfort
Ride . . . . ⊖
Noise . . . . ⊖
Driving position . . . . ⊖
Access . . . . ⊖
Controls and displays . . . . ◉
Fit and finish . . . . ⊖
Door top to ground, in. 55.5
Cargo area . . . . ○
Cargo volume, cu.ft. 35.5
Max. load, lb. 900

Seating
Front-seat comfort . . . . ⊖
Front shoulder room, in. 53.5
Front leg room, in. 42.0
Front head room, in. 5.0
Rear-seat comfort . . . . ⊖
Rear shoulder room, in. 53.5
Rear leg room, in. 28.0
Rear head room, in 5.0

Fuel economy . . . . ○
CU's overall mileage, mpg 21
CU's city/highway, mpg 15/28
CU's 150-mile trip, mpg 25
Annual fuel . . . . .705 gal./$1,410
Cruising range 370

RELIABILITY HISTORY

TROUBLE SPOTS	Subaru Forester							
	97	98	99	00	01	02	03	04
Engine	⊖	⊖	◉	◉	◉	◉	◉	◉
Cooling	◉	○	◉	◉	◉	◉	◉	◉
Fuel	◉	◉	○	◉	○	◉	◉	◉
Ignition	◉	⊖	◉	◉	◉	◉	◉	◉
Transmission	◉	○	◉	◉	◉	◉	◉	◉
Electrical	○	○	◉	◉	◉	◉	◉	◉
Air conditioning	◉	◉	◉	◉	◉	◉	◉	◉
Suspension	◉	◉	◉	◉	◉	◉	◉	◉
Brakes	○	○	◉	◉	◉	◉	◉	◉
Exhaust	⊖	◉	◉	◉	◉	◉	◉	◉
Paint/trim/rust	◉	⊖	◉	◉	◉	◉	◉	◉
Body integrity	◉	⊖	◉	◉	◉	◉	◉	◉
Power equipment	◉	◉	◉	◉	◉	◉	◉	◉
Body hardware	◉	◉	◉	◉	◉	◉	◉	◉
RELIABILITY VERDICT	−	−	−	✓	✓	✓	✓	✓

Expert • Independent • Nonprofit

Subaru Impreza

CR RECOMMENDED ✓

The Impreza serves up a supple ride and well-balanced handling, particularly the Top Pick WRX/WRX STi. The WRX's turbocharged 227-hp engine provides quick and effortless acceleration, especially at mid-rpm, and its well-tuned suspension offers agility with a compliant ride. The RS sedan, wagon, and Outback Sport make do with a 2.5-liter, 165-hp engine. The wagon's cargo volume is small. The Outback Sport rides stiffly and doesn't handle as well as other Imprezas. A score of Good in an IIHS offset-crash test is a plus. The ferociously quick 300-hp WRX STi is a performance bargain.

THE IMPREZA LINE
Body style:
sedan; wagon
Trim lines:
2.5 RS, Outback Sport, WRX, WRX STi
Base price range:
$18,095-$32,295

REPORT CARD

⊖	Predicted reliability
◉	Owner satisfaction
⊖	Predicted depreciation
◉	Accident avoidance
◉	Acceleration
⊖	Ride
⊖	Front seat comfort
⊖	Fuel economy

SPECIFICATIONS

Drive wheels AWD

Seating 2 front, 3 rear

Engines available
2.5-liter 4 (165 hp); 2.0-liter 4 turbo (227 hp); 2.5-liter 4 turbo (300 hp)

Transmissions available
5-speed manual; 6-speed manual; 4-speed automatic

Fuel
Fuel type . . . . .Regular or premium
EPA city/highway, mpg 18/24
Fuel refill capacity, gal. 15.9

Dimensions and weight
Length, in. 174
Width, in. 69
Wheelbase, in. 100
Curb weight, lb. 3,290
Percent weight, front/rear 58/42
Typical towing ability, lb. 2,000

SAFETY INFORMATION

Active safety features
Antilock brakes . . . . .Standard
Traction control . . . . .Not available
Stability control . . . . .Not available
Daytime running lights . . . . .Standard
Tire pressure monitor . . . . .Not available

Safety belts
Center-rear belt 3-point
Pretensioners, front/rear . . . . .Yes/no

Air bags
Occupant-sensing system . . . . .Not available
Side bags, front/rear . . . . .Optional/no
Inflatable curtain . . . . .Not available
Accident alert system . . . . .Not available

Crash tests
Gov't front-crash test, driver/front passenger . . . . . ⊖/◉
Gov't side-crash test, driver/rear passenger . . . . . . .NA/NA
IIHS offset crash test . . . . .Good
IIHS side crash test w/ side & curtain airbags . . . . .NA
IIHS side crash test w/o side & curtain airbags . . . . .NA

FROM THE TEST TRACK

Tested model
2004 WRX STi sedan AWD, 2.5-liter Four turbo, 6-speed manual

Tires as tested
Bridgestone Potenza RE070, size 225/45R17 90W

Acceleration . . . . ◉
0-30 mph, sec. 1.6
0-60 mph, sec. 5.2
Quarter mile, sec. 13.6
Quarter mile, mph 100
45-65 mph, sec. 3.1

Other findings
Transmission . . . . ⊖
Turning circle, ft. 40
Ground clearance, in. 5.0

Braking and handling
Braking . . . . ◉
Braking, dry pavement, ft. 123
Routine handling . . . . ◉
Emergency handling . . . . ◉
Avoidance maneuver, max. mph . . .54.0

Convenience and comfort
Ride . . . . ⊖
Noise . . . . ⊖
Driving position . . . . ⊖
Access . . . . ⊖
Controls and displays . . . . ◉
Fit and finish . . . . ⊖
Door top to ground, in. 50.5
Trunk . . . . ⊖
Luggage capacity . . . . .2+2
Max. load, lb. 830

Seating
Front-seat comfort . . . . ⊖
Front shoulder room, in. 52.5
Front leg room, in. 40.5
Front head room, in. 5.0
Rear-seat comfort . . . . ○
Rear shoulder room, in. 52.0
Rear leg room, in. 26.5
Rear head room, in 1.5

Fuel economy . . . . ⊖
CU's overall mileage, mpg 20
  CU's city/highway, mpg 15/26
  CU's 150-mile trip, mpg 22
Annual fuel . . . . .760 gal./$1,670
Cruising range 315

RELIABILITY HISTORY

TROUBLE SPOTS	Subaru Impreza Turbo							
	97	98	99	00	01	02	03	04
Engine						◉	◉	◉
Cooling						◉	◉	◉
Fuel						⊖	◉	◉
Ignition						◉	◉	◉
Transmission						⊖	◉	◉
Electrical						⊖	◉	◉
Air conditioning						◉	◉	◉
Suspension						◉	◉	◉
Brakes						⊖	◉	◉
Exhaust						◉	◉	◉
Paint/trim/rust						⊖	⊖	◉
Body integrity						○	⊖	◉
Power equipment						⊖	⊖	◉
Body hardware						⊖	◉	◉
RELIABILITY VERDICT						-	✓	✓

Subaru Legacy/Outback

RECOMMENDED ✓

The Legacy is a versatile, good-performing car with nimble routine handling. Steering feel and response are precise and communicative, and the ride is supple. Acceleration is a bit pokey with the standard 2.5i automatic. The GT and Outback XT are quick with the 250-hp turbocharged engine, but fuel economy suffers. Interior quality has been significantly upgraded. The GT is stimulating to drive, but at its handling limits it tends to slide its tail without much advance notice. Stability control is only available in the Outback 3.0 VDC. The Outback is a good SUV alternative.

THE LEGACY LINE
Body style:
sedan; wagon
Trim lines:
2.5i, 2.5i Limited, 2.5 GT, 2.5 GT Limited
Base price range:
$21,295-$29,795

REPORT CARD

⊖	Predicted reliability
⊖	Owner satisfaction
NA	Predicted depreciation
⊖	Accident avoidance
⊖	Acceleration
⊖	Ride
⊖	Front seat comfort
⊝	Fuel economy

SPECIFICATIONS

Drive wheels AWD

Seating 2 front, 3 rear

Engines available
2.5-liter 4 (168 hp); 2.5-liter 4 turbo (250 hp)

Transmissions available
5-speed manual; 4-speed automatic; 5-speed automatic

Fuel
Fuel type . . . . .Regular or premium
EPA city/highway, mpg 19/25
Fuel refill capacity, gal. 16.9

Dimensions and weight
Length, in. 186
Width, in. 68
Wheelbase, in. 105
Curb weight, lb. 3,540
Percent weight, front/rear 57/43
Typical towing ability, lb. 2,700

SAFETY INFORMATION

Active safety features
Antilock brakes . . . . .Standard
Traction control . . . . .Not available
Stability control . . . . .Not available
Daytime running lights . . . . .Standard
Tire pressure monitor . . . . .Not available

Safety belts
Center-rear belt 3-point
Pretensioners, front/rear . . . . .Yes/no

Air bags
Occupant-sensing system . . . . .Front
Side bags, front/rear . . . . .Standard/no
Inflatable curtain . . . . .Standard
Accident alert system .Available

Crash tests
Gov't front-crash test, driver/front passenger . . . . . .◑/◑
Gov't side-crash test, driver/rear passenger . . . .◑/◑
IIHS offset crash test . . . . .Good
IIHS side crash test w/ side & curtain airbags . . . .Marginal
IIHS side crash test w/o side & curtain airbags . . . . .NA

FROM THE TEST TRACK

Tested model
2005 2.5 GT Limited sedan AWD, 2.5-liter Four turbo, 5-speed automatic

Tires as tested
Bridgestone Potenza RE92, size 215/45ZR17

Acceleration . . . . ⊖
0-30 mph, sec. 3.1
0-60 mph, sec. 7.5
Quarter mile, sec. 16.0
Quarter mile, mph 90
45-65 mph, sec. 5.0

Other findings
Transmission . . . . ●
Turning circle, ft. 38
Ground clearance, in. 4.5

Braking and handling
Braking . . . . ⊖
Braking, dry pavement, ft. 140
Routine handling . . . . ●
Emergency handling . . . . ○
Avoidance maneuver, max. mph . . .51.5

Convenience and comfort
Ride . . . . ⊖
Noise . . . . ⊖
Driving position . . . . ⊖
Access . . . . ⊖
Controls and displays . . . . ●
Fit and finish . . . . ⊖
Door top to ground, in. 50.5
Trunk . . . . ○
Luggage capacity . . . . .3+2
Max. load, lb. 850

Seating
Front-seat comfort . . . . ⊖
Front shoulder room, in. 54.0
Front leg room, in. 41.0
Front head room, in. 2.5
Rear-seat comfort . . . . ⊖
Rear shoulder room, in. 53.0
Rear leg room, in. 28.0
Rear head room, in 2.0

Fuel economy . . . . ⊝
CU's overall mileage, mpg 18
CU's city/highway, mpg 11/27
CU's 150-mile trip, mpg 22
Annual fuel . . . . .855 gal./$1,880
Cruising range 340

RELIABILITY HISTORY

TROUBLE SPOTS	Subaru Legacy/Outback							
	97	98	99	00	01	02	03	04
Engine	◑	◑	○	◑	◑	◑	◑	◑
Cooling	◑	◑	◑	●	◑	●	●	●
Fuel	◑	◑	◑	●	◑	●	●	●
Ignition	●	◑	◑	●	●	●	●	●
Transmission	◑	●	●	●	●	●	●	◑
Electrical	◑	○	○	◑	◑	◑	◑	●
Air conditioning	◑	◑	●	●	●	●	◑	●
Suspension	●	◑	◑	●	◑	●	●	●
Brakes	◑	○	○	◑	◑	○	◑	◑
Exhaust	◑	●	●	●	●	●	●	●
Paint/trim/rust	◑	●	●	●	●	●	●	●
Body integrity	◑	◑	○	○	◑	○	◑	◑
Power equipment	◑	◑	◑	●	●	●	◑	●
Body hardware	◑	◑	◑	●	●	●	◑	●
RELIABILITY VERDICT	✓	✓	✓	–	–	✓	✓	

Suzuki Aerio

The Aerio replaced the unimpressive Esteem and the small Swift. It's available in sedan and four-door wagon/hatchback versions. The 2.0-liter four-cylinder was not particularly spirited or economical. It was upgraded to a 2.3-liter for '04. The ride is very stiff and uncomfortable. Handling is secure but not nimble. Like the Toyota Echo, the Aerio features a tall roofline that increases head room, offers easy access, and improves outward visibility. The digital instrument display, reminiscent of the early 1980s, has been replaced for 2005. The Aerio received a Poor rating in the IIHS side-impact-crash test.

THE AERIO LINE

Body style:
sedan; wagon
Trim lines:
S, LX, SX
Base price range:
$13,449-$17,249

REPORT CARD

○	Predicted reliability
NA	Owner satisfaction
●	Predicted depreciation
○	Accident avoidance
○	Acceleration
◒	Ride
⊖	Front seat comfort
⊖	Fuel economy

SPECIFICATIONS

Drive wheels Front or AWD

Seating 2 front, 3 rear

Engines available
2.3-liter 4 (155 hp)

Transmissions available
5-speed manual; 4-speed automatic

Fuel
Fuel type . . . . .Regular
EPA city/highway, mpg 25/31
Fuel refill capacity, gal. 13.2

Dimensions and weight
Length, in. 171
Width, in. 68
Wheelbase, in. 98
Curb weight, lb. 2,715
Percent weight, front/rear 61/39
Typical towing ability, lb. . . . . .NR

SAFETY INFORMATION

Active safety features
Antilock brakes . . . . .Optional
Traction control . . . . .Not available
Stability control . . . . .Not available
Daytime running lights . . . . .Standard
Tire pressure monitor . . . . .Not available

Safety belts
Center-rear belt 3-point
Pretensioners, front/rear . . . . .Yes/no

Air bags
Occupant-sensing system . . . . .Front
Side bags, front/rear . . . . .Standard/no
Inflatable curtain .Not available
Accident alert system . . . . .Not available

Crash tests
Gov't front-crash test, driver/front passenger . . . . . .NA/NA
Gov't side-crash test, driver/rear passenger . . . . . . .NA/NA
IIHS offset crash test . . . . .Good
IIHS side crash test w/ side & curtain airbags . . . . .Poor
IIHS side crash test w/o side & curtain airbags . . . . .NA

FROM THE TEST TRACK

Tested model
2003 GS sedan, 2.0-liter Four, 4-speed automatic

Tires as tested
Yokohama Geolandar G046, size P195/55R15 84V

Acceleration . . . .○
0-30 mph, sec. 3.5
0-60 mph, sec. 9.8
Quarter mile, sec. 17.5
Quarter mile, mph 81
45-65 mph, sec. 6.0

Other findings
Transmission . . . .◒
Turning circle, ft. 37
Ground clearance, in. 4.0

Braking and handling
Braking . . . .○
Braking, dry pavement, ft. 143
Routine handling . . . .◒
Emergency handling . . . .○
Avoidance maneuver, max. mph . . .51.5

Convenience and comfort
Ride . . . .◒
Noise . . . .○
Driving position . . . .◒
Access . . . .◒
Controls and displays . . . .◒
Fit and finish . . . .○
Door top to ground, in. 54.0
Trunk . . . .○
Luggage capacity . . . . .4+0
Max. load, lb. 895

Seating
Front-seat comfort . . . .◒
Front shoulder room, in. 54.0
Front leg room, in. 40.5
Front head room, in. 6.0
Rear-seat comfort . . . .○
Rear shoulder room, in. 53.0
Rear leg room, in. 28.0
Rear head room, in 2.0

Fuel economy . . . .◒
CU's overall mileage, mpg 25
CU's city/highway, mpg 18/32
CU's 150-mile trip, mpg 29
Annual fuel . . . . .610 gal./$1,220
Cruising range 360

RELIABILITY HISTORY

TROUBLE SPOTS	Suzuki Aerio							
	97	98	99	00	01	02	03	04
Engine							●	
Cooling							●	
Fuel							●	
Ignition							●	
Transmission							●	
Electrical						Insufficient data	●	Insufficient data
Air conditioning							●	
Suspension							●	
Brakes							●	
Exhaust							●	
Paint/trim/rust							○	
Body integrity							○	
Power equipment							●	
Body hardware							○	
RELIABILITY VERDICT							-	

● ◒ ○ ◒ ●
better ◄——► worse   See page 36 for more information.

Suzuki Forenza

This small sedan is called the Chevrolet Optra in Canada. The Forenza's low price may appear tempting, but it does not compete well in its class. The 2.0-liter four-cylinder engine delivers fairly slow acceleration and only so-so fuel economy. The Forenza corners reluctantly and does not inspire confidence when pushed to its limits. The ride is stiff and not well-controlled. Interior fit and finish is relatively good, and the rear seat is relatively roomy. We found it hard to find a Forenza with ABS. The Reno is the new hatchback version. The Forenza received a Poor rating in the IIHS side-crash test.

THE FORENZA LINE
Body style:
4-door hatchback; sedan; wagon
Trim lines:
S, LX, EX, Reno S, Reno LX, Reno EX
Base price range:
$13,449-$17,449

REPORT CARD

NA	**Predicted reliability**
NA	**Owner satisfaction**
NA	**Predicted depreciation**
○	**Accident avoidance**
◒	**Acceleration**
○	**Ride**
◒	**Front seat comfort**
○	**Fuel economy**

SPECIFICATIONS

Drive wheels Front

Seating 2 front, 3 rear

Engines available
2.0-liter 4 (126 hp)

Transmissions available
5-speed manual; 4-speed automatic

Fuel
Fuel type ....Regular
EPA city/highway, mpg 22/30
Fuel refill capacity, gal. 14.5

Dimensions and weight
Length, in. 177
Width, in. 68
Wheelbase, in. 102
Curb weight, lb. 2,840
Percent weight, front/rear 62/38
Typical towing ability, lb. ....NR

SAFETY INFORMATION

Active safety features
Antilock brakes ....Optional
Traction control ....Optional on wagon
Stability control ....Not available
Daytime running lights ....Standard
Tire pressure monitor ....Not available

Safety belts
Center-rear belt 3-point
Pretensioners, front/rear ....Yes/no

Air bags
Occupant-sensing system ....Side
Side bags, front/rear ....Standard/no
Inflatable curtain ....Not available
Accident alert system ....Not available

Crash tests
Gov't front-crash test, driver/front passenger ......NA/NA
Gov't side-crash test, driver/rear passenger ....NA/NA
IIHS offset crash test ....Acceptable
IIHS side crash test w/ side & curtain airbags ....Poor
IIHS side crash test w/o side & curtain airbags ....NA

FROM THE TEST TRACK

Tested model
2004 S sedan, 2.0-liter Four, 4-speed automatic

Tires as tested
Hankook Optimo H420, size P195/55R15 84V

Acceleration ....◒
0-30 mph, sec. 3.8
0-60 mph, sec. 11.3
Quarter mile, sec. 18.4
Quarter mile, mph 76
45-65 mph, sec. 7.2

Other findings
Transmission ....◒
Turning circle, ft. 36
Ground clearance, in. 5.0

Braking and handling
Braking ....○
Braking, dry pavement, ft. 147
Routine handling ....○
Emergency handling ....◒
Avoidance maneuver, max. mph ...49.5

Convenience and comfort
Ride ....○
Noise ....○
Driving position ....◒
Access ....○
Controls and displays ....◒
Fit and finish ....◒
Door top to ground, in. 51.0
Trunk ....○
Luggage capacity ....3+1
Max. load, lb. 875

Seating
Front-seat comfort ....◒
Front shoulder room, in. 55.0
Front leg room, in. 41.5
Front head room, in. 4.5
Rear-seat comfort ....○
Rear shoulder room, in. 53.0
Rear leg room, in. 28.0
Rear head room, in 3.0

Fuel economy ....○
CU's overall mileage, mpg 24
  CU's city/highway, mpg 16/35
  CU's 150-mile trip, mpg 29
Annual fuel ....625 gal./$1,250
Cruising range 385

RELIABILITY HISTORY

TROUBLE SPOTS	97 98 99 00 01 02 03 04
Engine	
Cooling	
Fuel	NOT
Ignition	
Transmission	ENOUGH
Electrical	
Air conditioning	DATA
Suspension	
Brakes	TO
Exhaust	
Paint/trim/rust	RATE
Body integrity	
Power equipment	
Body hardware	
RELIABILITY VERDICT	

Suzuki Grand Vitara/XL-7

CR RECOMMENDED ✓

Suzuki's line of small, truck-based SUVs includes the Grand Vitara and the extended-length XL-7. The 2.5-liter V6 is sluggish, hampered by a crude, unresponsive automatic. The XL-7 has a larger V6 and a five-speed automatic. A small third-row seat allows it to accommodate up to seven passengers in a pinch. The ride is stiff and rubbery. Handling is vague but secure in emergency maneuvers. The part-time four-wheel-drive system can't be used on dry pavement. The XL-7's offset-crash test was good, but the Grand Vitara received a Poor rating in the IIHS side-impact-crash test.

THE GRAND VITARA/XL-7 LINE
Body style:
4-door SUV; extended SUV
Trim lines:
LX, LX III, EX, EX III
Base price range:
$18,399-$27,799

REPORT CARD

○	Predicted reliability
●	Owner satisfaction
◒	Predicted depreciation
○	Accident avoidance
○	Acceleration
○	Ride
◒	Front seat comfort
●	Fuel economy

SPECIFICATIONS

Drive wheels Rear or part-time 4WD

Seating 2 front, 3 rear, 2 third

Engines available
2.5-liter V6 (165 hp); 2.7-liter V6 (185 hp)

Transmissions available
5-speed manual; 4-speed automatic; 5-speed automatic

Fuel
Fuel type . . . . .Regular
EPA city/highway, mpg 17/22
Fuel refill capacity, gal. 16.9

Dimensions and weight
Length, in. 187
Width, in. 70
Wheelbase, in. .110
Curb weight, lb. 3,590
Percent weight, front/rear 58/42
Typical towing ability, lb. 3,000

SAFETY INFORMATION

Active safety features
Antilock brakes . . . . .Optional
Traction control .Not available
Stability control .Not available
Daytime running lights . . . . .Standard
Tire pressure monitor . . . . .Available

Safety belts
Center-rear belt 3-point
Pretensioners, front/rear . . . . .Yes/no

Air bags
Occupant-sensing system . . . . .Not available
Side bags, front/rear . . . . .No/no
Inflatable curtain . . . . .Not available
Accident alert system . . . . .Not available

Crash tests
Gov't front-crash test, driver/front passenger . . . . .◒/○
Gov't side-crash test, driver/rear passenger . . . . . . .NA/NA
IIHS offset crash test . . . . .Good
IIHS side crash test w/ side & curtain airbags . . . . .NA
IIHS side crash test w/o side & curtain airbags . . . . . . .Poor

FROM THE TEST TRACK

Tested model
2002 XL-7 Touring extended SUV 4WD, 2.7-liter V6, 4-speed automatic

Tires as tested
Bridgestone Dueler H/T 687, size P235/60R16 99H

Acceleration . . . .○
0-30 mph, sec. 3.2
0-60 mph, sec. 10.0
Quarter mile, sec. 17.7
Quarter mile, mph 78
45-65 mph, sec. 6.6

Other findings
Transmission . . . .◒
Turning circle, ft. 41
Ground clearance, in. 5.5

Braking and handling
Braking . . . .○
Braking, dry pavement, ft. 145
Routine handling . . . .○
Emergency handling . . . .○
Avoidance maneuver, max. mph . . .52.0

Convenience and comfort
Ride . . . .○
Noise . . . .○
Driving position . . . .◒
Access . . . .◒
Controls and displays . . . .○
Fit and finish . . . .◒
Door top to ground, in. 61.5
Cargo area . . . .○
Cargo volume, cu.ft. 37.5
Max. load, lb. 1,170

Seating
Front-seat comfort . . . .◒
Front shoulder room, in. 52.5
Front leg room, in. 40.0
Front head room, in. 3.0
Rear-seat comfort . . . .○
Rear shoulder room, in. 53.0
Rear leg room, in. 25.0
Rear head room, in 4.5
Third-seat comfort . . . .●
Third shoulder room,in 29.5
Third leg room, in. 25.0
Third head room, in 4.0

Fuel economy
Fuel economy . . . .●
CU's overall mileage, mpg 17
CU's city/highway, mpg 12/22
CU's 150-mile trip, mpg 21
Annual fuel . . . . .870 gal./$1,745
Cruising range 320

RELIABILITY HISTORY

TROUBLE SPOTS	Suzuki Vitara, Grand Vitara, XL-7							
	97	98	99	00	01	02	03	04
Engine			○	○	○	●		
Cooling			●	●	●	●		
Fuel			○	○	◒	●		
Ignition			◒	◒	●	●		
Transmission			○	◒	●	●		
Electrical			○	○	◒	●		
Air conditioning			◑	◑	○	●		
Suspension			◒	◒	◒	◒		
Brakes			○	○	○	◒		
Exhaust			◒	●	◒	●		
Paint/trim/rust			○	○	○	○		
Body integrity			◑	◑	○	○		
Power equipment			○	○	○	●		
Body hardware			○	○	○	●		
RELIABILITY VERDICT			–	–	–	✓		

(Insufficient data)

Suzuki Verona

THE VERONA LINE
Body style:
sedan
Trim lines:
S, LX, EX
Base price range:
$17,449-$20,449

This is the successor to the Daewoo Leganza. Since GM bought Daewoo, these cars are sold through Suzuki—partly owned by GM. In Canada it is called the Chevrolet Epica. The 2.5-liter, 155-hp in-line six-cylinder is relatively quiet but no quicker than a competitor's four-cylinder. The Verona offers a lot of equipment and good fit and finish for a low price. Handling is reluctant with vague steering, but the ride is fairly comfortable. The automatic transmission is hesitant to downshift, blunting performance. The driving position is compromised by the steering wheel, which sits too far forward.

REPORT CARD

NA	**Predicted reliability**
NA	**Owner satisfaction**
NA	**Predicted depreciation**
⊖	**Accident avoidance**
○	**Acceleration**
⊖	**Ride**
⊖	**Front seat comfort**
◐	**Fuel economy**

SPECIFICATIONS

Drive wheels Front

Seating 2 front, 3 rear

Engines available
2.5-liter 6 (155 hp)

Transmissions available
4-speed automatic

Fuel
Fuel type ....Regular
EPA city/highway, mpg 20/28
Fuel refill capacity, gal. 17.2

Dimensions and weight
Length, in. 188
Width, in. 72
Wheelbase, in. 106
Curb weight, lb. 3,370
Percent weight, front/rear 59/41
Typical towing ability, lb. ....NR

SAFETY INFORMATION

Active safety features

Antilock brakes ....Standard (optional on S)
Traction control ....Optional on EX
Stability control ....Not available
Daytime running lights ....Standard
Tire pressure monitor ....Available

Safety belts

Center-rear belt 3-point
Pretensioners, front/rear ....Yes/no

Air bags

Occupant-sensing system ....Side
Side bags, front/rear ....Standard/no
Inflatable curtain ....Not available
Accident alert system ....Not available

Crash tests

Gov't front-crash test, driver/front passenger ......○/⊖
Gov't side-crash test, driver/rear passenger ....⊖/○
IIHS offset crash test ....Acceptable
IIHS side crash test w/ side & curtain airbags ....NA
IIHS side crash test w/o side & curtain airbags ....Poor

FROM THE TEST TRACK

Tested model
2004 LX sedan, 2.5-liter Six, 4-speed automatic

Tires as tested
Hankook Optimo H420, size P205/55R16 89H

Acceleration ....○
0-30 mph, sec. 3.6
0-60 mph, sec. 10.3
Quarter mile, sec. 17.8
Quarter mile, mph 79
45-65 mph, sec. 6.2

Other findings
Transmission ....○
Turning circle, ft. 38
Ground clearance, in. 5.0

Braking and handling
Braking ....⊖
Braking, dry pavement, ft. 130
Routine handling ....○
Emergency handling ....○
Avoidance maneuver, max. mph ...51.0

Convenience and comfort
Ride ....⊖
Noise ....⊖
Driving position ....○
Access ....⊖
Controls and displays ....⊖
Fit and finish ....⊖
Door top to ground, in. 51.5
Trunk ....○
Luggage capacity ....4+0
Max. load, lb. 900

Seating
Front-seat comfort ....⊖
Front shoulder room, in. 57.0
Front leg room, in. 40.5
Front head room, in. 4.0
Rear-seat comfort ....○
Rear shoulder room, in. 56.0
Rear leg room, in. 28.5
Rear head room, in 1.5

Fuel economy ....◐
CU's overall mileage, mpg 20
CU's city/highway, mpg 14/30
CU's 150-mile trip, mpg 23
Annual fuel ....750 gal./$1,500
Cruising range 365

RELIABILITY HISTORY

TROUBLE SPOTS	97 98 99 00 01 02 03 04
Engine	
Cooling	
Fuel	**NOT**
Ignition	
Transmission	**ENOUGH**
Electrical	
Air conditioning	**DATA**
Suspension	
Brakes	**TO**
Exhaust	
Paint/trim/rust	**RATE**
Body integrity	
Power equipment	
Body hardware	
RELIABILITY VERDICT	

Toyota 4Runner

CR RECOMMENDED ✓

The 4Runner is now the top-ranked SUV in its price class that is fit for serious off-roading. It's a big improvement over its predecessor, riding better than some car-based SUVs. Our tested V6 model delivered lively acceleration. Fuel economy was an unimpressive 16 mpg. Handling isn't nimble, but it is sound and secure with standard stability control. The interior feels substantial and is well-made. The power rear window and interior mirrors for reversing are nice touches. A third-row seat is a new option. The V6 gets a five-speed automatic for 2005, and the V8 receives more horsepower.

THE 4RUNNER LINE

Body style:
4-door SUV
Trim lines:
SR5, Sport, Limited
Base price range:
$27,795-$37,795

REPORT CARD

⊖	Predicted reliability
◉	Owner satisfaction
◉	Predicted depreciation
⊖	Accident avoidance
⊖	Acceleration
○	Ride
⊖	Front seat comfort
●	Fuel economy

SPECIFICATIONS

Drive wheels Rear, selectable, or permanent 4WD

Seating 2 front, 3 rear, 2 third

Engines available
4.0-liter V6 (245 hp); 4.7-liter V8 (270 hp)

Transmissions available
5-speed automatic

Fuel
Fuel type . . . . .Regular or premium
EPA city/highway, mpg 17/21
Fuel refill capacity, gal. 23.0

Dimensions and weight
Length, in. 189
Width, in. 74
Wheelbase, in. 110
Curb weight, lb. 4,345
Percent weight, front/rear 54/46
Typical towing ability, lb. 5,000

SAFETY INFORMATION

Active safety features
Antilock brakes . . . . .Standard
Traction control . . . . .Standard
Stability control . . . . .Standard
Daytime running lights . . . . .Optional
Tire pressure monitor . . . . .Available

Safety belts
Center-rear belt 3-point
Pretensioners, front/rear . . . . .Yes/yes

Air bags
Occupant-sensing system . . . . .Not available
Side bags, front/rear .Optional/no
Inflatable curtain . . . . .Optional
Accident alert system . . . . .Not available

Crash tests
Gov't front-crash test, driver/front passenger . . . .⊖/○
Gov't side-crash test, driver/rear passenger . . . . . .◉/○
IIHS offset crash test . . . . .Good
IIHS side crash test w/ side & curtain airbags . . . . .NA
IIHS side crash test w/o side & curtain airbags . . . . .NA

FROM THE TEST TRACK

Tested model
2003 SR5 4-door SUV 4WD, 4.0-liter V6, 4-speed automatic

Tires as tested
Dunlop AT20 Grand Trek, size P265/65R17 110S

Acceleration . . . . ⊖
0-30 mph, sec. 2.9
0-60 mph, sec. 8.2
Quarter mile, sec. 16.4
Quarter mile, mph 86
45-65 mph, sec. 5.2

Other findings
Transmission . . . . ◉
Turning circle, ft. 40
Ground clearance, in. 6.5

Braking and handling
Braking . . . . ⊖
Braking, dry pavement, ft. 132
Routine handling . . . . ○
Emergency handling . . . . ○
Avoidance maneuver, max. mph . . .46.5

Convenience and comfort
Ride . . . . ○
Noise . . . . ⊖
Driving position . . . . ⊖
Access . . . . ⊖
Controls and displays . . . . ⊖
Fit and finish . . . . ⊖
Door top to ground, in. 62.0
Cargo area . . . . ⊖
Cargo volume, cu.ft. 44.5
Max. load, lb. 1,035

Seating
Front-seat comfort . . . . ⊖
Front shoulder room, in. 58.0
Front leg room, in. 41.0
Front head room, in. 3.0
Rear-seat comfort . . . . ⊖
Rear shoulder room, in. 57.0
Rear leg room, in. 29.5
Rear head room, in 4.5
Fuel economy . . . . ●
CU's overall mileage, mpg 16
  CU's city/highway, mpg 11/22
  CU's 150-mile trip, mpg 19
Annual fuel . . . . .925 gal./$1,850
Cruising range 410

RELIABILITY HISTORY

TROUBLE SPOTS	Toyota 4Runner V6							
	97	98	99	00	01	02	03	04
Engine	◉	◉	◉	◉	◉	◉	◉	◉
Cooling	⊖	⊖	◉	◉	◉	◉	◉	◉
Fuel	◉	◉	⊖	◉	◉	◉	◉	◉
Ignition	◉	◉	◉	◉	◉	◉	◉	◉
Transmission	◉	◉	◉	◉	◉	◉	◉	◉
Electrical	○	○	◉	◉	◉	⊖	◉	◉
Air conditioning	◉	◉	◉	◉	◉	◉	◉	◉
Suspension	◉	⊖	◉	◉	⊖	◉	◉	◉
Brakes	○	⊖	⊖	◉	◉	◉	◉	◉
Exhaust	◉	◉	◉	◉	◉	◉	◉	◉
Paint/trim/rust	◉	⊖	◉	◉	◉	◉	◉	◉
Body integrity	⊖	⊖	⊖	⊖	◉	○	○	◉
Power equipment	○	○	⊖	◉	◉	◉	◉	◉
Body hardware	◉	⊖	◉	◉	◉	◉	◉	◉
RELIABILITY VERDICT	✓	✓	✓	✓	✓	✓	✓	✓

● ◉ ○ ⊖ ●
better ◀——▶ worse   See page 36 for more information.

Toyota Avalon

THE AVALON LINE
Body style:
sedan
Trim lines:
XL, Touring, XLS,
Limited
Base price range:
$26,350-$33,540

Toyota's largest sedan continues to embody roominess, convenience, quietness, and quality in this third-generation redesign. The Avalon has always been a sensible alternative to large domestic or upscale luxury sedans, and more so now. The outgoing model was refined and pampering. The new one, which arrived in February, is wider and has a more powerful V6 engine. The sumptuous rear seat can recline. Cabin access is easy and interior quality is commendable. Toyota has dropped the six-passenger version.

REPORT CARD

⊖	**Predicted reliability**
⊙	**Owner satisfaction**
NA	**Predicted depreciation**
NA	**Accident avoidance**
NA	**Acceleration**
NA	**Ride**
NA	**Front seat comfort**
NA	**Fuel economy**

SAFETY INFORMATION

Active safety features
Antilock brakes . . . . .Standard
Traction control . . . . .Included with stability
Stability control . . . . .Optional on XLS and Limited
Daytime running lights . . . . .Standard
Tire pressure monitor .Not available

Safety belts
Center-rear belt 3-point
Pretensioners, front/rear .Yes/no

Air bags
Occupant-sensing system . . . . .Not available
Side bags, front/rear .Standard/no
Inflatable curtain . . . . .Standard
Accident alert system . . . . .Not available

Crash tests
Gov't front-crash test, driver/front passenger . . . . . .NA/NA
Gov't side-crash test, driver/rear passenger . . . . .NA/NA
IIHS offset crash test . . . . .NA
IIHS side crash test w/ side & curtain airbags . . . . .NA
IIHS side crash test w/o side & curtain airbags . . . . .NA

SPECIFICATIONS

Drive wheels Front

Seating 2 front, 3 rear

Engines available
3.5-liter V6 (280 hp)

Transmissions available
5-speed automatic

Fuel
Fuel type . . . . .Regular
EPA city/highway, mpg 22/31
Fuel refill capacity, gal. 18.5

Dimensions and weight
Length, in. 197
Width, in. 73
Wheelbase, in. 111
Curb weight, lb. 3,545
Percent weight, front/rear . . . . .NA
Typical towing ability, lb. 1,000

ANOTHER LOOK

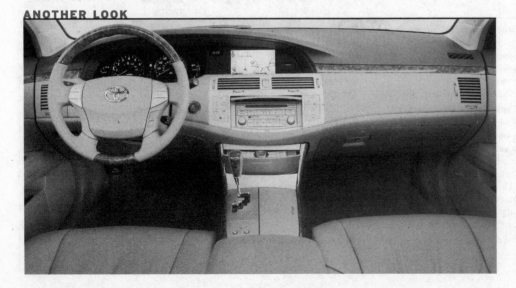

RELIABILITY HISTORY

TROUBLE SPOTS	97 98 99 00 01 02 03 04
Engine	
Cooling	NO
Fuel	
Ignition	
Transmission	DATA
Electrical	
Air conditioning	NEW
Suspension	
Brakes	MODEL
Exhaust	
Paint/trim/rust	
Body integrity	
Power equipment	
Body hardware	
RELIABILITY VERDICT	

Expert • Independent • Nonprofit

Toyota Camry

CR RECOMMENDED ✓

THE CAMRY LINE
Body style:
sedan
Trim lines:
Base, LE, SE, XLE
Base price range:
$18,195-$25,555

The Camry is among our top-rated family cars, thanks to its refinement, quietness, room, and ride comfort. For 2005 it received a minor update and a five-speed automatic transmission, which is smooth and responsive. Handling is predictable and secure. The XLE is fitted with grippier tires that improve handling and braking. The V6 is smooth and responsive; a larger 3.3-liter V6 powers the SE version. The lack of a telescoping steering wheel compromises the driving position for some drivers. The front seats are comfortable but could benefit from better thigh support. ABS is standard for 2005.

REPORT CARD

◉	Predicted reliability
◓	Owner satisfaction
◓	Predicted depreciation
○	Accident avoidance
○	Acceleration
◓	Ride
◓	Front seat comfort
○	Fuel economy

SPECIFICATIONS

Drive wheels Front

Seating 2 front, 3 rear

Engines available
2.4-liter 4 (160 hp); 3.0-liter V6 (210 hp); 3.3-liter V6 (225 hp)

Transmissions available
5-speed manual; 5-speed automatic

Fuel
Fuel type . . . . .Regular
EPA city/highway, mpg 24/34
Fuel refill capacity, gal. 18.5

Dimensions and weight
Length, in. 189
Width, in. 71
Wheelbase, in. 107
Curb weight, lb. 3,285
Percent weight, front/rear 59/41
Typical towing ability, lb. 2,000

SAFETY INFORMATION

Active safety features
Antilock brakes . . . . .Standard
Traction control . . . . .Included with stability
Stability control . . . . .Optional
Daytime running lights . . . . .Standard
Tire pressure monitor . . . . .Not available

Safety belts
Center-rear belt 3-point
Pretensioners, front/rear . . . . .Yes/no

Air bags
Occupant-sensing system .Front
Side bags, front/rear . . . . .Optional/no
Inflatable curtain . . . . .Optional
Accident alert system . . . . .Not available

Crash tests
Gov't front-crash test, driver/front passenger . . . . .◕/◓
Gov't side-crash test, driver/rear passenger . . . . . .◓/○
IIHS offset crash test . . . . .Good
IIHS side crash test w/ side & curtain airbags . . . . . .Good
IIHS side crash test w/o side & curtain airbags . . . . . .Poor

FROM THE TEST TRACK

Tested model
2005 LE sedan, 2.4-liter Four, 5-speed automatic

Tires as tested
Continental TouringContact AS, size P205/65R15 92T

Acceleration . . . .○
0-30 mph, sec. 3.4
0-60 mph, sec. 9.7
Quarter mile, sec. 17.6
Quarter mile, mph 81
45-65 mph, sec. 6.5

Other findings
Transmission . . . .◉
Turning circle, ft. 38
Ground clearance, in. 5.0

Braking and handling
Braking . . . .○
Braking, dry pavement, ft. 147
Routine handling . . . .◓
Emergency handling . . . .○
Avoidance maneuver, max. mph . . .50.0

Convenience and comfort
Ride . . . .◓
Noise . . . .◓
Driving position . . . .◓
Access . . . .◓
Controls and displays . . . .●
Fit and finish . . . .◓
Door top to ground, in. 52.5
Trunk . . . .○
Luggage capacity . . . . .4+1
Max. load, lb. 900

Seating
Front-seat comfort . . . .◓
Front shoulder room, in. 56.5
Front leg room, in. 41.0
Front head room, in. 3.0
Rear-seat comfort . . . .◓
Rear shoulder room, in. 56.0
Rear leg room, in. 28.5
Rear head room, in 3.5

Fuel economy . . . .○
CU's overall mileage, mpg 24
 CU's city/highway, mpg 16/34
 CU's 150-mile trip, mpg 28
Annual fuel . . . . .635 gal./$1,270
Cruising range 485

RELIABILITY HISTORY

TROUBLE SPOTS	Toyota Camry 4-cyl.							
	97	98	99	00	01	02	03	04
Engine	○	◓	◓	◓	●	●	●	●
Cooling	◓	◓	◓	◓	●	●	●	●
Fuel	◓	◓	◓	◓	●	●	●	●
Ignition	●	●	●	●	●	●	●	●
Transmission	●	●	●	●	●	●	●	●
Electrical	○	○	◓	◓	◓	●	●	●
Air conditioning	●	●	●	●	●	●	●	●
Suspension	◐	○	○	○	◓	◓	●	●
Brakes	○	○	○	○	◓	◓	●	●
Exhaust	◓	●	●	●	●	●	●	●
Paint/trim/rust	◓	◓	◓	◓	●	●	●	●
Body integrity	◓	◓	◓	◓	●	○	●	●
Power equipment	◓	◓	◓	◓	●	●	●	●
Body hardware	◓	◓	◓	◓	●	●	●	●
RELIABILITY VERDICT	✓	✓	✓	✓	✓	✓	✓	✓

● ◕ ○ ◓ ●
better ◀——▶ worse   See page 36 for more information.

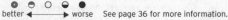

Toyota Camry Solara

CR RECOMMENDED ✓

The Solara, based on the current Camry, could pass for a Lexus since its styling is similar to the SC430's, and interior quality is impeccable. The standard engine is a 2.4-liter, 157-hp four-cylinder. A smooth and refined 3.3-liter, 225-hp V6 is optional. The V6 is mated to a gearbox that facilitates manual overrides. The ride is comfortable, but handling is not sporty. The rear seat is relatively roomy. The convertible model suffers from some body shake, but the top is well insulated.

THE CAMRY SOLARA LINE

Body style:
convertible; coupe
Trim lines:
SE, SE Sport, SLE
Base price range:
$19,320-$29,750

REPORT CARD

○	Predicted reliability
⊖	Owner satisfaction
NA	Predicted depreciation
⊖	Accident avoidance
⊖	Acceleration
○	Ride
⊖	Front seat comfort
○	Fuel economy

SPECIFICATIONS

Drive wheels Front

Seating 2 front, 3 rear

Engines available
2.4-liter 4 (157 hp); 3.3-liter V6 (225 hp)

Transmissions available
5-speed manual; 4-speed automatic; 5-speed automatic

Fuel
Fuel type .... Regular
EPA city/highway, mpg 20/29
Fuel refill capacity, gal. 18.5

Dimensions and weight
Length, in. .... .193
Width, in. .... .72
Wheelbase, in. .... .107
Curb weight, lb. 3,620
Percent weight, front/rear 60/40
Typical towing ability, lb. .... .NR

SAFETY INFORMATION

Active safety features
Antilock brakes .... .Standard
Traction control .... Included with stability
Stability control .... .Optional on SLE
Daytime running lights .... .Standard
Tire pressure monitor .... .Available

Safety belts
Center-rear belt 3-point
Pretensioners, front/rear .... .Yes/no

Air bags
Occupant-sensing system .... .Front
Side bags, front/rear .... .Standard/no
Inflatable curtain .... .Not available
Accident alert system .... .Not available

Crash tests
Gov't front-crash test, driver/front passenger ...... ●/●
Gov't side-crash test, driver/rear passenger .... NA/NA
IIHS offset crash test .... .NA
IIHS side crash test w/ side & curtain airbags .... .NA
IIHS side crash test w/o side & curtain airbags .... .NA

FROM THE TEST TRACK

Tested model
2005 SLE convertible, 3.3-liter V6, 5-speed automatic

Tires as tested
Bridgestone Turanza EL42, size P215/55R17 93V

Acceleration .... ⊖
0-30 mph, sec. 2.8
0-60 mph, sec. 7.5
Quarter mile, sec. 16.0
Quarter mile, mph .... .90
45-65 mph, sec. 5.2

Other findings
Transmission .... ●
Turning circle, ft. .... .39
Ground clearance, in. 4.5

Braking and handling
Braking .... ⊖
Braking, dry pavement, ft. .... .130
Routine handling .... ○
Emergency handling .... ○
Avoidance maneuver, max. mph 50.5

Convenience and comfort
Ride .... ○
Noise .... ○
Driving position .... ○
Access .... ○
Controls and displays .... ◉
Fit and finish .... ◉
Door top to ground, in. 51.0
Trunk .... ⊖
Luggage capacity .... .2+3
Max. load, lb. 755

Seating
Front-seat comfort .... ⊖
Front shoulder room, in. .. .55.5
Front leg room, in. .. .40.5
Front head room, in. .. .5.0
Rear-seat comfort .... ○
Rear shoulder room, in. 44.0
Rear leg room, in. 25.0
Rear head room, in 4.0

Fuel economy .... ○
CU's overall mileage, mpg .... .21
CU's city/highway, mpg 14/31
CU's 150-mile trip, mpg .... .25
Annual fuel .... .715 gal./$1,435
Cruising range .... .440

RELIABILITY HISTORY

TROUBLE SPOTS	Toyota Camry Solara							
	97	98	99	00	01	02	03	04
Engine		●	●	●	●	●		
Cooling		●	●	●	●	●		
Fuel		○	⊖	⊖	●	●		
Ignition		●	●	●	●	●		
Transmission		●	●	●	●	●		
Electrical		⊖	●	●	●	●		
Air conditioning		●	●	●	●	●		
Suspension		○	⊖	●	●	●		
Brakes		⊖	●	●	●	●		
Exhaust		●	●	●	●	●		
Paint/trim/rust		⊖	⊖	●	●	●		
Body integrity		⊖	⊖	○	○	○		
Power equipment		⊖	●	●	●	●		
Body hardware		⊖	●	●	●	●		
RELIABILITY VERDICT		✓	✓	✓	✓	✓		–

Expert • Independent • Nonprofit

Toyota Celica

CR RECOMMENDED ✓

THE CELICA LINE
Body style:
2-door hatchback
Trim lines:
GT, GT-S
Base price range:
$17,670-$22,335

W ith six speeds and relatively light weight, the Celica is a focused sporty coupe. Handling is capable, nimble, and secure, making the Celica fun to drive. The ride is pretty good for a sporty car, and the hatchback configuration adds versatility. The GT-S's 1.8-liter, 180-hp four-cylinder engine is a stronger performer than the GT's 140-hp version, but the difference is only apparent at very high rpm. Fuel economy is commendable considering the acceleration. 2005 is the last year for the Celica.

REPORT CARD

◉	Predicted reliability
⊖	Owner satisfaction
⊖	Predicted depreciation
◉	Accident avoidance
⊖	Acceleration
○	Ride
⊖	Front seat comfort
⊖	Fuel economy

SPECIFICATIONS

Drive wheels Front

Seating 2 front, 2 rear

Engines available
1.8-liter 4 (140 hp); 1.8-liter 4 (180 hp)

Transmissions available
5-speed manual; 6-speed manual; 4-speed automatic

Fuel
Fuel type . . . . .Regular or premium
EPA city/highway, mpg 23/32
Fuel refill capacity, gal. 14.5

Dimensions and weight
Length, in. 170
Width, in. 68
Wheelbase, in. .102
Curb weight, lb. 2,570
Percent weight, front/rear 62/38
Typical towing ability, lb. 2,000

SAFETY INFORMATION

Active safety features
Antilock brakes . . . . .Optional
Traction control . . . . .Not available
Stability control . . . . .Not available
Daytime running lights . . . . .Standard
Tire pressure monitor .Not available

Safety belts
Center-rear belt . . . . .NA
Pretensioners, front/rear .Yes/no

Air bags
Occupant-sensing system . . . . .Not available
Side bags, front/rear . . . . .Optional/no
Inflatable curtain . . . . .Not available
Accident alert system . . . . .Not available

Crash tests
Gov't front-crash test, driver/front passenger . . . . .⊖/⊖
Gov't side-crash test, driver/rear passenger . . . .○/NA
IIHS offset crash test . . . . .NA
IIHS side crash test w/ side & curtain airbags . . . . .NA
IIHS side crash test w/o side & curtain airbags . . . . .NA

FROM THE TEST TRACK

Tested model
2000 GT-S 2-door hatchback, 1.8-liter Four, 6-speed manual

Tires as tested
Yokohama Advan A-680, size 205/50R16 87V

Acceleration . . . .⊖
0-30 mph, sec. 2.9
0-60 mph, sec. 7.5
Quarter mile, sec. 16.0
Quarter mile, mph 89
45-65 mph, sec. 5.1

Other findings
Transmission . . . .⊖
Turning circle, ft. 36
Ground clearance, in. 5.5

Braking and handling
Braking . . . .⊖
Braking, dry pavement, ft. 130
Routine handling . . . .◉
Emergency handling . . . .⊖
Avoidance maneuver, max. mph . . .56.2

Convenience and comfort
Ride . . . .○
Noise . . . .○
Driving position . . . .⊖
Access . . . .○
Controls and displays . . . .◉
Fit and finish . . . .⊖
Door top to ground, in. 46.0
Trunk . . . .○
Luggage capacity . . . . .3+1
Max. load, lb. 725

Seating
Front-seat comfort . . . .⊖
Front shoulder room, in. 52.0
Front leg room, in. 41.5
Front head room, in. 2.0
Rear-seat comfort . . . .●
Rear shoulder room, in. 48.0
Rear leg room, in. 24.0
Rear head room, in 0.0

Fuel economy . . . .⊖
CU's overall mileage, mpg 28
CU's city/highway, mpg 21/36
CU's 150-mile trip, mpg 32
Annual fuel . . . . .540 gal./$1,185
Cruising range 430

RELIABILITY HISTORY

TROUBLE SPOTS	Toyota Celica							
	97	98	99	00	01	02	03	04
Engine	○			○	◉	◉	◉	
Cooling	◉			⊖	◉	◉	◉	
Fuel	◉			◉	◉	◉	⊖	
Ignition	◉			◉	◉	◉	◉	
Transmission	◉			⊖	◉	◉	◉	
Electrical	◉	Insufficient data	Insufficient data	◉	◉	◉	◉	Insufficient data
Air conditioning	⊖			◉	◉	◉	◉	
Suspension	◉			◉	◉	◉	◉	
Brakes	◉			◉	◉	◉	◉	
Exhaust	◉			◉	◉	◉	◉	
Paint/trim/rust	○			⊖	◉	◉	◉	
Body integrity	○			○	○	○	◉	
Power equipment	⊖			⊖	⊖	◉	◉	
Body hardware	⊖			⊖	◉	◉	◉	
RELIABILITY VERDICT	✓			✓	✓	✓	✓	

Toyota Corolla

CR RECOMMENDED ✓

THE COROLLA LINE
Body style:
sedan
Trim lines:
CE, S, LE, XRS
Base price range:
$13,780-$17,555

This Corolla is one of the better small sedans, with good head room and rear seat room. The ride is supple, and handling is responsive and secure. The driving position may be awkward for some, though, as the steering wheel might be too far away. The 1.8-liter engine delivers both responsive acceleration and very good fuel economy, even with the automatic. The cabin is fairly quiet except for some engine noise at high revs. Stability control is optional. We recommend getting the optional curtain airbags, since the Corolla rated Poor in the IIHS side-crash test without them.

REPORT CARD

◉	Predicted reliability
⊖	Owner satisfaction
○	Predicted depreciation
○	Accident avoidance
○	Acceleration
○	Ride
⊖	Front seat comfort
⊖	Fuel economy

SPECIFICATIONS

Drive wheels Front

Seating 2 front, 3 rear

Engines available
1.8-liter 4 (130 hp); 1.8-liter 4 (170 hp)

Transmissions available
5-speed manual; 6-speed manual; 4-speed automatic

Fuel
Fuel type . . . . .Regular or premium
EPA city/highway, mpg 29/38
Fuel refill capacity, gal. 13.2

Dimensions and weight
Length, in. 178
Width, in. 67
Wheelbase, in. .102
Curb weight, lb. 2,595
Percent weight, front/rear 61/39
Typical towing ability, lb. 1,500

SAFETY INFORMATION

Active safety features
Antilock brakes . . . . .Optional (standard on XRS)
Traction control . . . . .Included with stability
Stability control . . . . .Optional
Daytime running lights . . . . .Standard
Tire pressure monitor . . . . .Available

Safety belts
Center-rear belt 3-point
Pretensioners, front/rear . . . . .Yes/no

Air bags
Occupant-sensing system . . . . .Front
Side bags, front/rear . . . . .Optional/no
Inflatable curtain . . . . .Optional
Accident alert system .Not available

Crash tests
Gov't front-crash test, driver/front passenger . . . . . . ◐/◐
Gov't side-crash test, driver/rear passenger . . . . . . ◐/◑
IIHS offset crash test . . . . .Good
IIHS side crash test w/ side & curtain airbags . . .Acceptable
IIHS side crash test w/o side & curtain airbags . . . . . . .Poor

FROM THE TEST TRACK

Tested model
2003 LE sedan, 1.8-liter Four, 4-speed automatic

Tires as tested
Firestone FR690, size P195/65R15 89S

Acceleration . . . . ○
0-30 mph, sec. 3.7
0-60 mph, sec. 9.8
Quarter mile, sec. 17.5
Quarter mile, mph 82
45-65 mph, sec. 6.0

Other findings
Transmission . . . . ◉
Turning circle, ft. 38
Ground clearance, in. 5.0

Braking and handling
Braking . . . . ⊖
Braking, dry pavement, ft. 140
Routine handling . . . . ⊖
Emergency handling . . . . ○
Avoidance maneuver, max. mph . . .52.0

Convenience and comfort
Ride . . . . ○
Noise . . . . ⊖
Driving position . . . . ○
Access . . . . ⊖
Controls and displays . . . . ◉
Fit and finish . . . . ⊖
Door top to ground, in. 53.0
Trunk . . . . ○
Luggage capacity . . . . .4+1
Max. load, lb. 860

Seating
Front-seat comfort . . . . ⊖
Front shoulder room, in. 52.0
Front leg room, in. 40.0
Front head room, in. 5.0
Rear-seat comfort . . . . ○
Rear shoulder room, in. 53.0
Rear leg room, in. 27.0
Rear head room, in 2.0

Fuel economy . . . . ⊖
CU's overall mileage, mpg 29
CU's city/highway, mpg 20/39
CU's 150-mile trip, mpg 35
Annual fuel . . . . .515 gal./$1,035
Cruising range 430

RELIABILITY HISTORY

TROUBLE SPOTS	Toyota Corolla							
	97	98	99	00	01	02	03	04
Engine	●	●	●	●	●	●	●	●
Cooling	●	●	◐	●	◐	●	●	●
Fuel	●	◐	◐	◐	●	●	●	●
Ignition	●	●	◐	◐	●	●	●	●
Transmission	●	●	●	●	●	●	●	●
Electrical	○	◐	◐	●	●	●	●	●
Air conditioning	◐	●	●	●	●	●	●	●
Suspension	●	●	◐	◐	●	●	●	●
Brakes	○	○	◐	●	◐	●	●	●
Exhaust	●	●	●	●	●	●	●	●
Paint/trim/rust	○	◐	●	◐	●	●	●	●
Body integrity	●	○	◐	◐	◐	●	●	●
Power equipment	●	◐	◐	●	●	●	●	●
Body hardware	○	○	◐	●	◐	●	●	●
RELIABILITY VERDICT	✓	✓	✓	✓	✓	✓	✓	✓

Toyota Echo

RECOMMENDED ✓

THE ECHO LINE
Body style:
coupe; sedan
Trim lines:
–
Base price range:
$10,455-$10,985

The small Echo offers a commanding driving position and easy cabin access. With a manual transmission, the 1.5-liter engine provided spirited performance while returning 38 mpg in our testing. The shifter is a bit clunky, though. Handling is fairly responsive and secure, but body roll is pronounced when cornering. The ride is compliant. The roomy cabin has plenty of storage nooks, but the interior materials feel cheap. The speedometer is at the top center of the dashboard, which takes getting used to. Echos equipped with desirable antilock brakes can be hard to find. A redesign is due for 2006.

REPORT CARD

◉	Predicted reliability
⊖	Owner satisfaction
⊖	Predicted depreciation
○	Accident avoidance
○	Acceleration
○	Ride
⊖	Front seat comfort
◉	Fuel economy

SPECIFICATIONS

Drive wheels Front

Seating 2 front, 3 rear

Engines available
1.5-liter 4 (108 hp)

Transmissions available
5-speed manual; 4-speed automatic

Fuel
Fuel type .... Regular
EPA city/highway, mpg 34/41
Fuel refill capacity, gal. 11.9

Dimensions and weight
Length, in. 165
Width, in. 65
Wheelbase, in. 93
Curb weight, lb. 2,150
Percent weight, front/rear 60/40
Typical towing ability, lb. .... NR

SAFETY INFORMATION

Active safety features
Antilock brakes .... Optional
Traction control .... Not available
Stability control .... Not available
Daytime running lights .... Optional
Tire pressure monitor .... Not available

Safety belts
Center-rear belt 3-point
Pretensioners, front/rear .... Yes/no

Air bags
Occupant-sensing system .... Not available
Side bags, front/rear .... Optional/no
Inflatable curtain .... Not available
Accident alert system .... Not available

Crash tests
Gov't front-crash test, driver/front passenger ...... ○/◒
Gov't side-crash test, driver/rear passenger ...... ○/◒
IIHS offset crash test .... NA
IIHS side crash test w/ side & curtain airbags .... NA
IIHS side crash test w/o side & curtain airbags .... NA

FROM THE TEST TRACK

Tested model
2000 sedan, 1.5-liter Four, 5-speed manual

Tires as tested
Bridgestone Potenza RE92,
size P175/65R14 81S

Acceleration .... ○
0-30 mph, sec. 3.4
0-60 mph, sec. 9.8
Quarter mile, sec. 17.7
Quarter mile, mph 80
45-65 mph, sec. 6.5

Other findings
Transmission .... ⊖
Turning circle, ft. 35
Ground clearance, in. 4.5

Braking and handling
Braking .... ○
Braking, dry pavement, ft. 138
Routine handling .... ⊖
Emergency handling .... ○
Avoidance maneuver, max. mph ... 51.5

Convenience and comfort
Ride .... ○
Noise .... ○
Driving position .... ⊖
Access .... ⊖
Controls and displays .... ⊖
Fit and finish .... ○
Door top to ground, in. 54.5
Trunk .... ⊖
Luggage capacity .... 4+1
Max. load, lb. 775

Seating
Front-seat comfort .... ⊖
Front shoulder room, in. 52.5
Front leg room, in. 40.0
Front head room, in. 4.5
Rear-seat comfort .... ○
Rear shoulder room, in. 50.5
Rear leg room, in. 26.0
Rear head room, in 2.5

Fuel economy .... ◉
CU's overall mileage, mpg 38
  CU's city/highway, mpg 29/46
  CU's 150-mile trip, mpg 44
Annual fuel .... 400 gal./$795
Cruising range 495

RELIABILITY HISTORY

TROUBLE SPOTS	Toyota Echo							
	97	98	99	00	01	02	03	04
Engine				◉	◉	◉	◉	
Cooling				◉	◉	◉	◉	
Fuel				◉	◉	◉	◉	
Ignition				◉	◉	◉	◉	
Transmission				◉	◉	◉	◉	
Electrical				◉	◉	◉	◉	
Air conditioning				◉	◉	◉	◉	
Suspension				◉	◉	◉	◉	
Brakes				◒	◉	◉	◉	
Exhaust				◉	◉	◉	◉	
Paint/trim/rust				◒	◒	◉	◉	
Body integrity				◒	◉	◉	◒	
Power equipment				◉	◉	◉	◉	
Body hardware				◉	◉	◉	◉	
RELIABILITY VERDICT				✓	✓	✓	✓	

Insufficient data

Toyota Highlander

CR RECOMMENDED ✓

The well-rounded Highlander blends the virtues that appeal to most SUV buyers. It's similar to the Lexus RX330, though it's roomier, less costly, and has a third-row seat. A 2.4-liter, four-cylinder engine is standard; a smooth 3.3-liter V6 is available. The Highlander is quiet and roomy, with a comfortable ride and easy-to-use controls. Handling is sound and secure, though not particularly agile. A DVD rear-entertainment system is optional. Excellent offset-crash results as well as outstanding reliability and low depreciation round out this highly rated SUV. A hybrid arrives in summer 2005.

THE HIGHLANDER LINE

Body style:
4-door SUV
Trim lines:
Base, Limited, Hybrid
Base price range:
$24,280-$39,290

REPORT CARD

◕	Predicted reliability
◕	Owner satisfaction
◕	Predicted depreciation
⊖	Accident avoidance
⊖	Acceleration
⊖	Ride
⊖	Front seat comfort
◒	Fuel economy

SPECIFICATIONS

Drive wheels Front or AWD

Seating 2 front, 3 rear, 2 third

Engines available
2.4-liter 4 (160 hp); 3.3-liter V6 (230 hp);
3.3-liter V6 hybrid (268 hp)

Transmissions available
CVT; 4-speed automatic; 5-speed automatic

Fuel
Fuel type ....Regular
EPA city/highway, mpg 18/24
Fuel refill capacity, gal. 19.1

Dimensions and weight
Length, in. 184
Width, in. 72
Wheelbase, in. 107
Curb weight, lb. 4,035
Percent weight, front/rear 56/44
Typical towing ability, lb. 3,500

SAFETY INFORMATION

Active safety features
Antilock brakes ....Standard
Traction control ....Standard
Stability control ....Standard
Daytime running lights ....Optional
Tire pressure monitor ....Available

Safety belts
Center-rear belt 3-point
Pretensioners, front/rear ....Yes/no

Air bags
Occupant-sensing system ....Front
Side bags, front/rear ....Optional/no
Inflatable curtain ....Optional
Accident alert system ....Not available

Crash tests
Gov't front-crash test, driver/front passenger .....◕/◕
Gov't side-crash test, driver/rear passenger ....◕/◕
IIHS offset crash test ....Good
IIHS side crash test w/ side & curtain airbags ....NA
IIHS side crash test w/o side & curtain airbags ....NA

FROM THE TEST TRACK

Tested model
2004 Limited 4-door SUV AWD, 3.3-liter V6, 5-speed automatic

Tires as tested
Michelin Energy LX4, size 225/65R17 101S

Acceleration ....◒
0-30 mph, sec. 3.0
0-60 mph, sec. 8.8
Quarter mile, sec. 16.9
Quarter mile, mph 83
45-65 mph, sec. 6.1

Other findings
Transmission ....◕
Turning circle, ft. 40
Ground clearance, in. 7.0

Braking and handling
Braking ....⊖
Braking, dry pavement, ft. 137
Routine handling ....⊖
Emergency handling ....○
Avoidance maneuver, max. mph ...48.5

Convenience and comfort
Ride ....⊖
Noise ....⊖
Driving position ....⊖
Access ....◔
Controls and displays ....◔
Fit and finish ....⊖
Door top to ground, in. 61.0
Cargo area ....○
Cargo volume, cu.ft. 38.0
Max. load, lb. 1,160

Seating
Front-seat comfort ....⊖
Front shoulder room, in. 57.5
Front leg room, in. 41.0
Front head room, in. 4.0
Rear-seat comfort ....◕
Rear shoulder room, in. 57.0
Rear leg room, in. 29.5
Rear head room, in 4.0
Third-seat comfort ....●
Third shoulder room, in 53.5
Third leg room, in. 23.0
Third head room, in 1.5

Fuel economy ....◒
CU's overall mileage, mpg 19
  CU's city/highway, mpg 13/25
  CU's 150-mile trip, mpg 22
Annual fuel ....810 gal./$1,615
Cruising range 390

RELIABILITY HISTORY

TROUBLE SPOTS	Toyota Highlander			
	97 98 99 00	01	02	03 04
Engine		◕	◕	◕ ◕
Cooling		◕	◕	◕ ◕
Fuel		◒	◕	◕ ◕
Ignition		◕	◕	◕ ◕
Transmission		◕	◕	◕ ◕
Electrical		◕	◕	◕ ◕
Air conditioning		◕	◕	◕ ◕
Suspension		◕	◕	◕ ◕
Brakes		◒	◕	◕ ◕
Exhaust		◕	◕	◕ ◕
Paint/trim/rust		◕	◕	◕ ◕
Body integrity		◒	◒	◕ ◕
Power equipment		◕	◕	◕ ◕
Body hardware		◕	◕	◕ ◕
RELIABILITY VERDICT		✓	✓	✓ ✓

Toyota Land Cruiser

CR RECOMMENDED ✓

THE LAND CRUISER LINE
Body style:
4-door SUV
Trim lines:
–
Base price range:
$55,325

This big SUV is powered by a 4.7-liter V8 that provides good acceleration and exemplary smoothness. Although slightly less plush than its upscale Lexus LX470 cousin, at more than $55,000, it's hardly spartan. The interior is roomy, quiet, and well-finished. The ride is comfortable, and routine handling is sound though not agile. Standard stability control helps make the vehicle secure in emergency maneuvers. The four-wheel-drive system is permanently engaged—a major safety advantage. Good off-road performance is a strong suit, as is a 50/50-split forward-facing third-row seat.

REPORT CARD

◐	Predicted reliability
◓	Owner satisfaction
⊖	Predicted depreciation
○	Accident avoidance
○	Acceleration
⊖	Ride
⊖	Front seat comfort
●	Fuel economy

SPECIFICATIONS

Drive wheels Permanent 4WD

Seating 2 front, 3 rear, 3 third

Engines available
4.7-liter V8 (235 hp)

Transmissions available
5-speed automatic

Fuel
Fuel type . . . . .Premium
EPA city/highway, mpg 13/17
Fuel refill capacity, gal. 25.4

Dimensions and weight
Length, in. 193
Width, in. 76
Wheelbase, in. 112
Curb weight, lb. 5,435
Percent weight, front/rear 51/49
Typical towing ability, lb. 6,500

SAFETY INFORMATION

Active safety features
Antilock brakes . . . . .Standard
Traction control . . . . .Standard
Stability control . . . . .Standard
Daytime running lights . . . . .Standard
Tire pressure monitor . . . . .Not available

Safety belts
Center-rear belt 3-point
Pretensioners, front/rear . . . . .Yes/no

Air bags
Occupant-sensing system . . . . .Not available
Side bags, front/rear .Optional/no
Inflatable curtain . . . . .Optional with rollover
Accident alert system .Not available

Crash tests
Gov't front-crash test, driver/front passenger . . . . . .NA/NA
Gov't side-crash test, driver/rear passenger . . . . . . .NA/NA
IIHS offset crash test . . . . .NA
IIHS side crash test w/ side & curtain airbags . . . . .NA
IIHS side crash test w/o side & curtain airbags . . . . .NA

FROM THE TEST TRACK

Tested model
2001 4-door SUV 4WD, 4.7-liter V8, 4-speed automatic

Tires as tested
Michelin LTX M/S, size P275/70R16 114S

Acceleration . . . . ○
0-30 mph, sec. 3.3
0-60 mph, sec. 9.7
Quarter mile, sec. 17.4
Quarter mile, mph 79
45-65 mph, sec. 5.8

Other findings
Transmission . . . . ◐
Turning circle, ft. 42
Ground clearance, in. 8.5

Braking and handling
Braking . . . . ○
Braking, dry pavement, ft. 141
Routine handling . . . . ○
Emergency handling . . . . ⊖
Avoidance maneuver, max. mph . . .48.0

Convenience and comfort
Ride . . . . ◐
Noise . . . . ◐
Driving position . . . . ○
Access . . . . ○
Controls and displays . . . . ◑
Fit and finish . . . . ◑
Door top to ground, in. 66.5
Cargo area . . . . ⊖
Cargo volume, cu.ft. 50.0
Max. load, lb. 1,240

Seating
Front-seat comfort . . . . ⊖
Front shoulder room, in. 61.5
Front leg room, in. 40.0
Front head room, in. 3.5
Rear-seat comfort . . . . ⊖
Rear shoulder room, in. 61.0
Rear leg room, in. 29.0
Rear head room, in 4.5
Third-seat comfort . . . . ●
Third shoulder room, in 61.0
Third leg room, in. 26.0
Third head room, in 2.5

Fuel economy . . . . ●
CU's overall mileage, mpg 14
CU's city/highway, mpg 9/20
CU's 150-mile trip, mpg 18
Annual fuel . . . . .1,075 gal./$2,370
Cruising range 420

RELIABILITY HISTORY

TROUBLE SPOTS	Toyota Land Cruiser							
	97	98	99	00	01	02	03	04
Engine	◐	●	●	●	●	●	●	
Cooling	◐	●	●	●	●	●	●	
Fuel	●	◐	◐	◐	●	◐	●	
Ignition	◐	◐	●	●	◐	●	●	
Transmission	●	●	●	●	●	●	●	
Electrical	○	○	◐	◐	◐	◐	●	
Air conditioning	◐	◐	●	●	●	●	●	
Suspension	●	●	◐	●	●	●	●	
Brakes	●	◐	○	○	◐	◐	◐	
Exhaust	◐	●	◐	◐	●	●	●	
Paint/trim/rust	◐	●	●	◐	●	●	●	
Body integrity	◐	○	○	◐	◐	◐	◐	
Power equipment	◐	●	○	○	◐	●	●	
Body hardware	◐	●	○	◐	●	●	●	
RELIABILITY VERDICT	✓	✓	✓	✓	✓	✓		

Insufficient data

○ better ◐ ⊖ ● worse   See page 36 for more information.

Toyota MR2

CR RECOMMENDED ✓

The MR2 Spyder's light weight and midmounted 1.8-liter, 138-hp four-cylinder combine to provide brisk acceleration and excellent fuel economy. This well-balanced little sportster handles precisely and is fun to drive. Shifting the slick five-speed manual transmission is satisfying, too. A clutchless sequential manual is available. The manually operated soft top is easy to raise and lower. There's a tiny storage cubby behind the seats and a minuscule trunk in front, making this car a fun-to-drive toy rather than a long-haul companion. 2005 is the last year for the MR2.

THE MR2 LINE

Body style: convertible
Trim lines: None
Base price range: $25,145

REPORT CARD

⊙	Predicted reliability
NA	Owner satisfaction
⊖	Predicted depreciation
⊙	Accident avoidance
⊙	Acceleration
⊖	Ride
⊖	Front seat comfort
⊙	Fuel economy

SPECIFICATIONS

Drive wheels Rear

Seating 2 front

Engines available
1.8-liter 4 (138 hp)

Transmissions available
6-speed sequential; 5-speed manual

Fuel
Fuel type . . . . .Regular
EPA city/highway, mpg 25/30
Fuel refill capacity, gal. 12.7

Dimensions and weight
Length, in. 153
Width, in. 67
Wheelbase, in. .97
Curb weight, lb. 2,235
Percent weight, front/rear 43/57
Typical towing ability, lb. . . . . .NR

SAFETY INFORMATION

Active safety features
Antilock brakes . . . . .Standard
Traction control .Not available
Stability control .Not available
Daytime running lights . . . . .Standard
Tire pressure monitor .Not available

Safety belts
Center-rear belt . . . . .NA
Pretensioners, front/rear . . . . .Yes/NA

Air bags
Occupant-sensing system . . . . .Not available
Side bags, front/rear . . . . .No/NA
Inflatable curtain . . . . .Not available
Accident alert system .Not available

Crash tests
Gov't front-crash test, driver/front passenger . . . . . .NA/NA
Gov't side-crash test, driver/rear passenger . . . . .NA/NA
IIHS offset crash test . . . . .NA
IIHS side crash test w/ side & curtain airbags . . . . .NA
IIHS side crash test w/o side & curtain airbags . . . . .NA

FROM THE TEST TRACK

Tested model
2000 convertible, 1.8-liter Four, 5-speed manual

Tires as tested
Bridgestone RE040, size 185/55R15 81V (front), 205/50R15 85V (rear)

Acceleration . . . . ⊙
0-30 mph, sec. 2.3
0-60 mph, sec. 7.1
Quarter mile, sec. 15.6
Quarter mile, mph 88
45-65 mph, sec. 5.3

Other findings
Transmission . . . . ⊙
Turning circle, ft. 35
Ground clearance, in. 5.5

Braking and handling
Braking . . . . ⊙
Braking, dry pavement, ft. 125
Routine handling . . . . ⊙
Emergency handling . . . . ⊖
Avoidance maneuver, max. mph . . .54.5

Convenience and comfort
Ride . . . . ⊖
Noise . . . . ⊖
Driving position . . . . ⊖
Access . . . . ⊖
Controls and displays . . . . ⊙
Fit and finish . . . . ⊖
Door top to ground, in. 44.0
Trunk . . . . ●
Luggage capacity . . . . .0+0
Max. load, lb. 425

Seating
Front-seat comfort . . . . ⊖
Front shoulder room, in. 51.5
Front leg room, in. 41.0
Front head room, in. 3.5

Fuel economy
CU's overall mileage, mpg 31
  CU's city/highway, mpg 25/36
  CU's 150-mile trip, mpg 34
Annual fuel . . . . 490 gal./$975
Cruising range 400

RELIABILITY HISTORY

TROUBLE SPOTS	97 98 99 00 01 02 03 04
Engine	
Cooling	
Fuel	NOT
Ignition	
Transmission	ENOUGH
Electrical	
Air conditioning	DATA
Suspension	
Brakes	TO
Exhaust	
Paint/trim/rust	RATE
Body integrity	
Power equipment	
Body hardware	
RELIABILITY VERDICT	

Toyota Matrix

CR RECOMMENDED ✓

THE MATRIX LINE
Body style:
wagon
Trim lines:
Standard, XR, XRS
Base price range:
$14,860-$18,850

The Corolla-based Matrix is a tall wagon that can serve as an alternative to a small SUV. The 1.8-liter four-cylinder drones loudly and performs modestly. XRS models use a stronger version of this engine and come only with a manual transmission. Handling is nimble and the ride is compliant, if a little jittery. Access is very easy, and the rear seat is quite roomy. The driving position is so-so. The optional AWD system (available only with the automatic) works well but hurts acceleration and fuel economy. The rear seats fold to create a large, flat load floor. Stability control is optional for 2005.

REPORT CARD

⊖	**Predicted reliability**
○	**Owner satisfaction**
NA	**Predicted depreciation**
⊖	**Accident avoidance**
◒	**Acceleration**
⊖	**Ride**
⊖	**Front seat comfort**
○	**Fuel economy**

SPECIFICATIONS

Drive wheels Front or AWD

Seating 2 front, 3 rear

Engines available
1.8-liter 4 (123 hp); 1.8-liter 4 (130 hp); 1.8-liter 4 (170 hp)

Transmissions available
5-speed manual; 6-speed manual; 4-speed automatic

Fuel
Fuel type . . . . .Regular or premium
EPA city/highway, mpg 26/31
Fuel refill capacity, gal. 11.9

Dimensions and weight
Length, in. 171
Width, in. 70
Wheelbase, in. .102
Curb weight, lb. 2,985
Percent weight, front/rear 57/43
Typical towing ability, lb. 1,500

SAFETY INFORMATION

Active safety features
Antilock brakes . . . . .Opt. (std. on XRS, AWD)
Traction control . . . . .Included with stability
Stability control .Optional
Daytime running lights . . . . .Standard
Tire pressure monitor . . . . .Available

Safety belts
Center-rear belt 3-point
Pretensioners, front/rear . . . . .Yes/no

Air bags
Occupant-sensing system . . . . .Front
Side bags, front/rear .Optional/no
Inflatable curtain . . . . .Not available
Accident alert system .Not available

Crash tests
Gov't front-crash test, driver/front passenger . . . . . . ●/◐
Gov't side-crash test, driver/rear passenger . . . . . . ○/◐
IIHS offset crash test . . . . .NA
IIHS side crash test w/ side & curtain airbags . . . . .NA
IIHS side crash test w/o side & curtain airbags . . . . .NA

FROM THE TEST TRACK

Tested model
2003 XR wagon AWD, 1.8-liter Four, 4-speed automatic

Tires as tested
Goodyear Eagle RS-A, size P205/55R16 89H

Acceleration . . . . ◒
0-30 mph, sec. 4.1
0-60 mph, sec. 12.0
Quarter mile, sec. 18.8
Quarter mile, mph 74
45-65 mph, sec. 7.5

Other findings
Transmission . . . . ●
Turning circle, ft. 38
Ground clearance, in. 5.5

Braking and handling
Braking . . . . ◒
Braking, dry pavement, ft. 136
Routine handling . . . . ◒
Emergency handling . . . . ○
Avoidance maneuver, max. mph . . .51.5

Convenience and comfort
Ride . . . . ◒
Noise . . . . ○
Driving position . . . . ○
Access . . . . ●
Controls and displays . . . . ●
Fit and finish . . . . ◒
Door top to ground, in. 55.5
Cargo area . . . . ◒
Cargo volume, cu.ft. 28.0
Max. load, lb. 860

Seating
Front-seat comfort . . . . ◒
Front shoulder room, in. 53.0
Front leg room, in. 41.0
Front head room, in. 6.5
Rear-seat comfort . . . . ◒
Rear shoulder room, in. 52.0
Rear leg room, in. 28.0
Rear head room, in 5.5

Fuel economy . . . . ○
CU's overall mileage, mpg 24
  CU's city/highway, mpg 17/33
  CU's 150-mile trip, mpg 29
Annual fuel . . . . .625 gal./$1,250
Cruising range 315

RELIABILITY HISTORY

TROUBLE SPOTS	Toyota Matrix							
	97	98	99	00	01	02	03	04
Engine							●	●
Cooling							●	●
Fuel							●	●
Ignition							●	●
Transmission							●	●
Electrical							◒	◒
Air conditioning							●	●
Suspension							●	●
Brakes							●	●
Exhaust							●	●
Paint/trim/rust							●	●
Body integrity							○	◒
Power equipment							◒	●
Body hardware							●	●
RELIABILITY VERDICT							✓	✓

Toyota Prius

CR RECOMMENDED ✓

THE PRIUS LINE
Body style:
4-door hatchback
Trim lines:
–
Base price range:
$20,975

Toyota's second-generation Prius is unbeatable for its combination of economy, acceleration, and interior room. It couples a 1.5-liter gasoline engine with an electric motor, and it automatically switches between them or runs on both as needed. The car shuts the engine off at idle. We got an excellent 44 mpg overall in our tests. Shifts are automatic via a responsive continuously variable transmission (CVT). Regenerative braking recharges the battery while coasting or braking. Ride and handing are competent, though the steering feels vague. Access is easy. Reliability has been outstanding.

REPORT CARD

◒	Predicted reliability
◒	Owner satisfaction
NA	Predicted depreciation
○	Accident avoidance
○	Acceleration
◒	Ride
⊖	Front seat comfort
●	Fuel economy

SPECIFICATIONS

Drive wheels Front

Seating 2 front, 3 rear

Engines available
1.5-liter 4 hybrid (110 hp)

Transmissions available
CVT

Fuel
Fuel type . . . . .Regular
EPA city/highway, mpg 60/51
Fuel refill capacity, gal. 11.9

Dimensions and weight
Length, in. 175
Width, in. 68
Wheelbase, in. 106
Curb weight, lb. 2,950
Percent weight, front/rear 59/41
Typical towing ability, lb. . . . . .NR

SAFETY INFORMATION

Active safety features
Antilock brakes .Standard
Traction control .Standard
Stability control .Optional
Daytime running lights . . . . .Not available
Tire pressure monitor . . . . .Available

Safety belts
Center-rear belt .3-point
Pretensioners, front/rear . . . . .Yes/no

Air bags
Occupant-sensing system . . . . .Not available
Side bags, front/rear . . . . .Optional/no
Inflatable curtain .Optional
Accident alert system . . . . .Not available

Crash tests
Gov't front-crash test, driver/front passenger . . . . . . ◒/◒
Gov't side-crash test, driver/rear passenger . . . . ◒/◒
IIHS offset crash test . . . . .NA
IIHS side crash test w/ side & curtain airbags . . . . .NA
IIHS side crash test w/o side & curtain airbags . . . . . . .NA

FROM THE TEST TRACK

Tested model
2004 4-door hatchback, 1.5-liter Four hybrid, CVT

Tires as tested
Goodyear Integrity, size P185/65R15 86S

Acceleration . . . . ○
0-30 mph, sec. 3.7
0-60 mph, sec. 10.5
Quarter mile, sec. 18.1
Quarter mile, mph 78
45-65 mph, sec. 6.4

Other findings
Transmission . . . . ●
Turning circle, ft. 37
Ground clearance, in. 3.5

Braking and handling
Braking . . . . ○
Braking, dry pavement, ft. 143
Routine handling . . . . ◒
Emergency handling . . . . ○
Avoidance maneuver, max. mph . . .50.5

Convenience and comfort
Ride . . . . ◒
Noise . . . . ◒
Driving position . . . . ◒
Access . . . . ◒
Controls and displays . . . . ◒
Fit and finish . . . . ◒
Door top to ground, in. 53.0
Trunk . . . . ○
Luggage capacity . . . . .3+1
Max. load, lb. 825

Seating
Front-seat comfort . . . . ⊖
Front shoulder room, in. 55.0
Front leg room, in. 40.5
Front head room, in. 4.0
Rear-seat comfort . . . . ⊖
Rear shoulder room, in. 52.5
Rear leg room, in. 30.0
Rear head room, in 2.0

Fuel economy . . . . ●
CU's overall mileage, mpg 44
  CU's city/highway, mpg 35/50
  CU's 150-mile trip, mpg 48
Annual fuel . . . . .345 gal./$685
Cruising range 545

RELIABILITY HISTORY

TROUBLE SPOTS	Toyota Prius							
	97	98	99	00	01	02	03	04
Engine					●	●	●	●
Cooling					●	●	●	●
Fuel					○	◒	●	●
Ignition					●	●	●	●
Transmission					●	●	●	●
Electrical					○	○	○	●
Air conditioning					●	●	●	●
Suspension					○	○	○	●
Brakes					●	●	●	●
Exhaust					●	●	●	●
Paint/trim/rust					●	●	●	●
Body integrity					●	●	●	●
Power equipment					●	●	●	●
Body hardware					●	●	●	●
RELIABILITY VERDICT					✓	✓	✓	✓

Toyota RAV4

CR RECOMMENDED ✓

THE RAV4 LINE
Body style:
4-door SUV
Trim lines:
–
Base price range:
$18,750-$20,150

The RAV4 is one of our highest-rated small SUVs. The flexible, well-designed interior includes a rear seat you can fold and remove in halves. The noisy and slightly underpowered 2.0-liter engine was replaced with a smoother, stronger, and more pleasant 2.4-liter. The engine and automatic transmission work well together, and the AWD system does its job efficiently and unobtrusively on slippery pavement and limited off-road situations. Access and loading are very easy. Nimble handling and good fuel economy also add to the RAV4's appeal. ABS and stability control are standard.

REPORT CARD

◉	Predicted reliability
⊖	Owner satisfaction
◉	Predicted depreciation
⊖	Accident avoidance
○	Acceleration
○	Ride
⊖	Front seat comfort
○	Fuel economy

SPECIFICATIONS

Drive wheels Front or AWD

Seating 2 front, 3 rear

Engines available
2.4-liter 4 (161 hp)

Transmissions available
5-speed manual; 4-speed automatic

Fuel
Fuel type ....Regular
EPA city/highway, mpg 22/27
Fuel refill capacity, gal. 14.8

Dimensions and weight
Length, in. 167
Width, in. 68
Wheelbase, in. 98
Curb weight, lb. 3,135
Percent weight, front/rear 57/43
Typical towing ability, lb. 1,500

SAFETY INFORMATION

Active safety features
Antilock brakes ....Standard
Traction control ....Standard
Stability control ....Standard
Daytime running lights ....Optional
Tire pressure monitor ....Available

Safety belts
Center-rear belt 3-point
Pretensioners, front/rear ....Yes/no

Air bags
Occupant-sensing system ....Not available
Side bags, front/rear ....Optional/no
Inflatable curtain ....Optional
Accident alert system ....Not available

Crash tests
Gov't front-crash test, driver/front passenger .....◉/⊖
Gov't side-crash test, driver/rear passenger ....◉/⊖
IIHS offset crash test ....Good
IIHS side crash test w/ side & curtain airbags ....Good
IIHS side crash test w/o side & curtain airbags ....Poor

FROM THE TEST TRACK

Tested model
2004 4-door SUV AWD, 2.4-liter Four, 4-speed automatic

Tires as tested
Bridgestone Dueler H/T 687, size 215/70R16 99S

Acceleration ....○
0-30 mph, sec. 3.5
0-60 mph, sec. 9.9
Quarter mile, sec. 17.7
Quarter mile, mph. 78
45-65 mph, sec. 6.1

Other findings
Transmission ....⊖
Turning circle, ft. 37
Ground clearance, in. 6.0

Braking and handling
Braking ....⊖
Braking, dry pavement, ft. 142
Routine handling ....⊖
Emergency handling ....○
Avoidance maneuver, max. mph ...49.5

Convenience and comfort
Ride ....○
Noise ....○
Driving position ....⊖
Access ....⊖
Controls and displays ....◉
Fit and finish ....⊖
Door top to ground, in. 60.0
Cargo area ....○
Cargo volume, cu.ft. 36.5
Max. load, lb. 760

Seating
Front-seat comfort ....⊖
Front shoulder room, in. 55.0
Front leg room, in. 40.0
Front head room, in. 5.5
Rear-seat comfort ....⊖
Rear shoulder room, in. 53.5
Rear leg room, in. 26.0
Rear head room, in 5.0

Fuel economy ....○
CU's overall mileage, mpg 21
CU's city/highway, mpg 15/28
CU's 150-mile trip, mpg 24
Annual fuel ....710 gal./$1,420
Cruising range 330

RELIABILITY HISTORY

TROUBLE SPOTS	Toyota RAV4							
	97	98	99	00	01	02	03	04
Engine	○	◉	◉	◉	◉	◉	◉	◉
Cooling	◉	◉	◉	◉	◉	◉	◉	◉
Fuel	◉	○	◉	◉	◉	◉	◉	◉
Ignition	◉	◉	◉	◉	◉	◉	◉	◉
Transmission	◉	◉	◉	◉	◉	◉	◉	◉
Electrical	◉	◉	◉	◉	◉	◉	◉	◉
Air conditioning	◉	◉	◉	◉	◉	◉	◉	◉
Suspension	◉	◉	◉	◉	◉	◉	◉	◉
Brakes	○	○	◉	○	◉	◉	◉	◉
Exhaust	◉	◉	◉	◉	◉	◉	◉	◉
Paint/trim/rust	◉	◉	◉	◉	◉	◉	◉	◉
Body integrity	◉	○	◐	◉	○	○	◐	◉
Power equipment	◉	◉	◉	◉	◉	◉	◉	◉
Body hardware	◉	○	◉	◉	◉	◉	◉	◉
RELIABILITY VERDICT	✓	✓	✓	✓	✓	✓	✓	✓

◉ ◐ ○ ◐ ● better ⟵——⟶ worse See page 36 for more information.

Toyota Sequoia

CR RECOMMENDED ✔

THE SEQUOIA LINE
Body style:
4-door SUV
Trim lines:
SR5, Limited
Base price range:
$32,570-$45,060

The large Sequoia is based on Toyota's excellent Tundra pickup. The 4.7-liter V8 is very refined. Rear-wheel and selectable full-time four-wheel drive are available. With its third-row seat, it can accommodate up to eight passengers. The ride is stiff, and handling is ungainly but ultimately secure with the standard stability-control system. The Sequoia is roomier than the more exspensive Land Cruiser, but it does-n't ride as comfortably and has a less sophisticated 4WD sys-tem. 2005 brings more power and a five-speed automatic.

REPORT CARD

⊖	Predicted reliability
⊖	Owner satisfaction
◉	Predicted depreciation
○	Accident avoidance
○	Acceleration
○	Ride
⊖	Front seat comfort
●	Fuel economy

SPECIFICATIONS

Drive wheels Rear or selectable 4WD

Seating 2 front, 3 rear, 3 third

Engines available
4.7-liter V8 (282 hp)

Transmissions available
5-speed automatic

Fuel
Fuel type . . . . .Regular
EPA city/highway, mpg 15/18
Fuel refill capacity, gal. 26.0

Dimensions and weight
Length, in. 204
Width, in. 78
Wheelbase, in. 118
Curb weight, lb. 5,280
Percent weight, front/rear 52/48
Typical towing ability, lb. 6,200

SAFETY INFORMATION

Active safety features

Antilock brakes . . . . .Standard
Traction control . . . . .Standard
Stability control . . . . .Standard
Daytime running lights . . . . .Optional
Tire pressure monitor . . . . .Not available

Safety belts

Center-rear belt 3-point
Pretensioners, front/rear . . . . .Yes/no

Air bags

Occupant-sensing system . . . . .Front
Side bags, front/rear .Optional/no
Inflatable curtain . . . . .Optional with rollover
Accident alert system . . . . .Not available

Crash tests

Gov't front-crash test, driver/front passenger . . . . . .◒/◒
Gov't side-crash test, driver/rear passenger . . . . . . .NA/NA
IIHS offset crash test . . . . .NA
IIHS side crash test w/ side & curtain airbags . . . . . .NA
IIHS side crash test w/o side & curtain airbags . . . . . . .NA

FROM THE TEST TRACK

Tested model
2002 Limited 4-door SUV 4WD, 4.7-liter V8, 4-speed automatic

Tires as tested
Bridgestone Dueler H/T 689, size P265/70R16 111S

Acceleration . . . . ○

0-30 mph, sec. 3.5
0-60 mph, sec. 9.7
Quarter mile, sec. 17.5
Quarter mile, mph 81
45-65 mph, sec. 5.8

Other findings

Transmission . . . . ◉
Turning circle, ft. 43
Ground clearance, in. 8.5

Braking and handling

Braking . . . . ○
Braking, dry pavement, ft. 146
Routine handling . . . . ○
Emergency handling . . . . ◒
Avoidance maneuver, max. mph . . .46.0

Convenience and comfort

Ride . . . . ○
Noise . . . . ◒
Driving position . . . . ◒
Access . . . . ◒
Controls and displays . . . . ◒
Fit and finish . . . . ◒
Door top to ground, in. 68.0
Cargo area . . . . ◒
Cargo volume, cu.ft. 59.0
Max. load, lb. 1,320

Seating

Front-seat comfort . . . . ◒
Front shoulder room, in. 62.0
Front leg room, in. 41.0
Front head room, in. 5.0
Rear-seat comfort . . . . ◒
Rear shoulder room, in. 62.0
Rear leg room, in. 32.0
Rear head room, in 4.0
Third-seat comfort . . . . ◒
Third shoulder room,in 61.0
Third leg room, in. 26.0
Third head room, in 3.0

Fuel economy . . . . ●

CU's overall mileage, mpg 15
CU's city/highway, mpg 11/20
CU's 150-mile trip, mpg 19
Annual fuel . . . . .985 gal./$1,970
Cruising range 455

RELIABILITY HISTORY

TROUBLE SPOTS	Toyota Sequoia							
	97	98	99	00	01	02	03	04
Engine					●	●	●	●
Cooling					●	●	●	●
Fuel					●	●	●	●
Ignition					◒	●	●	●
Transmission					●	●	●	●
Electrical					○	◒	○	●
Air conditioning					◒	◒	●	●
Suspension					●	●	●	●
Brakes					○	◒	◒	●
Exhaust					●	●	●	●
Paint/trim/rust					◒	◒	◒	●
Body integrity					◒	◒	◒	●
Power equipment					◒	◒	◒	●
Body hardware					◒	◒	◒	●
RELIABILITY VERDICT					✓	✓	–	✓

Expert • Independent • Nonprofit

Toyota Sienna

CR RECOMMENDED ✓

The Sienna is a very comfortable, well-detailed minivan that can easily pass for a Lexus. The fuel-efficient 3.3-liter V6 engine is smooth and strong, and the five-speed automatic is very slick. The flexible interior features a 60/40-split rear seat that folds flat into the floor. Handling is secure, predictable, and responsive, but it lacks the agility of the Honda Odyssey. Power-retractable second-row windows and a telescoping steering wheel are pluses. Some desirable options, such as power seats, are only available on the upscale XLE model. All-wheel drive is optional. Crash-test results are impressive.

THE SIENNA LINE

Body style:
minivan

Trim lines:
CE, LE, XLE, XLE Limited

Base price range:
$23,425-$37,695

REPORT CARD

⊖	Predicted reliability
◉	Owner satisfaction
⊖	Predicted depreciation
○	Accident avoidance
⊖	Acceleration
⊖	Ride
◉	Front seat comfort
◒	Fuel economy

SPECIFICATIONS

Drive wheels Front or AWD

Seating 2 front, 3 rear, 3 third

Engines available
3.3-liter V6 (230 hp)

Transmissions available
5-speed automatic

Fuel
Fuel type ....Regular
EPA city/highway, mpg 19/26
Fuel refill capacity, gal. 21.0

Dimensions and weight
Length, in. 200
Width, in. 77
Wheelbase, in. 119
Curb weight, lb. 4,365
Percent weight, front/rear 57/43
Typical towing ability, lb. 3,500

SAFETY INFORMATION

Active safety features
Antilock brakes ....Standard
Traction control ....Included with stability
Stability control ....Optional
Daytime running lights ....Optional
Tire pressure monitor ....Available

Safety belts
Center-rear belt 3-point
Pretensioners, front/rear ....Yes/no

Air bags
Occupant-sensing system ....Front
Side bags, front/rear ....Optional/no
Inflatable curtain ....Optional
Accident alert system ....Not available

Crash tests
Gov't front-crash test, driver/front passenger .....◒/◉
Gov't side-crash test, driver/rear passenger ......◉/◉
IIHS offset crash test ....Good
IIHS side crash test w/ side & curtain airbags ....NA
IIHS side crash test w/o side & curtain airbags ....NA

FROM THE TEST TRACK

Tested model
2005 XLE minivan, 3.3-liter V6, 5-speed automatic

Tires as tested
Bridgestone Turanza EL42, size P225/60R17 98T

Acceleration ....◒
0-30 mph, sec. 3.1
0-60 mph, sec. 8.6
Quarter mile, sec. 16.9
Quarter mile, mph 84
45-65 mph, sec. 5.8

Other findings
Transmission ....◉
Turning circle, ft. 39
Ground clearance, in. 5.5

Braking and handling
Braking ....○
Braking, dry pavement, ft. 142
Routine handling ....◒
Emergency handling ....○
Avoidance maneuver, max. mph ...49.0

Convenience and comfort
Ride ....◒
Noise ....◒
Driving position ....◒
Access ....◉
Controls and displays ....◒
Fit and finish ....◒
Door top to ground, in. 62.0
Cargo area ....◒
Cargo volume, cu.ft. 70.5
Max. load, lb. 1,280

Seating
Front-seat comfort ....◉
Front shoulder room, in. 64.0
Front leg room, in. 40.5
Front head room, in. 3.5
Rear-seat comfort ....◉
Rear shoulder room, in. 64.5
Rear leg room, in. 31.5
Rear head room, in 4.0
Third-seat comfort ....○
Third shoulder room, in 62.0
Third leg room, in. 25.0
Third head room, in 2.5

Fuel economy ....◒
CU's overall mileage, mpg 19
CU's city/highway, mpg 13/27
CU's 150-mile trip, mpg 23
Annual fuel ....800 gal./$1,600
Cruising range 450

RELIABILITY HISTORY

TROUBLE SPOTS	Toyota Sienna							
	97	98	99	00	01	02	03	04
Engine	◒	◒	◒	◉	◒	◉	◉	◉
Cooling	◉	◉	◉	◉	◉	◉	◉	◉
Fuel	◉	◒	◉	◉	◉	◉	◉	◉
Ignition	◉	◉	◉	◉	◉	◉	◉	◉
Transmission	◒	◒	◒	◒	◉	◉	◉	◉
Electrical	○	○	◒	◒	◒	◒	◉	◉
Air conditioning	◒	◒	◉	◉	◒	◉	◉	◉
Suspension	◒	◒	◒	◒	◒	◉	◉	◉
Brakes	○	○	○	○	○	◒	◉	◉
Exhaust	◉	◒	◉	◒	◉	◉	◉	◉
Paint/trim/rust	◒	◉	◒	◒	◒	◉	◉	◉
Body integrity	◒	◒	○	◒	◒	◒	◉	◉
Power equipment	○	○	○	○	○	◒	◒	◉
Body hardware	●	◒	○	○	○	◒	◉	◉
RELIABILITY VERDICT	✓	✓	✓	✓	✓	–	✓	✓

Toyota Tacoma

THE TACOMA LINE
Body style:
regular cab; extended cab; crew cab
Trim lines:
Base, PreRunner, X-Runner
Base price range:
$13,415-$23,870

The redesigned Tacoma is no longer a utilitarian workhorse. It shares its platform with the 4Runner and Lexus GX470 SUVs. In addition to more powerful engines, the Tacoma also features a contemporary rack and pinion steering system. The interior is roomier and has a better finish than its predecessor. The driving position has been greatly improved with the addition of a telescoping steering wheel. The ride is better, although it is by no means comfortable with the optional TRD suspension. The sporty X-Runner tops the line. Stability control is optional, but may be very hard to find.

REPORT CARD

⊖	Predicted reliability
New	Owner satisfaction
NA	Predicted depreciation
NA	Accident avoidance
NA	Acceleration
NA	Ride
NA	Front seat comfort
NA	Fuel economy

SPECIFICATIONS

Drive wheels Rear or part-time 4WD

Seating 2 front, 3 rear

Engines available
2.7-liter 4 (164 hp); 4.0-liter V6 (245 hp)

Transmissions available
5-speed manual; 6-speed manual; 4-speed automatic; 5-speed automatic

Fuel
Fuel type .Regular
EPA city/highway, mpg 17/20
Fuel refill capacity, gal. 21.1

Dimensions and weight
Length, in. 208
Width, in. 75
Wheelbase, in. 128
Curb weight, lb. 4,215
Percent weight, front/rear 58/42
Typical towing ability, lb. 6,500

SAFETY INFORMATION

Active safety features
Antilock brakes . . . . .Standard
Traction control . . . . .Included with stability
Stability control . . . . .Optional
Daytime running lights . . . . .Optional
Tire pressure monitor . . . . .Not available

Safety belts
Center-rear belt 3-point
Pretensioners, front/rear . . . . .Yes/no

Air bags
Occupant-sensing system . . . . .Front
Side bags, front/rear . . . . .Optional/no
Inflatable curtain . . . . .Optional
Accident alert system . . . . .Not available

Crash tests
Gov't front-crash test, driver/front passenger . . . . .◐/◐
Gov't side-crash test, driver/rear passenger . . . .◐/NA
IIHS offset crash test .NA
IIHS side crash test w/ side & curtain airbags . . . . .NA
IIHS side crash test w/o side & curtain airbags . . . . .NA

ANOTHER LOOK

RELIABILITY HISTORY

TROUBLE SPOTS	97 98 99 00 01 02 03 04
Engine	
Cooling	NO
Fuel	
Ignition	
Transmission	DATA
Electrical	
Air conditioning	NEW
Suspension	
Brakes	MODEL
Exhaust	
Paint/trim/rust	
Body integrity	
Power equipment	
Body hardware	
RELIABILITY VERDICT	

Toyota Tundra

CR RECOMMENDED ✓

Currently our top-rated full-sized pickup, the Tundra's Lexus-derived V8 is smooth and quiet. 2005 brings a larger and more powerful V8 and a new 4.0-liter V6. The ride is civilized, the cabin is quiet and roomy in the crew cab, and fit and finish is top-notch. The power-retractable rear window is a nice touch. The crew cab has one of the longer beds in its class. Four-wheel-drive versions perform well off-road. The extended-cab model has a cramped rear seat. Good offset-crash results are a considerable plus. Electronic stability control is available.

THE TUNDRA LINE

Body style:
regular cab; extended cab; crew cab
Trim lines:
Base, WT, SR5, StepSide, Limited
Base price range:
$16,055-$33,175

REPORT CARD

◉	Predicted reliability
◉	Owner satisfaction
◉	Predicted depreciation
○	Accident avoidance
⊖	Acceleration
○	Ride
⊖	Front seat comfort
●	Fuel economy

SPECIFICATIONS

Drive wheels Rear or part-time 4WD

Seating 3 front, 3 rear

Engines available
4.0-liter V6 (245 hp); 4.7-liter V8 (282 hp)

Transmissions available
6-speed manual; 5-speed automatic

Fuel
Fuel type . . . . .Regular
EPA city/highway, mpg 15/18
Fuel refill capacity, gal. 26.4

Dimensions and weight
Length, in. .230
Width, in. 77
Wheelbase, in. 141
Curb weight, lb. 5,095
Percent weight, front/rear 56/44
Typical towing ability, lb. 6,700

SAFETY INFORMATION

Active safety features
Antilock brakes . . . . .Standard
Traction control . . . . .Included with stability
Stability control . . . . .Optional
Daytime running lights . . . . .Optional
Tire pressure monitor . . . . .Not available

Safety belts
Center-rear belt 3-point
Pretensioners, front/rear . . . . .Yes/no

Air bags
Occupant-sensing system . . . . .Not available
Side bags, front/rear . . . . .Optional/no
Inflatable curtain . . . . .Optional
Accident alert system .Not available

Crash tests
Gov't front-crash test, driver/front passenger . . . . .⊖/◉
Gov't side-crash test, driver/rear passenger . . . . . . .NA/NA
IIHS offset crash test . . . . .Good
IIHS side crash test w/ side & curtain airbags . . . . .NA
IIHS side crash test w/o side & curtain airbags . . . . .NA

FROM THE TEST TRACK

Tested model
2004 SR5 crew cab 4WD, 4.7-liter V8, 4-speed automatic

Tires as tested
Bridgestone Dueler H/T 840, size P265/65R17 110S

Acceleration . . . .◔
0-30 mph, sec. 3.1
0-60 mph, sec. 8.8
Quarter mile, sec. 16.9
Quarter mile, mph 82
45-65 mph, sec. 5.2

Other findings
Transmission . . . .◔
Turning circle, ft. 50
Ground clearance, in. 9.5

Braking and handling
Braking . . . .◑
Braking, dry pavement, ft. 136
Routine handling . . . .○
Emergency handling . . . .◕
Avoidance maneuver, max. mph 47.0

Convenience and comfort
Ride . . . .○
Noise . . . .○
Driving position . . . .○
Access . . . .○
Controls and displays . . . .◑
Fit and finish . . . .◑
Door top to ground, in. 68.0
Cargo area . . . .○
Max. load, lb. 1,505

Seating
Front-seat comfort . . . .◑
Front shoulder room, in. 62.0
Front leg room, in. 40.0
Front head room, in. 6.0
Rear-seat comfort . . . .◑
Rear shoulder room, in. 61.0
Rear leg room, in. 30.5
Rear head room, in 5.5

Fuel economy . . . .●
CU's overall mileage, mpg 14
CU's city/highway, mpg 10/18
CU's 150-mile trip, mpg 17
Annual fuel . . . . .1,085 gal./$2,170
Cruising range 420

RELIABILITY HISTORY

TROUBLE SPOTS	Toyota Tundra							
	97	98	99	00	01	02	03	04
Engine				◉	◉	◉	◉	◉
Cooling				◉	◉	◉	◉	◉
Fuel				○	○	◑	◉	◑
Ignition				◉	◉	◉	◉	◉
Transmission				◉	◉	◉	◉	◉
Electrical				◉	◑	◉	◑	◉
Air conditioning				◉	◉	◉	◉	◉
Suspension				◉	◉	◑	◉	◉
Brakes				◑	○	○	◑	◉
Exhaust				◉	◉	◑	◉	◉
Paint/trim/rust				◉	◉	◉	◉	◉
Body integrity				◉	◉	◉	◉	◉
Power equipment				◉	◉	◉	◉	◉
Body hardware				◉	◉	◉	◉	◉
RELIABILITY VERDICT		✓	✓	✓		✓		✓

◉ ◕ ○ ◔ ●
better ◄——► worse   See page 36 for more information.

Volkswagen Golf

Though it's a well-designed small car, the Golf's reliability has remained below average. It handles nimbly and has a supple, quiet ride. The interior has a high-quality feel. The seats are firm and supportive, but the rear is cramped. The 2.0-liter, four-cylinder engine is responsive but noisy. The sporty GTI's 1.8-liter turbo is punchy and smooth. The turbodiesel Golf TDI with a manual transmission had excellent fuel economy. The sporty R32 is discontinued for 2005. A redesign (shown) shared with the new Jetta bows in the fall.

THE GOLF LINE
Body style:
2-door hatchback; 4-door hatchback
Trim lines:
GL, GL TDI, GLS, GLS TDI, GTI
Base price range:
$15,830-$22,330

REPORT CARD

◒	**Predicted reliability**
◒	**Owner satisfaction**
○	**Predicted depreciation**
NA	**Accident avoidance**
NA	**Acceleration**
NA	**Ride**
NA	**Front seat comfort**
NA	**Fuel economy**

SPECIFICATIONS

Drive wheels Front

Seating 2 front, 3 rear

Engines available
1.9-liter 4 turbodiesel (100 hp); 2.0-liter 4 (115 hp); 1.8-liter 4 turbo (180 hp); 2.8-liter V6 (200 hp)

Transmissions available
5-speed manual; 6-speed manual; 4-speed automatic; 5-speed automatic

Fuel
Fuel type . . .Regular or diesel or premium
EPA city/highway, mpg 24/31
Fuel refill capacity, gal. 14.5

Dimensions and weight
Length, in. 163
Width, in. 68
Wheelbase, in. .99
Curb weight, lb. 2,935
Percent weight, front/rear 61/39
Typical towing ability, lb. 1,000

SAFETY INFORMATION

Active safety features
Antilock brakes . . . . .Standard
Traction control . . . . .Included with stability
Stability control . . . . .Optional (std. on GTI VR6)
Daytime running lights . . . . .Standard
Tire pressure monitor .Not available

Safety belts
Center-rear belt 3-point
Pretensioners, front/rear . . . . .Yes/no

Air bags
Occupant-sensing system . . . . .Side
Side bags, front/rear . . . . .Standard/no
Inflatable curtain . . . . .Standard
Accident alert system . . . . .Available

Crash tests
Gov't front-crash test, driver/front passenger . . . . . .
Gov't side-crash test, driver/rear passenger . . . .
IIHS offset crash test. . . . . .Good
IIHS side crash test w/ side & curtain airbags . . . . .NA
IIHS side crash test w/o side & curtain airbags . . . . . . .NA

ANOTHER LOOK

RELIABILITY HISTORY

TROUBLE SPOTS	Volkswagen Golf 4-cyl. Turbo							
	97	98	99	00	01	02	03	04
Engine				○	○	○	○	
Cooling				○	●	◒	●	
Fuel				●	●	○	○	
Ignition				●	◒	●	○	
Transmission				◒	●	◒	◒	
Electrical				◒	●	●	○	
Air conditioning				◒	●	◒	◒	
Suspension				◒	●	◒	◒	
Brakes				◒	○	◒	◒	
Exhaust				○	◒	●	◒	
Paint/trim/rust				○	◒	●	○	
Body integrity				○	◒	◒	◒	
Power equipment				●	●	●	◒	
Body hardware				◒	●	◒	○	
RELIABILITY VERDICT		✗	✗	✗	–			

Insufficient data

Volkswagen Jetta

THE JETTA LINE
Body style:
sedan
Trim lines:
1.9, 2.5
Base price range:
$17,900-$21,385

The new Jetta arrived in March. Volkswagen has evolved it into a more upscale sedan that straddles the small and family sedan categories. Three different powertrains are offered. A 2.5-liter, 150-hp five-cylinder arrives first, followed by a 200-hp, 2.0-liter version, and then a four-cylinder diesel. The new Jetta rides comfortably and handles better than the previous generation. The interior is considerably roomier, but the 2.5-liter engine is a bit noisy, but the six-speed automatic is very smooth.

REPORT CARD

New	Predicted reliability
New	Owner satisfaction
NA	Predicted depreciation
NA	Accident avoidance
NA	Acceleration
NA	Ride
NA	Front seat comfort
NA	Fuel economy

SPECIFICATIONS

Drive wheels Front

Seating 2 front, 3 rear

Engines available
1.9-liter 4 turbodiesel (100 hp); 2.5-liter 5 (150 hp); 2.0-liter 4 turbo (200 hp)

Transmissions available
6-speed sequential; 5-speed manual; 6-speed automatic

Fuel
Fuel type . . .Regular or diesel or premium
EPA city/highway, mpg 22/30
Fuel refill capacity, gal. 14.5

Dimensions and weight
Length, in. 179
Width, in. 69
Wheelbase, in. 102
Curb weight, lb. 3,285
Percent weight, front/rear 60/40
Typical towing ability, lb. . . . . .NA

SAFETY INFORMATION

Active safety features
Antilock brakes . . . . .Standard
Traction control . . . . .Standard
Stability control . . . . .Standard, Opt. on Value Edition
Daytime running lights . . . . .Standard
Tire pressure monitor .Not available

Safety belts
Center-rear belt 3-point
Pretensioners, front/rear . . . . .Yes/no

Air bags
Occupant-sensing system . . . . .Side
Side bags, front/rear . . . . .Standard/No
Inflatable curtain . . . . .Standard
Accident alert system . . . . .Available

Crash tests
Gov't front-crash test, driver/front passenger . . . . .NA/NA
Gov't side-crash test, driver/rear passenger . . . . . .NA/NA
IIHS offset crash test . . . . .NA
IIHS side crash test w/ side & curtain airbags . . . . .NA
IIHS side crash test w/o side & curtain airbags . . . . .NA

ANOTHER LOOK

RELIABILITY HISTORY

TROUBLE SPOTS

	97 98 99 00 01 02 03 04
Engine	
Cooling	NO
Fuel	
Ignition	
Transmission	DATA
Electrical	
Air conditioning	NEW
Suspension	
Brakes	MODEL
Exhaust	
Paint/trim/rust	
Body integrity	
Power equipment	
Body hardware	
RELIABILITY VERDICT	

better ◄———► worse See page 36 for more information.

Volkswagen New Beetle

The New Beetle has a lot going for it except reliability. It rides well and handles nimbly. The 2.0-liter four-cylinder performs just adequately, but the 150-hp, turbocharged 1.8-liter engine is stronger, smoother, and quieter. An economical, if noisy, 100-hp turbodiesel is available as well. The front seats are firm and supportive. The rear seat, while tolerable for two children, is cramped for adults. The power-operated convertible top is well-insulated from wind noise. Though improved, reliability is still below average. The New Beetle received a Good in the IIHS offset test and a Poor in the side-crash test.

THE NEW BEETLE LINE
Body style:
2-door hatchback; convertible
Trim lines:
GL, GLS TDI, GLS
Base price range:
$16,570-$25,450

REPORT CARD

⊖	Predicted reliability
○	Owner satisfaction
○	Predicted depreciation
⊖	Accident avoidance
⊖	Acceleration
○	Ride
⊖	Front seat comfort
○	Fuel economy

SPECIFICATIONS

Drive wheels Front

Seating 2 front, 2 rear

Engines available
1.9-liter 4 turbodiesel (100 hp); 2.0-liter 4 (115 hp); 1.8-liter 4 turbo (150 hp)

Transmissions available
5-speed manual; 6-speed automatic

Fuel
Fuel type . . .Regular or diesel or premium
EPA city/highway, mpg 23/29
Fuel refill capacity, gal. 14.5

Dimensions and weight
Length, in. 161
Width, in. 68
Wheelbase, in. 99
Curb weight, lb. 3,280
Percent weight, front/rear 63/37
Typical towing ability, lb. . . . . .NR

SAFETY INFORMATION

Active safety features
Antilock brakes .Standard
Traction control . . . . .Included with stability
Stability control .Optional
Daytime running lights . . . . .Standard
Tire pressure monitor . . . . .Not available

Safety belts
Center-rear belt . . . . .NA
Pretensioners, front/rear . . . . .Yes/no

Air bags
Occupant-sensing system .Side
Side bags, front/rear . . . . .Standard/no
Inflatable curtain . . . . .Not available
Accident alert system . . . . .Not available

Crash tests
Gov't front-crash test, driver/front passenger . . . . . .⊖/⊖
Gov't side-crash test, driver/rear passenger . . . . .NA/NA
IIHS offset crash test . . . . .Good
IIHS side crash test w/ side & curtain airbags . . . . .Poor
IIHS side crash test w/o side & curtain airbags . . . . .NA

FROM THE TEST TRACK

Tested model
2005 GLS convertible, 1.8-liter Four turbo, 5-speed manual

Tires as tested
Goodyear Eagle RS-A, size 205/55R16 91H

Acceleration . . . . ⊖
0-30 mph, sec. 2.8
0-60 mph, sec. 8.2
Quarter mile, sec. 16.7
Quarter mile, mph 84
45-65 mph, sec. 5.5

Other findings
Transmission . . . . ⊖
Turning circle, ft. 37
Ground clearance, in. 5.0

Braking and handling
Braking . . . . ⊖
Braking, dry pavement, ft. 133
Routine handling . . . . ⊖
Emergency handling . . . . ⊖
Avoidance maneuver, max. mph . . .55.5

Convenience and comfort
Ride . . . . ○
Noise . . . . ○
Driving position . . . . ○
Access . . . . ⊖
Controls and displays . . . . ⊖
Fit and finish . . . . ⊖
Door top to ground, in. 53.5
Trunk . . . . ⊖
Luggage capacity . . . . .0+3
Max. load, lb. 770

Seating
Front-seat comfort . . . . ⊖
Front shoulder room, in. 52.0
Front leg room, in. 42.0
Front head room, in. 8.0
Rear-seat comfort . . . . ●
Rear shoulder room, in. 40.5
Rear leg room, in. 23.5
Rear head room, in 0.0

Fuel economy . . . . ○
CU's overall mileage, mpg 24
  CU's city/highway, mpg 18/29
  CU's 150-mile trip, mpg 28
Annual fuel . . . . .630 gal./$1,390
Cruising range 370

RELIABILITY HISTORY

TROUBLE SPOTS	Volkswagen New Beetle Turbo							
	97	98	99	00	01	02	03	04
Engine			⊖	○	○	⊖	●	●
Cooling			⊖	⊖	⊖	⊖	●	●
Fuel			●	⊖	○	⊖	●	●
Ignition			⊖	⊖	●	○	●	●
Transmission			⊖	⊖	⊖	⊖	●	●
Electrical	Insufficient data	Insufficient data	●	●	●	●	○	●
Air conditioning			⊖	⊖	⊖	⊖	⊖	●
Suspension			⊖	⊖	⊖	⊖	⊖	●
Brakes			○	○	⊖	⊖	⊖	●
Exhaust			⊖	⊖	○	○	⊖	●
Paint/trim/rust			●	⊖	⊖	⊖	⊖	●
Body integrity			○	○	○	○	⊖	○
Power equipment			●	⊖	⊖	○	○	●
Body hardware			●	⊖	⊖	○	○	○
RELIABILITY VERDICT			✗	✗	✗	-	✗	

Expert • Independent • Nonprofit

Volkswagen Passat

CR RECOMMENDED ✓

Although in its twilight, the Passat still has a smooth ride, elegant cabin, and extensive safety features. Cornering is competent. The front seats are comfortable and the interior has a quality feel. The rear is spacious. The 1.8-liter turbocharged engine is responsive but slow off the line with the automatic. The V6 is quiet and strong. AWD is available, but it makes the car slower and thirstier. Reliability of the AWD model dropped to below average. The diesel engine returned 28 mpg overall in our testing. The redesigned Passat goes on sale at the end of the summer.

THE PASSAT LINE

Body style:
sedan; wagon
Trim lines:
GL, GL TDI, GLS, GLS TDI, GLX
Base price range:
$22,070-$33,615

REPORT CARD

○	Predicted reliability
○	Owner satisfaction
⊖	Predicted depreciation
◉	Accident avoidance
⊖	Acceleration
⊖	Ride
◉	Front seat comfort
○	Fuel economy

SPECIFICATIONS

Drive wheels Front or AWD

Seating 2 front, 3 rear

Engines available
2.0-liter 4 turbodiesel (134 hp); 1.8-liter 4 turbo (170 hp); 2.8-liter V6 (190 hp)

Transmissions available
5-speed manual; 5-speed automatic

Fuel
Fuel type . . . . .Diesel or premium
EPA city/highway, mpg 19/27
Fuel refill capacity, gal. 16.3

Dimensions and weight
Length, in. 185
Width, in. 69
Wheelbase, in. 106
Curb weight, lb. 3,530
Percent weight, front/rear 61/39
Typical towing ability, lb. 2,000

SAFETY INFORMATION

Active safety features
Antilock brakes . . . . .Standard
Traction control . . . . .Standard
Stability control . . . . .Optional (std. on GLX)
Daytime running lights . . . . .Standard
Tire pressure monitor . . . . .Not available

Safety belts
Center-rear belt 3-point
Pretensioners, front/rear . . . . .Yes/yes

Air bags
Occupant-sensing system . . . . .Side
Side bags, front/rear . . . . .Standard/no
Inflatable curtain . . . . .Standard
Accident alert system . . . . .Available

Crash tests
Gov't front-crash test, driver/front passenger . . . . ◉/◉
Gov't side-crash test, driver/rear passenger . . . .◉/◖
IIHS offset crash test . . . . .Good
IIHS side crash test w/ side & curtain airbags . . . . .NA
IIHS side crash test w/o side & curtain airbags . . . . .NA

FROM THE TEST TRACK

Tested model
2003 GLX sedan, 2.8-liter V6, 5-speed automatic

Tires as tested
Continental ContiTouring Contact CH95, size 205/55R16 91H

Acceleration . . . . ⊖
0-30 mph, sec. 3.1
0-60 mph, sec. 8.8
Quarter mile, sec. 16.9
Quarter mile, mph 86
45-65 mph, sec. 5.5

Other findings
Transmission . . . . ◉
Turning circle, ft. 38
Ground clearance, in. 4.0

Braking and handling
Braking . . . . ⊖
Braking, dry pavement, ft. 136
Routine handling . . . . ⊖
Emergency handling . . . . ⊖
Avoidance maneuver, max. mph . . .54.5

Convenience and comfort
Ride . . . . ⊖
Noise . . . . ⊖
Driving position . . . . ⊖
Access . . . . ⊖
Controls and displays . . . . ⊖
Fit and finish . . . . ⊖
Door top to ground, in. 51.5
Trunk . . . . ⊖
Luggage capacity . . . . .3+2
Max. load, lb. 1,060

Seating
Front-seat comfort . . . . ◉
Front shoulder room, in. 56.0
Front leg room, in. 42.0
Front head room, in. 4.0
Rear-seat comfort . . . . ⊖
Rear shoulder room, in. 54.0
Rear leg room, in. 29.0
Rear head room, in 2.0

Fuel economy . . . . ○
CU's overall mileage, mpg 21
CU's city/highway, mpg 14/30
CU's 150-mile trip, mpg 25
Annual fuel . . . . .730 gal./$1,600
Cruising range 370

RELIABILITY HISTORY

TROUBLE SPOTS	Volkswagen Passat V6							
	97	98	99	00	01	02	03	04
Engine	⊖		⊖	⊖	○	●	●	●
Cooling	●		⊖	○	○	●	●	●
Fuel	●		○	○	○	●	⊖	●
Ignition	⊖		⊖	⊖	●	●	●	●
Transmission	⊖		⊖	○	⊖	⊖	⊖	●
Electrical	⊖		⊖	●	●	⊖	●	●
Air conditioning	⊖	Insufficient data	⊖	●	●	●	⊖	●
Suspension	⊖		⊖	○	⊖	⊖	●	●
Brakes	⊖		○	○	○	○	⊖	●
Exhaust	○		●	●	●	●	⊖	●
Paint/trim/rust	⊖		●	⊖	⊖	⊖	⊖	⊖
Body integrity	⊖		○	○	○	○	⊖	●
Power equipment	●		○	○	○	⊖	⊖	⊖
Body hardware	●		○	○	⊖	●	⊖	●
RELIABILITY VERDICT	✗		✗	✗	✗	–	–	✗

Volkswagen Phaeton

THE PHAETON LINE
Body style:
sedan
Trim lines:
V8, W12
Base price range:
$66,950-$96,100

The Phaeton is Volkswagen's first foray into the exclusive club of large, premium-luxury cruisers that includes the Audi A8, BMW 7 Series, Jaguar XJ, Lexus LS430, and Mercedes-Benz S-Class. The same 4.2-liter V8 from the A8 is in the base Phaeton, while a 6.0-liter, 12-cylinder engine powers the W12. All-wheel drive is standard, in addition to a long list of safety and high-tech gadgets. The Phaeton is very roomy, quiet, and comfortable. This heavy sedan rides on an adjustable air suspension that compensates for passenger load and driving style, as in the A8.

REPORT CARD

NA	Predicted reliability
NA	Owner satisfaction
NA	Predicted depreciation
NA	Accident avoidance
NA	Acceleration
NA	Ride
NA	Front seat comfort
NA	Fuel economy

SPECIFICATIONS

Drive wheels AWD

Seating 2 front, 3 rear

Engines available
4.2-liter V8 (335 hp); 6.0-liter 12 (420 hp)

Transmissions available
5-speed automatic; 6-speed automatic

Fuel
Fuel type ....Premium
EPA city/highway, mpg 15/22
Fuel refill capacity, gal. 23.8

Dimensions and weight
Length, in. 204
Width, in. 75
Wheelbase, in. 118
Curb weight, lb. 5,100
Percent weight, front/rear 55/45
Typical towing ability, lb. ....NA

SAFETY INFORMATION

Active safety features
Antilock brakes ....Standard
Traction control ....Standard
Stability control ....Standard
Daytime running lights ....Standard
Tire pressure monitor ....Available

Safety belts
Center-rear belt 3-point
Pretensioners, front/rear ....Yes/yes

Air bags
Occupant-sensing system ....Side
Side bags, front/rear ....Standard/no
Inflatable curtain ....Standard
Accident alert system ....Available

Crash tests
Gov't front-crash test, driver/front passenger ......NA/NA
Gov't side-crash test, driver/rear passenger ....NA/NA
IIHS offset crash test ....NA
IIHS side crash test w/ side & curtain airbags ....NA
IIHS side crash test w/o side & curtain airbags ....NA

ANOTHER LOOK

RELIABILITY HISTORY

TROUBLE SPOTS	97 98 99 00 01 02 03 04
Engine	
Cooling	**NOT**
Fuel	
Ignition	**ENOUGH**
Transmission	
Electrical	
Air conditioning	**DATA**
Suspension	
Brakes	**TO**
Exhaust	
Paint/trim/rust	**RATE**
Body integrity	
Power equipment	
Body hardware	
RELIABILITY VERDICT	

Volkswagen Touareg

THE TOUAREG LINE

Body style:
4-door SUV

Trim lines:
V6, V8

Base price range:
$37,140-$44,260

V olkswagen's first SUV is a luxurious unibody model developed with the Porsche Cayenne. The ride is compliant. The interior is very quiet. Handling is responsive but didn't shine at the limits. The 3.2-liter V6 is thirsty for premium fuel and struggles to move the 5,200-pound vehicle, so acceleration feels lethargic. The V8 is brawnier, but bumps the price considerably. For 2005 the V6 got 20 more horsepower. The cargo area is modest. Many controls are overly complicated. On the plus side it's one of the few car-based SUVs that's an impressive off-roader. First-year reliability was poor.

REPORT CARD

●	Predicted reliability
○	Owner satisfaction
NA	Predicted depreciation
○	Accident avoidance
◒	Acceleration
○	Ride
◉	Front seat comfort
●	Fuel economy

SPECIFICATIONS

Drive wheels AWD

Seating 2 front, 3 rear

Engines available
3.2-liter V6 (240 hp); 4.2-liter V8 (310 hp)

Transmissions available
6-speed automatic

Fuel
Fuel type . . . . .Premium
EPA city/highway, mpg 16/21
Fuel refill capacity, gal. 26.4

Dimensions and weight
Length, in. 187
Width, in. 76
Wheelbase, in. 112
Curb weight, lb. 5,210
Percent weight, front/rear 52/48
Typical towing ability, lb. 7,700

SAFETY INFORMATION

Active safety features

Antilock brakes . . . . .Standard
Traction control . . . . .Standard
Stability control . . . . .Standard
Daytime running lights . . . . .Standard
Tire pressure monitor . . . . .Available

Safety belts

Center-rear belt 3-point
Pretensioners, front/rear . . . . .Yes/yes

Air bags

Occupant-sensing system . . . . .Side
Side bags, front/rear . . . . .Standard/no
Inflatable curtain . . . . .Standard
Accident alert system . . . . .Available

Crash tests

Gov't front-crash test, driver/front passenger . . . . .◑/◑
Gov't side-crash test, driver/rear passenger . . . .◑/○
IIHS offset crash test . . . . .NA
IIHS side crash test w/ side & curtain airbags . . . . .NA
IIHS side crash test w/o side & curtain airbags . . . . .NA

FROM THE TEST TRACK

Tested model
2004 V6 4-door SUV AWD, 3.2-liter V6, 6-speed automatic

Tires as tested
Dunlop Grandtrek ST 8000, size 255/60R17 106H

Acceleration . . . . ◒
0-30 mph, sec. 4.2
0-60 mph, sec. 11.9
Quarter mile, sec. 18.8
Quarter mile, mph 76
45-65 mph, sec. 6.9

Other findings
Transmission . . . . ◒
Turning circle, ft. 38
Ground clearance, in. 7.0

Braking and handling
Braking . . . . ○
Braking, dry pavement, ft. 147
Routine handling . . . . ◒
Emergency handling . . . . ○
Avoidance maneuver, max. mph . . .47.5

Convenience and comfort
Ride . . . . ○
Noise . . . . ◒
Driving position . . . . ◒
Access . . . . ◒
Controls and displays . . . . ○
Fit and finish . . . . ◉
Door top to ground, in. 61.0
Cargo area . . . . ◒
Cargo volume, cu.ft. 35.5
Max. load, lb. 1,280

Seating
Front-seat comfort . . . . ◉
Front shoulder room, in. 57.5
Front leg room, in. 41.0
Front head room, in. 4.0
Rear-seat comfort . . . . ◒
Rear shoulder room, in. 57.5
Rear leg room, in. 27.0
Rear head room, in 4.5

Fuel economy . . . . ●
CU's overall mileage, mpg 15
  CU's city/highway, mpg 10/20
  CU's 150-mile trip, mpg 18
Annual fuel . . . . .1,025 gal./$2,255
Cruising range 435

RELIABILITY HISTORY

TROUBLE SPOTS	Volkswagen Touareg							
	97	98	99	00	01	02	03	04
Engine								◉
Cooling								◉
Fuel								◉
Ignition								◉
Transmission								◉
Electrical								◒
Air conditioning								◒
Suspension								◒
Brakes								◉
Exhaust								◉
Paint/trim/rust								◉
Body integrity								○
Power equipment								◒
Body hardware								○
RELIABILITY VERDICT								✗

● ◒ ○ ◑ ●
better ◀——▶ worse   See page 36 for more information.

Volvo S40/V50

THE S40/V50 LINE
Body style:
sedan; wagon
Trim lines:
2.4i, T5
Base price range:
$23,560-$29,385

The new S40 sedan and V50 wagon are significantly improved over the previous generation, sharing mechanical components with the Mazda3 and European Ford Focus. They corner fairly nimbly, but have a stiff ride. The standard 168-hp, 2.4-liter, five-cylinder engine sounds raspy. A stronger, turbocharged 218-hp engine powers the T5. Although externally smaller than the old model, the new one is roomier inside. The front seats are supportive, but the rear seat is very tight. All-wheel drive is available. The V50 wagon is small but versatile inside.

REPORT CARD

New	Predicted reliability
New	Owner satisfaction
NA	Predicted depreciation
◔	Accident avoidance
○	Acceleration
○	Ride
◔	Front seat comfort
○	Fuel economy

SPECIFICATIONS

Drive wheels Front or AWD

Seating 2 front, 3 rear

Engines available
2.4-liter 5 (168 hp); 2.5-liter 5 turbo (218 hp)

Transmissions available
5-speed manual; 6-speed manual; 5-speed automatic

Fuel
Fuel type . . . . .Regular
EPA city/highway, mpg 22/30
Fuel refill capacity, gal. 16.4

Dimensions and weight
Length, in. 176
Width, in. 70
Wheelbase, in. 104
Curb weight, lb. 3,245
Percent weight, front/rear 60/40
Typical towing ability, lb. 2,000

SAFETY INFORMATION

Active safety features
Antilock brakes . . . . .Standard
Traction control . . . . .Standard
Stability control . . . . .Optional
Daytime running lights . . . . .Standard
Tire pressure monitor .Not available

Safety belts
Center-rear belt 3-point
Pretensioners, front/rear .Yes/yes

Air bags
Occupant-sensing system . . . . .Front
Side bags, front/rear . . . . .Standard/no
Inflatable curtain . . . . .Standard
Accident alert system . . . . .Available

Crash tests
Gov't front-crash test, driver/front passenger . . . . . ◔/◑
Gov't side-crash test, driver/rear passenger . . . . . . ●/◑
IIHS offset crash test . . . . .Good
IIHS side crash test w/ side & curtain airbags . . .Acceptable
IIHS side crash test w/o side & curtain airbags . . . . .NA

FROM THE TEST TRACK

Tested model
2005 2.4i sedan, 2.4-liter Five, 5-speed automatic

Tires as tested
Michelin Energy MXV4, size 205/55R16 91V

Acceleration . . . . ○
0-30 mph, sec. 3.7
0-60 mph, sec. 9.4
Quarter mile, sec. 17.3
Quarter mile, mph 84
45-65 mph, sec. 6.0

Other findings
Transmission . . . . ◔
Turning circle, ft. 37
Ground clearance, in. 4.5

Braking and handling
Braking . . . . ◔
Braking, dry pavement, ft. 135
Routine handling . . . . ◔
Emergency handling . . . . ○
Avoidance maneuver, max. mph . . .52.0

Convenience and comfort
Ride . . . . ○
Noise . . . . ◔
Driving position . . . . ◔
Access . . . . ◔
Controls and displays . . . . ◔
Fit and finish . . . . ◔
Door top to ground, in. 51.5
Trunk . . . . ◑
Luggage capacity . . . . .2+4
Max. load, lb. 950

Seating
Front-seat comfort . . . . ◔
Front shoulder room, in. 55.0
Front leg room, in. 41.5
Front head room, in. 3.0
Rear-seat comfort . . . . ◑
Rear shoulder room, in. 53.5
Rear leg room, in. 28.0
Rear head room, in 1.5

Fuel economy . . . . ○
CU's overall mileage, mpg 23
CU's city/highway, mpg 14/36
CU's 150-mile trip, mpg 29
Annual fuel . . . . .655 gal./$1,310
Cruising range 450

RELIABILITY HISTORY

TROUBLE SPOTS	97 98 99 00 01 02 03 04
Engine	
Cooling	
Fuel	NO
Ignition	
Transmission	DATA
Electrical	
Air conditioning	NEW
Suspension	
Brakes	MODEL
Exhaust	
Paint/trim/rust	
Body integrity	
Power equipment	
Body hardware	
RELIABILITY VERDICT	

Volvo S60

CR RECOMMENDED ✓

THE S60 LINE
Body style:
sedan
Trim lines:
2.4, 2.5T, T5, R
Base price range:
$27,585–$37,735

A lthough a good car, the S60 falls short in its highly competitive class. It's neither very luxurious nor sporty. The turbocharged engine in the 2.5T model we tested delivered quick acceleration, especially in midrange. The interior is fairly quiet and the front seats are comfortable. The ride is quite stiff and handling is secure, though not particularly agile. The rear seat is cramped. Rearward vision is compromised by the coupelike styling and rear head restraints. The confusing radio controls have been simplified for 2005. All-wheel-drive versions are available, including a very quick R version.

REPORT CARD

◯	Predicted reliability
◯	Owner satisfaction
◑	Predicted depreciation
◯	Accident avoidance
◑	Acceleration
◯	Ride
◑	Front seat comfort
◯	Fuel economy

SPECIFICATIONS

Drive wheels Front or AWD

Seating 2 front, 3 rear

Engines available
2.4-liter 5 (168 hp); 2.5-liter 5 turbo (208 hp); 2.4-liter 5 turbo (257 hp); 2.5-liter 5 turbo (300 hp)

Transmissions available
5-speed manual; 6-speed manual; 5-speed automatic

Fuel
Fuel type . . . . Regular or premium
EPA city/highway, mpg 22/30
Fuel refill capacity, gal. 18.5

Dimensions and weight
Length, in. 180
Width, in. 71
Wheelbase, in. 107
Curb weight, lb. 3,465
Percent weight, front/rear 59/41
Typical towing ability, lb. 3,300

SAFETY INFORMATION

Active safety features
Antilock brakes . . . . .Standard
Traction control . . . . .Standard
Stability control . . . . .Optional (standard on T5, R)
Daytime running lights . . . . .Standard
Tire pressure monitor . . . . .Available

Safety belts
Center-rear belt 3-point
Pretensioners, front/rear . . . . .Yes/yes

Air bags
Occupant-sensing system . . . . .Not available
Side bags, front/rear . . . . .Standard/no
Inflatable curtain . . . . .Standard
Accident alert system . . . . .Not available

Crash tests
Gov't front-crash test, driver/front passenger . . . . . ◑/◑
Gov't side-crash test, driver/rear passenger . . . . . . ●/◑
IIHS offset crash test . . . . .Good
IIHS side crash test w/ side & curtain airbags . . . . .NA
IIHS side crash test w/o side & curtain airbags . . . . .NA

FROM THE TEST TRACK

Tested model
2004 2.5T sedan, 2.5-liter Five turbo, 5-speed automatic

Tires as tested
Continental ContiTouring Contact CH95, size 215/55R16 93H

Acceleration . . . . ◑
0-30 mph, sec. 2.9
0-60 mph, sec. 7.9
Quarter mile, sec. 16.1
Quarter mile, mph 90
45-65 mph, sec. 5.0

Other findings
Transmission . . . . ◑
Turning circle, ft. 42
Ground clearance, in. 5.0

Braking and handling
Braking . . . . ◑
Braking, dry pavement, ft. 140
Routine handling . . . . ◑
Emergency handling . . . . ◯
Avoidance maneuver, max. mph . . .50.5

Convenience and comfort
Ride . . . . ◯
Noise . . . . ◑
Driving position . . . . ◑
Access . . . . ◑
Controls and displays . . . . ◯
Fit and finish . . . . ◑
Door top to ground, in. 50.0
Trunk . . . . ◯
Luggage capacity . . . . .3+2
Max. load, lb. 890

Seating
Front-seat comfort . . . . ◑
Front shoulder room, in. 56.0
Front leg room, in. 42.0
Front head room, in. 4.0
Rear-seat comfort . . . . ◯
Rear shoulder room, in. 56.0
Rear leg room, in. 27.0
Rear head room, in 3.0

Fuel economy . . . . ◯
CU's overall mileage, mpg 22
CU's city/highway, mpg 14/35
CU's 150-mile trip, mpg 26
Annual fuel . . . . .690 gal./$1,380
Cruising range 445

RELIABILITY HISTORY

TROUBLE SPOTS	Volvo S60
	97 98 99 00 01 02 03 04
Engine	◯ ◯ ◯ ◯
Cooling	◯ ◯ ◯ ◯
Fuel	◑ ◑ ◑ ◑
Ignition	◯ ◯ ◯ ◯
Transmission	◯ ◯ ◯ ◯
Electrical	● ◯ ◑ ◑
Air conditioning	◯ ◑ ◯ ◯
Suspension	◑ ◑ ◑ ◑
Brakes	◑ ◑ ◑ ◑
Exhaust	◑ ◑ ◑ ◑
Paint/trim/rust	◯ ◑ ◯ ◑
Body integrity	◯ ◯ ◑ ◯
Power equipment	◯ ◯ ◑ ◑
Body hardware	◯ ◯ ◑ ◑
RELIABILITY VERDICT	– – ✓ –

◉ ◑ ◯ ◐ ●
better ◀———▶ worse   See page 36 for more information.

Volvo S80

THE S80 LINE
Body style:
sedan
Trim lines:
2.5T, T6, T6 Premier
Base price range:
$36,365-$49,150

The S80 is a roomy front- or all-wheel-drive sedan that is aging. The interior is quiet, and handling is very secure but not particularly nimble. The ride is too stiff at low speeds. The T6's turbocharged version offers quick and effortless acceleration. The front seats are comfortable, and the rear is roomy. The trunk is relatively large and has some well thought out details. The audio system's unintuitive controls have been improved for 2005. Crash-test results are outstanding. A wide turning circle hampers parking maneuvers. Reliability has once again dropped to below average.

REPORT CARD

⊖	Predicted reliability
○	Owner satisfaction
○	Predicted depreciation
◉	Accident avoidance
◉	Acceleration
○	Ride
⊖	Front seat comfort
⊖	Fuel economy

SPECIFICATIONS

Drive wheels Front or AWD

Seating 2 front, 3 rear

Engines available
2.5-liter 5 turbo (208 hp); 2.9-liter 6 twin-turbo (268 hp)

Transmissions available
4-speed automatic; 5-speed automatic

Fuel
Fuel type . . . . .Regular
EPA city/highway, mpg 19/26
Fuel refill capacity, gal. 21.1

Dimensions and weight
Length, in. 190
Width, in. 72
Wheelbase, in. 110
Curb weight, lb. 3,630
Percent weight, front/rear 59/41
Typical towing ability, lb. 3,300

SAFETY INFORMATION

Active safety features
Antilock brakes . . . . .Standard
Traction control . . . . .Standard
Stability control . . . . .Optional (standard on T6)
Daytime running lights .Standard
Tire pressure monitor . . . . .Available

Safety belts
Center-rear belt 3-point
Pretensioners, front/rear . . . . .Yes/yes

Air bags
Occupant-sensing system . . . . .Not available
Side bags, front/rear . . . . .Standard/no
Inflatable curtain . . . . .Standard
Accident alert system . . . . .Not available

Crash tests
Gov't front-crash test, driver/front passenger . . . . .◉/◉
Gov't side-crash test, driver/rear passenger . . . . . .◉/◉
IIHS offset crash test . . . . .Good
IIHS side crash test w/ side & curtain airbags . . . . .NA
IIHS side crash test w/o side & curtain airbags . . . . . . .NA

FROM THE TEST TRACK

Tested model
2004 T6 sedan, 2.9-liter Six twin-turbo, 4-speed automatic

Tires as tested
Michelin Pilot MXM4, size 225/50R17 94V

Acceleration . . . . ◉
0-30 mph, sec. 2.8
0-60 mph, sec. 6.9
Quarter mile, sec. 15.3
Quarter mile, mph 94
45-65 mph, sec. 4.5

Other findings
Transmission . . . . ⊖
Turning circle, ft. 42
Ground clearance, in. 5.5

Braking and handling
Braking . . . . ◐
Braking, dry pavement, ft. 136
Routine handling . . . .○
Emergency handling . . . .◐
Avoidance maneuver, max. mph . . .54.0

Convenience and comfort
Ride . . . .○
Noise . . . .○
Driving position . . . .○
Access . . . .○
Controls and displays . . . .○
Fit and finish . . . .○
Door top to ground, in. 51.5
Trunk . . . .○
Luggage capacity . . . . .3+2
Max. load, lb. 890

Seating
Front-seat comfort . . . . ◐
Front shoulder room, in. 58.5
Front leg room, in. 42.0
Front head room, in. 3.5
Rear-seat comfort . . . . ◐
Rear shoulder room, in. 56.5
Rear leg room, in. 30.0
Rear head room, in 4.5

Fuel economy . . . . ⊖
CU's overall mileage, mpg 19
CU's city/highway, mpg 12/29
CU's 150-mile trip, mpg 23
Annual fuel . . . . .800 gal./$1,600
Cruising range 455

RELIABILITY HISTORY

TROUBLE SPOTS	Volvo S80							
	97	98	99	00	01	02	03	04
Engine			◐	○	◐	◐	◐	◉
Cooling			◐	○	◐	◉	◉	◉
Fuel			●	●	◐	◐	◐	◉
Ignition			◐	◐	◐	◐	◐	◉
Transmission			◐	◐	◐	◐	○	◉
Electrical			●	●	◐	◐	◐	◉
Air conditioning			◐	◐	○	◐	◐	◉
Suspension			●	●	○	◐	◐	◉
Brakes			◐	○	○	◐	◐	◉
Exhaust			◐	◉	◉	◉	◉	◉
Paint/trim/rust			◐	◐	○	◐	◉	◉
Body integrity			◐	◐	◐	◐	◐	◉
Power equipment			◐	◐	○	◐	◐	◉
Body hardware			◐	◐	○	◐	◐	◉
RELIABILITY VERDICT			✗	✗	✗	✗	✗	-

Expert • Independent • Nonprofit

Volvo V70/XC70

CR RECOMMENDED ✓

The V70 is essentially a wagon version of the S60. It's spacious and useful, with large, comfortable seats and an optional small third-row seat. The turbocharged 2.5-liter engine is quick. But with all-wheel drive, both acceleration and fuel economy suffer. The unintuitive audio system has been improved for 2005. The XC70 model has all-wheel drive and a raised ride height. Its ride is less comfortable than the regular V70's, and the steering feels vague and imprecise. Reliability has been average. A very quick 300-hp, all-wheel-drive R version tops the range.

THE V70/XC70 LINE
Body style: wagon
Trim lines: 2.4, 2.5T, T5, XC70, R
Base price range: $29,130-$39,255

REPORT CARD

○	Predicted reliability
⊖	Owner satisfaction
⊖	Predicted depreciation
⊖	Accident avoidance
⊖	Acceleration
○	Ride
◉	Front seat comfort
⊜	Fuel economy

SPECIFICATIONS

Drive wheels Front or AWD

Seating 2 front, 3 rear, 2 third

Engines available
2.4-liter 5 (168 hp); 2.5-liter 5 turbo (208 hp); 2.4-liter 5 turbo (257 hp); 2.5-liter 5 turbo (300 hp)

Transmissions available
5-speed manual; 6-speed manual; 5-speed automatic

Fuel
Fuel type . . . . .Regular or premium
EPA city/highway, mpg 18/24
Fuel refill capacity, gal. 18.5

Dimensions and weight
Length, in. 186
Width, in. 73
Wheelbase, in. .109
Curb weight, lb. 3,815
Percent weight, front/rear 54/46
Typical towing ability, lb. 3,300

SAFETY INFORMATION

Active safety features
Antilock brakes . . . . .Standard
Traction control . . . . .Standard
Stability control . . . . .Optional (standard on T5, R)
Daytime running lights .Standard
Tire-pressure monitor . . . . .Available

Safety belts
Center-rear belt 3-point
Pretensioners, front/rear . . . . .Yes/yes

Air bags
Occupant-sensing system .Front
Side bags, front/rear . . . . .Standard/no
Inflatable curtain . . . . .Standard
Accident alert system . . . . .Not available

Crash tests
Gov't front-crash test, driver/front passenger . . ◉/◉
Gov't side-crash test, driver/rear passenger . . . ◉/◉
IIHS offset crash test . . . . .NA
IIHS side crash test w/ side & curtain airbags . . . . . . .NA
IIHS side crash test w/o side & curtain airbags . . . . . .NA

FROM THE TEST TRACK

Tested model
2001 XC wagon AWD, 2.4-liter Five turbo, 5-speed automatic

Tires as tested
Pirelli Scorpion, size 215/65R16 98H

Acceleration . . . . ⊖
0-30 mph, sec. 3.0
0-60 mph, sec. 8.6
Quarter mile, sec. 16.8
Quarter mile, mph 84
45-65 mph, sec. 5.9

Other findings
Transmission . . . . ⊖
Turning circle, ft. 40
Ground clearance, in. 6.0

Braking and handling
Braking . . . . ⊖
Braking, dry pavement, ft. 134
Routine handling . . . . ⊖
Emergency handling . . . . ○
Avoidance maneuver, max. mph . . .50.5

Convenience and comfort
Ride . . . . ○
Noise . . . . ⊖
Driving position . . . . ⊖
Access . . . . ⊖
Controls and displays . . . . ◉
Fit and finish . . . . ⊖
Door top to ground, in. 52.5
Cargo area . . . . ○
Cargo volume, cu.ft. 35.5
Max. load, lb. 1,075

Seating
Front-seat comfort . . . . ◉
Front shoulder room, in. 56.0
Front leg room, in. 43.0
Front head room, in. 3.5
Rear-seat comfort . . . . ⊖
Rear shoulder room, in. 56.5
Rear leg room, in. 28.5
Rear head room, in 3.5

Fuel economy . . . . ⊜
CU's overall mileage, mpg 18
CU's city/highway, mpg 12/26
CU's 150-mile trip, mpg 22
Annual fuel . . . . .830 gal./$1,660
Cruising range 380

RELIABILITY HISTORY

TROUBLE SPOTS	Volvo Cross Country, XC70							
	97	98	99	00	01	02	03	04
Engine								
Cooling								
Fuel								
Ignition								
Transmission								
Electrical								
Air conditioning								
Suspension								
Brakes								
Exhaust								
Paint/trim/rust								
Body integrity								
Power equipment								
Body hardware								
RELIABILITY VERDICT	X	X	X	X	-	X	-	

Volvo XC90

The XC90's best features include its flexible and comfortable interior, seven-passenger seating capacity, and impressive safety features. However, heavy weight, mediocre fuel economy, and powertrains that aren't overly powerful detract from the driving experience. A new model with a Yamaha-built, 4.4-liter V8 mated to a six-speed automatic brings significantly more power for 2005. The ride is fairly comfortable, with responsive and secure handling, thanks to standard stability control. The head-protection air bags cover the side windows of all three rows of seats. Reliability has been poor.

THE XC90 LINE
Body style:
4-door SUV
Trim lines:
2.5T, T6, V8
Base price range:
$35,290-$45,395

REPORT CARD

●	Predicted reliability
○	Owner satisfaction
NA	Predicted depreciation
○	Accident avoidance
○	Acceleration
⊖	Ride
⊖	Front seat comfort
●	Fuel economy

SPECIFICATIONS

Drive wheels Front or AWD

Seating 2 front, 3 rear, 2 third

Engines available
2.5-liter 5 turbo (208 hp); 2.9-liter 6 twin-turbo (268 hp); 4.4-liter V8 (311 hp)

Transmissions available
4-speed automatic; 5-speed automatic; 6-speed automatic

Fuel
Fuel type . . . . .Regular
EPA city/highway, mpg 15/20
Fuel refill capacity, gal. 19.0

Dimensions and weight
Length, in. 189
Width, in. 75
Wheelbase, in. 113
Curb weight, lb. 4,795
Percent weight, front/rear 53/47
Typical towing ability, lb. 5,000

SAFETY INFORMATION

Active safety features
Antilock brakes . . . . .Standard
Traction control . . . . .Standard
Stability control .Standard
Daytime running lights . . . . .Standard
Tire pressure monitor . . . . .Available

Safety belts
Center-rear belt 3-point
Pretensioners, front/rear . . . . .Yes/yes

Air bags
Occupant-sensing system . . . . .Not available
Side bags, front/rear . . . . .Standard/no
Inflatable curtain . . . . .Standard with rollover
Accident alert system . . . . .Not available

Crash tests
Gov't front-crash test, driver/front passenger . . . . . . ◐/◑
Gov't side-crash test, driver/rear passenger . . . . ◐/◑
IIHS offset crash test . . . . .Good
IIHS side crash test w/ side & curtain airbags . . . . .NA
IIHS side crash test w/o side & curtain airbags . . . . .NA

FROM THE TEST TRACK

Tested model
2003 T6 4-door SUV AWD, 2.9-liter Six twin-turbo, 4-speed automatic

Tires as tested
Michelin Pilot HX MXM4, size P235/60R18 102V

Acceleration . . . .○
0-30 mph, sec. 3.5
0-60 mph, sec. 9.4
Quarter mile, sec. 17.2
Quarter mile, mph 85
45-65 mph, sec. 5.6

Other findings
Transmission . . . .⊖
Turning circle, ft. 42
Ground clearance, in. 7.5

Braking and handling
Braking . . . .○
Braking, dry pavement, ft. 144
Routine handling . . . .⊖
Emergency handling . . . .○
Avoidance maneuver, max. mph . .50.5

Convenience and comfort
Ride . . . .⊖
Noise . . . .⊖
Driving position . . . .⊖
Access . . . .⊖
Controls and displays . . . .⊖
Fit and finish . . . .⊖
Door top to ground, in. 61.0
Cargo area . . . .⊖
Cargo volume, cu.ft. 38.0
Max. load, lb. 1,285

Seating
Front-seat comfort . . . .⊖
Front shoulder room, in. 58.0
Front leg room, in. 41.5
Front head room, in. 4.5
Rear-seat comfort . . . .⊖
Rear shoulder room, in. 56.5
Rear leg room, in. 25.5
Rear head room, in 4.5
Third-seat comfort . . . .●
Third shoulder room, in 54.0
Third leg room, in. 26.0
Third head room, in. 0.0

Fuel economy . . . .●
CU's overall mileage, mpg 15
CU's city/highway, mpg 9/25
CU's 150-mile trip, mpg 18
Annual fuel . . . . . .1,000 gal./$2,000
Cruising range 320

RELIABILITY HISTORY

TROUBLE SPOTS	Volvo XC90							
	97	98	99	00	01	02	03	04
Engine							●	●
Cooling							●	●
Fuel							●	●
Ignition							●	●
Transmission							○	●
Electrical							○	●
Air conditioning							◐	●
Suspension							○	●
Brakes							○	◐
Exhaust							●	●
Paint/trim/rust							●	●
Body integrity							○	◐
Power equipment							○	○
Body hardware							●	○
RELIABILITY VERDICT							✕	✕

Expert • Independent • Nonprofit